THE EUROPEAN UNION SERIES

General Editors: Neill Nugent, William E. Paterson

The European Union series provides an authoritative library on the European Union, ranging from general introductory texts to definitive assessments of key institutions and actors, issues, policies and policy processes, and the role of member states.

Books in the series are written by leading scholars in their fields and reflect the most up-to-date research and debate. Particular attention is paid to accessibility and clear presentation for a wide audience of students, practitioners, and interested general readers.

The series editors are **Neill Nugent,** Professor of Politics and Jean Monnet Professor of European Integration, Manchester Metropolitan University, and **William E. Paterson,** Founding Director of the Institute of German Studies, University of Birmingham and Chairman of the German British Forum. Their co-editor until his death in July 1999, **Vincent Wright,** was a Fellow of Nuffield College, Oxford University.

Feedback on the series and book proposals are always welcome and should be sent to Steven Kennedy, Palgrave Macmillan, Houndmills, Basingstoke, Hampshire RG21 6XS, UK, or by e-mail to s.kennedy@palgrave.com

---

General textbooks

Published

Forthcoming

Also planned

Series Standing Order (outside North America only)
ISBN 0–333–71695–7 hardcover
ISBN 0–333–69352–3 paperback
Full details from www.palgrave.com

Visit Palgrave Macmillan's
EU Resource area at
www.palgrave.com/politics/eu/

Debates on European Integration

A Reader

Edited by

Mette Eilstrup-Sangiovanni

First published 2006 by
PALGRAVE MACMILLAN
Houndmills, Basingstoke, Hampshire RG21 6XS and
175 Fifth Avenue, New York, N.Y. 10010
Companies and representatives throughout the world

PALGRAVE MACMILLAN is the global academic imprint of the Palgrave
Macmillan division of St. Martin's Press, LLC and of Palgrave Macmillan Ltd.
Macmillan® is a registered trademark in the United States, United Kingdom
and other countries. Palgrave is a registered trademark in the European
Union and other countries.

ISBN-13: 978–1–4039–4103–9   hardback
ISBN-10: 1–4039–4103–3   hardback
ISBN-13: 978–1–4039–4104–6   paperback
ISBN-10: 1–4039–4104–1   paperback

This book is printed on paper suitable for recycling and made from fully
managed and sustained forest sources.

A catalogue record for this book is available from the British Library.

A catalog record for this book is available from the Library of Congress.

10 9 8 7 6 5 4 3 2 1
15 14 13 12 11 10 09 08 07 06

Printed and bound by
Creative Print & Design (Wales), Ebbw Vale

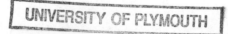

Contents

List of Tables

List of Figures

Preface

European integration theory is a vibrant field. The five decades that have passed since the birth of the European Coal and Steel Community (ECSC) in 1952 have seen a steady proliferation of scholarship dedicated to answering the question of how and why integration in Europe has come about. Yet, more than half a century of study has failed to produce much agreement about the proper explanation for the evolution of European integration. Indeed, it is tempting to agree with Alan Milward's reflection that 'the intention [of Western European governments] of voluntarily achieving political unification . . . remains one of the most ill-understood aspects of recent history and present historical life' (2000:2).

At a time when the political significance of the European Union (EU) is increasing both internally, due to EU decision-making impacting more and more on areas of domestic life, and externally, due to the Union's enhanced scope for external action, it seems more important than ever to understand the origins and nature of European integration. To this end, this book collects and analyses a number of seminal theoretical works which have shaped the field of European integration studies and which continue to serve as bedrock for theoretical work on integration. The idea took shape during my first years of teaching a course entitled 'The History and Politics of European Integration' at the University of Cambridge. Although many of my students were chiefly interested in acquiring a better factual understanding of the EU's various institutions, including their formal competences and the role of different social actors within them, and were not initially theoretically inclined, our seminar discussions nonetheless kept circling back to major theoretical works. The role and function of specific institutions and actors can rarely be understood through purely empirical knowledge. Descriptive accounts of European integration are always grounded in a particular set of assumptions about the way the world operates. For example, it is often argued that integration has constituted a security system for Europe. The creation of supranational institutions such as the ECSC and the European Economic Community (EEC) was needed to safely reintegrate a defeated Germany into the European family of nations. Yet, this account is not an unbiased statement of truth. It relies upon a set of theoretical propositions that proclaim the centrality of security and 'grand' intergovernmental bargains to the conduct of European politics. Other scholars argue that integration has been driven chiefly by economic motives – above all by a desire to stimulate intraregional trade and investment. These are not merely issues of empirical disagreement; they reflect differing assumptions about key actors and the environment within which action takes place (Rosamond 2000:5). For this reason, a full understanding of European integration requires us to unmask and evaluate the underlying theoretical assumptions which inform descriptive accounts.

This book has two main goals. The first is to introduce the major theoretical works which have shaped the field of European integration studies since its inception, and to offer a critical analysis both of individual works and of the broader theoretical perspectives of which they form a part. To highlight the contributions of individual works, I have placed them in the context of both extant and contemporary writings and have supplemented them with extensive introductory comments, which reflect on their theoretical input in critical and hopefully novel ways. Moreover, to illustrate how individual works relate to broader theoretical perspectives, I have consulted a wide range of sources which are not usually included in overviews of European integration theory. By doing so, I hope to further the debate among different explanations for European integration. The second goal is to illustrate how European integration studies have developed in dialogue with other disciplines. Throughout its development, the field of European integration studies has imported insights from other social sciences such as international relations, comparative politics, international political economy, sociology and international law. For example, the work of Karl Deutsch, who pioneered the so-called 'communication theory' of integration during the 1950s, drew on concepts from sociology, anthropology and social psychology. More recently, the development of critical and constructivist approaches in international relations during the 1990s have left an important mark on European integration theory. At the same time, the study of European integration has also provided important inputs into other disciplines. The emergence of the first integration theories in the 1950s and 1960s revolutionized the study of International Relations (IR) by calling attention to non-state, transnational actors. During the 1970s, European integration studies were a pioneering site for the development of theories of international regimes and interdependence. Europe has also served as a rich testing ground for theoretical concepts developed in other contexts, such as theories of custom unions, optimal currency areas, etc. The works collected in this volume demonstrate, I believe, that European integration theories have been most successful when they have engaged other disciplines, using insights from related fields to shed light on various aspects of the integration process, and/or treating the EU as a laboratory for developing and testing theories of general applicability in domestic and international politics. It is my hope, therefore, that this book may serve as an inspiration to future European integration theorists to remain open to theoretical influences from the broader fields of political science and international studies.

This book has taken a while to put together. I owe a great deal of thanks to Steven Kennedy, my publisher at Palgrave Macmillan for his support and patience during the process, and to William Paterson and anonymous reviewers for their comments on earlier drafts. I also wish to thank the Jean Monnet Centre at the University of Cambridge for financial support for this project. Finally I owe a big thank you to Andrea Sangiovanni for his comments and encouragement throughout the process.

METTE EILSTRUP-SANGIOVANNI

A note on the editing of the texts

[. . .] within the text indicates that one or more words or sentences have been omitted from a paragraph

[. . . .] at the left margin indicates that one or more paragraphs have been omitted

Some references made in original works which did not have their sources given are marked here with an asterisk.

Introduction

Why do states integrate? What leads independent states to pool sovereignty in larger political communities? The origins and consequences of international integration have been a topic of political and scholarly debate at least since the beginning of the modern state system. During the seventeenth, eighteenth and nineteenth centuries, scholars sought to explain the emergence of regional unions such as the Dutch Republic, the Swiss Confederation and the German *Zollverein* by pointing to the economic benefits of regional free trade, the need to balance against external military threats, and the requirement of arbitration mechanisms to preserve peace among member states. Others advocated integration as a general means to abolish global anarchy and war. Famous blueprints for international federations designed to eliminate war among states were devised by Enlightenment thinkers such as the Abbé de Saint-Pierre (1712–17), Jean-Jacques Rousseau (1761) and Immanuel Kant (1795). In the late nineteenth and early twentieth centuries many intellectuals and politicians passionately advocated world federation as a way to escape violent struggles propagated by nationalism and to promote the rule of law among states.

For many scholars and politicians in the twentieth century, the main impetus to integration came from World War I. The horrors of the war led people to search for some form of international authority which could regulate interstate relations. Initially, the focal point was the newly created League of Nations. However, when the League collapsed, political attention turned to devising alternative, post-national, schemes whereby peace could be organized. These efforts gave rise to the so-called 'pre-theories' of integration: 'federalism', 'functionalism' and 'transactionalism'. Developed before the actual advent of integration in Europe (or elsewhere), the pre-theories of integration were heavily normative and prescriptive. Their goal was not to explain variation in existing processes of integration but to devise blueprints for future projects. Like their eighteenth- and nineteenth-century predecessors, the chief aim was the elimination of war. Federalists sought to delegate power 'upwards' to a central authority in order to secure peace. Functionalists, on the other hand, rejected the idea of concentrating power in a new political authority on the grounds that it would merely reproduce the dangers of nationalism at a higher level. Instead, they advocated a sideways dispersal of authority to international orga-

1

nizations and functional agencies, thereby undermining allegiance to the nation state. Transactionalists, finally, offered a vision of integration that was essentially compatible with the continuation of sovereign statehood. The goal was not to banish the sovereign state but to end the 'state of war' between nations through the creation of international 'security communities' in which member states – due to feelings of shared identities – would no longer regard war as a possible policy tool.

The focus of the integration pre-theories was on devising ideal designs for worldwide international integration. Since the mid-1950s, however, scholarly debates about the causes and benefits of integration have centred primarily on a concrete (and geographically more limited) political experiment: the European Communities/European Union. While the pre-theories of integration were concerned with devising hypothetical schemes for international cooperation on the basis of normative considerations, the emergence of institutions of economic integration in post-war Europe offered political scientists a real setting in which to 'observe the actual processes whereby political actors move beyond the nation-state as a basic framework for action' (Lindberg 1963: 4). The birth of the European Coal and Steel Community (ECSC) in 1952 and the European Economic Community (EEC) in 1958 triggered wide-ranging scholarly debates about the conditions leading to the successful emergence of supranational institutions like the High Authority of the ECSC. At the centre of the controversy were a series of questions regarding the origins and future direction of the European Communities. Were the major determinants of integration essentially economic, social or political? What was the end point of the integration process? Would Europe develop into a federation? Or would the Community remain effectively an international regime? Finally, was European integration a unique phenomenon – a historically contingent outcome of two world wars, which had torn asunder the continent and destroyed the foundations of the European nation state – or was integration in Europe a harbinger of a more general trend toward the organization of the world into larger regional blocs?

Perhaps ironically, the early European integration theories were primarily developed by American scholars (though many of them – like Carl Friedrich and Karl Deutsch – were European refugees who settled in the United States). The post-war behavioural revolution in American social science led to a focus on theoretically orientated research rather than the more historically and normatively orientated approaches which tended to dominate European academia. Social theories were seen as 'scientific' devices for generating testable hypotheses which could be verified through empirical research. In this context, the experiment in European integration offered an ideal site both to test existing theories – of peaceful community building, of economic integration, of nation-building, etc. – and to develop new theoretical perspectives. The dominance of American perspectives was also facilitated by the fact that American political scientists tended to enjoy generous funding for projects, which were likely to be useful to US policy makers. The peaceful integration of Europe was seen as such a project.

Among the most influential theories of the time was neofunctionalism, developed by Ernst Haas, Leon Lindberg and others. Taking their starting point in the experiences of the ECSC and EEC, neofunctionalists sought to explain how economic cooperation would spread from one sector to another and would generate demand for political integration. Their main argument was that the creation of supranational institutions would advance integration by pointing states in the direction of joint interests. This argument was opposed by intergovernmentalists who denied any independent causal role for supranational institutions. State executives, they argued, remain the chief arbiters of integration and the interests of national governments tightly circumscribe the authority and influence of supranational organizations. This dispute between supranationalists and intergovernmentalists has been a permanent fixture of debates on European integration since the 1960s and continues to shape the field today through revised versions of the classic integration theories. For example, the period following the completion of the Single European Act in 1987 and the Treaty of Maastricht in 1992 saw a revival and refinement of neofunctionalism as well as the introduction of a new form of 'liberal intergovernmentalism', which affirms the dominance of governmental actors but extends classic intergovernmentalism by theorizing the domestic origins of state preferences. Another recent perspective – 'new institutionalism' – also bears on the supranationalist/intergovernmentalist debate by stressing the role of institutions as important players in the integration process rather than passive tools in the hands of state executives.

The dispute between supranationalists and intergovernmentalists over the role and impact of regional institutions is no longer the only fault line in European integration debates, however. During the past 15 years, a number of rival perspectives have emerged which challenge established integration theories. The late-1980s saw the (re-)emergence of perspectives drawn from comparative politics. Unlike IR-based theories which focus on explaining why states collaborate, comparative political scientists argue that integration in Europe has advanced so far that the EU must be studied as a *polity* rather than an instance of international cooperation. Analytical tools developed in the context of the study of IR are therefore seen to be inappropriate. Another crucial development has been the introduction in the mid-1990s of constructivist and critical perspectives on integration. In contrast to 'rationalist' theories such as neofunctionalism and intergovernmentalism, which

Table 1 *Major theoretical approaches to regional integration*

Phase/Approach	Main Themes	Integrative dynamic	End product
Phase I: Normative pre-integration theories 1920s–1960s			
Federalism		Intergovernmental constitutional bargaining or convention of a constituent assembly	Federal state
Functionalism	Why is integration desirable? How can it best be designed and promoted?	Creation of international functional organizations which take over key functions of nation states	International web of depoliticized functional agencies
Transactionalism		Learning and socialization through communication	International security community
Phase II: Explanatory integration theories 1950s onwards			
Neofunctionalism	Why does integration take place? How can specific integration outcomes be explained?	Spillover of cooperation from purely technical to increasingly political sectors	Supranational political community
Intergovern-mentalism		Converging national interests form basis for intergovernmental treaty bargains	International organization
Phase III: Neo-institutionalist and governance approaches 1980s onwards			
New institutionalist approaches			
a) *Rational institutionalism*		Institutions enable and constrain the actions of self-interested actors. Institutions intervene between actors' (exogenous) preferences and behaviour	

Table 1 *continued*

Phase/Approach	Main Themes	Integrative dynamic	End product
b) *Historical institutionalism*	What is the impact of EC/EU institutions on European governance and integration?	Integration is shaped by increasing returns and unintended consequences of existing institutional arrangements. Institutions are *intervening* as well as *independent* variables which constrain and define actors' preferences	International organization/supranational community
c) *Sociological institutionalism*		Institutions are constitutive for actors' identities and interests. Institutions are *independent* variables which constitute preferences and behaviour	
Comparative and Governance Approaches	What kind of political system is the EU? How can EU political processes be described and understood?	Informal integration which may or may not be captured in formal treaty bargains	A European 'polity'

Phase IV: Constructivist and critical perspectives 1990s onwards

Constructivist and critical perspectives	How does integration develop? How does integration affect the identities and interests of social actors?	Socialization through the diffusion of ideas, norms and institutions and through discursive processes	International society or polity based on shared and mutually constituted identities and meanings

emphasize material incentives for integration, constructivists stress the role of 'intersubjectivity' and 'socialization mechanisms' in driving integration. Over time, they argue, integration changes agents' identities and consequently alters their interests and behaviour. Rationalist theories, which tend to treat state interests as exogenous to interaction fail to appreciate the transformative effect of integration on state identities and therefore paint a much too static and simplistic picture of the integration process. Finally, during the 1990s a number of alternative perspectives such as feminist and post-structuralist theories, as well as normative theories of citizenship, have been applied to the study of integration, adding to the theoretical breadth of the field.

This reader aims to provide an introduction to key theoretical debates about the origins, nature, process and implications of integration in Europe. The goal is to illustrate the historical origin and development of rival theoretical perspectives on integration and to take stock of the discipline. Several excellent books have been published in recent years which offer detailed interpretative accounts of the major theoretical approaches to integration (see e.g. Rosamond 2000; Wiener and Diez 2004). My intention is not to duplicate such textbook overviews of integration theory. Rather, I wish to present, in their original form, some of the most influential scholarly works that have grounded and shaped the academic debate on integration in Europe over the past 50 years and to show how they relate to each other. There are two main reasons for collecting these works in a reader. First, while contemporary scholars make frequent reference to classic studies of integration and incorporate key insights from previous works, past theoretical frameworks are rarely explored in any detail. As new generations of theorists build on extant theories, part of the nuance of earlier work is lost as complex arguments are reduced to a few stylized points. Moreover, as we accept certain insights into mainstream debate, we often forget the alternatives. For example, as neofunctionalism became the leading theory of European integration in the 1950s and 1960s, the earlier functionalist approach to international organization was largely forgotten. With it scholars lost sight for many years of some of the key questions which animated functionalist debate, such as the possibility of specifying and satisfying welfare needs outside a participatory political framework. Revisiting past theoretical frameworks and tracing their influence on contemporary work is not merely of antiquarian and historical interest. A basic contention of this book is that past integration theories hold great relevance for evaluating and broadening contemporary scholarship.

A second reason for collecting major theoretical works on regional integration in a reader is the collective insights they hold for those who wish to understand the development of EU institutions and policies. Theoretical accounts offer an interpretation of the history and rationale behind key institutional developments in the EU and distil practical lessons for future efforts at deepening integration. Integration theory also holds crucial lessons for scholars and policy makers interested in other forms of international cooperation and organization. Theories of European integration not only throw light on the European experience but also provide insights concerning more general questions of the pre-conditions for, the motivations toward, and the impacts of international institutional cooperation. Indeed, as the following chapters illustrate, the study of European integration has traditionally been a harbinger of future theoretical trends in the wider field of IR, such as theories of international regimes, interdependence and transnational relations. Moreover, as Andrew Moravcsik (1997) observes, the EU today provides a rich laboratory for studying issues only just emerging elsewhere, such as international regulatory governance, binding inter-state legislative procedures, and multilevel governance.

This introductory chapter begins by discussing the meaning of the term 'integration'. It then continues with some thoughts on the extent to which theoretical concepts developed in the context of European integration studies are applicable also to other instances of regional or international cooperation and organization. It concludes with a brief overview of the structure of the book.

The Meaning of Integration

In order to evaluate different integration theories we must first arrive at a clear understanding of what is meant by 'integration'. This is by no means a straightforward task. There is no consensus definition of 'regional integration'. In fact, much of the scholarly debate revolving around integration in Europe and elsewhere is attributable to the fact that people mean different things when they use the concept. According to one of the first integration scholars, Karl Deutsch, integration refers to 'the probability that conflicts will be resolved peacefully'. As such, it is a *condition* or a *state of affairs*. Others have found it more helpful to define integration as a *process*. According to Ernst Haas conceptualizations of integration as a condition fail to provide us with the necessary tools to make a clear distinction between the situation prior to integration and the situation prevailing during the process, thus obscuring the role of social change. He therefore defines integration as 'the process whereby political actors in several distinct national settings are persuaded to shift their loyalties, expectations and political activities toward a new centre, whose institutions possess or demand jurisdiction over the pre-existing national states' (Haas 1958c: 627). The end result of this process, he suggests, is 'a new political community, superimposed over the pre-existing ones' (Haas 1968:16).

A third definition that also views integration as a process but avoids presupposing a specific end point is offered by another prominent neo-functionalist scholar, Leon Lindberg, who defines integration simply as 'the development of devices and processes for arriving at collective decisions by means other than autonomous action by national governments'. On this definition, political integration refers to the practices of *sharing* and *delegating* decision-making and can be achieved without moving toward a new 'political community' as defined by Haas (Lindberg 1963: 5–6). This definition is closer in spirit to conceptualizations preferred by most intergovernmentalist scholars who tend to focus on political manifestations of integration (i.e. the development of institutions for joint decision-making) rather than social integration and who do not envision movement toward a central, federal-type polity.

Scholars have differed not only on whether to define integration as a condition or a process but also on the substantive content of that process or condition. In other words, what does it mean to say that a region is either integrating or integrated? Is the nature of integration *political* unification, *economic* unification, or a combination of the two? Or is the content of integration a change in *social* attitudes – a growing feeling of common identity? Different theories propose different answers to this question. Broadly speaking, definitions and conceptualizations fall into three main categories: (1) studies focused on the attitudes and opinions of elites and other groups in members states; (2) studies focused on transactions – whether physical (such as economic exchange) or communicative – between member states; and (3) studies emphasizing the growth of political institutions at the community level (see Caporaso 1971: 229). Some definitions span several of these categories. For example, Haas's definition of integration as 'the process whereby political actors in several distinct national settings are persuaded to shift their loyalties, expectations and political activities toward a new centre' lumps together several potential indicators of integration: shifting loyalties (a social process), political activities (a political process), and the substitution of new institutions for traditional governance structures (institution-building). The problem with such broad-ranging definitions is that they may obscure the relationship between different indicators (Nye 1968a: 858). Do changing loyalties make political integration possible? Or do loyalties change as a result of the building of new political institutions? How can we discover the relationship between attitudinal change and political integration if the two are built into the same concept?

The lack of agreement on how to define integration has led to much critical self-reflection among students of integration (see e.g. Haas 1970, 1971: 18; Lindberg 1963; Nye 1968a; Puchala 1972). The fact that analysts work with different conceptions of both the process and outcome of integration, it is argued, makes it difficult to compare their findings. Whereas some studies emphasize the building of new institutions, others focus on elite interests, and yet others on changing popular and elite identities. What constitutes a key indicator of integration on one model may be irrelevant to another. Moreover, as Ernst Haas (1971: 18) points out, the lack of agreement on the dependent variable – integration – makes it difficult to identify and justify a set of relevant independent variables and to explore their hypothesized interdependence. So long as scholars insist on separate definitions, it is difficult to advance collective knowledge.

The difficulties of defining integration are most famously described by Donald Puchala (1972: 268) who likened the study of integration to the tale of a group of blind men trying to discover what an elephant looks like. Each blind man touched a different part of the animal, and each concluded that the elephant had the shape of the part he had touched. The man who felt the trunk concluded that an elephant must be tall and slender and so forth. As a result, they all reached very different conclusions about its appearance and they carried on a fervent debate. Puchala's much cited analogy aptly illustrates the problem of different starting points for analysis. Yet, while it is certainly important to be conscious of the fact that different approaches conceptualize integration differently and therefore depart from different analytical starting points, the argument made here is that this is not per se a problem for the collective generation of knowledge. After all, few concepts in political science are subject to a consensus definition. The meaning of concepts such as 'revolution', 'democracy' or even 'war' or 'peace' is passionately contested. Different approaches may look at different dimensions or manifestations of the phenomenon of integration but this does not mean they are doomed to talk past one another. In Puchala's account, problems of collective learning arise because each blind man is convinced that the entire animal must look like the part he is examining. Each man is seeking to extrapolate from a few rudimentary observations to a definition of the nature of the whole beast. If instead the men exchanged information about the various starting points for their investigations, they might be able to combine their knowledge and piece together a larger picture that would look more like the actual elephant. To some degree this is what is happening in current integration studies. At the time Puchala presented his critique, the field was dominated by a small number of 'grand theories', each of which relied on a few basic assumptions, in order to generalize about integration as a whole. Today, there appears to be a move away from competing grand theories toward middle-range theories that try to capture particular processes and outcomes. Such theories hold the promise of being more easily combined to provide a fuller picture of the subject of integration.

International Organization, Political System or *sui generis*?

Different definitions of integration reflect different theoretical and disciplinary interests. In the context of European studies, they also reflect different answers to the question: Of what is European integration an instance? Is the EU an international institution similar to but more institutionally advanced than other international institutions such as the UN, WTO or NATO? Or is European integration a unique phenomenon not replicated anywhere else in the world?

Clearly, this is a question with considerable implications for how to study and theorize about the EU. Broadly speaking, scholars divide into two main camps; those who view European integration as a singular phenomenon and those who view it as an instance of a more general class of phenomena. Those belonging to the first group tend to describe the EU as a unique adventure, emerging from an exceptional set of geopolitical and historical circumstances. For example, leading historian of European integration, Alan Milward, has declared that 'the EC is the product of a set of specific historical events, from whose study no long-run trends or predictions about the future of government or of countries can be safely deduced' (1992: 20). The upshot of this view is that European integration requires its own specialized theory. One often hears that, for example, the historical backdrop of European integration and the density and complexity of its institutional base makes integration in Europe qualitatively different from cooperation elsewhere in the world and hence rules out a comparative basis for theorizing its effects and causes.

Treating European integration as *sui generis*, however, gives rise to several methodological problems. First, if the EU is truly unique then theoretical propositions will be difficult to test in the EU context because of the well-known problems of testing hypotheses on a single case (Pollack 1997b). This predicament is often referred to as the $n = 1$ problem. Second, as Milward suggests, if the EU is exceptional this implies that any findings to emerge from EU studies will not be generalizable beyond Europe to other settings. It is partly in response to such methodological challenges that many scholars have sought to conceptualize European integration as part of a larger class of phenomena. We can identify at least three distinct ways in which they have done so. First, some have conceptualized integration as an instance of nation-building. This was the approach favoured by Karl Deutsch and his colleagues at Princeton (Deutsch 1953a, 1953b; Deutsch et al. 1957). International political unification, they suggested, is a phenomenon quite similar to the growth of nation states. Both the welding of tribes into peoples, the welding of peoples into nations, and the welding of nations into international communities follow a similar pattern of development, starting with the growth of communication grids, evolving through increasing interactions and communication, and leading to the development of joint perspectives and identities. Hence valuable lessons can be learned from comparing cases of nation-building and regional integration.

A second option, popular among IR theorists, is to view the EU as an instance of an international organization or regime, which can be compared at the macro level with other international organizations. There are at least two ways in which one can think of European integration from the point of view of the study of international organization. First, the EU may be treated as an instance of an international regime orientated toward economic and political cooperation. In this way, the EU can usefully be studied alongside other international organizations such as the OECD or the WTO. Second, the European project can be studied more specifically as an instance of regionalism in the global economy (see Puchala 1997; Marks 1997). As such it can be linked to the emergence and growth of other schemes for regional economic integration, such as the North American Free Trade Agreement (NAFTA), the Asian Pacific Economic Cooperation (APEC), the Arab League and Mercosur. In both cases, the questions guiding research on the EU will be similar to the questions guiding the general study of international organizations, namely: Why do states cooperate? What factors explain specific cooperative outcomes?

A third option is to treat the EU not as an instance of international cooperation but as a 'polity'. This is the position taken by a growing number of comparative political scientists. As integration has advanced over the past 50 years, they argue, the EU's complex institutional structure has come to resemble that of a modern nation state more than a conventional international regime. The relevant level of comparison, therefore, is not to other international organizations but to domestic political systems.

The disposition to treat the EU either as *sui generis* (an N of 1) or to search for a comparative basis (N > 1) has varied greatly over time and across different segments of the field of integration studies. As we shall see in parts I and II, historical-comparative studies were quite common among early integration theorists. In *Political Community and the North Atlantic Area* (1957) (see Chapter 3) Karl Deutsch and his colleagues drew on the experiences of multinational empires such as the Austro-Hungarian Empire, federal nation states such as Switzerland and Germany, and international organizations like NATO to examine the processes of international community formation. In *The Uniting of Europe* (1958a) (see Chapter 4) Ernst Haas studied integration processes in the context of the Nordic Council, NATO and the Western European Union (WEU), and in *Beyond the Nation State* (1964) he analysed the International Labour Organization (ILO) to discover the dynamics of international integration. Haas and Schmitter (1964) applied neofunctionalist theory to Latin America and Joseph Nye in *International Regionalism* (1968b) and *Peace in Parts* (1971b) undertook cross-regional comparative studies of integration efforts in the Americas, East Africa and the Middle East. After the mid-1970s, however, studies of regional and international integration were increasingly conducted within the narrow context of the European Communities. The efforts of particularly neofunctionalist scholars to extend their theoretical framework to regions outside Europe failed to generate results. Entities such as Mercosur, the Association of Southeast Asian Nations (ASEAN) and Asia-Pacific Economic Cooperation (APEC) proved simply too dissimilar from the EC to serve as a basis for systematic comparison. As a result, Haas declared that neofunctionalism could only be addressed at explaining a specific, time-bound, and non-recurrent event: the integration of post-war Western Europe.

The result of treating European integration as *sui generis* was that, over time, integration studies came to be viewed increasingly as a separate subfield of the study of IR. To many observers this has been a detrimental development. The lack of engagement with other fields, they charge, has hindered theoretical advancement by closing off the discipline from rich theoretical developments in international and comparative politics (see e.g. Haas 1975, 1976; Hooghe 2003; Moravcsik 1997). It is partly in reaction to such charges that scholars since the mid-1990s have sought in various ways to readjoin European integration studies to the general study of IR and comparative politics. One move has been to argue that European integration can in fact be studied alongside other instances of regional integration. An example of this approach is Walter Mattli's *The Logic of Regional Integration* (1999) in which he uses variation in integration processes across regions and across history to gain clues as to what drives the process. Another move has been to break down the European integration process into separate underlying dimensions, which can be studied alongside other similar cases (see Marks 1997; Moravcsik 1997; Pollack 1997b). This approach is exemplified by the work of Andrew Moravcsik who applies general theories of international relations and international political economy to explain particular aspects of the European integration process (preference formation, interstate bargaining, institutional design, etc.). Finally, a growing number of scholars have invoked policy-making perspectives, developed largely in the context of domestic politics to explain discrete processes and phenomena associated with European integration such as parliamentary voting behaviour, regulatory policy making, transnational interest group formation, public opinion, etc. These trends bode well for the future of the field, opening up new possibilities for theoretical advancement through comparative studies.

Content and Plan of the Book

The aim of this book is to provide an introduction to the key works which have fuelled and shaped theoretical debate on European integration. In selecting representative works I have given precedence to those interventions I feel best illuminate underlying theoretical disputes. The list of works featured and discussed in this book obviously does not provide an exhaustive introduction to the field of integration theory. First, there are several theoretical perspectives outside the mainstream of current EU studies which cannot be dealt with at any length here. I do not, for example, discuss feminist theories or those normative theories that address issues of citizenship or nationalism. Also, within each of the represented debates only a few works have been singled out for reproduction, leaving aside many valuable contributions. To give the reader a sense of the wider debates, each part opens with an introduction to the selected works that highlights their specific theoretical contribution and places them in the context of contemporary scholarship. A short guide to further reading allows the reader to explore the subjects covered in more detail. Individual scholarly contributions then follow, in almost all cases slightly edited to fit the format of the book.

The focus of this book is on integration *theory*. My aim is not to duplicate narratives about the historical development of European integration. Rather, I wish to explore how such developments have been reflected in social and political theory. However, academic ideas and debate can seldom be divorced from the social reality in which they emerge. Indeed, scholarly work on European integration is often closely bound up with the unfolding history of the EC. To facilitate understanding of this interplay, the reader may wish to consult one of the many available chronologies of the historical evolution of European integration. A chronology of European integration can be found on the EU resource area on Palgrave Macmillan's web site at http://www.palgrave.com/politics/eu/chronology.asp

The book is divided into six parts, each of which examines a major theoretical debate. The chronological presentation of arguments grouped into discrete 'debates' may seem to suggest a linear, unidirectional development of the field, with theory development advancing from one 'grand debate' to the next. For purposes of presentation this is a useful depiction. Yet, in reality, the distinction between various debates is often less clear-cut than this division suggests, with ideas being introduced, forgotten or rejected, and then reintroduced. For example, the so-called 'comparativist turn' in regional integration studies in the late 1980s was to a large degree anticipated by neofunctionalist scholarship in the 1960s and 1970s. Similarly, transactionalist scholars during the 1950s foreshadowed many themes taken up by constructivists in the 1990s. I seek to bring out such nuances in the discussion and analysis of theoretical contributions at the beginning of each part.

I begin, in Part I, by examining the early pre-theories of integration, federalism, functionalism and transactionalism. Developed during the interwar period and in the years immediately following World War II, these approaches respond in various ways to the experience of violent conflict and to the political and economic crisis of the post-war European nation state. Each approach imputed violent conflict to the anarchical nature of the interstate system and each focused on reducing the likelihood of war through the building of regional or international communities.

Part II looks at the development of neofunctionalist theory during the 1950s and 1960s and presents the intergovernmentalist critique formulated by, among others, Stanley Hoffmann (1958, 1964, 1966) and Roger Hansen (1969). Three main issues are at stake in this debate: How does integration proceed? How far can it go (i.e. can it extend from economic to security-related issues)? What is the role of supranational actors in moving the process along?

Part III illustrates the continuation of the long-standing debate between neofunctionalists and intergovernmentalists in the wake of agreement on the Single European Act (1987). This part also discusses the introduction of two so-called 'new institutionalist' perspectives – rational choice institutionalism and historical institutionalism – which advance the neofunctionalist/intergovernmentalist debate by examining the specific conditions under which institutions may shape policy outcomes (A third form of institutionalism – sociological institutionalism – is discussed in Part V).

Parts IV and V turn to more recent approaches to integration. Part IV examines the (re-)introduction of comparative politics perspectives which maintain that the EU is best studied as a form of polity rather than as an instance of international cooperation. This part also discusses the introduction of 'multilevel governance' approaches, which conceive of the EU as a unique 'postmodern' governance system. Part V provides an overview of recent constructivist and critical approaches. In contrast to the rationalist basis of most traditional integration theories these approaches focus on the relevance of ideas, norms and identities for international politics and examine the interaction of agents and structure.

Part VI concludes and looks to the future of European integration studies. In addition to the closing reflections of the editor, this final part features a short essay by Ben Rosamond, which addresses some common analytical problems in the field and discusses the merits of looking to classical integration theories as a basis for future theoretical innovation.

PART I

Interwar and Post-war Ideas of Europe

Featured works

- Altiero Spinelli and Ernesto Rossi (1944) *For a Free and United Europe. A Draft Manifesto* (Edizioni del Movimento Italiano per la Federazione Europe).

- David Mitrany (1943) 'A Working Peace System: An Argument for the Functional Development of International Organization', reprinted in Mitrany (1975) *The Functional Theory of Politics* (London: Martin Robertson & Co.).

- Karl Deutsch et al. (1957) *Political Community and the North Atlantic Area: International Organization in the Light of Historical Experience* (Princeton: Princeton University Press).

Pre-theories of International Integration

Numerous thinkers over the centuries have advocated international integration as a solution to universal anarchy and war. Saint-Pierre, Rousseau and Kant are frequently cited as intellectual ancestors of integration theory. However, the direct forerunners of modern integration theories are the classic 'pre-theories' of integration – federalism, functionalism and transactionalism – developed during the interwar and early post-war period.

The years following World War I were marked by considerable activism in support of European unity. New institutions for economic integration sprang forth, including a European Customs Union in 1924 and an International Steel Cartel among German, French and British producers in 1926. At the same time, ideas for political union spread among intellectual elites. Some groups advocated integration as a way to restore Europe's global position. The destruction of the war and the surge in American political and economic power had raised fears about Europe's competitive advantage, thereby increasing the appeal of a continental union. Others took a broader outlook. For them integration was a way to rule out war. Often found among members of the peace movement and the political left, such proponents of integration tended to look beyond Europe to an international federation, whether Atlantic-centred or universal in outlook. A prominent example is Clarence Streit, *Union Now: A Proposal for a Federal Union of Democracies of the North Atlantic* (1939).

It is against the backdrop of these political currents that the first theories of integration were born. Developed in the wake of World War I, the early theories of integration show a deep awareness of the dangers of nationalism and economic protectionism. War is seen as an inevitable product of an international system that divides peoples into self-reliant states and lets them compete unhindered for scarce resources. The focus is therefore on devising strategies for replacing international anarchy with some form of international society that regulates interstate relations. Three features unite the classic pre-theories of integration. First, they all embark from the observation that the problems of contemporary society have taken on dimensions that reach beyond the nation state and call for solutions at an international level.

17

Second, the pre-theories share a faith in the ability of international institutions to suppress conflict. The non-rational, violent aspects of human nature can be controlled, it is hoped, by appropriate institutional or social structures. Third, they all look beyond Europe as a locus for integration. While European unity is often endorsed as a starting point for a process of international integration, the ultimate goal is worldwide rather than regional governance.

Beyond these similarities, however, the pre-theories differ greatly in their visions of the end goal of integration and their prescriptions for how to get there. Federalists want to transfer the sovereignty of individual states to a central authority. The goal is a contractual world government that would reduce the risk of war by abolishing the existence of the sovereign state. To functionalists, the formula for peace is not federation but a gradual expansion of economic cooperation among states. By improving economic welfare, it is thought, one can remove an important pretext for international conflict. Transactionalists, by contrast, offer a sociologically grounded vision of integration. Their aim is to end interstate conflict though the formation of international 'security communities' in which feelings of trust and mutual identification means that member states will no longer consider war. We thus see in this early debate a distinction between 'constitutional' (political), 'functional' (economic) and 'sociological' conceptions of integration – distinctions that continue to mark the field today.

Federalism

Federalism – from its early origins to recent applications – remains the most candidly political and activist of the classical integration theories. Espoused by political leaders such as Altiero Spinelli, Alcide de Gasperi, Paul-Henri Spaak and Walter Hallstein, post-war European federalism presents itself more as a political movement than a theoretical approach. Even those theorists who were concerned with describing and explaining patterns of federal integration, such as Carl Friedrich (1953, 1964), were often active in drafting constitutions for federal unions, thereby crossing the line to political activism (Haas 1970: 624). Today, federalist ideals continue to inform political visions of the EU. For example, the 1992 Treaty of European Union (TEU) is seen by many as a first step toward a future federal Europe, and federal ideas also permeated the more recent Convention on the Future of Europe (2002–2003).

The origins of federalist thought are long and complex. As Rosamond (2000: 25) notes, the federalist legacy amounts to a mixture of governing schemes contrived by political philosophers and activists from the Enlightenment to the present, as well as practical lessons drawn from existing federal states like the United States, Germany, Switzerland and Canada. It is no surprise, therefore, that definitions of federalism vary. However, three common traits can be identified. First, all definitions of federalism rely on a division of powers between two or more levels of government. Typically, this division leads to a partitioning of functions between a federal core and its constituent units. The policy areas commonly reserved for the central government are foreign affairs, defence and macroeconomic policy, whereas member states often retain the power to act autonomously in areas of public policy, such as transport, education and public health. Second, in contrast to a league or confederation where the supranational government is chosen by and accountable to member states, in federal systems the central authority operates directly upon citizens (Friedrich 1964: 14; King 1982). Third, all definitions stress that the central government must come into being as a result of the voluntary transfer of powers from constituent members rather than through the use of force. This element explicitly separates federalism from 'universal monarchy' or empire.

Political philosophers have justified federalism on moral grounds arguing that it promotes liberty by allowing freedom of action for small groups or units and that it enables unity in pluralist societies by letting territorial or cultural communities be self-governing while at the same time facilitating collaboration between them to solve common problems (Burgess 2000: 25). Others have viewed it as a way for small polities to pool power resources in order to be able to survive external threats or to compete more effectively against foreign powers (e.g. Forsyth 1996; Riker 1994). Both motives have been frequently used to justify federation in Europe. As an approach to international organization, however, classical federalism presents itself first and foremost as a method to abolish war. The basic premise is that the existence of a multitude of sovereign states guided by principles of self-help and balance of power is a primary cause of war. The only way to rule out conflict is therefore to combine states into ever-larger units.

The federal approach to international organization gained wide popularity in interwar Europe. Among the first to popularize the ideal of a federal Europe was Count Coudenhove-Kalergi (1894–1972), publicist and founder of the Pan-Europa Movement. Born and raised in Austria, Coudenhove-Kalergi was deeply influenced by the collapse of the Austro-Hungarian empire after World War I, which persuaded him that federation was the only way to keep Europe from further disintegration. In his book *Pan Europe* (1923), Coudenhove-Kalergi put forward a vision of a 'United States of Europe' based on a republican constitution. This union would be one of five regional unions under the League of Nations and would not only ensure peaceful relations within Europe but also serve to enhance Europe's position vis-à-vis other regional groups, in particular the Pan-American Union. Another federalist pioneer was the Marquess of Lothian (Philip Kerr, 1882–1940). In contrast to Coudenhove-Kalergi's European focus, Kerr was committed to international federalism. A co-founder of the Federal Union Movement, his essay 'Pacifism Is not Enough nor Patriotism either' (1935) is considered one of the key texts in the history of international federalism. In it we find a clear assertion of the federalist conviction that growing international interdependence runs counter to the sovereign independence of states. We also see manifest the idea that the primary cause of war is not nationalism or ideological conflict among states but the existence of the sovereign state itself.

Whereas the interwar federalist movement was confined to a small intellectual and political elite, the horrors of World War II gave added impetus to federalist ideas – whether European or international in outlook. A federal solution to the problem of post-war peace found particular support among the European resistance movements. During the war, anti-fascist resistance groups in many countries devised schemes for European federation. (For an excellent selection of such plans see Lipgens, 1985). Among the most prominent figures of the post-war federalist movement was former communist and member of the Italian resistance, Altiero Spinelli. Confined by Mussolini to the island of Ventotene he and fellow prisoner Ernesto Rossi drafted the manifesto *For a Free and United Europe* (1944) (see Chapter 1) in which they argued that the ideology of national independence, once a powerful stimulus to progress and social solidarity within states, had degenerated into totalitarianism and imperialist doctrine. The manifesto – which later became the action programme for the Italian *Movimento Federalista Europeo* founded by Spinelli in 1943 – concluded that the division of Europe into separate nation states was a key cause of war and called for a European federation.

Federalists believe that international federation – i.e. the creation of a constitutional rule-making authority that divides power between federal, national and local authorities – is the only means to achieve peace and prosperity. The best way to tame power is by ensuring that it is not vested in any one institution or geographic point but is divided between many centres so as to create a system of 'checks and balances'. However, they differ profoundly on the methods to be used in achieving a federal state. Classic federalists tend to favour a rapid constitutional approach. On this view, political integration is seen as a dramatic act of constitutional revolution, initiated by political elites and decided through formal rules (Pentland 1975:12). Not all share this radical, top-down perspective, however. Another perspective – espoused in particular by Altiero Spinelli and fellow Italian federalist Mario Albertini – holds that integration must be cultivated as a broad popular, indeed a revolutionary, movement (see Levi 1991: 222;

Pistone 1991: 351–4; Spinelli and Rossi 1944). On this view, a precondition for federal union is the existence of a popular movement that puts pressure on elites to transfer power to a higher authority. Without such pressure from below, a federal government cannot claim to be a legitimate representative of the people. A third approach is 'incremental' or 'functional' federalism. Often associated with Jean Monnet, the French government official and architect of the ECSC, incremental federalism views political integration not as a result of radical constitutional change but as a gradual process of reciprocal adaptation of national institutions. By forging special functional links between states in a way that does not directly challenge national sovereignty, federalism can be slowly introduced (Burgess 2000; Pinder 1986; also Spinelli 1968). This gradual approach to federal union is close in spirit to neofunctionalism (see Part II), and won increasing repute among post-war federalists as hopes for the rapid political unification of Europe were dashed with the failure of the European Defence Community (EDC) and European Political Community (EPC) in 1954. It is important to note, however, that even on an incremental federalist view, integration remains a constitutional process, forged by formal rules, and dominated by political elites.

The emphasis on formal political and constitutional change puts federalism directly at odds with functionalism. Where functionalists depict integration as a process of growing economic, social and technical cooperation in areas removed from political oversight, federalists firmly reject the idea that it is possible to integrate specific sectors – economic, social or scientific – of international society without creating a common democratic government to manage such cooperation (Levi 1991: 222; Pistone 1991: 355). They also deny the transactionalist conjecture that sociological change by itself can trigger political unity. On a federalist view, economic cooperation and sociological change are anticipated results of political integration – not a necessary or sufficient precondition for it (see Spinelli 1968: 11).

As an approach to international organization, federalism has come under severe criticism. Writers in the realist tradition such as E. H. Carr (1939, 1945), Hans Morgenthau (1948), and Stanley Hoffmann (1956) warned against the utopian belief that there is a fundamental harmony of interest among nations that can be embodied in a world state or a series of regional federal unions. They cautioned that while world government might theoretically be conducive to peace, it would be precarious in the absence of the emergence of an underlying 'world community' – an unlikely prospect given the present strength of national loyalties (Morgenthau 1948: 341–50). They also questioned the idea that existing nation states would willingly surrender sovereignty to a new political authority. It would be a mistake to label such views 'anti-integrationist'. State-centrists like Hoffmann and Carr accepted the normative ideal of integration but urged caution: pushing too far too fast would have negative consequences as governments, jealous of their sovereignty, would turn their back on international institutions. Only by respecting the bounds of state sovereignty could one build effective international organizations for keeping peace and advancing economic growth (see Hoffmann 1956: 365). As such, their views are more compatible with the functionalist ideal of integration, as we shall see below.

Another line of criticism concerns the feasibility of federation. Is it really possible to create international unity simply through an act of institution building? Has history not clearly demonstrated that multi-national federations have a tendency to collapse, as did the Austro-Hungarian Empire, the USSR and Yugoslavia? (See in particular Malcolm 1995. It can be objected that the 'multinational federations' to which Malcolm refers were not true federations. However, his point about the difficulty of creating and sustaining political cohesion among different national groups still stands). And even if multinational federa-tion can endure is it not naive to believe that simply combining states into larger units will remove the risk of war? As Mitrany (1948: 351) points out, while federation may bring peace within a group, there is no evidence that it contributes to peace between it and other groups (see also Claude 1956; Forsyth 1996). Even a world federation would not banish war, since there would be plenty of opportunities for civil strife among various subunits.

Viewed as a theoretical approach, federalism suffers from a lack of both descriptive and interpretative power. For federalism the main focus is on the end product of integration rather than the means by which to get there. This has often implied greater focus on the design of federal institutions than on understanding the dynamics of the inte-gration process. As Haas observes, a major premise of federalist theory is that the needs of peoples will (or ought to?) result in the creation of federal regimes (1970: 624). There is no explicit focus on the antecedent conditions or causal factors that contribute to integration. A federative process essentially comes about because of a conviction among elites in various countries that union is advantageous – how this conviction arises and is spread among elites is left unexplained. Or as Noel Malcolm quips, many federalists seem to believe in a 'kind of cartographic mysticism that intuits that certain large areas of the map are crying out to merge as single geopolitical units' (1995: 53). Such critiques are largely justified in regard to early federalist writings. Yet, later studies often take a less ideological starting point. Wheare (1963) identifies a set of antecedent conditions for successful federation, including a need for common defence, economies of scale and prior political association. Riker (1994) explains the formation of federations in terms of the perceived costs and benefits to states of aggregating resources and Friedrich (1964) explicitly advocates a focus on 'federalising processes' rather than on preferred constitutional outcomes.

As a guide to European integration, federalism has had a mixed success. In the early 1950s there was a widespread sense that European integration was a first step toward a federal Europe (Forsyth 1996: 26; MacMahon 1955). In particular, the negotiations for a European Defence Community (EDC) which began in 1950, and the related proposal for a European Political Community (EPC), seemed to offer a quick route to federal union (see Spinelli, 1966: 19). With the collapse of the EDC and EPC, however, the mood changed. It became increasingly clear that while European integration might be a precursor of federalism, it was not itself an instance of a federalizing process (Forsyth 1996: 26). Early efforts to establish an openly federal 'United States of Europe' appeared to have reached too far too fast, thereby awakening the hesitations and reservations of too many actors. As a result, many federalists drew the conclusion that a functionalist approach based on incremental moves toward closer cooperation in strictly functional areas stood a better chance of realizing the goal of a United Europe.

Since the 1980s federalist theory has enjoyed a partial revival. This was in part triggered by the European Parliament's adoption in February 1984 of a draft treaty on the creation of a European Union. The provisions of the draft treaty – which was drawn up by the so-called 'Crocodile group' with Spinelli as its coordinating rapporteur and was passed by a large majority in Parliament (237 votes for, 32 against, 34 abstentions) – included Union citizenship, cooperation on justice and home affairs, a coordinated foreign and security policy, a European monetary system, abolition of unanimity in the Council, and a system of financial equalization between regions – all steps that would make the EC more akin to a federal state. As a result, scholars again turned their attention to federalist theory. For example, Pinder (1986) insists that federalism continues to be a valid framework for understanding the dilemmas facing modern nation states and for designing institutional solutions to international problems. The pressures of interdependence means that the logical end result of European integration is a federal union – even if the process lasts half a century or more. Indeed, he argues, the single market programme was a crucial step toward a federal Europe, and even a potential catalyst for greater unity in the world (Pinder 1993: 61–6; also Elazar 1998). To Sbragia (1992), by contrast, federal theory offers an important analytical tool for understanding how the EC operates as a polity. The EC may not be a classic federation but by conceiving it as a federal system of sorts (with authority dispersed across local, national and regional levels) we can draw comparisons to other federal politics. This will help us gain a better understanding of the way territorial politics play themselves out in the Community. This comparative federalist approach is discussed in more detail in Part IV.

Functionalism

Like federalists, functionalists sought to theorize the conditions for world peace. But in contrast to the federalist vision of a constitutional settlement that reins in conflict by dividing authority between a centre and its units, functionalism offers a strategy for peace based on promoting international cooperation in non-controversial, technical and economic areas. Developed by David Mitrany in the 1930s, functionalist integration theory holds that, in an interdependent world, international organizations arranged according to functional tasks are better placed to solve universal technical and economic problems, and provide social services, than nation states. Once created, international functional organizations will gradually take over the core welfare functions of governments, thereby winning the allegiance of domestic societies and undermining the basis of national frontiers. The result is a gradual shift from a balance-of-power system built around sovereign states to a system whose units are non-territorial, functional and technocratic agencies. Like its federalist counterpart, functionalism offers a formula for international organization rather than a theory of integration (Groom and Taylor 1975: 1). In the words of Mitrany, 'the functional approach is an attempt . . . to offer a practical line of action that might overcome the deep-seated division between the needs of material unity and stubborn national loyalties' (1943: 126).

The intellectual lineage of functionalism can be traced back to the classical liberal economic philosophy of the nineteenth century, which held that trade and material progress were fundamentally contrary to war. An important inspiration for Mitrany's ideas was the work of British liberal economist Norman Angell (other important influences were Hobhouse and Laski). In his famous book *The Great Illusion* (1910), Angell argued that economic interdependence made war irrational and that growing transnational economic links would lead states to eschew armed conflict. Mitrany built directly on these ideas. Like Angell, he saw the promotion of welfare as a primary means to prevent war: 'Give people a moderate sufficiency of what they need and ought to have and they will keep the peace: this has been proved time and time again nationally, but it has not yet been tried internationally'.

But where Angell saw economic interdependence as a direct instigator of peace, Mitrany saw it merely as an *opportunity* for peace that could be realized only through the creation of international planning agencies designed to serve common welfare goals (Ashworth 1999: 85). What Mitrany had in mind was not a federal world state or a series of regional federal unions. He was quick to point out that political federations would merely reproduce the sins of the nation state at a higher level. Rather what was needed was a complete rethinking of the way the world was governed. He wanted to reorientate us away from comprehensive political designs (whether national, regional or international) toward a system of function-specific international organizations, which linked together particular activities and interests, one at a time, according to need and acceptability (see Mitrany 1965: 135).

As a practical approach to international organization, Mitrany's functionalism was strongly inspired by the growth in international functional organizations at the end of the nineteenth century, such as the International Telegraphic Union (1865), the International Postal Union (1874) and the commissions controlling navigation on the Danube. 'Working smoothly and efficiently for the interests of the world at large' rather than for individual states (Mitrany 1932: 89–90), these were prime examples of the kind of international cooperation Mitrany was after. He also drew on the lessons of Allied cooperation during World War I. In particular, Sir Arthur Salter's (1919, 1921) analysis of inter-allied cooperation was a substantial influence (see Mitrany 1969: 17–18). In his work, which Mitrany later edited for the Carnegie Endowment's 'Economic and Social History of the First World War', Salter describes how the transatlantic supply line during the war was organized essentially along functional lines. Collaboration was governed by close links between the relevant departmental organizations of the Allies, such as transport or munitions. Decisions were made by direct communication between experts rather than via intergovernmental negotiations. The effect, he notes, was that issues were rarely politicized. If there was any conflict of interest, it was a conflict between different services rather than between different countries (Salter 1919:20). To Salter this was a model for future international cooperation.

Building on these ideas, Mitrany's early work laid out the key principles that went into his functional theory. In 1932 he gave the Dodge lectures at Yale University where he presented for the first time his functional principle of international organization. Published under the title 'The Progress of International Government' (1932) the lecture laid the ground for the famous booklet 'A Working Peace System', which first appeared in 1943 (see Chapter 2). Written before the end of World War II and the post-war boom in economic and functional cooperation, the lecture provides a clear vision of functional cooperation and identifies the twin 'revolutionary changes' that Mitrany believed were transforming international relations in a functional direction. The first was technological progress. Mitrany observed that by the twentieth century, developments in communication, industry and warfare had raised political, social and moral issues that could only be dealt with on a global scale. The second change was the growing role of the state in the provision of welfare for the individual. A defining trend of the twentieth century was that people were focusing less on military security and more on social security and welfare. The result was increasing pressure on the state as more and more functions were pressed upon it by society (Mitrany 1932: 86–97). Politically these trends were moving in critical opposition. On the one hand, the greater role of the state in providing welfare for its citizens required centralized economic planning. On the other hand, economic interdependence meant that welfare needs could no longer be satisfied by economic activity within the state but became reliant on forces outside it. Mitrany saw in this schism a danger and an opportunity. The danger was that states, in striving for economic self-sufficiency, would turn more nationalist than ever. This had been the case after 1919 when major tasks of reconstruction had been left to individual states and created a basis for a new form of rabid economic nationalism (Mitrany 1939: 171). Mitrany sought to impress the urgency of the conflict on his readers, and to promote functional integration as the only way forward from it. The fundamental contradiction between interdependence and national welfare provision meant that, in the long run, the growth of national welfare programmes would produce pressure toward the transfer of welfare functions to international organizations where they would be better fulfilled (Mitrany 1932: 97, 1941: 107).

During World War II, these ideas matured. At the beginning of the war, Mitrany wrote a memorandum entitled 'Agenda of Peace-Making' (1939) in which he argued that problems of reconstruction would be more numerous and complex than after the last war and would force advances in international cooperation. The war, he predicted, would trigger a wave of 'social nationalism' as publics disillusioned with the wartime performance of their regimes would demand increased security and social welfare. To Mitrany, this presented a new opportunity to fulfil the functionalist vision. To retain political control, he argued, the Allies would have to quickly jump-start economic and social life. To do so they would be forced to rely on international cooperation (1939: 173, 1969: 19). According to some later students of European integration, this is precisely what happened. Alan Milward (1992; see introduction to Part III) argues that post-war integration has been the result of policymakers searching for ways to ensure the successful implementation of national welfare programmes. He thus confirms Mitrany's prediction that growing demands for welfare provision would create pressure toward integration. But whereas Mitrany hoped that social and economic integration would lead to the demise of the state, the result, according to Milward, has been to 'rescue the nation-state' by allowing it to satisfy public demands more effectively.

A recurrent theme in Mitrany's work is his critique of federalism, which also features strongly in the article below (see also Mitrany 1941, 1965). Mitrany saw at least three fundamental fallacies in the federalist agenda. First, he rejected the 'utopianism' of ideas for world federation. He pointed out that existing federal states such as Germany or Switzerland were essentially national federations, built on historical elements of kinship and shared history. Their experience could not be replicated at the international level, which was more diverse and complex. Second, he criticized the rigidity of a constitutional approach to international organization. To Mitrany, the best way to tackle socio-economic problems was through administration not legislation. Federal polities were ill equipped to deal with the complexities and fluidity of modern economic and social life, which required the capacity to adapt to constantly changing circumstances (1971: 540). To illustrate this he turned to a federalist icon, the USA. He described how Roosevelt had to fight the Supreme Court to implement the New Deal in 1933 (Mitrany 1943: 35, 1965: 60). Crucial to American economic success, the New Deal had been implemented only with great difficulty due to the constitutional inflexibility of the American federal system. A world federation would be even more rigid since it would concentrate control over many functions in different environments in a single centre where they would be subject to political conflict and deadlock. Finally, a world federation would not secure peace. To Mitrany, the federalist espousal of political means to arrive at clearly political goals was more likely to produce conflict than peace. One cannot provide a political solution to problems of divisive interests in the absence of an underlying socio-psychological community (Taylor 1968: 89). Such a community cannot be imposed from above but must be built, step-by-step, via cooperation to solve common problems of non-controversial, economic and social character. In other words, integration must be depoliticized.

While Mitrany rejected ideas for world federation as impractical, he was equally critical of plans for more limited regional unions. To Mitrany, 'anything that throws a fixed territorial framework around a social-technological activity amputates the working principles and frustrates the very purpose of the action, no matter at what level of jurisdiction – provincial or national, federal or regional' (1975: 256). Functional regions, he stressed, are not geographical entities like Western Europe, but practical areas such as railway transport, aviation, shipping or epidemic control (1941: 111–16). He also warned that regionalism held the seeds to a new form of nationalism. To stimulate internal unity, regional unions would have to create a sense of outer danger. Interwar pan-Europeanists and post-war federalists had exploited anti-Americanism and Bolshevism to increase intra-European loyalty (1930: 475, 1965: 125). Mitrany felt that such strategies would not lead beyond nationalism but would give birth to new inter-regional divisions (Mitrany 1948: 351; see also Salter 1929: 93).

Associated chiefly with the work of Mitrany, functionalism gained a substantial following in the early post-war period with scholars focusing in particular on the specialized agencies of the UN and the ECSC as foundations for international functional cooperation (see e.g. Mance 1946; White 1949). Later contributors to the approach include Patrick Sewell (1966), and Paul Taylor (1968, 1975a, 1975b). But Mitrany's approach was also a target of intense criticism, in particular by scholars identifying themselves as 'neofunctionalists' (see Part II). Much of this criticism centred on the apolitical, technocratic nature of functionalism. Functionalism moves by tackling non-political, technical problems and by basing its solutions on a universal 'common good'. The basic premise is that international conflict can be tamed by delegating tasks to technical experts. Being interested in problem solving rather than power, experts can be expected to achieve agreement where statesmen will fail. Experience suggests, however, that technical and economic matters are not always non-controversial but may be subject to political and cultural conflict. Experts evidently do not always agree, and special interests may be as prevalent in expert communities as among the constituents they represent. (For a critique along these lines see Haas 1964: 11–13 and Claude 1956: 387).

Functionalism was also faulted for ignoring the significance of political boundaries. As Hans Morgenthau, a leading realist scholar, pointed out, the belief that the superior performance of international organizations will lead people to abandon loyalty to the state is naive: whereas in war the common interest in victory might temporarily enable functional cooperation, in peacetime what the nation has to offer in terms of contributions to individual welfare outweighs by far the benefits to be derived from international functional agencies (Morgenthau 1948: 335).

A final line of criticism pushed mainly by federalists centred on democratic oversight. Mitrany's vision of technocratic planning implied government by experts, and would hence be undemocratic (Sewell 1966: 42). Yet, Mitrany himself saw no contradiction between expert government and a democratic basis for politics. In his vision, control by national governments and parliaments would be replaced with control by international functional assemblies consisting of representatives of government and professional bodies. Such functional representation would offer a valid remedy for the growing power and insulation of the administrator by 'bringing together those who know with the things they know', and would ultimately be more sensitive to constituents' needs than a parliamentary system (Mitrany 1965: 140; also Ashworth 1999: 93–103). The problem with this position is that it pays no attention to the generation and representation of interests. How do functional assemblies determine what needs to represent? How do they prioritize among different constituencies and interests? Or as James Mayall (1975: 254) notes, 'if the state, and hence the criterion of national interests, are dissolved, how and to whom do...needs present themselves?' As we shall see in Part IV, this argument recurs in various guises in recent debates over democratic legitimacy in the EU.

'A Working Peace System', reproduced in Chapter 2, is clearly a normative document, setting out an agenda for international change. Yet, as David Mutimer (1992: 23) points out, it could also be read to imply a functional *explanation* of integration: that is, the supply of functional organs at the international level is explained by the need to solve a growing number of transnational technical problems. In this text, Mitrany portrays functionalism as a form of 'federalism by instalments'. Note, however, that in many other writings he explicitly denies that a species of federation is an ultimate end goal of integration, projecting instead a global web of technical administrative agencies.

Transactionalism

Transactionalism or 'communication theory' focuses on the social rather than political or economic dimensions of integration. In contrast to federalism, the transactionalist approach does not presuppose a specific legal and institutional framework. In contrast to functionalism, it does not concern itself with the satisfaction of practical welfare needs, but rather with the conditions necessary to create and maintain a sense of community among the populations of different countries (Pentland 1975: 36). Pioneered by Karl Deutsch and his colleagues in the 1950s, transactionalism views integration as a process of cultural assimilation, leading to the formation of international 'security communities' (a concept first introduced by van Wagenen in 1952) in which peoples are linked in bonds of mutual trust and identification, and in which war is no longer considered possible. Simply stated, Deutsch's vision of integration as the formation of security communities relies on the notion that international transactions – communication, migration, mutual services, military collaboration, even tourism – trigger processes of social-psychological learning which in turn produce common identities and trust among social actors.

In the transactionalist model, integration has two key dimensions. The first is a process of *social* integration, leading to the formation of 'pluralistic' security communities. In such communities states retain their legal independence but interactions are guided by feelings of 'we-ness' and by 'dependable expectations of peaceful change' (Deutsch 1969: 122; van Wagenen 1965). An example of a pluralistic security community is Norway and Sweden, where neither have in recent memory imagined solving political conflicts by force. The second dimension is a process of *political* integration. Once pluralistic community formation has taken place, political elites may opt to build common supranational institutions, thereby producing 'amalgamated' security communities (essentially federal unions) (Deutsch et al. 1957: 6; Puchala 1970a: 184). However, amalgamation is not a necessary or per se desirable outcome. Indeed, Deutsch felt that pluralistic security communities were a more likely, more viable, and, because of their greater durability, more effective way of promoting international peace than political unions (Deutsch 1969: 122). He cautioned that premature efforts to achieve unified government without first attaining a high level of social integration would be self-defeating and might increase rather than mitigate conflict. This would be especially true if a centralized 'federal' authority was established prematurely, since the break-up of federations often leads to civil war. Moreover, he warned, the political unification of unequal partners may institutionalize the inequality and give a cachet of legitimacy to the exploitation of the weak by the strong (Merritt and Russett 1981: 9–10).

Deutsch's approach to international integration is firmly rooted in the study of nationalism and nation-building. Growing up in a multinational state, Czechoslovakia, which suffered a great deal during the war, Deutsch was drawn to the study of nationalism and the formation of large-scale communities (Merritt and Russett 1981: 6). In his first published works, *Nationalism and Social Communication* (1953a) and 'The Growth of Nations' (1953b) he explored theoretical and empirical linkages between communication patterns and national community. He presented a new model of a 'nation' or 'people' as a 'community of social communication', in which membership essentially consists in the ability and inclination to communicate more effectively, and on a wider range of subjects, with members of one large group than with outsiders (Deutsch 1953a: 70–1). He also introduced the concept of 'social mobilization' as the process whereby people become uprooted from their traditional communities and become available for new patterns of communication and behaviour. This process, he argued, increases the likelihood of integration (i.e. the formation of new pluralistic communities) among people who already share the same language, have compatible value systems, mutually responsive elites, and adequate communication channels.

In the pioneering study, *Political Community and the North Atlantic Area* (1957) (see Chapter 3) Deutsch and his Princeton colleagues apply these ideas to study community-building processes in this area. Through detailed examination of historical cases of integration and disintegration they describe the key features of political integration in the North Atlantic area from the eighteenth to the twentieth century. They find that community formation depends less on formal structures of joint decision-making (as argued by federalists) and more on a development of mutual sympathy, trust and loyalties; in short, of a 'we-feeling', which results in mutual perception of needs and mutual responsiveness in the process of decision-making (Deutsch et al. 1957: 36). By comparing individual cases with respect to a range of indicators, they attempt to generalize the conditions favourable to integration. They find that the formation of political communities depend less on geopolitical factors such as a common external threat and more on the complementarity of value systems and high levels of mutual responsiveness.

Associated chiefly with the work of Deutsch and his Princeton colleagues in the 1950s, transactionalism won wide support among American political scientists throughout the 1950s and 1960s and even into the 1970s. Contributors to the approach include Bruce Russett (1963, 1970, 1971), Helen Feldstein (1967), Theodore Caplow and Kurt Finsterbusch (1968), and Donald Puchala (1970a, 1970b, 1981). A major reason for the popularity of the approach was its 'scientific' character, which enticed scholars to use the newest technological developments in data collection and analysis. A champion of the behavioural revolution in American political science, Deutsch stressed the need to test theoretical conjectures against empirical data. To him, integration was a quantitative concept that could be directly observed and measured. As a result, his works assembled and analysed a large amount of statistical data on population movements, language assimilation and the flow of international transactions such as trade and mail. In *Nationalism and Social Communication* he shows that it is possible to empirically ascertain the existence of national communities by observing people's communication behaviour. The same logic is applied to international community formation, which Deutsch argues can be measured by the volume, context and scope of international transactions over multiple ranges of social, economic, cultural and political areas (Deutsch 1954; Puchala 1970b: 742–3). To ascertain whether integration has taken place, Deutsch uses a statistical tool called the 'index of relative acceptance', which measures the ratio of extra-regional relative to intra-regional communication and transactions. Integration is indicated by a higher volume and range of communications between community members than between members and outsiders (1956: 149). The more varied and numerous the transactions among a group of states, the more pronounced and solid the international community is likely to be (Deutsch 1969: 101).

The idea that states can learn to govern their mutual relations without giving up sovereignty to supranational institutions (i.e. without 'amalgamation') has made the transactionalist approach popular with policymakers and scholars (Pentland 1975: 13–14). Yet problems of operationality have weakened the approach as a theoretical tool. While transactionalists emphasize the study of manifest transaction flows – ranging from flows of trade, mail, travel, migration, to the exchange of university students and translations of books – critics have charged that evidence of increasing transactions is not a good indicator of 'integration' because it does not directly measure the growth of community or sense of mutual obligation, which may lag far behind interactions. Another problem related to measurement is the relativistic character of Deutsch's concept of integration. As Inglehart (1968: 121) observes, Deutsch's estimation of integration is based on zero-sum assumptions. More integration within Europe presupposes relatively fewer transactions with the rest of the world. This makes it impossible to determine whether the world as such is becoming more integrated.

Even if we accept that transactions are a valid indicator of integration, this makes transaction analysis a descriptive rather than an explanatory tool. As Puchala (1970b: 762) argues, transaction flows may reflect regional integration but they do not necessarily *cause* integration – indeed they may be *caused by* integration. This points to a deeper problem in transactionalism, namely the failure to specify a theoretical relationship between transaction flows and social assimilation on the one hand and political change on the other. Transactionalism holds that, under certain conditions, processes of social assimilation lead to integration. Yet, as critics contend, the paradigm never specifies the causal relationship between social assimilation and political change (see Fisher 1969: 288–9; Haas 1970: 626; Hoffmann 1963: 526; Inglehart 1968: 122; Nye 1968a). As Fisher (1969) notes, social assimilation is a psychological variable relating to the attitudes of mass publics, whereas political integration (whether in the form of pluralistic or amalgamated security communities) can be described as a variable relating primarily to the behaviour of political elites. With the exception of Bruce Russett (1963), who looks at how the existence of an Anglo-American security community affects the behaviour of individual decision-makers, most transactionalists seem satisfied with demonstrating covariance between social assimilation at the mass level and the growth of political communities. This leaves open the question of how the attitudes of mass populations become the basis for altered government policies.

The Pre-theories and the Development of European Integration Studies

The integration pre-theories have had enormous impact on the later study of regional integration and more broadly of international relations. The emergence of European integration theories introduced into IR a new paradigm which challenged the dominant realist view of the sovereign state as the only significant actor in international relations. At a time when the discipline of IR seemed fixed on the notion that conflict was the beginning and the end of the subject matter of IR, integration theorists drew attention to collaboration for welfare ends as an important aspect of contemporary interstate relations (Puchala 1981: 148). Individual integration theories left a significant imprint on the further study of international organization. Mitrany's functionalist ideas were instrumental in drawing attention to the significance of non-governmental actors in IR and were a precursor for major approaches to international cooperation, including interdependence theory, transnationalism and regime theory (Taylor 1975b: xviii). Deutsch's transactionalist perspective has been an important source of inspiration, not only to those working in comparative political science, which Deutsch's work was mainly associated with, but also for sociologically orientated IR-scholarship. For example, members of the English School and scholars working in a social-constructivist perspective have resurrected the concept of security communities to describe islands of international society that achieve the status of 'mature anarchy' or 'zones of peace' due to their high interaction capacity and dense networks of common rules and norms (see e.g. Adler and Barnett 1998; Buzan 1991; van Wagenen 1965: 21). Federalism has also left its mark on international organization studies. Many present scholars employ variants of federalism to study international institution-building (see e.g. Elazar 1998, Sbragia 1992).

The pre-theories also influenced the empirical development of European integration. Jean Monnet's pragmatic approach to integration and Robert Schuman's avowal that 'Europe will not be built all at once . . . it will be built by concrete achievements which create de facto solidarity' are direct reflections of Mitrany's functionalist strategy. Federalist ideology was another crucial inspiration for the EC founding fathers. As Perry Anderson (1996: 4) observes, 'a customs union, even equipped with an agricultural fund, did not require a supranational Commission armed with powers of executive direction, a High Court (and) a Parliament . . . The actual machinery of the Community is inexplicable without . . . the federalist vision of Europe developed by Monnet and his circle'. (On the influence of federalist ideas on European integration, see also Burgess 2000; Forsyth 1996: 40). Yet, despite their influence on the actual integration process, the development of the EC ultimately disappointed the hopes of classic integration scholars. Mitrany strongly criticized the Community for both its 'federalist' and 'regional' fallacies: the emphasis on centralized, federal institutions was unsuitable, and the creation of a European regional union risked having a divisive role internationally (Mitrany 1965: 226). Federalists, by contrast, found that the Community was not federal enough. Spinelli in 1957 wrote an article entitled 'The mockery of the Common Market' in which he predicted that the EC would fail because of the lack of central rule-making authority. To Deutsch, the European Community simply failed to qualify as an instance of integration. Keeping to his emphasis on transaction flows and social assimilation rather than the building of political institutions, Deutsch concluded that, by 1957, integration in Europe had effectively come to a halt. Once you controlled for growth in prosperity, increases in transactions among EC members after 1957 were no larger than would be predicted from a random probability model (Deutsch 1966: 355, 1969: 123). These observations, of course, called into question the basic assumptions of the pre-theories about what drives integration: whereas federalist sentiment and social assimilation in Europe remained low, institution-building flourished. Yet, the growth of functional organs did not appear to reduce loyalties to the nation state or quell political conflict such as functionalists predicted. These shortcomings in the face of empirical developments led to important theoretical modifications, which are the topic of the following chapters.

Further Reading

Federalism

Karmis, D. and Norman, W. (eds) (2005) *Theories of Federalism. A Reader* (Basingstoke: Palgrave). This reader brings together the most significant writings on federalism from the seventeenth century to the present.

Spinelli, A. (1966) *The Eurocrats* (Baltimore: Johns Hopkins Press). This is an important federalist perspective on the workings and shortcomings of the EC institutions during the early phases of integration.

Bosco, A. (ed.) (1991) *The Federal Idea. The History of Federalism from Enlightenment to 1945* (London: Lothian Foundation Press). An important collection of contemporary essays discussing the history and theory of federalism in a European context.

Burgess M. (2000) *Federalism and the European Union: The Building of Europe, 1950–2000* (London: Routledge). This book provides an excellent discussion of the influence of federalist ideas on the political and institutional development of the EC/EU.

Pinder, J. (1986) 'European Community and the Nation State: A Case of a Neo-federalism', *International Affairs*, 62(1), 41–54. In this article Pinder makes a case for a new kind of 'neo-federal' Europe.

Functionalism

Salter, A. (1919) 'The Organisation of the League of Nations' in W. Arnold-Forster (ed.) *Sir Arthur Salter: The United States of Europe and Other Papers*. This is a highly interesting perspective on international organization, which provides one of the clearest expressions of functionalist thought in interwar political writings.

Mitrany, D. (1975) *The Functional Theory of Politics* (London: Martin Robertson & Co.). This book contains a complete collection of Mitrany's main works with a commentary by Mitrany himself.

Claude, I. (1956) *Swords Into Ploughshares: The Problems of Progress of International Organization* (London: University of London Press). A classic study of the growth of international organizations in the interwar and early post-war period, containing an excellent discussion and critique of the functionalist perspective.

Ashworth, L. (1999) *Creating International Studies. Angell, Mitrany and the Liberal Tradition* (Aldershot: Ashgate). An excellent introduction to the liberal tradition in international studies, which traces the influence of classical liberal ideas on functionalist theory.

Groom, A.J.R. and Taylor, P. (eds) (1975) *Functionalism. Theory and Practice in International Relations* (London: University of London Press). This volume provides a comprehensive overview of the development and influence of functionalist theory on the study of international relations.

Transactionalism

Deutsch, K. (1969) *Nationalism and its Alternatives* (New York: Alfred A. Knopf). In this work Deutsch uses transaction analysis to theorize the factors driving political integration at the national as well as regional levels.

Russett, B. M. (1963) *Community and Contention: Britain and America in the Twentieth Century* (Cambridge: Cambridge University Press). An often overlooked example of transactionalist theory applied to the Anglo-American security community.

Merritt, R. and Russett, B. (eds) (1981) *From National Development to Global Community: Essays in Honor of Karl W. Deutsch* (London: George Allen and Unwin). This collection of essays with contributions by, among others, Donald Puchala offers a comprehensive review and critique of Deutsch's work on integration.

Realism

Carr, E. H. (1945) *Nationalism and After* (London: Macmillan). One of the best examples of the realist critique of 'utopian' ideals of international integration.

Chapter 1

For a Free and United Europe.
A Draft Manifesto

Altiero Spinelli and Ernesto Rossi*

I   The Crisis of Modern Civilization

The equal right of all nations to organize themselves into independent
States has been established. Every people, defined by its ethnic, geographical, linguistic and historical characteristics, was expected to find
the instrument best suited to its needs within a State organization
created according to its own specific concept of political life, and with
no outside intervention. The ideology of national independence was a
powerful stimulus to progress. It helped overcome narrow-minded
parochialism and created a much wider feeling of solidarity against
foreign oppression. It eliminated many obstacles hindering the free
movement of people and goods. Within the territory of each new State,
it brought the institutions and systems of the more advanced societies
to more backward ones. But with this ideology came the seeds of capitalist imperialism which our own generation has seen mushroom to the
point where totalitarian States have grown up and world wars have
been unleashed.

Thus the nation is no longer viewed as the historical product of co-
existence between men who, as the result of a lengthy historical
process, have acquired greater unity in their customs and aspirations
and who see their State as being the most effective means of organizing
collective life within the context of all human society. Rather the
nation has become a divine entity, an organism which must only consider its own existence, its own development, without the least regard
for the damage that others may suffer from this. The absolute sovereignty of national States has led to the desire of each of them to domi-

---

* The full-length version of this manifesto was drawn up by Altiero Spinelli and Ernesto
Rossi in 1941 when they were both interned on the island of Ventotene. The present text was
translated by the Altiero Spinelli Institute for Federalist Studies, and is reprinted with the
kind permission of the same institute. The text has been slightly abbreviated, as indicated, to
fit the format of this volume.

nate, since each feels threatened by the strength of the others, and considers that its 'living space' should include increasingly vast territories that give it the right to free movement and provide self-sustenance without needing to rely on others. This desire to dominate cannot be placated except by the hegemony of the strongest State over all the others.

As a consequence of this, from being the guardian of citizens' freedom, the State has been turned into a master of vassals bound into servitude, and has all the powers it needs to achieve the maximum war-efficiency. Even during peacetime, considered to be pauses during which to prepare for subsequent, inevitable wars, the will of the military class now holds sway over the will of the civilian class in many countries, making it increasingly difficult to operate free political systems. Schools, science, production, administrative bodies are mainly directed towards increasing military strength. . . .

Totalitarian States are precisely those which have unified all their forces in the most coherent way, by implementing the greatest possible degree of centralization and autarky. They have thus shown themselves to be the bodies most suited to the current international environment. It only needs one nation to take one step towards more accentuated totalitarianism for the others to follow suit, dragged down the same groove by their will to survive.

II   Post-war Tasks. European Unity

Germany's defeat would not automatically lead to the reorganization of Europe in accordance with our ideal of civilization. In the brief, intense period of general crisis (when the States will lie broken, when the masses will be anxiously waiting for a new message, like molten matter, burning, and easily shaped into new moulds capable of accommodating the guidance of serious internationalist minded men), the most privileged classes in the old national systems will attempt, by underhand or violent methods, to dampen the wave of internationalist feelings and passions and will ostentatiously begin to reconstruct the old State institutions. Most probably, the British leaders, perhaps in agreement with the Americans, will try to push things in this direction, in order to restore balance-of-power politics, in the apparent immediate interests of their empires.

The question which must be resolved first, failing which progress is no more than mere appearance, is the definitive abolition of the division of Europe into national, sovereign States. The collapse of the majority of the States on the continent under the German steam-roller has already given the people of Europe a common destiny: either they will all submit to Hitler's dominion, or, after his fall, they will all enter a revolutionary crisis and will not find themselves separated by, and entrenched in, solid State structures. Feelings today are already far more disposed than they were in the past to accept a federal reorganization of Europe. The harsh experience of recent decades has opened the eyes even of those who refused to see, and has matured many circumstances favourable to our ideal.

All reasonable men recognize that it is impossible to maintain a balance of power among European States with a militarist Germany enjoying equal conditions with other countries, nor can Germany be broken up into pieces or held on a chain once it is conquered. We have seen a demonstration that no country within Europe can stay on the sidelines while the others battle: declarations of neutrality and non-aggression pacts come to nought. The uselessness, even harmfulness, of organizations like the League of Nations has been demonstrated: they claimed to guarantee international law without a military force capable of imposing its decisions and respecting the absolute sovereignty of the member States. The principle of non intervention turned out to be absurd: every population was supposed to be left free to choose the despotic government it thought best, in other words virtually assuming that the constitution of each individual States was not a question of vital interest for all the other European nations. The multiple problems which poison international life on the continent have proved to be insoluble: tracing boundaries through areas inhabited by mixed populations, defence of alien minorities, seaports for landlocked countries, the Balkan Question, the Irish problem, and so on. All matters which would find easy solutions in the European Federation, just as corresponding problems, suffered by the small States which became part of a vaster national unity, lost their harshness as they were turned into problems of relationships between various provinces.

Moreover, . . . dissolution of the French army and the disintegration of the French Republic itself at the first serious collision with the German forces (which, it is to be hoped, will have lessened the chauvinistic attitude of absolute Gallic superiority), and in particular the awareness of the risk of total enslavement are all circumstances that will favour the constitution of a federal regime, which will bring an end to the current anarchy. Furthermore, it is easier to find a basis of agreement for a European arrangement of colonial possessions since England has accepted the principle of India's independence and since France has potentially lost its entire empire in recognizing its defeat.

To all of this must be added the disappearance of some of the most important dynasties, and the fragility of the basis which sustains the ones that survive. It must be taken into account that these dynasties, by considering the various countries as their own traditional appanage, together with the powerful interests backing them, represented a serious obstacle to the rational organization of the United States of Europe, which can only be based on the republican constitution of federated countries. And, once the horizon of the old Continent is superseded, and all the peoples who make up humanity are included in a single design, it will have to be recognized that the European Federation is the only conceivable guarantee ensuring that relationships with American and Asiatic peoples will work on the basis of peaceful co-operation, writing for a more distant future when the political unity of the entire world will become possible.

Therefore, the dividing line between progressive and reactionary parties no longer coincides with the formal lines of more or less democracy, or the pursuit of more or less socialism, but the division falls along a very new and substantial line: those who conceive the essential purpose and goal of struggle as being the ancient one, the conquest of national political power, and who, although involuntarily, play into the hands of reactionary forces, letting the incandescent lava of popular passions set in the old moulds, and thus allowing old absurdities to arise once again, and those who see the main purpose as the creation of a solid international State, who will direct popular forces towards this goal, and who, even if they were to win national power, would use it first and foremost as an instrument for achieving international unity.

With propaganda and action, seeking to establish in every possible way the agreements and links among the individual movements which are certainly in the process of being formed in the various countries, the foundation must be built now for a movement that knows how to mobilize all forces for the birth of the new organism which will be the grandest creation, and the newest, that has occurred in Europe for centuries; in order to constitute a steady federal State, that will have at its disposal a European armed service instead of national armies; that will break decisively economic autarkies, the backbone of totalitarian regimes; that will have sufficient means to see that its deliberations for the maintenance of common order are executed in the individual federal states, while each State will retain the autonomy it needs for a plastic articulation and development of political life according to the particular characteristics of the various peoples.

If a sufficient number of men in the main European countries understand this, then victory will soon fall into their hands, since both circumstances and opinion will be favourable to their efforts. They will have before them parties and factions that have already been disqualified by the disastrous experience of the last twenty years. Since it will be the moment for new action, it will also be the moment for new men: the MOVEMENT FOR A FREE AND UNITED EUROPE.

III   Post-war Duties. Reform of Society

A free and united Europe is the necessary premise to the strengthening of modern civilization as regards which the totalitarian era is only a temporary setback. As soon as this era ends the historical process of struggle against social inequalities and privileges will be restored in full. All the old conservative institutions that have hindered this process will either have collapsed or will be teetering on the verge of collapse. The crisis in these institutions must be boldly and decisively exploited.

In order to respond to our needs, the European revolution must be socialist, i.e. its goal must be the emancipation of the working classes and the creation of more humane conditions for them. The guiding light in determining what steps need to be taken, however, cannot simply be the utterly doctrinaire principle whereby private ownership of the material means of production must in principle be abolished and only temporarily tolerated when dispensing with it entirely. Wholesale nationalization of the economy under State control was the first, utopian form taken by the working classes' concept of their freedom from the yoke of capitalism. But when this State control is achieved, it does not produce the desired results but leads to a regime where the entire population is subservient to a restricted class of bureaucrats who run the economy.

The truly fundamental principle of socialism, vis-à-vis which general collectivization was no more than a hurried and erroneous inference, is the principle which states that, far from dominating man, economic forces, like the forces of nature, should be subject to man, guided and controlled by him in the most rational way, so that the broadest strata of the population will not become their victims. The huge forces of progress that spring from individual interests, must not be extinguished by the grey dullness of routine. Otherwise, the same insoluble problem will arise: how to stimulate the spirit of initiative using salary differentials and other provisions of the same kind. The forces of progress must be extolled and extended, by giving them increasing opportunities for development and employment. At the same time, the tracks guiding these forces towards objectives of greatest benefit for all society must be strengthened and perfected.

Private property must be abolished, limited, corrected, or extended according to the circumstances and not according to any dogmatic principle. This guiding principle is a natural feature in the process of forming a European economic life freed from the nightmares of militarism or national bureaucratism. Rational solutions must replace irrational ones, even in the working class consciousness. With a view to indicating the content of this principle in greater detail, we emphasize the following points while stressing the need to assess the appropriateness of every point in the programme and means of achieving them in relationship to the indispensable premise of European unity . . .

The time has now come to get rid of these old cumbersome burdens and to be ready for whatever turns up, usually so different from what was expected, to get rid of the inept among the old and create new energies among the young. Today, in an effort to begin shaping the outlines of the future, those who have understood the reasons for the current crisis in European civilization, and who have therefore inherited the ideals of movements dedicated to raising the dignity humanity, which were shipwrecked either on their inability to understand the goal to be pursued or on the means by which to achieve it have begun to meet and seek each other.

The road to pursue is neither easy nor certain. But it must be followed and it will be!

Chapter 2

A Working Peace System: An Argument for the Functional Development of International Organization

David Mitrany*

I   The General Problem

The need for some new kind of international system was being widely canvassed before the war, as the League of Nations found itself frustrated in its attempts to prevent aggression and to organize peace. Some blamed this failure on the irresponsibility of small states; others ... rather on the egoism of the Great Powers. Still others imputed the League's failure more directly to weaknesses in its own constitution and machinery: the proper ingredients were there, but only inadequately. It was especially among those who held this view that the idea of a wide international federation began to be embraced as a new hope.

Federation is indeed the only alternative to a League tried so far for linking together a number of political units by democratic methods. It would mean an association much closer than was the League, and its advocacy therefore takes it for granted that the League failed because it did not go far enough. In what way would federation go farther? Federation would be a more intensive union of a less extensive group – the constitutional ties would be closer; secondly, certain activities would be more definitely and actively tied together. More definite common action is clearly the end – the formal arrangements which the federalists put in the forefront would be merely a necessary adjunct, to ensure the reliable working of the federal undertakings. And that is as it should be, for, leaving formal arguments aside, it is plain that the League failed not from overstrain but from inaction. It might have

---

* The full-length version of this article was first published in 1943 by the *Royal Institute for International Affairs* (Chatham House, London), and is reprinted with permission. The text has been slightly edited, as indicated, to fit the format of this volume.

done more about sanctions, but that would not have been enough; even if the League's action for 'security' had been more fearless, that would not by itself have sufficed to give vitality to an international system that was to last and grow. To achieve that end such a system must in some important respects take over and co-ordinate activities hitherto controlled by the national state, just as the state increasingly has to take over activities which until now have been carried on by local bodies; and, like the state, any new international authority could under present conditions not be merely a police authority.

We realize now that the League failed because, whatever the reasons, it could not further that process of continuous adjustment and settlement which students of international affairs call 'peaceful change.' But they themselves, taking the form for the substance, all too often thought of it mainly as a matter of changing frontiers. We shall have to speak of this again, but what peaceful change should mean, what the modern world, so closely inter-related, must have for its peaceful development is some system that would make possible automatic and continuous social action, continually adapted to changing needs and conditions, in the same sense and of the same general nature as any other system of government. Its character would be the same, for certain purposes, only the range would be new. It is in that sense that the League's work has in truth been inadequate and ineffective, as one may readily see if one reflects whether a change of frontiers now and then would really have led to a peaceful and co-operative international society.

A close federation is supposed to do just what the League proved unable to do, and in a set and solid way. But, to begin with, can we take a system which has worked well in one field and simply transplant it to another, so much wider and more complex? Federations have still been national federations; the jump from national states to international organization is infinitely more hazardous than was the jump from provincial units to national federations. None of the elements of neighborhood, of kinship, of history, are there to serve as steps. The British Empire is bound closely by old ties of kinship and history, yet no one would suggest that there is among its parts much will for federation. Yet, apart from this matter of whether the federal idea has any great prospects, there is the more important question whether it would have any great virtues in the international sphere. If the evil of conflict and war springs from the division of the world into detached and competing political units, will it be exorcised simply by changing or reducing the lines of division? Any political reorganization into separate units must, sooner or later, produce the same effects; any international system that is to usher in a new world must produce the opposite effect of subduing political division. As far as one can see, there are only two ways of achieving that end. One would be through a world state which would wipe out political divisions forcibly; the other is the way discussed in these pages, which would rather overlay political divisions with a spreading web of international activities and agencies, in which and through which the interests and life of all the nations would be gradually integrated. That is the fundamental change to which any effective international system must aspire and contribute: to make international government co-extensive with international activities. A League would be too loose to be able to do it; a number of sectional federations would, on the contrary, be too tight to be welded into something like it; therefore when the need is so great and pressing, we must have the vision to break away from traditional legalistic ideas and try some new way that might take us without violence towards that goal. The beginnings cannot be anything but experimental; a new international system will need even more than national systems a wide freedom of continuous adaptation in the light of experience. It must care as much as possible for common needs that are evident, while presuming as little as possible upon a social unity which is still only latent and unrecognized. As Mr. Winant well said in a lecture at Leeds in October 1942: 'We must be absolute about our principal ends (justice and equality of opportunity and freedom), relative and pragmatic about the mechanical means used to serve those ends.'

The need for a pragmatic approach is all the greater because we are so clearly in a period of historical transition. When the state itself, whatever its form and constitution, is everywhere undergoing a deep social and political sea-change, it is good statesmanship not to force the new international experiments into some set established form, which may be the less relevant the more respectable it is, but to see, above all, that these experiments go with and fit into the general trend of the time.

. . . .

II   The Perplexities of Federation

The defects of continental and ideological unions

Perhaps as good a way as any to seek an answer to that question, essential as a starting point, is to examine some of the main aspects and implications of the schemes proposed. For the past year or so it has been widely suggested that a federal scheme alone can meet our need, and a number of actual schemes have been put on paper. How effective would these federal schemes be, and where would they lead us politically? Before examining more definite aspects, however, it would be well to look in passing at one or two of the general propositions in which those schemes are often wrapped. As is the way of wrappings, they only obscure the substance of the contents, but these general propositions help to reveal the conception which lies behind the schemes and so its fitness for our needs.

One of the most persistent of these propositions is the attempt to distinguish between a 'union of peoples' as against a 'union of states.' Federation, it is insisted, must be a union of peoples, to escape the 'fundamental flaw in the League in its being made of States as members.' We must refrain from indulging in the nice speculation as to what, under this conception, is the state; and of how the state would be separated from the people and the people detached from their state. We must take the federalists on their own ground, which is that to create something good and lasting we must unite not the chief political units but the several political societies – the peoples – themselves. What peoples, one is led to ask, and how? Clearly, they must be united as whole communities – we cannot pick and choose parts of them; we must take the whole of each nation, as now organized, with its groups and sections, without discriminating between classes and parties, and so on. That means that we include not only those who believe in the union, but also those, who assuredly must exist, if only as a minority, who do not; and given the democratic process, that minority may at any time become a majority. What will happen to the union of 'peoples' if some of the new majorities begin to tug at the common bonds? A union of peoples means, in effect, the union of political groups, and these and their attitude are bound to alter, or could be made to alter easily with the powerful means for stirring up popular currents which are now available. Here again there is the same harking back to the outlook and conditions of the nineteenth century, when 'popular' was supposed to be all that was fair and reliable. Now that we have had some experience of what totalitarian dictators can do with popular opinion, either by usurping it or by corrupting it, we must look for some foundation that is not so easily changed by propaganda or shattered if abused by some particular group or unit.

That concern with dogmatic forms and appearances comes out still more strongly in the basis suggested for selecting the federal members. There are only two criteria of selection: one essentially geographical, the other essentially ideological, in the broader sense of that term. A Pan-American or European federation would be of the first type, and would cut across ideological divisions; an Anglo-Saxon or a 'democratic' federation would be of the second type, and would cut across natural geographical divisions. What would be the effects and implications of these alternatives?

(a) Continental unions

There has been much talk in recent years of the need for 'continental' unions. The Germans have argued for a Monroe doctrine for Europe, and the Japanese for one for Asia, while in the home of that doctrine Pan-Americanism has grown some solid roots. Americans have naturally denounced the misuse of their doctrine by Nazi and Japanese; the Monroe doctrine was meant to protect the states of the Americas, not to subject them to the strongest among them. The factor which has been and remains the chief obstacle to Pan-Americanism, fear of domination by the major partner, Germany and Japan have regarded as the proper condition for a continental union. Such a demand is in itself almost a proof that there is no real unity in Europe or Asia, as there is none in the Western Hemisphere. Yet it is a realistic anticipation of a relationship that would be well-nigh inevitable in existing circumstances, until the factor of power shall have been tamed; and the closer the union the more inevitably would it be dominated by the more powerful member. That is a first objection to schemes for continental union.

In the second place, the Roman peace within such unions, even if tolerable to those subject to it, in no way promises to be also a contribution to world peace. One of the most constant lessons of political experience suggests that such aggregations would be flushed with a new sense of power, as they would be provided with a greater ability to use it. A few years ago, when the Pan-European idea was in fashion, its chief exponent had a fleeting moment of intuitive sincerity. The Pan-European movement, wrote Kalergi, 'is not a movement for world peace but for union, similar to the movements for German and Italian union in the nineteenth century. The movements for union were inwardly also movements for peace'. But outwardly? The German Empire was not satiated when it had united the congeries of small Germanic states. A full-fledged Pan-American union would at best be strongly isolationist. There is little promise of peace in the mere change from the rivalry of Powers and alliances to the rivalry of whole continents, tightly organized and capable of achieving a high degree of, if not actual, self-sufficiency. Continental unions would have a more real chance than individual states to practise the autarky that makes for division.

Further, without that promise of peace such unions could not bring with them a promise of continued social well-being. But there is in any case no assurance – and that is the third objection – that a European federation especially would bring its peoples prosperity. Schemes of this kind have been mooted more than once during the nineteenth century, but then Europe was in effect the political stage of the world. Economic relations with the rest of the world were yet modest, and so was general intercourse; communications were clumsy, the exchange of goods and ideas was limited, and Europe was, and felt, much of a unit *vis-a-vis* a vast exotic outer world. Since then powerful centres of social life have developed also in the other continents, and that has led not to segregation. but to an ever greater and varied economic and social interdependence of all peoples and lands. What therefore might have amounted to a fairly self-contained international, if European, society if those earlier plans had been adopted, in our time would mean rather the cutting up of a somewhat loose but living world system. The advocates of continental unions have often argued that a universal system would skip a stage in the political evolution of the world. 'Just as the idea of national unity was a postulate of the nineteenth century,' wrote Kalergi, 'so is the idea of continental unity a postulate of the twentieth century.' The analogy is more revealing than valid. There is a fictitious naturalness about these continental units. None of them has in fact that unity of type and purpose which drew men of one nation together, and if such unions would tie up certain strands they would tear up many more, and more promising ones. The problems which now divide the national states would almost all crop up again in any territorial realignment; their dimensions would be different, but not their evil nature. Yet if the analogy is fallacious, its use is significant. It shows that those who use it cannot break away from the conception which can see political society only as territorially closed units, aiming at being politically and economically self-contained. In so far as they have to admit that existing limits are holding up social progress-though their concern is admittedly more with military security-they can think merely of stretching that conception, but not of going beyond it or outside it.

(b) *'Ideological' unions*

Since the battle of the ideologies, which has played havoc with the League, a different type of federation has been urged upon us not a geographical, but what one might call a sympathetic federation, with, as a conspicuous example, Mr. Streit's first proposal for the federation of fifteen democracies. This criterion of selection would obviate the evident lack of unity of outlook of continental unions, but it assumes in the countries concerned a democratic unity which is seldom there. It would abandon to their fate democratic sections in the states excluded, while taking in in the states included non-democratic sections which would be a weakness in, and a latent threat to, the new body politic. The French Canadians are one example of such discordant groups, and such dissident minorities, as we have said, may at times become majorities. France, which was to be one of the pillars of Mr. Streit's scheme, is a somewhat different case in point. What would happen if one or more members were to go fascist and so lose their qualification for membership? And what if, at the same time, countries formerly fascist were to go democratic? Would the first be turned out and the second taken in? Federation under present conditions means a fairly close organization, political and economic; to revise the membership perhaps every few years would mean to disrupt periodically those very factors which would be the life-blood of the union. Or, if that is to be avoided and the original union kept together, either its ideological basis would have to be jettisoned or it would have to be maintained by force. That would almost turn the union into a Holy Alliance that would be led to stifle the democratic process in the house of its members in order to keep up the democratic dogma in its own constitution.

. . . .

. . . Clearly, there is here a gross but fundamental confusion as to the real issue involved. The criterion of selection is made to rest on existing or professed democratic form, whereas the only test that could satisfy is that of democratic performance. . . The performance which matters in international affairs is that which concerns and affects the sphere of international relations. A democratic federation would not lead to peace if some of its members, while democratically governed, were in the wider sphere to break the rules of democratic conduct. Abyssinia was destroyed by fascist Italy, but it was democratic Italy that laid hands on Tripoli and the Dodecanese; and a presumably democratic Poland it was that seized Vilna. Some other countries, though not democratically governed according to current definition, like Portugal, or Turkey under Kemal, may behave democratically in their international relations. Which of the two would make the better constituent of a democratic international system?

In the years immediately before the war the USSR was more ready to uphold the League's system of security than many a democratic member, while she had no part in the work of the ILO. Japan, on the other hand, remained a member of the ILO even after she had resigned from the League. Should they have been excluded from what they were willing to do because they were not doing everything else? This is another aspect of the same question, cases of a partial sharing in international action, which shows how difficult it must be, and even damaging, to insist on orthodoxy. In every case what matters is a readiness to co-operate for avoiding conflict and for advancing the task of common well-being. That is all one can ask and all one need ask. The very end of political organization is to make it possible that people with differing views and divergent sentiments should yet work together peacefully for common ends. Law and order have never meant a mere declaration of faith, but a line of conduct. In national society life is divided into public and private spheres; even in the public sphere the citizen may hold and speak any views as long as he does not willfully obstruct its course, i.e. as long as he behaves democratically. That dichotomy is a fundamental trait of liberal democracy; it is totalitarian doctrine that denies the right to a difference of outlook, even in matters not of common concern. Nor is it otherwise in existing federations. There is much variation in the several parts of the United States in regard to press and censorship, the right of meeting and association, franchise qualifications, etc.; more recently the intent and spirit of the Federal labour laws have been greatly cramped by restrictive legislation in a score of states; nor would anyone claim that the states of the cotton belt are governed democratically. Farther north, Quebec shows many a democratic flaw, while Alberta has, in a different direction, tried to go a way of her own. Yet in both countries federal activities are developing fast and progressively; it would indeed be true to say that it is in the widening of that common field that the democratic process is best satisfied and expressed. What justification is there for expecting more and asking more in international society? If anything, our initial demands must be more modest there, both because international bonds are more tenuous, and because innate differences between the parts are more marked and more sensitive. Clearly, the ideological criterion of selection, in any case difficult to define, would be as invidious as it is irrelevant in principle.

Common defects of sectional unions

While territorial or continental groupings, therefore, would lean upon an unreal unity of outlook and interest, ideological groupings would cut across certain real and natural interests. In Europe, and still more in the Western Hemisphere, they would break up, for instance, what are in effect natural units for security, and so would tend to grow the habits of a grand alliance rather than of a collective system of law and order.

Apart from such particular defects, all sectional schemes have certain defects in common. What, above all, would be their relations with outside groups, and their effect upon them? Pan-Europa, as we know, was in practice to be a separate organization, with a point directed against Russia and against the United States. A 'democratic' federation would of set purpose have a point against non-democratic Powers; just as the Axis, in spite of the Anti-Comintern Pact, was led by its ideology to turn rather against the liberal democratic states. The first effect of any such sectional grouping, therefore, must be to force those left outside to join together in some counter-group. 'Such seems the disposition of man,' said Dr Johnson, 'that whatever makes a distinction produces rivalry.' Continental unions would almost have to invent extraneous danger or antagonism so as to stimulate internal unity; ideological unions would, of course, have such bogies ready made. We should be thrown back upon a balance of power between groups that would be much more formidable than those which broke the back of the European Concert in 1914, or than the Axis and counter-Axis groups of recent years.

To obviate that danger, those who realize it propose that sectional unions should be linked up into a wider association, probably a universal League. But the mere fact of association will not lay the danger; it will all depend on the nature of the sectional units and on their relation to the wider body. Now, federal schemes imply a fairly close organization of joint activities and interests of member states. Security, economic and social development, all require under present conditions, whatever the unit of organization, centralized planning and control. The closer the organization of the sectional unions, the sharper will be their division from other similar unions, and the more tenuous their links with any universal body. It is useless to hope and to prescribe that relations with other groups should be liberal and co-operative. Finance, production, defence, etc., cannot be organized tightly in a sectional unit, and at the same time be open on equal terms to other units. Even so relatively mild a step as the Ottawa preferential arrangement helped to divide the British Empire from the rest of the world; while in the opposite sense the close economic ties which are growing up now between Canada and America, should they persist after the war in their present limited character, would loosen in a corresponding degree Canada's ties with the Empire. The organization of a federal group would have to be rigid, arid so therefore will be its relations with other similar units. It is not possible to change the structure of such planned economy, or system of defence, continuously. Therefore the closer federal unit would in fact be the active dominant unit in political and social life, inevitably with privileges for its members and restrictions against non-members. In so far as successful it would engender a group patriotism, thus in the end reproducing in all political essentials the relationship which has existed between states and the League rather than that between a state and its local bodies, or that of a federation to its members. The centre of gravity of the new international life, that is, would again be misplaced, unless the scope and authority of the smaller units were to be correspondingly lesser than those of the wider grouping – and in that case they could not be close federations.

Between the conception of a universal league or association and that of sectional unions there is, therefore, a difference not merely of degree, but of essence. The sectional units would proceed in the old way through a definition of a limited territory, the other through the organization of certain common interests; and while the first would organize within their limits with the inevitable tendency to differentiate between members and outsiders, the second would select and organize certain activities for the opposite purpose of integrating with regard to them the interests and actions of all. That is precisely the urgent task which is facing us, and which would test the effectiveness of any new international system: to make international government co-extensive with international activities . . .

. . . .

III   The Functional Alternative

General considerations

Can these vital objections be met, and the needs of peace and social advance be satisfied, through some other way of associating nations for common action? The whole trend of modern government indicates such a way. That trend is to organize government along the lines of specific ends and needs, and according to the conditions of their time and place, in lieu of the traditional organization on the basis of a set constitutional division of jurisdiction of rights and powers. In national government the definition of authority and the scope of public action are now in a continuous flux, and are determined less by constitutional norms than by practical requirements. The instances are too many and well-known to need mentioning; one might note only that while generally the trend has been towards greater centralization of services, and therefore of authority, under certain conditions the reverse has also occurred, powers and duties being handed over to regional and other authorities for the better performance of certain communal needs. The same trend is powerfully at work in the several federations, in Canada and Australia and especially in the United States, and in these cases it is all the more striking because the division of authority rests on written constitutions which are still in being and nominally valid in full. Internationally, too, while a body of law had grown slowly and insecurely through rules and conventions, some common activities were organized through *ad hoc* functional arrangements and have worked well. The rise of such specific administrative agencies and laws is the peculiar trait and indeed the foundation of modern government.

A question which might properly be asked at the outset in considering the fitness of that method for international purposes is this: Could such functions be organized internationally without a comprehensive political framework? Let it be said, first, that the functional method as such is neither incompatible with a general constitutional framework nor precludes its coming into being. It only follows Burke's warning to the sheriffs of Bristol that 'government is a practical thing' and that one should beware of elaborating constitutional forms 'for the gratification of visionaries.' In national states and federations the functional development is going ahead without much regard to, and sometimes in spite of, the old constitutional divisions. If in these cases the constitution is most conveniently left aside, may not the method prove workable internationally without any immediate and comprehensive constitutional framework? If, to cite Burke again, it is 'always dangerous to meddle with foundations,' it is doubly dangerous now. Our political problems are obscure, while the political passions of the time are blinding. One of the misfortunes of the League experiment was that a new institution was devised on what have proved to be outdated premises. We might also recollect that of the constitutional changes introduced in Europe after the last war, fine and wise though they may have been, none has survived even a generation. How much greater will that risk of futility be in post-war Europe, when the nations will be split much worse than in 1919 within and between themselves? We know now even less about the dark historical forces which have been stirred up by the war, while in the meantime the problems of our common society have been distorted by fierce ideologies which we could not try to bring to an issue without provoking an irreconcilable dogmatic conflict. Even if action were to be to some extent handicapped without a formal political framework, the fact is that no obvious sentiment exists, and none is likely to crystallize for some years, for a common constitutional bond.

In such conditions any pre-arranged constitutional framework would be taken wholly out of the air. We do not know what, if anything, will be in common – except a desperate craving for peace and for the conditions of a tolerable normal life. The peoples may applaud declarations of rights, but they will call for the satisfaction of needs. That demand for action could be turned into a historic opportunity. Again, we might take to heart what happened in the USA in 1932–33, and think of what chances the Roosevelt administration would have had to achieve unity, or indeed to survive, if instead of taking immediate remedial action they had begun by offering constitutional reforms – and that where a common system was already in being. A timid statesman might still have tried to walk in the old constitutional grooves. Mr. Roosevelt simply stepped over them. He grasped both the need and the opportunity for centralized practical action. Unemployment, the banking collapse, flood control, and a hundred other problems had to be dealt with by national means if they were to be dealt with effectively and with lasting results.

The significant point in that emergency action was that each and every problem was tackled as a practical issue in itself. No attempt was made to relate it to a general theory or system of government. Every function was left to generate others gradually, like the functional subdivision of organic cells; and in every case the appropriate authority was left to grow and develop out of actual performance. Yet the new functions and the new organs, taken together, have revolutionized the American political system. The federal government has become a national government, and Washington for the first time is really the capital of America. In the process many improvements in the personnel and machinery of government have come about, and many restrictive state regulations have melted away. More recently there has been heard the significant complaint that the ties between cities and their states are becoming looser, while those with the national government become ever stronger. No one has worked to bring this about, and no written act has either prescribed it or confirmed it. It has been a purely functional development at every point. A great constitutional transformation has thus taken place without any changes in the Constitution. There have been complaints, but the matter-of-course acceptance has been overwhelming. People have gladly accepted the service when they might have questioned the theory. The one attempt at direct constitutional revision, to increase and liberalize the membership of the Supreme Court, was bitterly disputed and defeated. Yet that proposal involved in effect much less of a constitutional revolution than does the experiment of the Tennessee Valley Authority. The first would not have ensured any lasting change in. the working of American government, whereas the second has really introduced into the political structure of the United States a new regional dimension unknown to the Constitution.

In many of its essential aspects – the urgency of the material needs, the inadequacy of the old arrangements, the bewilderment in outlook – the situation at the end of this war will resemble that in America in 1933, though on a wider and deeper scale. And for the same reasons the path pursued by Mr. Roosevelt in 1933 offers the best, perhaps the only, chance for getting a new international life going. It will be said inevitably that in the United States it was relatively easy to follow that line of action, because they were in fact one country, with an established constitution. Functional arrangements could be accepted, that is, because in many fields the federal states had grown in the habit of working together. That is no doubt true, but not the most significant point of the American experiment; for that line was followed not because the functional way was so easy but because the constitutional way would have been so difficult. Hence the lesson for unfederated parts of the world would seem to be this – if the constitutional path had to be avoided, for the sake of effective action, even in a federation which already was a working political system, how much less promising must it be as a starting mood when it is a matter of bringing together for the first time a number of varied, and sometimes antagonistic, countries? But if the constitutional approach, by its very circumspectness, would hold up the start of a working international system, bold initiative during the period of emergency at the end of the war might set going lasting instruments and habits of a common international life. And though it may appear rather brittle, that functional approach would in fact be more solid and definite than a formal one. It need not meddle with foundations: old institutions and ways may to some extent hamper reconstruction, but reconstruction could begin by a common effort without a fight over established ways. Reconstruction may in this field also prove a surer and less costly way to revolution. As to the new ideologies, since we could not prevent them we must try to circumvent them, leaving it to the growth of new habits and interests to dilute them in time. Our aim must be to call forth to the highest possible degree the active forces and opportunities for co-operation, while touching as little as possible the latent or active points of difference and opposition.

There is one other aspect of the post-war period which has been much discussed and which has a bearing on this point, and which helps to bring out the difference in outlook between the two methods contrasted here. Much has been heard of a suggestion that when the war ends we must have first a period of convalescence, and that the task of permanent reorganization will only come after that. It is a useful suggestion, in so far as it may help to clear up certain practical problems. But it could also be misleading and even dangerous, if the distinction were taken to justify either putting off the work of international government, or differentiating between the agencies by which the new international activities are to be organized into nurses for convalescence and mentors for the new life. A clean division in time between two such periods in any case is not possible, for the period of 'convalescence' will be different for different activities and ends; but, above all, except for such direct and exceptional consequences of the war as demobilization and the rebuilding of damaged areas, the needs of society will be the same at once after the war as later on. The only difference will be the practical one of a priority of needs, the kind of difference which might be brought about by any social disturbance – an epidemic or an earthquake or an economic crisis – and the urgency of taking action. For the rest, one action and period will merge into the other, according to circumstances. Seed and implements will be as urgent for ensuring the food supply of Europe and Asia as the actual distribution of relief, and indeed more urgent if the war should end after a harvest. Again, both relief and reconstruction will depend greatly on the speedy reorganization and proper use of transport, and so on.

Both circumstances point again to the advantage of a functional practice, and to the disadvantage, if not the impossibility, of a comprehensive formal attempt at organization. To obtain sufficient agreement for some formal general scheme would, at best, not be possible without delay; at the same time, action for relief and reconstruction will have to start within the hour after the 'cease fire'. The alternatives would be, if a comprehensive constitutional arrangement is desired and waited for, to put the immediate work either in the hands of temporary international agencies, or to leave it to the individual states. The one, in fact, would prepare for the other. Except in matters of relief – the distribution of food, fuel, and clothing and also medical help – *ad hoc* temporary agencies could have no adequate authority or influence; all of what one might call the society-building activities, involving probably considerable planning and reorganization within and between the several countries, would fall upon the individual states again, as in 1919, when they competed and interfered rather than cooperated with each other, to the loss of them all. Yet it is vital that international activity should be from the outset in the same hands and move in the same direction after the war as later, otherwise the chances of building up an international system would be gravely prejudiced. It is certain that one of the chief reasons for the failure of the League was that it was given a formal authority and promissory tasks for the future, while the immediate, urgent, and most welcome tasks of social reconstruction and reform were left to be attended to by national agencies; later efforts to retrieve that mistake only led to a series of barren economic conferences; as by that time the policy of each country was set hard in its own mould. It is inevitable with any scheme of formal organization that the national states should have to re-start on their own, and natural therefore that refuge should be sought in the idea of a period of convalescence; while the full-fledged scheme is worked out and adopted. But functional authorities would not need such political hospitalization, with its arbitrary and dangerous division of stages; they would merely vary, like any other agency everywhere and at any time, the emphasis of their work in accordance with the changing condition of their task, continuing to control and organize transport, for instance, after they had rebuilt it, and in the same way taking each task in hand with a plan and authority for continuing it. The simple fact is that all that re-starting of agriculture and industry and transport will either be done on some pre-arranged common programme, or it will have to be done, for it could not wait, on disjointed local plans; it will be done either by pre-established international agencies, or it will have to be done by local national agencies – and the agencies which will act in the supposed convalescence period will be those to gather authority and acceptance unto themselves.

. . . .

The broad lines of functional organization

The problem of our generation, put very broadly, is how to weld together the common interests of all without interfering unduly with the particular ways of each. It is a parallel problem to that which faces us in national society, and which in both spheres challenges us to find an alternative to the totalitarian pattern. A measure of centralized planning and control, for both production and distribution, is no longer to be avoided, no matter what the form of the state or the doctrine of its constitution. Through all that variety of political forms there is a growing approximation in the working of government, with differences merely of degree and of detail. Liberal democracy needs a re-definition of the public and private spheres of action. But as the line of separation is always shifting, under the pressure of fresh social needs and demands, it must be left free to move with those needs and demands and cannot be fixed through any constitutional re-statement. The only possible principle of democratic confirmation is that public action should be undertaken only where and when and in so far as the need for common action becomes evident and is accepted, for the sake of the common good. In that way controlled democracy could yet be made the golden mean whereby social needs might be satisfied as largely and justly as possible, while still leaving as wide a residue as possible for the free choice of the individual.

That is fully as true for the international sphere. It is indeed the only way to combine as well as may be international organization with national freedom. We have already suggested that not all interests are common to all, and that the common interests do not concern all countries in the same degree. A territorial union would bind together some interests which are not of common concern to the group, while it would inevitably cut asunder some interests of common concern to the group and those outside it. The only way to avoid that twice-arbitrary surgery is to proceed by means of a natural selection, binding together those interests which are common, where they are common, and to the extent to which they are common. That functional selection and organization of international relations would extend, and in a way resume, an international development which has been gathering strength since the latter part of the nineteenth century. The work of organizing international public services and activities was taken a step further by the League, in its health and drug control work, in its work for refugees, in the experiments with the transfer of minorities and the important innovations of the League loan system, and still more through the whole activity of the ILO. But, in addition, many activities and interests in the past had been organized internationally by private agencies – in finance and trade and production, etc., not to speak of scientific and cultural activities. In recent years some of these activities have in various countries been brought under public national control; indeed in totalitarian countries all of them. In a measure, therefore, the present situation represents a retrogression from the recent past: self-sufficiency has spread from economics to the things of the mind, and while flying and wireless were opening up the world, many old links forged by private effort have been forcibly severed. It is unlikely that most of them could be resumed now except through public action, and if they are to operate as freely as they did in private hands, they cannot be organized otherwise than on a non-discriminating functional basis.

What would be the broad lines of such a functional organization of international activities? The essential principle is that activities would be selected specifically and organized separately, each according to its nature, to the conditions under which it has to operate, and to the needs of the moment. It would allow, therefore, all freedom for practical variation in the organization of the several functions, as well as in the working of a particular function as needs and conditions alter. Let us take as an example the group of functions which fall under communications, on which the success of post-war reconstruction will depend greatly. What is the proper basis for the international organization of *railway* systems? Clearly, it must be European, or rather, *continental,* North-American, and so on, as that gives the logical administrative limit of co-ordination. A division of the continent into separate democratic and totalitarian unions would not achieve the practical end, as political division would obstruct that necessary co-ordination; while British and American participation would make the organization more cumbrous without any added profit to the function. As regards shipping, the line of effective organization which at once suggests itself is *international,* or inter-continental, but not universal. A European union could not solve the problem of co-ordination without the co-operation of America and of certain other overseas states. *Aviation* and *broadcasting,* a third example in the same group, could be organized effectively only on a *universal* scale, with perhaps subsidiary regional arrangements for more local services. Such subsidiary regional arrangements could in fact be inserted at any time and at any stage where that might prove useful for any part of a function; devolution according to need would be as easy and natural as centralization, whereas if the basis of organization were political every such change in dimension would involve an elaborate constitutional re-arrangement. Similarly, it could be left safely to be determined by practical considerations whether at the points where functions cross each other-as rail and river transport in Europe, or civil flying in Europe and America-the two activities should be merely coordinated or put under one control.

These are relatively simple examples. The functional co-ordination of production, trade and distribution evidently would be more complex, especially as they have been built up on a competitive basis. But the experience with international cartels, with the reorganization of the shipping, cotton and steel industries in England, not to speak of the even wider and more relevant experience with economic co-ordination in the two world wars, they all show that the thing can be done, and that it has always been done on such functional lines. No fixed rule is needed, and no rigid pattern is desirable for the organization of these functional strata.

A certain degree of fixity would not be out of place, however, in regard to the more *negative* functions, especially those related to 'law and order,' but also to any others of a more formal nature, and which are likely to remain fairly static. Security, for instance, could be organized on an interlocking regional basis; and the judicial function likewise, with a hierarchy of courts, the wider acting as courts of appeal from the more local courts. Yet even in regard to security, and in addition to regional arrangements, the elasticity inherent in functional organization may prove practicable and desirable, if only in the period of transition. Anglo-American naval co-operation for the policing of the seas may prove acceptable for a time, and it would cut across physical regions; agreement on a mineral sanction would of necessity mean common action by those countries which control the main sources; and other such combinations might be found useful for any particular task in hand. That is security only for defence; security arrangements were conceived usually on a geographical basis because they were meant to prevent violence, and that would still be the task of sanctions, etc., based on some regional devolution. But in addition there is a growing functional devolution in the field of social security – in connection with health, with the drug and white slave traffic, with subversive movements, etc. In all that important field of social policing it has been found that co-ordination and co-operation with the police of other countries on functional lines, varying with each task, was both indispensable and practicable. There is no talk and no attempt in all this to encroach upon sovereignty, but only a detached functional association which works smoothly and is already accepted without question.

However that may be, in the field of more *positive* active functions – economic, social, cultural – which are varied and ever-changing in structure and purpose, any devolution must, like the main organization, follow functional lines. Land transport on the Continent would need a different organization and agencies should the railways after a time be displaced by roads; and a Channel tunnel would draw England into an arrangement in which she does not at present belong, with a corresponding change in the governing organ.

Here we discover a cardinal virtue of the functional method – what one might call the virtue of technical self-determination. The functional *dimensions*, as we have seen, determine themselves. In a like manner the function determines its appropriate *organs*. It also reveals through practice the nature of the action required under the given conditions, and in that way the *powers* needed by the respective authority. The function, one might say, determines the executive instrument suitable for its proper activity, and by the same process provides at need for the reform of that instrument at every stage. This would allow the widest latitude for variation between functions, and also in the dimension or organization of the same functional needs and conditions change. Not only is there in all this no need for any fixed constitutional division of authority and power, prescribed in advance, but anything beyond the most general formal rules would embarrass the working of these arrangements.

The question of wider co-ordination

The question will be asked, however, in what manner and to what degree the various functional agencies that may thus grow up would have to be linked to each other, and articulated as parts of a more comprehensive organization. It should be clear that each agency could work by itself, but that does not exclude the possibility of some of them or all being bound in some way together, if it should be found needful or useful to do so. That indeed is the test. As the whole sense of this particular method is to let activities be organized as the need for joint action arises and is accepted, it would be out of place to lay down in advance some formal plan for the co-ordination of the several functions. Co-ordination, too, would in that sense have to come about functionally. Yet certain needs and possibilities can be foreseen already now, though some are probable and others only likely, and it may help to round off the picture if we look into this aspect briefly.

1. *Within the same group* of functions probably there would have to be co-ordination either simply for technical purposes or for wider functional ends, and this would be the first stage towards a wider integration. To take again the group concerned with communications-rail, road, and air transport in Europe would need *technical* co-ordination in regard to time-tables, connections, etc. They may need also a wider *functional* co-ordination if there is to be some distribution of passenger and freight traffic for the most economic performance-whether that is done by a superior executive agency or by some arbitral body, perhaps on the lines of the F.C.C. in America. Sea and air traffic across the Atlantic or elsewhere, though separately organized probably would also benefit from a similar type of co-ordination. Again, various mineral controls, if they should be organized separately, would need some coordination; though this arbitrary grouping of 'minerals' would be less to the point than the co-ordination of specific minerals and other products with possible substitutes-of crude oil with synthetic oil, of crude rubber with synthetic rubber, and so on.

2. The next degree or stage might be, if found desirable, the coordination of *several groups* of functional agencies. For instance, the communications agencies may not only work out some means of acting together in the distribution of orders for rolling stock, ships, etc.; but they could or should work in this through any agencies that may have come into being for controlling materials and production, or through some intermediary agency as a clearing house. There is no need to prescribe any pattern in advance, or that the pattern adopted in one case should be followed in all the others.

3. The co-ordination of such working functional agencies with any *international planning* agencies would present a third stage, and one

that brings out some interesting possibilities, should the ideas for an International Investment Board or an International Development Commission, as an advisory organ, come to fruition. One can see how such a Development Commission might help to guide the growth of functional agencies into the most desirable channels, and could watch their inter-relations and their repercussions. And an Investment Board could guide, for instance, the distribution of orders for ships, materials, etc., not only according to the best economic use, but also for the purpose of ironing out cyclical trends. It could use, according to its nature, its authority or its influence to make of such orders a means additional to international public works, etc., for dealing with periods or pockets of unemployment. Co-ordination of such a general kind may in some cases amount almost to arbitration of differences between functional agencies; regional boards or councils like those of the Pan-American Union might be used to adjust or arbitrate regional differences.

4. Beyond this there remains the habitual assumption, as we have already said, that international action must have some overall *political authority* above it. Besides the fact that such a comprehensive authority is not now a practical possibility, it is the central view of the functional approach that such an authority is not essential for our greatest and real immediate needs. The several functions could be organized through the agreement, given specifically in each case, of the national governments chiefly interested, with the grant of the requisite powers and resources; whereas it is clear, .to emphasize the previous point, that they could not allow such organizations simply to be prescribed by some universal authority, even if it existed. For an authority which had the title to do so would in effect be hardly less than a world government; and such a strong central organism might develop a tendency to take unto itself rather more authority than that originally alloted to it, requiring in its turn the checks and balances used in federal systems, but which would be difficult to provide in any loose way. If issues should arise in the functional system which would call either for some new departure or for the interpretation of existing arrangements, that could be done only in council by all the governments concerned. In so far as it may be desired to keep alive some general view of our problems, and perhaps a general watch over the policies of the several joint agencies, some body of a representative kind, like the League Assembly or the Governing Body of the ILO, could meet periodically, perhaps elected by proportional representation from the assemblies of the various states. Such an assembly, in which all the states would have a voice, could discuss and ventilate general policies, as an expression of the mind and will of public opinion; but it could not actually prescribe policy, or this might turn out to be at odds with the policy of governments. Any line of policy

recommended by such an assembly would have to be pressed and secured through the policy-making machinery of the various countries themselves.

These then are the several types and grades of co-ordination which might develop with the growth of functional activities. But there is, finally, in the political field also the problem of security, admittedly a crucial problem, for on its being solved effectively the successful working of the other activities will depend. At the same time, the general discussion of functional organization will have served to bring out the true place and proportion of security, as something indispensable but also as something incapable by itself of achieving the peaceful growth of an international society. It is in fact a separate function like the others, not something that stands in stern isolation, overriding all the others. Looking at it in this way, as a practical function, should also make it clear that we would not achieve much if we handled it as a one-sided limited problem – at present too often summed up in 'German aggression.' German aggression was a particularly vicious outgrowth of a bad general system, and only a radical and general change of the system itself will provide continuous security for all. In this case, also, it would be useful to lay down some formal pledges and principles as a guiding line, but the practical organization would have to follow functional, perhaps combined with regional, lines. That is all the more necessary as we know better now how many elements besides the purely military enter into the making of 'security'. The various functional agencies might, in fact, play an important role in that wider aspect of security: they could both watch over and check such things as the building of strategic railways, or the accumulation of strategic stocks in metals or grains. Possibly they could even be used, very properly and effectively, as a first line of action against threatening aggression, by their withholding services from those who are causing the trouble. They could apply such preventive sanctions more effectively than if these were to wait upon the agreement and action of a number of separate governments, and they could do so as part of their established duties, arid therefore with less of the political reactions caused by political action.

Representation in control

One aspect that is likely to be closely examined is that of the structure of the functional controls, and here again the initial difficulty will be that we shall have to break away from attractive traditional ideas if we are to work out the issue on its merits. It is not in the nature of the method that representation on the controlling bodies should be democratic in a political sense, full and equal for all. Ideally it may seem that all functions should be organized on a worldwide scale, and that all states should have a voice in control. Yet the weight of reality is on the side of making the jurisdiction of the various agencies no wider than the most effective working limits of the function; and while it is understandable that all countries might wish to have a voice in control, that would be really to hark back to the outlook of political sovereignty. In no functional organization so far have the parties interested had a share in control as 'by right' of their separate existence – neither the various local authorities in the London Transport Board, nor the seven states concerned in the T.V.A., nor the states of the world in the B.I.S. And in any case, in the transition from power politics to a functional order we could be well satisfied if the control of the new international organs answered to some of the merits of each case, leaving it to experience and to the maturing of a new outlook to provide in time the necessary correctives. The new method would have in this regard certain very solid merits: (i) Any claim to a share in control would have to be justified by a corresponding and evident capacity for performance; (ii) by that test smaller states could also qualify and the participants in control would vary, thus avoiding an exclusive accumulation of influence by a few countries; (iii) the same test again would govern not only the fact of participation in control, but also the extent of the powers of control in each case; (iv) and the performance would be practical and measurable, with a periodical balance-sheet, more definite and more suitable for examination than the reports to the League's Mandatcs Commission, through which the work and the policy of each agency could be closely checked. Czechs and Swiss may possibly dislike not having a direct part in the control of an International Shipping Board, and it is true that as consumers they would run a certain risk, as with such a monopolistic Board they could not drive the bargains that are possible when shipping is run by a number of competing private undertakings. Still, in this case also they would have no direct voice in control, and would be equally powerless against a shipping cartel, whereas the organization of shipping as a recognized common service would give them a standing in court, so to speak, with a right to bring open plaint for any particular grievances and even to criticize on general grounds any failings of the service. To this might be added that from all past experience a personnel which would be largely technical and permanent is likely to develop both a professional pride and a vested interest in good performance. That is an important point, and one that helps to bring out in this case, too, how formal ideas of equality may actually stand in the way of practical achievement. For 'equal representation' involves not only the presence but also the character of representation; it is not merely a matter of being represented, but clearly of being represented by people of one's own choice and who will express one's particular interests. The demand for equal share in control is only too likely to lead to that for an equal or proportional share in personnel, and that would be to build up within the various agencies a mass of national groups rather than a detached international civil service. Yet the growth of such a service would be the best insurance against any possible abuses, just as the functional method itself, by concentrating all attention on a practical public service, is likely more than anything else to breed a new conscience in all those concerned with such international activities.

This line of action would help to develop also another factor that is needed for the good working of any such experiment, namely, an international outlook and opinion. The very fact that it would concentrate attention on practical issues and activities would give people a better chance than the habitual political arguments to judge it on its merits. And as it would be natural to vary the seat of the various agencies, placing it in each case at a convenient centre for the particular function, people in many parts of the world would have before their eyes a piece of international government in action . . .
. . . .

IV   Through Functional Action to International Society

The way of national selection

One cannot insist too much that such gradual functional developments would not create a new system, however strange they might appear in the light of our habitual search for a unified formal order. They would merely rationalize and develop what is already there. In all countries social activities, in the widest sense of the term, are organized and reorganized continually in that way. But because of the legalistic structure of the state and of our political outlook, which treat national and international society as two different worlds, social nature, so to speak, has not had a chance so far to take its course. Our social activities are cut off arbitrarily at the limit of the state and, if at all, are allowed to be linked to the same activities across the border only by means of uncertain and cramping political ligatures. What is here proposed is simply that these political amputations should cease. Whenever useful or necessary the several activities would be released to function as one unit throughout the length of their natural course. National problems would then appear, and would be treated, as what they are, the local segments of general problems . . .

. . . There is nothing incompatible between the two conceptions: the functional arrangements might indeed be regarded as organic elements of a federalism by installments. But such a federalism if it came would be the solid growth of a natural selection and evolution, tested and accepted by experience, and not a green-table creation, blown about and battered by all the winds of political life. A functional organization does not crack if one of the participants tries political or social experiments of his own. Nor would indeed its existence be in jeopardy, as would be that of a sectional federation, if one of the members were to secede altogether. If the seceding member or members should happen to be pivotal factors in certain activities the result might be serious, but even then only the particular function affected would be endangered, while the others could go on . . .

Politically the method would have the strength which comes from free growth. No country need be forced to come in, and no country would be forced to stay out. Countries would come in for those functional activities in which they would be entitled to participate by the weight of their interests and resources, but all countries would benefit from the performance of a general service, even if they had no part in its control. On the other hand, no one would share in power who did not share in responsibility. This good democratic postulate could be reinforced by democratic representation; the functional structure could be made a union of peoples, not of states, but of the people directly concerned in any specific function, by giving them functional representation somewhat on the lines of the governing organs of the ILO.

The future lies clearly with a more liberal and systematic development on these lines. Not all activities can, or need be, so organized. But in all essential activities we could advance from our present position effectively and without delay if we would but put out of our minds the old political argument between political centralism and political devolution, which were the concomitants of the passive Liberal state, and follow a line more closely fitting the actual progress of our communal life. Instead of breaking up government mechanically into a pyramid of subordinate territorial areas, we need for our new ends rather to dissect its tasks and relevant authorities on lines that correspond to and fit those tasks. Instead of keeping up the old and barren attempt to establish a formal and fixed division of sovereignty and power, a division which changing conditions continually puts out of joint, we could with a little insight and boldness distribute power in accordance with the practical requirements of every function and object. Instead, that is, of asking *by whom* should sovereignty and power be exercised, we should rather ask *upon what* objects they should be exercised; or, to put it in other words, the real question is not 'who are the rightful authorities,' but rather 'what are the rightful ends – and what the proper means for them?' Authority would derive from the performance of a common task and would be conditioned by it, and not from the possession of a separate 'right' . . .

. . . .

The Tasks Ahead

. . . .

The task that is facing us is how to build up the reality of a common interest in peace. But with a revolutionary element injected into war that demands also a new sense of peace. Not a peace that would keep the nations quietly apart, but a peace that would bring them actively together; not the old static and strategic view of peace, but a social view of it. As General Smuts said in a recent speech: 'this is the social century.' Or one might say that we must put our faith not in a protected peace but in a working peace; it would indeed be nothing more nor less than the idea and aspiration of social security taken in its widest range. The number of problems which take on a world character is growing apace, partly because we have a better understanding of them – and know that with economics; as with epidemics and drugs, the evil must be attacked at the source and therefore through international action but also because of their technical peculiarities. Such is the nature of all the wonderful technical inventions that each harbours within it as much a threat as a promise. That was so with the steamship and still more with the submarine; and while flying and wireless bring comforts, they also bring fears – one threatens to interfere with the domestic safety of every people, and the other with its domestic sentiments and peace of mind. And airplanes and broadcasts cannot simply be denied access by a sovereign authority as was possible with ships and trains and telegraph; they drop upon us from the skies. Hence these contacts which crowd upon us from all directions can be as much a source of conflict as of co-operation; they must be built up in friendship for common use, or they will grow foul around us in suspicion and competition.

Empire and League having failed to find a way to an active international unity, because outstripped in different ways by the growth of social life, some reformers would now try federation; yet the very number and variety of the schemes proposed, limited territorially or ideologically, show that a scheme that might bring all peoples together cannot even be thought of. Federation, like other political formations, carries a Janus head which frowns division on one side in the very act of smiling union on the other. The idea which would look upon the United Nations as the grouping of the future is more spacious but less solid; it would break up the world upon no sounder basis than the chance alliance of war, and such a miscellaneous grouping on the basis of political equality would hardly suit the needs of executive action in the great tasks ahead. The growth of new administrative devices, and especially of planned public action, must be followed up also in the international sphere if the latter is to be more than a shadow. The organization of all social activities on an universal scale and on such lines is not yet practicable. Federal schemes, though they take account of the new factor, are logical only on a limited scale, at the expense of general unity. There remains the functional method. It is by no means free of difficulties, but these are on the whole mechanical difficulties which one could hope to overcome, and not political difficulties that spring from the very act of creation of the new organization.

. . . .

Chapter 3

Political Community and the North Atlantic Area: International Organization in the Light of Historical Experience

Karl W. Deutsch et al.*

The Problem

We undertook this inquiry as a contribution to the study of possible ways in which men some day might abolish war. From the outset, we realized the complexity of the problem. It is difficult to relate 'peace' clearly to other prime values such as 'justice' and 'freedom'. There is little common agreement on acceptable alternatives to war, and there is much ambiguity in the use of the terms 'war' and 'peace'. Yet we can start with the assumption that war is now so dangerous that mankind must eliminate it, must put it beyond serious possibility. The attempt to do this may fail. But in a civilization that wishes to survive, the central problem in the study of international organization is this: How can men learn to act together to eliminate war as a social institution?

This is in one sense a smaller, and in another sense a larger, question than the one which occupies so many of the best minds today: how can we either prevent or avoid losing 'the next war'? It is smaller because there will, of course, be no chance to solve the long-run problem if we do not survive the short-run crisis. It is larger because it concerns not only the confrontation of the nations of East and West in the 20th century, but the whole underlying question of relations between political units at any time. We are not, therefore, trying to add to the many words that have been written directly concerning the East–West struggle of the 1940–1950s. Rather, we are seeking new light with

---

* Reproduced from Karl W. Deutsch et. al. (1957) *Political Community and the North Atlantic Area: International Organization in the Light of Historical Experience* (Princeton: Princeton University Press). The text has been slightly edited, as indicated, to fit the format of this volume. Some peripheral footnotes have been omitted.

which to look at the conditions and processes of long-range or permanent peace, applying our findings to one contemporary problem which, though not so difficult as the East-West problem, is by no means simple: peace *within* the North Atlantic area.

. . . .

We are dealing here with political communities. These we regard as social groups with a process of political communication, some machinery for enforcement, and some popular habits of compliance. A political community is not necessarily able to prevent war within the area it covers: the United States was unable to do so at the time of the Civil War. Some political communities do, however, eliminate war and the expectation of war within their boundaries. It is these that call for intensive study.

We have concentrated, therefore, upon the formation of 'security-communities' in certain historical cases. The use of this term starts a chain of definitions, and we must break in here to introduce the other main links needed for a fuller understanding of our findings.

A SECURITY-COMMUNITY is a group of people which has become 'integrated':

By INTEGRATION we mean the attainment, within a territory, of a 'sense of community' and of institutions and practices strong enough and widespread enough to assure, for a 'long' time, dependable expectations of 'peaceful change' among its population.

By SENSE OF COMMUNITY we mean a belief on the part of individuals in a group that they have come to agreement on at least this one point: that common social problems must and can be resolved by processes of 'peaceful change'.

By PEACEFUL CHANGE we mean the resolution of social problems, normally by institutionalized procedures, without resort to large-scale physical force.

A security-community, therefore, is one in which there is real assurance that the members of that community will not fight each other physically, but will settle their disputes in some other way. If the entire world were integrated as a security-community, wars would be automatically eliminated. But there is apt to be confusion about the term 'integration'.

In our usage, the term 'integration' does not necessarily mean only the merging of peoples or governmental units into a single unit. Rather, we divide security-communities into two types: 'amalgamated' and 'pluralistic'.

By AMALGAMATION we mean the formal merger of two or more previously independent units into a single larger unit, with some type of common government after amalgamation. This common government may be unitary or federal. The United States today is an example of the amalgamated type. It became a single governmental unit by the formal merger of several formerly independent units. It has one supreme decision-making center.

The PLURALISTIC security-community, on the other hand, retains the legal independence of separate governments. The combined territory of the United States and Canada is an example of the pluralistic type. Its two separate governmental units form a security-community without being merged. It has two supreme decision-making centers. Where amalgamation occurs without integration, of course a security-community does not exist.

Since our study deals with the problem of ensuring peace, we shall say that any political community, be it amalgamated or pluralistic, was eventually SUCCESSFUL if it became a security-community – that is, if it achieved integration – and that it was UNSUCCESSFUL if it ended eventually in secession or civil war.

Perhaps we should point out here that both types of integration require, at the international level, some kind of organization, even though it may be very loose. We put no credence in the old aphorism that among friends a constitution is not necessary and among enemies it is of no avail. The area of practicability lies in between.

Integration is a matter of fact, not of time. If people on both sides do not fear war and do not prepare for it, it matters little how long it took them to reach this stage. But once integration has been reached, the length of time over which it persists may contribute to its consolidation.

It should be noted that integration and amalgamation overlap, but not completely. This means that there can be amalgamation without integration, and that there can be integration without amalgamation. When we use the term 'integration or amalgamation' in this book, we are taking a short form to express an alternative between integration (by the route of either pluralism or amalgamation) and amalgamation

Table 2   *Security communities*

	Non-Amalgamation	Amalgamation
Integration	Pluralistic Security-Community	Amalgamated Security-Community
	Example (Norway-Sweden today)	Example: (USA today)
Non-Integration	Pluralistic Security-Community	Amalgamated but not Security-Community
	Example (USA-USSR today)	Example (Habsburg Empire 1914)

short of integration. We have done this because unification movements in the past have often aimed at both of these goals, with some of the supporters of the movements preferring one or the other goal at different times. To encourage this profitable ambiguity, leaders of such movements have often used broader symbols such as 'union', which would cover both possibilities and could be made to mean different things to different men.

One of our basic premises is that whatever we can learn about the process of forming security-communities should be helpful in an indirect way not only to planners, but also to existing international organizations. If the way to integration, domestic or international, is through the achievement of a sense of community that undergirds institutions, then it seems likely that an increased sense of community would help to strengthen whatever institutions – supranational or international – are already operating. When these institutions are agencies for enforcement of the public will, we encounter that ancient and tantalizing puzzle: who policies the police? Can we make certain that agreements freely entered into, will be reliably enforced or peacefully changed? Until we can do this, war may be called upon to do the job, liquidating the disputing parties instead of the dispute.

Everyone knows that political machinery already exists for reaching international decisions, and that these decisions cannot always be enforced after they are decided upon. Likewise, judicial machinery also exists which could be used for settling any international dispute without force; but states cannot be brought before a court against their will, nor made to abide by its judgment. It is equally true that enforcement or compliance can be achieved for a time without willing acceptance, as in the case of a strong state against a weak one. But without steady acceptance by large numbers of people, compliance is bound to be ineffective or temporary.

A situation of compliance, then, presupposes general agreement about something. Perhaps the 'something' has to be the substance of the matter being complied with, or perhaps merely the legitimacy of the enforcing agent, or even the rightfulness of the procedure being used. Once men have attained this condition of agreement with regard to a social institution for enforcement of the public will, and have stabilized this condition that institution would seem to be reliably supported: the police are effectively policed. This kind of institution – perhaps the most crucial of all – represents the force organized on behalf of the community. In our terms, a sense of community would have been achieved to a high degree – perhaps high enough to be considered as integration.

. . . .

The Integrative Process: Some General Characteristics

For purposes of exposition, we have divided our findings into two parts: first, general changes in our way of thinking about political integration; and second, specific findings about the background conditions and the dynamic characteristics of the integrative process. In this chapter, we shall first discuss our general findings. Our more specific findings will follow in later sections . . .

1   Re-examining some popular beliefs

To begin with, our findings have tended to make us increasingly doubtful of several widespread beliefs about political integration. The first of these beliefs is that modern life, with rapid transportation, mass-communications, and literacy, tends to be more international than life in past decades or centuries, and hence more conducive to the growth of international or supranational institutions. Neither the study of our cases, nor a survey of more limited data from a larger number of countries, has yielded any clear-cut evidence to support this view. Nor do these results suggest that there has been inherent in modern economic and social development any unequivocal trend toward more internationalism and world community.

This is particularly true of political amalgamation. The closer we get to modern conditions and to our own time, the more difficult it is to find any instances of successful amalgamation of two or more previously sovereign states. Thus far we found not a single full-fledged modern social-service state that has successfully federated or otherwise merged with another . . .

. . . .

Another popular belief that our findings make more doubtful is that the growth of a state, or the expansion of its territory, resembles a snowballing process, or that it is characterized by some sort of bandwagon effect, such that successful growth in the past would accelerate the rate of growth or expansion of the amalgamated political community in the future. In this view, as villages in the past have joined to make provinces, and provinces to make kingdoms, so contemporary states are expected to join into ever-larger states or federations. If this were true, ever-larger political units would appear to be the necessary result of historical and technological development. Our findings do not support this view. While the successful unification of England facilitated the later amalgamation of England and Wales, and this in turn facilitated the subsequent amalgamation of England and Wales with Scotland in the union of the two kingdoms. The united kingdom of Britain did not succeed in carrying through a successful and lasting amalgamation with Ireland. Nor could it retain its political amalgamation with the American colonies . . .

. . . .

Another popular notion is that a principal motive for the political integration of states has been the fear of anarchy, as well as of warfare among them. According to this view, men not only came to look upon war among the units concerned as unpromising and unattractive, but also as highly probable. For they came to fear it acutely while believing it to be all but inevitable in the absence of any strong superior power to restrain all participants. Consequently, according to this theory, one of the first and most important features of a newly-amalgamated security-community was the establishment of strong federal or community-wide laws, courts, police forces, and armies for the enforcement against potentially aggressive member states and member populations. Beliefs of this kind parallel closely classic reasoning of Thomas Hobbes and John Locke; and some writers on federalism or on international organization, have implied a stress on legal institutions and on the problem coercing member states. Our findings suggest strong qualifications for these views. The questions of larger-community police forces and law enforcement, and of the coercion of member states, turned out to be of minor importance in the early stages of most of the amalgamated security-communities we studied.

. . . .

2 General findings

Among our positive general findings, the most important seems to us that both amalgamated security-communities and pluralistic security-communities are practicable pathways to integration. In the course of our research, we found ourselves led by the evidence to attribute a greater potential significance to pluralistic security-communities than we had originally expected. Pluralistic security-communities turned out to be somewhat easier to attain and easier to preserve than their amalgamated counterparts . . .

A The strengths of pluralism

The somewhat smaller risk of breakdown in the case of pluralistic security-communities seems indicated by an examination of the relative numbers of successes and failures of each type of security-community. We can readily list a dozen instances of success for each type. Cases of successful amalgamated security-communities would be, for instance: United States since 1877; England since the 17th century; England-Wales since 1512; England-Scotland since 1707; Germany since 1871; Italy since 1859; France Since at least the late-19th century; Canada since 1867; the Netherlands since 1831; Belgium since 1831; Sweden since 1815; and Switzerland since 1848. Cases of successful pluralistic security-communities include: United States between 1781–1789; England-Scotland between the late 1560s and 1707; Prussia and the

German states except Austria between 1815 and 1866–1871; Norway-Sweden since 1907; Switzerland between 1291 and 1847; United States-Canada since the 1970s; United States-Mexico since the 1930s; United States-United Kingdom as early as 1871, or certainly since the end of the century; United Kingdom-Netherlands since perhaps 1815; Denmark-Sweden since the late nineteenth or early twentieth century; Denmark-Norway since the same time; and France-Belgium since some time in the 19th century. An example of an emerging pluralistic security-community might be England-Ireland since 1915.

On the other hand, we find a sharp contrast in the number of failures for each type. We have found only one case of a pluralistic security-community which failed in the sense that it was followed by actual warfare between the participants, and it is doubtful whether a pluralistic security-community existed even in that case: this was the relationship of Austria and Prussia within the framework of the German Confederation since 1815. . . . In contrast to this single instance of failure of a pluralistic security-community, we can readily list seven cases of amalgamated security-communities that failed: the United States in 1861; England-Ireland in 1918; Austria-Hungary in 1918; Norway-Sweden in 1905; Metropolitan France with a series of revolutions and wars between 1789 and 1871; Metropolitan France and Algeria in the 1950s; and Spain including the Catalan and Basque populations in the 1930s. A number of these wars were fought with a bitterness that might have proved fatal to both contestants if they had possessed present-day weapons of mass destruction.

On balance, therefore, we found pluralistic security-communities to be a more promising approach to the elimination of war over large areas than we had thought at the outset of our inquiry.

But this relative superiority of a pluralistic security-community as a more easily attainable form of integration has limited applications. It worked only in those situations in which the keeping of the peace among the participating units was the main political goal overshadowing all others. This goal has been the main focus of our study. In our historical cases, however, we found that men have often wanted more: they have wanted a political community that would not merely keep the peace among its members but that would also be capable of acting as a unit in other ways and for other purposes. In respect to this capacity to act – and in particular, to act quickly and effectively for positive goals – amalgamated security-communities have usually been far superior to their pluralistic counterparts. In many historical cases men have preferred to accept the somewhat greater risk of civil war, or of war among the participating units, in order to insure this greater promise of joint capacity for action. It is only today, in the new age of nuclear weapons, that these risks and gains must be reevaluated. Now a pluralistic security-community may appear a somewhat safer device than amalgamation for dealing with man's new weapons.

B   *The thresholds of Integration*

Our second general finding concerns the nature of integration. In our earliest analytical scheme, we had envisaged this as an all-or-none process, analogous to the crossing of a narrow threshold. On the one side of this threshold, populations and policy-makers considered warfare among the states or political units concerned as still a serious possibility, and prepared for it; on the other side of the threshold they were supposed to do so no longer. We expected to apply two broad kinds of tests to the presence or absence of integration – that is, the existence or nonexistence of a security-community – among particular states or territories.

One of these tests was subjective, in terms of the opinions of the political decision-makers, or of the politically relevant strata in each territory. These had to be inferred from many kinds of historical evidence in the past, or from samples or surveys in present-day situations obtained by well-known methods of studying public opinion . . .

The other kind of test was essentially objective and operational. It replaced the recording of opinions by the measurement of the tangible commitments and the allocation of resources with which people backed them: how large preparations were made specifically for the possibility of war against any other group within the wider community . . .

. . . .

Somewhat contrary to our expectations, however, some of our cases taught us that integration may involve a fairly broad zone of transition rather than a narrow threshold; that states might cross and recross this threshold or zone of transition several times in their relations with each other; and that they might spend decades or generations wavering uncertainly within it.

Thus we found that states could maintain armed forces which were potentially available for warfare against each other, but which were not specifically committed to this purpose. The American state militias from 1776 to 1865 and the forces of the Swiss cantons from the 13th to the 19th centuries, seem to have been available for such purposes if the political temper of their respective communities had warranted such employment, as it did on a few occasions. It would thus be extraordinarily difficult to say just in which year warfare between the Protestant and Catholic cantons ceased to be a practical political possibility after 1712, or when it again became temporarily a practical possibility between 1815 and 1847; or just when integration within the United states was lost in the period between 1820 and 1861, and ware between North and South became a substantial possibility . . .

. . . .

C   Communication and the sense of community

Integration has proved to be a more continuous process than our earliest analytical scheme had suggested; but it continues to be characterized by important thresholds. Within this framework of our revised general concept of integration, we have arrived at a somewhat deeper understanding of the meaning of 'sense of community'. It appears to rest primarily on something other than verbal assent to some or many explicit propositions. The populations of different territories might easily profess verbal attachment to the same set of values without having a sense of community that leads to political integration. The kind of sense of community that is relevant for integration, and therefore for our study, turned out to be rather a matter of mutual sympathy and loyalties; of 'we-feeling', trust, and mutual consideration; of partial identification in terms of self-images and interests; of mutually successful predictions of behavior, and of cooperative action in accordance with it – in short, a matter of a perpetual dynamic process of mutual attention, communication, perception of needs, and responsiveness in the process of decision-making. 'Peaceful change' could not be assured without this kind of relationship.

. . . .

D   Growth around core areas

As such a process of integrative behavior, sense of community requires some particular habits of political behavior on the part of individuals and some particular traditions and institutions on the part of social groups and of political units, such as provinces or states.

These habits, in turn, are acquired by processes of social learning. People learn them in the face of background conditions which change only slowly, so that they appear at any moment as something given – as political, economic, social, or psychological facts that must be taken for granted for the purposes of short-range politics. The speed and extent of this learning of habits of integrative political behavior are then influenced in each situation by these background conditions, as well as by the dynamics of the particular political process – the particular movement toward integration. Some of our more specific findings deal with the importance of certain background conditions in each area studied, while others deal with the successive stages of the integrative political process that occurred.

The outcome, then, of the integrative process among any particular group of countries depends on the interplay of the effects of background conditions with moving political events. One aspect of this interplay deserves to be singled out for particular attention. It is the matter of political, economic, and social capabilities of the participating political units for integrative behavior.

Generally, we found that such integrative capabilities were closely related to the general capabilities of a given political unit for action in the fields of politics, administration economic life, and social and cultural development. Larger, stronger, more politically, administratively, economically, and educationally advanced political units were found to form the cores of strength around which in most cases the integrative process developed.

Political amalgamation, in particular, usually turned out to be a nuclear process. It often occurred around single cores, as in the case of England, Piedmont, Prussia, and Sweden. Each of these came to form the core of a larger amalgamated political community . . .

E   The need for rising capabilities

The extent of integrative capabilities which already existed in the individual political units at the beginning of a major drive toward amalgamation thus turned out to be very important for the future development of the process. But another step was no less important: the further increase of these capabilities in the course of the movement toward amalgamation. The presence or absence of growth in such capabilities played a major role in every integrative process we studied, and particularly in every case of an amalgamation movement.

Generally, amalgamation did not come to pass because the government of the participating units had become weaker or more inefficient; nor did it come to pass because men had been forced to turn away from these increasingly incapable organizations to the building of a larger and less decrepit common government. Rather, amalgamation occurred after a substantial increase in the capabilities of at least some of the participating units, or sometimes of all of them. Examples are the increase in the capabilities of the American colonies before 1789, and in the capabilities of Prussia before 1871. The increase in the capabilities of the political organizations or governments of the individual states, cantons, principalities, and the like, formed a major element in the dynamic political process leading to amalgamation in each instance.

Such capabilities relevant to integration were of two broad kinds. One was related to the capacity to act of a political unit – such as its size, power, economic strength, administrative efficiency, and the like. The other kind was related to the ability of a unit to control its own behavior and to redirect its own attention. More accurately, this means the ability of its political decision-makers and relevant political elites to redirect and control, their own attention and behavior so as to enable rulers to receive communications from other political units which were to be their prospective partners in the integrative process. It means, further, the ability to give these messages from other political units adequate weight in the making of their own decisions, to perceive the needs of the populations and elites of these other units, and to respond to them quickly and adequately in terms of political or economic action. The first kind of capabilities – those related to the capacity to act and to overcome external obstacles – are closely linked to what we often call power; the second kind are linked to what we propose to call responsiveness.

The two kinds of capabilities obviously overlap. Power that cannot be controlled by the governments or political communities who try to exercise it is likely to dwindle soon by dissipation or to be checked by growing external resistance; and responsiveness would remain a matter of mere intention, lacking the measure of power required to put the intended responses into practical effect. Yet we found that power and responsiveness were not quite equal in importance. Once a moderate measure of power had been achieved, the capabilities relating to the responsiveness of a political unit and its rulers seemed to be of crucial importance to the success or failure of integration.

. . . .

F   The race between capabilities and loads

Another set of data we found to be of crucial importance pertained to the burdens thrown upon the tangible and intangible resources of political units by the requirements of establishing or maintaining either an amalgamated or a pluralistic security-community. Such loads or burdens, as we have called them, were of many kinds. They included military or financial burdens, drains on manpower or wealth; the burden of risk from political or military commitments; costs of social and economic readjustments, such as at the establishment of a customs union; and similar burdens of a material kind. But they also included intangible burdens upon government, which could be visualized as somewhat similar to traffic loads of vehicles at a road intersection or of messages at a telephone exchange. In the cases of crossroads or switchboards, the flow of vehicles or messages requires more than a certain volume of material facilities for its accommodation; it also requires a certain number of decisions which must be made in a limited amount of time by the traffic officer who controls traffic at the inter-section, or by the persons or apparatus that control the flow of calls through the telephone exchange.

It is this burden, imposed by the traffic load of messages and signals upon the attention-giving and decision-making capabilities of the persons or organizations in control, that has close parallels in the burden of government upon rulers. It is a burden upon the attention-giving, information-processing, and decision-making capabilities of administrators, political elites, legislatures, or electoral majorities. Thus the failure of the British Parliament to respond quickly and ade-quately to the disastrous Irish famine of 1846 was not caused primarily by any lack of material or financial resources to provide relief. Rather, the failure was one of adequate attention, perception, and decision-making to meet the burdens of responsibility which the Parliament had taken upon itself under the terms of Anglo-Irish union. It was nonetheless a failure that was to have far-reaching effects upon the future of Anglo-Irish relations.

Political amalgamation in general tended to increase the load of demands upon the material resources and the decision-making capabilities of governments, since decisions for larger areas and populations had to be made by fewer central institutions. The success or failure of amalgamation, then, depended in considerable part upon the relationship of two rates of change: the growing rate of claims and burdens upon central governments as against the growing – in some instances, the insufficiently growing – level of capabilities of the governmental institutions of the amalgamated political community. The load of communications, demands, and claims upon the capabilities of government was also growing from independent causes – such as the increasing complexity of economic life, the increasing level of popular expectations in terms of living standards, social opportunities, and political rights, and the increasing political activity of previously passive groups and strata. Hence the outcome of the race between the growth of loads and capabilities sometimes remained precarious for a longer period, or it changed from one period to another.

. . . .

The Importance of Background Conditions

In general, our cases have left us impressed with the importance of certain background conditions for the success or failure of the integrative process. The influence of background conditions appears to be larger, and the opportunities for decisive action by political leaders or movements appear to be somewhat more limited, than we had thought at the beginning of our study.

To be sure, we found that the importance of a few background conditions had been somewhat overrated. Certain conditions which had often been considered as essential for the establishment of an amalgamated security-community turned out to be helpful to that end but not essential to it. Such helpful but nonessential conditions included previous administrative and/or dynastic union; ethnic or linguistic assimilation; strong economic ties; and foreign military threats. While all of these turned out to be helpful to integration, none of them appeared to be essential since each of them was absent in the successful establishment of at least one amalgamated security-community. Thus no previous administrative union had linked the Italian states for almost

1500 years. No ethnic or linguistic assimilation had wiped out the differences between the language groups of Switzerland. No strong economic ties existed between England and Scotland, or Norway and Sweden, or among the Italian states, prior to their union in each case. And no unusual foreign military threat played any important role in the adoption of the Swiss federal constitution in 1848, or in the union between England and Wales.

. . . .

Some essential requirements for the establishment of amalgamated security-communities

A number of conditions appear to be essential, so far as our evidence goes, for the success of amalgamated security-communities – that is, for their becoming integrated . . .

1. *Values and Expectations.* The first group of essential conditions deals with motivations for political behavior, and in particular with the values and expectations held in the politically relevant strata of the political units concerned. In regard to values, we found in all our cases a compatibility of the main values held by the politically relevant strata of all participating units . . .

. . . .

Values were most effective politically when they were not held merely in abstract terms, but when they were incorporated in political institutions and in habits of political behavior which permitted these values to be acted on in such a way as to strengthen people's attachment to them. This connection between values, institutions, and habits we call a 'way of life', and it turned out to be crucial. In all our cases of successful amalgamation we found such a distinctive way of life – that is, a set of socially accepted values and of institutional means for their pursuit and attainment, and a set of established or emerging habits of behavior corresponding to them. To be distinctive, such a way of life has to include at least some major social or political values and institutions which are different from those which existed in the area during the recent past, or from those prevailing among important neighbors. In either case, such a way of life usually involved a significant measure of social innovation as against the recent past.

Putting the matter somewhat differently, we noted in our cases that the partial shift of political habits required in transferring political loyalties from the old, smaller political units, at least in part, to a new and larger political community has only occurred under conditions when also a great number of other political and social habits were in a state of change. Thus we find that the perception of an American people and an American political community, as distinct from the individual 13 colonies, emerged between 1750 and 1790. This occurred at the same time as the emergence of a distinct American way of life clearly different from that of most of the people of Great Britain or French Canada . . .

In regard to expectations, we found that in all our cases amalgamation was preceded by widespread expectations of joint rewards for the participating units, through strong economic ties or gains envisaged for the future . . .

. . . .

Some non-economic expectations also turned out to be essential. In all our cases of successful amalgamation we found widespread expectations of greater social or political equality, or of greater social or political rights or liberties, among important groups of the politically relevant strata – and often among parts of the underlying population – in the political units concerned.

2. Capabilities and Communication Processes. Values and expectations not only motivate people to performance, but the results of this performance will in turn make the original values and expectations weaker or stronger. Accordingly, we found a number of essential conditions for amalgamation which were related to the capabilities of the participating units or to the processes of communication occurring among them. The most important of these conditions was an increase in the political and administrative capabilities of the main political units to be amalgamated. Thus the amalgamation of Germany was preceded by a marked increase in the political and administrative capabilities of Prussia from 1806 onward, and by a lesser but still significant increase in the corresponding capabilities of Bavaria and of other German states. Similarly, there were important increases in the capabilities of Piedmont in the course of the last decades preceding Italian unification. In the case of the American colonies, considerable increases in the capabilities of American state governments after 1776, and particularly the adoption of important and effective state constitutions by Pennsylvania, Virginia, Massachusetts, and other states, paved the way for the Articles of Confederation and later for federal union.

Another essential condition for amalgamation, closely related to the increase in capabilities, is the presence of markedly superior economic growth, either as measured against the recent past of the territories to be amalgamated, or against neighboring areas. Such superior economic growth did not have to be present in all participating units prior to amalgamation, but it had to be present at least in the main partner or partners vis-a-vis the rest of the units to be included in the amalgamated security-community. The higher economic growth rates of England, Prussia, and Piedmont, both immediately before and during amalgamation, are conspicuous examples.

Another essential requirement for successful amalgamation was the presence of unbroken links of social communication between the political units concerned, and between the politically relevant strata within them. By such unbroken links we mean social groups and institutions which provide effective channels of communication, both horizontally among the main units of the amalgamated security-community and vertically among the politically relevant strata within them. Such links thus involve always persons and organizations.

. . . .

Another essential condition, related to the preceding one, is the broadening of the political, social, or economic elite, both in regard to its recruitment from broader social strata and to its continuing connections with them. An example of such a broadening of the elite was the emergence of a new type of political leader among the landowners of Virginia, such as George Washington, who retained the respect of his peers and at the same time also knew, well before the American Revolution, how to gain the votes of poorer farmers and frontiersmen . . .

3. *Mobility of Persons.* Another condition present in all our cases of successful amalgamation was the mobility of persons among the main units, at least in the politically relevant strata. It is quite possible that this condition, too, may be essential for the success of amalgamation . . .

4. *Multiplicity and Balance of Transactions.* We also found that it was not enough for a high level of communication and transactions to exist in only one or two topics, or in one or two respects, among two or more political units if their amalgamation was to be successful. Rather it appeared that successfully amalgamated security-communities require a fairly wide range of different common functions and services, together with different institutions and organizations to carry them out. Further, they apparently require a multiplicity of ranges of common communications and transactions and their institutional counterparts. Thus the unification of Germany on the political level in 1871 had been prepared by the setting up of common institutions in regard to customs policies, to postal matters, and to the standardization of commercial laws; and beyond the sphere of politics, amalgamation had been prepared by a multiplicity of common institutions in cultural, educational, literary, scientific, and professional affairs...

Two other conditions may well turn out to be essential for the success of amalgamation, but these will have to be investigated further. The first of them is concerned with the balance in the flow of communications and transactions between the political units that are to be amalgamated, and particularly with the balance of rewards between the different participating territories . . . In the course of studying cases of successful amalgamation, we found that is was apparently important for each for the participating territories or populations to gain some valued services or opportunities . . .

The second condition follows from the preceding one. It was not essential that the flow of rewards . . . should balance at any moment, but it seems essential that they should balance some over some period of time . . .

5. *Mutual Predictability of Behavior.* A final condition that may be essential for the success of amalgamation may be come minimum amount of mutual predictability to behavior. Members of an amalgamated security-community – and, to a lesser extent, of a pluralistic security-community – must be able to expect from one another some dependable interlocking, interchanging, or at least compatible behavior; and they must therefore be able, at least to that extent, to predict one another's actions. Such predictions may be based on mere familiarity. In this way, the Vermonters or English-speaking Canadians may know what to expect to their French-Canadian neighbors and to what extent to rely on them, even through they do not share their folkways and culture and do not know what it feels like to be a French-Canadian. Even so, familiarity may be sufficiently effective to permit the development of an attitude of confidence and trust . . .

. . . .

6. *Summary.* Altogether we have found nine essential conditions for an amalgamated security-community: (1) mutual compatibility of main values; (2) a distinctive way of life; (3) expectations of stronger economic ties or gains; (4) a marked increase in political and administrative capabilities of at least some participating units; (5) superior economic growth on the past of at least some participating units; (6) unbroken links of social communication, both geographically between territories and sociologically between different social strata; (7) a broadening of the political elite; (8) mobility of persons, at least among the politically relevant strata; and (9) a multiplicity of ranges of communication and transaction. And we have found indications that three other conditions may be essential: (10) a compensation of flows of communications and transactions; (11) a not too infrequent interchange of group roles; and (12) considerable predictability of behavior.

. . . .

Special Features of Pluralistic Security-communities

In regard to the problem of a pluralistic security-community, we found that its attainment would be favored by any conditions favorable to the success of an amalgamated security-community, and that it was sometimes hindered by conditions or processes harmful to the latter. Pluralistic security-communities sometimes succeeded, however, under far less favorable conditions than the success of an amalgamated government would have required; and they sometimes survived unfavorable or disintegrative processes which would have destroyed an amalgamated political community. The survival of the Swiss Confederation under the relatively unfavorable conditions of the 17th and 18th centuries is a case in point. Another is the survival of the

Scandinavian pluralistic security-community under the strains of and stresses of two world wars.

. . . .

Of the twelve conditions that appeared to be essential for the success of an amalgamated security-community, or at least potentially so, only two or possibly three were found to be very important for a pluralistic security-community as well. The first of these was the compatibility of major values relevant to political decision-making. The second was the capacity of the participating political units or governments to respond to each other's needs, messages, and actions quickly, adequately, and without resort to violence. In the case of a pluralistic security-community, such capabilities for political responsiveness required in each participating state a great many established political habits, and of functioning political institutions, favoring mutual communication and consultation. To be effective, such habits and institutions had to insure that messages from other member governments or units would not merely be received, but would be understood, and that they would be given real weight in the process of decision-making. A third essential conditions for a pluralistic security-community may be mutual predictability of behavior; this appears closely related to the foregoing. But the member states of a pluralistic security-community have to make joint decisions only about a more limited range of subject matters, and retain each a far wider range of problems for autonomous decision-making within their own borders. Consequently, the range and extent of the mutual predictability of behavior required from members of a pluralistic security-community is considerable less than would be essential for the successful operation of an amalgamated one.

. . . .

The Issue of Functionalism as a Pathway to Amalgamation

Our finding that the bringing together of the necessary background conditions for amalgamation in our cases resembled an assembly-line process, suggests indirectly an answer to an old question: does merging of one or more governmental functions among two or more political units promote progress toward later over-all amalgamation of their governments? Or, on the contrary, does what we shall call functional amalgamation impede such overall amalgamation by inadequate performance of the few already amalgamated functions? Does it take the wind from the sails of the movement for full-scale amalgamation by making the few already amalgamated functions serve adequately the main needs which had supplied most of the driving power for the over-all amalgamation movement?

Before we answer this question, we must say exactly what we mean by functionalism. As we are using the term here, it includes all cases of partial amalgamation, where some governmental functions are delegated by the participating units on a low or a high level of decision-making. Whether a particular function or institution is so important that its pooling with another government would have the effect of overall amalgamation rather than partial – and thus take it out of the field of functionalism – depends on the importance of this particular function of institution in the domestic politics of the participating units . . .

. . . .

How helpful, then, has functionalism been? We have found, first of all, that overall amalgamation can be approached functionally and by steps, with successful overall amalgamation at the end. This occurred in the cases of Germany with the Zollverein (of which, significantly, Austria was not a member); the United States with the common administration of Western lands under the Articles of Confederation; the Swiss cantons since the 14th century, and the common citizenship between Geneva, Bern, and Fribourg, and later other Swiss cantons from the 16th century onward; finally, between England and Wales and England and Scotland before the union of crowns preceding full amalgamation. In all these cases amalgamation eventually was successful. But functional amalgamation was also proposed and rejected among the Italian states in the 1840s, and eventually amalgamation was achieved without its aid. Moreover, functional amalgamation took place in at least three of our cases that were eventually unsuccessful: there was the union of crowns between Austria, Bohemia, and Hungary from 1526 onward; there was the union of crowns between Norway and Sweden in 1814; and there were various forms of partial amalgamation between England and Ireland before 1801.

These examples are taken from a sample collection of historical cases and situations in which instances of successful amalgamation outnumber the unsuccessful ones by more than two to one. From this it should be clear that the historical evidence in favor of functionalism is quite inconclusive.

It seems safest to conclude that the issue of functionalism has been greatly overrated. Functionalism, it appears, is a device that has been widely used both in successful and in unsuccessful movements toward amalgamation, somewhat as functional devolution and decentralization have been used in successful and in unsuccessful attempts at secession. The outcome in all such situations seems mostly to have been the result of other conditions and other processes – depending largely on whether functionalism mainly was associated with experiences of joint rewards or of joint deprivations – with functionalism in itself doing little to help or to harm . . .

Perhaps the most that can be said for functionalism as approach to integration is that it seems less hazardous than a sudden attempt at overall amalgamation . . .

. . . .

PART II

Theorizing the Common Market: Neofunctionalism and its Critics

Featured works

- Ernst Haas (1968) *The Uniting of Europe: Political, Social and Economic Forces 1950–1957*, 2nd edn (Stanford: Stanford University Press).

- Leon Lindberg (1963) *The Political Dynamics of European Economic Integration* (Stanford: Stanford University Press).

- Stanley Hoffmann (1966) 'Obstinate or Obsolete? The Fate of the Nation-State and the Case of Western Europe', *Daedalus*, 95(3).

- Roger Hansen (1969) 'Regional Integration: Reflections on a Decade of Theoretical Efforts', *World Politics*, 21(2).

Neofunctionalism and its Critics

Given their prescriptive nature and orientation toward broad international organizations like the League of Nations and the UN, the integration pre-theories proved ill-suited to explaining the process of economic integration that began in Western Europe in the early 1950s. By the mid-1950s, a new body of scholarship emerged, mainly among American political scientists, which took its starting point in the direct empirical study of the emerging economic institutions of the European Communities. According to Rosamond, 'neofunctionalism can be read at one level as a theory provoked entirely by the integrative activity among the original six member states' (Rosamond 2000: 10). Yet, while neofunctionalism was undoubtedly stimulated by the emergence of the EC, it was also tied to broader theoretical trends that were not directly related to the birth of the Community. Like transactionalism, neofunctionalism was a product of the behaviouralist turn in American social science after World War II (Taylor 1975b: xiii). Behaviouralism implied a rejection of the descriptive focus on institutional forms entailed in early integration theories in favour of a focus on political behaviour and processes. It also implied an embrace of the methodological rigour associated with the natural sciences. Social theories were no longer seen as blueprints for desired forms of social organization but as 'scientific' devices for generating testable hypotheses, which could be verified through empirical research. Fuelled by a desire to construct a general scientific explanation of the process of integration, neofunctionalists set out to test and reformulate functionalist principles in the context of regional institutions like the ECSC, Euratom, the EEC and NATO.

This introduction focuses on the development of neofunctionalist theory from the mid-1950s to the 1970s. Neofunctionalist studies during this period are numerous and span a wide group of authors. I will discuss and display only a small segment of this scholarship (see the suggestions for further reading for a fuller account). In particular, I focus on the work of Ernst Haas, Leon Lindberg, Stuart Scheingold, Philippe Schmitter and Joseph Nye as the leading representatives of neofunctionalism. Their work has been and continues to be a momentous influence on European integration studies and international relations in general. I also look at major critiques levelled against neofunctionalism. The most serious challenge came from a group of so-called 'intergovernmentalists'. Rooted in the tradition of classic realist authors like E. H. Carr and Hans Morgenthau, they warned that the neofunctionalist prediction of a gradual 'spillover' from economic cooperation to political union was mistaken. While governments might cooperate on uncontroversial economic and technical issues (so-called 'low politics'), they would never delegate control of sensitive or 'high political areas' such as foreign affairs and security to a supranational institution. National sovereignty would therefore remain a key determinant of international politics. This critique from intergovernmentalists led to substantial modification and reformulation of neofunctionalism during the 1960s and early 1970s before the theory was finally declared obsolete.

The Origins of Neofunctionalism

Neofunctionalism, as developed by Ernst Haas and others in the late 1950s and 1960s, presents the first comprehensive theory of regional integration. Whereas functionalists emphasized the virtues of a united Europe in terms of welfare and peace, neofunctionalists sought to 'dissect the actual integration *process* in order to derive propositions about its nature' (Haas 1958a: xii). Unlike its predecessor, then, neofunctionalism does not offer a 'manual' for integration but aspires to construct a systematic predictive theory of international political integration. Yet it is also normative. Despite presenting itself as a positive theory, neofunctionalism is infused with a strong normative commitment to the integration of Europe (Mutimer 1992: 33).

The central focus of neofunctionalism is the relationship between economic and political integration. Simplified, the premise is that integration in economic and functional sectors will lead to pressure for political integration due to 'spillovers' and 'unintended consequences' that occur when states discover that integration in one functional area impacts upon their interdependent activities in other related areas. The theory assigns a key role to supranational organizations in providing the dynamic for further integration. In the first instance, integration in economic sectors increases the volume of trade and transactions across borders. These transactions in turn create problems, which can only be solved by a supranational bureaucracy. Once supranational institutions are created, industry groups and other social interests organize on a regional level to put pressure on the new bureaucracy which itself acts as a pressure group for further integration (Nye 1966: 18). Gradually, the loyalties and expectations of citizens will become focused on the new centre and a new political union is born.

This argument shares much in common with classical functionalism. Like functionalists, neofunctionalists maintain that integration is a logical response to the complexities of modern economic life. Growing economic interdependence implies that to continue to perform its functions adequately, the nation state is under pressure to delegate certain functions to regional and international institutions. There are, however, key differences from classic functionalism. First, while functionalists view integration as an inescapable outcome of historical forces that drive the state to supply more and more functions and thereby impel it to enter into a network of international functional institutions, neofunctionalists merely assume that once such institutions are created they will tend to promote integration – even if this was not an original purpose of creating them (Milward and Sørensen 1993: 2). Second, integration on a neofunctionalist view is rooted in the self-interest of political actors rather than a universal concern for the advancement of welfare. What drives integration is the perception of individual actors that they stand to benefit from supranational rather than national solutions: not a collective dedication to a 'common good' (Haas 1964: 230–8; Lindberg 1963: 293). The emphasis on political self-interest leads neofunctionalists to reject the technological determinism of functionalism. In the neofunctionalist version, integration is advanced less by functional pressures or technological change *as such*, but more by the interaction of political forces – politicians, interest groups, political parties, and even governments – who seek to exploit these pressures in pursuit of their own interests (Haas 1964: 101).

A third difference from functionalism relates to the end result of integration. While functionalists visualize an international community in which authority is dispersed among separate functional organizations, neofunctionalists look to the creation of a central political authority. In his seminal work *The Uniting of Europe* (see Chapter 4) Haas defines integration as 'the process whereby political actors in several distinct national settings are persuaded to shift their loyalties, expectations and political activities towards a new centre' The result is 'a new political community, superimposed over the pre-existing ones' (1958a: 16). This focus on central political institutions is close in spirit to federalism. Indeed, many argue that, from a normative standpoint, neofunctionalism can be read as an attempt to apply the functionalist method of incremental change in the service of the federalist goal of building large-scale political communities (Ashworth 1999: 104; Taylor 1968). It is important to note, though, that Haas and his followers did not expressly share in the ideology of federalism. As Haas saw it, 'supranational organs are essential to prevent governments from going back on their promises to integrate and to administer, free from national interference, the transitional rules for the gradual introduction of free trade' (1968: 458). Supranational institutions, in other words, are viewed as rational solutions to collective action problems emanating from economic co-operation rather than expressions of 'cultural' or 'political' unity'.

A final characteristic of neofunctionalism that sets it apart from classic functionalism is its regional focus. The social, economic and political forces that neofunctionalists point to as movers of integration all have a regional dimension (Haas 1964: 49). Whereas classic functionalism is a theory of post-territorial governance, neofunctionalism is therefore essentially a theory of regionalism (Rosamond 2000: 69).

The Integration Process: Converging Expectations, 'Spillover' and 'Supranational Entrepreneurship'

Neofunctionalist accounts of integration are rooted in a pluralist interpretation of politics. Drawing on the prevailing pluralist theories of systems theorists such as Talcott Parsons and David Easton, neofunctionalists conceive of the state as an arena in which different interest groups compete for influence and power within a framework of overarching consensus (Haas 1958a: 5 and Chapter 4). According to this theory, integration is an inherently conflictual and highly political process in which various organized interests strive to gain individual advantage. The upshot is a model of integration based on 'converging expectations' rather than shared notions of 'a common good' (Haas 1958b: 448). Whereas functionalists and federalists rely on an emerging consensus on social and economic questions, neofunctionalists argue that there need not be a harmony of interest for political integration to proceed. Rather, they assume that integration is likely to be supported by governments, political parties, interest groups and regional institutions for distinctly different reasons (Lindberg 1963: 107–8). As Haas (1964: 39) puts it:

> I do not deny that men, on occasion, may agree on the common good. I wish to stress merely that these convergences of opinion cannot be relied upon to operate all the time or even with reasonable frequency. Since societies and organisations, however, show a capacity for survival even in the absence of a demonstrable and continuous devotion to a generally accepted common good, we must posit a more basic consensual tie than such agreement ... [W]e may think of modern nation-states as communities whose basic consensus is restricted to agreement on the procedure for maintaining order and settling disputes among groups, for carrying out well-understood functions. Unlike that of the Functionalist, this conception presupposes agreement merely on the means for achieving welfare, but not on the content of laws and policies, not on the substance of the functions.

There is a clear element of 'hidden hand' logic to this account of integration. Haas's theory of interest politics borrows directly from classical Liberals like Smith, Bentham and Mill to whom individual economic interests are strictly divorced from any imputed concern with general welfare or social order (see Haas 1964: 32–3). A key insight of classical Liberalism is that the 'general good' may emerge from unplanned, uncoordinated, and plainly egotistic individual behaviour. To Haas, this assumption of separate and even competing purposes converging to produce general welfare provided a more realistic basis for a theory of integration than either the utopian functionalist vision of technocratic progress based on a generally accepted 'common good' or the federalist vision of 'cultural unity'. In respect to the birth of the EEC he argues:

> The Federalists were wrong: it was not cultural unity but economic advantage that proved to be an acceptable shared goal among the Six. Each of the Six, for individual national reasons and not because of a clear common purpose, found it possible and desirable to embark on the road of economic integration using supranational institutions ... Converging economic goals embedded in the bureaucratic, pluralistic, and industrial life of modern Europe provided the crucial input (Haas, 1968: xix).

For Haas, then, integration is driven, not by a collective commitment to a common good but by the separate yet intersecting self-interests of economic and political actors (Haas 1958b: 448). But which actors matter? Public opinion at large is unimportant. The bureaucratized nature of European states means that decisions are made by leadership, that is, by elites (Haas 1958a: 17). In addition to policy makers, economic elites (unions, trade and professional associations, business and financial lobbies, etc.) are the most important. It is primarily through their selfish striving for economic benefits that integration is launched and moved forward.

The pluralist model of politics yields several distinct propositions about the conditions in which integration is most likely to flourish. First, it is expected that ideological diversity and fragmentation of interests domestically promote integration. As Haas argues, 'fragmentation of beliefs makes possible a realignment of loyalties at the supranational level, because groups in each country are partisans of thought patterns having their parallels in groups across the border' (1968: 158). Or put differently, neofunctionalists expect that political and ideological fragmentation at the national level will be resolved by the substitution of 'national interests' for new patterns of group and individual interests at the regional level (see Milward and Sørensen 1993: 4). Second, the emphasis on separate but converging aims implies that broad-ranging initiatives are often more likely to succeed than narrow ones. Integration, to progress, has to satisfy a plurality of rival interests. The more issues involved, the easier it is to exchange concessions and strike compromises across policy areas. Or as Haas puts it, 'a new treaty needs merely to be so constructed as to contain a large variety of otherwise unrelated provisions and thus appeal to a large enough constituency to establish another converging pattern of support' (1968: 290). Finally, pluralism gives primacy to incremental decision-making or integration 'by stealth'. As Haas comments, in a pluralist setting, 'the functionalist must choose a strategy that will unite many and alienate few'. 'He can only move in small steps and without a clear logical plan, because if he moved in bold steps and in masterful fashion he would lose the support of many' (1964: xxiii). Pluralism therefore privileges the step-by-step approach to integration favoured by functionalists over the sweeping constitutional approach advocated by federalists.

Spillover

Under conditions of converging interests, how does the actual integration process unfold? Perhaps the most important concept in the neofunctionalist explanation of the integration is the idea of 'spillover'. In its most general formulation, spillover refers to a logic whereby initial steps toward integration trigger endogenous economic and political dynamics which provide an impetus for further integration. There are several aspects of the logic of spillover. The first, *functional* spillover, is based on the premise that different economic sectors are highly interdependent, and that integration in one sector may create problems that can only be resolved through further integration in other, related, sectors. For example, Haas (1958a) shows how integration in coal and steel had a 'backwash' effect in less industrialized localities leading to demands for redistributive policies within the Community – an objective never faced by the architects of the ECSC. Similarly, Lindberg (1963: 6) predicts that the removal of tariff barriers among EEC members will make it difficult in the long run to resist coordination of economic and taxation policies, even if governments initially had no intention to harmonize those policies.

Political spillover, by contrast, occurs because economic and social integration influences the political aspirations of major societal groups in participating states. As integration proceeds, actors become aware that their interests can no longer be adequately served at the national level. Industrial groups and political parties organize across borders in order to influence the new decision-making centres. These adaptations create a further impulse for centralization of decision-making (Haas 1958a: 9–10 and ch.11; Lindberg 1963: 94, 101).

A third form of spillover – *cultivated* spillover – stresses the role of supranational institutions such as the European Commission in promoting integration. The Commission, because it represents the 'general interest', is well placed to mediate among national viewpoints by advancing impartial compromise proposals (Lindberg 1963: 210, 278). Whereas state-to-state bargaining often results in 'lowest-common-denominator solutions', supranational institutions can help states resolve conflicts by working out a solution 'at a higher level' where more interests can be accommodated. Referred to as 'upgrading the common interest' this tactic usually implies the expansion of the mandate of a supranational agency (Haas 1960: 368). Supranational actors may also help redefine negotiation conflicts by including other – often functionally unrelated – negotiation subjects (so-called 'issue-linkage') or by offering direct compensations for concessions ('side-payments') (see Lindberg and Scheingold 1970: 118; Schmitter 1969: 163). The reason the Commission can do these things effectively is, first that it has a monopoly of policy initiative; second that it enjoys a special legitimacy as the only actor that can claim to speak from a truly 'European' point of view; and third that it has a mastery of 'objective' technical expertise with regard to European-wide questions (Haas 1968: 524; Lindberg and Scheingold 1970: 129).

The neofunctionalist literature is strewn with examples of integration being advanced by creative supranational entrepreneurship. Lindberg (1963) links successful integration in the early 1960s to the extraordinary 'ingenuity' and 'skill' of the European Commission under its first President, Walter Hallstein. Ross (1995) highlights the particular skill of Jacques Delors in securing agreement on both the Single European Act and the Treaty of European Union. Note, however, that effective supranational entrepreneurship depends on conflicts of interest among member states. If state preferences were perfectly aligned, there would be no need for supranational mediation. Diverging state preferences are what allow supranational arbiters to step in and seek to 'upgrade the common interest'. Disagreement also creates opportunities for expanding the scope of integration via side-payments: the more that preferences diverge, the larger the side-payments that are needed to create a pro-integration coalition, and the greater the possibility for extending integration to new sectors and thereby widening the mandate of supranational institutions (Lindberg and Scheingold 1970: 118; Schmitter 1969: 163). Hence, somewhat counter-intuitively, low-level conflicts of interests are seen as an important vehicle for furthering integration.

Neofunctionalism in Comparative Perspective

Initially formulated in the late 1950s, neofunctionalism during the 1960s and early 1970s underwent substantial modification. Changes to the theory were in part a response to the slowdown in European integration during the 1960s as well as to the theoretical criticism launched by intergovernmentalist scholars. However, they were also a reaction to unsuccessful efforts to apply the theory comparatively outside Western Europe. Most of the foundational neofunctionalist texts were developed in a European context and based on detailed studies of the functioning of major EC institutions. Haas, in Chapter 4 of this book, explores the link between economic and political integration in the context of the ECSC; Lindberg, in Chapter 5, studies the role of supranational entrepreneurship in the negotiation of the EEC; and Lindberg and Scheingold (1967, 1970) examine the birth of the Common Agricultural Policy. So long as the focus rested on the EC, empirical developments appeared largely to corroborate neofunctionalist expectations regarding spillover and supranational entrepreneurship. A next step, however, took the theory beyond Europe. The search for a generalizable explanation of integration led neofunctionalists to seek to apply the theory to a wider group of regional settings. In his article 'International Integration: The European and Universal Process' (1961) Haas applied neofunctionalist principles to explain integration in the Soviet Bloc, among the Arab States and in the Americas. In *Beyond the Nation-State* (1964) he examined the contribution of the International Labour Organization (ILO) to integration at the international level. Haas and Schmitter (1964) analysed processes of integration in Latin America, and Nye (1966, 1968a, 1968b, 1971a, 1971b) set out a conceptual framework for the comparative study of regional integration, which he applied to Africa, the Middle East, Latin America and Europe. Applications outside Europe were rarely successful, however. Integration in other regions of the world appeared to advance at a far slower pace than in Europe. This impelled neofunctionalists to focus on the factors that made Europe especially propitious for integration. Parametric variables such as the fact that all the member states were democracies with a high degree of social pluralism, high levels of industrial and economic development, and compatibility of major elite values, as well as the fact the external security of the region was being safeguarded by another international organisation, had to be incorporated into the theory (see especially Haas and Schmitter 1964; Schmitter 1970).

The attention given to a wider set of background variables that had to be satisfied before integration could succeed meant that neofunctionalism grew more accurate as a description of European integration. Yet, the location of the necessary background conditions for integration also highlighted the limited scope of the theory. Neofunctionalism was geared toward explaining integration among a regional grouping of liberal democratic polities with advanced industrial economies that also found themselves closely allied in security terms. The highly contingent nature of the theory meant that it had reduced applicability outside Europe (see Haas 1970, 1976). As a result, scholars largely turned away from comparative studies and toward the exclusive study of the EC and its institutions. This limited focus, however, came at a cost. As many critics have charged, due to the well-known problems of testing hypotheses on a single case, a theory so closely bound up with the empirical study of a specific instance of integration could not generate systematic generalizations.

The Intergovernmentalist Critique

While regional developments beyond Europe failed to corroborate neofunctionalist expectations, the trajectory of integration among the six EC members also presented a challenge for the theory. Early neofunctionalism assumed a certain degree of 'automaticity' in spillover (or at least it presupposed that the integration process would tend toward continual expansion rather than contraction). Although they acknowledged that successful spillover depended on the continued commitment of member states to integration, Haas and his colleagues assumed that – once integration was underway – the alternatives open to any state would gradually be limited because withdrawal would imply a sacrifice of economic advantage (Haas 1958b: 454; Lindberg 1963: 11). Hence, any problems arising from integration would be solved through more rather than less co-operation. Initially, developments in the EC seemed to vindicate these predictions. When neofunctionalism was formulated – roughly between 1956 and 1964 – the ECSC had already spilled over into the EEC and Euratom (Tranholm-Mikkelsen 1992: 7). The theory soon came under strain from empirical developments, however. The French veto of British membership in 1963, and French President General de Gaulle's boycott of the central Community institutions in 1965 (the so-called 'Empty Chair Crisis') dealt a blow to neofunctionalist expectations of an automatic progression from a common market to economic union and finally to political union. The collapse of the Bretton Woods system in the early 1970s unleashed a period of national protectionism, which further undercut expectations regarding spillover from the Common Market. The sudden slowdown of integration and the apparent reassertion of nationalist sentiment triggered widespread self-criticism among neofunctionalist scholars. It also led to an upsurge in state-centred or 'intergovernmentalist' scholarship, which was strongly critical of neofunctionalism.

The intergovernmentalist critique was based on three key assertions, all rooted in the intellectual tradition of realism. First, in contrast to the neofunctionalist emphasis on the role of non-state actors in providing the dynamic for integration, intergovernmentalists pointed to the continued dominance of the nation state and of national interests. Second, they insisted that states remain the sole arbiters of their external policies. The pluralist image of the European policy process as a complex network comprising a multitude of national, transnational and supranational participants was rejected in favour of a more conventional picture of governments carefully aggregating domestic positions at the national level before negotiating internationally (Webb 1977: 18). This image rested on two underlying premises. First, it was presupposed that European issues are the prerogative of foreign offices and therefore remain insulated from the domestic political processes in which national interest groups participate. Second, it was assumed that member states come to the negotiation table in Brussels with coordinated and coherent negotiation positions which are subsequently relatively resistant to pressure by organized interests or institutions operating at the supranational level (Hodges 1972: 25).

The third key assertion was that intergovernmentalists rejected the notion of spillover. The spillover logic suggests that integration is driven by unintended consequences. As Haas argued, integration is 'the unexpected outcome of initial decisions whose long-term consequences have not been adequately understood by the parties involved' (Haas 1970: 627). By contrast, intergovernmentalists saw integration as resulting from the purposive behaviour of states. States do not enter blindly into international agreements. Rather, they carefully judge the likely results of alternative agreements. Agreements that do not satisfy the long-term aspirations of member states will tend to be undone. Whenever and wherever integration occurs, therefore, it is because member states have willed it.

Among the foremost critics of neofunctionalism was Stanley Hoffmann. In a series of articles (1963, 1964, 1965b, 1966, 1982) he challenged the neofunctionalist prophecy of a gradual transfer of power from the nation state to a new European entity. Neofunctionalists, Hoffmann contended, had been too optimistic about the potential for spillover from economic to political integration due to two main fallacies. First, by focusing too closely on the internal dynamics of the integration process they had neglected the wider context – international as well as domestic – in which integration takes place. States are subject to different external pressures and calculate differently how to respond to such constraints. As a result, the attraction of regional cooperation is frequently offset by the tug of global forces. For example, US involvement in European security pulled EC members in different directions, leading some to favour closer Atlantic ties at the expense of European collaboration while prompting others to push for closer integration as a way to diminish dependence on the Americans. Neofunctionalism also ignored the possibility of diverging political developments at the domestic level. In pluralistic societies political power may at times fall into the hands of individuals or groups who do not share the values of elites in other member states, or disagree on how those values should be realized. A case in point, of course, was de Gaulle's rise to power in France.

Hoffmann further chastised neofunctionalism for failing to draw a distinction between 'high' and 'low' politics. 'Low politics' is concerned with interests that are representative of only a negligible fraction of a nation's resources. It mainly refers to welfare policies. 'High politics', by contrast, has at its core 'the vital interests of national diplomacy and strategy'. The fact of diverging interests implies that integration can only work in the domain of low politics (Hoffmann 1963: 530–31). As long as integration affects only welfare issues, states may be willing to compromise to reach agreement. Once the process reaches issues, which affect the realm of power and high politics as well as the realm of welfare, agreement becomes difficult if not impossible. Integration will then come to a halt (Hoffmann 1964: 89, 1965b: 84).

The upshot of these observations, Hoffmann argued, is that the EC cannot be usefully analysed in the traditional terms of integration theory, which assumes that member states are engaged in the formation of a new, supranational political entity superseding old nations (see Hoffmann 1966). Rather, the Community should be conceived as an international regime – a set of norms, rules and decision-making procedures – designed to reduce the transaction costs of co-operation on a variety of issue-areas rendering mutual and unambiguous benefits to its member states (Hoffmann 1982: 33, 1983).

Another prominent intergovernmentalist critic was Roger Hansen. Building on Hoffmann's analysis, Hansen (Chapter 7 of this book) deepened the critique of neofunctionalism by pointing to problems of application both in Europe and the less-developed world. Economic developments in Europe revealed serious limitations in the concept of spillover, he argued. The Common Market had secured massive economic gains without producing pressure to move toward political union (1969: 249). A likely explanation was that economic benefits had been equitably spread among the Six thereby avoiding 'distributive crises' that might have aided spillover by creating opportunities to 'redefine interests at a higher level' (1969: 253). The concept of spillover was even less helpful when applied outside Europe. Whereas in Europe, the equitable distribution of benefits had hindered 'politicization' of economic integration, in less developed countries the backwash effects of integration had led to 'over-politicization' resulting in deadlock. The reason, argued Hansen, is that economic integration among less-developed countries is best conceptualized in terms of 'high politics' and is thus less susceptible to integration.

The critique of neofunctionalism launched by Hoffmann and others formed the basis for a distinctive intergovernmentalist approach to European integration, which continues to dominate the field today (see

Part III). Intergovernmentalism and neofunctionalism are diametrically opposed both in terms of the emphasis they place on the role of supranational institutions vs state interests, and insofar as neofunctionalism views integration as a result of gradual and unobtrusive exchanges among a multitude of actors whereas intergovernmentalism stresses grand treaty-making bargains among state executives (Webb 1977: 18). The most radical contrast to neofunctionalism, however, is the intergovernmentalist denial of the uniqueness of the EC as a framework for international cooperation (ibid.). To neofunctionalists, European integration is about building a new political community, which will supersede existing nation states. To intergovernmentalists, on the other hand, the EC is best conceived as an international regime designed to reduce transaction costs of cooperation among its members (see e.g. Hoffmann 1982; Moravcsik 1998). Accordingly, the fundamental question animating intergovernmentalist scholarship on European integration is not 'what explains the emergence of a new supranational political community?' but the more general question 'why do states cooperate?'

Revised Neofunctionalism

The slowdown in European integration and the barrage of criticism from state-centric scholars like Hoffmann and Hansen led to extensive revision of neofunctionalism. In the second edition of *The Uniting of Europe* (1968), Haas suggested several modifications of the theory to enable it to better account for empirical developments. First, the assumed superiority of incremental economic decision-making over crucial policy choices should be modified to reflect the possibility that integration could be halted by the emergence of 'dramatic political actors' such as General de Gaulle, whose actions were ideologically motivated (Haas, 1968: xxiii). Greater attention should be given to changes in the international system which might influence patterns of regional cooperation (1968: xxiv–xxvi). The concept of spillover was also overhauled. Whereas neofunctionalists initially had relied on a certain degree of determinism in spillover, the weight of empirical evidence now led them to conclude that spillover was not a given but only one of several possible developments. New models were developed in which functional interdependence and goal frustration could lead not only to 'spillover' but also to 'spill-around' (an increase in the scope but not the level of integration) and 'spill-back' (a decrease in either the scope or level of integration) (see Lindberg and Scheingold 1970: 137; Nye 1970: 805; Schmitter 1970: 846). At the same time it was acknowledged that the activist role assigned to supranational institutions had been somewhat exaggerated: while the role of the

Commission was often crucial to achieving agreement, it appeared contingent upon personal factors, that is, who occupied the presidency, and on how much support he received from key member states (Schmitter 2004: 55).

Despite reformulation, however, neofunctionalism seemed to have lost much of its appeal. Scholars continued to find problems with its application both in Europe and elsewhere. By 1975, Haas explicitly confirmed the 'obsolescence' of neofunctionalist models by suggesting that theories of regional integration were becoming increasingly irrelevant to explaining state behaviour within regional organizations (Haas 1975, 1976). Neofunctionalism, he observed, rested on two core assumptions which no longer held true. First, it assumed a constant objective – the attainment of a political community – by gradual steps. Second, it assumed a regional focus for cooperation. Yet, the 12 members of the EC did not show a commitment to any 'final' set of institutions, nor did they display a firm commitment to regionalism. Instead links with external actors were increasingly interfering with regional institutionalization (1976: 183–99). What appeared to be happening was that regional integration was being taken over by broader dimensions of international economic interdependence. Haas therefore concluded that, rather than an attempt to build a regional political union, the policies and institutions of the EC illustrated an attempt to deal with growing international interdependence (or what he called 'turbulence'). The upshot, he argued, was that regional integration ought 'to be subordinated to a general theory of interdependence'. This verdict signalled the temporary demise of regional integration theory. Whereas a small group of mainly European scholars continued the study of regional integration processes, most IR scholars redirected their energies to the broader study of international interdependence and regimes (see e.g. Haas 1976, 1980, 1982; Nye 1977). Here they frequently continued to draw on neofunctionalist concepts to explain the relation between growing interdependence and international cooperation.

The Neofunctionalist Legacy

Neofunctionalism has been by far the most influential theory of European integration. As Rosamond observes, for many 'integration theory' and 'neofunctionalism' are virtual synonyms (2000: 50). Although the theory ultimately fell into disrepute, neofunctionalism made several lasting contributions to the study of regional and international cooperation. Not only did neofunctionalism itself make a comeback as a favoured explanation for the revival of European integration in the 1980s but, as we shall see in subsequent chapters, new theoret-

ical directions such as liberal intergovernmentalism, multi-level gover
nance, neo-institutionalism and constructivism all import key neofunctionalist assumptions.

Two of these theoretical contributions deserve to be highlighted.
First, neofunctionalism played a crucial role in reminding us that the
state cannot be viewed as a unitary actor in international politics. By
pointing to the importance of pluralistic structures in integrating states,
and by specifying the social and economic groups thought to be carriers of integration, neofunctionalism focused attention on the role of
domestic politics. Haas himself repeatedly stressed that a fully-fledged
theory of integration would have to incorporate an explicit theory of
domestic interest politics to account for 'convergences' of interests.
Other theorists also stressed domestic politics. Scheingold (1970) called
for a comparative analysis of the distributional effects of integration
among different domestic groups as a way to account for variation in
integration. Puchala (1975: 507) drew attention to the fact that successful integration depends not only on joint decision-making at the
regional level but also on the subsequent ability of national governments to implement those decisions in the face of resistance from
domestic polities and societies. Yet, despite calling attention to the significance of domestic politics, neofunctionalism failed in providing a
coherent theory of interest politics. At the end of the day, most classic
neofunctionalist writings focused on 'process' dynamics such as functional and cultivated spillover while lacking theoretical micro-foundations – i.e. assumptions specifying the nature of key domestic actors,
their preferences, how they form coalitions at the domestic and international level, etc. – which would allow them to specify the link
between domestic determinants and regional outcomes. (For a critique
along these lines see Moravcsik 1993a, 1998.) The specific link
between domestic and international politics was therefore left to be
drawn by a later generation of scholars.

A second major contribution was to conceptualize the EC as a political system. Neofunctionalism took 'political community' as the dependent variable. Yet, it implicitly recognized that political community
must also be an independent variable. After all, the logic of spillover is
based on the notion that community outputs affect the attitudes and
expectations of politically relevant groups in ways that lead them to
favour further integration. Integration is portrayed as a two-way
process in which national groups seek to shape 'federal' or 'supranational' decisions but in turn come under pressure to conduct themselves in accordance with doctrines originating from the new central
institutions (Haas 1968). Thus, the functioning of the EC polity – its
institutional capacity, operating procedures, decision-making processes
and ideological framework – became an important object of study.
Lindberg (1965, 1966, 1967) and Lindberg and Scheingold (1970)

offered some of the earliest attempts at conceptualizing the EC as a political system. Similarly, Puchala (1975: 507) conceived of the EC as a 'multi-layered political system', which governs the behaviour of political actors across local, national and regional levels. Their basic insight – that integration constitutes an independent as well as a dependent variable and that the EC can be studied not only as the end product of an integrative process but also as a political system in its own right – is at the heart of current comparative politics and 'governance' approaches to integration, and is discussed in Part IV.

Intergovernmentalist critiques of neofunctionalism also left an important mark on European integration studies. Whereas neofunctionalists focused attention on supranational institutions, state-centrists like Hoffmann and Hansen reminded us that the process of integration is set in motion by political decisions made by states. Supranational organizations should therefore not be conceived as autonomous actors, capable of pushing their own agenda. They are created to serve the interests of nation states and will flourish only as long as states perceive that they fulfil their purpose. This potent critique of the role of supranational authority set the stage for a prolonged debate between 'supranationalists' and 'intergovernmentalists' in the European context, and between 'neo-institutionalists' and 'neo-realists' in the wider field of IR about the causal significance of international institutions. This debate is the subject of the next part.

Further Reading

Neofunctionalism

Haas, E. (1964) *Beyond the Nation-State: Functionalism and International Organization* (Stanford: Stanford University Press). A classic text in which Haas explores the functional basis of the ILO and its contribution to international integration.

Haas, E. (1976) 'Turbulent Fields and the Theory of Regional Integration', *International Organization*, 30(2), 173–212. An interesting analysis of regional integration theory in which Haas discusses the shortcomings of neofunctionalist theory in the face of rising global interdependence.

Haas, E. and Schmitter, P. (1964) 'Economics and Differential Patterns of Political Integration: Projections about Unity in Latin America', *International Organization*, 18(4), 705–37. In this widely cited article Haas and Schmitter seek to apply neofunctionalist principles to explain the development of integration in Latin America.

Lindberg, L. and Scheingold, S. (1970) *Europe's Would-Be Polity: Patterns of Change in the European Community* (Englewood Cliffs,

NJ: Prentice-Hall). This classic study is among the first to conceptualize the EC as a comprehensive political system. Provides an excellent overview of neofunctionalist scholarship at the time.

Puchala, D. (1972) 'Of Blind Men, Elephants, and International
Integration', *Journal of Common Market Studies*, 10(3), 267–84. A
classical reading, focusing on the problem of 'grand theorizing' in
the field of European integration.

Intergovernmentalism

Hoffmann, S. (1964) 'The European Process at Atlantic
Crosspurposes', *Journal of Common Market Studies*, 3. In this
article Hoffmann explores the potential negative impact of external
political factors on the European integration process.

Hoffmann, S. (1982) 'Reflections on the Nation-state in Western
Europe Today', *Journal of Common Market Studies*, 21(1–2),
21–37. A standard intergovernmentalist critique of the neofunctionalist ideal of 'depoliticized' integration. The article calls attention to
the importance of external factors in the integration process and
elaborates on Hoffmann's earlier distinction between 'high' and
'low' politics.

Chapter 4

The Uniting of Europe: Political, Social and Economic Forces 1950–1957

Ernst B. Haas*

Community and Integration

Two major opposing trends have come to characterise international relations at the end of the Second World War: while some twenty new states have made their appearance since 1945, with every indication that the process will gain even more momentum, a network of international organisations has sprung up countering the full impact of this multiplication of sovereignties. Whether in the realm of political relations or specific functional tasks, whether at the universal or the regional level, contacts and associations among governments, private groups and individuals have been institutionalised as never before. Whereas the trend in Africa and Asia is toward the evolution of ever more political groupings aspiring to statehood, the process in Europe and in the Atlantic area tends toward the limitation of sovereign independence, the growth of more rather than less formal bonds among national communities and perhaps toward the substitution of a new federal organism for the present national state.

New states may grow up as the result of the splintering of an existing political community – or an empire – as well as from the merger of hitherto distinct and independent entities. In both processes the evolution of 'national consciousness' is held to be the crucial factor. Loyalty to the established font of authority wanes as a feeling of separate identity takes possession of the group clamouring for new forms of political organisation. Yet we know little about the constituents of this process. While it is possible frequently to specify the content of the

---

* Reproduced from Ernst Haas (1968) *The Uniting of Europe: Political, Social and Economic Forces* 1950–1957, 2nd edn. (Stanford, CA: Stanford University Press), chapter 1, (reproduction by the kind permission of Peter Haas). The text has been slightly edited, as indicated, to fit the format of this volume. References have been changed to Harvard citation style wherever possible. Some peripheral footnotes have been omitted.

new doctrine of national consciousness it is far more difficult to explain who originates, propagates, expands and accepts it. More difficult still is the question of why the doctrine originates and why it gains – or fails to gain – acceptance. How and why does national loyalty tend to coincide with the territorial boundaries of the state? Is it inherent in political evolution that it must be so? Is it natural and inevitable that India, Ghana or Belgium are characterised by a sense of national identity which extends to their frontiers but not beyond?

The process of development of a political community, therefore, is but little understood in terms of the analytical standards and criteria of observation with which the social scientist today works. While much work is being done in the study of this process among the nascent political entities in underdeveloped areas, much less attention has been paid to the reverse process of community formation through international organisation, among western industrial states. This is true in all fields of trans-state activity, whether intergovernmental at the level of formal diplomacy, intergovernmental at the level of informal discussion by experts, 'supranational' or federal. Each of these is a device to arrive at collective decisions by means other than unlimited action by a national government. Each is a means for peacefully unifying diverse groups in common action. Yet detailed data on how – if at all – cohesion is obtained through these processes is lacking.

International relations in contemporary western Europe provide a living laboratory of these processes at work. The Organisation for European Economic Co-operation (OEEC) at the level of intergovernmental contacts, the Council of Europe as an inter-parliamentary forum, the system of Scandinavian co-operation and the Western European Union as a mixture of the two, and the European Coal and Steel Community (ECSC) as a quasi-federal government in two economic sectors, provide landmarks in the process of substituting collective action for decisions by governments acting in isolation. It is time that these efforts be examined to judge if and how 'political community' results from measures of 'political integration'.

Basic Definitions: Political Community

The systematic study of the process of community formation through organisations of this type necessitates the explicit stating of an ideal type appropriate to the known institutional setting of western Europe. Here, the existing national states *are* political communities. While they seem to enjoy the unquestioning 'loyalty' of their citizens – with the exception of dedicated Communists as distinguished from the mass of Communist voters – they are by no means monolithic units. Pluralism of groups, values and institutions is the hallmark of western European political life. Nor, as past history and contemporary developments indicate, are these existing states immutable entities. Belgium came into existence in 1830; Germany federated in 1870; the bloody history of boundary changes is well remembered by the present generation. The existing political communities are neither so homogeneous internally as to speak with one united voice on national or international issues nor preordained historically as to constitute 'natural' units.

'Loyalty' was singled out as a crucial term in this definition and it must be specified further in operational terms. A population may be said to be loyal to a set of symbols and institutions when it habitually and predictably over long periods obeys the injunctions of their authority and turns to them for the satisfaction of important expectations. In part the existence of such sentiments can be tested by the regularity of popular compliance with fundamental government decisions; and in part it is subject to verification by the kind of attitude testing of perceptions of mutuality of aspirations made familiar by post-1945 surveys (see Deutsch et al. 1957: 36). *Political community, therefore, is a condition in which specific groups and individuals show more loyalty to their central political institutions than to any other political authority, in a specific period of time and in a definable geographic space.* In this study, this condition will be the one toward which the process of 'political integration' is supposed to lead.

Group conflict is a given and expected form of conduct in the nations under study. French, German or Italian policy emerges as the result of this conflict. Hence a larger political community, composed of the nations now still separate and distinct, may well be expected to display the same traits. Hence our ideal type of community formation will assume group conflict as given on the level of the present national units as well as in the larger community which may emerge. In fact, the competing activities of permanently organised interest groups and of political parties are singled out as the significant carriers of values and ideologies whose opposition, identity or convergence determines the success or failure of a transnational ideology.

If group conflict is one central characteristic of political community so is the existence of a commonly accepted body of belief. Despite the opposition of ideologies and their adherents, consensus exists to a sufficient degree in the contemporary national units to preclude recourse to civil war and revolt. The ideal type of political community implicit in this study assumes, therefore, that the condition toward which the process of integration is expected to lead is one in which a sufficient body of general consensus imposes limitations upon the violence of group conflict. These limitations are the basic agreement on the *means* for settling differences, even if consensus as to *ends* of political action can be achieved only at such high levels of abstraction as to be irrelevant to the analysis of political conduct. Stated in constitutional terms, the agreement on the means of political action is equivalent to the acceptance of the doctrine of respect for the rule of law. Official decisions, once made according to procedural rules accepted as binding by all, are carried out.

For purposes of this discussion, the beliefs common to otherwise antagonistic groups will be labelled the 'nationalism' of a given community, while the doctrines peculiar to a group will be referred to as 'ideology.' Nationalism is composed of values and claims acceptable to the great bulk of the population while also setting it apart from the values and claims of other political communities. At the socio-cultural level of attitudes and beliefs our political community is held together despite the internal strife of the constituent groups by the general acceptance of national identity, of nationalism, which manifests itself primarily in the consensus on the means for achieving agreement on policy.

. . . .

This picture of political community differs in some essential respects from the kindred concept of 'security community' proposed by some contemporary students of nationalism and community formation (Deutsch 1953a, 1954; van Wagenen 1952). In both formulations, the absence of violence as a means of political action among the participating groups is given a central place. Deutsch's concept, however, does not insist on the presence of a specified institutional structure, contenting itself with the consecration of non-violent means of achieving social change as the major criterion differentiating 'community' from ordinary international relations. The scheme here used, by contrast, makes the existence of political institutions capable of translating ideologies into law the cornerstone of the definition. While the co-existence of conflict and harmony within the same social system can no doubt be achieved without the attributes of a single statehood, the deliberate creation and perpetuation of a new national consciousness can hardly be expected to come about without the presence of formal governmental institutions and practices. Since the possession of such a consciousness is considered a criterion of political community, the techniques for realising and maintaining it must be posited as necessary to the ideal type.

These are the central characteristics of pluralistic nations in contemporary western Europe and at the same time the earmarks of our model of political community. In clearly positing an extreme scheme, rather than an intermediate one permitting of violence-free conduct short of the attainment of statehood by the entities under study, it is intended to furnish a precise yardstick for the analysis of governmental and group conduct in western Europe in the effort to determine now to what extent the condition of political community has been or is likely to be reached.

Political community, as here defined, need not presuppose the emergence of a federal state, though this is one possibility and certainly the aim of many contemporary European statesmen and thinkers. While a central government is essential institutionally and a collective national consciousness socially, the constitutional form which will qualify for the ideal type may be that of a unitary, a federal or even a confederate arrangement. ... Normally the type of confederation represented by international organisations in which only states are subjects and governments are vested with a power of veto does not approach our definition of community. A structure could emerge, however, in which a compulsory and binding judicial system is combined with a majoritarian legislative device, supervising the work of a central administration of restricted powers but with direct jurisdiction over groups and individuals, while many major decisions are still made at the level of intergovernmental negotiations. If in such a system governments negotiate and compromise so that one or several severely modify their position in the effort to arrive at a binding common agreement of profound consequence, the resulting habitual pattern of reaching consensus could well fit into the definition of political community, though representing neither the typical unitary nor federal categories of constitutions.

Hence the institutional criteria of 'political community' as here defined combine the separate features posited by Deutsch and his associates. They analyse in terms of two types: 'amalgamated' and 'pluralistic' security communities. The former correspond essentially to unitary or federal states while the latter comprise relationships between sovereign states from which the possibility of recourse to force has been banished. ... While my definition would exclude 'pluralistic security communities' of this type because of the absence of judicial, administrative and legislative ties and because of the scarcity of institutionalised relations among private groups, our concept of 'political community' is nevertheless broader than Deutsch's 'amalgamated security community' because it includes the possibility of a constant flow of obedience to central decisions made by intergovernmental agencies (Deutsch et al 1957: 3–21).

. . . .

Having stated the ideal type of political community, our task is the assessment of empirical data in an effort to determine whether and why developments leading to the evolution of a community are taking place. General estimates of the existence or absence of loyalty other than to the national state do not suffice. Hence a number of indicators of community sentiment will be discussed here, applicable specifically to the study of how interest groups, political parties and governments act in a supranational setting.

Community sentiment would be considered to flourish if:

1. Interest groups and political parties at the national level endorse supranational action in preference to action by their national gov-

ernment, or if they are divided among themselves on this issue. Only the case of unanimous national opposition to supranational action could be considered incompatible with community sentiment.

2. Interest groups and political parties organise beyond the national level in order to function more effectively as decision-makers *vis-a-vis* the separate national governments or the central authority and if they define their interests in terms larger than those of the separate national state from which they originate.

3. Interest groups and political parties, in their efforts at supranational organisation, coalesce on the basis of a common ideology, surpassing those prominent at the national level.

4. Interest groups and political parties, in confronting each other at the supranational level, succeed in evolving a body of doctrine common to all, or a new nationalism (i.e., 'supranationalism').

5. Interest groups, political parties *and* governments show evidence of accepting the rule of law in faithfully carrying out supranational court decisions, administrative directives and rules even when they oppose these, instead of obstructing or ignoring such decisions; further, when opposing federal policy, they channel their objections through the legal avenues provided instead of threatening or practising secession.

6. Governments negotiate with one another in good faith and generally reach agreement, while not making themselves consistently and invariably the spokesmen of national interest groups; further, community sentiment would seem to prevail if governments give way in negotiations when they find themselves in a minority instead of insisting on a formal or informal right of veto.

Clearly, only a collection of saints could be expected to display positively all these indicators of community sentiment at the outset of a process of integration. In order to qualify as a true political community, however, all the above indicators must be positively established before the condition defined in our scheme has been met. Given a series of pluralistic assumptions, any establishment of sentiment confined to parties alone, or to interest groups, or to governments considered in isolation from their subjects, would fall short of the final condition posited.

. . . .

Basic Definitions: Political Integration

Our definition of political community relies not so much on 'objective criteria' as on an assessment of the conduct of groups, individuals and governments. On a more abstract level, the criteria singled out as crucial to the definition result from habitual behaviour patterns: they are not superimposed by the observer upon the social scene. The same rule governs the definition of the second key term used in this study, 'political integration.' Conceived not as a condition but as a *process,* the conceptualisation relies on the perception of interests and values by the actors participating in the process. Integration takes place when these perceptions fall into a certain pattern and fails to take place when they do not. If pluralism is considered an inherent part of the ideal type of political community, pluralistic processes of decision-making and interest perception, naturally, are considered equally essential attributes of the process of political integration.[1]

Before a firm definition or scheme can be stated, it must be recognised that integration in Western Europe has thus far been essentially confined to economic measures. Hence it is necessary to establish the meaning of 'economic integration' as that term is generally used in the nexus of European politics. Following Gehrels and Johnston (1955), the possible general definition as 'the presence of important economic links between a group of countries' must be rejected as too vague operationally. The development of such links can and does result from organisations, such as OEEC, which do not pretend to represent or aim at political community. Economic aspects of integration, if relevant to the evolution of community, must possess these characteristics: (1) agreement for gradual but complete elimination of tariffs, quotas and exchange controls on trade among the member countries; (2) abandonment of the right to restore trade restrictions on a unilateral basis for the duration of the agreement, regardless of difficulties that may arise; (3) joint action to deal with problems resulting from the removal of trade barriers within the community and to promote more efficient utilisation of the resources of the area; (4) some degree of harmonisation of national policies that affect price structures and the allocation of resources (for example, social security and agricultural programmes) and of monetary and fiscal policies; and (5) free, or at least freer, movement of capital and labour.

But economic integration, however defined, may be based on political motives and frequently begets political consequences. The existence of political motives is a matter for empirical research and, in western Europe, is clearly established. More hypothetical formulations are required to deal with the problem of political consequences. Thus it may be posited that economic integration unaccompanied by the growth of central institutions and policies does *not necessarily* lead to political community since no pressure for the reformulation of expectations is exercise. Free trade, therefore, cannot be automatically equated with political integration; nor can the interpenetration of national markets be so considered. If economic integration merely implied the removal of barriers to trade and fails to be accompanied by new centrally made fiscal, labour, welfare and investment measures, the relation to political integration is not established. If, however, the integration of a specific section (e.g., coal and steel), or of economics generally (e.g., the 'General Common Market') goes hand in hand with the gradual extension of the scope of central decision-making to take in economic pursuits not initially 'federated', the relation to the growth of political community is clear. It must be stressed, moreover, that the degree of 'success' achieved as measured by purely economic standards – growth in the value and volume of trade, business earnings, wage levels, etc. – is not necessarily an index of political success. Economic dissatisfaction may go hand in hand with demands for more federal political action. Unequal distribution of economic benefits may give rise to political opposition where none existed before. Hence the measure of political success inherent in economic integration lies in the demands, expectations and loyalties of the political actors affected by the process, which do not logically and necessarily follow from statistical indices of economic success.[2]

The decision to proceed with integration or to oppose it rests on the perception of interests and on the articulation of specific values on the part of existing political actors. Rather than relying on a scheme of integration which posits 'altruistic' or 'idealistic' motives as the conditioners of conduct, it seems more reasonable – assuming the pluralistic basis of politics here used – to focus on the interests and values defended by the major groups involved in the process, experience showing that these are far too complex to be described in such simple terms as 'the desire for Franco-German peace' or the 'will to a United Europe'. As the process of integration proceeds, it is assumed that values will undergo change, that interests will be redefined in terms of a regional rather than a purely national orientation and that the erstwhile set of separate national group values will gradually be superseded by a new and geographically larger set of beliefs.

The scheme, finally, assumes that the process of integration will yield a new national consciousness of the new political community, uniting the erstwhile nations which had joined. If the content of nationalism at the level of the former nation had been posited as the overlapping and agreement on principle of the multitude of separate group ideologies, the same conception applies at the level of the new community. As the beliefs and aspirations of groups undergo change due to the necessity of working in a transnational institutional framework, mergers in values and doctrine are expected to come about, uniting groups across former frontiers. The expected overlapping of these group aspirations is finally thought to result in an accepted body of 'national' doctrine, in effect heralding the advent of a new nationalism. Implied in this development, of course, is a proportional diminution of loyalty to and expectations from the former separate national governments.

Shifts in the focus of loyalty need not necessarily imply the immediate repudiation of the national state or government. Multiple loyalties have been empirically demonstrated to exist, either because no conflict is involved between various foci or because the political actor manages psychologically to ignore or sublimate a conflict even if it does exist 'objectively.' In fact some psychologists suggest that attachment to new foci of loyalty, such as international or supranational organisations, may come about by a threefold process in which attachments to the new centre exist side by side with continued deference to the established foci. New loyalties may come into existence as end values, i.e., the new order is desired as an end in itself. Secondly, new loyalties may develop merely in response to a pressure for conformity exercised by the new centre of power. Thirdly – and most importantly for the study of political integration in a framework of consensus – new loyalties are thought to grow haphazardly in their function as intermediary means to some ultimate end, perhaps the same end also fought for in the context of the established national loyalties. Groups and individuals uncertain of their ability to realise political or economic values in the national framework may thus turn to supranational agencies and procedures, without being attracted by 'Europeanism' as such. If the process of developing dual loyalties via this mechanism continues for a sufficiently protracted period, the new central institutions may ultimately acquire the symbolic significance of end values.

A process of political integration, stated in these general terms, is susceptible of detailed investigation only if a set of specific indicators is provided as well. Integration being a process over time, certain identical questions can be raised for purposes of analysis at regular intervals. Care must be taken that indicators of integration are designed with specific reference to the scope of activity of the organisation studied: the reactions of groups concerned with the production, processing, manufacturing and marketing of coal and steel in the instance of the ECSC.

Put in terms of questions, these indicators are proposed for a periodic analysis of development toward the end of political community:

1. What is the position of key interest groups, political parties and governments toward the proposal to integrate a given sector or to federate, or to the treaty formalising such a step? Can the position taken be correlated with the economic expectations of the actors, their political fears or hopes, their satisfaction or dissatisfaction with the national political context, their ideologies or their notion of the national interest?

Having established the initial positions of these groups, the next step in the process of establishing indicators is to sort out the patterns of agreement, opposition and convergence. At the national level, groups may favour integration because they agree in their definition of interests on the basis of identical values: the case of identity of aspirations. They may also agree on the ends of a policy of integration, arriving at this stage, however, on the basis of different values and interests. This constitutes the case of convergence of interests. Finally, groups may oppose integration, either for identical or convergent reasons. Accurate analysis demands that we establish clearly the starting positions as the process gets under way.

2. After the advent of new central institutions, can shifts in position among political parties, interest groups and governments be noted? Shifts for more integration as well as in opposition thereto must, of course, be considered. The indicators would include the same range of questions posed in the effort to define the characteristics of political community. How can shifts be correlated with the ideologies and expectations listed above? . . .

However, the framework of analysis shifts in the second step. While positions taken at the national level still require attention, these must be contrasted with claims made at the level of the new institutions. If new patterns of identities, convergence or opposition are in evidence, the effort must be made to determine whether they originate at the national or the 'supranational' levels.

3. Periodically, the basic question of whether the conditions identified with political community have been realised must be raised. The question can be answered in terms of the indicators for political community presented above.

Such conclusions can be reached only on the basis of again sorting out group values and political demands and structuring them in terms of points of identity. By relating the findings back to earlier positions defended and correlating these with political activity within the frameworks of national government and federal institutions, more definite conclusions with respect to the impact of specific measures of integration on the evolution of ideology and nationalism can be advanced.

We can now state a formal definition of political integration, as used in our ideal type. *Political integration is the process whereby political actors in several distinct national settings are persuaded to shift their loyalties, expectations and political activities toward a new centre, whose institutions possess or demand jurisdiction over the pre-existing national states.* The end result of a process of political integration is a new political community, superimposed over the pre-existing ones.

Before a formal analysis can be made, however, it is essential to specify who the political actors are. It is as impracticable as it is unnecessary to have recourse to general public opinion and attitude surveys, or even to surveys of specific interested groups, such as business or labour. It suffices to single out and define the political elites in the participating countries, to study their reactions to integration and to assess changes in attitude on their part. In our scheme of integration, 'elites' are the leaders of all relevant political groups who habitually participate in the making of public decisions, whether as policy-makers in government, as lobbyists or as spokesmen of political parties. They include the officials of trade associations, the spokesmen of organised labour, higher civil servants and active politicians.

The emphasis on elites in the study of integration derives its justification from the bureaucratised nature of European organisations of long standing, in which basic decisions are made by the leadership, sometimes over the opposition and usually over the indifference of the general membership. This gives the relevant elites a manipulative role which is of course used to place the organisation in question on record for or against a proposed measure of integration.

A further important justification for the elite approach to the study of integration lies in the demonstrable difference in attitudes held at the leadership levels of significant groups, as contrasted with the mass membership . . .

. . . .

Having so far focused on the perceptions and activities of politically significant groups and their elites, it remains to state the role assigned to institutions and structured belief patterns in our ideal type of political integration. Groups put forward interdependent sets of values – ideologies – in their struggle with other groups for political prominence. In a given political community, these ideologies merge and overlap to permit the existence of a set of beliefs held by almost all citizens. But since group action at all levels of political activity hinges around action by governmental institutions, the relationship assumed between beliefs and institutional conduct must be made explicit.

During the initial stages of any process of political integration, the nationalism established in each of the participating countries is still supreme. The decision to join in or to abstain from the proposed steps of integration is defended in terms of national values by each interested group. Once the institutions associated with the step of integration are established, however, a change is likely to take place. The ideologies defended by national groups are likely to influence – and perhaps shape – the values and ideology of the officials manning the new institution. Certainly no effort will be spared to make the attempt at shaping. However, a reverse process of gradually penetrating national ideologies can also be supposed to get under way. Decision-makers in the new institutions may resist the effort to have their beliefs and policies dictated by the interested elites, and advance their own prescription. Or the heterogeneity of their origins may compel them to fashion doctrines and develop codes of conduct which represent an amalgamation of various national belief systems or group values. A two-way process is likely to result in any case: influence originating from national sources seeking to shape 'federal' or 'supranational' decisions and efforts to make national groups conduct themselves in accordance with doctrines originating from the new central institutions. If permitted to operate for any length of time, the national groups now compelled to funnel their aspirations through federal institutions may also be constrained to work within the ideological framework of those organs. Eventually, the transformed doctrines will again be utilised to influence the federal decision-makers, who in turn will have to react in one or both of the approaches sketched above.

It is evident, therefore, that a complex pattern of interaction between national ideologies on the one hand and the beliefs of the office-holders in the central institutions on the other will come about. The eventual changes produced at the national level will constitute one of the indicators of the degree of integration as the process continues, while the analysis of this interaction is one of the crucial problems of this study – and of any study of political integration . . .
. . . .

Notes

1 See Deutsch et al. 1957 for the use of 'objective criteria' in the discussion of community and integration, such as the volume of economic transaction, the volume of social communication and the adequacy of the communications network to carry the 'integration load'. These devices are developed as indicators of the potentiality inherent in certain *communities* in the effort to integrate, in Deutsch 1953a.
2 For a thoughtful exploration of the relation between political federalism and economic integration, see Diebold 1955. Diebold stresses that federalism does not of itself imply a specific economic policy leading to integration of separate economies. Nor is federation a *sine qua non* for the achievement of economic integration. However, the attainment of specific welfare standards in a larger market would almost automatically compel some kind of central action even if the initial plan of economic unity did not provide for it. It is demonstrative of the close link between political and economic motives in contemporary western Europe that the draft treaty for the establishment of the European Political Community also included a provision for the establishment of a General Common Market within ten years. Later developments saw the shelving of the political scheme but the resuscitation of the economic plank with the expectation that it would lead eventually to more political centralism.

Chapter 5

The Political Dynamics of European Economic Integration

Leon N. Lindberg*

Political Integration: Definitions and Hypotheses

The Europe that gave birth to the idea of the nation-state appears to be well on the way to rejecting it in practice. The Treaty establishing the European Economic Community (EEC), signed in Rome on March 25, 1957, represents the latest in a series of steps designed to break down the bastions of European national separatism. Its six signatories, France, Germany, Italy, Belgium, the Netherlands, and Luxembourg, were already members of the European Coal and Steel Community (ECSC), whose foundation in 1952 had created a common market restricted to coal and steel. The experience with this first effort at sector integration led ultimately to the creation of the EEC as well as the European Atomic Energy Community (Euratom).

It soon became evident that integration by sectors could only yield limited results. Its restricted scope, unconnected with the other parts of the economic and financial system, ruled out any large-scale activities and made it impossible to achieve an overall equilibrium. To sweep away from Europe protectionism and economic nationalism with their resulting high production costs, high costs of living and economic stagnation, a different approach was required, a wide attack in more than one dimension as it were; it must have the depth of integration and the wide scope of a freeing of trade. This approach was provided first by the Beyen Plan and then by the Spaak Report, which marked the first step towards the Common Market (Deniau 1960: 6).

The EEC has as its primary goal the creation of an area in which goods, people, services, and capital will be able to circulate freely. To achieve this, a customs union is created, but a customs union in which

* Reproduced by kind permission of Stanford University Press from Lindberg, Leon N. (1963) *The Political Dynamics of European Economic Integration* (Stanford, CA: Stanford University Press). Copyright © 1963 by the Board of Trustees of the Leland Stanford Jr. University. The text has been slightly edited, as indicated, to fit the format of this volume. References have been changed to Harvard citation style wherever possible. Some notes have been omitted.

attention is devoted not only to barriers between states, but to economic, financial, and social reactions that may take place in the Member States. The main purpose is the abolition of trade barriers, tariffs, and quotas which is to be accomplished more or less automatically during a twelve to fifteen-year transition period . . .

The economic and social significance of these developments is certainly far-reaching – one need only read the newspapers to confirm this. For the political scientist, too, they are of consuming interest, for here he can observe the actual processes whereby political actors move beyond the nation-state as a basic framework for action, appearing finally to realize the oft-proclaimed 'fact' of the international interdependence of nations. Forces are at work in Western Europe that may alter the nature of international relations, as well as offer promise of a fuller and more prosperous life for the inhabitants of the region.

The stated goal of the EEC is the creation of a customs union and ultimately the achievement of a significant measure of economic integration. The fundamental motivation is political. It is, in the words of the Treaty, to establish 'an ever closer union among the European peoples' (EEC Treaty, Preamble). Our concern will be with the political *consequences* of economic integration. We shall try to measure the extent to which the creation of the EEC and the activities which take place in its framework give rise to the phenomenon of political integration. Whereas in terms of commercial policy the establishment of the EEC is 'already the most important event of this century', its vast political significance is still only a potential (Frank 1961: 292).

Political Integration

What, then, do we mean by political integration? Some writers define it as a *condition,* and others as a *process.* In the works of Karl Deutsch, integration refers to the probability that conflicts will be resolved without violence . . .

. . . .

Haas insists that we should look at political integration as a *process:*

> Political integration is the process whereby political actors in several distinct national settings are persuaded to shift their loyalties, expectations and political activities toward a new centre, whose institutions possess or demand jurisdiction over the pre-existing national states. The end result of a process of political integration is a new political community, superimposed over the pre-existing ones (Haas 1958a: 16).

In Haas's work, this definition is rigorously tied to an ideal-type analysis in which the institutions of the ECSC are compared to those of an ideal federal-type system. This kind of heuristic device is certainly above reproach and did in fact yield extremely valuable results. My own investigations, however, have led me to adopt a more cautious conception of political integration, one limited to the development of devices and processes for arriving at collective decisions by means other than autonomous action by national governments. It seems to me that it is logically and empirically possible that collective decision-making procedures involving a significant amount of political integration can be achieved without moving toward a 'political community' as defined by Haas. In fact, use of this type of ideal, or model, analysis may well direct the researcher to a different set of questions and a different interpretation of the data collected:

> European integration is developing, and may continue so for a long time, in the direction of different units. . . . We can only speculate about the outcome, but a forecast of the emergence of a pluralistic political structure, hitherto unknown, might not be wholly erroneous. Such a structure might very well permit to a great extent the participating nations to retain their identity while yet joined in the organizations that transcend nationality (Schokking and Anderson 1960: 388).

For the purpose of this study, political integration will be defined as a *process,* but without reference to an end point. In specific terms, political integration is (1) the process whereby nations forgo the desire and ability to conduct foreign and key domestic policies independently of each other, seeking instead to make *joint decisions* or to *delegate* the decision-making process to new central organs (Haas 1960: 2); and (2) the process whereby political actors in several distinct settings are persuaded to shift their expectations and political activities to a new center.[1]

Although this dual definition lacks the analytical clarity and precision of model analysis, it is, I believe, appropriate to the problem at hand. Not only does it provide us with a set of interrelated indicators by means of which to judge the experience of the EEC, but it specifies what I take to be the process of political integration. The first part of the definition refers to two modes of decision-making which are, in my opinion, intimately related, the existence of delegated decision-making being a basic precondition for progress in shared decision-making. The processes of *sharing* and of *delegating* decision-making are likely to affect the governmental structure in each state involved, creating new internal problems of coordination and policy direction, especially between Ministries of Foreign Affairs and such specialized ministries as

Economic Affairs, Agriculture, and Labor that are accustomed to regarding their spheres as wholly or primarily of domestic concern. States with traditions of representative and parliamentary government are also faced with the problem created by the development of decision-making centers whose authority derives from an international, rather than a national, consensus.

The second part of the definition refers to the patterns of behavior shown by high policy-makers, civil servants, parliamentarians, interest-group leaders, and other elites. Here our attention is directed to the perceptions and resulting behavior of the political actors in each of the states involved. The relationship between this set of indicators and those referring to governmental decision-making is very close. By the nature of the process, government policy-makers and civil servants are involved increasingly in the new system of decision-making: they attend meetings of experts, draft plans, and participate in an overall joint decision-making pattern. Similarly, as the locus of decision-making changes, so will the tactics of groups and individuals seeking to influence the decision-making process. They may oppose the change, but once made they will have to adjust to it by changing their tactics, or their organization, or both, to accommodate to the new situation. In Haas's words: 'Conceived not as a condition but as a *process,* the conceptualisation [of political integration] relies on the perception of interests...by the actors participating in the process. Integration takes place when these perceptions fall into a certain pattern and fails to take place when they do not.' Moreover, 'as the process of integration proceeds, it is assumed...that interests will be redefined in terms of regional rather than a purely national orientation' (Haas 1958a: 11, 13).

So much for defining the concept of political integration. The problem now is to try to spell out how it can be made to occur in actual life. Since there have been numerous efforts at transnational organization and cooperation that have not had political results of this kind, political scientists have tried to identify constant background, or environmental, factors or conditions upon which political integration is contingent. Thus Deutsch isolates the following conditions as essential or helpful for a pluralistic or amalgamated security-community: initially compatible value systems, mutually responsive elites, adequate communications channels, a commitment to a 'new way of life', and the existence of a 'core area'. (Deutsch et al. 1957: 12–13). Similarly, Haas calls for a pluralistic social structure, a high level of economic and industrial development, and a modicum of ideological homogeneity (Haas 1961: 375).

But the examination of background factors or conditions does not help us account completely for the *process* of political integration, nor does it permit differentiation between the situation prior to integration and the situation prevailing during the process. Accordingly, it is necessary to try to identify some additional variable factors to specify *how* political integration occurs. On the basis of Haas's researches and my own experiences in Western Europe, I suggest that the process of political integration requires the following conditions: (1) Central institutions and central policies must develop. (2) The tasks assigned to these institutions must be important enough and specific enough to activate socioeconomic processes to which conventional international organizations have no access. (3) These tasks must be inherently expansive. (4) The Member States must continue to see their interests as consistent with the enterprise.

Central Institutional Development

Central institutions are required in order to *represent* the common interests which have brought the Member States together, and in order to *accommodate* such conflicts of interest as will inevitably arise. In discussing the institutions of the EEC, I prefer to avoid the concept of 'supranationality' and to focus instead on the extent to which the Community institutions are enabled to deal directly with fields of activity, rather than merely influencing the actions of individual governments in respect of these fields. There are four main aspects to be considered.

1. North, Koch, and Zinnes seek to distinguish between compromise and 'true integration,' both seen as ways of dealing with conflict (1960: 367-72). Both depend upon *reducing the intensity* of the conflict by uncovering its sources, and by taking the demands of both sides and breaking them into their constituent parts. Each party to the conflict is forced to re-examine and re-evaluate its own desires against those of the other party and against the implications of the total situation. True integration is achieved when a solution has been found in which 'both desires have found a place', in which the interests of the parties 'fit into each other'. I suggest that the central institutions of the EEC, by isolating issues and identifying common interests, may play a crucial role here in 'precipitating unity'.

2. The integrative impact of the central institutions will depend in part upon the *competencies* and *roles* assigned to them. Much, however, depends upon whether or not the institutions make full use of their competencies and upon *how they define their role*. The literature on organizational decision-making suggests some relevant questions in this context. What formal and informal decision-making and relational patterns will develop? What patterns of commitment will be enforced by organizational imperatives, by the social character of the personnel, by 'institutionalization,' by the social and cultural environment, and by centers of interest generated in the course of action and decision? I suggest that the early years of the existence of

these institutions will be significant in determining their long range competence, that patterns of internal differentiation and conflicting values will develop, that organizational behavior will be conditioned by the necessity of adjusting to the environment, and that co-optation will be used as a tactic to head off opposition.
3. Central institutions lacking real competency to affect policy-making directly may develop a *consensus* that will influence those national or international decision-makers who do determine policy.
4. Finally, the patterns of interaction engendered by the central institutions may affect *the overall system* in which they operate; in other words, these institutions may have latent effects that contribute to political integration. As Alger points out, participants in the activities of central institutions may develop multiple perspectives, personal friendships, a camaraderie of expertise, all of which may reflect back upon the national governments and affect future national policy-making (Alger 1961). Such latent effects, however, are significant only if the individuals concerned are influential at the national level, *and* if their activities in the central institutions involve significant policy-making.

Elite Activation

Thanks to the efforts of the so-called 'group theorists', political scientists today know that any analysis of the political process must give a central place to the phenomena of group conflict, to the beliefs, attitudes, and ideologies of groups participating in the process of policy formation. If political integration, as we have defined it, is going on, then we would expect to find a change in the behavior of the participants. Consequently we must identify the aims and motives of the relevant political groups, the conditions of their emergence, and the means by which they seek and attain access to centers of political power.

One of the main obstacles to political integration has been the fact that international organizations lack direct access to individuals and groups in the national communities involved. 'Short of such access, the organization continues to be no more than a forum of intergovernmental consultation and cooperation.' (Haas and Whiting 1956: 443).

Actors with political power in the national community will restructure their expectations and activities only if the tasks granted to the new institutions are of immediate concern to them, and only if they involve a significant change in the conditions of the actors' environment. Several patterns of reaction may be expected:

1. Individual firms may undertake measures of self-protection or adjustment in the form of cartels to limit competition, the conclusion of agreements, and so on.
2. Groups may change their political organization and tactics in order

to gain access to, and to influence, such new central decision-making centers as may be developing.
3. These activities may act back upon the central institutions and the Member States by creating situations that cannot be dealt with except by further central institutional development and new central policies. An example would be a developing need for antitrust legislation in response to an evolving network of agreements between firms in several countries.
4. Such activities may also have latent effects of the kind already described, operative under the same conditions.

Inherently ExpansiveTasks

Here is a problem of central importance because changes in the policy needs of the Member States create definite phases in the life of international organizations. To remedy this, the task assigned to the institutions must be inherently expansive and thus capable of overcoming what Haas calls 'the built-in autonomy of functional contexts'.

Lessons about integrative processes associated with one phase do not generally carry over into the next because the specific policy context . . . determines what is desired by governments and tolerated by them in terms of integrative accommodations . . . There is no dependable, cumulative process of precedent formation leading to ever more community-oriented organizational behavior, unless the task assigned to the institutions is inherently expansive, thus capable .of overcoming the built-in autonomy of functional contexts and of surviving changes in the policy aims of Member States (Haas 1961: 376).

This is the principle involved in the concept of 'spillover'. In its most general formulation, 'spill-over' refers to a situation in which a given action, related to a specific goal, creates a situation in which the original goal can be assured only by taking further actions, which in turn create a further condition and a need for more action, and so forth. The concept has been used by Haas to show that integrating one sector of the economy – for example, coal and steel – will inevitably lead to the integration of other economic and political activities. We shall formulate it as follows: the initial task and grant of power to the central institutions creates a situation or series of situations that can be dealt with only by further expanding the task and the grant of power. Spillover implies that a situation has developed in which the ability of a Member State to achieve a policy goal may depend upon the attainment by another Member State of one of its policy goals. The situation may show various features:

1. The dynamics of spillover are dependent upon the fact that support for any given step in integration is the result of a convergence of goals and expectations. These often competing goals give rise to

competing activities and demands, which may be the basis of further convergence leading to further integration.

2. Lack of agreement between governments may lead to an expanded role for the central institutions; in other words, Member States may delegate difficult problems.

3. At the level of elite groupings, demands and expectations for further actions may be expressed as a result of partial actions taken by the central institutions.

4. The activities of the central institutions and nonofficial elites may create situations that cannot be dealt with except by further central institutional development and new central policies.

5. Far-reaching economic integration, involving all sectors of the economy, as in the EEC, may offer great scope for spill-over between sectors. Conflicts over further integration in a given sector, involving disparate national interests, may be resolved by bargains between such sectors (e.g., agriculture and energy).

6. Participation in a customs union will probably elicit reactions from nonmember states, a situation which may create problems that can be resolved only by further integration or by expanding the role of the central institutions.

Continuity of National Policy Aims

'Spillover' assumes the continued commitment of the Member States to the undertaking. The Treaty of Rome was the result of a creative compromise, a convergence of national aspirations. Political and economic integration cannot be expected to succeed in the absence of a will to proceed on the part of the Member States. Granted that it would be difficult for a state to withdraw from the EEC, it must be stressed that little could be done to move beyond minimal obligations if one or several states were to maintain a determined resistance. It seems likely, however, that with the operation of the other integrative factors, the alternatives open to any Member State will gradually be limited so as to reduce dependence upon this factor. For the will to proceed need not have a positive content. Given only a general reluctance to be charged with obstruction, or to see the enterprise fail, the stimulus to action can be provided by the central institutions or by other Member States.

The way in which decisions are made, in which conflicts of interest among the Member States are resolved, will be of definitive importance for political integration, because the kind of accommodation that prevails will indicate the nature of the positive convergence of pro-integration aims, and of the extent to which the alternatives open to national decision-makers may have been limited by participation in the enterprise. In this connection we may ask the question: Under what conditions does conflict produce a stronger bond between the parties than that which existed before? (North, Koch and Zinnes 1960: 355). Moreover, as already mentioned, the mode of accommodation is directly correlated to the developmental potential of the central institutions.

Conflicts between states may be resolved on the basis of 'the minimum common denominator', by 'splitting the difference', or by 'upgrading common interests' (Haas 1961: 36, 78). The 'minimum common denominator' type, characteristic of classical diplomatic nego-tiations, involves relatively equal bargainers who exchange equal con-cessions while never going beyond what the least cooperative among them is willing to concede. Accommodation by 'splitting the difference' involves a similar exchange of concessions, but conflicts are ultimately resolved somewhere between the final bargaining positions, usually because of the mediatory role performed by a secretariat or expert study groups, or out of deference to third-party pressure such as might be institutionalized in 'parliamentary diplomacy'. This implies 'the existence of a continuing organization with a broad frame of reference, public debate, rules of procedure governing the debate, and the state-ment of conclusions arrived at by some kind of majority vote' (ibid.). Although such mediating organs may not be able to define the terms of agreement, they do participate in setting limits within which the ulti-mate accommodation is reached. Accommodation on the basis of 'upgrading common interests', whether deliberately or inadvertently, depends on the participation of institutions or individuals with an autonomous role that permits them to participate in actually defining the terms of the agreement. It implies greater progress toward political integration, for it shows that the parties succeeded in so redefining their conflict so as to work out a solution at a higher level, which almost invariably implies the expansion of the mandate or task of an international or national governmental agency. In terms of results, this mode of accommodation maximizes . . . the 'spillover' effect of inter-national decisions: policies made pursuant to an initial task and grant of power can be made real only if the task itself is expanded, as reflected in the compromises among the states interested in the task (ibid. 368).

This last type comes closest to what North, Koch, and Zinnes call 'true integration'.

. . . .

General Conclusions

We are now in a position to advance some conclusions about the actual and potential impact of the EEC on decision-making patterns in the 'Europe of the Six' . . .

Have the Six abandoned the desire and ability to conduct foreign and key domestic policies independently of each other, seeking instead to make joint decisions or to delegate the decision-making process to new central institutions? We have seen that in signing the Rome Treaty, these six countries committed themselves to establishing 'the foundations of an ever closer union among the European peoples' (EEC Treaty, Preamble) in the form of 'a Common Market and progressively approximating the economic policies of the Member States, to promote throughout the Community a harmonious development of economic activities, a continuous and balanced expansion, an increased stability, an accelerated raising of the standard of living and closer relations between its Member States' (ibid.: Art. 2). The obligations accepted by the Member States are at times specified in the greatest detail for every particular, and at times stated only in the most vague and general terms. Thus whereas the features of the customs union (tariff and quota elimination, and the establishment of the common external tariff) are spelled out in detail with respect to *goals, policies, and rules*, the elaboration of policies regarding such matters as transport, competition, mobility of labor and services, state aids and state trading, capital movements and capital transfers, agriculture, and general commercial law is left to the central institutions, with only broad goals or policy alternatives stated in the Treaty. The central institutions are therefore endowed with a potentially far-reaching legislative power that can be exercised without the necessity of obtaining ratification from national parliaments.

Our analysis of this institutional system, and of decision-making in it, has revealed that there is a subtle mixture of delegated and shared policymaking. A vast and complex multinational bureaucracy has evolved, composed of national and Community civil servants and politicians. Policymaking, or the pattern of bargaining and exchanging of concessions that it has come to mean, involves not only six governments, but also an autonomous representative of the interests of the Community as a whole, the Commission. The Commission enjoys some unique advantages by virtue of its ability to embody the authority of a Community consensus. It can claim to speak for the common interests of all six countries, and has repeatedly demonstrated its capacity to precipitate unity by taking divergent demands and breaking them into their constituent parts, thus obliging each party to a conflict to re-examine its position in the perspective of the common interest.

The Commission has performed its supervisory functions (regarding the customs union provisions) diligently and at the same time with prudence, preferring to achieve government compliance by using persuasion than by exercising its power to bring suits before the Court of Justice, although this, too, has been done. In making policy proposals to the Council of Ministers, it has sought to engage national civil servants in policy preparation, yet it has not defined the interests of the Community as an average of those of the Member States. Instead, it has vigorously defended its own role as spokesman for Community interests, and has sought to expand this role in its specific proposals. It has grasped the initiative repeatedly in acting as a mediator or broker between the Member States in the Council of Ministers, as well as in the many special committees set up to achieve the maximum consensus possible below the ministerial level (e.g., the Committee of Permanent Representatives, the Special Committee on Agriculture, and the Rey Committee).

The Council of Ministers clearly considers itself a Community institution and not an intergovernmental body. Most issues that reach it involve basic conflicts of interest among Member States. Each member tries to influence the content of the final decision as much as it can, but all are agreed on the necessity of mutual concessions, since the normal practice is to exclude the possibility of not reaching an agreement at all. Agreements are reached on issues involving basic conflicts of interest when the cost of further delay becomes too great. Thus the pressures on the Community from GATT, the British, and the EFTA were largely responsible for forcing the Member States to come to quick agreements on the level of the common external tariff and List G, on acceleration, and on basic policy toward the outside world. In all these cases further procrastination or discussion would have called into question the integrity of the EEC itself. Such pressures also arise within the Community as different elites seek to achieve their own goals through action at the Community level, e.g., the initiation by business groups of the movement for accelerating the Treaty timetable, and the demands from French and Dutch agriculture for rapid implementation of the common agricultural policy.

Conflict resolution in the Council usually follows an upgrading-of-common-interests pattern, although other elements may be injected. This lack of clarity is due to the interpenetration of roles to which we have devoted so much attention. While the Council may reach agreement on the basis of a text submitted by the Commission, this text may itself incorporate a 'splitting of the difference' from a lower level. The three types of conflict resolution we have employed are abstract types, and for the most part we can discuss only the *extent* to which a given decision approximates the abstract standard. The crucial ingredients are two: first, the participation of an institutionalized mediator with autonomous powers; and, second, a continued commitment of the Member States to the enterprise, and hence to the necessity of ultimately reaching a decision. We have already noted that the Commission participates as a *de facto* seventh member in all meetings of the Council and of its preparatory bodies. Here its role depends on the fact that the bulk of the work of the Council is based on a prior proposal from the Commission, the terms of which cannot be changed by the Council except by unanimity, or *by agreement between the Council and the Commission.* Even where the Treaty does not assign this role to the Commission the same pattern has prevailed. Thus the Member States asked the Commission to prepare the common position on the free trade area, as well as the proposals on acceleration, precisely because they could not come to an agreement without its services. Once these tasks had been conferred, it was extremely difficult for the Council to resist the proposals made by the Commission. Moreover, it has proved far easier for Member States to give in to the Commission than it would have been for the Germans to give in to the French or vice versa; in other words, in justifying their actions, both to themselves and to their respective governments, Ministers have been able to defend major concessions on the ground that they were made in the interests of the Community.

The European Parliamentary Assembly and the Economic and Social Committee have been tangential to this evolving policy-making process. A procedural and substantive consensus is well developed in the EPA, and it possesses an important moral influence as a result of its strong pro-integration majority. At this stage, however, it seems to serve as little more than a sounding board for the Commission. In spite of its determined efforts to influence the policy-making process, there is little evidence that it has been successful. As we have seen, many in the EPA have been highly critical of the institutional developments we have described, partly, at least, because they felt their own role was being diminished. It is something of a paradox that one reason for the relative impotence of the EPA may be the strong dedication of the great majority of its members to a maximum of political and economic integration. In the present situation, and as long as these values are still relatively precarious, this forces it to give support to the Commission and to Community solutions even when its policy demands have not been met . . .

It was our expectation that as the Six began to share or delegate decision-making, political actors in these countries would begin to restructure their activities and aspirations accordingly. This has been most striking at the level of high policy-makers and civil servants, for the EEC policy-making process, by its very nature, engages an ever-expanding circle of national officials. There is strong evidence that this sort of interaction contributes to a 'Community-mindedness', by broadening perspectives, developing personal friendships, and fostering a camaraderie of expertise, all of which come from being involved in a joint problem-solving operation. Such developments can be expected to occur in a rough correlation to the frequency of contact. Thus they are more marked in the Committee of Permanent Representatives, which meets twice a week or more and is in constant contact with European integration affairs, than in one of the committees of customs experts that meet once or twice a year. We may expect, however, that more and more officials will become deeply involved as the Community continues to negotiate common policies or coordinated and harmonized policies. This has certainly been the case in agriculture. As these negotiations proceed, we may expect to see accelerated the incipient processes whereby the distinction between domestic affairs and foreign affairs becomes eroded. Thus the technical ministers (transport, agriculture, economic and financial affairs, etc.) are already finding it necessary to meet on a regular basis and to extend their discussions beyond the obligations of the Rome Treaty.

There is also ample evidence of a restructuring of activities and expectations at the level of nonofficial political actors, although its incidence is less striking, owing primarily to the overall phasing of the Treaty timetable. For the most part, the effect of the Treaty to date has been negative in the sense that it has involved the elimination of tariffs and quotas, and of obstacles to the free establishment of professions and services, and so on. Nevertheless, individual firms and groups of firms have certainly responded to their perceptions of the economic advantages to be gained from the creation of a large free market. They have also taken steps to protect themselves from what they take to be the possible disadvantages of the new market. This indicates that the Common Market has been accepted and that economic circles have come to define their interests in terms of it . . .

At the level of political organization and action, there is great surface activity, but in general it cannot be said that the coming of the Common Market has basically altered the behavior of national interest groups. The bulk of interest-group activity remains oriented toward national goals. But there is a great deal of new transnational contact: witness the creation of 222 EEC-level interest groups and the fairly regular participation of representatives of national interest groups in the ESC. Interest-group leaders are being involved in a pattern of interaction similar to that described for national officials. There is an unparalleled amount of traveling, meeting, and exchanging of views. Organizations that in the past balked at paying for the expenses of one delegate to some international meeting may now help to maintain a large, expensive staff in Brussels for the purpose of trying to influence the Community institutions. Yet these activities are not as yet oriented to any really significant joint problem-solving. Most of the EEC-level interest groups are merely liaison groups with essentially secretarial functions and no real role to play in coordinating national group views.

The most notable exception to these generalizations has been in the sector of agriculture, in which the immediate interests of agricultural producers, agricultural workers, and all the industries concerned with the transformation, trade, or marketing of agricultural products are involved. Here the incidence of political activity has been the highest, and here, too, EEC-level interest groups have begun to play a significant role. This leads us to anticipate that as the Community moves to major undertakings in other sectors of the economy, nationally organized interest groups will be compelled to channel more of their political activities through EEC-level groups, if only to establish some new constituency relationship and maintain routes of access to the policy-making process. This will doubtless also force them to engage in some kind of a negotiating process designed to achieve concerted action at this level.

It has been said that these developments are misleading, that they are merely a reflection of good times and could be overturned if there were an economic slump. It is maintained that integration is the product of an accidental and temporary marriage of convenience that nobody has been hurt yet, and that support will disappear as soon as the shoe begins to pinch. Our findings lead us to reject such a judgment. Significant national powers have been thrust into a new institutional setting in which powerful pressures are exerted for 'Community' solutions: that is, solutions which approximate the upgrading-of-common-interests type. Our case studies have revealed that important and divergent national interests have been consistently accommodated in order to achieve a decision.

Two important and related factors that might limit continued political integration have been singled out: namely, the autonomy of functional contexts, and the possibility of a major policy reversal on the part of one or several Member States. Experience over the first three years has confirmed our original hypotheses about the inherently expansive nature of the tasks assigned to the EEC. The case studies have illustrated in a striking fashion the operation of the spillover principle. Community policies have resulted from a pattern of concession, a pattern that confirms the expansive potentialities inherent in the Treaty by virtue of its broad scope and generality. Practically all governments, parties, and groups perceive some likely advantage from the EEC. The reaction of business groups to the Common Market was more favorable than anyone had dared to hope. Much of the same can be said of farmers' and peasants' organizations.

Even General de Gaulle has come to consider at least some version of the Community of the Six as economically and politically indispensable to his vision of France's destiny. His substantive policies with regard to internal EEC affairs have supported the Treaty of Rome. In fact, the French have been among the most insistent that the Common Market be realized more quickly. We have also noted that on a number of occasions the positions taken by the French were closest to those of the

Commission. This has not implied that the long-range goals of the two are identical, related, or even necessarily compatible. As the following statement shows, de Gaulle continues to view the Commission as 'mere technicians', useful for France but certainly not to be endowed with the chief role in integration: 'These bodies have their technical value, but they have not, and cannot have, any political authority or consequently be effective' (de Gaulle 1960: 10). And, again, 'In Europe, legitimate power is the power which comes from national sovereignty, and against this power arbitrary outside tyrannies like the so-called "supranational" institutions can do nothing' (Debre 1960: 12). Nevertheless, in most EEC negotiations the French have accepted the developing procedural code of the Treaty. They have demonstrated a willingness to make concessions and have accepted the initiatory and brokerage activities of the Commission. But they have resisted direct efforts to increase the competence or prestige of the Commission, except when this seemed a necessary price for substantive agreement.

We have not argued that integration is supported for identical reasons, but for converging ones. The convergence of these pro-integration aims and expectations may be grouped as follows:

Integration as political unification. This group consists of a relatively small number of strategically placed 'Europeans' in all walks of life and in all countries, mostly in Christian-Democratic parties, but some of them in Socialist parties, particularly in Belgium and the Netherlands; a majority of EPA members; the Commission; Adenauer, Schuman, Pella, Wigny, Romme, and Spaak; and Monnet and various 'federalists'.

Integration as economic unification. This group is composed of Socialist and Christian-Democratic parties and trade unions in all countries; other groups which consider themselves in a marginal position at the national level, or which have come to the conclusion that comprehensive welfare or planning programs cannot be achieved at the national level; Belgian industry; and Dutch agriculture.

Integration as economic and political cooperation. This head covers de Gaulle and the UNR; center parties in France; agricultural groups in France, Belgium, Italy, and Luxembourg; and high-cost industry in all countries.

Integration as free trade. Here we have free-trade-oriented parties; Liberals in Italy, Belgium, and the Netherlands; the FDP, the DP, and the Erhard wing of the CDU; low-cost and highly efficient industry in all countries, especially in Germany and the Netherlands; and commerce in all countries.

The case studies have graphically demonstrated that none of these broad 'visions', of a united Europe could be realized in practice without the others gaining some measure of realization as well . . .

. . . .

Can we then say that the alternatives open to national policy-makers have been so dramatically narrowed as to eliminate the possibility of a failure or breakdown of the EEC? There is always the possibility of a calamity. I refer to something short of the ultimate calamity of global nuclear war: e.g., Soviet trade overtures and a clear offer of reunification would severely strain Germany's devotion to European integration; France could be plunged into chaos when de Gaulle leaves the scene; a government of the extreme right or left could conceivably come to power in France, or of the extreme left in Italy. Barring this kind of occurrence, it would seem almost impossible for a nation to withdraw entirely from integration. The political and economic advantages are probably too compelling, and the processes too well-advanced. Moreover, the ability of any nation to exercise a formal veto over joint decision-making will be still further reduced as time goes on.
. . . .

To say it is unlikely that any Member State will withdraw from the EEC is not to say the process of political integration could not be slowed down and perhaps arrested. It is important to keep in mind the nature and limits of the conclusions we have drawn. Our main findings have concerned the nature and functioning of the EEC institutional system and the procedural code governing its decisions. This code is based upon willingness to compromise national positions and to confer certain tasks on central institutions that act in the name of the Community. Such willingness can be premised on one or both of two factors: a slowly emerging concept of 'the rules of the game' of the Community, in which case one might be able to speak of a Community consensus; or a particular pattern of interest convergence.

A society generates support for a political system in two ways: through outputs that meet the demands of the members of society; and through the processes of politicization . . . through which attachments to a political system become built into the . . . members of a society. . . When the basic political attachments become rooted or institutionalized, we say that the system has become accepted as legitimate. . . . What I am suggesting here is that support resting on a sense of legitimacy . . . provides a necessary reserve if the system is to weather those frequent storms when the more obvious outputs of the system seem to impose greater hardships than rewards (Easton 1961: 93–4).

Both kinds of support underlie European integration, although it has been the convergence of interests and the interdependence of concrete goals, that have been crucial. Integration is rooted in interest, in the perception of the actors that they can better satisfy their aspirations in this new framework. What is striking about the Treaty of Rome and the first years of the EEC is the *scope* of the tasks assigned to the central institutions, and the extent to which these tasks appear to be inherently expansive; that is, the extent to which integrative steps in one functional context spill over into another. An ever-widening circle of actors finds this system to be an effective, logical, and appropriate framework in which to pursue its goals, and this is one essential feature of a community.

. . . .

Notes

1 This definition is adapted from Haas (1958a: 12). I have preferred to limit it to shifts in political expectations and activities, and to exclude shifts in values and any reference to a political Community end point, since it seems premature to undertake a study of value changes, even if an efficient way of measuring them could be devised. Changes in values can be expected to come about only as a result of new patterns of political expectations and activities.

Chapter 6

Obstinate or Obsolete? The Fate of the Nation-State and the Case of Western Europe

Stanley Hoffmann*

I

The critical issue for every student of world order is the fate of the nation-state. In the nuclear age, the fragmentation of the world into countless units, each of which has a claim to independence, is obviously dangerous for peace and illogical for welfare. The dynamism which animates those units, when they are not merely city-states of limited expanse or dynastic states manipulated by the Prince's calculations, but nation-states that pour into their foreign policy the collective pride, ambitions, fears, prejudices, and images of large masses of people, is particularly formidable. An abstract theorist could argue that any system of autonomous units follows the same basic rules, whatever the nature of those units. But in practice, that is, in history, their substance matters as much as their form; the story of world affairs since the French Revolution is not merely one more sequence in the ballet of sovereign states; it is the story of the fires and upheavals propagated by nationalism. A claim to sovereignty based on historical tradition and dynastic legitimacy alone has never had the fervor, the self-righteous assertiveness which a similar claim based on the idea and feelings of nationhood presents: in world politics, the dynastic function of nationalism is the constitution of nation-states by amalgamation or by splintering, and its emotional function is the supplying of a formidable good conscience to leaders who see their task as the achievement of nationhood, the defense of the nation, or the expansion of a national mission.

This is where the drama lies. The nation-state is at the same time a

---

* Reproduced by kind permission of MIT Press Journals from Stanley Hoffmann (1966), 'Obstinate or Obsolete? The Fate of the Nation-State and the Case of Western Europe', *Daedalus*, 95(3), 862–915. © 1966 by the American Academy of Arts and Sciences. The text has been slightly edited, as indicated, to fit the format of this volume. References have been changed to Harvard citation style where possible. Some peripheral footnotes have been omitted.

form of social organization and – in practice if not in every brand of theory – a factor of international non-integration; but those who argue in favor of a more integrated world, either under more centralized power or through various networks of regional or functional agencies, tend to forget Auguste Comte's old maxim that *on ne detruit que ce qu'on remplace:* the new 'formula' will have to provide not only world order, but also the kind of social organization in which leaders, elites, and citizens feel at home. There is currently no agreement on what such a formula will be (see Aron 1962: ch. 11; Emerson 1962: ch. 19); as a result, nation-states – often inchoate, economically absurd, administratively ramshackle, and impotent yet dangerous in international politics – remain the basic units in spite of all the remonstrations and exhortations. They go on *faute de mieux* despite their alleged obsolescence; indeed, not only do they profit from man's incapacity to bring about a better order, but their very existence is a formidable obstacle to their replacement.

If there was one part of the world in which men of good will thought that the nation-state could be superseded, it was Western Europe. One of France's most subtle commentators on international politics has recently reminded us of E. H. Carr's bold prediction of 1945: 'we shall not see again a Europe of twenty, and a world of more than sixty independent sovereign states' (Carr 1965: 51 quoted in Hassner 1965: 499–528). Statesmen have invented original schemes for moving Western Europe 'beyond the nation-state', (Hass 1964) and political scientists have studied their efforts with a care from which emotional involvement was not missing. The conditions seemed ideal. On the one hand, nationalism seemed at its lowest ebb; on the other, an adequate formula and method for building a substitute had apparently been devised. Twenty years after the end of World War II – a period as long as the whole interwar era – observers have had to revise their judgments. The most optimistic put their hope in the chances the future may still harbor, rather than in the propelling power of the present; the less optimistic ones, like myself, try simply to understand what went wrong.

My own conclusion is sad and simple. The nation-state is still here, and the new Jerusalem has been postponed because the nations in Western Europe have not been able to stop time and to fragment space. Political unification could have succeeded if, on the one hand, these nations had not been caught in the whirlpool of different concerns, as a result both of profoundly different internal circumstances and of outside legacies, and if, on the other hand, they had been able or obliged to concentrate on 'community-building' to the exclusion of all problems situated either outside their area or within each one of them. Domestic differences and different worldviews obviously mean diverging foreign policies; the involvement of the policy-makers in issues among which 'community-building' is merely one has meant a deepening, not a decrease, of those divergencies. The reasons follow: the unification movement has been the victim, and the survival of nation-states the outcome, of three factors, one of which characterizes every international system, and the other two only the present system. Every international system owes its inner logic and its unfolding to the *diversity* of domestic determinants, geo-historical situations, and outside aims among its units; any international system based on fragmentation tends, through the dynamics of unevenness (so well understood, if applied only to economic unevenness, by Lenin) to reproduce diversity. However, there is no inherent reason that the model of the fragmented international system should rule out by itself two developments in which the critics of the nation-state have put their bets or their hopes. Why must it be a diversity of nations? Could it not be a diversity of regions, of 'federating' blocs, superseding the nation-state just as the dynastic state had replaced the feudal puzzle? Or else, why does the very logic of conflagrations fed by hostility not lead to the kind of catastrophic unification of exhausted yet interdependent nations, sketched out by Kant? Let us remember that the unity movement in Europe was precisely an attempt at creating a regional entity, and that its origins and its springs resembled, on the reduced scale of a half-continent, the process dreamed up by Kant in his *Idea of Universal History* (see Hoffmann 1965a).

The answers are not entirely provided by the two factors that come to mind immediately. One is the legitimacy of national self-determination, the only principle which transcends all blocs and ideologies, since all pay lip service to it, and provides the foundation for the only 'universal actor' of the international system: the United Nations. The other is the newness of many of the states, which have wrested their independence by a nationalist upsurge and are therefore unlikely to throw or give away what they have obtained only too recently. However, the legitimacy of the nation-state does not by itself guarantee the nation-state's survival in the international state of nature, and the appeal of nationalism as an emancipating passion does not assure that the nation-state must everywhere remain the basic form of social organization, in a world in which many nations are old and settled and the shortcomings of the nation-state are obvious. The real answers are provided by two unique features of the present international system. One, it is the first truly *global* international system: the regional subsystems have only a reduced autonomy; the 'relationships of major tension' blanket the whole planet, the domestic polities are dominated not so much by the regions problems as by purely local and purely global ones, which conspire to divert the region's members from the internal affairs of their area, and indeed would make an isolated treatment of those affairs impossible. As a result, each nation, new or old, finds itself placed in an orbit of its own, from which it is quite difficult to move away: for the attraction of the regional forces is offset by the pull of all the other forces. Or, to change the metaphor, those nations that coexist in the same apparently separate 'home' of a geographical region find themselves both exposed to the smells and noises that come from outside through all their windows and doors, and looking at the outlying houses from which the interference issues. Coming from diverse pasts, moved by diverse tempers, living in different parts of the house, inescapably yet differently subjected and attracted to the outside world, those cohabitants react unevenly to their exposure and calculate conflictingly how they could either reduce the disturbance or affect in turn all those who live elsewhere. The adjustment of their own relations within the house becomes subordinated to their divergences about the outside world; the 'regional subsystem' becomes a stake in the rivalry of its members about the system as a whole.

However, the coziness of the common home could still prevail if the inhabitants were forced to come to terms, either by one of them, or by the fear of a threatening neighbor. This is precisely where the second unique feature of the present situation intervenes. What tends to perpetuate the nation-states decisively in a system whose universality seems to sharpen rather than shrink their diversity is the new set of conditions that govern and restrict the rule of force: Damocles' sword has become a boomerang, the ideological legitimacy of the nation-state is protected by the relative and forced tameness of the world jungle. Force in the nuclear age is still the 'midwife of societies' insofar as revolutionary war either breeds new nations or shapes regimes in existing nations; but the use of force along traditional lines, for conquest and expansion – the very use that made the 'permeable' feudal units not only obsolete but collapsed and replaced them with modern states often built on 'blood and iron' – has become too dangerous. . . . Thus agglomeration by conquest or out of a fear of conquest fails to take place. The new conditions of violence tend even to pay to national borders the tribute of vice to virtue: violence which dons the cloak of revolution rather than of interstate wars, or persists in the form of such wars only when they accompany revolutions or conflicts in divided countries, perversely respects borders by infiltrating under them rather than by crossing them overtly. Thus all that is left for unification is what one might call 'national self-abdication' or self-abnegation, the eventual willingness of nations to try something else; but precisely global involvement hinders rather than helps, and the atrophy of war removes the most pressing incentive. What a nation-state cannot provide alone – in economics, or defense – it can still provide through means far less drastic than hara-kiri.

These two features give its solidity to the principle of national self-determination, as well as its resilience to the UN. They also give its present, and quite unique, shape to the 'relationship of major tension': the conflict between East and West. This conflict is both muted and universal – and both aspects contribute to the survival of the nation-state. As the superpowers find that what makes their power overwhelming also makes it less usable, or rather usable only to deter one another and to deny each other gains, the lesser states discover under the umbrella of the nuclear stalemate that they are not condemned to death, and that indeed their nuisance power is impressive – especially when the kind of violence that prevails in present circumstances favors the porcupine over the elephant. The superpowers experience in their own camps the backlash of a rebellion against domination that enjoys broad impunity, and cannot easily coax or coerce third parties into agglomeration under their tutelage. Yet they retain the means to prevent other powers from agglomerating away from their clutches. Thus, as the superpowers compete, with filed nails, all over the globe, the nation-state becomes the universal point of salience, to use the new language of strategy – the lowest common denominator in the competition.

Other international systems were merely conservative of diversity; the present system is profoundly conservative of the diversity of nation-states, despite all its revolutionary features. The dream of Rousseau, concerned both about the prevalence of the general will – that is, the nation-state – and about peace, was the creation of communities insulated from one another. In history, where 'the essence and drama of nationalism is not to be alone in the world' (Hassner 1965: 523), the clash of non-insulated states has tended to breed both nation-states and wars. Today, Rousseau's ideals come closer to reality, but in the most un-Rousseauan way: the nation-states prevail in peace, they remain unsuperseded because a fragile peace keeps the Kantian doctor away, they are unreplaced because their very involvement in the world, their very inability to insulate themselves *horn* one another, preserves their separateness. The 'new Europe' dreamed by the Europeans could not be established by force. Left to the wills and calculations of its members, the new formula has not jelled because they could not agree on its role in the world. The failure (so far) of an experiment tried in apparently ideal conditions tells us a great deal about contemporary world politics, about the chances of unification movements elsewhere, and about the functional approach to unification. For it shows that the movement can fail not only when there is a surge of nationalism in one important part, but also when there are differences in assessments of the national interest that rule out agreement on the shape and on the world role of the new, supranational whole.

. . . .

II

. . . .

Western Europe in the postwar years has been characterized by three features which have affected all of its nations. But each of those features has nevertheless affected each of the six nations in a different way because of the deep differences that have continued to divide the Six.

1. The first feature – the most hopeful one from the viewpoint of the unifiers – was the temporary demise of nationalism. In the defeated countries – Germany and Italy – nationalism had become associated with the regimes that had led the nations into war, defeat, and destruction. The collapse of two national ideologies that had been bellicose, aggressive, and imperialistic brought about an almost total discredit for nationalism in every guise . . .

However, the demise of nationalism affected differently the various nations of the half-continent. On the one hand, there were significant differences in national consciousness. If nationalism was low, patriotic sentiment was extremely high in liberated France. The circumstances in which the hated Nazis were expelled and the domestic collaborators purged amounted to what I have called elsewhere a rediscovery of the French political community by the French (Hoffmann et al. 1963): the nation seemed to have redeemed its 'cohesion and distinctiveness'. On the contrary, in Germany especially, the destruction of nationalism seemed to have been accompanied by a drop in national consciousness as well: what was distinctive was guilt and shame; what had been only too cohesive was being torn apart not by internal political cleavages, but by partition, zones of occupation, regional parochialisms blessed by the victors. The French national backbone had been straightened by the ordeal, although the pain had been too strong to tempt the French to flex nationalistic muscles; the German national backbone appeared to have been broken along with the strutting jaw and clenched fist of Nazi nationalism. Italy was in slightly better shape than Germany, in part because of its Resistance movements, but its story was closer to the German than to the French.

However, there were other elements in the national situation, besides patriotic consciousness, that also affected differently the various nations' inclination to nationalism. The defeated nations – Germany in particular – were in the position of patients on whom drastic surgery had been performed, and who were lying prostrate, dependent for their every movement on the surgeons and nurses. Even if one had wanted to restore the nation to the pinnacle of values and objectives, one could not have succeeded except with the help and consent of one's guardians – who were not likely to give support to such a drive; in other words, the situation itself set the strictest limits to the possibility of any kind of nationalism, expansive or insulating. The lost territories

were beyond recuperation; a healing period of 'repli' comparable to
that which had marked the early foreign policy of the Third Republic
was not conceivable either. One could not get anything alone, and anything others could provide, while limited, would be something to be
grateful for.

On the other hand, France and, to a lesser extent (because of their
much smaller size), Belgium and Holland were not so well inoculated.
For, although the prevalence of the nation meant little in the immediate European context, it meant a great deal in the imperial one: if the
circumstances of the Liberation kept national consciousness from
veering into nationalism in one realm, the same circumstances tended
to encourage such a turn with respect to the colonies. Cut down to size
in Europe, these nations were bound to act as if they could call upon
their overseas possessions to redress the balance; accustomed, through
their association of nationalism with Nazi and Fascist imperialism, to
equate chauvinism only with expansion, they would not be so easily
discouraged from a nationalism of defense, aimed at preserving the
'national mission' overseas. . . . The French . . . suffered almost at once
from dis-imperial dyspepsia, and the long, losing battle they fought
gave rise continuously to nationalist tantrums of frustration and rage.
Moreover, the French inclination to nationalism was higher because of
an internal component of the national situation as well: there was in
France one political force that was clearly nationalist, that had indeed
presided over the Liberation, given whatever unity they had to the
Resistance movements, and achieved in the most impressive way a
highly original convergence of Jacobin universalist nationalism and of
'traditionalist', right-wing, defensive nationalism – the force of General
de Gaulle. His resignation had meant, as Alfred Grosser (1965: 12)
suggests, the defeat of a doctrine that put not only a priority mark on
foreign affairs but also a priority claim on *Notre Dame la France*. The
incident that had led to his departure – a conflict over the military
budget – had been symbolic enough of the demise of nationalism
referred to above. But his durability, first as a political leader, later as a
'capital that belongs to all and to none', reflected a lasting nostalgia for
nationalism; and it was equally symbolic that the crisis which returned
him to power was a crisis over Algeria.

2. The second feature common to all the West European national
institutions, yet affecting them differently, was the 'political collapse of
Europe'. Europe did not merely lose power and wealth: such losses can
be repaired, as the aftermath of World War I had shown. Europe, previously the heart of the international system, the locus of the world
organization, the fount of international law, fell under what de Gaulle
has called 'the two hegemonies'. The phrase is, obviously, inaccurate
and insulting: one of those hegemonies took a highly imperial form,
and thus discouraged and prevented the creation in Eastern Europe of

any regional entity capable of overcoming the prewar national rivalries. Nothing is to be gained; however, by denying that US hegemony
has been a basic fact of life. American domination has indeed had the
kinds of 'domination effects' any hegemony produces: the transfer of
decision-making in vital matters from the dominated to the dominator
breeds a kind of paternalism in the latter, and irresponsibility (either in
the form of abdication or in the form of scapegoatism) in the former.
But the consequences of hegemony vary according to its nature. The
peculiar nature of this domination has also had unique consequences –
better and worse than in the classical cases. One may dominate
because one wants to and can; but one may also dominate because one
must and does: by one's weight and under the pressures of a compelling situation. This has been America's experience: its hegemony
was 'situational', not deliberate.

The effects have been better than usual, insofar as such hegemony
restricted itself to areas in which European nations had become either
impotent or incapable of recovery by self-reliance. It left the dominated
with a considerable freedom of maneuver, and indeed prodded them
into recovery, power recuperation, and regional unity; it favored both
individual and collective emancipation. But the effects have been worse
precisely because this laxity meant that each party could react to *this*
common feature of the national situations (that is, American hegemony) according to the distinctive *other* features of his national situation, features left intact by the weight and acts of the US, by contrast
with the USSR. American domination was only one part of the picture.
Hence the following paradox: both America's prodding and the individual and collective impotence of Western European nations, now
reduced to the condition of clients and stakes, ought logically to have
pushed them into unity-for-emancipation – the kind of process Soviet
policy discouraged in the other half of Europe. But the very margin of
autonomy left to each West European nation by the US gave it an
array of choices: between accepting and rejecting dependence, between
unity as a weapon for emancipation and unity as merely a way to
make dependence more comfortable. It would have been a miracle if
all the nations had made the same choice; the diversity of national situations has ultimately prevailed. To define one's position toward the US
was the common imperative, but each one has defined it in his own
way.

At first, this diversity of domestic outlooks and external positions did
not appear to be an obstacle to the unification movement. As Ernst
Haas has shown (1958a), the movement grew on ambiguity, and those
who accepted American hegemony as a lasting fact of European life as
well as those who did not could submerge their disagreement in the
construction of a regional entity that could be seen, by the former, as
the most effective way for continuing to receive American protection

and contributing to America's mission and, by the latter, as the most effective way to challenge American predominance. However, there are limits to the credit of ambiguity. The split could not be concealed once the new entity was asked to tackle matters of 'high politics' – that is, go beyond the purely internal economic problems of little impact or dependence on the external relationship to the US.[1] It is therefore no surprise that this split should have disrupted unification at two moments – in 1953–54, when the problem of German rearmament was raised; and in 1962–65, when de Gaulle's challenge of the US became global.

. . . .

3. The divisions and contradictions, described above were sharpened by the third common feature, which emerged in the mid-1950s and whose effects have developed progressively since: the nuclear stalemate between the superpowers. The impact of the 'balance of terror' on the Western alliance has been analyzed so often and well (see especially Kissinger 1965) that nothing needs to be added here; but what is needed is a brief explanation of how the two splits already discussed have been worsened by Europe's gradual discovery of the uncertainties of America's nuclear protection (now that the US could be devastated too), and how some new splits appeared. For to the extent to which the stalemate has loosened up a previously very tight situation – tight because of the threat from the East and the ties to the US – it has altogether sharpened previous differences in national situations *and* increased the number of alternatives made available to elites and statesmen. Greater indeterminacy has meant greater confusion.

First, the split between French 'resistance' and German 'resignation' has become deeper. The dominant political elites in Germany have interpreted the new national situation created by the balance of terror as merely adding urgency to their previous calculation of interest. The nuclear stalemate was, given Germany's position, deemed to increase the danger for the West: the US was relatively less strong, the Soviet Union stronger, that is, more of a threat. . . . If America's monopoly was broken, if America's guarantee was weakened thereby, what was needed in a world that was not willing to let Germany rearm with nuclear weapons, in a continent that could not really develop a nuclear force of its own capable of replacing America's and of matching Russia's – was a German policy so respectful of America's main concerns, and also so vigilant with respect to the Soviet Union, that the US would both feel obligated to keep its mantle of protection over Germany and not be tempted into negotiating a detente at Germany's expense. German docility would be the condition for, and counterpart of, American entanglement . . .

In France, on the contrary, the balance of terror reinforced the attitude of resistance: what had always been a goal – emancipation – but had in fact been no more than a hope, given the thickness of the iron curtain, the simple rigidity of the superpowers' policies in the days of Mr. Dulles, and Europe's inability to affect the course of events, now became a possibility; for the giants' stalemate meant increased security for the less great (however much they might complain about the decrease of American protection and use it as a pretext, their lament coexisted with a heightened feeling of protection against war in general). What the Germans saw as a liability was an opportunity to the French. Germany's situation, its low national consciousness, incited most German leaders to choose what might be called a 'minimizing' interpretation of the new situation; France's situation, its high national consciousness and, after 1958, the doctrine of its leader, incited French political elites to choose a 'maximizing' interpretation. The increasing costs of the use of force made this use by the superpowers less likely, American protection less certain but also less essential, Europe's recovery of not merely wealth but power more desirable and possible – possible since the quest for power could be pushed without excessive risk of sanctions by the two giants, desirable since power, while transformed, remains the moving force and *ultima ratio* of world politics. This recovery of power would help bring about the much desired prevalence of polycentrism over bipolarity.

. . . .

This long discussion of the different responses to common situations has been necessary in reaction to the dominant approach to European integration which has focused on process. The self-propelling power of the process is severely constrained by the associates views and splits on ends and means. In order to go 'beyond the nation-state', one will have to do more than set up procedures in adequate 'background' and 'process conditions'. For a procedure is not a purpose, a process is not a policy.

III

However, since it is the process of European integration that is its most original feature, we must examine it also (see Hoffmann 1963: 3–31, 1964). We have been witnessing a kind of race, between the logic of integration set up by Monnet and analyzed by Haas, and the logic of diversity, analyzed above. According to the former, the double pressure of necessity (the interdependence of the social fabric, which will oblige statesmen to integrate even sectors originally left uncoordinated) and of men (the action of the supranational agents) will gradually restrict the freedom of movement of the national governments by turning the national situations into one of total enmeshing. In such a milieu, nationalism will be a futile exercise in anachronism, and the national consciousness itself will, so to speak, be impregnated by an awareness of the higher interest in union. The logic of diversity, by contrast, sets limits to the degree to which the 'spillover' process can limit the freedom of action of the governments; it restricts the domain in which the logic of functional integration operates to the area of welfare; indeed, to the extent that discrepancies over the other areas begin to prevail over the laborious harmonization in welfare, even issues belonging to the latter sphere may become infected by the disharmony which reigns in those other areas. The logic of integration is that of a blender which crunches the most diverse products, overcomes their different tastes and perfumes, and replaces them with one, presumably delicious juice. One lets each item be ground because one expects a finer synthesis: that is, ambiguity helps rather than hinders because each 'ingredient' can hope that its taste will prevail at the end. The logic of diversity is the opposite: it suggests that, in areas of key importance to the national interest, nations prefer the certainty, or the self-controlled uncertainty, of national self-reliance, to the uncontrolled uncertainty of the untested blender; ambiguity carries one only a part of the way. The logic of integration assumes that it is possible to fool each one of the associates some of the time because his overall gain will still exceed his occasional losses, even if his calculations turn out wrong here or there. The logic of diversity implies that, on a vital issue, losses are not compensated by gains on other (and especially not on other less vital) issues: nobody wants to be fooled. The logic of integration deems the uncertainties of the supranational function process creative; the logic of diversity sees them as destructive past a certain threshold: Russian roulette is fine only as long as the gun is filled with blanks. Ambiguity lures and lulls the national consciousness into integration as long as the benefits are high, the costs low, the expectations considerable. Ambiguity may arouse and stiffen national consciousness into nationalism if the benefits are slow, the losses high, the hopes dashed or deferred. Functional integration's gamble could be won only if the method had sufficient potency to promise a permanent excess of gains over losses, and of hopes over frustrations. Theoretically, this may be true of economic integration. It is not true of political integration (in the sense of 'high politics').

The success of the approach symbolized by Jean Monnet depended, and depends still, on his winning a triple gamble: on goals, on methods, on results. As for goals, it is a gamble on the possibility of substituting motion as an end in itself, for agreement on ends. It is a fact that the transnational integrationist elites did not agree on whether the object of the community-building enterprise ought to be the construction of a new super-state – that is, a federal potential nation, *a la* USA, more able because of its size and resources to play the traditional game of power than the dwarfed nations of Western Europe – or whether the object was to demonstrate that power politics could be overcome through cooperation and compromise, to build the first example of a radically new kind of unit, to achieve a change in the nature and not merely in the scale of the game. Monnet himself has been ambiguous on this score; Hallstein has been leaning in the first direction, many of Monnet's public relations men in the second (see e.g. Kohnstamm 1964). Nor did the integrationists agree on whether the main goal was the creation of a regional 'security-community', (Deutsch et al. 1957) that is, the pacification of a former hotbed of wars, or whether the main goal was the creation of an entity whose position and might could decisively affect the course of the cold war in particular, of international relations in general. Now, it is perfectly possible for a movement to feed on its harboring continental national-ists as well as anti-power idealists, inward-looking politicians and outward-looking politicians – but only as long as there is no need to make a choice. Decisions on tariffs did not require such choices. Decisions on agriculture already raise basic problems of orientation. Decisions on foreign policy and membership and defense cannot be reached unless the goals are clarified. One cannot be all things to all people all of the time.

As for methods, there was a gamble on the irresistible rise of supra-national functionalism. It assumed, first, that national sovereignty, already devalued by events, could be chewed up leaf by leaf like an artichoke. It assumed, second, that the dilemma of governments having to choose between pursuing an integration that ties their hands and stopping a movement that benefits their people could be exploited in favor of integration by men representing the common good, endowed with the advantages of superior expertise, initiating proposals, propped against a set of deadlines, and using for their cause the tech-nique of package deals. Finally, it was assumed that this approach would both take into account the interests of the greater powers and prevent the crushing of the smaller ones. The troubles with this gamble have been numerous. One, even an artichoke has a heart, which remains intact after the leaves have been eaten. It is of course true that a successful economic and social integration would considerably limit the freedom governments would still enjoy in theory for their diplo-macy and strategy; but why should one assume that they would not be aware of it? As the artichoke's heart gets more and more denuded, the governments' vigilance gets more and more alerted. To be sure, the second assumption implies that the logic of the movement would prevent them from doing anything about it: they would be powerless to save the heart. But, two, this would be true only if governments never put what they consider essential interests of the nation above the particular interests of certain categories of nationals, if superior exper-tise were always either the Commission's monopoly or the solution of the issue at hand, if package deals were effective in every argument, and, above all, if the governments' representatives were always determined to behave as a 'community organ' rather than as the agents of states that are not willing to accept a community under any conditions. Finally, functional integration may indeed give lasting satisfaction to the smaller powers, precisely because it is for them that the ratio of 'welfare politics' to high politics is highest, and that the chance of gaining benefits through intergovernmental methods that reflect rather than correct the power differential between the big and the small is poorest; but this is also why the method is not likely *a la longue* to satisfy the bigger powers as much: facing them, the supranational civil servants, for all their skill and legal powers, are a bit like Jonases trying to turn whales into jellyfish. Of course, the idea – ultimately – is to move from an essentially administrative procedure in which supranational civil servants enter a dialogue with national ministers, to a truly federal one in which a federal cabinet is responsible to a federal parliament; but what is thus presented as a linear progress may turn out to be a vicious circle, since the ministers hold the key to the transformation, and may refuse it unless the goals are defined and the results already achieved are satisfactory.

There was a gamble about results as well. The experience of integration would entail net benefits for all, and bring about clear progress toward community formation. Such progress could be measured by the following yardsticks: in the realm of interstate relations, an increasing transfer of power to the new common agencies, and the prevalence of solutions 'upgrading the common interest' over other kinds of compromises; in the realm of transnational society, an increasing flow of communications; in the area of national consciousness – which is important both for interstate relations, because (as seen above) it may set limits to the statesmen's discretion, and for transnational society, because it affects the scope and meaning of the communication flows – progress would be measured by increasing compatibility of views about external issues. The results achieved so far are mixed: negative on the last count (see below), limited on the second, and marked on the first by features that the enthusiasts of integration did not expect. On the one hand, there has been some strengthening of the authority of the Commission, and in various areas there has been some 'upgrading of common interests'. On the other hand, the Commission's unfortunate attempt to consolidate those gains at de Gaulle's expense, in the spring of 1965, has brought about a startling setback for the whole enterprise; moreover, in their negotiations, the members have conspicuously failed to find a common interest in some vital areas (energy, England's entry), and sometimes succeeded in reaching apparently 'integrating' decisions only after the most ungainly, traditional kind of bargaining, in which such uncommunity-like methods as threats, ultimatums, and retaliatory moves were used. In other words, either the ideal was not reached, or it was reached in a way that was both the opposite of the ideal and ultimately its destroyer. If we look at the institutions of the Common Market as an incipient political system for Europe, we find that its authority remains limited, its structure weak, its popular base restricted and distant.[2]

It is therefore not surprising if the uncertainty about results already achieved contributes to uncertainty about future prospects. For the very divisions among the partisans of integration make it hard to predict where the 'Monnet method' would lead, if the process were to continue along the lines so fondly planned by the French 'inspirator'. Would the enterprise become an effective federation, gradually turning the many into one, or would it lead to a mere facade behind which all the divergences and rivalries would continue to be played out? It is at least remarkable that Gaullist and American fears should converge in one respect: de Gaulle has consistently warned that the application of the supranational method to the area of high politics would lead not to a strong European entity, but to a dilution of national responsibility whose only beneficiary would be the US; incapable of defining a coherent policy, the 'technocrats' would leave the decisions in vital areas to the US, at least by default. On the contrary, many Americans have come to believe, on the basis of some of EEC's actions in the realm of tariffs and trade, that a united Europe would be able to challenge US leadership much more effectively than the separate European states ever could. The truth of the matter is that nobody knows: a method is not a policy, a process is not a direction; the results achieved so far are too specialized, and the way in which they have been reached is too bumpy, to allow one to extrapolate and project safely. The face of a united Europe has not begun to emerge; there are just a few lines, but one does not know whether the supranational technique would finally give to Western Europe the features of a going concern, or those of a Fourth Republic writ large – the ambitions of a world power, or the complacency of parochialism. The range of possibilities is so broad, the alternatives are so extreme, that the more the Six move into the stormy waters of high politics, the less not only they but also the outside powers, such as the US, which may be affected by their acts are willing to extend the credit of hope and to make new wagers: neither Gaullist France nor the present US leadership is willing to risk a major loss of control. Contrary to the French proverb, in the process of functional integration, only the first steps do not cost much.

There are two important general lessons one can draw from a study of the process of integration. The first concerns the limits of the functional method: its very (if relative) success in the relatively painless area in which it works relatively well lifts the participants to the level of issues to which it does not apply well any more – like swimmers whose skill at moving quickly away from the shore suddenly brings them to the point where the waters are stormiest and deepest, at a time when fatigue is setting in, and none of the questions about ultimate goal, direction, and length of swim has been answered. The functional process was used in order to 'make Europe'; once Europe began being made, the process collided with the question: 'making Europe, what for?' The process is like a grinding machine that can work only if someone keeps giving it something to grind. When the users start quarreling and stop providing, the machine stops. For a while, the machine worked because the governments poured into it a common determination to integrate their economies in order to maximize wealth; but with their wealth increasing, the question of what to do with it was going to arise: a technique capable of supplying means does not *ipso facto* provide the ends, and it is about those ends that quarrels have broken out. They might have been avoided if the situation had been more compelling – if the Six had been so cooped up that each one's horizon would have been nothing other than his five partners. But this has never been their outlook, nor is it any more their necessity. Each one is willing to live with the others, but not on terms too different from his own; and the Six are not in the position of the three miserable prisoners of *No Exit*. Transforming a dependent 'subsystem' proved to be one thing; defining its relations to all other subsystems and to the international system in general has turned out to be quite another – indeed, so formidable a matter as to keep the transformation of the subsystem in abeyance until those relations can be defined.

The model of functional integration, a substitute for the kind of instant federation which governments had not been prepared to accept, shows its origins in important respects. One, it is essentially an administrative model, which relies on bureaucratic expertise for the promotion of a policy defined by the political authorities, and for the definition of a policy that political decision-makers are technically incapable of shaping – something like French planning under the Fourth Republic. The hope was that in the interstices of political bickering the administrators could build up a consensus; but the mistake was to believe that a formula that works well within certain limits is a panacea – and that even within the limits of 'welfare politics' administrative skill can always overcome the disastrous effects of political paralysis or mismanagement (cf. the impact of inflation, or balance of payment troubles, on planning). Two, the model assumes that the basic political decisions, to be prepared and pursued by the civil servants but formally made by the governments, would be reached through the process of short-term bargaining, by politicians whose mode of operation is empirical muddling through, of the kind that puts immediate advantages above long-term pursuits: this model corresponds well to the nature of parliamentary politics with a weak Executive, for example, the politics of the Fourth Republic, but the mistake was to believe that all political regimes would conform to this rather sorry image, and also to ignore the disastrous results which the original example produced whenever conflicts over values and fundamental choices made mere empirical groping useless or worse than useless (cf. decolonization) (along similar lines, see Rosenstiel 1962).

The second lesson is even more discouraging for the advocates of functionalism. To revert to the analogy of the grinder, what has happened is that the machine, piqued by the slowing down of supply, suddenly suggested to its users that in the future the supplying of grinding material be taken out of their hands and left to the machine. The institutional machinery tends to become an actor with a stake in its own survival and expansion. The same thing happens often enough within a state whose political system is ineffective. But here we deal not with one but with six political systems, and the reason for the ineffectiveness of the Council of Ministers of the Six may be the excessive toughness, not the weakness, of the national political systems involved. In other words, by trying to be a force, the bureaucracy here, inevitably, makes itself even more of a stake that the nations try to control or at least to affect . . .

IV

We must come now to the balance sheet of the 'European experiment'. The most visible aspect is the survival of the nations. To be sure, they survive transformed: first, swept by the advent of the 'age of mass consumption', caught in an apparently inexorable process of industrialization, urbanization, and democratization, they become more alike in social structure, in economic and social policies, even in physical appearance; there is a spectacular break between a past which so many monuments bring to constant memory, and a rationalized future that puts these nations closer to the problems of America's industrial society than to the issues of their own history. Second, these similarities are promoted by the Common Market itself: it is of no mean consequence that the prospect of a collapse of the Market should have brought anguish to various interest groups, some of which had fought its establishment: the transnational linkages of businessmen and farmers are part of the transformation. Third, none of the Western European nations is a world power any longer in the traditional sense, that is, in the sense either of having physical establishments backed by military might in various parts of the globe, or of possessing in Europe armed forces superior to those of any non-European power.

And yet they survive as nations. Let us go back to the criteria of integration listed above. On foreign and defense policies, not only has no power been transferred to common European organs, but France has actually taken power away from NATO, and, as shown in part two, differences in the calculations of the national interest have, if anything, broadened ever since the advent of the balance of terror. As for intra-European communications, research shows that the indubitably solid economic network of EEC has not been complemented by a network of social and cultural communications; the links between some of those societies and the US are stronger than the links among them. Indeed, even in the realm of economic relations, the Common Market for goods has not been completed by a system of pan-West European enterprises: enterprises that find themselves unable to compete with rivals within EEC often associate themselves with American firms rather than merge with such rivals. Finally, views about external issues, far from becoming more compatible, appear to reflect as well as to support the divergent definitions of the national interest by the statesmen. French elite opinion puts Europe ahead of the North Atlantic partnership, deems bipolarity obsolete, is overwhelmingly indifferent or even hostile to the US, and is still highly suspicious of Germany; only a minority comes out in favor of a genuine political federation of Western Europe and thinks that US and French interests coincide. German elite opinion puts the North Atlantic entente ahead of Europe, believes that the world is still bipolar, is overwhelmingly favorable to the US, deems US and German interests in agreement, is either favorably inclined toward France or at least not hostile, and shows a majority in favor of a European federation. There is no common European outlook. Nor is there a common 'project', a common conception of either Europe's role in world affairs or Europe's possible contribution to the solution of the problems charac-teristic of all industrial societies.

It is important to understand where the obstacles lie. To some extent, they lie in the present condition of national consciousness. I mentioned earlier that there were at the start considerable differences from country to country . . .

. . . .

And yet, if the 'national consciousness' of the European nations could be isolated from all other elements of the national situation, one would, I think, conclude that the main reasons for the resistance of the nation-state lie elsewhere.

They lie, first of all, in the differences in national situations, exacer-bated by the interaction between each of the Six and the present inter-national system. Earlier, we have looked at concrete instances of such differences; let us return to them in a more analytic way. One part of each national situation is the purely *domestic* component. In a modern nation-state, the very importance of the political system, in the triple sense of functional scope, authority, and popular basis, is already a

formidable obstacle to integration. It is comparatively easier to overcome the parochialism of a political system which, being of the night-
watchman variety, has only a slender administrative structure, whose
power consists of punishing, rather than rewarding, with the help of a
tiny budget, and whose transmission belts to the mass of the people are
few and narrow, than it is to dismantle the fortress of a political
system which rests on 'socially mobilized' and mobilizing parties and
pressure groups, and handles an enormous variety of social and economic services with a huge bureaucracy. To be sure, it was the hope
and tactic of Monnet to dismantle the fortress by redirecting the allegiance of parties and pressure groups toward the new central institutions, by endowing the latter with the ability to compete with the
national governments in the setting up of social services. In other
words, the authority of the new European political system would
deepen as its scope broadened and its popular basis expanded. The
success of this attempt at drying up the national ponds by diverting
their waters into a new, supranational pool depended on three prereq-
uisites which have not been met: with respect to popular basis, the
prevalence of parties and pressure groups over Executives; with respect
to scope, the self-sustaining and expanding capacity of the new central
bureaucracy; with respect to both scope and popular basis, the development of transnational political issues of interest to all political forces
and publics across boundary lines. The modern Executive establishment has one remarkable feature: it owes much of its legitimacy and its
might to the support of popularly based parties and pressure groups,
but it also enjoys a degree of autonomy that allows it to resist pressures, to manipulate opposition, to manufacture support. Even the
weak Fourth Republic has evaded pressure toward 'transnationalism'
and diluted the dose of 'bargaining politics' along supranational lines.
The civil servants' careers are still made and unmade in the national
capitals. Above all, each nation's political life continues to be dominated by 'parochial' issues: each political system is like a thermos
bottle that keeps warm, or lukewarm, the liquid inside. The European
political process has never come close to resembling that of any
Western European democracy because it has been starved of common
and distinctive European issues. It is as if, for the mythical common
man, the nation-state were still the most satisfying – indeed the most
rewarding – form of social organization in existence (see Emerson
1962). As for what it can no longer provide him with by itself, the
state can still provide it without committing suicide, through cooperation, or the citizens can go and find it across borders, without any need
to transfer their allegiance – or else there is, in any event, no guarantee
that any form of social organization other than a still utopian world
state could provide it . . .
. . . .

Thus, the national situations have multiplied the effects of differences between the shapes of the various national consciences. But the resistance of the nation-state is not due only to the kind of loan of life that its inevitable entanglement in international affairs and the idle motion left by its past provide even to nations with a low national consciousness. It is due also to the impact of the revival of nationalism in France. Even without de Gaulle the differences analyzed above would have slowed down integration and kept some fire in the nation's stoves. But the personal contribution of de Gaulle to the crisis of integration has been enormous. Not only has he raised questions that were inescapable in the long run, earlier and more pungently than they would have been otherwise, but he has also provided and tried to impose his own answers. His impact is due to his style as well as to his policies. The meaning of de Gaulle has been a change in French policy from ambivalence toward supranational integration to outright hostility; from a reluctance to force one's partners to dispel the ambiguities of 'united Europe' to an almost gleeful determination to bring differences out into the open; from a tendency to interpret the national situation as oppressively difficult to a herculean effort at improving all its components in order to push back limits and maximize opportunities. The meaning of de Gaulle has also been a change in the national situations of the others, leading to a sharpening of antagonisms and to a kind of cumulative retreat from integration . . .

. . . .

V

This long balance sheet leaves us with two sets of questions: What are the prospects in Western Europe? What generalizations can one draw from the whole experience? As for the prospects, what precedes reads perhaps too much like a post-mortem. Is there no chance for the European Community? Is it condemned to be, at best, a success in the economic realm but a fiasco in 'high politics', something like a hydra with one single body but a multitude of heads? It would be presumptuous indeed to read hope out of court. One of the decisive elements in the movement's 'spillback', de Gaulle's nationalism, may not outlive him. His successors may have a less sweeping vision and may make exactly the opposite gamble from his – that is, prefer the risks of the common enterprise, whose rewards might be high if it works, to the dividends of national action; they could indeed attempt to revive the Monnet concept of Europe, and even to overcome the deficiencies of functionalism by a leap into more genuinely federal institutions. Moreover, whereas de Gaulle has had the backing of a parliamentary majority hostile to supranational integration and has exerted the kind of rule that parties and pressure groups do not affect much anyhow, his successors may depend for domestic support and survival precisely on those parties and pressure groups which had started to weave a transnational fabric. Should this be the case, the 'Europe of the Six', instead of being as close as it now is to the traditional model of inter-state relations, might move again toward the other ideal-type, that of political community-building, so well described by Ernst Haas, who sees in it the wave of the future.

Whereas in the case of a revival of German nationalism, the prospect of failure may not be enough to deter an attempt, here I would main-tain that an attempt would not be tantamount to success. In the first place, while nothing (not even the Common Market) is irreversible, no important event leaves the world unmarked, and after the event one can never pick up the pieces as if nothing had happened: this, which is true of the Common Market, is true also of General de Gaulle. It will not be easy to sweep under the rug the curls of dust he has willfully placed in the sunlight; it will not be easy to ignore the kinds of ques-tions he has asked, even if his answers are rejected, precisely because they are the questions any European enterprise would have faced sooner or later. Second, even the passing of his nationalism might not transform the national situations of the European nation-states so deeply that all the cleavages discussed here would suddenly disappear. For, even if all the political leaders of Western Europe had once again the same non-nationalist approach, the differences in the national situ-ations would still lead to divergent definitions of the national interests. In particular, the problem of nuclear weapons control and command in a grouping divided between nuclear 'have-nots' and nuclear 'haves' may prove to be as intractable, and to raise as much of an obstacle to community-formation among Western Europeans, as in the Atlantic alliance. The ideal conditions not merely for the resumption but for the success of a forward march would be a transformation of Germany's external situation and of France's domestic one. If the search for a détente should lead the US to put a rapprochement with the USSR ahead of its bonds to West Germany, and if it became clear in West Germany, as a result, both that security is neither the most urgent problem nor entirely provided any more by the US, and that reunifica-tion cannot be obtained from and through the US; if, in addition, such disappointment with the US does not encourage West German leader-ship to follow a nationalist path, or if an attempt by West Germany to obtain for itself from Moscow what its allies had failed to provide for her should end in frustration, then – at last – West Germany might be willing to accept a foreign policy close to de Gaulle's 'European Europe' with its indifference to regimes and ideologies, its repudiation of the cold war outlook, its opening to the East, and its cautious promise of eventual reunification at the cost of border limitations and arms restrictions. In other words, on the German side, what would be required would be a 'polycentric', yet non-nationalist, reading of the external situation. This would be likely to happen if at the same time France had given up her nationalist interpretation of 'polycentrism', and become again more humble, more willing to trust the Community organs, more in need of adopting European integration as a goal in itself. Such a possibility would exist if, domestically, the impervious stability of de Gaulle's regime were to be replaced not merely with a political system whose Executive would lean on an 'integrationist' party majority, but with the kind of instability that both prevents political leaders from acting on the world stage as if they were its managers and pressures them into seeking a European solution, or alibi, for their difficulties. Europe as Germany's least frustrating framework, Europe as the best compensation for Frances domestic troubles, a Europe following Monnet's approach toward de Gaulle's objectives: it may appear like a dream; it cannot be dismissed. But whether it has a chance depends essentially on *when* the General's nationalism will pass from the scene, on *what* degree of cooperation among the nations of Western Europe there will be at that time, on *whether* a new attempt by Britain to join the Community would introduce additional complications, on *what* the US policy in Europe will be; the chance depends on the timely convergence of too many variables to be counted on.

Against such a chance, there is too big a range of obstacles. Here is where the European experience is of general significance.

1. A first set of remarks deals with the conditions which the national situations of the units engaged in an attempt to integrate must meet, lest the attempt be unsuccessful. Those situations ought to be similar; but a generalization of this kind is almost worthless: what matters is the nature of the similarity.

a. Insofar as domestic circumstances are concerned, two conditions are essential. The first one is obvious at first sight, much less so upon reflection: the units must be political communities, not in a substantive sense (common values and goals, *a la* Rousseau) but in a formal one (the existence of intense communications and of common habits and rules across regional differences as well as across the borders of ethnic groups, tribes, or classes);[3] in other words, transnational integration presupposes integration within the units.[4] These units need not be nation-states, in the sense of communities endowed with external sovereignty under international law; but conversely, if a newly independent state is merely a shell within which there is no community yet, the cleavages that divide the population into separate communities will prove to be decisive obstacle to trans-state integration: domestic integration is a prerequisite to the kinds of flows of transactions and of ideas which trans-state integration requires and will of necessity be the primary goal of any leader who tries to be more than the representative of the dominant sect, class, tribe, or ethnic group. This explains why, for so many countries of Latin America, Latin American integration remains a chimera, and also why it has been so difficult in Africa and in Asia to move beyond the nation-state: in many cases, the state is there, but not yet the nation.

The second condition concerns the structure of society and of the political system in units that are political communities. The students of integration have rightly stressed the importance of pluralistic social structures and elite groups in the units that try to integrate. But success depends on more than a similarity of such structures: It requires the simultaneous presence in the Executive of leaders who represent those sections of the elites that advocate union and whose power depends on the support of the integrationist elites and groups. To the extent to which many of the new states – those whose capacity to become viable nation-states is most dubious – are single-party states with so-called charismatic (or should one say authoritarian?) leaders, this internal condition for unification is missing.

b. Insofar as external conditions are concerned, what matters is not that the units be in 'objectively' similar situations at the time when integration begins and while it proceeds. What matters is 'subjective' similarity – a similarity that is not the scholar's assertion, but the policy-maker's conviction. The implication, which is crucial, is that one must examine more than the relation of each unit to the international system at the moment. Even if this relation is the same for all the units involved, one must go beyond: One must also determine whether the units come to this moment and place from similar origins and through similar itineraries, whether they are likely to proceed from this moment and place toward similar destinations. 'Objective' similarity is disembodied – removed from time and space. The similarity that matters is a similarity in the way in which different statesmen interpret a whole historical and geographical experience and outline the future in the light of this experience. Integration means a common choice of a common future . . .

. . . .

2. A second set of remarks concerns the meaning of integration. It has become possible for scholars to argue both that integration is proceeding and that the nation-state is more than ever the basic unit, without contradicting each other, for recent definitions of integration 'beyond the nation-state' point not toward the emergence of a new kind of political community, but merely toward an 'obscur[ing of] the boundaries between the system of international organizations and the environment provided by member states'. (Haas, 1964: 29). There are two important implications.

a. The first one is, not so paradoxically, a vindication of the nation-state as the basic unit. So far, anything that is 'beyond' is 'less': that is, there are cooperative arrangements with a varying degree of autonomy, power, and legitimacy, but there has been no transfer of allegiance toward their institutions, and their authority remains limited, conditional, dependent, and reversible. There is more than a kernel of truth in the Federalist critique of functional integration: functionalism tends to become, at best, like a spiral that coils ad infinitum. So far, the 'transferring [of] exclusive expectations of benefits from the nation-state to some larger entity' (Haas and Schmitter 1964: 705–37, 710) leaves the nation-state both as the main focus of expectations, and as the initiator, pace-setter, supervisor, and often destroyer of the larger entity: for in the international arena the state is still the highest possessor of power, and while not every state is a political community there is as yet no political community more inclusive than the state.[5] To be sure, the military function of the nation-state is in crisis; but, insofar as the whole world is 'permeable' to nuclear weapons, any new type of unit would face the same horror, and, insofar as the prospect of such horror makes war more subdued and conquest less likely, the decline of the state's capacity to defend its citizens is neither total nor sufficient to force the nation-state itself into decline. The resistance of the nation-state is proven not only by the frustrations of functionalism but also by both the promise and the failure of Federalism. On the one hand, Federalism offers a way of going 'beyond the nation-state,' but it consists in building a new and larger nation-state. The scale is new, not the story, the gauge not the game. Indeed, the Federalist model applies to the 'making of Europe' the Rousseauistic scheme for the creation of a nation: it aims at establishing a unit marked by central power and based on the general will of a European people. The Federalists are right in insisting that Western Europe's best chance of being an effective entity would be not to go 'beyond the nation-state', but to become a larger nation-state in the process of formation and in the business of world politics: that is, to become a sovereign political community in the formal sense at least. The success of Federalism would be a tribute to the durability of the nation-state; its failure so far is due to the irrelevance of the model. Not only is there no general will of a European people because there is as of now no European people, but the institutions that could gradually (and theoretically) shape the separate nations into one people are not the most likely to do so. For the domestic problems of Europe are matters for technical decisions by civil servants and ministers rather than far general wills and assemblies (a general will to prosperity is not very operational). The external problems of Europe are matters for executives and diplomats. As far the common organs set up by the national governments, when they try to act as a European executive and parliament, they are both condemned to operate in the fog maintained around them by the governments and slapped down if they try to dispel the fog and reach the people themselves. In other words, Europe cannot be what some of nations have been: a people that creates its state; nor can it be what some of the oldest states are and many of the new ones aspire to be: a people created by the state. It has to wait until the separate states decide that their peoples are close enough to justify the setting up of a European state whose task will be the welding of the many into one; and we have just examined why such a joint decision has been missing. The very obstacles which make the Federalist model irrelevant to nations too diverse and divided also make all forms of union short of Federalism precarious. Functionalism is too unstable for the task of complete political unification. It may integrate economies, but either the nations will then proceed to a full political merger (which economic integration does not guarantee) – in that case the federal model will be vindicated at the end, the new unit will be a state forging its own people by consent and through the abdication of the previous separate states, but the conditions for success described above will have to be met – or else the national situations will remain too divergent, and functionalism will be merely a way of tying together the preexisting nations in areas deemed of common interest. Between the cooperation of existing nations and the breaking in of a new one there is no stable middle ground. A federation that succeeds becomes a nation; one that fails leads to secession; half-way attempts like supranational functionalism must either snowball or roll back.

  b. But the nation-state, preserved as the basic unit, survives transformed. Among the men who see in 'national sovereignty' the Nemesis of mankind, those who put their hopes in the development of regional superstates are illogical, those who put their hopes in the establishment of a world state are utopian, those who put their hopes in the growth of functional political communities more inclusive than the nation-state are too optimistic. What has to be understood and studied now – far more than has been done and certainly far more than this essay was able to do – is, rather than the creation of rival communities, the transformation of 'national sovereignty': it has not been superseded, but to a large extent it has been emptied of its former sting; there is no super-shrew, and yet the shrew has been somewhat tamed. The model of the nation-state derived from the international law and relations of the past, when there was a limited number of players on a stage that was less crowded and in which violence was less risky, applies only fitfully to the situation of today. The basic unit, having proliferated, has also become much more heterogeneous; the stage has shrunk, and is occupied by players whose very number forces each one to strut, but its combustibility nevertheless scares them from pushing their luck too hard. The nation-state today is a new wine in old bottles, or in bottles that are sometimes only a mediocre imitation of the old; it is not the same old wine. What must be examined is not just the legal capacity of the sovereign state, but the *de facto* capacity at its disposal: granted the scope of its authority, how much of it can be used, and with what results? There are many ways of going 'beyond the nation-state', and some modify the substance without altering the form or creating new forms. To be sure, as long as the old form is there, as long as the nation-state is the supreme authority, there is a danger for peace and far welfare; Gullivers tied by Lilliputians rather than crushed by Titans can wake up and break their ties. But Gullivers tied are not the same as Gullivers untied. Wrestlers who slug it out with fists and knives, prisoners in a chain gang, are all men; yet their freedom of action is not the same. An examination of the international implications of 'nation-statehood' today and yesterday is at least as important as the ritual attack on the nation-state.

3. A final remark concerns the future of integration. Prospects of genuine unification would improve if the international system created the conditions and incentives for moving 'beyond the nation-state'. In a world in which, on the one hand, many more units had succeeded in becoming genuine nations with pluralistic structures, in which, *on* the other hand, a return to multipolarity had resulted both in greater autonomy for the subsystems and in a resurrection of interstate war (in the form of limited conventional war or even geographically limited nuclear conflicts), the conditions of unification would be met, at least in some parts of the world: a less universal and intense involvement, a more compelling threat, greater internal harmony might allow the nation-state to supersede itself. But even so, the result might simply be the agglomeration of many smaller nation-states into fewer, bigger ones; and there are more things in the heaven and earth of possible international futures than in any philosophy of international relations.

Notes

1 See Hoffmann 1965b: 85–101. The very success of internal economic integration raised those external issues far earlier than many expected. (Cf. Britain's application for membership, the problem of external commercial policy.)

2 Under authority, I include three distinct notions: autonomy (the capacity to act independently of the governments, and particularly the financial capacity), power (control over acts of others), and legitimacy (being accepted as the rightful center of action).

3 I find Haas's definition of a political community (Haas 1958a:5) ('a condition in which specific groups and individuals show more loyalty to their central political institutions than to any other political authority') not very helpful in the case of states marked by severe domestic cleavages; there might be more loyalty to the center than to any other political authority merely because there is no other *political* authority, and yet one would still not be in the presence of anything like an integrated society.

4 The distinctions I suggest are like marks on a continuum. 1. At one end, there are *cooperative arrangements* whose institutions have no autonomy from the various governments (OECD, the UN in most respects) . . . 2. Then there are *entities* which have *central institu-*

tions endowed with some authority, in the sense of legal autonomy from the components and legal power all over the territory of the entity, but which are *not* political communities in the formal sense, because of drastic discontinuities in communications and transactions among the components, or because the cleavages within the entity deprive in fact the central institutions of autonomy or of much effective power (that is, states such as the Congo or certain Latin American states; supranational entities like the EEC, and, within the limits of effective military integration, NATO). Such entities may be astonishingly resilient if they are states, endowed with international personality and institutions that have a formal monopoly of force or at least a superiority of force over internal challenges; but if these entities are supranational (and especially when they are not merely a way of disguising the hegemony of one of the component members), they are likely to be highly unstable (see below) precisely because the entity's 'central' institutions are likely to be constantly challenged by the central institutions of the component states, endowed with external sovereignty as well as with superior force. In other words, supranational entities will tend either to retrogress toward stage 1 or to progress toward stage 3. 3. Next come entities which are *political communities* in the *formal* but not in the substantive sense: that is, their central institutions have autonomy and power, there are common habits, and the rules that come from above are enforced across internal barriers, but the central institutions are not endowed with legitimacy all over the territory, and the habits and rules are not based on common values concerning the polity; this is the case of many nation-states, which have 'national consciousness' but are not political communities in the last sense. 4. Here I refer to nation-states whose central institutions are altogether autonomous, effectively powerful and legitimate, and whose society has share values concerning the polity. These are political communities in the *substance* sense. . . . The difference between stage 3 and stage 4 is largely a difference in the level and scope of consensus. I would reserve the term nation to states in those two stages.

5 One could argue that the entity of the Six, insofar as its functional scope is concerned (that is, the realm of welfare, which is certainly a significant part of politics) is a political community in the formal sense. My own analysis of political realities (by contrast with the law of the treaties that established the three communities) is more pessimistic; although I admit that because of the Commission's role the entity of the Six came close to being a political community in the formal sense, recent events have underlined the precariousness of the Commission's autonomy and power.

Chapter 7

Regional Integration: Reflections on a Decade of Theoretical Efforts

Roger D. Hansen*

The appearance of major studies by Karl Deutsch and Ernst Haas in the late 1950s won for integration theory a prominent position among the contemporary approaches to the study of international relations. A decade later its achievements are very much a matter of debate. While many students of integration theory have been led, by disappointment with results, to focus their attention on smaller and more manageable units, such as local communities and city-suburb relations, others continue investigations at the international level (see Jacob and Toscano 1964).

Among the latter group the so-called 'neofunctionalists' have been particularly prominent, largely because of the favorable reception accorded to Haas's *The Uniting of Europe*. For some time Europe remained the focal point for most of the works on regional integration, but in the past several years the application of integration theory to Latin America, Africa, and Asia has become increasingly fashionable. During the course of these endeavors Haas and Philippe Schmitter have developed a conceptual framework that they suggest will illuminate the process of regional integration in the European environment and in less developed areas of the world as well. Since Haas has studied integration efforts in both industrial and nonindustrial settings and has attempted to devise a conceptual approach applicable to both, an investigation of some of the limitations it entails provides a fairly accurate assessment of the present neofunctional contribution to regional integration theory. This is true for two reasons: Haas is one of the

* Reproduced by kind permission of The Johns Hopkins University Press from Hansen, Roger D. (1969) 'Regional Integration: Reflections on a Decade of Theoretical Efforts', *World Politics*, 21(2), 242–71. © The Johns Hopkins University Press. The text has been edited, as indicated, to fit the format of this volume. A summary of the Haas 1968 article has been left out, since that article is reproduced in full in Chapter 4. References have been changed to Harvard citation style wherever possible. Some peripheral footnotes have been omitted.

most thoughtful and sophisticated theorists of regional integration; and most, though not all, of his major concepts and conclusions complement and confirm those of other leading students in the field (see e.g. essays by Deutsch, and Etzioni 1964).

A Model of Regional Integration

'Does the economic integration of a group of nations automatically trigger political unity? Or are the two processes quite distinct, requiring deliberate political steps because purely economic arrangements are generally inadequate for ushering in political unity?' (Haas and Schmitter 1964). The Haas-Schmitter model is specifically addressed to the question of the automaticity of the link between economic and political integration; and their thesis is that 'under moderns conditions the relationship between economic and political union has best be treated as a continuum.' (ibid.: 261). Why? In order to portray the Haas-Schmitter views most fully and fairly, their answer is presented with no intervening interpretation:

Linkages between economic objectives and policies, on the one hand, and political consequences of a disintegrative or integrative nature, on the other, are of a 'functional' character: they rest very often on indirection, on unplanned and accidental convergence in outlook and aspiration among the actors, on dialectical relations between antagonistic purposes. They also frequently contain elements of creative personal action by administrators who seize upon crises, the solution of which upgrades common interests among the actors; hence they include an organizational component which may, depending on the organization, be of dominant significance. Integration can be conceived as involving the *gradual politicization* of the actors' purposes which were initially considered 'technical' or 'noncontroversial'. Politicization implies that the actors, in response to the initial purposes, agree to widen the spectrum of means considered appropriate to attain them. This tends to increase the controversial component, i.e., those additional fields of action which require political choices concerning how much national autonomy to delegate to the union. Politicization implies that the actors seek to resolve their problems so as to upgrade common interests and, in the process, delegate more authority to the center. It constitutes one of the properties of integration – the intervening variable between economic and political union – along with the development of new expectations and loyalties on the part of organized interests in the member nations. (Ibid.: 261–2, italics added).

The authors define a successful political union as a regional entity upon which actors bestow a 'significant portion of their loyalties'.

They posit that a successful union implies an end to threats of revolt or secession even though the scope of central control continues to be extended. 'In other words, a political union can be said to exist when the politicized decision-making process has acquired legitimacy and authority.' (Ibid.: 265–6).

Having developed the dynamic of *politicization,* Haas and Schmitter construct three sets of observable variables 'which seem to intervene more or less consistently between the act of economic union and the possible end product we label political union' (Ibid.: 266). They consist of *background variables* (size of member-units, rates of inter-unit transactions, extent of social pluralism within the units, and elite complementarity), *variables at the moment of economic union* (degree of shared government purposes, and powers delegated to the union), and *process variables* (decision-making style, post-integration rates of transactions, and the adaptability of governments in situations of disappointment and crisis). High, mixed, or low ratings are to be determined for each set of variables as they are applied to the study of any regional grouping. The higher the scores, the more likely it is that an economic union will automatically be transformed into a form of political union. 'Because a spillover is likely to occur in these cases [i.e., cases of high scores for all three sets of variables], the functional adaptation to its implications is likely to be 'automatic' in the sense that the participating actors will make the kinds of decisions which will safeguard their collective economic welfare . . .' (ibid.: 274). The lower the scores, the less the automaticity and the more difficult the move from economic to political union.

With the exception of the final variable – adaptability in crises – all are familiar in the literature of regional integration and need not be discussed here. A further word should be said about the adaptability measurement, however, because it involves an issue of some importance to our following analysis of the Haas-Schmitter scheme and Haas's original theoretical observations upon the course of European integration. Haas has consistently maintained that economic integration will have more spillover into a broad range of political issues than will any other functional approach – i.e., that economic issues and policies are less 'autonomous' than others. The process of spillover from economic integration will not only lead to *gradual politicization,* but also to occasional *crises.* 'Crisis is the creative opportunity for realizing [the] potential to redefine aims at a higher level of consensus.' (Ibid.: 273). Thus, a low degree of autonomy characterizing modern industrialized economic sectors and the propensity for economic integration involving such economies to engender crises are crucial assumptions in Haas's 'expansive logic of economic integration', and will be analyzed below.

. . . .

A Critique

The theoretical and empirical weaknesses in the model may best be illustrated by applying it to the process of integration first in Western Europe, and then in less developed regions of the world. The Haas treatment of European integration might be sketched thus: Within the European economy limited sectoral agreements so increase trade flows and ensuing common problems that a supranational bureaucracy develops to deal with them, and an ever-broadening number of economic activities are touched by growing supranational jurisdiction. Industrial groups also organize at the new regional level in order to influence the emerging power centers. Over time these centers of jurisdiction are granted increasing powers; political loyalties, following in the wake of economic interests, gradually attach themselves to the new supranational entities. As Haas recently summarized his early views:

> The superiority of step-by-step economic decisions over crucial political choices is assumed as permanent; the determinism implicit in the picture of the European social and economic structure is almost absolute. Given all these conditions, we said, the progression from a politically inspired common market to an economic union, and finally to a political union among states, is automatic (Haas 1967: 327).

The major question that has arisen over the Haas analysis (and prognosis) is the necessary extent of the political ramifications of economic union in the Western European case. As Etzioni suggests, 'how far [spillover] carries unification before it is exhausted is a question whose answer is as yet largely unknown.' (Etzioni 1964: 54). Much recent criticism of the dialectic of spillover simply points to the obvious fact that the pace of European integration has diminished (for contrasting views on the present pace of and prospects for Western European integration, see Inglehart 1967; Deutsch 1966; Deutsch et al. 1967). To the extent that the 'logic of economic integration' as expounded by Haas and other functionalists suggested an inevitability about the eventual political unification of Europe of the Six, this type of criticism appears to have at least temporary validity. Most of it, however, analyzes *what* has happened rather than *why* it has happened, thereby contributing little to a better understanding of the integration process in industrially and politically developed regions. Of much greater importance, and therefore considered in some detail below, is a theoretical critique developed by Stanley Hoffmann and others. In addition, economic theory and economic events in the Western European setting suggest some limitations to the spillover thesis that heretofore have been ignored or overlooked.

Economic analysis, both theoretical and empirical, is most helpful, however, in calling into question the relevance of the Haas-Schmitter model to the understanding of the connections between economic and political integration in Latin America and other semi-industrial and nonindustrial regions. One perceptive student of regional integration in African and Latin American settings has suggested that in many under-developed areas

> much that in the European context would be simple welfare poli-
> tics becomes tinged with emotive and symbolic content that is
> usually associated with national security politics. One consequence
> . . . is that there is less opportunity for autonomous bureaucrats to
> go quietly about the business of integration in 'noncontroversial'
> spheres. . . . If the problem in most underdeveloped areas is one of
> premature 'overpoliticization', then it is not helpful for compara-
> tive study to conceive of the integration process as 'gradual politi-
> cization'.' (Nye 1965: 870–84).

A discussion of the theory and practice of economic integration in such unions as the Central American and East African common markets will both substantiate the objection raised by Nye and suggest the necessity of some major revisions in present neofunctional approaches as applied to economically less developed regions.

Western Europe: 'High' Politics and the International System

Stanley Hoffmann recently wrote of Europe of the Six that

> the failure (so far) of an experiment tried in apparently ideal condi-
> tions tells us a great deal about contemporary world politics, about
> the chances of unification movements elsewhere, and about the func-
> tional approach to unification. For it shows that the movement can
> fail not only when there is a surge of nationalism in one important
> part, but also when there are differences in assessments of the national
> interest that rule out agreement on the shape and on the world role of
> the new, supranational whole . . . (Hoffmann 1966: 867).
> . . . .

The Hoffmann analysis . . . raises two major issues with regard to the present neofunctionalist literature on regional integration. The first involves the interaction between what we might label the endogenous and the exogenous variables – between the region engaged in integra-tion schemes on the one hand, and the international environment on the other. The second involves the distinction between high and low politics. Is the traditional view of a discontinuity between the two preferable to the continuum proposed by Haas and Schmitter? The answer to both questions will of course be conditioned as much by one's particular interest in and approach to the study of international relations as by the inherent merits and demerits of present regional integration theory itself. There is evidence to suggest, however, that the neofunctionalist approach should be significantly modified if it is to deal effectively with the range of issues raised by Hoffmann and others.

We shall argue below that the Haas-Schmitter model suffers from a serious theoretical inadequacy in its dealing with regional integration schemes in less developed areas: it does not attempt to isolate and measure those exogenous factors in the international environment that affect the integration *process*. Moreover, its theory is so constructed that questions about the interaction between subsystem and macro-system do not generally appear relevant to the outcome of integration effort beyond the initial analysis of 'elite complementarity'. It makes no systematic attempt to locate and measure the effects of international environment changes on elite perceptions within the regional union over time. In the European case, those who approach the study of integration from a different conceptual viewpoint – e.g., that of historical sociology and systems analysis – also raise the same general issue. Hoffmann . . . traces much of the failure of spillover to the diversity of national situations in Western Europe and the intimate connection between the region and the bipolar relationship of major tension that has structured the international system since the end of World War II (Hoffmann 1966: 868). These interacting variables engendered Hoffmann's 'logic of diversity', which soon challenged Haas's 'logic of integration' (i.e., spillover) in the race for Europe's future. While much empirical work remains to be done in order to test the relevance of the variables suggested by Hoffmann and others who employ somewhat similar modes of conceptualization, the limitations inherent in the neofunctionalist approach should encourage further efforts in that direction.

Haas himself has recently recognized that 'something is missing' in his exploration of the integration process in Western Europe (Haas 1958a: 327). But he does not view the inadequacy of his original theory as a product of its disregard for the interaction between exogenous and endogenous variables. Rather he continues to focus exclusively on aspects internal to regional integration experiments, and concludes that he underestimated the 'built-in limits' of pragmatic interest politics concerned with economic welfare.

Pragmatic interests, simply because they are pragmatic and not reinforced with deep ideological or philosophical commitment, are ephemeral . . . And a political process which is built and projected from pragmatic interests, therefore, is bound to be a frail process, susceptible to reversal. And so integration can once more develop into disintegration (Ibid.: 327–8.)

The halting of the gradual move toward political union in Western Europe followed the rejection by De Gaulle's EEC partners of his bid for a common foreign and defense policy, and his subsequent failure to lure the Bonn government away from its Washington moorings. It appears that at this point the General was unwilling to allow the Community to pass into its third stage, which would have instituted a process of decision-making by a majority-vote method in the Council of Ministers. Although not all of his reasons are yet known, the outcome of his stand during the 1965 crisis was to restrain effectively the movement toward supranationality within the Six. Thus the integration movement, based on 'pragmatic politics', was stalled by the opposition of one member state whose government viewed increased supranationality as detrimental to its own conception of a proper European foreign policy and defense posture.

Haas develops the following matrix to encompass his amended views of regional integration:

Table 3   *Aims of nongovernmental elites*

		Dramatic-Political	Incremental-Economic
Aims of Statesmen	Dramatic-Political	Integration either direct and smooth; or impossible	Integration erratic and reversible
	Incremental-Economic	Integration erratic and reversible	Integration gradual but automatic

The trouble with Haas's amended approach is that it offers many possibilities without suggesting how we are to account for any of them. What situations, events, pressures are conducive to the dramatic-political integrative leadership of a Bismarck, a Cavour? When will similarly motivated elites appear? To say, as Haas does, that 'reliance on high politics demands either a statesman of this calibre or a widely shared normative elite consensus'(Haas 1958a: 328) and that 'in most actual situations in which regional integration is desired, neither ingredient is present in sufficient quantity' (ibid.) may indicate something about the general distribution of an integration effort's basic ingredients. However, such static observations are of limited value in explaining, for any given case, either the initial 'mix' of the variables or the dynamic process itself.

The appearance of a De Gaulle remains a mystery within the context of the Haas approach, and Haas still refers to France as the 'deviant case' within the Six (ibid.: 319). In terms of the contrasting Hoffmann paradigm, the interaction of international system characteristics and the process of European integration suggests the inevitability of such 'deviance' as perceptions change on the part of one actor or another. Thus, while Haas's amended theory is surely strengthened by his recognition that 'integration and disintegration as two rival social processes are simultaneously at work', (ibid.: 315) it still seems too isolated from external variables that may well help to account for the variety of outcomes observed. In some cases, as will be suggested below, certain 'compelling' international environmental pressures may trigger and sustain integration efforts; in others, the minimum degree of interaction between system and regional subsystem may enhance the prospects for success.

. . . .

Western Europe: The Economic Limitations of Spillover

The increasingly comprehensive paradigms for the study of regional integration . . . clearly suggest that the neofunctionalist approach has failed to comprehend some major relevant variables. Another weakness of the Haas model is that it has overweighted one of its own primary concepts, that of spillover from the economic to the political sector. An analysis of the economic achievements of the EEC to date reveals two characteristics that have helped to weaken the logic of spillover. The first is that the Common Market can operate so as to produce major economic gains without moving from customs union to political union. The second is that the benefits of economic integration in the Common Market have been equitably spread among the member units, thus avoiding to a considerable extent a series of 'distribution crises' that might well have aided the spillover process.

Expanding the size of the market open to producers within the EEC has permitted the achieving of economies of scale resulting from mass production and product specialization; it has also induced greater competition. Further, increased rates of regional investment, both domestic and foreign, have been engendered by the move toward free trade within the Six and the establishment of a common external tariff.

A recent Brookings study of the Common Market concludes that its economic achievements have been very substantial.

The conditions requisite for a successful customs union are all present: the members are advanced countries at an almost equivalent level of industrialization; they have long been major trading partners and have common geographical borders; they are all heavily engaged in international trade and some of them had high tariffs originally, allowing much scope for rationalization. Furthermore, the EEC began during a period of economic prosperity, which made the required economic adjustments easier. In turn, because the EEC was successful, economic prosperity was prolonged and enhanced. Thus there has occurred an interaction between income growth and international trade in a 'virtuous circle' often sought but seldom achieved (Krause 1967: 20).

Intra-EEC trade 'grew at a truly remarkable compound annual rate of 17% between 1958–9 and 1965.' (ibid.: 21). Investment rates rose substantially in each country, as did GNP growth rates and the inflow of foreign capital.

Of vital importance in understanding the limitations to the logic of spillover in this setting is the recognition that these very substantial benefits have been achieved without much movement toward greater supranational jurisdiction. Economists have long recognized that customs unions among developed countries can deliver a substantial economic payoff for a very limited price in terms of the surrender of national sovereignty. In a theoretical work written in 1960, Bela Balassa concluded that 'an inter-governmental approach appears to be sufficient to ensure satisfactory operation of an economic union without a unification of the institutional structure . . .' (Balassa 1961: 272). Krause, in his new study of the EEC, confirms the Balassa view:

> Economic integration requires coordination of many economic policies and this involves essentially political decisions, but formal political institutions may not be needed to bring this about. Governments do not need to be told, for instance, that excessive inflation in an open economy quickly leads to difficulties for themselves and their trading partners. They can see for themselves the rapidly deteriorating balance of payments, and pressures immediately arise for corrective actions. A 'hidden hand' toward policy coordination is directed by the market mechanism and it has proven to be very effective with the EEC (Krause 1967: 24).

And Krause's analysis of the workings of the Common Market led him to the following conclusion: 'What is certain is that political integration will occur only as a result of a positive political decision to bring it about, not as a result of economic pressures alone (ibid.: 24).

The final observation to be made with reference to the workings of the EEC and the process of spillover is that the gains from economic integration were spread among the Six in such a way that no major 'distribution crises' arose, thus depriving the spillover process of opportunities in which to 'redefine aims at a higher level of consensus'. While the bitter contest over a common agricultural policy might be characterized as a problem of distribution of benefits – French agricultural gains balanced against German manufacturing gains – this particular issue had its origin in the Messina negotiations. It *did not arise* as an unexpected crisis resulting from integration; rather, like the ghost of

Hamlet's father, it appeared in the first act and never ventured far from the stage. The other major crisis faced among the Six, involving various British bids for membership in the EEC, has had little to do with economic issues.[2]

Economic theory suggests why the 'hidden hand' of the marketplace helped to minimize the problem of an equitable distribution of economic gains from free trade among the EEC countries. It is worth investigating because it also provides us with a frame of reference for understanding the quite different experience with economic integration among less developed countries.

Economists have noted that economic integration efforts are often accompanied by two contrasting types of results; Myrdal has labeled one set 'spread effects', and the other 'backwash effects'. (Myrdal 1957: ch. 3). *Spread effects* are those that tend to minimize income disparities within a market area; they include such factors as increased demand in more developed centers for the products of the less developed periphery and the transmission to the latter of technological knowledge, improved skills, and capital. *Backwash effects* include the movement of capital and skilled labor toward the more advanced centers, and the concentration in them of new industries, thus tending to increase regional disparities in levels of economic development.

For the purpose of this essay, the relevant point of these theoretical observations is that spread effects, which are likely to reduce regional disparities on the average, predominate in a union of developed economies (Balassa 1961: 204). Highly developed price systems permit the exploitation of cost differences; existing industrial structures in each country allow all to benefit from the effects of increasing intra-industry specialization; infrastructure similarities discourage the concentration of foreign investments in any single member-unit; and the existence of highly developed transport and communications facilities promotes intra-regional exchange. Factors such as these have often been cited as contributing, for example, to the decline of disparities in income among various regions of the United States. They have undoubtedly helped to minimize both the number and the magnitude of crises in the EEC and, in doing so, to limit the opportunities for an active spillover process.

In contrast, backwash effects play a far greater role in unions of underdeveloped countries; the more marked the initial disparities in such a union, the more the backwash effects tend to predominate.

> With an imperfect price system, primitive transportation facilities, and an uneven distribution of social and economic overhead in these areas, *agglomerative tendencies* assume importance. These are related to the availability of overhead capital, skilled labor and linked industrial processes, when the latter not only provide ready

markets and low-cost inputs but also contribute to future improvements through the exchange of technological information and induced technical change. (Balassa 1965: 123, italics added).

In retrospect, we may tentatively suggest that three factors led to an overestimation of the expansiveness of functional integration in Europe of the Six. They were, first, a failure to relate the process of regional integration closely enough to relevant international system factors; second, a tendency to deny rather than to investigate the discontinuity between high and welfare politics proclaimed by traditionalists; and third, a failure to recognize that sizeable (and equitably distributed) economic gains would result from a common market *coordinated* by sovereign states rather than managed by ceaselessly expanding supranational authorities.

Regional Integration among less Developed Countries

Backwash effects and their tendency to aggravate existing disparities in levels of development in Latin American, African, and Asian regional economic integration experiments sharply limit the relevance of the Haas-Schmitter model as applied to these areas of the world. As Nye points out, integration involving less developed countries seems to produce not 'gradual politicization', but 'overpoliticization'. A brief discussion of the two most comprehensive economic integration attempts among such countries at present – the East African and the Central American common markets – will substantiate this observation.

The East African common market originated with a customs union between Kenya and Uganda in 1917; Tanganyika became the third member in 1927. Despite its longevity, the common market was in a state of collapse by 1965. The severe frictions among the three newly independent African states arose over the issue of the distribution of the benefits from economic integration. Uganda and Tanganyika argued that all the gains were going to Kenya, and cited the following indicators: Kenya was supplying well over 60% of the intraregional exports; its trade surplus with the other members was substantial and growing; and it was steadily enhancing its position as the industrial center of the union. Kenya was producing 70% of the manufactures of the common market and exporting a growing percentage of them to the two relatively less developed member countries . . .

The failure of the integration scheme to spread its benefits equitably produced growing frictions and demands for reform, including explicit threats of withdrawal by Tanganyikan government officials. The most significant result was the Kampala Agreement of 1964, which included a provision to allocate selected major industries to each of the three member countries, and another to ensure an equitable distribution of other manufacturing establishments through a complex system of inducements. When the Agreement failed to produce immediate results Tanzania began to restrict regional imports, over the heated protests of Kenyan industrial and governmental circles. Growing trade restrictions, together with the decision to dissolve the region's monetary union and establish three national central banks, 'provoked a general fear that the common market and common service agreements might be completely destroyed' (Wionczek 1967: 839).

The crisis produced another, more comprehensive attempt to resolve the existing disputes over the issue of *balanced economic growth* in the union. In East Africa, as in Central America, the concept of balanced growth has to do not so much with GNP growth rates as with an increasingly equitable distribution of industry throughout the union and generally balanced increases in intra-regional trade. The results of the Philip Commission's efforts to reach a compromise settlement were the signing in June, 1967, and the putting into effect, as of December 1, 1967 of the Treaty of East African Cooperation – 'an ingenious effort to eliminate the causes of past frictions among the member countries'(ibid.: 840). Among the major devices marshalled by the Treaty to achieve a balanced industrial spread in the region are programs for fiscal incentives, transfer taxes, an East African Development Bank, and industrial licensing laws. Whether or not the scheme succeeds, its intricacy and comprehensiveness are symbolic of the political sensitivity in less developed countries to the problem of 'equal distribution', and especially to the insistence of each on the right to an 'industrial sector', however limited.

The Central American Common Market is less than a decade old, but the explosive political issue of 'balanced economic development' *(desarrollo economico equilibrado)* surfaced as soon as the freeing of internal trade and the formation of a uniform external tariff began to affect trade flows and the location of new industry in the region. In Central America the two 'less developed' member countries are Honduras and Nicaragua; the latter qualifies only in the sense that its manufacturing sector is somewhat smaller than those in the three 'advanced' member countries – Guatemala, El Salvador, and Costa Rica. The issues raised by Honduras and Nicaragua are the same as those set forth by Uganda and Tanzania: the backwash effects accompanying membership in the Central American Common Market are limiting their economic (particularly industrial) development. And their evidence is the same: growing trade deficits with the more advanced member countries, loss of tariff revenues resulting from the freeing of trade, and the increasing concentration of industry in the more advanced industrial centers of Guatemala City, San Salvador, and San Jose (Costa Rica).

. . . .

The Central Americans, like the East Africans, have attempted to cope with the issue of balanced development through a regional development bank that lends generously to the less developed members, through licensing arrangements that encourage domestic and foreign investors to locate new plants in the less industrialized member states, and through various other forms of preferential treatment. However, all such attempts are inadequate to overcome the agglomerative tendencies associated with the backwash effects of economic integration in less developed regions. This is true even in regions like Central America where the disparities in the economic structures are not very pronounced, and for at least three reasons. First, the more advanced member countries are too short of resources for their own development programs to do much by way of aiding fellow-members. Second, governmental elites in the more developed countries do not wish to supply such assistance; nor are the vested interests in those countries particularly receptive to any such channeling of resources or to agreements granting others preferential treatment. Third, the factors contributing to the lagging performance of a member country in these unions are often such that financial resources alone cannot restore anything resembling a balance except in the very long run. In the case of Honduras, for example, impediments to development are more political, administrative, and 'human-resource' – oriented than are those of its neighbors; only years of slow and marginal improvements at these levels of development will permit Honduras to benefit from the advantages of economic integration on anything like an equal basis with other member countries (see Hansen 1967, chs. 4 and 5 for a more detailed discussion).

The evidence from the East African and Central American cases clearly suggests that, for less developed countries, economic integration is better conceptualized in terms of high politics than its welfare equivalent in Western Europe. Indeed, this might have been surmised on *a priori* grounds. The traditionalists have always maintained that the core of high politics lay in the realm of foreign and defense policy. But it is clear that in the present international system there is a very high correlation between industrialization and the capacity (though, in the nuclear age, not always the immediate inclination) of states to engage in high politics; indeed, industrialization might be considered as a prerequisite to any meaningful high-political role performance. It enables a state to produce essential military and technological components of foreign and defense policies at the 'hardware' level, and to finance and supply foreign aid and other capital exports at the level of 'software'.[3] Western European nations could afford to treat economic integration as a matter of welfare politics without foreclosing their high-politics option because each started from a significantly industrialized base. The case is quite other in the less developed regions of the world. And while few – if any – of the countries in these areas will make it to center court, some will obviously become *regional* powers. For this reason it is not surprising that growing industrial concentration in Kenya or Guatemala should represent a concern for Tanzania or Honduras going beyond the level of welfare politics. This would seem to be especially true for an area like Central America, with a history of regional military conflict and attempts at hegemony by the regional 'great power', i.e., Guatemala. In an industrialized area like Western Europe, economic integration, by distributing benefits equitably, will not intensify regional hierarchy; indeed, spread effects may tend to diminish it. In contrast, economic integration has *exactly the opposite effect* in underdeveloped regions of the world . . .

The East African and Central American experiences confirm the observation that 'instant politicization' characterizes economic integration in the less developed world. The findings sharply limit the relevance of the Haas-Schmitter model – one that would have us view economic and political union as a continuum, and gradual politicization as the mode of movement along that continuum. It can, of course, be asserted that despite the heated frictions and high politics of these two common markets, both are still in operation – and generally at increasingly comprehensive levels of economic integration. This is quite true, and we shall argue below that the odds in favor of their continuation may be somewhat better than recent crises suggest. However, such a conclusion is derived from a line of reasoning that has virtually no relation to the Haas-Schmitter model, a model that can hardly incorporate in its present form the high politics of industrial development noted above.

The Future of Regional Integration in less Developed Areas: Theory and Practice

Thus far we have dealt with some of the theoretical limitations involved in the literature on regional integration of less developed areas, but not upon its prognostications for the future of present and pending experiments. In these concluding comments we will alter our focus in an attempt to answer two questions: How does the current literature on regional integration assess the probabilities for success of integration schemes in Latin America, Africa, and Asia? Do the existing concrete examples of such regional integration confirm theoretical conclusions, or do they suggest the need for alteration?

Virtually all of the present writing is pessimistic about the future of integration schemes among less developed countries. Etzioni, for example, tentatively suggests that limited horizons, lack of administrative and political skills, and preoccupation with problems of domestic modernization all represent major barriers to successful integration efforts (Etzioni 1964: 318–21). Hoffmann regards fully integrated units ('political communities') and pluralistic social structures within them as essential requisites for successful regional integration, and observes that the lack of such structures in many Latin American countries reduces integration to 'a chimera' (1966: 904–5). Deutsch's 'capabilities' approach also produces pessimistic observations on regional integration among underdeveloped nations. In most such states domestic 'loads', derived from as well as necessitating social, political, and economic change, are already overstraining capabilities. In these circumstances it is difficult to imagine that a growth in the capacity for 'responsiveness' among member units to each others' needs will keep pace with the increasing burdens imposed by integration schemes. Finally, Haas argues that

> because the modern 'industrial-political' actor fears that his way of life cannot be safeguarded without structural adaptation, he turns to integration; by the same token, political actors who are neither industrial, nor urban, nor modern in their outlook . . . seek refuge in national exclusiveness. Thus, countries dominated by a non-pluralistic social structure are poor candidates for participation in the integration process. Even if their governments do partake at the official level, the consequences of their participation are unlikely to be felt elsewhere in the social structure (Haas 1961: 106).

Haas and Schmitter, in their studies of LAFTA, seem to confirm this pessimism. Applying their scheme of variables, they conclude that the area is 'an unlikely candidate for international community formation . . .' (Haas and Schmitter 1965–6: 7). They account for the fact that LAFTA has not entirely collapsed by the appearance of two 'functional equivalents': – the bargaining principle of 'reciprocity', and the role of Latin America's *tecnicos.* The reciprocity principle entails the willingness of parties to recognize duties as well as rights – specifically in the LAFTA case the willingness to see that benefits from integration are equitably shared. The *tecnicos,* the region's economists/civil servants, are portrayed as playing a role in LAFTA similar to that undertaken by integration-oriented civil servants in Western Europe (ibid.: ch. 5). The Haas-Schmitter prediction, however, remains generally pessimistic about the prospects for Latin American integration.

. . . .

Against this general background, however, the continued functioning of the East African and Central American economic integration schemes poses an interesting question: How have they managed to survive in the face of the difficulties suggested both by political and by economic theory?

. . . .

Several relevant factors emerge as we shift our attention from an exclusively regional focus to the interaction between these regional groupings and the international environment within which they are functioning. An analysis of the structure of the international system and the transnational forces of change within it indicates why these particular states have turned to economic integration rather than seeking Haas's 'refuge in national exclusiveness'. It has long been recognized that a high degree of external 'compellingness' can promote integration, that external threats often lead to a corresponding tightening of cooperative bonds. We have already noted that the degree of international stability inherent in the bipolar balance that emerged by the 1960s lessened the external pressures for European integration. France (like China) could better afford the risks of reasserted national autonomy within the interstices of the superpower confrontation. In contrast, two elements in the present international system enhance the degree of compellingness for economic integration among the countries of Central America and East Africa.

The first involves a particular characteristic of the present international economic system – generally referred to as 'sluggish' world demand for many primary commodities – and its effect upon the prospects for economic growth in small countries whose economic performances are heavily dependent upon the export of such items . . .
. . . .

Two specific complaints have been developed with regard to such dependence. The first concentrates on the fact that primary commodity trade has historically proved particularly vulnerable to marked short-term fluctuations of price and earnings. Where these products represent a substantial portion of national income, the effect of such fluctuations on economic performance can be significant. Furthermore, when countries are implementing development programs in which foreign exchange is a limiting factor, sudden shortfalls in export earnings can, by restricting imports, produce major bottlenecks and thus retard development.

A second – and much more important – complaint focuses not on fluctuations in primary commodity export earnings, but on the long-term trends for such commodities. It argues that growth in demand for many primary commodities will be slow and therefore unreliable as an impetus to economic development . . .
. . . .

The issue of sluggish demand for many traditional exports of the less developed countries has been analyzed in detail on many occasions, and the effort to separate fact from fiction need not be repeated here. What is relevant for our purposes is that elites in countries like those of Central America have been convinced by some overstated economic arguments that their continued dependence upon the export of a few primary products condemns them to economic instability and slow rates of growth. Furthermore, even a most judicious weighing of the evidence leads to the general conclusion that 'the limited possibilities of expanding the exports of primary products would appear as a constraint to the acceleration of economic growth in the less developed countries' (Balassa 1965: 67. For a general discussion of the degree of primary commodity export dependence in Central America, see Hansen 1967: chs. 1, 2). This is particularly true for traditional Central American exports, while it would not be true for other primary products like fruits, certain vegetables, and beef, for which income-elasticities of demand are significantly higher. As these countries seek to diversify their economies through industrialization, major impediments to efficient production imposed by the size of their domestic markets on the one hand and the difficulties of exporting manufactured goods on the other most often result in inefficient structures of production, balance-of-payment difficulties, and economic stagnation.

Problems posed by export dependence and by the limitations of microscopic domestic markets were major compelling factors in the Central American decision to attempt economic integration. And in less than a decade the results are striking: over 95% of the items listed in the Central American tariff schedule are entitled to free trade within the region; over 98% are covered by a common external tariff; regional trade has grown by close to 400%, rising from 6% of total Central American imports to close to 20% by 1968. It is interesting to note in the face of this impressive effort that more than twenty official attempts at political unification of the region have failed dismally since the disintegration of the original Central American Federation over a century ago.

In East Africa a major attempt at political unification in 1963 failed as well; yet economic union persists despite regional dissension. Here the explanation is similar, but with a variation: Economic union was a pre-independence achievement. When faced with the realization that the common market was disintegrating (1965–66), elites in each member country recognized the compellingness of the situation. For Kenya, it lay in the fact that her protected access to Tanzania and Uganda provided the Kenyan manufacturing sector with its major foreign markets; without them Kenya's economy would face mounting structural difficulties. For the other two members, compellingness involved not present markets for manufactures so much as potential markets. They, even more than Kenya, needed the protection of the union's common external tariff to foster incipient manufacturing sectors. The bargain struck in June, 1967, and made operative in December cannot be explained in its entirety by this commitment to industrialization; without it, however, the course of events is inexplicable.

. . . .

If a final illustration of the interaction between international system and regional integration is needed, the issues raised at the United Nations Conference on Trade and Development provide us with one. A major impediment to rapid economic growth within many less developed countries is that their domestic markets are too small to support efficient industrialization. If they were able to export their industrial products to the West, this bottleneck could be overcome. However, as many recent studies have shown, the levels of effective tariff protection in the United States and Western Europe are generally very high for just those industrial products the less developed countries are now manufacturing in quantity. This, then, is another important sense in which the international economic system is compelling Latin America and other regions toward various patterns of integration. Furthermore, given the internal conflicts engendered by common markets in such regions, it can surely be hypothesized that if the West were to abolish the tariffs in question – for example, those on textiles, leather goods, sporting goods, and bicycles – or to grant significant trade preferences to the less developed countries, movements toward regional integration in Asia, Africa, and Latin America would probably experience a major setback (see Patterson 1965; Johnson 1966). Faced with the lure of the West's markets, less developed countries would probably conclude that the costs of regional integration far outweighed its benefits. Thus transnational forces – in this instance trade patterns and the process of industrialization – can be both integrating and disintegrating in nature. Unless and until regional integration theory is amended to take account of such variables, it will continue to present only a partial picture of the total process.

The use of the word 'model' two paragraphs above should be disclaimed immediately. No systematic attempt to construct an alternative approach has been included in this critique of the neofunctionalist paradigm of regional integration. Nor is it suggested that the Haas-Schmitter model, which has provided the focus for much of the preceding discussion, is not a valuable contribution to our understanding of the integration process. An examination of this literature in the light of present empirical evidence does suggest, however, that major attention should be paid to two sets of unresolved questions.

First, just how expansive is 'the logic of economic integration'? Theoretical and empirical issues raised here suggest that the 'hidden hand' of the marketplace in economic integration schemes among advanced economies with increasingly competent monetary and fiscal policy tools may operate to diminish the number of distribution crises, limit spillover into politics, and promote the coordination of sovereign national policies rather than the emergence of supranational institutions. Conversely, the 'logic of economic integration' among less developed countries – as suggested by economic analysis and confirmed empirically – may generally substitute over-politicization for gradual politicization, significantly diminishing the relevance of current neo-functionalist theory. Finally, if high and low politics are still best conceptualized as discontinuous, how does spillover affect changing perceptions of the former category?

Second, what is the theoretically appropriate manner of relating the process of regional integration to the international environment in which it operates? The lower the degree of regional autonomy in the present international system, the more necessary will it be for present theoretical approaches that concentrate on what we have labeled *endogenous* regional factors – or variables, in the Haas-Schmitter sense – to incorporate *exogenous* factors in a systematic manner. Events in the Western European, Latin American, and East African cases considered above reflect a dynamic interaction between an internal regional dialectic, analyzed by present theory, and changing international environmental pressures relatively unexplored in current neofunctionalist literature. Resolving the problem may prove theoretically and empirically formidable; ignoring it will hamper productive research.

. . . .

Notes

1 It may not be accidental that most successful instances of African integration occurred under colonial rule, which imposed a type of subsystem autonomy, and that the US's experiment in federation was undertaken during a period when the Atlantic Ocean implied extended periods of isolation from – rather than involvement at – the center of world politics.

2 The crisis over agriculture, for that matter, was an issue less of economics than of politics. All commentators on the 1965 confrontation concur that the moment was chosen by De Gaulle to press the issues of structure in and direction of the Community.

3 Again the crucial issue is elite perception. Even though there are often more satisfactory approaches to economic development than intensified programs of industrialization, elites in most less developed countries don't believe it.

PART III

The 1992-Project: Supranationalism vs Intergovernmentalist Bargaining

Featured works

- Wayne Sandholtz and John Zysman (1989) '1992: Recasting the European Bargain', *World Politics*, 42(1).

- Anne-Marie Burley and Walter Mattli (1993) 'Europe before the Court: A Political Theory of Legal Integration', *International Organization*, 47(1).

- Geoffrey Garrett (1995) 'The Politics of Legal Integration in the European Union', *International Organization*, 49(1).

- Andrew Moravcsik (1993a) 'Preferences and Power in the European Community: A Liberal Intergovernmentalist Approach', *Journal of Common Market Studies*, 31(4).

- Paul Pierson (1996) 'The Path to European Integration: A Historical Institutionalist Analysis', *Comparative Political Studies*, 29(2).

The 1992-Project, the Revival of Neofunctionalism and the Liberal Intergovernmentalist Challenge

The late 1970s and early 1980s were periods of 'Euro-pessimism'. As Ben Rosamond (2000: 98) notes, 'not only had 'integration theory' apparently failed, but also the widespread perception took root that little of substance was occurring within the Communities themselves'. During the 1970s, an adverse economic climate and the accession of new, more reluctant member states put a brake on integration (Tranholm-Mikkelsen 1992: 7). New initiatives in the fields of transport and social policy – areas in which one might expect spillover from the common market – were stillborn. As the European integration process ground to a halt, scholars turned their attention to the study of international interdependence and regimes.

By the early 1990s, however, a renewed academic interest in the phenomenon of integration had taken hold. This coincided with several new Community initiatives. The Single European Act (SEA) in 1986 set out a timetable for completing the Community's internal market by the end of 1992 and reformed Community decision-making. It also extended the formal scope of the EC in fields such as regional policy, environmental protection, and some aspects of social policy. This was followed by a commitment in Maastricht in 1991 to move towards the long-standing objective of economic and monetary union. The unexpected success of institutional change within the Community was reinforced by the collapse of the Soviet empire in Eastern Europe. The position of Europe in world politics was rapidly changing, making efforts to deepen integration among European countries once again a phenomenon to attract interest from scholars across the fields of international relations, comparative politics and international law.

One consequence of the revival of integration was a reawakening of neofunctionalist scholarship. For those working in a neofunctionalist tradition, the 1992-initiative offered proof of an integrationist impulse fuelled by supranational leadership. This observation triggered a wave of 'new' neofunctionalist scholarship which focused on the role of central institutions in the integration process. This scholarship advanced two basic claims. First, supranational institutions play a crucial role in the day-to-day operation of the EC. Second, not only the

Commission but also the European Court of Justice are fundamentally pro-integration actors that exercise their authority in such a way as to continuously push for 'more Europe'. As a result of their activism, the integration process often escapes the collective control of member states.

The sudden progress of integration also led to an upsurge in intergovernmentalist theorizing. The state-centric critique of the 1960s had been largely 'negative'. As Keohane and Hoffmann (1991: 9) remark, early critics of neofunctionalism often resorted to mere description of events that contradicted neofunctionalist predictions without any attempt to put an alternative theory in its place. By the early 1990s, however, intergovernmentalists began to develop competing accounts of the integration process, which were based on firm microlevel assumptions about the nature of national interests. State preferences were no longer taken as exogenous 'givens' but were derived from specific assumptions about the nature of key actors, their interests and the constraints facing them. In line with developments in the wider field of IR, the domestic level was increasingly brought into state-centric theories by reflecting on how state preferences are influenced by societal inputs (see e.g. Bulmer 1983; Huelshoff 1994; Moravcsik 1991). At the same time, scholars began to advance more explicit hypotheses about the role of external factors, thereby moving toward the construction of comprehensive theoretical accounts that combined domestic, regional and international variables to explain the core of European integration.

The upsurge in both neofunctionalist and state-centric scholarship launched a decade of debate between so-called 'supranationalist' and 'intergovernmentalist' interpretations of the sources of institutional change within the Communities, which is the subject of this part. This debate tracked wider debates in the field of IR about the role and autonomy of international institutions. Indeed, many scholars partaking in the debate did not see themselves as theorizing exclusively about European integration but as generating and testing hypotheses about international cooperation, which could be generalized to other settings. In other words, the EU was increasingly treated, not as a phenomenon *sui generis,* but as an instance of an international regime – albeit it an unusually developed and multifaceted one.

The tendency to treat the EU as a form of international regime also characterized a third theoretical development of the 1980s and 1990s, namely the introduction of so-called 'new institutionalist' perspectives. These include both 'rational', 'historical' and 'sociological' forms of institutionalism. While they differ in scientific world view, research design, and in their assumptions about the role of institutions for both preference-formation and action, 'new' institutionalist analyses all share the basic premise that 'institutions matter' in the integration process. Although integration may be initiated by agreement among governments, institutions – once established – take on a life of their own and define rules and norms which constrain state action (Puchala 1999: 318). The key to understanding integration therefore lies in understanding the structure and influence of European institutions. Yet, most new institutionalists stop short of accepting the neofunctionalist premise that supranational institutions, rather than states, are the primary movers of integration. Instead they seek to account for variation in the relative autonomy of institutional actors over time and across policy areas to determine the specific conditions in which institutions may be influential. As such, they may often be said to occupy a middle ground between the intergovernmentalist and supranationalist positions. This part focuses on rational choice and historical forms of institutionalism. Part V takes up sociological institutionalism.

A New Neofunctionalism

In theoretical terms, a direct consequence of agreement on the SEA was to fuel a wave of 'new' neofunctionalist scholarship. The conclusion of the Single Act in the fall of 1985 followed closely upon the instatement of a new decisive Commission under the leadership of Jacques Delors, thereby ostensibly confirming the importance of supranational entrepreneurship (see Peterson and Bomberg 1993; Ross 1995; Sandholtz 1993; Stone Sweet and Sandholtz 1998). Functional spillover also seemed to be in play. It was plausible, for example, to argue that the removal of tariff barriers within the Common Market had generated pressure for harmonization of product standards across the Community thereby prompting the move from a common to a single market (see e.g. Corbey 1995; on functional spillover see also Laursen 1990; Lodge 1989; Sandholtz, 1996; Stone Sweet and Sandholtz 1997; Taylor 1989).

Two of the most emphatic pleas for reviving neofunctionalism were made by Tranholm-Mikkelsen (1992) and Burley and Mattli (1993: see Chapter 9 of this book). Mikkelsen argues that, although neofunctionalism cannot provide a full understanding of European integration, the 'new dynamism' of the EC since 1985 reveals important elements of neofunctionalist logic. For example, he points to functional links between 'negative' (de-regulatory) and 'positive' (re-regulatory) integration. As barriers to trade go down, new regulation is often required to even out the economic consequences. He also finds evidence of political spillover insofar as domestic interest groups have reorientated their expectations toward the 1992-project. Cultivated spillover, finally, is displayed by the activist role of the Delors Commission (1991: 12–15).

Burley and Mattli focus more narrowly on the role of the European Court. They find that the legal integration of the Community corresponds remarkably closely to Haas's original neofunctionalist model. The technical complexity of EC law makes it difficult for politicians to foresee the consequences of Court decisions. Law therefore provides a 'technical' or 'functional' domain that circumvents the direct clash of political interests and allows self-interested supranational and sub-national actors (such as national courts and judges) to advance integration without significant interference by national governments (1993: 45). Court decisions also have spillover effects insofar as European legislation leads to a gradual shift in the expectations of government institutions and private actors participating in the legal system (1993: 43–4). This argument, which forms part of a wider wave of 'legal institutionalist' scholarship that swept the field during the 1990s, constitutes a particularly important amendment to neofunctionalism. As we saw in Part II, neofunctionalists concentrated mainly on interdependencies rooted in production and trade. These were areas in which the Commission was seen as crucial for mediating national interests. They paid much less attention to the significance of decisions taken by the ECJ. By contrast, Burley and Mattli – along with other legal scholars – suggest that the EC legal system may in fact be the domain in which neofunctionalist arguments regarding cultivated spillover work best. (On the role of the ECJ in furthering integration, see also Alter 1998; Stone Sweet 1994, 2000, 2004; Weiler 1982).

Taken together the arguments by Mikkelsen and Burley and Mattli build a strong case for the continued relevance of key neofunctionalist concepts such as functional and cultivated spillover. Nonetheless, scholars urging a revival of neofunctionalism faced a difficult challenge in explaining the timing of new integration initiatives. If spillover and supranational entrepreneurship were responsible for the 1992-project why had it not occurred sooner? How, in other words, could explanations based on spillover account for the apparent 'stop-and-go' nature of integration? Dorette Corbey's (1995) 'dialectical functionalist' model provides a creative answer to this question. She argues that when integration proceeds in one sector, member states seek to compensate for their loss in sovereignty by protecting adjacent sectors against EU intervention, thereby heralding a 'stop' phase. As states shift their national interventions to adjacent policy areas, however, they generate increased policy competition in those areas, which eventually becomes self-defeating. To reduce the negative effects of competition, they turn to renewed integration: the next 'go' phase (1995: 253–4). Spillover-driven integration, therefore, is not a smooth process but one that is punctuated by periods of stagnation.

Despite such creative efforts at rescuing the concept of spillover, however, support for neofunctionalist theory remained guarded. As

Keohane and Hoffmann (1991: 3) observed, the success of the SEA generally came as a surprise to scholars in the field, and 'what was unpredicted by analysts working with established theories cannot, in general, be adequately explained *post hoc* through the use of such theories'. Few scholars therefore argued for a wholesale resurrection of neofunctionalism. Most pleaded for appropriating certain elements – such as cultivated spillover – while also taking into account intergovernmentalist insights about the importance of external factors. An excellent example of this approach is the analysis by Sandholtz and Zysman (1989: see Chapter 8 of this book), which is often credited with reopening the debate on neofunctionalism. They contend that the 1992-project was triggered by a shift in the international distribution of economic power, which created pressure for European market reform. Yet, they argue, the SEA cannot be understood simply as a response to exogenous pressure. Two other factors were necessary as well. The first was the effective political leadership of the Commission in liaison with transnational organized industry. The second was the coming to power of market-orientated governments in many member states thereby creating a domestic political environment receptive to reform (1989: 95–7). The result is a theoretically eclectic argument in which external economic competition and vigorous supranational entrepreneurship combine with a favourable constellation of domestic interests in key member states to induce change. This argument is consistent with the equally multifarious analysis by Keohane and Hoffmann (1991) who likewise identify the main sources behind the 1992-initiative as 'external pressure', 'effective supranational entrepreneurship' and 'converging trends of domestic political change' – all of which had to coincide for integration to proceed. (For similar arguments, see also Cameron 1992; Sandholtz 1993.) Although such arguments diverge in crucial ways from neofunctionalism (most importantly by stressing global factors rather than functional spillover as the trigger of institutional change), the weight given to the role of the Commission and to transnational business interests implies that traditional neofunctionalist concerns remain pivotal.

A New Intergovernmentalism

The new dynamism in the EC also sparked new variants of intergovernmentalism. In sharp contrast to the neofunctionalist emphasis on the role of supranational bureaucracies in furthering integration, intergovernmentalists insist that supranational institutions cannot pressure or coax states into accepting a pace of integration that does not harmonize with their national interests. As we saw in the last chapter, intergovernmentalists assume that states value sovereignty and resist granting open-ended concessions of authority to international institutions. Yet, they accept that states may at times choose to pool or delegate decision-making powers within international institutions in order to improve the efficiency of interstate bargaining and secure compliance with agreements. The issue is often put in terms of 'principal agent' theory: States may delegate powers to supranational 'agents', but only under strict oversight and subject to definite limitations on the power of supranational administrators. Integration is therefore seen as a careful compromise, balancing the need for efficient international cooperation on the one hand with the desire to preserve national autonomy on the other.

Two strands of intergovernmentalist theory contributed to the study of European integration during the 1990s. The first, 'realist intergovernmentalism', continued the lineage from classical realists like Carr and Morgenthau. The essence of realist intergovernmentalism is the link between international cooperation and underlying national security interests (Gowa 1994; Grieco 1988, 1999). One version sees integration in post-war Europe as a function of intra-European geopolitical concerns such as the peaceful reintegration of West Germany (Baun 1996; Eilstrup-Sangiovanni and Verdier 2005; Grieco 1995; Pedersen 1998). On this view, the main motivation behind integration has been to institute a lasting safeguard against renewed conflict among European states. For example, Pedersen (1998) portrays integration as a strategy of 'soft hegemony' whereby a comparatively weak regional power seeks to assert its influence through cooperation rather than outright domination. Eilstrup-Sangiovanni and Verdier (2005) show that smaller states can use integration as a way of 'binding' a rising regional hegemony and preventing it from reaching a dominant position in the future. And Grieco (1995) offers a realist explanation for EMU which holds that Germany chose cooperation in order to prevent 'balancing' against it in the monetary sphere, while its weaker neighbours chose to 'bandwagon' to gain influence on German policy. A second version depicts integration as a direct function of the bipolar conflict. On one hand, post-war integration among European states is presented as a way to strengthen the western alliance against the Soviet threat. On the other hand, the 'shadow cast by the superpowers' is said to have provided a 'protective mantle' under which European states could cooperate without the fear that the greater advantage of one would be translated into military force to be used against the others (Joffe 1984; Mearsheimer 1990: 47; Waltz 1979, 1986: 58). The upshot of this version of realism is that European integration is ephemeral; in the absence of both a powerful external threat and a bipolar international structure, integration is destined eventually to relapse (Mearsheimer 1990: 47).

The second and more widely discussed strand of intergovernmentalism is 'liberal intergovernmentalism' (LI). LI is most closely associated with the work of Andrew Moravcsik (1991, 1993a, 1998). As Schimmelfennig notes, LI is often characterized as 'a theoretical "school" with no "disciples" and a single "teacher"' (2004: 75). It must be stressed, however, that Moravcsik's version of LI is a variant of a larger class of international political economy (IPE) approaches which can be classified as both 'liberal' and 'intergovernmentalist' (e.g. Austin and Milner 1999; Mann 1993; Martin 1993, 2000; Mattli 1999; Milner 1997; Milward 1992). Three features distinguish LI from traditional, realist, intergovernmentalism. First, LI acknowledges the importance of domestic politics in the formulation of state preferences. Second, LI follows neoliberalism in viewing institutions as necessary for international cooperation. Third, LI explains integration, not as a function of geopolitical concerns, but as a product of growing economic interdependence: changes in the structure of the global economy are seen to increase the benefits to economic exchange, thereby putting pressure on governments to facilitate economic cooperation through institutionalization. In the remainder of this section, I will first give a brief overview of the main assumptions and propositions of LI as formulated in the work of scholars like Alan Milward and Andrew Moravcsik. I will then turn to some of the major criticisms that have been raised against this prominent approach.

General assumptions of liberal intergovernmentalism

Two theoretical fundamentals distinguish the LI approach to integration. First, LI is an application of a wider class of IR-theories known as rationalist institutionalism to the study of European integration. Although LI was introduced before the general institutionalist turn in European studies, it shares the same basic assumptions as 'new' rationalist institutionalist approaches to integration. The core assumption of rationalist institutionalism is that states are *rational* actors that calculate the utility of alternative courses of action and select the one(s) that maximize their individual utility, taking into account the constraints imposed by the preferences and actions of others. International institutions, on this view, embody the converging preferences of national governments that perceive they can better achieve their individual (self-interested) goals through institutionalized cooperation than through unilateral action. Second, LI defines states as *unitary* actors insofar as it assumes that regional policy making is determined primarily by state executives while domestic actors play no independent role in international negotiations. In contrast to most versions of rational institutionalism, however, LI does not treat state preferences as fixed or exogenous 'givens'. Rather it invokes a commercial liberal approach, which depicts foreign economic policy as a function of market incentives facing domestic economic actors. The basis of this approach is a pluralist model, in which governments aggregate the preferences of domestic groups into a consistent preference order before negotiating internationally. Integration, on this model, is not determined solely by shifts in the global economy but reflects the impact of such shifts on the constellation of preferences at the domestic level (see Milner 1997; Moravcsik 1998: 3).

The foundation of liberal intergovernmentalism was laid in two influential studies by historian Alan Milward (1984, 1992). He charged that conventional accounts of European integration had overstated the negative impact of integration on the state; the effect of integration had been to *reassert* the power of the nation state, not to undermine it. He began with the observation that most Western European states were so weakened by their experiences over the period of 1929–45 (the Great Depression of 1929–32 and World War II) that they more or less had to recreate themselves as functioning units in the immediate post-war period (Milward and Sørensen 1993: 5). To reassert their capacity to rule effectively, European governments had to show themselves responsive to a broad range of societal demands. However, growing interdependence meant that the policies and social reforms needed could only be advanced through an international framework. Integration therefore constituted a way to 'rescue' the European nation state by creating economic and political conditions that would ensure the continued allegiance of its citizens (Milward 1992: 27).

Milward's analysis introduced many of the salient elements elaborated in later intergovernmentalist studies by Moravcsik and others. Most important was the insight that integration does not challenge state autonomy but that sovereignty may be preserved or even strengthened through integration. Another central insight was that institutionalization is motivated by a desire to enhance the credibility of inter state bargains. Sovereign states, argued Milward, ideally prefer not to cede authority to international bodies. The reason they may nonetheless accept integration is that it renders agreements irreversible. In the European context, what was needed to ensure economic growth was a credible commitment to free trade. Post-war European states were diverting a substantial share of their long-term investment to the development of manufactured exports. They would not risk doing so without guarantees that trade barriers would remain lowered and markets opened for their exports. The framework of the European Common Market offered such a guarantee (Milward and Sørensen 1993: 12).

Moravcsik's version of liberal intergovernmentalism

Milward's central insight – that European integration is a function not of geopolitical concerns or supranational manipulation of state interests but of a plain desire by European governments to enhance socio-economic stability by expanding intra-European trade and economic cooperation – is elaborated by Andrew Moravcsik (1991, 1993a, 1998). His magnum opus, *The Choice for Europe: Social Purpose and State Power from Messina to Maastricht* (1998), seeks to explain the 'grand treaty-making bargains' through which European integration has evolved. Like Milward, he finds that, 'at its core, European integration has been dictated by a need to adapt, through policy co-ordination, to increasing economic interdependence'. In particular, he argues, European integration can be analysed as a successful intergovernmental regime designed to reduce negative economic externalities from policies pursued by foreign governments through negotiated policy coordination (1993a: 474; 1998: 35).

The most conspicuous feature of Moravcsik's approach is his explicit effort to 'normalize' European integration. European integration, he maintains, is sufficiently similar to general international politics that it can be studied and explained using general theories of IR. He divides the integration process into three stages – preference formation, interstate negotiation and institutional choice – each of which can be explained using general theories of foreign economic policy, rationalist bargaining and functionalist regime theory. The first stage presents a *liberal* theory of national preference formation. At this stage, foreign policy goals are formulated in response both to the constraints and opportunities imposed by economic interdependence and to shifting pressure from domestic constituents (Moravcsik 1998: 35–9). The domestic preferences that matter most in the context of European integration are those of organized producer groups who stand to gain or lose directly from the freeing of trade and who therefore tend to mobilize strongly around European issues. Note, however, that while the main function of government in Moravcsik's framework is to aggregate the (predominantly economic) demands of domestic interest groups he also allows for some discretion by state executives to pursue broader ideological or geostrategic goals. The ability of executives to follow their own agenda varies with the intensity of domestic preferences: in situations where domestic groups are strongly mobilized and hold clear preferences over alternative policies, government policies tend simply to reflect the balance of societal forces. In situations where societal pressure is ambiguous (e.g. because the net costs and benefits of a policy are uncertain) or divided, however, politicians acquire discretion for independent action on the basis of ideological leanings (Moravcsik 1998: 486).

The second stage draws on rationalist bargaining theory to explain the substantive outcomes of interstate negotiations. At this level national executives are the supreme actors – (societal actors exert influence only through the domestic political structures of member states). A core claim of rationalist bargaining theory is that international negotiation outcomes reflect the relative bargaining power of states, which is in turn a function of the relative value that governments place on reaching agreement. The more a government values agreement compared to reverting to the status quo, the less credible is its threat to walk away from the bargaining table if it does not get its preferred outcome, and, therefore, the more concessions it will have to make in order to gain backing for its preferred outcome (1993a: 499; 1998: 62).

To explain the third stage, the creation and design of international institutions, Moravcsik draws on a functional account of institution building (Keohane 1984). Functional regime theory argues that states create international institutions both to reduce the transaction costs associated with international negotiation (the costs of identifying issues, exchanging information, negotiating bargains, codifying agreements, etc.) and to overcome second-order problems of monitoring and enforcement. Moravcsik accepts both premises, but whereas standard functional regime theory focuses primarily on the desire to reduce the transaction costs of interstate negotiations (Keohane 1984) Moravcsik places greater emphasis on the need to enhance the credibility of interstate bargains. The transaction costs of international negotiations are generally low relative to the potential gains from cooperation, he argues. The main rationale for delegating decision-making authority to international institutions is therefore not to reduce the costs of agreement but to solve subsequent problems of compliance (Moravcsik 1999a, 1998: 73–4, 1993a: 512). Briefly stated, then, the general argument of Moravcsik's LI is as follows:

> EU integration can best be understood as a series of rational choices made by national leaders. These choices responded to constraints and opportunities stemming from the economic interests of powerful domestic constituents, the relative power of each state in the international system, and the role of institutions in bolstering the credibility of interstate commitments (Moravcsik 1998: 18).

Moravcsik's version of LI improves on existing intergovernmentalist accounts in several ways. First, by combining a rationalist theory of interstate bargaining with an explicit theory of a domestic preference formation he is able to account for variation in state preferences over time and across issue areas. Second, by drawing on functionalist regime theory he provides a more plausible explanation for institutional design; EU institutions are not merely temporary reflections of great power alliance politics, but their creation and design are explained by the need to enhance the credibility of inter-state bargains in the area of free trade. The main target of Moravcsik's writings, however, is neofunctionalism and – in his later work – historical institutionalism (see especially Moravcsik 1999a). He categorically rejects the neofunctionalist premise that supranational institutions play a crucial role in furthering integration. Successful supranational entrepreneurship presupposes that central institutions have fuller and more reliable information about the nature and intensity of national preferences and about the consequences of integration than member states do and therefore can mediate between opposing national positions. It also presupposes that institutions lower the transaction costs associated with policy initiation and negotiation. By contrast, Moravcsik's rationalist framework depicts a world of interstate bargaining in which both policy initiatives and information are plentiful, in which states have good knowledge about the preferences and constraints of other states, and where the transaction costs of negotiation are low relative to the gain of cooperation (1998: 52–61). In such a world, governments have plenty of incentives to provide the leadership necessary for successful negotiations and do not depend on supranational institutions to reach efficient bargaining solutions (1999a: 269–70). Moravcsik also rejects the notion that integration proceeds via unintended consequences. To neofunctionalists (and to many institutionalists) the implications of integration are somewhat unpredictable and institutions therefore may end up constraining states in ways that are unforeseen and undesired by the states that design them. For intergovernmentalists like Moravcsik, by contrast, state executives are not only in full control of the integration process, they are also entirely foresighted when it comes to predicting its implications. To the extent that supranational institutions are capable of acting against the short-term preferences of governments it is only because governments have wanted it so as a means to ensure efficient enforcement of treaty obligations (see also Garrett 1995: Chapter 10 of this book).

It is worth dwelling for a moment on the relationship of LI to neofunctionalism. Moravcsik is categorical in his rejection of the supranationalist elements of neofunctionalism. However, it is worth noting that his theory of domestic interest politics is in fact quite close in spirit to the neofunctionalist model. Like neofunctionalists he adopts a pluralist model that takes the commercial interests of domestic economic elites as a key driving force for integration. And like neofunctionalists he assumes that integration moves forward whenever the interests of economic elites in major states converge. He also joins neofunctionalists in assuming that uncertain and vaguely stated integration initiatives are more likely to succeed, since they engender less domestic opposition (1993a: 490). His theory appears to subsume functional spillover; indeed, the premise that integration presents a way to adapt to increasing economic interdependence suggests that integration may well 'spill over' from one functional area to another – only such spillover is not automatic or deterministic but is circumscribed by the economic preferences of key member states, as is also the case in later neofunctionalist writings. To some extent, then, LI may be said to build on neofunctionalism but to give it a more sophisticated and rigorous theoretical underpinning. Yet, two fundamental differences remain: First, in neofunctionalism, subnational and transnational groups are seen to act directly in regional politics, whereas in LI they act only through state executives who aggregate and filter their interests. Second, whereas neofunctionalism ascribes a high degree of autonomy to supranational institutions in determining the trajectory of integration, LI insists that integration reflects the collective will of member state governments whereas central institutions play merely a 'subservient' role.

Critiques of liberal intergovernmentalism

The main strength of LI lies in drawing together theories of domestic preference formation, interstate bargaining, and institutional choice to explain the core of European integration. Yet, LI has often been criticised for focusing too narrowly on explaining the major treaty-making bargains in the history of European integration without considering incremental changes that occur over time via judicial or administrative policies (see e.g. Jacthenfuchs and Kohler-Koch 2004; Friis 1998; Peterson 1995a; Wincott 1995). As Scharpf quips, a study that considers only intergovernmental negotiations subject to unanimity is bound to conclude that the preferences of national governments shape outcomes (Scharpf 1999: 165). This does not, however, rule out that supranational and transnational actors are decisive when it comes to shaping day-to-day policymaking. One response to this line of criticism would be to deem it unfair. As Schimmelfennig (2004: 81) suggests, it is unreasonable to fault LI for not being able to explain all of EU politics, in particular its day-to-day policymaking under the first pillar, since Moravcsik explicitly limits the scope of LI to international treaty negotiations and other issues of unanimous decision-making. Yet, this defence may not be adequate. To Moravcsik, integration is the product of a series of high-profile interstate bargains, which establish basic features of institutional design and set the agenda for intervening periods of 'consolidation'. Yet, many critics argue that processes of institution-formation go on between interstate bargaining and that formal treaty rules are often a reaction to 'informal integration' (institutional changes that occur in between treaty-bargains) – to capture or constrain it (Friis 1998; Hix 2002; Marks 1993; Rosamond 2000: 130; Stacey and Rittberger 2003: 859). The relevant critique of LI is therefore not simply that a focus on so-called 'major events' is not exhaustive of the phenomenon of European integration, but rather that any account of major events will remain inadequate without taking into account the smaller, day-to-day advances, which set the stage for formal treaty bargains.

Critics have also challenged the notion that governments are firmly in the driver's seat during intergovernmental negotiations. For example, Beach (2005) finds evidence that EU institutions play a significant role even in the most intergovernmental forums: the Intergovernmental Conferences (IGCs) which tackle fundamental issues such as treaty reform or enlargement. The reason, he argues, is that complex multilateral negotiating situations such as IGCs are characterized by high bargaining costs and are frequently plagued by coordination problems, which can prevent parties from finding and agreeing upon mutually acceptable outcomes. Supranational leadership can help to lower the costs of bargaining and help states choose between several acceptable bargains. Institutional leadership is most likely to matter when institutions possess strong material resources and informational advantages, when the issues being negotiated are technically complex, and when the distribution of governmental preferences create broad zones of agreement within which supranational entrepreneurs can influence outcomes on the margin (Beach 2005, ch. 2). This reasoning simply amounts to a restatement of neofunctionalist arguments about the informational and positional advantages of supranational institutions. A more interesting point raised by Beach in relation to LI concerns the dynamics of state-to-state bargaining. Member states' bargaining power, Beach suggests, is not merely a function of their relative preference intensity as Moravcsik claims but also depends on the way they play their cards. In other words, strategy matters! This claim introduces an additional dimension into inter-state negotiations; whereas LI assumes that governments are all 'efficient' negotiators and that the only variable relevant to explaining bargaining outcomes is therefore the relative value they place on reaching agreement, Beach suggests that negotiation outcomes may vary as a result of the relative skilfulness of governments' strategic choices.

A second important critique of LI is that it is too heavily biased towards economic policies. The major case studies conducted by Moravcsik (as well as by Mattli, Milner and Martin) all focus on issues of economic integration. One would therefore expect economic concerns to have shaped government preferences (Scharpf 1999: 165). Yet initiatives such as the European Political Cooperation (EPC) or the Common Foreign and Security Policy (CFSP) are not easily explained by reference to economic concerns. Moravcsik's response to this line of criticism is to concede that some integration measures are not a direct response to economic interdependence but may be driven by broader strategic or ideological concerns. Thus, his explanation of CFSP points to weak domestic constraints on governments, which allowed them to pursue broader idiosyncratic goals (1993a: 494). There is a danger, however, that such an explanation becomes *ad hoc*. If governments do more than just respond to societal pressure, then it becomes necessary to expand the assumptions of the theoretical framework to account for executive preferences – whether macroeconomic, geostrategic or ideological – independently of societal demands. LI as it stands largely treats executive preferences as a residual factor, which helps to account for otherwise unexplained variation in outcomes.

New Institutionalism

The third theoretical development addressed in this introduction is the inception of a body of literature known as 'the new institutionalism'. New institutionalist analyses draw on general theories of domestic and international institutions to explain the development of integration. In reality, the new institutionalism consists not of one but many institutionalisms. The most prominent forms are 'rational-choice', 'historical' and 'sociological' institutionalism. However, one can also identify other forms such as 'legal' and 'epistemic' institutionalism. (For reviews of the new institutionalisms in European studies see Aspinwall and Schneider 2000, 2001; Jupile and Caporaso 1999; Pollack 1996, 2004). The key feature of new institutionalist approaches is that they focus on EU institutions not only as outcome variables whose origin and design needs explanation, but also as independent and/or intervening variables which crucially affect actors' strategies and goals in the area of integration.

Like many approaches to European integration the new institutionalism – whether in its rationalist, historical or sociological form – did not originate in the field of European studies but reflected a growing interest during the 1980s among political scientists and students of international relations in studying the effects of institutions on political processes (see e.g. March and Olson 1989; Thelen and Steinmo 1992). As one of the most densely institutionalized settings in the world, however, the EU offers a particularly ideal place to study the effects of institutions on political behaviour. Hence, the 'institutionalist turn' in political science quickly caught hold among 'Europeanists' and also helped to attract a new generation of political scientists and IR-scholars to the study of European integration. This section examines the new institutionalisms in rational choice and historical analysis and their application to the study of the EU. Sociological institutionalism is dealt with in Part V.

Rational choice-institutionalism

The rational-choice approach to the study of institutions grew out of the efforts by American political scientists to understand the role of US congressional institutions (see Riker 1986; Shepsle 1979, 1986). Simplified, they found that while there are strong efficiency incentives for 'principals' (such as subnational legislators) to delegate authority for implementing and adjudicating policy to institutional 'agents', the facts of agenda-setting power and inflexible decision-making rules imply that such delegation may result in giving institutional agents significant influence over policy. One of the first scholars to apply a rational-choice model to study the EU was Fritz Scharpf (1988). In his pioneering work on 'joint decision-traps' in the EU and other federal systems, he observed that certain decision-rules (such as unanimity voting through which a single state may block reforms desired by other members) produces a situation in which a given institution or policy, once instituted, will remain fixed, even in the face of changing policy preferences. Since then, a number of students have used the approach to study the role of EU institutions in shaping the policy outputs of EU governance (e.g. Garrett 1992a, 1995; Garrett and Weingast 1993; Majone 2000; Pollack 1996, 1997a; Tsebelis 1994, 1995a, 1996; Tsebelis and Garrett 1996, 2001a, 2001b;).

Rational-choice institutionalism (RCI) shares much in common with liberal intergovernmentalism insofar as it views states as instrumentally rational, unitary actors, and in its emphasis on credible commitments. Like LI, RCI takes a broadly functional approach to institutional design; institutions are created by states because states benefit from the functions performed by them. A particularly important function of institutions is that they reduce transaction costs and solve problems of incomplete contracting, monitoring and enforcement. It is important to note that RCI regards preference formation as exogenous to the institutional venue. Institutions are seen to provide constraints and opportunity structures for strategic actors to achieve their independently derived goals; they do not shape these goals (North 1990). This does not mean, however, that institutions are mere reflections of underlying national preferences and power. Rather, institutions are seen as crucial in distributing decision-making power among competing actors. As Garrett and Tsebelis (1996: 294) argue, 'different [institutional] procedures, by giving the power to propose and the power to veto to different actors, systematically lead to different outcomes'. Political outcomes, therefore, cannot be explained without careful study of the EU's institutions.

Rational-choice analysts have examined the workings of all four major institutions at the Union level – the Council, Commission, Parliament and Court – and the ways in which they interact. These studies address two general sets of questions. First, why and under what conditions will member-state 'principals' delegate power to supranational 'agents'? Second, to what extent are agents empowered by such delegation to act in an autonomous manner? A good illustration of a rational-choice approach applied to legal integration is the work of Geoffrey Garrett (1992a and 1995: see Chapter 10 in this book). Whereas Burley and Mattli argue that the European Court has

succeeded in advancing integration at the expense of national sovereignty, and even die-hard intergovernmentalists like Moravcsik
concede that ECJ rulings often transcend what was foreseen and
desired by member states, Garrett argues that the growth of EU law is
explicable in terms of the interests of member states. Governments
could, if they wished, either ignore ECJ decisions or amend the legal
order through treaty revision. When they refrain from doing so it is
because an activist Court provides an efficient solution to problems of
incomplete contracting and enforcement of EU treaty obligations. The
ECJ for its part behaves like a strategic actor who realizes that its
power is contingent on the acquiescence of member states and therefore refrains from making decisions that it foresees states will not generally approve of (see Garrett 1992a; 1995; Garrett and Weingast
1993; Garrett et al. 1998; Tsebelis and Garrett 2001a).

Garrett's analysis provides an excellent illustration of the rationalist
premise that the EU's institutional order evolves through strategic interaction between member states and institutions. It also illustrates the intergovernmentalist premise that institutions serve to realize the interests of
member states while having little or no independent effect on political
outcomes. It must be noted, however, that many rational institutionalists
feel his model exaggerates the degree of member-state control. Garrett's
analysis presupposes the availability of effective control mechanisms
(such as legislative overruling and budget cuts) whereby states can 'rein
in' institutional actors whose behaviour has ceased to track state preferences. Yet, many rational-choice institutionalists argue that institutions
tend to be considerably more 'sticky' than his analysis implies for several
reasons. First, passing new legislation is expensive. Moreover, the fact
that social actors tend to adjust to and invest in institutions implies that
there may be significant adaptation costs associated with reform. Second,
uncertainties about the effects of reform may lead states to favour
existing institutions. Finally, decision-rules such as qualified majority or a
unanimity vote may allow a subset of members to block reform against
the will of other members. The result is that institutions that are suboptimal from the point of view of collective state interests may endure
because the expected gains from reform are outweighed by the costs, or
because there are uncertainties about the effects of change (Keohane
1984: 102–3; Shepsle 1989: 144). This does not imply that institutions
are permanently 'locked in' but, as Pollack (1996: 438) argues, it suggests
that institutions cannot simply be assumed to reflect the underlying preferences and power of states at any given time.

Another strand of RCI focuses on agenda-setting power as a source
of institutional influence (e.g. Pollack 1996, 1997a; Tsebelis 1994,
1995a, 1996; Tsebelis and Garrett 1996, 2001b). Building again on
studies of US congressional committees, rational-choice analysts argue
that delegation of policy initiative to the Commission and Parliament

enables these institutions to accelerate and shape integration because it is often more costly for national decision-makers to modify than to accept their proposals. Taking into account variation in voting rules and amendment procedures, they seek to specify under what conditions powers of proposal may enable supranational agents to advance policies closer to their own ideal point than to the collective ideal point of member governments. An example of this approach is Pollack's analysis of the agenda-setting powers of the Commission (1997a). Drawing upon principal-agent analysis, he argues that the Commission can exploit differing preferences among its multiple principals (member states) to pursue its own preferences. The extent of the Commission's agenda-setting power depends on the decision-rules governing new legislation. Its influence is greatest where the voting rule is some form of majority, and where the amendment rule is restrictive – in other words, where it is easier for states to agree to adopt the Commission's proposal than to amend it (Pollack 1996: 451; see also Tsebelis and Garrett 2001b: 367–9).

One of the key strengths of the rational-choice approach to international institutions is to specify under what conditions member-state principals can or cannot constrain the unintended effects of delegation to institutional agents. Yet, rational-choice analyses also have limitations. Leaving aside metatheoretical or methodological critiques, which reject the very assumption of instrumental rationality, two concrete points of criticism are often raised against rational-choice models. The first regards the implausibility of exogenous preference formation. As Sandholtz (1996), points out EU member states do not form their preferences in isolation and then attempt to realize them at the EU level. Instead preferences are constantly evolving through interstate bargaining and interaction at the regional level. The inability of RCI to accommodate changes in preferences that occur during bargaining constitutes a serious blind spot in rationalist analyses. Moreover, the difficulty of specifying preference functions in advance with any precision tends to render prediction as opposed to post hoc explanation impossible (Sandholtz and Stone-Sweet 1998). A second criticism is that RCI analyses privilege the study of formal institutions at the expense of the informal, transnational policy networks studied by students of sociological institutionalism and multilevel governance (see Pollack 1996: 453). Integration is not driven solely by formal rules of interaction but also by the informal rules and norms that develop among actors over time and constrain policy choices. The inability to account for such constraints is a serious shortcoming of RCI.

Historical Institutionalism

Whereas rational-choice institutionalism views institutions as more or less efficient instruments for realizing the long-term preferences of states, historical institutionalism (HI) focuses on how institutions develop over time and affect the position of states in ways that are often unintended or undesired by their creators. A distinguishing feature of HI is that it accepts basic intergovernmentalist assumptions about the primacy of national governments in the creation and reform of international institutions. Institutions, it is argued, are created by instrumentally motivated states to serve their collective interests. Over time, however, 'increasing returns' and 'lock-in' effects imply that institutions often become entrenched and difficult to alter even in the face of a changing policy environment (Bulmer 1994; Hall and Taylor 1996: 942; Pierson 1996: 126; Pollack 1996: 430). Some historical institutionalists go a step further, claiming that state preferences themselves may be shaped and altered over time by prior institutional choices.

A fundamental premise of HI is that institutional development is subject to increasing returns (a concept borrowed from economics). Simply stated, the argument is that institutions induce self-reinforcing or positive feedback processes that make reversals of direction increasingly unattractive over time. This is true for two reasons. First, institutional decision-rules such as unanimity may create a barrier to reform. Second, societal actors (including governments) adapt to new rules through learning and make investments based on the expectation that these rules will continue, thereby increasing the cost of policy change. As Pierson (2000: 259) argues:

> In contexts of complex social interdependence, new institutions and policies are costly to create and often generate learning effects, co-ordination effects, and adaptive expectations. Institutions and policies may encourage individuals and organisations to invest in specialised skills, deepen relationships with other individuals and organisations, and develop particular political and social identities. These activities increase the attractiveness of existing institutional arrangements relative to hypothetical alternatives. As social actors make commitments based on existing institutions and policies, their cost of exit from established arrangements generally rises dramatically.

The effect of increasing returns is a dynamic of so-called 'path dependence', which implies that 'once a country or region has started down a track, the costs of reversal may be high and will tend to increase over time. There will be other choice points, but the entrenchments of certain institutional arrangements obstruct an easy reversal of the initial choice' (Levi quoted in Pierson 2000: 251–2). One implication of path dependence is that earlier events matter more than later ones; given high costs of change, an initial choice of 'path' will significantly constrain later actions. Path dependence therefore justifies a turn to history to discover how initial choices determine subsequent political developments. Another implication is 'path inefficiency'. Although institutions may start out by offering efficient solutions to given social problems, in the long run, the outcome that becomes 'locked in' may generate lower payoffs than a foregone alternative would have.

The foremost example of HI applied to the EU is Pierson's (1996) article 'The Path to European Integration' (see Chapter 12; for an elaborate treatment of the logic of increasing returns, see Pierson 2000). Starting from intergovernmentalist premises about member-state control and efficient institutions at the time of institutional design, he argues that, over time, 'gaps' may occur in member-state control of the integration process for four reasons. First, institutional actors frequently use the authority delegated to them to advance their own interests. Second, the need to secure re-election means that national decision-makers tend to focus on the immediate consequences of their actions while discounting long-term effects. Third, the density and complexity of issues dealt with by the EC implies a significant potential for unintended consequences as actions in one area can have unforeseen effects in other areas. Finally, policy preferences may shift over time leading to a divergence between state interests and prior institutional choices. Once gaps emerge states find it difficult to regain control for two principal reasons. First, decision-rules in the EU create a barrier to reform by allowing treaty reform only by unanimous voting. Second, societal actors adapt to new rules through learning and make investments based on the expectation that these rules will continue, thereby increasing the cost of policy change (Pierson 1996).

The sources of 'gaps' in member-state control that are highlighted by Pierson's article are close to neofunctionalist assumptions. Essentially, he is arguing that member states have imperfect control over the integration process due to a combination of technical complexity, supranational entrepreneurship and unintended consequences. What distinguishes Pierson's analysis from neofunctionalism is that he offers stronger analytical foundations to account for microlevel constraints on member-state control. Also, Pierson's argument, unlike neofunctionalism, does not treat institutional lock-in and path-dependent behaviour as a constant feature of integration but rather as a variable that changes across different kinds of political institutions and policies. Some institutions and policies, he argues, may be quite easily subject to sanctions and reversals by member states, whereas others – specifically those that generate far-reaching adaptive effects among larger numbers of people – are more difficult to change.

Pierson's version of HI overlaps significantly with rational-choice institutionalism insofar as he emphasizes actor intentionality and optimal institutional design in the short term. As a result, some scholars do not consider HI as a distinct and competing school of thought but rather as a variant of rational-choice theory, emphasizing the importance of institutional inertia, sequencing and path dependence in the integration process (see Pollack 2004: 141). It is important to note, however, that not all historical institutionalists depart from rational-choice assumptions. Some take a more sociological starting point, focusing on the ways in which actors internalize institutional constraints. They argue that the institutional context shapes not only the strategic incentives facing states but also the very goals that states pursue. On this view, institutions are resistant to redesign, ultimately, because they structure the very choices about reform that states are likely to make (see e.g. Armstrong and Bulmer 1997; Hall and Taylor 1996: 940; Thelen and Steinmo 1992: 8). Such accounts have more in common with sociological institutionalism (see Part V).

HI offers an important critique of functionalist explanations of institutional design, which tend to explain institutions as uniquely efficient solutions to given social problems (Keohane 1984: 81). As Pierson observes, the institutions in existence at a given point in time may reflect the unintended consequences of earlier institutional decisions made by actors with imperfect information and short time horizons. Hence 'rather than assume relative efficiency as an explanation [for institutional design] we have to go back and look' (Pierson 2000: 263–4). This is good advice but it also points to a scope limitation in HI. HI suggests that institutional starting points matter greatly for future political developments but it does not tell us much about why given institutions are chosen in the first place. Nor, for that matter, does it tell us much about why and how institutions change over time. By focusing explicitly on endogenous sources of institutional stability and change, HI fails to accommodate exogenous sources of preferences. As a result, HI is far better equipped to explain the persistence and stability of institutions than to account for change (Stacey and Rittberger 2003: 867). Second, one must be careful not to exaggerate the effect of institutional lock-in. As Pollack warns, 'Not every EC decision represents a joint-decision trap, since many such decisions either expire . . . or can be amended by qualified majority . . . and not every EC policy creates massive micro-level adaptations' (1996: 443). Hence, he suggests, we do best to acknowledge that control by member states may vary considerably across states and issue-areas, and over time according to the control mechanisms introduced by states (1996: 448). The implication is that while HI may be relevant in some areas, it will be much less relevant in others.

Intergovernmentalism vs Supranationalism: A Dependent Variable Problem?

The debate between intergovernmentalists and supranationalists has been a permanent fixture of European integration studies since the 1970s. This debate has often taken the form of a stalemate with neofunctionalists asserting and intergovernmentalists denying any important causal role for supranational institutions in the integration process (Pollack 1997b). The introduction of new institutionalist perspectives offers some promise of overcoming this impasse. As Marc Pollack, argues:

> the primary virtue of the new institutionalism in rational choice theory . . . is that it allows us to transcend the intergovernmentalist-neofunctionalist debate by acknowledging the initial primacy of the member states and, proceeding from this point, to generate a series of hypotheses about supranational autonomy and influence more precise than those generated by either neofunctionalist or intergovernmentalist theory' (Pollack 1997a: 101).

In other words, the leading question is no longer whether institutions matter but in what conditions they matter and how they make their influence felt.

A significant achievement of the debate between intergovernmentalists and supranationalists during the 1990s is the theoretical plurality and methodological rigour it brought to the study of integration. A key strength of both LI and new institutionalist theories lies in deriving explanations for different dimensions of the integration process from general theories of domestic and international politics thereby facilitating more rigorous testing and generalization of results. Despite its analytical rigour, however, the debate seems to suffer to some extent from a 'dependent variable problem'. As Puchala notes:

> historical institutionalists by and large do not explain the same behaviour as intergovernmentalists attempt to explain. Most of the issues and policy processes examined by them have to do with secondary or follow-on rule-making and implementation, or, in Moravcsik's phrasing, the EC's 'everyday' legislation delegated to the EU institutions as a result of the prior intergovernmental decisions . . . Therefore, we should expect, and intergovernmentalists may well accept, that EU institutions would be and should be effective in the realms of delegated competence (Puchala 1999: 324).

This observation may seem to suggest a division of labour, whereby intergovernmentalists explain the 'history-making' bargains while supranationalists concentrate on accounting for 'informal integration'. Yet this straightforward compromise does not suffice to mediate between the two positions, since, as we have seen, it is possible to argue that formal integration (treaty-making bargains) is a reaction to underlying processes of informal integration (institutional change that occurs in between treaty bargains). If this is the case, then we need a theory that accounts for the interplay between informal and formal integration in order to explain the development of the EU. To some extent this is the ambition of some recent governance theories, which are reviewed in Part IV.

Further Reading

New neofunctionalism

Tranholm-Mikkelsen, J. (1992) 'Neofunctionalism: Obstinate or Obsolete?', *Millennium: Journal of International Studies*, 20(1), 1–22. A good review article, which discusses the continued relevance of neofunctionalism to European integration.

Sandholtz, W. and Stone Sweet, A. (eds) (1998) *European Integration and Supranational Governance* (Oxford: Oxford University Press). An important collection of essays, offering a range of new perspectives on the continued relevance of neofunctionalist concepts for the analysis of European integration.

Hoffmann, S., and Keohane, R. (eds) (1991) *The New European Community: Decision-making and Institutional Change* (Boulder, CO: Westview Press). A splendid collection of essays offering several perspectives (neofunctionalist as well as intergovernmentalist) on the phenomenon of institutional change during the 1980s.

Realist and liberal intergovernmentalism

Mearsheimer, J. (1990) 'Back to the Future: Instability in Europe after the Cold War', *International Security*, 15, 5–56. This article is one of the best examples of a traditional, realist approach applied to contemporary European integration.

Milward, A. (1992) *The European Rescue of the Nation-State* (London: Routledge). This important book examines the social and economic origins of European integration and famously argues that integration reaffirms the authority of the nation state.

Moravcsik, A. (1993) 'Preferences and power in the European Community. A Liberal Intergovernmentalist Approach' *Journal of Common market Studies* 31(4), 473–524. An earlier statement of Moravcsik's liberal intergovernmentalist theory, which he later elaborates and subjects to more rigorous testing in his book *The Choice for Europe*.

Moravcsik, A. (1999a) 'A New Statecraft? Supranational Entrepreneurs and International Cooperation', *International Organization*, 53(2), 267–306. This important article offers a detailed discussion and rejection of neofunctionalist assumptions regarding supranational entrepreneurship.

New institutionalism

Tsebelis, G. (1994) 'The Power of the European Parliament as a Conditional Agenda Setter', *American Political Science Review* 88(1), 128–42. A rational-choice institutionalist analysis of the growing agenda-setting powers of the European Parliament.

Hall, P. and Taylor, R. (1996) 'Political Science and the Three New Institutionalisms', *Political Studies*, 44(5), 936–57. An excellent review article, which outlines the main institutionalist approaches in political science: rational-choice, historical and sociological institutionalism.

Aspinwall, M. and Schneider, G. (eds) (2001) *The Rules of Integration: Institutionalist Approaches to the Study of Europe* (New York: Manchester University Press). This collection of essays features a number of excellent institutionalist analyses of the European Union.

Pollack, M. (2003) *The Engines of European Integration: Delegation, Agency and Agenda-setting in the EU* (New York: Oxford University Press). A comprehensive analysis of the reasons why states delegate powers to supranational organizations and of the resulting agency and agenda-setting powers of supranational agents.

Beach, D. (2005) *The Dynamics of European Integration: Why and When EU Institutions Matter* (Basingstoke: Palgrave Macmillan). This book traces the deepening and widening of the EU from the mid-1980s to the present, investigating the role and impact of the Commission, the EP and the Council Secretariat. Beach finds that EU institutions do matter vis-à-vis governments even in intergovernmental settings such as IGCs but that their influence varies according to their leadership resources and strategies.

Chapter 8

1992: Recasting the European Bargain

Wayne Sandholtz and John Zysman*

Under the banner of '1992', the European Communities are putting in place a series of political and business bargains that will recast, if not unify, the European market. This initiative is a disjunction, a dramatic new start, rather than the fulfillment of the original effort to construct Europe. It is not merely the culmination of the integration begun in the 1950s, the 'completion' of the internal market. The removal of all barriers to the movement of persons, capital, and goods among the twelve member states (the formal goal of the 1992 process) is expected to increase economies of scale and decrease transaction costs. But these onetime economic benefits do not capture the full range of purposes and consequences of 1992. Dynamic effects will emerge in the form of restructured competition and changed expectations. Nineteen ninety-two is a vision as much as a program – a vision of Europe's place in the world. The vision is already producing a new awareness of European strengths and a seemingly sudden assertion of the will to exploit these strengths in competition with the United States and Japan. It is affecting companies as well as governments. A senior executive of Fiat recently declared, 'The final goal of the European "dream" is to transform Europe into an integrated economic continent with its specific role, weight and responsibility on the international scenario vis-à-vis the US and Japan' (Signorini 1989: 6).

But why has this process begun, or begun again, now? In this article, we propose that changes in the international structure triggered the 1992 process. More precisely, the trigger has been a real shift in the distribution of economic power resources (crudely put, relative American decline and Japanese ascent). What is just as important is that European elites perceive that the changes in the international

* Reproduced by kind permission of The Johns Hopkins University Press from Wayne Sandholtz, and John Zysman (1989) '1992: Recasting the European Bargain', *World Politics*, 42(1), 95–128. © The Johns Hopkins University Press. The text has been slightly edited, as indicated, to fit the format of this volume. References have been changed to Harvard citation style wherever possible. Some peripheral footnotes have been omitted.

setting require that they rethink their roles and interests in the world. The United States is no longer the unique source of forefront technologies; in crucial electronics sectors, for example, Japanese firms lead the world. Moreover, Japanese innovations in organizing production and in manufacturing technologies mean that the United States is no longer the most attractive model of industrial development. In monetary affairs, some Europeans argue that Frankfurt and Tokyo, not Washington, are now in control. In short, shifts in relative technological, industrial, and economic capabilities are forcing Europeans to rethink their economic goals and interests as well as the means appropriate for achieving them. American coattails, they seem to have concluded, are not a safe place when the giant falters and threatens to sit down.

While economic changes have triggered the 1992 process, security issues may shape its outcomes. Europe's economic relationship with the United States has been embedded in a security bargain that is being reevaluated. This is not the first reassessment of the alliance, but it is the first time that it takes place against the backdrop of Soviet internal reform and external overtures to dismantle the symbols of the cold war. The point is that the security ties that underpinned US-European economic relations are being reconsidered in Europe. But we need not look deeply into the security issues to understand the origins of the 1992 movement, though some believe that the nuclear horse-trading at Reykjavik accelerated the 1992 process (Baron 1989: 88). Eventually, the economic and security discussions will shape each other.

We hypothesize that structural change was a necessary, though not a sufficient, condition for the renewal of the European project. It was a trigger. Other factors were equally necessary and, in combination, sufficient. First, 1992 emerged because the institutions of the European Communities, especially the Commission, were able to exercise effective policy leadership. International structural shifts and a favorable domestic setting provided a motive and an opportunity for restarting the Communities. The Commission played the role of policy entrepreneur. The renewed drive for market unification can be explained only if theory takes into account the policy leadership of the Commission. To be sure, the Commission did not act alone; a transnational industry coalition also perceived the need for European-level action and supported the Commission's efforts. The Commission, aided by business, was able to mobilize a coalition of governmental elites that favored the overall objective of market unification. Member governments were receptive to the 1992 initiatives because of the domestic political context in the member states, which had altered in ways that made European-level, market-oriented initiatives viable. The most important elements of the domestic political setting were the failure of existing, purely national economic strategies, the decline (or transformation) of the left, and the presence of vigorously market-oriented governments on the right. Without these shifts, an EC-based response to the changing international structure would have been politically impossible.

We therefore propose to analyze 1992 in terms of elite bargains formulated in response to international structural change and the Commission's policy entrepreneurship . . .

. . . .

Explaining 1992: Alternative Approaches

Analysis of the 1992 project in Western Europe could follow anyone of three broad approaches, each with a different focus. One approach would look to the internal dynamics of the integration process itself, as in integration theory. A second would concentrate on the domestic politics behind the regional agreements. The third approach, for which we argue, focuses on elite bargains in response to the challenges and opportunities posed by international and domestic changes. The analysis of elite bargains incorporates the strengths of the other two approaches while avoiding their major weaknesses. Although we have no intention of elaborating three different theoretical frameworks, we will briefly describe what appear to be the chief shortcomings of the integration theory and domestic politics approaches.

Consider integration theory. Instead of a single theory, there were numerous permutations, each employing different concepts and definitions (see Puchala 1972). But what distinguished integration theory from other, traditional analyses of international politics was that it assigned causal significance to the process of integration itself. Indeed, a genuine integration theory would have to posit some specific political effects stemming from the internal logic of integration. This was the contribution of neofunctionalist integration theories, which were in turn partly inspired by the functionalist theory of David Mitrany (1943).

. . . .

For a number of reasons, we do not believe that integration theories are well suited for analyzing the 1992 movement. The major weaknesses were recognized by the integration theorists themselves; two of their criticisms are most relevant to the concerns of this paper. (1) The internal logic of integration cannot account for the stop-go nature of the European project. One possibility, suggested by Lindberg and Scheingold, is that the Community attained many of its objectives, which led to 'the disappearance of many of the original incentives to integrate.' (Lindberg and Scheingold 1970: 23). The question then becomes, why did the renewed drive for the single internal market emerge in the mid-1980s and why did it rapidly acquire broad support among governments and business elites? (2) Even where the Community did not meet expectations or where integration in one area pointed out problems in functionally related areas, national leaders could frequently opt for national means rather than more integration. That is, even in issue areas where the pressure for spillovers should have been strong, national means appeared sufficient and were preferred. In the 1960s, efforts to establish a common transport policy fell flat because national policies appeared adequate to interested parties (ibid.: 179). During the 1970s, the Commission's efforts on behalf of broad Community science and technology planning (the Spinelli and Dahrendorf plans) got nowhere because governments perceived science and technology as areas in which national policies could and should be pursued. The national option always stands against the EC option and frequently wins.

An explanation rooted in the domestic politics of the various European countries is a second possible approach to explaining 1992. Certainly the shift of the socialist governments in France and Spain toward market-oriented economic policies (including privatization and deregulation) was essential for acceptance of the 1992 movement. The Thatcher government in the U.K. could also support measures that dealt primarily with reducing regulations and freeing markets. Thus, the favorable domestic political context was one of the necessary conditions that produced 1992.

But domestic politics cannot carry the full analytical burden, for three main reasons. (1) An argument based on domestic politics cannot answer the question, why *now?* Such an argument would have to account for the simultaneity of domestic developments that would induce states to act jointly. Attention to changes in the international context solves that problem. International changes posed challenges and choices to all the EC countries at the same time. (2) The political actors that figure in analyses of European domestic politics have not yet been mobilized in the 1992 project, though perhaps that is now beginning. Although the political parties and the trade unions now talk about 1992 (and will act in the future as the social dimension moves to the top of the agenda), they were not involved in the discussions and bargains that started the process. Governments (specifically, the national executives) and business elites initiated and defined 1992 and have moved it along. (3) An argument based on domestic politics cannot explain *why* domestic political changes produced the 1992 movement. The project did not bubble up spontaneously from the various national political contexts. On the contrary: leadership for 1992 came from outside the national settings; it came from the Commission.

The third approach to analyzing 1992 is the one we advance in this paper. It focuses on elite bargains formed in response to changes in the international structure and in the domestic political context. The postwar order of security and economic systems founded upon American leadership is beginning to evolve after a period of relative US decline and Japanese ascent. These developments have led Europeans to reconsider their relations with the United States and within the EC. The international and domestic situations provided a setting in which the Commission could exercise policy entrepreneurship, mobilizing a transnational coalition in favor of the unified internal market.

The 1992 movement (as well as the integration of the 1950s) can be fruitfully analyzed as a hierarchy of bargains. Political elites reach agreement on fundamental bargains embodying basic objectives; subsidiary bargains are required to implement these objectives. The fundamental bargains agreed upon for 1992 are embodied in the Single European Act (SEA) and in the Commission's White Paper which outlined specific steps toward the unified internal market. The SEA extended majority voting in the Council and cleared the way politically for progress toward unifying the internal market. Endorsement of the Commission's proposals in the White Paper represents agreement on the fundamental objective of eliminating barriers to the movement of persons, goods, and capital. The specific measures proposed by the Commission (some 300 of them) can be thought of as implementing bargains. Further implementing bargains have yet to be considered in areas like the monetary system, taxation, and social policy.

The original European movement can be seen in terms of this framework.[1] The integration movement was triggered by the wrenching structural changes brought about by World War II; after the war, Europe was no longer the center of the international system, but rather a frontier and cushion between the two new superpowers.[2] Political entrepreneurship came initially from the group surrounding Robert Schuman and Jean Monnet. The early advocates of integration succeeded in mobilizing a transnational coalition supportive of integration; the core of that coalition eventually included the Christian Democratic parties of the original Six, plus many of the Socialist parties (Yondorf 1965).

The fundamental objectives of the bargains underlying the European Coal and Steel Community (ECSC) and the expanded European Communities were primarily two: (1) the binding of German industry to the rest of Europe so as to make another war impossible, and (2) the restarting of economic growth in the region. These objectives may have been largely implicit, but they were carried out by means of a number of implementing bargains that were agreed upon over the years. The chief implementing bargains after the ECSC included the Common Market, the Common Agricultural Program, the regional development funds,[3] and, most recently, the European Monetary System (EMS).

The fundamental external bargain made in establishing the Community was with the United States; it called for (certainly as remembered now in the US) national treatment for the subsidiaries of foreign firms in the Common Market. That is, foreign (principally American) firms that set up in the Community could operate as if they were European. American policy makers saw themselves as willing to tolerate the discrimination and potential trade diversion of a united Europe because the internal bargain of the EEC would contribute to foreign policy objectives. Not only was part of Germany tied to the West, but sustained economic growth promised political stability. All of this was framed by the security ties seen as necessary on both sides of the Atlantic to counter the Soviet Union.

The European bargains – internal and external – were made at the moment of American political and economic domination. A bipolar security world and an American-directed Western economy set the context in which the European bargain appeared necessary. Many expected the original Community to generate ever more extensive integration. But the pressures for spillover were not that great. Economics could not drive political integration. The building of nation-states remains a matter of political projects. Padoa-Schioppa has put it simply and well: 'The cement of a political community is provided by indivisible public goods such as "defence and security". The cement of an economic community inevitably lies in the economic benefits it confers upon its members.' (Padoa-Schioppa 1987). The basic political objectives sought by the original internal bargain had been achieved: the threat of Germany was diminished and growth had been ignited. When problems arose from the initial integrative steps, the instruments of national policy sufficed to deal with them. Indeed, the Community could accommodate quite distinct national social, regulatory, and tax policies. National strategies for growth, development, and employment sufficed.

Several fundamental attributes of the economic community that emerged merit emphasis, as they prove important in the reignition of the European project in the mid-1980s. First, the initial effort was the product of governmental action, of intergovernmental bargains. Second, there was the partial creation of an internal market; that is a reduction, but not an elimination, of the barriers to internal exchange. The success of this initiative was suggested by the substantial increase in intra-European trade. Third, and equally important, there was toleration of national intervention; in fact, in the case of France such intervention was an element of the construction. There was an acceptance of national strategies for development and political management. Fourth, the European projects were in fact quite limited, restricted for the most part to managing retrenchment in declining industries and easing dislocations in the rural sector (and consequently managing the politics of agriculture) through the Common Agricultural Policy. There were several significant exceptions, including the European Monetary System that emerged as a Franco-German deal to cope with exchange-rate fluctuations that might threaten trade relations; however, the basic principle of national initiative persisted. Fifth, trade remained the crucial link between countries. Joint ventures and other forms of foreign direct investment to penetrate markets continued to be limited. Sixth, American multinationals were accepted, if not welcomed, in each country.

When the global context changed, the European bargains had to be adjusted for new realities. Wallace and Wessels have argued that 'even if neither the EC or EFTA had been invented long before, by the mid-eighties some form of intra-European management would have had to be found to oversee the necessary economic and industrial adjustments' (Wallace and Wessels 1989: 4).

The Political Meaning of Changing Economic Structures

Changing international economic structures altered the choices and constraints facing European elites. Europe's options shifted with the changes in relative economic power resources. The relative position of the United States declined, prior to 1970, as its trade partners reconstructed themselves and developed. Gaps closed in technology, wealth, and productivity. The US now has difficulty controlling its own economic environment, let alone structuring the system for others. The changed international setting is equally a story of the emergence of Japan, which has grown into the second-largest economy of the world, overtaking all of the individual European nations and even the Soviet Union. The significance of Japan's rise is frequently hidden rather than revealed by data about its growing share of world gross domestic product and its booming exports. The substantial consequences of the international changes are qualitative as well as quantitative. They alter the political as well as the economic choices for Europe. It is not a matter of trade quantities or economic well-being, though it may eventually be viewed in that way. For now, the problem is one of control and influence. To capture the essence of the phenomenon, we note shifts in technology, money, and trade.

In this essay we cannot trace out in detail the strategic consequences for governments and corporations of the multiple manifestations of this structural change. Let us take technology, for example. European elites (both in government and in business) face new choices regarding the acquisition of advanced technologies not developed at home. Japan has assumed a leading position in a number of key high-technology sectors, especially in electronics. By 1988, total Japanese electronics production virtually equaled that of the United States, and in 1989 should surpass it. Competition in semiconductors (one market segment in electronics) suggests both the changes and the shifting European choices. In 1985, a Japanese company, NEC, became the world's largest producer of semiconductors. A year later, Japan's total world market share for integrated circuits surpassed that of the United States for the first time, at just over 45%. Japanese producers emerged suddenly and now dominate the market for memory chips, a product sold in enormous volume and one that serves to drive the advances in production technology . . .

. . . .

The Europeans have responded aggressively to break their dependence on the US and Japan, as key microelectronics technologies acquire ever greater commercial significance. At the core of the effort are joint development programs for DRAMS [dynamic random access memories] and for microprocessors. The Mega project launched jointly by Philips and Siemens to develop state-of-the-art DRAM production processes and the Joint European Semiconductor Silicon (JESSI) project for microprocessors that includes SGS-Thomson as well as Siemens and Philips are straightforward responses to the changed structure of global markets in this critical sector.

In the second arena – monetary matters – after decades of a dollar-based fixed exchange-rate system and a managed system that still revolves around the dollar, a system is beginning to emerge in which US policy is increasingly dictated by Tokyo if not Frankfurt. The dollar remains the financial core of the world system, but because of America's huge and growing debt, the dollar remains the basis of the system by the choice of others, not so much by American decisions. Japan's export boom has put immense financial resources under Japanese control. Japan has already assumed a more powerful position in the International Monetary Fund (IMF), with American agreement, and unsuccessfully sought a greater role in the World Bank. Japanese funds are now a key part of plans to ease the debt crisis of the third world. For Europeans, decisions in Tokyo will have as much or more impact on monetary conditions as decisions taken in Washington or New York. Perhaps the EMS will soon need to be conceived as a mark zone moving in relation to the yen. The dollar is no longer the obvious sole choice for the world's reserve currency. At any rate, the structure of monetary and current relations has changed, and therefore the choices and constraints for European elites have changed also.

A third arena is trade. For most of the postwar period, the US has been the leader in a system of free trade and multilateralism. Now, although the executive branch maintains the rhetoric of free trade, the new US trade bill has adopted a different logic and carries veiled protectionist threats. Furthermore, the percentage of American trade covered by bilateral agreements has risen in the last years. At the same time, Japan has emerged as a major exporter to Europe while its markets remain difficult to penetrate; it is not as open as the American market was. Consequently, a unified EC market has become vitally important for European development. The structure of Europe's trade environment has changed in recent years, and so have the choices and challenges for European government and business elites.

In sum, the choices for European elites in technology, money, and trade have changed. Previously, the options had centered on the US. If Europe could not lead in technology, at least it could acquire it relatively easily from the US. If Europe could not structure financial rules to its liking, at least it could accommodate to American positions. If Europe was not first, it was second, and a series of individual bargains by governments and companies could suffice. However, it would be quite another matter to be third. To be dependent on Japan in monetary and technology matters, without the integrated defense and trade ties that link the Atlantic partners, was a different problem. The new international structure required new bargains.[4]

The structural changes we have been depicting do not 'cause' responses. Structural changes pose challenges and opportunities. They present choices to decision makers. Three broad options, individually or in combination, were open to the countries of the EC. First, each nation could seek its own accommodation through purely national strategies; but, for reasons we explore below, going it alone appeared increasingly unpalatable. Second, Europe could adjust to Japanese power and shift ties from the US to Japan. But the Japanese option had significant counts against it: (1) there were no common security interests with Japan to undergird the sorts of relations Europe has had with the United States; and (2) Japan has so far been unwilling to exercise a vigorous leadership role in the international system. The third option was that Europe could attempt to restructure its own position to act more coherently in a changing world. The international changes did not produce 1992; they provoked a rethinking. The 1992 project emerged because the domestic context was propitious and policy entrepreneurs fashioned an elite coalition in favor of it.

Political Entrepreneurship: Understanding the Changing Bargains

The surprisingly sudden movement by governments and companies toward a joint response does not have a clear and simple explanation. Uncertainty abounds. In a situation so open, so undefined, political science must rediscover the art of politics. The 1992 movement cannot be understood as the logical response to the situation in which actors and groups found themselves, and cannot therefore be understood through such formal tools as theories of games or collective action. Neither the payoff from nor preferences for any strategy were or are yet clear.[5] European choices have been contingent on leadership, perception, and timing; they ought to be examined as an instance of elites constructing coalitions and institutions in support of new objectives.[6]

This is not a story of mass movements, of pressure groups, or of legislatures. In the 1950s, the European project became a matter of party and group politics. In the 1980s, the EC institutions were not the object of debate; they were a political actor. Indeed, the Commission exercised leadership in proposing technical measures for the internal market that grabbed the attention of business and government elites, but were (in the initial stages at least) of little interest to the organs of mass politics. The governments and business elites had already been challenged by the international changes in ways that the parties and unions had not been. Some business and government leaders involved in 1992 are, in fact, trying to sidestep normal coalition politics in order to bring about domestic changes.

Consequently, any explanation of the choice of Europe and its evolution must focus on the actors – the leadership in the institutions of the European Community, in segments of the executive branch of the national governments, and in the business community (principally the heads of the largest companies) – and what they have achieved.[7] These are the people who confronted the changes in the international environment and initiated the 1992 process. Each of these actors was indispensable, and each was involved with the actions of the others. The Community remains a bargain among governments. National governments – particularly the French – have begun to approach old problems in new ways and to make choices that are often unexpected. The Commission itself is an entrenched, self-interested advocate of further integration, so its position is no surprise. The multinationals are faced with sharply changed market conditions, and their concerns and reactions are not unexpected. The initiatives came from the EC, but they caught hold because the nature of the domestic political context had shifted. The interconnections and interactions among them will almost certainly defy an effort to assign primacy, weight, or relative influence.

In this section, we first address the domestic political context that prepared the ground for the Commission's plans. We then look at the Commission's initiatives, and finally at the role of the business elite in supporting the 1992 project.

The question is why national government policies and perspectives have altered. Why, in the decade between the mid-1970s and the mid-1980s, did European governments become open to European-level, market-oriented solutions? The answer has two parts: the failure of national strategies for economic growth and the transformation of the left in European politics. First, the traditional models of growth and economic management broke down. The old political strategies for the economy seemed to have run out. After the growth of the 1960s, the world economy entered a period of stagflation in the 1970s. As extensive industrialization reached its limits, the existing formulas for national economic development and the political bargains underpinning them had to be revised. Social critics and analysts in fact defined the crisis as the failure of established formulas to provide even plausible guides for action (Cohen 1983). It was not simply that the price of commodities rose, but that the dynamics of growth and trade changed (see Zysman 1983: ch. 1).

Growth had been based on the shift of resources out of agriculture into industry; industrial development had been based on borrowing from abroad the most advanced technologies that could be obtained and absorbed. Suddenly, many old industrial sectors had to be closed, as in the case of shipbuilding. Others had to be transformed and reorganized, factories continuously upgraded, new machines designed and introduced, and work reorganized. The arguments that eventually emerged held that the old corporate strategies based on mass production were being forced to give way to strategies of flexibility and adaptability (see Hall 1987; Sabel and Piore 1984). Despite rising unemployment, the steady pace of improvement in productivity, coupled with the maintenance and sometimes reestablishment of a strong position in production equipment in vital sectors, suggested that Europe's often distinctive and innovative approaches to production were working. However, that was only to come toward the end of the decade. In short, during the 1970s, national executive and administrative elites found themselves facing new economic problems without adequate models for addressing them.

The 1970s were therefore the era of Europessimism. Europe seemed unable to adjust to the changed circumstances of international growth and competition after the oil shock. At first, the advanced countries stumbled, but then the United States and Japan seemed to pick themselves back up and to proceed. Japan's growth, which had originally been sustained by expansion within domestic markets, was bolstered by the competitive export orientation of major firms in consumer durables. New approaches to manufacturing created substantial advantages. In the United States, flexibility of the labor market – meaning the ability to fire workers and reduce real wages – seemed to assure jobs, albeit in services and often at lower wages, despite a deteriorating industrial position in global markets. Japan experienced productivity growth; the United States created jobs. Europe seemed to be doing neither and feared being left behind by the US-Japanese competition in high technology.

For Europe, the critical domestic political issue was jobs, and the problem was said to be labor market rigidity. In some sense that was true, but the rigidities did not lie exclusively or even primarily with the workers' attitudes. They were embedded in government policy and industrial practice. In most of Western Europe, the basic postwar political bargain involved governmental responsibility for full employment and a welfare net. Consequently, many European companies had neither the flexibility of their American counterparts to fire workers or reduce wages, nor, broadly across Europe, the flexibility Japan displayed in redeploying its labor force. As unemployment rose, the old growth model built on a political settlement in each country was challenged – initially from the left by strategies of nationalization with state investment, and then from the right by strategies of deregulation with privatization. The political basis, in attitude and party coalition, for a more market-oriented approach was being put in place.

. . . .

[Thus] the second aspect of the changed domestic political context was the shift in government coalitions in a number of EC member-states. Certainly the weakening of the left in some countries and a shift from the communist to the market-socialist left in others helped to make possible a debate about market solutions (including unified European markets) to Europe's dilemma. In Latin Europe, the communist parties weakened as the era of Euro-communism waned. Spain saw the triumph of Gonzalez's socialists, and their unexpected emergence as advocates of market-led development and entry into the Common Market. Italy experienced a weakening of the position of the communists in the complex mosaic of party positioning. In France, Mitterrand's victory displaced the communists from their primacy on the left. The first two years of the French socialist government proved crucial in turning France away from the quest for economic autonomy. After 1983, Mitterrand embraced a more market-oriented approach and became a vigorous advocate of increased European cooperation. This had the unexpected consequence of engendering independence for the state-named managers of nationalized companies. When the conservative government of Jacques Chirac adopted deregulation as a central policy approach, a second blow was dealt to the authority of the French state in industry. In Britain and Germany, the Labour and Social Democratic parties lost power as well as influence on the national debate.

Throughout Europe the corporatist temptation waned; that is, management of the macro-economy by direct negotiations among social groups and the government no longer seemed to work. In many union and left circles an understanding grew that adaptation to market processes would be required. (As the 1992 movement progressed, unions in most countries became wary that the European 'competitive imperative' might be used to justify policies that would restrict their influence and unwind their positions and gains (Hall 1987: 28). As a counterpoint on the right, Thatcher began to fear a bureaucratized and socialized Europe.)

In an era when deregulation – the freeing of the market – became the fad, it made intuitive sense to extend the European internal market as a response to all ailments. Moreover, some governments, or some elites within nations, can achieve purely domestic goals by using European agreements to limit or constrain national policy choices. The EMS is not only a means of stabilizing exchange rates to facilitate trade, but also a constraint on domestic politics that pushes toward more restrictive macroeconomic policies than would otherwise have been adopted. There is little doubt that the course of the social experiment in 1981 would have been different if France had not been a member of the EMS, which required formal withdrawal from commitments if a country wanted to pursue independent expansionary policies. In a different vein, some Italians use the threat of competitive pressures as a reason to reform the administration. As one Italian commentator put it, 'Europe for us will be providential... The French and Germans love 1992 because each thinks it can be the key country in Europe. The most we can hope for is that 1992 straightens us out' (Revzin 1988: 1).

In any case, in Europe we are watching the creation of like-minded elites and alliances that at first blush appear improbable – such as Mitterrand and Thatcher committed to some sort of European strategy. These elites are similar in political function (though not in political basis) to the cross-national Christian Democratic alliance that emerged in support of the original Community after World War II in Germany, France, and elsewhere. European-level, market-oriented solutions have become acceptable.

This was the domestic political soil into which the Commission's initiatives fell. Traditional models of economic growth appeared to have played themselves out, and the left had been transformed in such a way that socialist parties began to seek market-oriented solutions to economic ills. In this setting, the European Community provided more than the mechanisms of intergovernmental negotiation. The Eurocracy was a standing constituency and a permanent advocate of European solutions and greater unity. Proposals from the European Commission transformed this new orientation into policy, and, more importantly, into a policy perspective and direction. The Commission perceived the international structural changes and the failure of existing national strategies, and seized the initiative.

To understand how the Commission's initiatives led governments to step beyond failed national policy, let us examine the case of telematics, the economically crucial sector combining microelectronics, computers, and telecommunications . . .

In telematics, European collaboration emerged when the Commission, under the leadership of Etienne Davignon, struck an alliance with the twelve major electronics companies in the EC. Because of the mounting costs and complexity of R&D, rapid technological and market changes, and the convergence of hitherto separate technologies (e.g., computing and telecommunications), these twelve companies were motivated to seek interfirm partnerships. Although such partnerships were common with American firms, the possibilities within Europe had not been explored. The twelve firms designed the European Strategic Programme for Research and Development in Information Technology (ESPRIT) and then sold it to their governments. The RACE program (Research for Advanced Communicationstechnologies in Europe) emerged via a similar process (for more detail, see Sandholtz 1989: ch. 7–8). In short, the Community's high-technology programs of the early 1980s took shape in a setting in which previous national policies had been discredited, the Commission advanced concrete proposals, and industry lent essential support. In a sense, the telematics cases prefigure the 1992 movement and display the same configuration of political actors: the Commission, certain political leaders and specific agencies within the national governments, and senior business leaders.

The Commission again took the initiative with the publication of its 'White Paper' in June 1985. The initiative should be seen as a response to the stagnation of the Community enterprise as a result of, among other things, the budget stalemates. When Jacques Delors took office as president of the European Commission in 1985, he consciously sought an undertaking, a vision, that would re-ignite the European idea. The notion of a single market by 1992 caught the imagination because the need for a broader Europe was perceived outside the Commission. Helen Wallace and Wolfgang Wessels suggest that if the EEC and the European Free Trade Association (EFTA) had not existed by the late 1980s, they would have had to be invented (Wallace and Wessels 1989). Or, as was the case, reinvented.

The White Paper set out a program and a timetable for the completion of the fully unified internal market (Emerson 1988).[8] The now famous set of three hundred legislative proposals to eliminate obstacles to the free functioning of the market, as well as the analyses that led up to and followed it, expressed a clear perception of Europe's position (Cecchini 1988; Emerson 1988; Padoa-Schioppa 1987). European decline or the necessities of international competitiveness (choose your own phrasing) require – in this view – the creation of a continental market.

The White Paper's program had the political advantage of setting forth concrete steps and a deadline. The difficult political questions could be obscured by focusing on the mission and by reducing the issues to a series of apparently technical steps. Advocates of market unification could emphasize highly specific, concrete, seemingly innocuous, and long overdue objectives rather than their consequences (*Economist* 9 July, 1988: 6, 8). In a sense, the tactic is to move above and below the level of controversy. The broad mission is agreed to; the technical steps are unobjectionable. Of course, there is a middle ground where the questions of the precise form of Europe, the allocation of gain and pain in the process, become evident. A small change in, say, health and safety rules may appear unimportant, but may prove to be the shelter behind which a national firm is hiding from European and global competitors. Here we find the disputes about outcomes, both in terms of market results and of social values. Obscuring the issues and interests was crucial in developing Europe the first time, one might note, and has been instrumental once again.

Implementation of the White Paper required a separate initiative: the limitation, expressed in the SEA, of national vetoes over Community decisions. At its core, the Community has always been a mechanism for governments to bargain. It has certainly not been a nation-state, and only a peculiar kind of federalism. Real decisions have been made in the Council by representatives of national governments. The Commissioners, the department heads, are drawn from a pool nominated by the governments. Broader representative institutions have played only a fictive (or, more generously, a secondary) role. Moreover, decisions taken by the Council on major issues had to be unanimous, providing each government with a veto. For this reason, it has been painfully difficult to extend the Community's authority, to change the rules of finance, or to proceed with the creation of a unified market and change the rules of business in Europe. The most reluctant state prevailed. Furthermore, domestic groups could block Community action by persuading their government to exercise the veto.

Many see the SEA as the most important amendment to the Treaty of Rome since the latter was adopted in 1957.[9] This act has replaced the Luxembourg Compromise (which required decisions to be taken by unanimity) with a qualified majority requirement in the case of certain measures that have as their object the establishment and functioning of the internal market. The national veto still exists in other domains, but most of the three hundred directives for 1992 can be adopted by qualified majority. As a result, disgruntled domestic interest groups have lost a source of leverage on their governments; the national veto no longer carries the clout it once did. Perhaps equally important, the SEA embodies a new strategy toward national standards that were an obstacle to trade within the Community. Previously, the EEC pinned its hopes on 'harmonization', a process by which national governments would adopt 'Euronorms' prepared by the Commission. The SEA instead adopts the principle affirmed in the famous Cassis de Dijon case. That principle holds that standards (for foodstuffs, safety, health, and so on) that prevail in one country must be recognized by the others as sufficient.

The third actor in the story, besides the governments and the Commission, is the leadership of the European multinational corporations. In a number of ways, they have experienced most directly some of the consequences of the international economic changes. They have acted both politically and in the market. The White Paper and the SEA gave the appearance that changes in the EC market were irreversible and politically unstoppable. Businesses have been acting on that belief. Politically, they have taken up the banner of 1992, collaborating with the Commission and exerting substantial influence on their governments. The significance of the role of business, and of its collaboration with the Commission, must not be underestimated. European business and the Commission may be said to have together bypassed national governmental processes and shaped an agenda that compelled attention and action.

Substantial support for the Commission's initiatives has come from the Roundtable of European Industrialists, an association of some of Europe's largest and most influential corporations, including Philips, Siemens, Olivetti, GEC, Daimler Benz, Volvo, Fiat, Bosch, ASEA and Ciba-Geigy. Indeed, when Jacques Delors, prior to assuming the presidency of the Commission in 1985, began campaigning for the unified internal market, European industrialists were ahead of him. Wisse Dekker of Philips and Jacques Solvay of Belgium's Solvay chemical company in particular were vigorously arguing for unification of the ECS fragmented markets. In the early 1980s, a booklet published by Philips proposed urgent action on the internal market. 'There is really no choice', it argued, 'and the only option left for the Community is to achieve the goals laid down in the Treaty of Rome. Only in this way can industry compete globally, by exploiting economies of scale, for what will then be the biggest home market in the world today: *the European Community home market*' (Europe 1990: 5).

It is hard, though, to judge whether the business community influenced Europe to pursue an internal market strategy or was itself constituted as a political interest group by Community action. Business began to organize in 1983, when the Roundtable of European Industrialists was formed under the chairmanship of Pehr Gyllenhammer, of Volvo. Many of the original business discussions included senior Community bureaucrats; in fact, Etienne Davignon reportedly recruited most of the members of the original group. The executives constituting the Roundtable (numbering 29 by mid-1987) were among the most powerful industrialists in Europe, including the non-EEC countries. The group initially published three reports: one on the need for development of a Europe-wide traffic infrastructure, one containing proposals for Europe's unemployment crisis, and one,

Changing Scales, describing the economies of scale that would benefit European businesses in a truly unified market (van Tulder and Junne 1988: 214–5).

The European Roundtable became a powerful lobby vis-a-vis the national governments. One member of the Delors cabinet in Brussels has declared, 'These men are very powerful and dynamic . . . when necessary they can ring up their own prime ministers and make their case' (ibid.: 215, n. 8). Delors himself has said, 'We count on business leaders for support' (Krause 1988: 24). Local and regional chambers of commerce have helped to establish about fifty European Information Centers to handle queries and publicize 1992.[10] In short, the 1992 process is repeating the pattern established by ESPRIT: major businesses have allied with the Commission to persuade governments, which were already seeking to adapt to the changed international structure.

At the same time that the business community has supported the political initiatives behind the 1992 movement, it has been acting in the market place. A series of business deals, ventures, and mergers form a critical part of the 1992 movement. Even if nothing more happens in the 1992 process, the face of business competition in Europe is being changed. The structure of competition is being altered.

There has been a huge surge in joint ventures, share-swapping, and mergers in Europe. Many are justified on the grounds of preparing for a unified market, some for reasons of production and marketing strategies, and some as a means of defense against takeovers (Forman 1988: A26). But much of the movement is a response to business problems that would exist in any case. Still, the process has taken on a life of its own. The mergers provoke responses in the form of other business alliances; the responding alliances appear more urgent because of the political rhetoric. As the Europeans join together, American and Japanese firms scurry to put their own alliances in place and to rearrange their activities.

. . . .

These deals clearly represent decisions by major companies to join together on a European scale in order to position themselves for global competition. In many sectors, as Stephen Cohen points out, 1992 may consist fundamentally of these business alliances and mergers; that is, even if the process is limited to these alliances, big business in Europe will have been transformed. The moves by major business will affect smaller businesses, including transport, and the political form and position of Europe. The business deals also represent a change in governmental attitudes to accept and encourage that process. The pace of European mergers was accelerating in the mid-1980s; in 1987, it became a rush. Perhaps not by accident, that is the year in which the political initiatives for a unified market became fully believable.

. . . .

The External Bargain: Open Trade and a Regional Economy

The 1992 process may have been sparked by a change in global structure; its outcome is certain to shape both the organization and the regimes of the international system in the coming decades. The advanced countries are likely to become three trading regions organized around the United States, Japan, and the European Community. Indeed, Western Europe and the United States each represent about one-quarter of the global GDP, and Japan about one-eight. Whether the regions remain open or become closed to each other, and whether they encourage direct foreign investment rather than trade, remains to be seen . . .

. . . .

There are two competing images of Europe. One image is Europe as a set of small- and medium-sized countries that have opened themselves to the global economy and must adjust to it. The other image is of the European nations moving over the last thirty years from inter-linked national economies to a regional economy. In the second view, the countries of Europe are, together, no longer passive takers in the system; they are able to shape their international environment. The new Europe, as Lafay and Herzog emphasize, really lies between these two images. It consists of one tight bloc, the Community, and a looser confederation, the European Free Trade Association. Increasingly, the EFTA appears to be adjusting to the recent EEC initiatives (Wallace and Wessels 1989). What the mechanism may be – from status quo through full membership – does not much matter for the central argument here. Europe will be concerned with itself. The political boundaries are beginning to correspond to the existing pattern of economic and trade policies.

This shift does not mean that Europe will become a fortress, but in itself the creation of a politically unified trade region, capable of coherent action, is significant. It does mean that Europe will now consciously develop joint policies to benefit the Community, policies in which internal considerations are primary. The direction that Europe's external policy takes will depend as much on choices made by its trading and financial partners as on its own predilections and internal politics. The structural shifts that compel European adjustments are also changing American and Japanese trade policies; these changes will alter Europe's choices in their turn.

. . . .

Conclusion

Europe is throwing the dice. It is confronted with a change in the structure of the international economy, with emerging Japanese and dwin-

dling American power and position. It feels the shift in Asian competi
tive pressure in industry and finance. The problems are no longer those
of American production in Europe, but of Japanese imports and production displacing European production. More importantly perhaps,
Europe also feels the shift in rising Japanese influence in the monetary
and technology domains. The industrial and governmental presump-
tions and deals with which Europe has operated are changing or will
change. Indeed, Europeans may have to construct a coherent political
presence on the global stage in order to achieve the most attractive
accommodation to the new order.

We hypothesize that change in the international economic structure
was necessary for the revival of the European project. A full-fledged
test of this proposition will require detailed analysis of the perceptions
and beliefs of those who participated in launching the 1992 movement.
We have mentioned other analytical approaches – based on integration
theory and domestic politics – that appear logically unsuited to
explaining 1992. Of course, these approaches are not really alternatives. There are functional links among some of the bargains being
struck, and domestic factors clearly shaped governmental responses to
the international changes. But tests of alternative explanations often
create a false sense of scientism by setting individually weak explanations against each other and finding 'confirmation' by denying the
worst of them. Competing explanations often represent different types
of explanation, different levels of analysis. In the end, it is not a matter
of which one is better, but of whether the right questions are being
asked. This article is an effort to frame the proper questions and
propose analytical links among them.

We argue that structural situations create the context of choice and
cast up problems to be resolved, but they do not dictate the decisions
and strategies. In other words, the global setting can be understood
in neorealist terms, but the political processes triggered by changes in
the system must be analyzed in other than structural terms. The
choices result from political processes and have political explanations. In this case, the process is one of bargains among nations and
elites within the region. The political process for implementing these
bargains is labeled 'Europe 1992', a complex web of intergovernmental bargains and accommodations among the various national
business elites.

In the first half of this essay, we showed why 1992 has so far been a
project of elites; in the second half, we suggested that the elites are
unlikely to maintain that monopoly. The commitment of the governments to the process, the fundamental bargain, is expressed by the end
of the single-nation veto system, which changed the logic of
Community decision making. Europe's states have thrown themselves
into the drive for a unified market, unleashing business processes that

in themselves are recasting the terms of competition within Europe. The terms of the final bargains are open.

The effort to reshape the European Communities has so far been guided by three groups: Community institutions, industrial elites, and governments. The Commission proposes and persuades. Important business coalitions exercise indispensable influence on governments. Governments are receptive because of changes in the world economy and shifts in the domestic political context. The domestic context has changed in two key ways: (1) with the failure of traditional models of growth and purely national strategies for economic management; and (2) with the defeat of the left in some countries, and with its transformation because of the weakening of communist parties in others. These changes opened the way for an unlikely set of elite alliances. In this context, EC initiatives began to demonstrate that there were joint European alternatives to failed national strategies. The telematics programs were one precursor. Delors built on the budding sense of optimism and gave energy and leadership to the notion of a genuine single market. Whether a broader range of political groups will become involved is an open issue, one that may determine both whether the process continues and what form it takes.

The outcomes are quite unknowable, dependent on the timing and dynamics of a long series of contingent decisions. But the story, and consequently the analysis, concerns political leadership in creating a common European interest and then constructing a set of bargains that embody that understanding. Many of the choices are simply calculated risks, or perhaps explorations that will be entrenched if they work and refashioned if they don't. Even if we could predict the outcomes of any single choice with a high degree of confidence, the sequencing of diverse decisions and their cumulative effects would be impossible to foresee. It would be ironic if 1992 succeeded formally but economic rejuvenation did not follow. In any case, Europe's choices – particularly the possibility of a coherent Western Europe emerging as an actor on the global stage – will powerfully influence the world economic system, and perhaps the security system as well.

Notes

1 We have no intention of providing a detailed history of the EEC; that story has been well told many times. We seek only to show that the major elements of that history fit the analytical framework we are proposing here.

2 Many of the early students of European integration recognized that structural changes caused by the war were crucial in triggering the process. See e.g. Lindberg and Scheingold 1970, especially ch. 1.

3 The regional development funds had a precursor in development programs created at Italy's insistence in 1956. They acquired more importance after the accession of Britain

and Ireland, and have become vital elements of the EC bargain since the addition of Greece, Spain, and Portugal.

4 Again, we are not the first to suggest that external, international forces trigger changes in regional integration politics. Joseph Nye (1965: 882–3) proposed that 'outside actors or events' could act as 'catalysts' in regional integration efforts, and that drastic changes in the international environment had been crucial in bringing about European integration.

5 Strategic games are useful heuristic devices that can help us reason about structured situations by clarifying the logic of interaction. In this instance, whatever the general methodological case, substantial investment in specifying and manipulating a multi-player, multi-issue game will have limited payoffs in our understanding of 1992. Indeed, the crucial analytic issues must be resolved long before a set of games can even be devised. Games of strategic interaction require preference functions for each player. With 1992, decision makers do not possess the intellectual means to foresee alternative outcomes, much less rank them. Game theory, as even its most enthusiastic proponents recognize, cannot yet deal with changing preferences. Given all of these lacunae and uncertainties, game models of the international interactions involved in 1992 cannot possibly capture the political dynamics that matter. Behind the games are the crucial factors: political strategies, constraints, and leadership.

   Nor is this really a problem for theories of collective action as traditionally conceived in political science. The problem is not one of inducing actors to contribute to the production of a collective good (i.e., avoiding free riders). The institutional structure of the community compels participation and shared leadership. At issue are the areas that should be opened to joint policy making and the institutional arrangements that might prove acceptable to the parties. Not only are there substantial risks and costs for all, but imposing European decisions on domestic politics requires domestic political action by the national executive, not just acquiescence in the European Commission and Council of Ministers. There are, in other words, multiple layers of politics.

6 This is not a matter of elite learning that can be explained by theories of learning. Our proposition would clearly be that what has altered behavior is changed circumstances, not increased knowledge. By knowledge we mean formally specified relationships (information and theories about it) that suggest what outcomes will result from what causes. It is not a better understanding of an existing situation, but the discovery of a new situation that is at issue. The necessary ingredient for adaptation is therefore vision and leadership, an image of arrangements or relationships that will respond to new tasks, and the skill to mobilize diverse groups to construct that future. Rather than greater technically rooted knowledge, it is politically founded insight that is called into play.

7 We have attempted (without fully succeeding) to distinguish between the politics of coalitions and the role of institutions in shaping the present response. In the first European movement that established the ECSC and then the EEC, there were no European institutions shaping and activating the players. Now there are, and the game is consequently quite different. The most important 'spillover' probably lies in the creation of a permanent advocate of more extensive integration as well as a permanent location for it.

8 The White Paper proposals can be grouped into sets, as follows: 1. Liberalization of government procurement; essentially opening national procurement to outside bidders. 2. Technical norms, by which the largest number of proposals set technical standards that otherwise preclude movement of goods through Europe. 3. Transport services. 4. Agricultural border taxes and subsidies. 5. National restrictions in the community's external trade relations; these matters are not strictly an element of the 'internal bargain', but are included here for the sake of completeness. 6. Abolition of fiscal frontiers, there being no longer a need to assess taxes at the border. 7. Financial services, including banking, stock markets, and related services and insurance, with the bold aim of creating a European capital market.

9 This view is sometimes expressed in EEC materials lauding 1992. Not everyone would agree; they would cite budget initiatives in 1970 and 1975 and the direct election of the EP. We cite the SEA because it rejects the national veto.

10 Another business group collaborating with the Commission and actively promoting the 1992 process is the Union of Industrial and Employers' Confederations in Europe (UNICE), which includes over thirty industrial associations from throughout Europe. The secretary general of UNICE, Zygmunt Tyszkiewicz, described the union's working groups and lobbying as follows: 'Nine-tenths of our work comprises the regular, invisible interchange of ideas between our experts and the EC Commission's civil servants' (Krause 1988: 24).

Chapter 9

Europe before the Court: A Political Theory of Legal Integration

Anne-Marie Burley and Walter Mattli*

European integration, a project deemed politically dead and academically moribund for much of the past two decades, has re-emerged as one of the most important and interesting phenomena of the 1990s. The pundits are quick to observe that the widely touted 'political and economic integration of Europe' is actually neither, that the '1992' program to achieve the single market is but the fulfillment of the basic goals laid down in the Treaty of Rome in 1958, and that the program agreed on for European monetary union at the Maastricht Intergovernmental Conference provides more ways to escape monetary union than to achieve it. Nevertheless, the 'uniting of Europe' (Haas 1958a) continues. Even the self-professed legion of skeptics about the European Community (EC) has had to recognize that if the community remains something well short of a federal state, it also has become something far more than an international organization of independent sovereigns (see e.g. Keohane and Hoffmann 1990: 280–1).

An unsung hero of this unexpected twist in the plot appears to be the European Court of Justice (ECJ). By their own account, now confirmed by both scholars and politicians, the thirteen judges quietly working in Luxembourg managed to transform the Treaty of Rome (hereafter referred to as 'the treaty') into a constitution. They thereby laid the legal foundation for an integrated European economy and polity. (The definitive account of the 'constitutionalization' of the treaty is Stein 1981. For a more recent account from an ECJ judge, see Mancini 1989). Until 1963 the enforcement of the Rome treaty, like that of any other international treaty, depended entirely on action by

* Reproduced by kind permission of MIT Press Journals from Anne-Marie Burley and Walter Mattli (1993) 'Europe before the Court: A Political Theory of Legal Integration', *International Organization*, 47(1), 41–76. © 1993 by the World Peace Foundation and the Massachusetts Institute of Technology. The text has been slightly edited, as indicated, to fit the format of this volume. Wherever possible, references have been changed to Harvard citation style. Some peripheral footnotes have been omitted.

the national legislatures of the member states of the community. By 1965, a citizen of a community country could ask a national court to invalidate any provision of domestic law found to conflict with certain directly applicable provisions of the treaty. By 1975, a citizen of an EC country could seek the invalidation of a national law found to conflict with self-executing provisions of community secondary legislation, the 'directives' to national governments passed by the EC Council of Ministers. And by 1990, community citizens could ask their national courts to interpret national legislation consistently with community legislation in the face of undue delay in passing directives on the part of national legislatures.

The ECJ's accomplishments have long been the province only of lawyers, who either ignored or assumed their political impact.[1] Beginning in the early 1980s, however, a small coterie of legal scholars began to explore the interaction between the Court and the political institutions and processes of the EC. However, these approaches do not explain the *dynamic* of legal integration. Further, they lack micro-foundations. They attribute aggregate motives and interests to the institutions involved to illustrate why a particular outcome makes theoretical sense, but they fail to offer a credible account of why the actual actors involved at each step of the process might have an *incentive* to reach the result in question.

On the other side of the disciplinary divide, political scientists studying regional integration in the 1950s and 1960s paid, surprisingly, little attention to the role that supranational *legal* institutions may play in fostering integration (a noteworthy exception is Scheingold 1965). Even more puzzling is that much of the recent literature on the EC by American political scientists continues to ignore the role courts and community law play in European integration (the one major exception is Garrett 1992a. See also Garrett and Weingast 1993.).

We seek to remedy these deficiencies by developing a first-stage theory of the role of the Court in the community that marries the insights of legal scholars in the area with a theoretical framework developed by political scientists. We argue that the legal integration of the community corresponds remarkably closely to the original neo-functionalist model developed by Ernst Haas in the late 1950s.[2] By legal integration, our dependent variable, we mean the gradual penetration of EC law into the domestic law of its member states. This process has two principal dimensions. First is the dimension of formal penetration, the expansion of (1) the types of supranational legal acts, from treaty law to secondary community law, that take precedence over domestic law and (2) the range of cases in which individuals may invoke community law directly in domestic courts. Second is the dimension of substantive penetration, the spilling over of community legal regulation from the narrowly economic domain into areas dealing with issues such as occupational health and safety, social welfare, education, and even political participation rights.[3] Cutting across both these categories is the adoption of principles of interpretation that further the uniformity and comprehensiveness of the community legal system.

We find that the independent variables posited by neofunctionalist theory provide a convincing and parsimonious explanation of legal integration. We argue that just as neofunctionalism predicts, the drivers of this process are supranational and subnational actors pursuing their own self-interests within a politically insulated sphere.[4] The distinctive features of this process include a widening of the ambit of successive legal decisions according to a functional logic, a gradual shift in the expectations of both government institutions and private actors participating in the legal system, and the strategic subordination of immediate individual interests of member states to postulated collective interests over the long term.

Law functions as a mask for politics, precisely the role neofunctionalists originally forecast for economics. The need for a 'functional' domain to circumvent the direct clash of political interests is the central insight of neofunctionalist theory. This domain could never be completely separated from the political sphere but would at least provide a sufficient buffer to achieve results that could not be directly obtained in the political realm. Law, as Eric Stein recognized, is widely perceived by political decision makers as 'mostly technical', and thus lawyers are given a more or less free hand to speak for the EC Commission, the EC Council of Ministers and the national governments (Stein 1981: 3). The result is that important political outcomes are debated and decided in the language and logic of law. Further, although we make the case here for the strength of neofunctionalism as a framework for explaining *legal* integration – an area in which the technicality of the Court's operation is reinforced by the apparent technicality of the issues it addresses – the principle of law as a medium that both masks and to a certain extent alters political conflicts portends a role for the Court in the wider processes of economic and even political integration.

This specification of the optimal preconditions for the operation of the neofunctionalist dynamic also permits a specification of the political *limits* of the theory, limits that the neofunctionalists themselves recognized. The strength of the functional domain as an incubator of integration depends on the relative resistance of that domain to politicization. Herein, however, lies a paradox that sheds a different light on the supposed naivete of 'legalists'. At a minimum, the margin of insulation necessary to promote integration requires that judges themselves appear to be practicing law rather than politics. Their political freedom of action thus depends on a minimal degree of fidelity to both substantive law and the methodological constraints imposed by legal reasoning. In a word, the staunch insistence on legal realities as distinct from political realities may in fact be a potent political tool.

. . . .

Legal and Political Theories of Juridical Contribution to European Integration

In this section we review the main themes and conclusions of two sets of approaches inquiring about the role of the ECJ in European integration. Most of the European legal literature begins and ends with law, describing a legalist world that is hermetically closed to considerations of power and self-interest. A handful of 'contextualists' do go further in an effort to place law in a broader political context. As an explanation of the actual process of legal integration, legalism fails for assuming that law can operate in a political vacuum. The contextual approaches are a considerable improvement in this regard and often yield a treasure trove of valuable information about the Court, but ultimately, they offer only hypotheses about underspecified relationships between law and politics.

The writings of American political scientists on European integration are equally unsatisfactory. Realism, the dominant paradigm in the field of international relations, assumes away the relevance of supranational institutions. Thus, the ECJ has received perfunctory attention at best – a most unsatisfactory state in light of the data that have accumulated over the past three decades. Nevertheless, even those writers most sympathetic to a neofunctionalist point of view have overlooked the Court's contribution to integration.

Legal approaches

Legalism: pure law

Legalism is an approach to the study of the ECJ that denies the existence of ideological and sociopolitical influences on the Court's jurisdiction. Microfoundational explanations of the roles of individual actors give way to an all-purpose emphasis on the 'rule of law'. Martin Shapiro put the essence of legalism as follows: 'The Community [is presented] as a juristic idea; the written constitution as a sacred text; the professional commentary as a legal truth; the case law as the inevitable working out of the correct implications of the constitutional text; and the constitutional court as the disembodied voice of right reason and constitutional teleology' (Kaiser 1965: 39–40; Shapiro 1980: 538).

Legalism is embraced by the vast majority of European legal scholars specializing in EC law. Its appraisal of the Court's substantive contribution to European integration and of its juridical method of treaty interpretation is unanimously positive. Charges of judicial activism, that is, of undue judicial policymaking, are either denied[5] or viewed as a necessary stand against the complete disintegration of the community. This argument, known as the 'ruin' – or the 'or else' – justification, runs as follows: The political actors in the community, confronted with unexpected problems, often are unable or unwilling to stick to their treaty obligations. In such moments, the Court dutifully intervenes and temporarily assumes policymaking leadership to prevent the rapid erosion of the community, 'a possibility that nobody really envisaged, not even the most intransigent custodian of national sovereignty' (Mancini 1989: 600; see also Barav 1980; Bettati 1989; Everling 1984c; Lecourt 1976; Pescatore 1974; Rasmussen 1986).

Legalists thus uniformly view the ECJ as a great boon to European integration. The Court acts based upon its vast formal powers and according to its treaty-based duty to exploit those powers to their utmost.[6] It thereby scrupulously observes the inherent limitations of the community's judicial function (Rasmussen 1986: 195-6, n. 127).

Contextualism: law and politics

A few legal scholars recently have extended their analytic focus and proposed to substitute a law-politics duality for the 'rule of law'. They endeavor to analyze the reciprocal relationship between the legal and political spheres in European integration.[7] These approaches suffer generally from two problems: first, the nature of the relationship is often fuzzy and claims of cause and effect are qualified so as to be rendered almost empty. Second, the incentives for action are not spelled out. We briefly review the conclusions of three studies in the contextualist tradition.

Joseph Weiler juxtaposes the ECJ and EC law – or 'normative supranationalism' – squarely on one side, and community politics – or 'decisional supranationalism' – on the other (Weiler 1981). Normative supranationalism describes the process of integration in the legal sphere, that is, the growth in scope and depth of community law and policies. Weiler claims that 'from a juridical point of view . . . certain fundamental facets of the supranational system took crucial, even revolutionary strides ahead' during the first decade of the EEC (ibid.: 270). Paradoxically, during that same period, a decline of decisional supranationalism set in. The member states grew unwilling to entrust the execution of policies to the EC Commission and instead channeled most of the community work through a growing number of intergovernmental committees within the Council of Ministers.

Weiler suggests that the decline of decisional supranationalism was at least partly caused by the rapid deepening of normative supranationalism. To this extent, the Court has had 'a negative effect' (ibid.: 291) on decisional supranationalism.[8]

The most outspoken work critical of the Court to date is Hjalte Rasmussen's *On Law and Policy in the European Court of Justice*. The methodology underlying Rasmussen's discussion is similar to that of Weiler. However, the focus is geared more toward the interface of the law and the Court's judicial pro-EC policymaking. At the outset, Rasmussen observes that 'it is widely known but rarely recorded in print that even firm believers in a federal Europe occasionally are baffled by the Court's strong and bold pro-Community policy preference' (Rasmussen 1986: 3). This leads him to examine the extent of judicial policymaking and its impact on the process of European integration. Rasmussen acknowledges that judicial activism may well be a 'social good' as long as it agrees with the wishes of the majority of the member states (ibid.: 8). However, applied to the ECJ of the 1960s and 1970s, his conclusions are strongly negative. He notes that the Court was guided by its own rigid policy preferences and repeatedly went 'way beyond the textual stipulations [of the treaty] leaving behind it a variety of well-merited, legal-interpretative principles' (ibid.: 12) thus severing its world from the 'world of the real events' (ibid.: 13). This alienation produced, at times, disruptions and stoppages in the political decision-making process and endangered the Court's judicial authority and legitimacy.

. . . .

Political science theories

Realism

Realism is the antithesis of legalism. From a realist perspective, supranational organizations such as the ECJ are essentially ineffectual at forcing upon sovereign states a pace of integration that does not conform to the states' own interests and priorities. The ECJ's role is best described as fulfilling an essentially 'technical serviant' role (Weiler 1982). Faced with a dispute, legal technocrats simply apply treaty provisions and rules formulated by the policymaking organs of the EC. Judicial interpretation, according to this model, is nothing more than a translation of these rules into operational language, devoid of political content and consequence (Taylor 1983: 280).

Realists view the notion of supranational community law as an absurdity, on the ground that 'if a national legislature decided to limit the effect of a Communities' regulation, or to nullify it, and if this intention was made plain to the national courts by the legislature . . . the national courts would not apply the Communities' law' (ibid.:

284). In short, realism asserts the primacy of national politics over community law and emphasizes the limits that the member states have imposed upon their involvement in community affairs 'which stops well short of any grant of sovereignty to the regional institutions' (ibid.: 294).

An example of a critique of the legalist approach that agrees with the realist premises is Stuart Scheingold's *The Law in Political Integration* (1971) Scheingold revisits the claim of the federalizing role of the Court. He finds that the impact of judicial decisions upon the substance of community policy has been 'rather modest. . . . By and large, the Court of Justice has operated as a validator of decisions . . . rather than as a policymaker' (ibid.: 16). He finds no hard evidence that the Court has contributed *directly* to the capacity of imposing 'constitutional' solutions on difficult problems. Thus, he concludes that the 'legal process *seems* to incorporate the member-states into a federal system. But the political process is basically consensual and pays more than lip service to the autonomy and integrity of national units in decision-making' (ibid.: 3, emphasis added). Nonetheless, Scheingold grants the possibility that the Court has had an *indirect* impact on European integration. He explains that by repeatedly and vigorously asserting federal prerogatives, the Court was 'feeding into the symbiotic relationship emerging between Community institutions and existing national structures-mobilizing national elites, enlisting national institutions in behalf of Community goals, and generally blurring the lines which divide(d] one set of structure from the other' (ibid. For a related argument on the virtues of 'federal rhetoric', see Pryce 1987).

Neorationalism

Geoffrey Garrett's and Barry Weingast's studies are two rare examples by political scientists that deal explicitly with the ECJ (Garrett 1992a; Garrett and Weingast 1993). They rely on a 'rationalist' approach to the study of institutions, one that proceeds from the basic realist premises of sovereign and unitary actors but which accepts a role for institutions based on rational choice and game theoretic studies of cooperation (see Keohane 1988).

Garrett begins with the proposition that the Court is in fact able to impose constraints on national political authorities within the community (Garrett 1992a: 556). Its continued ability to play such a role, however, does not result from any autonomous power. Rather, the maintenance of the community legal system is actually 'consistent with the interests of member states' (ibid.: 557). Member states' continuing collaboration within the EC indicates that they value the gains from effective participation in the internal market more highly than the potential benefits of defecting from community rules (see Garrett

1992a: 540, 557; Garrett and Weingast 1993: 27). However, due to the complexity of the community system, the incentives for unilateral defection may be considerable, especially if cheating is hard for other governments to spot or if the significance of defection is difficult to evaluate. Logically, if cheating is endemic, there are no gains from cooperation. It is thus in the member states' selfish interest to delegate some authority to the ECJ to enable it to *monitor* compliance with community obligations, to facilitate 'the logic of retaliation and reputation in iterated games' (Garrett and Weingast 1993: 27) or, more broadly, to create a shared belief system about cooperation and defection in the context of differential and conflicting sets of individual beliefs that would otherwise inhibit the decentralized emergence of cooperation (ibid.: 13). The ECJ performs a further valuable role for the member states: it mitigates the *incomplete contracting problems* by applying the general rules of the Rome treaty to a myriad of unanticipated contingencies, thus obviating the costly need for the actors to make exhaustive agreements that anticipate every dispute that might arise among them (Garrett 1992a: 557; Garrett and Weingast 1993: 27–8).

These various benefits notwithstanding, however, the Court would still not be worth the costs it imposes on individual member states unless 'it faithfully implement[s] the collective internal market preferences of [Community] members' (Garrett 1992a: 558). Garrett concludes that the ECJ, and the domestic courts that follow its judgments, meets this criterion as well, on the ground that its rulings 'are consistent with the preferences of France and Germany' (ibid.: 559). This assertion is simply wrong. Garrett cites one case in support of his thesis, the Court's 1979 ruling in *Cassis de Dijon,* in which the Court reached a ruling consistent with Germany's export interests. Yet, in that case, as in five other landmark constitutional cases, the German government argued explicitly and strongly against the Court's ultimate position. Indeed, Germany's lawyers put forth views opposed to those of the Court more often than any other country (see Stein 1981: 25). The French government did not make an appearance in any of these cases but battled the Court ferociously in other forums (see discussion of the *Sheepmeat* cases below). Further, there is absolutely no evidence that the Court actually attempts, as Garrett and Weingast contend, to track the positions of the member states. Stein argues that the Court follows the lead of the *commission,* using it as a political bellwether to ascertain how far member states can be *pushed* toward the Court and the commission's vision of maximum integration.

With the luxury of hindsight and the ability to manipulate the analysis at a very high level of generality, it is easy to assert that a particular decision was 'in the interests' of a particular state. Indeed, since the Garrett and Weingast approach assumes that states will only comply with judicial decisions if in fact those decisions are in their interests, they have an obvious incentive to deduce interest-compatibility from compliance. More generally, since the last five years have been a period in which all the principal EC member states have strongly supported continued integration, judicial decisions that retrospectively can be seen to have strengthened integration seem automatically congruent with the interests of those states. What we know is that at the time a particular case is brought, different governments strongly disagree as to its outcome. Over time, however, they tend to accept the Court's position and regard the path chosen as inevitable. *It is precisely this process that needs to be explained.* Here neorationalism is at a loss. Neofunctionalism is in its element.

. . . .

A Return to Neofunctionalism

An account of the impact of the Court in terms that political scientists will find as credible as lawyers must offer a political explanation of the role of the Court from the ground up. It should thus begin by developing a political theory of how the Court integrated its own domain, rather than beginning with legal integration as a fait accompli and asking about the interrelationship between legal and political integration. The process of legal integration did not come about through the 'power of the law', as the legalists implicitly assume and often explicitly insist on. Individual actors – judges, lawyers, litigants – were involved, with specific identities, motives, and objectives. They interacted in a specific context and through specific processes. Only a genuine political account of how they achieved their objectives in the process of legal integration will provide the basis for a systematic account of the interaction of that process with the political processes of the EC.

Such an account has in fact already been provided, but it has never been applied to the Court as such. It is a neofunctionalist account.

. . . .

A Neofunctionalist Jurisprudence

The advent of the first major EC crisis in 1965, initiated by De Gaulle's adamant refusal to proceed with certain aspects of integration he deemed contrary to French interests, triggered a crescendo of criticism against neofunctionalism. The theory, it was claimed, had exaggerated both the expansive effect of increments within the economic sphere and the 'gradual politicization' effect of spillover (Nye 1965).

Critics further castigated neofunctionalists for failing to appreciate the enduring importance of nationalism, the autonomy of the political sector, and the interaction between the international environment and the integrating region (Hoffmann 1963, 1966).

Neofunctionalists accepted most of the criticism and engaged in an agonizing reassessment of their theory. The coup de grace, however, was Haas's publication of *The Obsolescence of Regional Integration Theory,* in which he concluded that researchers should look beyond regional integration to focus on wider issues of international interdependence (Haas 1975, 1976).

With the benefit of greater hindsight, however, we believe that neofunctionalism has much to recommend it as a theory of regional integration. Although it recognizes that external shocks may disrupt the integration process (Haas and Schmitter 1964: 710), it boasts enduring relevance as a description of the integrative process *within a sector*. The sector we apply it to here is the legal integration of the European Community.

The creation of an integrated and enforceable body of community law conforms neatly to the neofunctionalist model. In this part of the article we describe the phenomenon of legal integration according to . . . neofunctionalist categories . . . : actors, motives, process, and context. Within each category, we demonstrate that the distinctive characteristics of the ECJ and its jurisprudence correspond to neofunctionalist prediction. We further show how the core insight of neofunctionalism – that integration is most likely to occur within a domain shielded from the interplay of direct political interests – leads to the paradox that actors are best able to circumvent and overcome political obstacles by acting as nonpolitically as possible. Thus in the legal context, judges who would advance a pro-integration 'political' agenda are likely to be maximally effective only to the extent that they remain within the apparent bounds of the law.

Actors: a specialized national and supranational community

On the supranational level, the principal actors are the thirteen ECJ judges, the commission legal staff, and the six advocates-general, official members of the Court assigned the task of presenting an impartial opinion on the law in each case. Judges and Advocates-General are drawn from universities, national judiciaries, distinguished members of the community bar, and national government officials (see Brown and Jacobs 1977). Judges take an oath to decide cases independently of national loyalties and are freed from accountability to their home governments by two important facets of the Court's decision-making process: secrecy of deliberation and the absence of dissenting opinions.

A quick perusal of the Treaty of Rome articles concerning the ECJ suggests that the founders intended the Court and its staff to interact primarily with other community organs and the member states. Articles 169 and 170 provide for claims of noncompliance with community obligations to be brought against member states by either the commission or other member states. Article 173 gives the Court additional jurisdiction over a variety of actions brought against either the commission or the council by a member state, by the commission, by the council, or by specific individuals who have been subject to a councilor commission decision directly addressed to them.

Almost as an afterthought, Article 177 authorizes the Court to issue 'preliminary rulings' on any question involving the interpretation of community law arising in the national courts. Lower national courts can refer such questions to the ECJ at their discretion; national courts of last resort are required to request the ECJ's assistance. In practice, the Article 177 procedure has provided a framework for links between the Court and subnational actors – private litigants, their lawyers, and lower national courts.[9] From its earliest days, the ECJ waged a campaign to enhance the use of Article 177 as a vehicle enabling private individuals to challenge national legislation as incompatible with community law. The number of Article 177 cases on the Court's docket grew steadily through the 1970s, from a low of 9 in 1968 to a high of 119 in 1978 and averaging over 90 per year from 1979 to 1982 (Rasmussen 1986: 245). This campaign has successfully transferred a large portion of the business interpreting and applying community law away from the immediate province of member states.[10]

As an additional result of these efforts, the community bar is now flourishing. Groups of private practitioners receive regular invitations to visit the Court and attend educational seminars. They get further encouragement and support from private associations such as the International Federation for European Law, which has branches in the member states that include both academics and private practitioners. Smaller practitioners' groups connected with national bar associations also abound (see Brown and Jacobs 1977: 180–1). The proliferation of community lawyers laid the foundation for the development of a specialized and highly interdependent community above and below the level of member state governments. The best testimony on the nature of the ties binding that community comes from a leading EC legal academic and editor of the *Common Market Law Review*, Henry Schermers. In a recent tribute to a former legal advisor to the commission for his role in 'building bridges between [the Commission], the Community Court and the practitioners', Schermers wrote:

> Much of the credit for the Community legal order rightly goes to the Court of Justice of the European Communities, but the Court will be the first to recognize that they do not deserve all the credit. Without the loyal support of the national judiciaries, preliminary

questions would not have been asked nor preliminary rulings followed. And the national judiciaries themselves would not have entered into Community law had not national advocates pleaded it before them. For the establishment and growth of the Community legal order it was essential for the whole legal profession to become acquainted with the new system and its requirements. Company lawyers, solicitors and advocates had to be made aware of the opportunities offered to them by the Community legal system (Schermers 1990).

In this tribute, Schermers points to another important set of subnational actors: community law professors. These academics divide their time between participation as private consultants on cases before the court and extensive commentary on the Court's decisions. In addition to book-length treatises, they edit and contribute articles to a growing number of specialized journals devoted exclusively to EC law.[11] As leading figures in their own national legal and political communities, they play a critical role in bolstering the legitimacy of the Court.

Motives: the self-interest of judges, lawyers, and professors

The glue that binds this community of supra- and subnational actors is self-interest. In the passage quoted above, Schermers speaks of making private practitioners aware of the 'opportunities' offered to them by the community legal system. The Court largely created those opportunities, providing personal incentives for individual litigants, their lawyers, and lower national courts to participate in the construction of the community legal system. In the process, it enhanced its own power and the professional interests of all parties participating directly or indirectly in its business.

Giving individual litigants a personal stake in community law

The history of the 'constitutionalization' of the Treaty of Rome, and of the accompanying 'legalization' of community secondary legislation, is essentially the history of the direct effect doctrine. And, the history of the direct effect doctrine is the history of carving individually enforceable rights out of a body of rules apparently applicable only to states. In neofunctionalist terms, the Court created a pro-community constituency of private individuals by giving them a direct stake in promulgation and implementation of community law. Further, the Court was careful to create a one-way ratchet by permitting individual participation in the system only in a way that would advance community goals.

The Court began by prohibiting individuals from seeking to annul legal acts issued by the Council of Ministers or the EC Commission for exceeding their powers under the Treaty of Rome. As noted above,

Article 173 of the treaty appears to allow the council, the commission, the member states, and private parties to seek such an injunction. In 1962, however, the Court held that individuals could not bring such actions except in the narrowest of circumstances.[12] A year later the Court handed down its landmark decision in *Van Gend & Loos,* allowing a private Dutch importer to invoke the common market provisions of the treaty directly against the Dutch government's attempt to impose customs duties on specified imports.[13] *Van Gend* announced a new world. Over the explicit objections of three of the member states, the Court proclaimed:

> the Community constitutes a *new legal order* . . . for the benefit of which the states have limited their sovereign rights, albeit within limited fields, and *the subjects of which comprise not only Member States but also their nationals.* Independently of the legislation of the Member States, Community law *therefore not only imposes obligations on individuals but it also intended to confer upon them rights which become part of their legal heritage.* These rights arise not only where they are expressly granted by the Treaty, but also by reason of obligations which the Treaty imposes in a clearly defined way upon individuals as well as upon the Member States and upon the institutions of the Community.[14]

The Court effectively articulated a social contract for the EC, relying on the logic of mutuality to tell community citizens that since community law would impose new duties of citizenship flowing to an entity other than their national governments, which had now relinquished some portion of their sovereignty, they must be entitled to corresponding rights. Beneath the lofty rhetoric, however, was the creation of a far more practical set of incentives pushing toward integration. Henceforth importers around the community who objected to paying customs duties on their imports could invoke the Treaty of Rome to force their governments to live up to their commitment to create a common market.

The subsequent evolution of the direct effect doctrine reflects the steady expansion of its scope. . . . After vociferous protest from national courts,[15] the Court did balk temporarily at granting horizontal effect to community directives – allowing individuals to enforce obligations explicitly imposed by council directives on member states against other individuals – but has subsequently permitted even these actions where member governments have failed to implement a directive correctly or in a timely fashion.[16]

Without tracking the intricacies of direct effect jurisprudence any further, it suffices to note that at every turn the Court harped on the benefits of its judgements for individual citizens of the community. In

Van Duyn, for instance, the Court observed: 'A decision to this effect (granting direct effect to community directives) would undoubtedly strengthen the legal protection of individual citizens in the national courts' (*Van Duyn*: 1342). Conversely, of course, individuals are the best means of holding member states to their obligations:

> Where Community authorities have, by directive, imposed on Member states the obligation to pursue a particular course of conduct, the useful effect of such an act would be weakened if individuals were prevented from relying on it before their national courts and if the latter were prevented from taking it into consideration as an element of Community law. (Ibid.: 1348. For a discussion of more recent cases in which the Court explicitly has carved out individual rights in the enforcement of community directives see Curtin 1990).

The net result of all these cases is that individuals (and their lawyers) who can point to a provision in the community treaties or secondary legislation that supports a particular activity they wish to undertake – from equal pay for equal work to a lifting of customs levies – can invoke community law and urge a national court to certify the question of whether and how community law should be applied to the ECJ. When litigants did not appear to perceive the boon that had been granted them, moreover, the Court set about educating them in the use of the Article 177 procedure (see Mancini 1989: 605–6; also Pescatore 1974: 99; Rasmussen 1986: 247). The Court thus constructed a classically utilitarian mechanism and put it to work in the service of community goals. Citizens who are net losers from integrative decisions by the councilor the commission cannot sue to have those actions declared ultra vires. But citizens who stand to gain have a constant incentive to push their governments to live up to paper commitments.[17] As Haas argued in 1964, a successful international organization can achieve 'growth through planning . . . only on the basis of stimulating groups and governments in the environment to submit new demands calling for organizational action' (Haas 1964: 128).

Courting the national courts

The entire process of increasing the use of the Article 177 procedure was an exercise in convincing national judges of the desirability of using the ECJ. Through seminars, dinners, regular invitations to Luxembourg, and visits around the community, the ECJ judges put a human face on the institutional links they sought to build.[18] Many of the Court's Article 177 opinions reinforced the same message. It was a message that included a number of components designed to appeal to the self-interest primarily of the lower national courts. It succeeded ultimately in transforming the European legal system into a split system, in which these lower courts began to recognize two separate and distinct authorities above them: their own national supreme courts, on questions of national law, and the ECJ, on questions of European law. Judge Mancini explains quite candidly that the ECJ needed the 'cooperation and goodwill of the state courts' (Mancini 1989: 605).[19]

Shapiro expresses surprise at the willingness of lower national courts to invoke Article 177 against the interests of their own national supreme courts, noting that lower court judges 'must attend to their career prospects within hierarchically organized national judicial systems' (Shapiro 1991: 127). Weiler offers several explanations, beginning with the legitimacy of ECJ decisions conferred by the national prestige of individual judges and the precise reasoning of the opinions themselves. He ultimately concludes, however, that the 'legally driven constitutional revolution' in the EC is 'a narrative of plain and simple judicial empowerment' (Weiler 1991: 2426). And further, that 'the EC system gave judges at the lowest level powers that had been reserved to the highest court in the land'. For many, 'to have de facto judicial review of legislation...would be heady stuff' (ibid.).

Perhaps the best evidence for this 'narrative of empowerment' comes from the ECJ itself. Many of the opinions are carefully crafted appeals to judicial ego. In *Van Gend & Loos* itself the Belgian and Dutch governments had argued that the question of the application of the Treaty of Rome over Dutch or Belgian law was solely a question for the Belgian and Dutch national courts. The ECJ responded by announcing, in effect, that the entire case was a matter solely between the national courts and the ECJ, to be resolved without interference from the national governments. When the Belgian government objected that the question of European law referred by the national court could have no bearing on the outcome of the proceedings, the ECJ piously responded that it was not its business to review the 'considerations which may have led a national court or tribunal to its choice of questions as well as the relevance which it attributes to such questions.' (*Van Gend & Loos*: 22). In this and subsequent direct effect cases the ECJ continually suggested that the direct effect of community law should depend on judicial interpretation rather than legislative action.[20]

Finally, in holding that a national court's first loyalty must be to the ECJ on all questions of community law[21] the Court was able simultaneously to appeal to national courts *in their role* as protectors of individual rights – a very effective dual strategy.[22] Such argumentation simultaneously strengthens the force of the Court's message to national courts by portraying the construction of the European legal system as simply a continuation of the traditional role of European courts and, indeed, liberal courts everywhere: the protection of individual rights against the state. At the same time, as discussed above, the Court strengthens its own claim to perform that role, building a constituency beyond the Brussels bureaucracy.

Reciprocal empowerment

This utilitarian depiction of the integration process must include the ECJ itself. It is obvious that any measures that succeed in raising the visibility, effectiveness, and scope of EC law also enhance the prestige and power of the Court and its members, both judges and advocates general. In addition, however, by presenting itself as the champion of individual rights and the protector of the prerogatives of lower national courts, the ECJ also burnishes its own image and gives its defenders weapons with which to rebut charges of antidemocratic activism. Rasmussen points out that the encouragement to use Article 177 procedure meant that the Court visibly sided with 'the little guy', the underdog against state bureaucracies, 'the "people" against the "power-elite"' (Rasmussen 1986: 245). Strikingly enough, this is a characterization with which Judge Koenrad Lenaerts essentially concurs (see Lenaerts forthcoming*).

The empowerment of the ECJ with respect to the national courts is more subtle. While offering lower national courts a 'heady' taste of power, the ECJ simultaneously strengthens its own legal legitimacy by making it appear that its own authority flows from the national courts. It is the national courts, after all, who have sought its guidance; and it is the national courts who will ultimately *decide* the case, in the sense of issuing an actual ruling on the facts. The ECJ only 'interprets' the relevant provision of community law, and leaves it for the national court to apply it to the facts of the case. In practice, of course, the ECJ frequently offers a virtual template for the subsequent lower court decision (for specific examples, see Everling 1984c: 1299–1301). But, the all-important fiction is preserved.

Finally, the empowerment of the ECJ simultaneously empowers all those who make their living by analyzing and critiquing its decisions. Here community law professors and their many assistants join with members of the community bar to form a communitywide network of individuals with a strong stake in bolstering the Court's prestige. On the most basic level, the growing importance of community law translates into a growing demand for professors to teach it and hence, funding for chaired professorships.[23] The holders of these chairs are likely, in turn, to aspire to become judges and advocates general themselves, just as many current judges and advocates general are likely to return to the professorate when their terms expire. This is a neofunctionalist interest group par excellence.

Process

. . . the neofunctionalist description of the actual process of integration focused on three major features: functional spillover, political spillover, and upgrading of common interests. All three dynamics are clearly present in the building of the EC legal system.

Functional spillover: the logic of law

Functional spillover presupposes the existence of an agreed objective and simply posits that the jurisdiction of the authorities charged with implementing that objective will expand as necessary to address whatever obstacles stand in the way. This expansion will continue as long as those authorities do not collide with equally powerful countervailing interests. Alternatively, of course, one objective might conflict with another objective. Such limits define the parameters within which this 'functionalist' logic can work.

In the construction of a community legal system, such limits were initially very few, and the functional logic was very strong. Judge Pierre Pescatore has attributed the ECJ's success in creating a coherent and authoritative body of community law to the Court's ability – flowing from the structure and content of the Treaty of Rome – to use 'constructive methods of interpretation' (Pescatore 1974: 89–90). One of the more important of those methods is the 'systematic method', drawing on 'the various systematic elements on which Community law is based: general scheme of the legislation, structure of the institutions, arrangement of powers, . . . general concepts and guiding ideals of the Treaties. Here is a complete 'architecture', coherent and well thought out, *the lines of which, once firmly drawn, require to be extended*' (ibid.: 87, emphasis added). Interpretation according to the systematic method means filling in areas of the legal structure that logically follow from the parts of the structure already built.

A well-known set of examples confirms the power of this functional logic as applied by the ECJ. After *Van Gend & Loos,* the next major 'constitutional' case handed down was *Costa v. Enel,* which established the supremacy of community law over national law. In plain terms, *Costa* asserted that where a treaty term conflicted with a subsequent national statute, the treaty must prevail. Predictably, Judge Federico Mancini justifies this decision by reference to the ruin argument (Mancini 1989: 600). He argues further, however, that the supremacy clause 'was not only an indispensable development, it was also a logical development' (ibid.). Students of federalism have long recognized that the clash of interests between state and federal authorities can be mediated in several ways: either (1) by allowing state authorities to implement federal directives at the time and in the manner they desire, or (2) by allowing both state and federal authorities to legislate directly, which entails formulating guidelines to establish a hierarchy between the two. On this basis, Mancini (and Eric Stein before him) points out that *because* the Court had 'enormously extended the Community power to deal directly with the public' in *Van Gend & Loos,* it now became logically necessary to insist that community law must prevail over member state law in cases of conflict (ibid.: 601). In short, the 'full impact of direct effect' can only be realized 'in combination with' the supremacy clause (see Weiler 1991: 2414).

The evolution of community law also has manifested the substantive broadening typical of functional spillover. EC law is today no longer as dominantly economic in character as in the 1960s (Nugent 1989: 151). It has spilled over into a variety of domains dealing with issues such as health and safety at work, entitlements to social welfare benefits, mutual recognition of educational and professional qualification, and, most recently, even political participation rights. Two notable examples are equal treatment with respect to social benefits of workers, a field developed almost entirely as a result of Court decisions (for further reading, see Leleux 1982), and the general system of community trademark law – again formed entirely by the Court's case law. In both areas the Court gradually extended its reach by grounding each new decision on the necessity of securing the common market.

Political spillover: 'transnational incrementalism'

The neofunctionalists argued that integration was an adaptive process of gradually shifting expectations, changing loyalties, and evolving values (see Haas 1958a: 12, 1961: 366). In trying to explain why member states responded positively to the Court's legal innovations, Joseph Weiler writes:

> it is clear that a measure of transnational incrementalism developed. Once some of the highest courts of a few Member States endorsed the new constitutional construct, their counterparts in other Member States heard more arguments that those courts should do the same, and it became more difficult for national courts to resist the trend with any modicum of credibility. (Weiler 1991: 2425).

Beyond the Court's specific machinations, however, law operates as law by shifting expectations. The minute a rule is established as 'law', individuals are entitled to rely upon the assumption that social, economic, or political behavior will be conducted in accordance with that rule. The creation and application of law is inherently a process of shifting expectations. A major function of a legal rule is to provide a clear and certain standard around which expectations can crystallize. As long as those actors to which the Court's decisions are directed –

member state governments, national courts, and individuals – accept one decision as a statement of the existing law and proceed to make arguments in the next case from that benchmark, they are shifting their expectations. This is precisely the process that court watchers, even potentially skeptical ones, have identified. Hjalte Rasmussen demonstrates that even governments overtly hostile to the Court's authority do not seek to ask the Court to overturn a previous ruling but rather accept that ruling as a statement of the law and use it as a point of departure for making arguments in subsequent cases. After reviewing an extensive sample of briefs submitted to the Court by member governments, Rasmussen was unable to find even one instance in which a member state suggested that a prior precedent be overruled (Rasmussen 1986: 275–81).

This finding is particularly striking given that states do often strongly object to a proposed interpretation or application of a particular legislative term in its briefs and arguments *prior* to a particular decision.[24] One of the most celebrated instances of member state defiance of the Court is the *Sheepmeat* case. This represented the culmination of a line of precedents in which the Court had held repeatedly that the treaty prohibited intra-EC agricultural trade restrictions created by national market organizations for specific products.[25] The French government fought bitterly against this position at every turn but after losing in the first two cases, it chose to argue in the third for a delay in implementing its obligations – rather than to dispute the earlier decisions by the Court that had established those obligations in the first place (for a more detailed account of these cases, see Rasmussen 1986: 281–4, 338–45).

Upgrading common interests

For the neofunctionalists, upgrading common interests referred to a 'swapping mechanism' dependent on the services of an 'institutionalized autonomous mediator'. The Court is less a mediator than an arbiter and has no means per se of 'swapping' concessions. What it does do, however, is continually to justify its decisions in light of the common interests of the members as enshrined in both specific and general objectives of the original Rome treaty. The modus operandi here is the 'teleological method of interpretation', by which the court has been able to rationalize everything from direct effect to the preemption of member state negotiating power in external affairs in every case in which the treaty grants internal competence to community authorities.[26] All are reasoned not on the basis of specific provisions in the treaty or community secondary legislation but on the accomplishment of the most elementary community goals set forth in the Preamble to the treaty.

According to Judge Pescatore, the concepts employed in the teleological method include 'concepts such as the customs union, equality of treatment and non-discrimination, freedom of movement, mutual assistance and solidarity, economic interpenetration and finally economic and legal unity as the supreme objective' (Pescatore 1974: 88) . . .

Rhetorically, these formulas constantly shift the analysis to a more general level on which it is possible to assert common interests – the same common interests that led member states into the community process in the first place. French sheepfarmers might fight to the death with British sheepfarmers, but the majority of the population in both nations have a common interest in 'the free movement of goods'. 'Upgrading the common interest', in judicial parlance, is a process of reasserting long-term interest, at least as nominally perceived at the founding and enshrined in sonorous phrases, over short-term interest. In the process, of course, to the extent it succeeds in using this method to strengthen and enhance community authority, the Court does certainly also succeed in upgrading its own powers.

Context: the (apparent) separation of law and politics

The effectiveness of law in the integration process – as Haas predicted for economics – depends on the perception that it is a domain distinct and apart from politics. Shapiro has argued, for instance, that the Court, aided and abetted by its commentators, has derived enormous advantage from denying the existence of policy discretion and instead hewing to the fiction, bolstered by the style and retroactivity of its judgments. An absolute division between law and politics, as between economics and politics, is ultimately impossible. Nevertheless, just as Haas stressed that overt political concerns are less *directly* engaged in economic integration, requiring some time for specific economic decisions to acquire political significance, so, too, can legal decision-making function in a relative political vacuum. Although the political impact of judicial decisions will ultimately be felt, they will be more acceptable initially due to their independent nonpolitical justification.

The importance of undertaking integration in a nominally nonpolitical sphere is confirmed by the underlying issues and interests at stake in the nascent debate about judicial activism in the community. As periodic struggles over the proper balance between judicial activism and judicial restraint in the United States have demonstrated, assertions about the preservation of the legitimacy and authority necessary to uphold the rule of law generally have a particular substantive vision of the law in mind (see e.g. Shapiro 1978). In the community context, the response to Rasmussen's charge of judicial activism reveals that the substantive stakes concern the prospects for the Court's self-professed task, integration. In heeding widespread advice to maintain a careful balance between applying community law and articulating and defending community ideals, the Court is really preserving its ability to camouflage controversial political decisions in 'technical' legal garb.

Maintaining the fiction

The European legal community appears to understand the importance of preserving the Court's image as a nonpolitical institution all too well. The dominant theme in scholarship on the Court in the 1970s and 1980s was reassurance that the Court was carrying out its delicate balancing act with considerable success (see Dumon 1976: 51–3; Green 1969: 26–33, 498; Mann 1972: 508–15; Scheingold 1965: 263–85; Stein 1981). Rasmussen describes a widespread refusal among community lawyers and legal academics to criticize the Court on paper. The consensus seems to be that overt recognition of the Court's political agenda beyond the bounds of what 'the law' might fairly be said to permit will damage the Court's effectiveness (for a discussion of 'the oral tradition' of criticism that European scholars refuse publicly to acknowledge, see Rasmussen 1986: 147-8, 152–4). Commenting on the same phenomenon, Shapiro has observed that the European legal community understands its collective writings on the Court as a political act designed to bolster the Court. By denying the existence of judicial activism and thus removing a major potential locus of opposition to the Court, they promote an institution whose pro-community values accord with their own internalized values (Shapiro 1980: 542).

The Court itself has cooperated in burnishing this nonpolitical image. Pescatore set the tone in 1974, contending that the first reason for the 'relative success of Community case law' is 'the wide definition of the task of the Court as custodian of law' (1974: 89). And certainly the Court has carefully crafted its opinions to present the results in terms of the inexorable logic of the law. To cite a classic example, in the *Van Gend & Loos* decision, in which the Court singlehandedly transformed the Treaty of Rome from an essentially nonenforceable international treaty to a domestic charter with direct and enforceable effects, it cast its analysis in the following framework: 'To ascertain whether the provisions of an international treaty extend so far in their effects it is necessary to consider the spirit, the general scheme, and the wording of those provisions' (*Van Gend & Loos*).

. . . .

Transforming the political into the legal

Court watchers have long understood that the ECJ uses the EC Commission as a political bellwether. In any given case, the ECJ looks to the commission's position as an indicator of political acceptability to the member states of a particular result or a line of reasoning.[27] From the Court's own perspective, however, the chief advantage of following the commission is the 'advantage of objectivity', resulting from the commission's supranational perspective (Pescatore 1974: 80). In neofunctionalist terms, the Court's reliance on what Pescatore characterizes as 'well-founded information and balanced legal evaluations', as 'source material for the Court's decisions' allows it to cast itself as nonpolitical by contrasting the neutrality and objectivity of its decision-making processes with the partisan political agendas of the parties before it.

Relatively less attention has been paid to the role of the commission in depoliticizing potentially inflammatory disputes among the member states. Judge Pierre Pescatore credits the procedure set forth in Article 169 (whereby the *commission* initiates an action against a member state for a declaration of default on a community legal obligation) with defusing the potential fireworks of an Article 170 proceeding, in which one state would bring such a charge directly against another (ibid.: 80–2). By allowing default proceedings to be initiated by 'an institution representative of the whole, and hence objective both by its status and by its task', this device 'permits the Member States more easily to accept this process of control over their Community behavior and the censure which may arise for them from the judgments of the Court' (ibid.: 82). Against this backdrop, it is of signal importance that the Court itself actively and successfully encouraged the increased use of the Article 169 procedure (see Rasmussen 1986: 238–40).

This perspective reveals yet another dimension of the Court's encouragement of the Article 177 procedure. The increased use of Article 177 shifted the vanguard of community law enforcement (and creation) to cases involving primarily *private* parties. It thus further removed the Court from the overtly political sphere of direct conflicts between member states, or even between the commission and member states. The political implications of private legal disputes, while potentially very important, often require a lawyer's eye to discern. Following Haas's description of economic integration, Article 177 cases offer a paradigm for the 'indirect' penetration of the political by way of the legal.

Law as a mask

The above discussion of context reveals that the neofunctionalist domain is a domain theoretically governed by a distinct set of nonpolitical objectives, such as 'the rule of law' or 'economic growth and efficiency', and by a distinctive methodology and logic. These characteristics operate to define a purportedly 'neutral' zone in which it is possible to reach outcomes that would be impossible to achieve in the political arena. Neofunctionalists also insisted, however, that this neutral zone would not be completely divorced from politics. On the contrary, 'economic' – or, in our case, 'legal' – decisions inevitably would acquire political significance. This gradual interpenetration was the mechanism by which economic integration might ultimately lead to political integration.

The key to understanding this process is that even an economic decision that has acquired political significance is not the same as a 'purely'
political decision and cannot be attacked as such. It retains an independent 'nonpolitical' rationale, which must be met by a counter-argu-
ment on its own terms. Within this domain, then, contending political
interests must do battle by proxy. The chances of victory are affected
by the strength of that proxy measured by independent nonpolitical
criteria.

From this perspective, law functions both as mask and shield. It
hides and protects the promotion of one particular set of political
objectives against contending objectives in the purely political sphere.
In specifying this dual relationship between law and politics, we also
uncover a striking paradox. Law can only perform this dual political
function to the extent it is accepted as law. A 'legal' decision that is
transparently 'political,' in the sense that it departs too far from the
principles and methods of the law, will invite direct political attack. It
will thus fail both as mask and shield. Conversely, a court seeking to
advance its own political agenda must accept the independent constraints of legal reasoning, even when such constraints require it to
reach a result that is far narrower than the one it might deem politically optimal.

In short, a court's political legitimacy, and hence its ability to
advance its own political agenda, rests on its legal legitimacy. This
premise is hardly news to domestic lawyers. It has informed an entire
school of thought about the US Supreme Court.[28] It also accords with
the perception of ECJ judges of how to enhance their own effectiveness, as witnessed not only by their insistence on their strict adherence
to the goals of the Treaty of Rome but also by their vehement reaction
to charges of activism. Mancini again: 'If what makes a judge "good"
is his awareness of the constraints on judicial decision-making and the
knowledge that rulings must be convincing in order to evoke obedience, the Luxembourg judges of the 1960s and 1970s were obviously
very good' (Mancini 1989: 605).

What is new about the neofunctionalist approach is that it demonstrates the ways in which the preservation of judicial legitimacy shields
an entire domain of integrationist processes, hence permitting the
accretion of power and the pursuit of individual interests by specified
actors within a dynamic of expansion. Moreover, the effectiveness of
'law as a mask' extends well beyond the ECJ's efforts to construct a
community legal system. To the extent that judges of the European
Court do in fact remain within the plausible boundaries of existing
law, they achieve a similar level of effectiveness in the broader spheres
of economic, social, and political integration.

Implications and Conclusions

The Maastricht treaty

The Maastricht Treaty on European Union reflects a determination on the part of the member states to limit the ECJ. The Court is entirely excluded from two of the three 'pillars' of the treaty: foreign and security policy and cooperation in the spheres of justice and home affairs. In addition, a number of specific articles are very tightly drafted to prevent judicial manipulation. For instance, in the provisions on public health, education, vocational training, and culture, the treaty provides that the council shall adopt necessary measures to achieve the common objectives set forth, '*excluding any harmonization of the laws and regulations of the Member States*' (TEU, Art. 126–9). This explicit prohibition of harmonization is an effort to ensure that the expedited decision-making procedures under Article 100 for the completion of the internal market cannot be interpreted to apply to those additional substantive areas. On the other hand, another amendment allows the Court for the first time, at the commission's request, to impose a lump-sum or penalty payment on a member state that fails to comply with its judgment (TEU, Art. 143).

At first glance, the Maastricht provisions appear to confirm the Garrett-Weingast theory of the Court. The member states chose to strengthen the Court's power to monitor and punish defections from those areas of the treaty where it exercises jurisdiction; they chose to exclude it altogether in areas of lesser political consensus. Yet, Garrett and Weingast conclude that the single most important factor behind the maintenance of the community legal system is not the Court's performance of monitoring and incomplete contracting functions but rather the alignment of its judgements with the interests of the member states holding the balance of power in the community. If so, and if indeed the Court ensures the protection of its authority and legitimacy by assiduous fidelity to state interests rather than to the law, then why worry? Why should not the member states permit unrestricted jurisdiction, secure in the knowledge that the political constraints on the Court are safeguard enough? In areas of member state consensus, the Court will follow that consensus; in areas of continuing disagreement at least among the big states, the Court could be expected to decline jurisdiction or to decide on a technicality.

The answer can only be that the Court does have the power to pursue its own agenda, and that the personal incentives in the judicial and legal community, as well as the structural logic of law, favor integration. Further, the autonomy of the legal domain means that once started down a particular path, the Court's trajectory is difficult to monitor or control. It can be slowed by countermeasures carefully constructed on its own terms; the exclusion of harmonization, for instance, can be understood as a direct check on spillover crafted in legal language and according to legal rules. However, only exclusion provides certainty. Such exclusion will indeed stop the integration process in those areas; as fully admitted by neofunctionalists, neofunctionalism is a stochastic process, sensitive to political constraints. Absent such extreme measures, however, when not specifically cabined, the neofunctionalist dynamic does indeed produce incremental but steady change.

. . . .

In conclusion, neofunctionalism offers a genuine political theory of an important dimension of European integration. It is a theory that should be equally comprehensible and plausible to lawyers and political scientists, even if European judges and legal scholars resist it for reasons the theory itself explains. Previously, those who would argue for the force of the law had to forsake 'political' explanations, or at least explanations satisfactory to political scientists. Conversely, most of those seeking to construct a social scientific account of the role of the Court typically have eschewed 'fuzzy' arguments based on the power of law. We advance a theory of the interaction of law and politics that draws on both disciplines, explaining the role of law in European integration as a product of rational motivation and choice. Lawyers seeking to offer causal explanations, as well as political scientists trying to explain legal phenomena, should be equally satisfied.

Notes

1 This apparent indifference to larger political questions has been so profound as to earn reproach even from a member of the ECJ itself. Judge Ulrich Everling offered his own account of the relationship between the Court and the member states in 1984, beginning, 'The central problem of the European Community is the tension which exists between it and its Member States'. He further observed in a footnote that 'this problem is largely ignored and underestimated in the legal literature'. See Everling 1981, 1984a: 215, 1984b.

2 After reviewing the events of the late 1980s and the new flurry of interest in the literature, Keohane and Hoffmann resurrected neofunctionalism and restored it to the agenda of EC research, reminding their readers of its more sophisticated aspects (1990: 286ff). In the same article, drawing on the work of Joseph Weiler and Renaud Dehousse, Keohane and Hoffmann also acknowledge that the 'Community legal process has a dynamic of its own', (1990: 278). They fail to put these two insights together, however. An argument that neofunctionalists mistakenly overlooked the ECJ is found in Schmitter, forthcoming.

3 A quantitative illustration of the growing importance of community law is the number of cases referred to the ECJ by domestic courts. The number jumped from a low of 9 in 1968 to a high of 119 in 1978.

4 Legal integration does not necessarily need to take place within the framework of supranational institutions, although that is our focus here. For a non-institutional analysis of the dynamics of legal integration among liberal states, see Burley 1992.

5 Justice Lord Mackenzie Stuart writes: 'It is the Treaties and the subordinate legislation which have a policy, and which dictate the ends to be achieved. The Court only takes note of what has already been decided' (Stuart 1977: 77. For a similar argument, see Lecourt 1976: 237).

6 Writers in this tradition point frequently to Art. 4 of the Rome treaty, which lists the court as one of the institutions to carry out the tasks entrusted to the community by member states who, according to the treaty's preamble, are 'determined to lay the foundations of an ever closer union among the people of Europe'. (*Treaties Establishing the European Communities* (1987)).

7 This approach was pioneered by Scheingold (1965) in a study of the early Court (1953 to the early 1960s) when it served as the judicial arm of the ECSC and in 1957 extended its activities to the EEC and the Atomic Energy Community.

8 In his most recent article, Weiler retreats from his earlier causal proposition, claiming instead to offer a 'synthesis and analysis . . . in the tradition of the "pure theory of law" with the riders that "law" encompasses a discourse that is much wider than doctrine and norms and that the very dichotomy of law and politics is questionable'. See Weiler 1991: 2409. As a newly self-proclaimed legalist, Weiler avoids the difficulties of empirical proof. He borrows two concepts from Hirschman's *Exit, Voice, and Loyalty-Responses to Decline in Firms, Organizations, and States* (1970). The concept of *exit* describes the mechanism of organizational abandonment in the face of unsatisfactory performance; *voice* describes the mechanism of intraorganizational correction and recuperation. Weiler claims that the process by which community norms and policy hardened into binding law with effective legal remedies constitutes 'the closure of Selective Exit' in the EEC. This in turn increased the importance of voice. Crucially, Weiler adds: 'Instead of simple (legal) cause and (political) effect, this subtler process was a circular one. On this reading, the deterioration of the political supranational decisional procedures, the suspension of majority voting in 1966, and the creation and domination of intergovernmental bodies such as COREPER [the Committee of Permanent Representatives] and the European Council constituted the political conditions that allowed the Member States to digest and accept the process of constitutionalization' (see ibid.: 2428–9). The direct causal sequence of his earlier work is now reversed, and his conclusion as to the ultimate nature of the Court's impact on the integration process is equivocal, simultaneously recognizing the positive contributions of the Court and warning against the dangers of excessive judicial activism.

9 It may seem odd to characterize lower national courts as subnational actors, but as discussed below, much of the Court's success in creating a unified and enforceable community legal system has rested on convincing lower national courts to leapfrog the national judicial hierarchy and work directly with the ECJ (see Volcansek 1986; Usher 1981).

10 The Court's rules allow member states to intervene to state their position in any case they deem important, but this provision is regularly underutilized.

11 Prominent examples include *The Common Market Law Review, The European Law Review, Yearbook of European Law, Legal Issues of European Integration, Cahier de Droit Europeen, Revue trimestrielle de Droit Europeen,* and *Europarecht.* A vast number of American international and comparative law journals also publish regular articles on European law.

12 See Case 25/62, *Plaumann & Co. v. Commission of the EEC, European Court Reports* (ECR), 1963, p. 95. See also Rasmussen, 1980: 112–27.

13 Case 26/62, N.V. *Algemene Transport & Expeditie Ondememing Van Gend & Loos v. Nederlandse Administratie der Belastingen, ECR,* 1963: 1.

14 Ibid.: 12, emphasis added.

15 *Bundesfinanzhof* decision of 25 April 1985 (VR123/84), Entscheidungen des Bundesfinanzhofes, vol. 143: 383. The decision was quashed by the *Bundesverfassungsgericht* (the German Constitutional Court) in its decision of 8 April

1987 (2 BvR 687/85), [1987] *Recht der Internationalen Wirtschaft* 878. See also the *Cohn Bendit* case, *Conseil d'Etat,* 22 December 1978, Dalloz, 1979: 155.

16 See Case 152/84, *Marshall v. Southhampton and South West Hampshire Area Health Authority (Teaching), Common Market Law Review,* vol. 1, 1986: 688; and Case 152/84, *ECR,* 1986: 737. On the relationship between *Marshall* and *Marleasing,* See Rasmussen forthcoming*.

17 More prosaically, but no less effectively for the construction of a community legal system, the Art. 177 procedure offers 'clever lawyers and tacticians...the possibility of using Community law to mount challenges to traditional local economic restrictions in a way which may keep open a window of trading opportunity whilst the legal process grinds away'. In a word, delay. See Gormley 1990.

18 Rasmussen describes a 'generous information campaign', as a result of which a steadily increasing number of national judges traveled to the *Palais de Justice,* at the ECJ's expense, for conferences about the court and the nature of the Article 177 procedure. See Rasmussen 1986: 247.

19 In this regard, Volcansek (1986: 264–6) offers an interesting discussion of the various 'follow-up mechanisms' the ECJ employed to further an ongoing partnership with the national courts, including positive feedback whenever possible and gradual accommodation of the desire occasionally to interpret community law for themselves.

20 See, e.g., *Lütticke,* p. 10, where the ECJ announced that the direct effect of the treaty article in question depends solely on a finding by the national court: see also Case 33/76 *Rewe-Zentralfinanz Gesellschaft and Rewe-Zentral AG v. Landwirtschaftskammer für das Saarland, ECR,* 1989, p. 1998; and Case 45/76 *Coment BV v. Produktschap voor Siegewassen, ECR,* 1976: 2052–3.

21 Case 106/77, *Amministrazione delle Finanze dello Stato v. Simmenthal S.p.A.* [1978] *ECR,* 629.

22 Ibid.: 643.

23 The 'Jean Monnet Action', a program of the European Commission, has recently created 57 new full-time teaching posts in community law as part of a massive program to create new courses in European integration.

24 As is now widely recognized, Belgium, Germany, and the Netherlands all filed briefs strongly objecting to the notion of direct effect in *Van Gend & Loos.* None subsequently suggested revisiting that decision.

25 The first of these cases was Case 48/74, *Mr. Charmasson v. Minister for Economic Affairs and Finance, ECR,* p. 1383, involving a suit by a French banana importer challenging import restrictions imposed by the French banana market organization; the second was the *Potato* case, Case 231/78,*Commission v. UK, ECR,* 1979, p. 1447, an action by the commission against Britain for the activities of its potato market organization in which the French government supported the British position against the interests of its own potato exporters. The final installment in this saga was a challenge by the commission against the French again, this time for restrictions on sheepmeat from Britain. See Case 232/78, *Commission v. France, ECR,* 1979, p. 2729.

26 Case 22/70, *Commission of the European Communities v. Council of the European Communities, ECR,* 2170 1971:363.1971, p. 363.

27 The classic study documenting this proposition is Eric Stein (1981: 25). Out of ten landmark cases, Stein found only two in which the Court had diverged from the Commission.

28 The most notable proponents of this approach to American judicial politics were Justice Felix Frankfurter and his intellectual protege Alexander Bickel. See Bickel 1970.

Chapter 10

The Politics of Legal Integration in the European Union

Geoffrey Garrett*

Developments in the European Union (EU) since the mid-1980s have generated considerable debate on the dynamics of the pooling of sovereignty and concomitant reductions in the authority of national governments. While most attention has been paid to the EU's internal market and monetary integration, its legal system is the clearest manifestation of burgeoning supranationalism. European law has 'direct effect' in national jurisdictions (that is, it applies even if it has not been incorporated into domestic law). It also has supremacy over conflicting domestic laws. The 1958 Treaty of Rome and its subsequent amendments (the 1987 Single European Act and the 1993 Treaty on European Union) operate as a de facto constitution. Finally, the European Court of Justice (ECJ) exercises judicial review not only over interactions between member states but also over the behavior of governments within their national boundaries.

In a recent article in this journal, Anne-Marie Burley and Walter Mattli offer a neofunctionalist account of this remarkable legal system (Burley and Mattli 1993). They assert that the Court of Justice has been the prime mover in European legal integration and that national governments passively have accepted the court's lead. European law, they argue, operates both as a 'mask' that conceals the real effects of legal integration and as a 'shield' that effectively insulates the legal system from political tampering by member governments. In turn, Burley and Mattli contend that this explanation is superior to what they term the 'neorationalist' accounts that I have given in this journal, and elsewhere with Barry Weingast (see Garrett 1992a; Garrett and Weingast 1993). From this perspective, member governments could, if they so chose, either ignore ECJ decisions or amend the legal order

* Reproduced by kind permission of MIT Press Journals from Geoffrey Garrett (1995) 'The Politics of Legal Integration in the European Union', *International Organization*, 49(1), 171–81. © 1995 by the IO Foundation and the Massachusetts Institute of Technology. The original text is reproduced in full. Where possible, references have been changed to Harvard citation style. Some peripheral footnotes have been omitted.

through multilateral action. The fact that governments have done neither to any important degree thus implies that the extant order serves their interests.

Burley and Mattli claim that these neorationalist propositions lack empirical support. In many important cases, individual governments have fought vehemently against – but then ultimately accepted – adverse rulings by the Court of Justice. Furthermore, neither the SEA nor the Treaty on European Union significantly curtailed the power of the court. In explaining these developments, Burley and Mattli argue 'neorationalism is at a loss. Neofunctionalism is in its element'.

I do not wish to reiterate the general argument made by Weingast and me that the legal order is accepted by member governments because it mitigates the incomplete contracting and monitoring problems that would otherwise hinder the realization of mutual gains from trade liberalization. Rather, I focus here on the behavior of national governments and the Court of Justice in specific cases, as the first step to developing a theory of legal integration with strong microfoundations.

With respect to national governments, I argue that while there are incentives for governments to argue against decisions that declare national practices to be illegal restrictions of EU trade (because trade barriers benefit specific sectors while the costs of protection are widely diffused), this does not mean that governments invariably want to ignore ECJ rulings once they are made (on the first point see Magee et al. 1989). Rather, governments must weigh the costs of accepting the court's decision against the benefits derived from having an effective legal system in the EU (in terms of enhancing the efficacy of the internal market). The costs of acquiescence vary with the economic size and political clout of the adversely affected sectors. The benefits of accepting a decision are a function of the magnitude of the country's economic gains from the internal market. Where the broader benefits a government derives from having an effective legal system underpinning the internal market outweigh the specific domestic costs associated with the court's ruling in a given case, the government's rational strategy will be to accept the decision. I argue that this was precisely the calculation made by the German government in the landmark 1979 case *Cassis de Dijon,* which Burley and Mattli claim is an important example of the inadequacies of the rational government perspective (Burley and Mattli 1993: 51. For the text of *Cassis de Dijon,* see Case 120/78, 1979).

I then extend this line of reasoning by arguing that the Court of Justice is also a strategic rational actor. The justices' primary objective is to extend the ambit of European law and their authority to interpret it. However, they understand that their power is not based on the letter of the EC's treaties but rather depends critically on the continuing acquiescence of national governments. As a result, the court's judicial activism is constrained by the reactions they anticipate from member governments to their decisions. From the court's perspective, the best decisions are those that both expand European law and enhance the court's reputation for constraining powerful member governments. Viewed in this light, one should expect cases similar to *Cassis* to be common, whereas the court is much less likely to take decisions it anticipates that powerful governments would not abide.

Burley and Mattli's Argument

Burley and Mattli's argument consists of three elements. First, the evolution of the European legal system was not foreseen by the signatories to the Treaty of Rome. Second, the primary mechanism for the expansion of European law has been the co-opting of member states' judges (and lawyers) by the ECJ. Finally, national governments have been unable to resist this accretion of authority because the court has couched its behavior in technical and apolitical terms, going no further than faithfully implementing EC treaties.

At one level, the first proposition is incontrovertible: the direct effect and supremacy doctrines were not written into the Rome treaty but were espoused by the Court of Justice in the 1960s and 1970s. It should be remembered, however, that the signatories did choose to create a very powerful legal system – even if the court later built on this foundation.[1] With respect to Burley and Mattli's second proposition, it is true that judges in member states often support the Court of Justice's accretion of power because the doctrines of direct effect and supremacy give domestic judges powers of judicial review that they would otherwise not possess. Some national high courts, however, do exercise judicial review in the purely domestic context, most notably, France's top administrative court, the Conseil d'Etat, and Germany's constitutional court, the Bundesverfassungsgericht. Furthermore, these two courts have chosen on occasion not to follow decisions of the ECJ, which has in turn prompted the court to temper its activism to regain the support of these key national courts. The relationship between national courts and the ECJ is complex and space does not permit a fuller discussion of this issue here (but see Goldman 1993).

In this essay, I concentrate on Burley and Mattli's final claim: that the European legal system is not in the interests of member governments but that they have been unable to reorient the system in accordance with their preferences. One could try to counter this assertion by showing that member governments have, in fact, altered the legal system to constrain the court. But as Burley and Mattli show, although the power of the ECJ was somewhat circumscribed in the SEA and at Maastricht, its fundamental role in the European legal system was not altered (1993: 73–4). Some argue that treaty revision has not been necessary because governments have been able effectively to evade European laws of which they disapprove (see Caporaso and Keeler 1993; Noll 1992). But while compliance with European law is far from perfect, there can be no gain-saying that a surprisingly large number of adverse ECJ decisions are followed by national governments (Garrett 1992a: 555–6).

If member governments have neither changed nor evaded the European legal system, then from a so-called rational government perspective it must be the case that the existing legal order furthers the interests of national governments. To substantiate this claim, one could rely on the general propositions about monitoring and incomplete information that I have developed with Weingast. Burley and Mattli, however, do not take strong exception to these arguments. Rather, they stress, correctly, that the ECJ frequently has taken decisions that were opposed by powerful member governments, and that these governments subsequently have accepted the court's rulings. The next section analyzes this phenomenon.

The German Government and 'Cassis de Dijon'

The facts and importance of *Cassis de Dijon* are well-known. The case helped establish 'mutual recognition' – products that can be sold in one member state be freely available in all others – as the basic principle for trade liberalization in Europe. (For a recent critique of the conventional wisdom about the importance of the *Cassis* decision itself in the completion of the internal market, see Alter and Meunier-Aitsahalia 1994). The Court of Justice ruled that a German regulation blocking the sale of the French liqueur because it did not fit into any accepted German category of alcoholic beverage was an illegal restriction of trade. The German government argued hard in support of its regulatory barrier, but it did not convince the ECJ that there was any acceptable reason to override the principle of free trade (such as protecting the health of German citizens). After the court's decision was taken, the government accepted it and Cassis is now freely available in Germany. Burley and Mattli cite this as a clear instance of the mismatch between rational government precepts and the operation of the EU legal system.

In contrast, I argue that the German government's behavior can easily be explained in terms of its rational self-interest. Consider the government's calculations before the case was decided. The primary cost of a ruling against the German government would have been the political fallout from the loss of market share for adversely affected domestic alcohol producers. These costs were unlikely to be large since not all segments of the German alcohol sector would be hurt by the importation of Cassis. The impact on powerful wine and beer producers would have been minimal. The only firms likely to suffer were those making fortified wines and low-alcohol liqueurs, and these constitute a tiny part of the German economy. The indirect costs of the *Cassis* decision arguably were significantly higher. If all sheltered sectors of the German economy viewed the government's behavior in *Cassis* as a signal of its broader intentions with respect to trade policy, and if these sectors were economically and politically powerful, this would have been a significant constraint on the government. However, the portion of the economy that would be adversely affected in the short term by trade liberalization is smaller in Germany than in any other union member (Smith and Wanke 1993: 537–46). Furthermore, Germany has been able effectively to insulate from EC tampering some of the most important sectors that would be hurt by free trade – such as the public utilities and the financial institutions (Soskice and Vitols 1993; Woolcock et al. 1991). On the other hand, exporters are both economically important and politically influential in Germany, and public support for further European integration was very strong in the late 1970s.

Thus, even on a generous interpretation, the potential costs of the *Cassis* decision for the German government were not large. But this does not mean that there were no incentives for the government to fight hard in the ECJ, particularly if the government anticipated that it would eventually lose the case. The government then could credibly claim not only that it was prepared to fight for the protection of German industry (to attract or maintain the support of the sheltered sectors of the economy) but also that it was a 'good European' (because it accepted that the legal system was the appropriate arbiter in trade disputes, even when this had deleterious consequences for Germany).

After the Court of Justice ruled, however, the strategic calculus of the German government changed dramatically. Germany is the most competitive economy in Europe. As a result, national economic performance would benefit greatly from the removal of further barriers to trade across the continent. Accepting the court's decision would increase the efficacy of German efforts to push for more trade liberalization among member states that benefit less from it ('we are prepared to accept free trade even when it harms segments of our economy in the short run. So should you'). Moreover, if the German government believed that the rule of law and the authority of the ECJ were important to completing the internal market – as Weingast and I argue – the government had every incentive not to undermine the court's authority by visibly flouting one of its decisions. One might even suggest that the Court has tended to act as a de facto agent of the German government by vigorously prosecuting the free trade cause but without extending its reach into other areas of more concern to Germany, such as financial deregulation. It would obviously be better for the German government to have the court rather than the government further the free trade cause (lest the government be accused of bullying).

In sum, the German government's behavior *in Cassis* was wholly rational. The potential domestic political costs of accepting the decision were small because of the weakness of the adversely affected groups, and the government could lessen these even further by fighting the case. In contrast, the potential economic costs of flouting the court's decision – prejudicing the future of free trade in Europe – were substantial in virtue of Germany's preeminent competitive position. The government's strategy of fighting hard in the court but accepting the ultimate decision sent two desirable signals. Domestically, the government indicated its willingness to support sheltered sectors that would be harmed by freer trade. Internationally, the German government underlined its commitment to reciprocal trade liberalization across Europe by accepting a decision that apparently hurt it.

The Government-ECJ Game

It would be unwise to base the case for the analytic power of rational choice merely on *Cassis*. However, space does not allow for a detailed examination of other court cases. Instead, I outline a general model for government-ECJ interactions that suggests why the *Cassis* pattern (the court's ruling against a relatively unimportant sector in a powerful member state) is quite common.

Assume for the moment that the ECJ has made a trade liberalization decision that will hurt a sheltered sector of a national economy. How

Market share and political clout of industry potentially harmed by court decision

		High	Low
Benefit to national economy of trade liberalization	*High*	Justify evasion	Accept
	Low	Overt evasion	Conceal evasion

Figure 1   *Government reponses to adverse decisions by the European Court of Justice*

should the government respond to the decision? Two situations are straightforward, as can be seen in Figure 1. First, where the adversely affected sectors are domestically weak (as in *Cassis*) and the national economy benefits greatly from freer trade in Europe (which is generally the case for the EC's northern core), one should expect governments to accept adverse court decisions. The diametrically opposite case is that in which the harmed sectors are large and powerful (for instance, public utilities) in a country that gains little in the short run from the internal market (typically true for the less developed economies of southern Europe). Here, governments would more likely be prepared to ignore court decisions because the domestic costs of accepting them far outweigh any immediate gains from trade liberalization.

Government behavior is more difficult to predict in the remaining two cells where the domestic and external incentives push in different directions. The government's dilemma is less severe when a decision would affect only a small sector of a less developed economy and the benefits of participation in the internal market in the short term are limited. This is common in southern Europe, and governments often try to conceal evasion and to plead implementation problems if they are caught. The stakes are much higher where the domestic costs of accepting a decision are great, but so, too, are the benefits the national government might reap from trade liberalization in Europe more generally. This would likely be the situation if the court were to rule against implicit barriers to trade in northern Europe provided, for example, by preferential public procurement policies. Here, it would be virtually impossible for the government fully to accept the decision. But on the other hand, one should expect the government to minimize the damage done to the authority of the court and free trade in Europe – either by trying covertly to evade the decision or, if this is not possible, by claiming that the circumstances surrounding the case are exceptional and affect vital national interests.

It is at this point that the strategic behavior of the court needs to be included in the analysis. Up until now, I have focused on the response of governments to court decisions. But as Burley and Mattli acknowledge, the court's thinking is influenced by the reactions it anticipates from member governments: 'the ECJ uses the EC Commission as a political bellwether. In any given case, the ECJ looks to the commission's position as an indicator of the political acceptability to the member states of a particular result or a line of reasoning' (1993: 71). This is because the justices understand that their ability to preside over a powerful European legal system is not written in stone (the EU's treaties do not form a formal constitution). Even though there is no evidence of member governments choosing not to re-appoint justices who fail to do their bidding, the effective authority of the court is contingent upon individual governments neither undermining its legitimacy by flouting its decisions nor weakening its formal powers through treaty revision.[2]

On what basis should the court make its decisions? Legal scholars concentrate on precedent and treaty interpretation. It is clear, however, that in most cases pertaining to the free movement of goods, services, capital, and people (the 'four freedoms' at the core of the EU), there is no coherent legal basis to inform court behavior. The reason for this is the coexistence of contradictory articles in the Rome treaty. Article 30 states that 'quantitative restrictions on imports and all measures having equivalent effect . . . shall be prohibited'. However, Article 36 states that this principle can be violated where the restriction of trade can be 'justified on grounds of public morality, public policy, or public security ... [or] the protection of national treasures.' These exceptions are vague and potentially of wide scope. At maximum, Article 36 could be construed as suggesting that protection is justified where this is consistent with the government's 'public policy' agenda.

When should we expect the court to rule on the basis of Article 30 (free trade) or Article 36 (restricting trade)? ECJ behavior will likely be conditioned by its expectations about the likely responses of member governments. Three different outcomes can be envisaged (see Figure 2). The first is that typified by *Cassis de Dijon*. The court makes an adverse decision (that is, following Article 30) against an unimportant sector in a powerful member state because it expects that the government will accept the decision. Such cases are ideal from the court's perspective because they allow the ECJ to extend its authority – both in terms of the ambit of European law and its reputation for being able to enforce its decisions even against governments from powerful member states without jeopardizing its legitimacy.

The second scenario concerns court decisions against governments from less powerful member states. Given the short-run costs of free trade for these governments, there is a good chance that they will evade the court's decisions (either covertly or, if necessary, overtly),

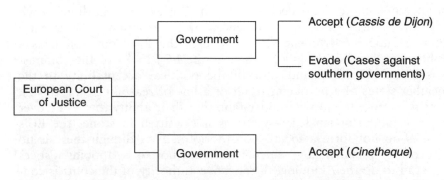

Figure 2 *The European Court of Justice–government game, with applicable*

and this probability increases with the importance of the adversely affected domestic sectors. Should one expect the court to follow Article 30 in such cases? Using the logic of the previous paragraph, one would probably answer no. However, in many instances the court's vigilance in prosecuting for free trade might increase its support among the northern core of the EU that benefits greatly from trade liberalization. Thus, there may be incentives for the court to make adverse decisions against southern member states even if the justices suspect that such decisions will be evaded.

Finally, when the court knows that an adverse decision against an important sector in a powerful member state not only will likely be evaded but also that this behavior will threaten its credibility and power, one should expect the ECJ not to challenge the government (by accepting the existing protectionist behavior under Article 36). A clear recent instance of such a decision is the *Cinetheque* case (*Cinetheque*, 1 CMLR/365, 1986). In this case, a suit was brought against a French government regulation stipulating that films cannot be sold on video-tape until one year after their release in cinemas. The French government argued that this regulation was designed to maintain the French film industry in the face of competition from English-language producers (primarily from the United States), and that the domestic film industry was an essential part of the fabric of French life. The Court of Justice accepted this argument even though the government's practice was a clear violation of free trade. The reason for the court's behavior is clear: it understood that protecting the domestic film industry was a 'no go' area for the French government. Even though the economic size of the sector was small, its symbolic importance was manifestly great.[3] As a result, the ECJ knew that the French government would not abide by a decision to remove this trade protection, and thus the rational course of action for the court was not to rule against the existing restrictive trade practice.

Understanding ECJ-government interactions in these game-theoretic terms sheds considerable light on the evolution of the European legal system. From this perspective, it is not at all surprising that Burley and Mattli can point to numerous court rulings against powerful member governments that the governments subsequently abide. Where the adversely affected domestic sectors are unimportant (as in *Cassis*) the court can further its interests by ruling against the government because it understands that the government is very likely ultimately to accept the decision. But where a powerful government has a strong vested interest in protecting a sector of its economy (as in *Cinetheque*), the court is much less likely to challenge an existing barrier to trade. And in such cases there is no reason for the involved government not to accept the decision. These cases may be less noteworthy for those looking for examples of the erosion of national sovereignty in Europe, but from a gametheoretic perspective they are just as important because they delineate the limits on ECJ power and the importance of national governments to legal integration.

Conclusion

In this short essay, I have argued that one cannot reject neorationalist accounts of European legal integration merely by observing that the Court of Justice often makes decisions that powerful member governments protest but subsequently accept. This behavior is the preferred strategy of governments where the short-run domestic costs of accepting the adverse decision are outweighed by the broader benefits the country derives from trade liberalization in Europe. In other circumstances, national governments should be less likely to acquiesce in adverse ECJ decisions-when the country gains little (at least in the short run) from trade liberalization or when the court's ruling harms a large segment of the domestic economy.

However, viewing legal integration in rational choice terms should not be limited to the decisions of national governments. The Court of Justice is also a strategic actor that takes into account the anticipated responses of national governments before it decides cases brought before it. The court likely will rule against governments in cases where it expects the government ultimately to accept the decision. And the incentives for the court to so act increase when the government is from a powerful member state – in virtue of the enhanced reputation the court would earn from successfully constraining the behavior of a strong government within its own borders. From a game-theoretic perspective, it is not surprising that the *Cassis* pattern recurs quite frequently in Europe; such cases are in the interests both of powerful governments and of the Court of Justice. Thus, the trajectory of legal integration in Europe can be explained in rational choice terms, without recourse to Burley and Mattli's critical assumptions about the ignorance of governments and the innate power of 'the law' – both of which have become increasingly untenable with the heightened visibility and politicization of European law in the past fifteen years.

Notes

1 Articles 169 and 170 allow for cases to be brought in the Court of Justice against national governments for violating their treaty obligations. Art. 171 explicitly states that members must comply with ECJ decisions. Art. 177 encourages national courts to request from the ECJ preliminary rulings on the application of European law to domestic cases. See *Treaties Establishing the European Communities*.

2 The Justices of the ECJ hold renewable six-year terms. Each member government selects one justice; they jointly choose one additional justice.
3 The importance the French government attaches to the film industry was demonstrated graphically in the end game to the Uruguay Round.

Chapter 11

Preferences and Power in the European Community: A Liberal Intergovernmentalist Approach

Andrew Moravcsik*

I Introduction

The European Community (EC) is the most successful example of institutionalized international policy co-ordination in the modern world, yet there is little agreement about the proper explanation for its evolution. From the signing of the Treaty of Rome to the making of Maastricht, the EC has developed through a series of celebrated intergovernmental bargains, each of which set the agenda for an intervening period of consolidation. The most fundamental task facing a theoretical account of European integration is to explain these bargains. Today many would revive neo-functionalism's emphasis on *sui generis* characteristics of EC institutions, in particular the importance of unintended consequences of previous decisions and the capacity of supranational officials to provide leadership.

This article joins the debate by reasserting the self-critique, advanced almost two decades ago by Ernst Haas and other leading neo-functionalists, who suggested that European integration can only be explained with reference to general theories of international relations. The basic claim of this article is that the EC can be analysed as a successful intergovernmental regime designed to manage economic interdependence through negotiated policy co-ordination. Refinements and extensions of existing theories of foreign economic policy, intergovernmental negotiation, and international regimes provide a plausible and generalizable explanation of its evolution. Such theories rest on the assumption that state behavior reflects the rational actions of governments constrained at home by domestic societal pressures and abroad by their

* Reproduced by kind permission of Blackwell Publishing from Andrew Moravcsik (1993) 'Preferences and Power in the European Community: A Liberal Intergovernmentalist Approach', *Journal of Common Market Studies*, 31(4), 473–524. The text has been edited slightly, as indicated, to fit the format of this volume. Some footnotes have been omitted.

strategic environment. An understanding of the preferences and power of its Member States is a logical starting point for analysis. Although the EC is a unique institution, it does not require a *sui generis* theory.
. . . .

II   From Pre-theory to Theory

1   The limitations of neo-functionalism

. . . .

Despite the richness of its insights, neo-functionalism is today widely regarded as having offered an unsatisfactory account of European integration (Cornett and Caporaso 1992; Haas 1975; Hansen 1969; Hoffmann 1966; Keohane and Hoffmann 1991; Keohane and Nye 1975; Taylor 1983; Webb 1983). The most widely-cited reason is empirical: neo-functionalism appears to mispredict both the trajectory and the process of EC evolution. Insofar as neofunctionalism advances a clear prediction about the trajectory of the EC over time, it was that the technocratic imperative would lead to a 'gradual', 'automatic', and 'incremental' progression toward deeper integration and greater supranational influence (Haas 1964: 70; 1967: 327; 1976: 176). Instead, however, the process of Community-building has proceeded in fits and starts through a series of intergovernmental bargains. Nor has the process by which integration takes place supported the neo-functionalist view. Integration has only intermittently spilled over into related sectors and policies and, at least until recently, the autonomous influence of supranational officials has increased slowly and unevenly, if at all.

While empirical critiques of neo-functionalism are not without merit, they should not be overstated. To be sure, the empirical evidence does not seem to confirm the stress placed by neo-functionalism on political spillover and the autonomy of supranational officials. But other premises, particularly the focus on economic interests, may still be viable. It remains plausible, for example, to argue that integration is a distinctive policy response of modem welfare states to rising economic interdependence.

A more incisive criticism of neo-functionalism is theoretical, namely that it failed to generate an enduring research programme because it lacked a theoretical core clearly enough specified to provide a sound basis for precise empirical testing and improvement. Only the early variants of neo-functionalism predicted a steady development toward federalism. Faced with the failure of European integration to advance steadily, and variation in integration across issues, time-periods or countries ('spillback', 'spill-around', 'encapsulation'), however, neofunctionalism provided no clear direction for revision.[1]

As a result, further development in neo-functionalist theory seemed to converge toward an increasingly complex and indeterminate ideal-typical description of the single case of the EC. Increasing numbers of epicyclical modifications and alternative causal mechanisms were introduced, until the predictions became so indeterminate as to preclude precise testing. Descriptions of alternative causal mechanisms proliferated, some diametrically opposed to the theory's initial focus on technocratic management and economic planning. The uneven development of the EC in the 1960s, for example, was interpreted as a result of the influence of 'dramatic political actors', of which de Gaulle was the archetype – an account theoretically unrelated to Haas's earlier predictions and, moreover, empirically unsatisfying, since the malaise outlasted de Gaulle's presidency. By the end of the 1960s, almost any process of decision-making among democratic states was consistent with the theory (Lindberg and Scheingold 1971).

Underlying neo-functionalism's failure to develop predictions about variations in the evolution of the EC was its lack of grounding in underlying general theories of domestic and international political economy. In international political economy (IPE), as in other social phenomena, it is widely accepted that prediction and explanation, particularly over time, require theories that elaborate how self-interested actors form coalitions and alliances, domestically and internationally, and how conflicts among them are resolved. Such theories must be derived independently of the matter being studied, in the sense that they require a set of restrictive microfoundations – assumptions specifying the nature of the fundamental social actors, their preferences, and the constraints they face. In this regard, neo-functionalism is both oddly apolitical and lacking in any aspiration to generality, in that it advances long-term predictions about the future of the EC without underlying, more specific theories that identify the decisive determinants of politicians' choices among competing alternatives. While stressing the domestic politics of economic policy co-ordination, neo-functionalism lacks an equivalent to modern theories of trade policy, which explain government choices on the basis of models of pressure from predictable distributional coalitions. Neo-functionalism, as Lindberg and Scheingold put it, describes domestic processes, but 'says little about *basic causes*' of variation in national demands for integration (Lindberg and Scheingold 1970: 284, emphasis in original). Neo-functionalist analyses of international bargaining point to the existence of dynamics such as log-rolling, compromise, and upgrading the common interest through linkage and supranational mediation, but offer no explanation – except the variable skill of supranational leaders – of how governments choose among them.

Neo-functionalism's *ad hoc* approach eventually detached it from rich currents in general theories of IPE over the past two decades (cf.

Keohane and Nye 1975). With the exception of a few studies of (largely unsuccessful) attempts at regional integration among developing countries, the EC came to be treated as a *sui generis* phenomenon, thereby impeding efforts at theoretical generalization.[2] This was based in large part on the *a priori* expectation that Europe would develop in a federal direction, which led neofunctionalists to stress the uniqueness of its institutional structure, rather than analogies to other forms of interstate co-operation. The possibility of explaining integration in terms of theories of interdependence, regimes or other generalizable phenomena was thereby lost, while the potential for useful comparison and theoretical development remained limited (Pentland 1973: 189–94). For this reason, neo-functionalism remains today an inductively derived ideal-type, rather than a general theory – in the words of its creator, a pre-theory of regional integration.

2   The legacy of neo-functionalism

The success of the EC in recent years has fuelled efforts among scholars to resurrect neo-functionalist models, in particular those that stress the unintended consequences for Member States of leadership exercised by supranational actors including Commission officials and European parliamentarians (Pederson 1992; Peterson and Bomberg 1993; Ross 1992; Sandholtz 1992). This body of work repeats many neo-functionalist themes, if sometimes by other names. Yet current efforts to resurrect neo-functionalism rarely address the *conclusions that neo-functionalists themselves drew* about the weaknesses of their approach, nor do they consider the implications for current theory-building of theoretical developments in international relations (IR) theory over the intervening two decades. The functionalist legacy, combined with contemporary theories of IPE, suggests at least three important conclusions.

First, by 1975 leading neo-functionalists were nearly unanimous in arguing that 'regional integration theory', which had sought to explain the progress of the EC along the *sui generis* path toward a future federalist endpoint should be supplemented, perhaps supplanted, by a *general* theory of national policy responses to international interdependence. Rather than focusing on the future aspirations that make the EC unique, neo-functionalists argued that the emphasis should be on generalizable aspects of the current activities of the EC. Recognizing the central importance of economic management among those activities, Haas came to believe that 'the study of regional integration should be both included in and subordinated to the study of changing patterns of interdependence' (Haas 1975).

In the language of modern theories of IPE, this implies that the EC should be treated as an international regime designed to promote policy co-ordination. As Hoffmann, Haas's erstwhile critic asserted in

1982, 'the best way of analyzing the EEC is . . . as an international regime (Hoffmann 1982: 33). International regimes promulgate principles, norms, rules and decision-making procedures around which actor expectations converge in given issue-areas, through which 'the actions of separate individuals or organizations – which are not in pre-existing harmony – [are] brought into conformity with one another through a process of negotiation . . . often referred to as policy co-ordination' (Keohane 1984: 51; Krasner 1983: 1). Regime theory provides a plausible starting point for analysis – a set of common conceptual and theoretical tools that can help structure comparisons with other international organizations, as well as internal comparisons among different cases of EC policy-making. At the same time, however, contemporary regime analysis requires refinement to take account of the unique institutional aspects of policy co-ordination within the EC, as evidenced by the depth of its purported goals, the richness of the networks it sustains, and, above all, the solidity of its supranational legal identity (Keohane and Hoffmann 1991).

Second, the neo-functionalist legacy suggests that explanations of integration require stronger underlying theories of variation in substantive, as well as institutional, outcomes. The neo-functionalists were concerned overridingly with 'tracing progress toward a terminal condition called *political community* – the evolution of a unique, potentially federal political structure in Europe that would prevent war and guarantee peaceful change' (Haas 1961; Lindberg and Scheingold 1970: 99). Accordingly, they limited their definition of integration almost exclusively to institutional characteristics of the EC – the scope and institutional form of common decision-making. This discouraged attention to distributional conflicts in the EC over issues such as the level of external tariffs, agricultural prices, or regulatory harmonization, which require attention to the substantive measures of policy co-ordination. An instructive example is the creation of the CAP in the 1960s. While the neo-functionalists emphasize the Commission's success in creating a policy *formally* under the control of the EC, they overlook the fact that it was a defeat for the Commission's original *substantive* proposal, which foresaw a prudently limited, self-financing, relatively low-price regime.[3]

A broader definition of European integration might consider four dimensions of policy co-ordination: (1) the *geographical scope* of the regime; (2) the *range* of issues in which policies are co-ordinated; (3) the *institutions* of joint decision-making, implementation and enforcement; (4) the *direction and magnitude of substantive domestic policy adjustment*. These four elements may be thought of as different dimensions of the same underlying variable, namely policy co-ordination. While the first three are similar to those employed by neofunctionalists, the fourth – the direction and magnitude of substantive policy adjustment – is based on the view that policy co-ordination is most significant where it imposes greater adjustment on domestic policy. Since the costs and benefits of the necessary adjustments generally vary across countries, the measure also helps in the analysis of distributional conflict.

Third, by the 1970s, many neo-functionalists had concluded that unicausal theories are unable to account for EC policy-making. More than one theory is required (Cornett and Caporaso 1992; Pentland 1973: 189–94; Puchala 1972). Modern theories of IPE suggest a number of empirical, theoretical and philosophical reasons, discussed in more detail in the next section, to treat the need for multicausal explanation as a *general* principle. Empirically robust explanations of international policy co-ordination are likely to incorporate, at a minimum, theories of both national preference formation and intergovernmental negotiation, each grounded in explicit assumptions about actor preferences, constraints and choices (Moravcsik 1992b). The vagueness of neo-functionalist predictions suggest, moreover, that only such theories can explain, rather than simply describe, the evolution of the EC. Only by meeting these criteria, most neo-functionalists felt, could scholars move from 'pre-theory' to theory.

3 Liberal intergovernmentalism and the rationality assumption

Rather than resurrecting neo-functionalism, the approach introduced here takes seriously the self-criticisms of neo-functionalists examined above. They point toward a conception of the EC more closely in line with contemporary theories of IPE. Such theories suggest that the EC is best seen as an international regime for policy co-ordination, the substantive and institutional development of which may be explained through the sequential analysis of national preference formation and intergovernmental strategic interaction.

This section proposes a framework within which to construct such an explanation, termed 'liberal intergovernmentalism'. Liberal intergovernmentalism builds on an earlier approach, 'intergovernmental institutionalism', by refining its theory of interstate bargaining and institutional compliance, and by adding an explicit theory of national preference formation grounded in liberal theories of international interdependence (Moravcsik 1991). Various specific points seek to refine and extend the existing literature, but the result is broadly consistent with current theories of IPE, in particular endogenous tariff theory, negotiation analysis, and functional explanations of international regimes.

At the core of liberal intergovernmentalism are three essential elements: the assumption of rational state behaviour, a liberal theory of national preference formation, and an intergovernmentalist analysis of interstate negotiation. The assumption of rational state behaviour provides a general framework of analysis, within which the costs and benefits of economic interdependence are the primary determinants of national preferences, while the relative intensity of national preferences, the existence of alternative coalitions, and the opportunity for issue linkages provide the basis for an intergovernmental analysis of the resolution of distributional conflicts among governments. Regime theory is employed as a starting point for an analysis of conditions under which governments will delegate powers to international institutions.

Much contemporary IR-theory is based on the assumption of state rationality. State action at any particular moment is assumed to be minimally rational, in that it is purposively directed toward the achievement of a set of consistently ordered goals or objectives.[4] Governments evaluate alternative courses of action on the basis of a utility function. The approach taken here departs decisively, however, from those theories in IR, most notably realist and neo-realist approaches, which treat states as 'billiard balls' or 'black boxes' with fixed preferences for wealth, security or power. Instead, governments are assumed to act purposively in the international arena, but on the basis of goals that are defined domestically. Following liberal theories of IR, which focus on state-society relations, the foreign policy goals of national governments are viewed as varying in response shifting pressure from domestic social groups, whose preferences are aggregated through political institutions. National interests are, therefore, neither invariant nor unimportant, but emerge through domestic political conflict as societal groups compete for political influence, national and transnational coalitions form, and new policy alternatives are recognized by governments. An understanding of domestic politics is a precondition for, not a supplement to, the analysis of the strategic interaction among states (Moravcsik 1991, 1992b).

The model of rational state behaviour on the basis of domestically-constrained preferences implies that international conflict and co-operation can be modelled as process that takes place in two successive stages: governments first define a set of interests, then bargain among themselves in an effort to realize those interests. Metaphorically, these two stages shape demand and supply functions for international co-operation. A domestic preference formation process identifies the potential benefits of policy co-ordination perceived by national governments (demand), while a process of interstate strategic interaction defines the possible political responses of the EC political system to pressures from those governments (supply). The interaction of demand and supply, of preference and strategic opportunities, shapes the foreign policy behaviour of states.[5]

This conception of rationality suggests that parsimonious explanations of international conflict or co-operation can be constructed by employing two types of theory sequentially: a theory of national preference formation *and* a theory of interstate strategic interaction. Unicausal explanations of European integration, which seek to isolate either demand or supply are at best incomplete and at worst misleading ... Explaining the emergence in 1978–9 of the European Monetary System, for example, requires that we understand both the convergence of macroeconomic policy preferences, which led European governments to favour monetary co-ordination, *and* the determinants of the outcomes of the tough interstate bargaining that took place over the precise terms under which it would take place.

Thus liberal intergovernmentalism integrates within a single framework two types of general IR-theory often seen as contradictory: a liberal theory of national preference formation and an intergovernmentalist analysis of interstate bargaining and institutional creation.[6] In the sections that follow, these sequential components are developed in more detail.

III Liberalism, National Preference Formation and the Demand for Integration

1 Liberalism and state-society relations

The theory of national preference formation set out in this section is liberal in inspiration. Liberal theories of IR focus on the effect of state-society relations in shaping national preferences. They assume that private individuals and voluntary associations with autonomous interests, interacting in civil society, are the most fundamental actors in politics. State priorities and policies are determined by politicians at the head of the national government, who 'are embedded in domestic and transnational civil society, which decisively constrains their identities and purposes'.[7] The most fundamental influences on foreign policy are, therefore, the identity of important societal groups, the nature of their interests, and their relative influence on domestic policy. Groups that stand to gain and lose a great deal per capita tend to be the most influential. The identity, interests, and influence of groups vary across time, place and, especially, issue-area, according to the net expected costs and benefits of potential foreign policies. The factors that determine the identity, interests and influence of domestic groups are themselves both domestic and transnational. In this sense, 'second image reversed' theories, which assume that international constraints create patterns of societal interests that influence governments via the 'transmission belt' of domestic politics, are characteristically liberal.[8] But so are theories that stress purely domestic state-society relations, due to the nature of domestic political and socio-economic institutions.

Groups articulate preferences; governments aggregate them. For lib erals, the relationship between society and the government is assumed to be one of principal-agent; societal principals delegate power to (or otherwise constrain) governmental agents. The primary interest of governments is to maintain themselves in office; in democratic societies, this requires the support of a coalition of domestic voters, parties, interest groups and bureaucracies, whose views are transmitted, directly or indirectly, through domestic institutions and practices of political representation. Through this process emerges the set of national interests or goals that states bring to international negotiations.

This is not to say that all foreign policy proposals begin with direct pressure from pluralist groups, only that state leaders must construct governing coalitions out of influential groups with specific interests. Sometimes the influence of societal groups is indirect. In economic affairs, for example, some firms and groups, particularly those with fixed investments and assets, may seek to influence governments directly, exercising the option of voice, others, particularly those with more mobile investments and assets, may find it less expensive to shift investments to alternative activities or jurisdictions, exercising the option of 'exit' (Bates and Lien 1985; Hirschman 1970; Lindblom 1977; Magee et al. 1989: 13, 93, 102). In the liberal view, even the latter constraint ultimately rests on the desire of politicians to avoid imposing costs on – and thereby alienating – those social groups whose support maintains them in office.

Yet the interests of societal groups are not always sharply defined. Where societal pressure is ambiguous or divided, governments acquire a range of discretion. While domestic societal groups impose a basic constraint on governments the nature and tightness of this constraint varies with the strength and intensity of pressures from social groups. At times the principal-agent relationship between social pressures and state policies is tight; at times, 'agency slack' in the relationship permits rational governments to exercise greater discretion.[9]

The liberal focus on domestic interests and state-society relations is consistent with a number of plausible motivations for government to support (or oppose) European integration. These include federalist (or nationalist) beliefs, national security concerns and economic interests . . . Elsewhere these alternative specifications of liberal theory are tested against one another (Moravcsik 1992a); here the focus is on motivations that stem from economic interdependence and the ways in which they constrain governmental preferences in international negotiations.

2 Interdependence, externalities and co-operation

At the core of liberal theories of economic interdependence lies the claim that increasing transborder flows of goods, services, factors, or pollutants create 'international policy externalities' among nations, which in turn create incentives for policy co-ordination. International policy externalities arise where the policies of one government create costs and benefits for politically significant social groups outside its national jurisdiction. Where the achievement of domestic governmental goals depends on the policies of its foreign counterparts, national policies are interdependent and policy externalities can arise (Cooper, 1986: 292–3).

National governments have an incentive to co-operate where policy co-ordination increases their control over domestic policy outcomes, permitting them to achieve goals that would not otherwise be possible. This situation arises most often where co-ordination eliminates negative international policy externalities ... Negative policy externalities occur where the policies of one nation imposes costs on the domestic nationals of another, thereby undermining the goals of the second government's policies. Examples include protectionist barriers against flows of foreign goods and capital, competitive devaluation, and lax domestic environmental pollution standards. Each of these policies may impose costs on foreign nationals, thereby undermining the policy goals of foreign governments ...

In the modern international political economy, policy co-ordination has two major purposes, each of which aims at removing a negative policy externality. The first is the accommodation of economic interdependence through *reciprocal market liberalization*. Restrictions on imports and exports are not simply of interest to domestic societal groups, but to their counterparts abroad as well. The liberalization of the movement of goods, services and factors of production may promote modernization and a more efficient allocation of domestic resources, favouring producers in internationally competitive sectors and owners of internationally scarce factors of production. Restrictions on imports of goods and factors impose policy externalities on potential foreign exporters, investors and immigrants.

The second major purpose of economic policy co-ordination is policy harmonization in order to assure the continued provision of public goods for which the state is domestically responsible, such as socio-economic equality, macroeconomic stability and regulatory protection. National welfare provision, monetary policy, labour market controls, product regulation and many other domestic policies rely for their effectiveness on the separation of markets for goods, services, factors and pollutants. Where economic interdependence links jurisdictions, divergent national policies may undermine each other's effectiveness. Co-ordinated (or common) policies may therefore result in greater de facto control over domestic policy outcomes than unilateral efforts (Cooper 1972).

Contrary to the beliefs often attributed to them, liberals do not argue that cooperation to achieve trade liberalization and the common provision of public goods is inevitably supported by all governments. The vulnerability of governments to negative externalities may vary greatly: some are able to sustain effective policies autonomously, others remain vulnerable to negative externalities from policies abroad. While the latter have an incentive to support international policy co-ordination, those that produce negative externalities or benefit from the positive externalities of others have an incentive to free ride on the domestic policies of their neighbours, rather than cooperate (Keohane and Nye 1989: 12ff). Only where the policies of two or more governments create negative policy externalities for one another, and unilateral adjustment strategies are ineffective, inadequate or expensive, does economic interdependence create an unambiguous incentive to co-ordinate policy.[10]

3   The distributional consequences of policy co-ordination

Even where agreements are mutually beneficial, governments often have different preferences concerning the distribution of the benefits, leading to conflict over the precise terms of co-operation.[11] The costs and benefits of policy-coordination are often unevenly distributed among and within nations rendering nearly inevitable a measure of international and domestic conflict between winners and losers. To the extent that it takes domestic and international distributional conflict into account, liberal interdependence theory does not, as some have suggested, assume the existence of a harmony of interests or a simple correlation between potential transactions and co-operation. Nations and domestic groups that are disadvantaged by policy co-ordination are likely to oppose it. Only where governments can collectively overcome such opposition is co-operation possible. The distribution of expected net societal costs provides a means of predicting the nature of political conflict and co-operation in the EC, both internationally and domestically.[12]

Domestically, governments participating in international negotiations are both empowered and constrained by important societal groups, which calculate their interests in terms of the expected gains and losses from specific policies (Frieden 1991a; Gourevitch 1986; Milner 1988; Odell, 1982). Powerful groups disadvantaged by co-operation will seek to obstruct government policy, even where such policies generate net gains for society as a whole. To understand and predict the likelihood of international co-operation in any given instance, therefore, requires a more precise specification of domestic societal interests in particular issue-areas and the ways in which those interests constrain governments.

Societal pressure on national governments reflects not only the expected magnitude of gains and losses, but also the uncertainty and risk involved. The magnitude, certainty and risk of domestic distributional effects of policy coordination determines not only the goals of respective governments, but the extent to which governments can afford to be flexible in negotiation. At one extreme, where the net costs and benefits of alternative policies are certain, significant and risky, individual citizens and firms have a strong incentive to mobilize politically. In such circumstances, unidirectional pressure from cohesive groups of producers or organized private interests imposes a strict constraint on government policy. The prospects for international agreement will depend almost entirely on the configuration of societal preferences; in negotiations, governments have little flexibility in making concessions, proposing linkages, managing adjustment or otherwise settling on the 'lowest common denominator'. International agreement requires that the interests of dominant domestic groups in different countries converge; where they diverge, co-ordination is precluded. Such conditions are approximated in EC negotiations over agricultural prices, and EC bargaining positions are dictated by pressures from interest groups.

At the other extreme, where the net costs and benefits of alternative policies are diffuse, ambiguous or insignificant, and the risk is low, the societal constraints on governments are looser (cf. Buchanan and Tullock 1962: 789). Under such circumstances, leading politicians enjoy a wider range of de facto choice in negotiating strategies and positions. More than one policy is likely to be consistent with the basic desire of politicians to remain in government. The slack in the principal-agent relationship between society and the state permits governments to assume more political risk by taking a more 'enlightened' or longer-term view, balancing winners and losers to construct broader coalitions, accepting short-term losses for long-term gains, or pursuing more ideologically controversial goals.

4 Policy areas and national preferences in the EC

Different policy areas engender characteristic distributions of costs and benefits for societal groups, from which follow variations in patterns of domestic political mobilization, opportunities for governments to circumvent domestic opposition, and motivations for international co-operation.[13] EC policy areas can be divided into three categories on the basis of policy objectives: the liberalization of the exchange of private goods and services, the provision of socio-economic collective goods, and the provision of non-economic collective goods.

Commercial policy, market access and producer interests

At the core of the EC is its Internal Market. The most basic EC policies – including internal market policy, agricultural policy, competition policy, industrial policy, and research and development policy – are designed to liberalize or eliminate distortions in markets for private goods and services. Modern theories of commercial policy begin by assuming that individual and group support for liberalization and protection reflects, to a first approximation, the net expected costs and benefits of the policy change (Hillman 1989; Magee et al. 1989). Social groups with an intense interest in a given policy are more likely to mobilize than those with a weak interest, since higher per capita gains support the costs of locating, organizing, monitoring and representing concentrated groups. This tends to create a systematic political bias in favour of producers vis-à-vis those with more diffuse interests, such as tax-payers and individual consumers, or those with no direct access to the political process, such as foreign producers (Hillman 1989; Olson 1965). Following endogenous tariff theory, the approach employed here assumes that societal groups mobilized around commercial policy issues are composed almost exclusively of domestic producers, whether drawn from labour or capital, who organize by sector on the basis of calculations of net expected costs and benefits resulting from the introduction of new policies.[14]

Among producers, the net expected costs and benefits of liberalization reflect the following factors. First, *the extent to which individual producers profit from commercial liberalization depends most fundamentally on their competitive positions in domestic and international markets.*[15] Protectionist policies not only redistribute domestic wealth from consumers to sheltered producers, but also create negative policy externalities for exporters excluded from potential markets. Accordingly, exporters and multinational investors tend to support freer trade, which increases their profits; import-competing producers tend to oppose free trade, which undermines their profitability. Where adjustment is relatively costless or compensation between winners and losers can be arranged, distributional effects need not create opposition to free trade. Where adjustment and compensation are costly, however, a domestic prisoners dilemma among domestic veto groups – each of which seeks to be exempted from disadvantageous policy changes, leading to a suboptimal outcome for society as a whole – translates into an international prisoner's dilemma, in which each government seeks to shelter its weakest sectors from international market pressure. Policy co-ordination helps overcome these dilemmas by balancing the gains and losses of free trade within and across countries, thereby creating viable domestic coalitions in favour of liberalization.[16]

. . . .

Second, *cross-cutting or balanced patterns of interests internalize the costs and benefits of trade liberalization* to the same sets of firms and sectors, creating a cross-cutting set of interests that undermines opposition to liberalization. Most importantly, intra-industry trade and investment patterns reduce the net effects on the positions of individual producers and sectors.[17] Even producers facing substantial import-competition have an incentive to support free trade if loss of domestic market share is offset by exports, control over foreign producers, or receipts from foreign investments. The risk of a large loss is reduced as well. Producers of finished goods also form concentrated interest groups in favour of free trade in raw materials and intermediate inputs.

Third, *where the effects of policy changes are uncertain, organized opposition to government initiatives is diluted.* Uncertainty about the effects of cooperation arises where policies are stated vaguely, left to future negotiation, mediated by complex market processes, or applied in an unpredictable way across a population. Uncertain policies engender less opposition than those that are immediate, precise and targeted. Policies often become more controversial as specific provisions are negotiated and the real effects become evident – as occurred in implementing EC agricultural, transport and competition policy in the 1950s and 1960s.

In many cases, pressure from private economic interests is enough to convince governments to liberalize. Where the net expected costs and benefits to firms and sectors are significant, unambiguous and predictable for important segments of domestic producers, pressures from producer interests will impose a relatively tight constraint on state policy. Most agricultural sectors, as well as industries with chronic surplus capacity, are characterized by inter-industry trade patterns, uniform and calculable interests, and high fixed, irreversible investments and assets. Net commodity exporting countries demanded liberalization; net commodity importing countries resisted it. In the CAP, interstate bargains have been possible only on the basis of lowest common denominator log-rolling agreements in individual sectors, with the costs passed on to consumers and foreign producers. Direct pressure from producer interests in the EC has created and maintained a system of high agricultural prices and managed trade, regardless of the preferences of politicians.

In other cases, the decision to liberalize reflects not just pressure from narrow interests, but a broader calculation on the part of the government. When net expected costs are insignificant, ambiguous, balanced or uncertain, governments enjoy a greater autonomy from particularistic domestic groups that oppose co-operation, which they can employ to create support for broader societal goals. This they can do by negotiating international compromises and issue linkages, which creates viable coalitions by balancing winners against losers. By subsidizing the costs of adjustment, or by balancing losses of domestic market share with gains in foreign markets, they can also mute opposition to liberalization. Both agricultural trade liberalization in Germany and industrial trade liberalization in France were accompanied by large domestic subsidies to uncompetitive producers expressly designed to finance adjustment. The more governments are able to act independently of groups disadvantaged by a policy, thereby trading off gains and losses over a larger constituency, the more we should observe the compromises and 'upgrading the common interest' predicted by neo-functionalists. Whereas neo-functionalism stresses the autonomy of supranational officials, liberal intergovernmentalism stresses the autonomy of national leaders.

. . . .

Socio-economic public goods provision

EC policies are not limited to the co-ordination of explicit market liberalization policies, but include also the coordination of domestic policies designed to redress market failures or provide public goods, such as those that assure macroeconomic stability, social security, environmental protection, public health and safety standards, and an acceptable distribution of income. Rising economic interdependence often exacerbates the tension between uncoordinated national policies, the effectiveness of which often requires that either national markets be separated or national policies be harmonized (Cooper 1972). Transborder inflows of air and water pollution can undermine the effectiveness of national environmental policies; capital outflows can undermine the credibility of domestic monetary policy; 'social dumping' can undermine the competitiveness of industry and the viability of social compromises.

As with commercial policy, an incentive for international policy co-ordination exists when the configuration of domestic policies produces negative policy externalities – domestic problems that cannot be resolved through domestic regulation, because of interference from policies pursued by foreign governments – for more than one country: Negotiated policy co-ordination typically involves some surrender of domestic policy autonomy in exchange for a similar surrender on the part of other countries. Where domestic policy instruments remain effective, governments will continue to maintain them; but where governments have exhausted all cost-effective domestic means of achieving domestic policy targets, they have an incentive to turn to international coordination. Accordingly, policy co-ordination will typically be sought particularly by smaller governments, with little control over their domestic markets and high economic interdependence, and by those, generally with high levels of domestic public goods provision, whose policies are particularly vulnerable to disruption.

Many socio-economic public goods policies have important implications for international commerce. The effects of uncoordinated policies – exchange rate shifts, disparate production and product standards, or divergent social welfare policies – may distort or obstruct international commerce. Therefore, in contrast to pure commercial liberalization, the international co-ordination of such policies raises a 'two-dimensional' issue, in that governments must strike a balance between two independently valued policy targets: flows of economic transactions and levels of public goods provision. To the extent that governments are concerned about trade liberalization, the incentives for international and domestic co-operation and conflict will resemble those in issues of pure commercial policy. However, where governments are primarily concerned with the provision of domestic public goods, the level of conflict and co-operation among governments depends on the extent to which national policy goals are compatible. When governments have divergent macroeconomic, environmental and social goals, then co-ordination is likely to be costly and difficult. International conflict emerges over the division of the burden of adjustment. The more divergent national policies are to begin with, the greater the costs of co-operation. Nonetheless, where these costs are outweighed by the interest in reducing negative policy externalities, international policy co-ordination can help governments reach an optimal balance between increased market access and the maintenance of regulatory standards.[18]

Due to the 'two-dimensional' nature of the public goods issues, the range of mobilized interests is typically broader than in commercial policy. Whereas in pure commercial policy, the 'public interest' is pursued almost entirely by national governments, backed by broad coalitions of interested parties, the public interest is represented in public goods concerns by pressure from public interest groups and mass publics. Where existing domestic policy reflects widespread popular support, domestic regulations are likely to be resistant to the changes required to achieve international harmonization. Alongside producer interest, non-producers may either influence policy directly, as when environmental interest groups mobilize opposition, or punish or reward the government for the results of policy, as when voters respond to recent macroeconomic performance.

As in commercial policy, the level of constraint on governments varies, depending on the intensity and calculability of private interests. Policies involving the direct regulation of goods and production processes tend to engender strong mobilization of producer groups, while the co-ordination of policies to provide macroeconomic public goods, including pollution, inflation, unemployment and the aggregate distribution of income, generates a more diffuse pattern of societal interests. Most producers have more ambiguous and variable interests in public goods provision – e.g. the value of the currency the level of domestic inflation, or the aggregate level of pollution – than in issues of pure commercial policy. Where strong commercial or public interests are fulfilled in their demands for policy co-ordination, governments will act accordingly. Often, however, the results of negative externalities and policy failure are more diffuse, leading to a more general economic or regulatory crisis. In the latter case, governments may act without direct pressure from interested parties.

Macroeconomic policy provides an illustrative example. While groups do organize around the trade-related costs and benefits of monetary management (Frieden 1991b), these incentives are often offset by other concerns. While currency depreciation increases the competitiveness of domestically-produced tradeable goods, it also raises the costs of imported intermediate inputs and raw materials, as well as increasing the risk of longer-term inflation. Domestic monetary policy is influenced by the autonomy of domestic monetary institutions and the identity of the party in power, among other things. Recent steps toward European monetary integration, for example, reflect a set of national commitment to macroeconomic discipline imposed by the unsustainability of domestic policies in the face of increased international capital mobility. Only once domestic policies had converged substantially did more intensive international co-operation become conceivable. When they diverged the system once again came under pressure.

Political co-operation, EC institutions, and general income transfers

Some EC policies cannot be interpreted as direct responses to policy externalities imposed by economic interdependence. Some, such as a common foreign and security policy, aim to provide non-socio-economic collective goods; others, such as general European Community institutions and transnational (regional and structural) income transfers, exist either for their own sake or to facilitate other policies. Liberal theory suggests that fundamental constraints on national preferences will reflect the costs and benefits to societal actors; where these are weak, uncertain or diffuse, governments will be able to pursue broader or more idiosyncratic goals.

The costs and benefits created by *political co-operation* for private groups are diffuse and uncertain. Private producers take little interest in political cooperation, leaving domestic influence over the policy almost exclusively to partisan elites, with a secondary, intermittent constraint imposed by mass publics. The reasoning used to justify policies tends to be symbolic and ideological, rather than calculated and concrete. The inherent incalculability of gains and losses in these policy areas accounts for a troubling neo-functionalist anomaly, namely the manifest importance of ideologically motivated heads of state ('dramatic-political' actors) in matters of foreign policy and institutional reform. The difficulty of mobilizing interest groups under conditions of general uncertainty about specific winners and losers permits the positions of governments, particularly larger ones, on questions of European institutions and common foreign policy, to reflect the ideologies and personal commitments of leading executive and parliamentary politicians, as well as interest-based conceptions of the national interest. This may help explain the ability and willingness of national-ists like Charles de Gaulle and Margaret Thatcher to adopt an uncom-promising position toward the dilution of national sovereignty, as well as support by various European leaders for direct elections to the European Parliament, the creation of the European Council, and the quiet development of European Political Co-operation – each an issue in which the costs and benefits to organized interest groups is near impossible to calculate.

Similarly, the politics of decisions about *EC institutions* vary widely, depending on the nature of the decision-making process to be institu-tionalized. Where the consequences of institutional decisions are calcu-lable and concrete, national positions will be instrumental, reflecting the expected influence of institutional reforms on the realization of substantive interests. This is, for example, generally the case with deci-sions about majority voting on specific economic policies. Moreover, some delegations of power are viewed as necessary for the effective functioning of the EC. These institutions – to which we shall return in Section IV below – include common representation in international negotiation, the Commission's power of proposal under QMV, and enforcement of EC rules by the ECJ and the Commission.

The more general and less predictable the implications of decisions on the relative power of institutions, the larger the space for leading politicians and partisan elites to act on the basis of ideological predilec-tions. National interests would lead one to expect large, self-sufficient and uncompetitive countries, as well as those that hold outlier prefer-ences on questions of public goods provision, to be relatively unwilling to accept stronger supranational institutions, such as majority voting or a European Parliament. British and French policy provides some support for this view, but Italy's consistent federalism remains an exception. Similarly, smaller countries might be expected to support strong supranational power. The Benelux countries have indeed done so, yet Danish, Greek and Irish support has been less consistent. National parliamentary elites appear to play an important role in countries like Italy, Germany and the Netherlands, which support fed-eralist institutions.

Regional and structural policies – since they are neither significant enough to provide major benefits to the donors, nor widely enough distributed to represent a policy of common interest – are most plau-sibly interpreted as side payments extended in exchange for other poli-cies.

5 Conclusion

This section has employed and extended contemporary theories of IPE to predict the national preferences of EC Member States across three types of issues: commercial policy, socio-economic public goods provision, and other institutional, political or structural policies. In each case, the magnitude, distribution and certainty of net expected costs and benefits to private groups were employed to predict policy preferences of governments, as well as their range of relative autonomy vis-à-vis those domestic groups that oppose cooperation. This defines the demand for international cooperation; in the next section, we turn to the capacity of the international system to supply cooperation.

IV   Intergovernmentalism, Interstate Bargaining and the Supply of Integration

Intergovernmentalist theory seeks to analyse the EU as the result of strategies pursued by rational governments acting on the basis of their preferences and power. The major agenda-setting decisions in the history of the EC, in which common policies are created or reformed, are negotiated intergovernmentally, but can they be consistently explain in terms of a theory of interstate bargaining? Like many international negotiations, EC decisions of this kind can this be thought of as a game of co-ordination with distributional consequences – in other words, a bargaining game over the terms of co-operation (Garrett 1992b; Krasner, 1991; Sebenius 1991). The configuration of domestically determined national preferences defines a 'bargaining space' of potentially viable agreements, each of which generates gains for one or more participants. Governments, if they are to pursue a common policy, must collectively select one. The choice between different agreements often has important distributional consequences; governments are therefore rarely indifferent among them. Negotiation is the process of collective choice through which conflicting interests are reconciled.

Bargaining games raise two analytical problems. Lax and Sebenius (1986) refer to these as problems of 'creating' and 'claiming' value. They might be thought of also as co-ordination and bargaining aspects of strategic interaction. The first problem concerns the efficiency of negotiations. Negotiations create value by facilitating mutually beneficial exchanges, but excessive costs of identifying, negotiating and enforcing bargains may obstruct co-operation. Strategic behaviour may lead governments to withhold information about mutually beneficial bargains, negotiation may require costly threats, enforcement may be expensive or impossible. International institutions can help to ameliorate some of these problems by proposing potential agreements, providing rules for decision-making, and the adjudication of disputes. The second problem concerns the distributional implications of interstate bargaining. The choice of a specific outcome from among many possible ones determines the distribution of expected costs and benefits among national governments. Governments bargain hard for advantage. In order to explain bargaining outcomes, it is necessary to understand the factors that account for the relative power.

Creating and claiming value often occur simultaneously, but they can be divided for analytical purposes. In the following section, the focus is on the distributional implications. Strategic interaction is assumed to be efficient, the choice of agreements is restricted to those along the Pareto-frontier, and the analysis focuses on the international distribution of gains and losses. In the following section, in which the role of supranational institutions in assuring efficient bargaining outcomes is addressed, these assumptions are then relaxed.

Bargaining power and the intensity of preferences

Negotiation analysis has identified numerous factors that may influence the distributional outcomes of international bargaining, among them the nature of the alternative policies and coalitions, the level and symmetry of information, the extent of communication, the sequence of moves, the institutional setting, the potential for strategic misrepresentation of interests, the possibility of making credible commitments, the importance of reputation, the cost-effectiveness of threats and side-payments, and the relative preferences, risk-acceptance, expectations, impatience, and skill of the negotiating parties (Harsanyi 1977; Raiffa 1982). In the abstract, any of these factors might be important predictors of bargaining outcomes.

To generate precise and accurate predictions about a set of comparable cases, such as major EC decisions, detailed assumptions must be made about the situation in which the parties are bargaining . . .

The following three assumptions about interstate bargaining offer a plausible starting point for analysis of EC decision-making. First, intergovernmental co-operation in the EC is voluntary, in the sense that neither military coercion nor economic sanctions are threatened or deployed to force agreement. . . . Thus, fundamental decision in the EC can be viewed as taking place in a non-coercive unanimity voting system. Second, the environment in which EC governments bargaining is relatively information-rich. National negotiators are able to communicate at low cost and possess information about the preferences and opportunities facing their foreign counterparts, as well as the technical implications of policies that are of the greatest interest to them (Moravcsik 1993b). Third, the transaction costs of intergovernmental bargaining are low. Negotiations within the EC take place over a protracted period of time, during which member governments can extend numerous offers and counter-offers at relatively little cost. Side-payments and linkages can be made. Governments can credibly commit themselves to substantive policies through explicit institutional arrangements. Technically, it is possible to design efficient institutions to monitor and enforce any agreement at any desired level. (The assumption of low transaction costs is relaxed in a later section of this article.)

The assumption of a non-coercive, information-rich, deliberative, institutionalized setting may not be perfectly realized at all times during the history of the EC, but it is a reasonable first approximation of the context in which European governments typically negotiate. One implication of these assumptions is that bargaining outcomes should be efficient, in the sense that conflicts are generally resolved Pareto-optimally. Opportunities for useful bargains are exploited. Moreover, these assumptions reduce the importance of various factors that influence bargaining outcomes elsewhere, such as first mover advantages, strategic sequencing, strategic misrepresentation, the use of costly coercive threats, and the role of unilateral precommitments. EC negotiations can be viewed as a co-operative game in which the level of co-operation reflects patterns in the preferences of national governments.

Yet even in this relatively benign environment, relative power matters. Bargaining leverage stems most fundamentally from asymmetries in the relative intensity of national preferences, which reflect, according to the analysis in the previous section, the relative costs and benefits of agreements to remove negative externalities. In negotiating policy co-ordination, the terms will favour those governments able to remove negative externalities by opening markets to which others intensely desire, access, modifying policies others intensely desire to change, or distributing resources others intensely desire to share. The more intensely governments desire agreement, the more concessions and the greater effort they will expend to achieve it. The greater the potential gains for a government from co-operation, as compared to its best alternative policy, the less risk of non-agreement it is willing to assume and, therefore, the weaker its bargaining power over the specific terms of agreement.

Theories of bargaining and negotiation suggest three likely determinants of interstate bargaining power under such circumstances: (1) unilateral policy alternatives ('threats of non-agreement'); (2) alternative coalitions ('threats of exclusion'); and (3) the potential for compromise and linkage.

Unilateral alternatives and threats of non-agreement

A necessary condition for negotiated agreement among rational governments is that each perceive the benefits of co-operation as preferable to the benefits of the best alternative available to it. Where there exists a policy more desirable than co-operation, a rational government will forgo agreement. *The simple, but credible threat of non-agreement – to reject co-operation in favour of a superior alternative – provides rational governments with their most fundamental form of bargaining power.* The more attractive a government's policy alternatives – often termed 'outside options', 'reservation values', 'concession limits', or 'best alternatives to negotiated agreement (BATNAs)' – the less intense its preference for agreement and the greater its bargaining leverage.[19] Governments with attractive alternatives will not tolerate inconvenient agreements, while governments with unattractive alternatives gain from co-operation even if they have to compromise. Leaving aside for the moment alternative coalitions, linkages and side-payments, the 'threat of non-agreement' guarantees that the outcomes of rational bargaining must fall within a set of agreements, termed the 'feasible set', ranging from an outcome in which all the joint gains accrue to one country to those in which they accrue to another, that is, a set is bounded by the best policy alternatives available to governments. Only agreements within this set are viable.[20]

The most basic type of alternative is simply the unilateral policy that a government is able to pursue without an agreement, that is, under the institutional *status quo*. When bargaining on the basis of unilateral alternatives, governments have only one threat, that of non-co-operation. In negotiations over trade liberalization, for example, the bargaining power of unilateral alternatives stems from asymmetrical interdependence: governments that are less dependent on internal trade than their negotiating partners, and therefore stand to gain less from agreement, enjoy greater bargaining leverage. Thus, even if democratic governments rarely apply tactical or punitive sanctions, *implicit* sanctions – the credible threat to retain protection as the best alternative to agreement – remain a fundamental source of bargaining power. In negotiations over public goods policies, governments with greater domestic policy autonomy enjoy leverage over those whose policies are ineffective or vulnerable to external disruption. In both these bargaining situations, governments of large, prosperous, relatively self-sufficient countries tend to wield the most influence, because they gain relatively little from agreement, compared to their smaller, poorer, more open neighbours. The former can therefore afford to be more discriminating about the terms they will accept.

One implication of bargaining on the basis of the intensity of preferences is that the need to compromise with the least forthcoming government imposes the binding constraint on the possibilities for greater co-operation, driving EC agreements toward the *lowest common denominator*. Let us assume, for example, that European governments are selecting by unanimity vote among a set of possible agreements, arrayed in order of increasing divergence from the *status quo*. If each government favours agreements closest to its preferred point and is willing to accept only those agreements that it prefers to the *status quo*, it is the government with a preferred point closest to the *status quo* whose veto ultimately limits the extent of reform. A 'lowest common denominator' outcome does *not* mean that final agreements perfectly reflect the preferences of the least forthcoming government – since it is generally in its interest to compromise somewhat rather than veto an agreement – but only that the range of possible agreements is decisively constrained by its preferences.

The evolution of the EC illustrates the importance, but also some important implications of unilateral alternatives as determinants of interstate bargaining outcomes. In negotiations over the terms of European monetary integration since the late 1970s, Germany's alternative to negotiated agreement – *de facto* monetary autonomy – has been more attractive than the alternative of its neighbours, which is increasing dependence on the Bundesbank. As a result, the German government has been able to demand that monetary integration take place through convergence to Germany's low-inflation standard, without which Germany would have had little incentive to depart from the institutional *status quo*. Similarly, Britain has traditionally been viewed as indispensable to the credibility of European Political Co-operation. Its interests have been accommodated by those whose unilateral foreign policy options are limited, including Germany, Italy and many smaller states.

. . . .

Agreement at the lowest common denominator does not, however, inevitably mean adoption of the lowest possible common standard. In numerous cases, less environmentally conscious governments in Britain, Spain and elsewhere have accepted environmental product standards far higher than those prevailing domestically. Relatively high environmental and public health standards, such as high air pollution and recycling standards, do not disconfirm the prediction of lowest common denominator agreements. Some of these decisions reflect the dynamics of qualified majority voting, yet even under unanimity, these apparent anomalies are quite consistent with the model of bargaining on the basis of preference intensity, *if preferences are specified properly*. In the EC context, regulatory issues are often 'two-dimensional', linking commercial and public welfare concerns. High national standards operate as permissible non-tariff barriers under Article 36 of the Treaty of Rome. Often, the regulation of environmental product standards creates unexpected alliances, as illustrated by the cases of auto emissions standards, recycling laws for bottles and packaging, and standards for toxic chemicals (Levy 1991; Majone 1992c; Vogel 1992). Such regulations are thus more acceptable to business in Germany, Denmark and the Netherlands than they otherwise might be. Better yet, however, from the perspective of business in these high standard countries, much of which is multinational, would be an integrated market with high *EC* environmental standards. Produces in low standard countries would gain as well, since access to markets with high standards, but off by unilateral barriers, would thereby be assured. Far from sparking a race to the bottom, the creation of a single market under 'lowest common denominator' bargaining often creates incentives for the EC to harmonize at a high level.

Alternative coalitions and the threat of exclusion

Where the only alternatives to agreement are unilateral policies, EC negotiations over major reforms can be thought of as taking place within a unanimity voting system in which agreement requires that the minimal demands of each country be satisfied. Sometimes, however, the best alternative to agreement is not unilateral action, but the formation of an alternative coalition from which certain states are excluded. Where alternative coalitions are possible, a government must calculate the value of an agreement by comparing it not to unilateral policy options, but to its gain from alternative coalitions it would join or from 'going it alone...as [it] faces various coalitions' (Raiffa 1982: 253). *The existence of opportunities to form attractive alternative coalitions (or deepen existing ones), while excluding other parties, strengthens the bargaining power of potential coalition members* vis-à-vis *those threatened with exclusion.* In the EC context, such bargaining power may result either from the threat to co-operate with non-EC countries or, more common today, from the possibility of forming or deepening alternative institutions within Europe, while leaving some members behind – a 'two-track' or 'multi-speed' Europe (Moravcsik 1991). Such coalitional dynamics tend to favour large states, whose participation is necessary for viable coalitions, and governments with preferences close to the median of the EC, since they are potential members of more viable coalitions.

By creating negative policy externalities, the formation of an alternative coalition creates an incentive for recalcitrant governments to compromise. Due to the much greater market power involved, the threat of exclusion from a coalition is a more powerful incentive to co-operation than a single state's threat of non-agreement. To a much greater extent than unco-ordinated policies, alternative coalitions – for example an exclusive free trade arrangement – can create negative policy externalities for those left outside it. By diverting investment, credit, trade, political influence, or market confidence, exclusion from an alternative coalition may impose significant costs, even in the absence of military and economic coercion (Binmore and Dasgupta 1987: 9). Under these conditions, a government may seek to avoid exclusion by agreeing to terms of co-operation that leave it *worse off in absolute terms than the* status quo ante – although, of course, the agreement is Pareto-improving in the sense that the government is better off as compared to its position if the failure to reach agreement had led to the formation of an alternative coalition.

A number of major events in the history of the EC can be interpreted as responses to the threat of exclusion from an alternative coalition. The initial British response to the formation of the Common Market in the 1950s and 1960s is an illustrative example. The British government initially sought to undermine European integration by proposing an alternative free trade area. When this failed, the British sought to dilute the Common Market by negotiating a free trade deal directly with it, and subsequently formed a parallel organization, the European Free Trade Association (EFTA). Only when each of these strategies had failed did Britain finally apply for membership of the EC – only to find that the adjustment of other countries to the Common Market had shifted relative bargaining power even further against it. This is a case in which Britain, while it would have gained from membership, would nevertheless have preferred the *status quo ante*.

. . . .

Yet alternative coalitions do not always create negative externalities for excluded states and, therefore, pressure for geographical spillover. Where a policy of exclusion has *positive* externalities, a contrary dynamic occurs. Where free trade is assured, for example, governments with low social standards often have a clear incentive to free ride, rather than to compromise on common harmonized standards. This helps explain why the threat of exclusion was powerless to block the British government's striking last minute 'opt-out' of social policy at Maastricht. Exclusion from the social policy provisions of the Maastricht Treaty, insofar as it had any effect at all, promised to make British firms *more* competitive on a European market from which they cannot be excluded. The adoption of high EC social protection standards is thus likely to be possible only through linkage or side payments, which play such an important role in cementing co-operation with the Mediterranean countries.

The distinction between positive and negative externalities provides a means of predicting which policies are 'inherently expansive' – thus resolving an ambiguity in neo-functionalist theory. Where policy externalities are negative, non-members have an incentive to join the organization, which will lead them to compromise on common standards. Where policy externalities are positive, non-members have an incentive to free ride, rather than compromise, and agreements above the lowest common denominator are possible only through linkages and side payments, to which we now turn.[21] This not only helps to explain the dynamics of geographical expansion in the EC, but also the dynamics of current bargaining over regulatory issues.

Compromise, side-payments and linkage at the margin

Unilateral and coalitional policy alternatives define a range of viable agreements which all participants prefer to the *status quo*. Within that range, the precise point at which negotiators will compromise is more difficult to predict, particularly when more than two states are involved. In general, bargaining power will depend on the intensity of preference at the margin. Where uncertainty exists about the breakdown of negotiations or time pressure, concessions tend to come disproportionately from governments for which the failure to reach agreement would be least attractive – that is, from those governments which stand to lose the most if agreement is not reached. Where such uncertainty does not exist, the terms of the final agreement will reflect the relative intensity of preferences at the margin, which defines the shape of the feasible set: governments that place a greater value on concession at the margin will gain more from negotiations.[22]

More importantly for our purposes here, governments often have differential preference intensities across issues, with marginal gains in some issue-areas being more important to them than to other governments. Under these circumstances, it may be to the advantage of both parties to exchange concessions in issue-areas about which their preferences are relatively weak for concessions in other areas about which they care more. Even where a set of agreements, taken individually, would each be rejected by at least one national government, they may generate net advantages for all if adopted as a 'package deal' . . .

The major limitation on linkage strategies is domestic opposition. Linkages have important domestic distributional consequences. They tie together into package deals issues in which domestic groups benefit with those in which domestic groups lose. Package deals tend to create winners and losers in *all* countries that are party to them. Where domestic gains and losses produced by linkage are only imperfectly fungible through compensation across issues, linkage becomes a complex and politically risky strategy. Since losers tend to generate more political pressure than winners, for a domestic trade-off to be tolerable, adjustment costs to important domestic groups must be moderate or substantial compensation must be paid.

The importance of domestic costs and benefits suggests a number of predictions about linkage. First, linkages are most likely in areas where the preferences of domestic groups are not intense. Minor issues are more likely to be sacrificed to a linkage. Wherever possible, therefore, financial or symbolic side-payments between states, rather than linkages between substantive issues are employed. The Maastricht agreement was typical, in that issues implicitly linked to monetary policy included highly fungible resources, such as increases in structural funds, or symbolic issues, such as deletion of 'federalist' language and increased powers to the European Parliament. Second, package deals are most likely in the final stage of bargaining – that is, at the margin to balance gains and losses among issues in which all parties are close to being net beneficiaries – rather than among issues in which nations are large net winners and losers. Third, linkages are most likely between closely related issues – within, rather than between, sectors. Where the costs and benefits are internalized to sectors or firms, there is more possibility for producers to adjust, diversify, or to balance gains and losses, just as in the case of intra-industry trade. Sectoral organizations may neutralize opposition by aggregating sectoral support and opposition into a single position. Linkages between disparate sectors are most likely to occur where the possibilities for intra-issue compromise or linkage between related issues have been exhausted. Fourth, if linkages do impose real losses on domestic sectors, they are more likely to be effective when accompanied by domestic side-payments from governments to disadvantaged private groups. In the 1960s and 1970s, industrial subsidies in France and agricultural subsidies in Germany were explicitly designed to ease adjustment to liberalization.

Linkage is thus a politically costly, second-best strategy for integration. Linkages that attempt too much – such as the linkage between the Common Agricultural Policy and strong supranational institutions in the 1960s – are often unstable and are circumvented at a later stage. The limitations on linkage are illustrated by the purported linkage on which the EC is said to be founded, namely that between German access to French industrial markets and French access to German agricultural markets. While such a linkage existed on the margin, it was less central than is often asserted. Industrialists and farmers in both countries gained. French industry's objections to the Common Market were in fact relatively minor; by 1959, before tariff reductions had begun in earnest, they were already among the strongest supporters of acceleration. Opposition to a common agricultural policy came primarily from economic liberals in the German government, who opposed high prices, and farmers, who feared low prices. The final agreement left farmers in every country, including Germany, with higher average support prices than they had enjoyed previously. Those elements of the CAP price structure that most disadvantaged certain farmers were offset by domestic compensation and adjustment assistance. In the 1970s, any residual loss to German farmers was more than offset by the compensation for currency movements and the subsequent renationalisation of the CAP, leaving only division of the much smaller budgetary expenditures as an outstanding issue. In contrast to neo-functionalism, which viewed linkage as the core of the EC, it is seen here as a strategy best pursued on the margin and of lesser importance than intra-sectoral trade-offs. Linkages that impose large losses on important domestic groups are unstable.

So far this analysis has focused primarily on the sources of national preferences and the distributional outcomes of intergovernmental negotiations over commercial liberalization, domestic public goods provision, and general political and institutional questions. We turn now from an analysis of the distributional outcomes of intergovernmental bargaining to an analysis of its efficiency. Modern regime theory views international institutions as deliberate instruments to improve the efficiency of bargaining between states.

V Supranational Institutions and the Efficiency of Decision-making

Strong supranational institutions are often seen as the antithesis of intergovernmentalism. Wrongly so. The decision to join all but the most minimalist of regimes involves some sacrifice of national autonomy, which increases the political risk to each Member State, in exchange for certain advantages. In the intergovernmentalist view, the unique institutional structure of the EC is acceptable to national governments only insofar as it strengthens, rather than weakens, their control over domestic affairs, permitting them to attain goals otherwise unachievable.

EC institutions strengthen the power of governments in two ways. First, they increase the efficiency of interstate bargaining. The existence of a common negotiating forum, decision-making procedures, and monitoring of compliance reduce the costs of identifying, making and keeping agreements, thereby making possible a greater range of co-operative arrangements. This explanation relies on the functional theory of regimes, which focuses on the role of regimes in reducing transaction costs (Keohane 1984). However, in order to explain the unique level of institutionalization found in the EC, this body of theory must be extended to include the delegation and pooling of sovereignty. Second, EC institutions strengthen the autonomy of national political leaders *vis-à-vis* particularistic social groups within their domestic polity. By augmenting the legitimacy and credibility of common policies, and by strengthening domestic agenda-setting power, the EC structures a 'two-level game' that enhances the autonomy and initiative of national political leaders – often, as noted above, a prerequisite for successful market liberalization. With a few important exceptions, EC institutions appear to be explicable as the result of conscious calculations by Member States to strike a balance between greater efficiency and domestic influence, on the one hand, and acceptable levels of political risk, the other.

1 Supranational institutions and functional regime theory

Much of the institutional structure of the EC can be readily explained by the functional theory of regimes, which argues that where transaction costs – the costs of identifying issues, negotiating bargains, codifying agreements, and monitoring and enforcing compliance – are significant, international institutions may promote greater co operation by providing information and reducing uncertainty. In the conventional regime-theoretical view, EC institutions serve as a passive structure, providing a contractual environment conducive to efficient intergovernmental bargaining. As compared to *ad hoc* negotiation, they increase the efficiency of bargaining, facilitating agreements that could not otherwise be reached (Buchanan and Tullock 1962; Keohane 1984; Levy et al. 1992).

The functional regime theory view of international institutions as passive, transaction-cost reducing sets of rules readily explains the role of EC institutions as a framework for negotiating major decisions, from the Treaty of Rome to Maastricht. The *acquis communautaire* of the EC functions to stabilize a constantly evolving set of rules and expectations, which can only be altered by unanimous consent. Institutions promote international co-operation by providing a negotiating forum with bureaucratic institutions that disseminate information and policy ideas; a locus for representatives of business, political parties, national bureaucracies, and interest groups to discuss issues of common concern; joint decision-making procedures; a common set of underlying legal and political norms; and institutions for monitoring and defining national compliance. Greater information and predictability reduce the cost of bargaining and the risk of unilateral non-compliance. Like the GATT, the G-7 and other international regimes, EC institutions provide fora in which to craft linkages and side-payments that render policy co-ordination more viable domestically. Package deals linking regional funds and British entry or structural funds and the SEA were surely easier to reach within a common international institution. Yet the large political risk inherent in open-ended decisions about the future scope of EC activities means that Member States remain hesitant to delegate authority to supranational or majoritarian institutions. The essence of the EC as a body for reaching major decisions remains its transaction-cost reducing function, as explicated by contemporary regime theory.

When we turn from major constitutional decision-making to the process of everyday legislation, administration and enforcement, however, the EC seems to be a far more unusual international institution – more than a passive set of rules codifying previous decisions. The EC differs from nearly all other international regimes in at least two salient ways: by *pooling* national sovereignty through QMV rules and by *delegating* sovereign powers to semi-autonomous central institutions. These two forms of transferring national sovereignty are closely related. QMV, for example, not only makes the formal decision-making of any single government more dependent on the votes of its foreign counterparts, but also more dependent on agenda-setting by the Commission.

In order to understand the conditions under which Member States will forgo *ad hoc* decision-making under the unanimity rule in favour of a common agreement to pool or delegate sovereignty, contemporary regime theory must be extended. An insightful starting point, suggested by Garrett and Weingast in their analysis of the ECJ, is to view delegation as a response to the problem of incomplete contracting. Predicting the circumstances under which future contingencies will occur is often difficult and costly, sometimes impossible (Garrett & Weingast 1991). Where member governments have shared goals, but are unable or unwilling to foresee all future contingencies involved in the realization of common goals, they may have an incentive to establish common decision-making procedures or to empower neutral agents to propose, mediate, implement, interpret and enforce agreements.

The metaphor of incomplete contracting *per se,* while a useful starting assumption, fails to explain variation in either the level or the form of delegation (or pooling) of sovereignty. Delegation is, after all, only one of a number of possible responses to future uncertainty. Many unpredictable EC decisions – including the annual determination of CAP prices and the definition of new issues under Art. 235 – are neither delegated nor pooled; others – the determination of international negotiating positions and administered protection against third countries – are pooled, but not delegated. Elsewhere in the international system, delegation is even rarer, despite many cases of incomplete contracting. Even within the EC, governments often refuse to assume the political risk of delegation, preferring instead imperfect enforcement and inefficient decision-making, to the surrender of sovereignty. Incomplete contracting appears to be neither a necessary, nor a sufficient, condition for delegation.

What, then, distinguishes cases of delegation or pooling from cases of *ad hoc* unanimity voting? Following public choice analyses of domestic constitutional choice, intergovernmentalist theory views the decision to adopt QMV or delegation to common institutions as the result of a cost-benefit analysis of the stream of future substantive decisions expected to follow from alternative institutional designs. For individual Member States carrying gut such a cost-benefit calculation, the decision to delegate or pool sovereignty signals the willingness of national governments to accept an increased political risk of being outvoted or overruled on any individual issue in exchange for more efficient collective decision-making on the average.[23] Movement beyond unanimous voting and *ad hoc* negotiation for a class of decisions can thus be thought of as a means of deliberately encouraging implicit linkages across various related issues within an iterated game among governments. By facilitating linkages, delegation or pooling is likely to produce more decisions at a lower cost in time and energy than the laborious negotiation of *ad hoc* package deals. Compared to unanimity voting, delegation and pooling of sovereignty are more efficient, but less controlled forms of collective decision-making. Of the two, delegation involves greater political risk and more efficient decision-making, while pooling through QMV involves less risk, but correspondingly less efficiency.

Examining this trade-off more precisely, the following three conditions should encourage national governments to support a movement from unanimity to delegated or pooled decision-making: *(1) The potential gains from cooperation.* Where time pressure, previous failures to reach agreement, the desire to implement a prior decision, or a shift in national preferences requires more rapid decision-making, delegation or pooling is more likely. *Ceteris paribus,* the less attractive the *status quo* and the greater the expected gains from increased co-operation, the greater the corresponding incentive to pool or delegate. Levels of economic transactions and, in particular, intra-industry trade, which are higher among the EC countries than among any comparable set of industrialized countries, are likely to lead eventually to pressure for greater delegation and pooling 'of sovereignty. Where large numbers of similar decisions are involved, the efficiency gains are correspondingly greater (cf. Keohane 1983).

(2) The level of uncertainty regarding the details of specific delegated or pooled decisions. Lack of precise knowledge about the form, details and outcome of future decisions not only precludes more explicit contracts, as noted above, but also helps defuse potential opposition from those who would be disadvantaged by the implicit linkages. Where agreements can be foreseen, some governments and domestic groups would have more reason to prefer direct bargaining under unanimity, as occurred in setting the initial levels of the Common External Tariff and agricultural prices, in order to block policies disadvantageous to them.

(3) The level of political risk for individual governments or interest groups with intense preferences. Political risk can be understood as the probability of a large downside loss to a government or interest group. Risk-averse governments will assent to procedures where the scope and magnitude of expected and potential losses are minimized, given the goals of co-operation. Governments have an incentive to delegate authority only when there is little probability that the cumulative distributional effects of delegated or pooled decisions will be biased in an unforeseen way against the interests of any national government or major domestic group.[24] The form of third-party representation, agenda-setting and enforcement should involve the minimal transfer of sovereignty needed to achieve desired outcomes. One way to limit the scope of delegation and pooling, often employed in the EC, is to nest specific decisions inside a set of larger decisions already reached by unanimity, thereby both diversifying and limiting political risk.

Each of the three most important instances in which the Treaty of Rome delegates Member State authority to supranational officials – external representation, agenda-setting and enforcement – appears to fulfill these conditions.

External representation: Since the EC is a customs union with a common external tariff, negotiations with third countries require a single agent to represent common positions. In order for national governments to trust the agent, it must be perceived as neutral. While this requires that an agent be delegated, only limited independent decision-making for short periods of time is required to carry out designated tasks. Close monitoring and oversight by national governments is to be expected. In the common commercial policy of the EC, for example, the Commission represents the Community, but tight control is maintained by the Article 113 Committee. Only where time pressure in the midst of negotiations forces a rapid decision and national governments are deadlocked can supranational officials advance independent initiatives. These are still subject to *ex post* approval, but may transfer some marginal power to the Commission. In European Political Co-operation, where fewer decisions are taken and a common external position is viewed as less imperative, the EC is generally represented by the foreign ministers of its Member States.

Agenda-setting: Where a wide consensus exists on a broad substantive agenda, it can often be realized more efficiently by granting a measure of agenda-setting power to a supranational institution, in this case the Commission. As a reliable source of independent proposals, the Commission assures that technical information necessary for decision is available. More importantly, as a neutral arbiter, it provides an authoritative means of reducing the number of proposals to be considered. Majorities may exist for a number of alternative proposals on a single issue, with governments unable to reduce them to a compromise through their vetoes. This is particularly important where governments have sought to increase the efficiency of bargaining by employing QMV. In such circumstances, agenda-setting power can be decisive in deciding which proposal prevails. In the EC, delegating the power of proposal to the Commission provides a means of setting the agenda, thereby avoiding time-consuming or inconclusive 'cycling' between difficult proposals or an arbitrary means of proposal selection . . .[25]

Yet the ability to select among viable proposals grants the Commission considerable formal agenda-setting power, at least in theory. The power is particularly decisive when the *status quo* is unattractive, creating general support for joint action, yet there is considerable disagreement between national governments over what should replace it. Often a number of proposals might gain majority support, among which the Commission's choice is decisive. The most controversial cases of implementing the White Paper agenda, including a number in telecommunications, environmental and social policy, stand as examples. (For a similar analysis of parliamentary power, see Tsebelis 1992.)

Enforcement: The possibilities for co-operation are enhanced when neutral procedures exist to monitor, interpret and enforce compliance. Neutral enforcement permit governments to extend credible commitments, thus helping to overcome the almost inevitable interstate prisoner's dilemma of enforcement, whereby individual governments seek to evade inconvenient responsibilities, thereby undermining the integrity of the entire system. By taking the definition of compliance outside of the hands of national governments, a supranational, legal system strengthens the credibility of national commitments to the institution. The cost of such delegation, which goes beyond the monitoring functions of classical international regimes, is increased political risk. Functions of this type in the EC include competition policy, administered by the Commission, and the interpretation and application of EC law, carried out by the ECJ (Garrett and Weingast 1991).

In each of these three cases, there is a substantive commitment to the achievement of broad goals, while the political risk is small, insofar as each delegated decision is relatively insignificant. Perhaps most important, the scope of delegation is explicitly limited by national governments . . .

Of the three types of delegation, only the enforcement power of the ECJ appears to have resulted in a grant of independent initiative to supranational bodies beyond that which is minimally necessary to perform its functions – and beyond that which appears to have been foreseen by governments. The ECJ has constitutionalized the Treaty of Rome, built alliances with domestic courts and interest groups, preempted national law in important areas, and opened new venues for Commission initiative, as in cases like *ERTA* in common commercial policy, and *Cassis de Dijon* in technical harmonization.

The expansion of judicial power in the EC presents an anomaly for the functional explanation of delegation as a deliberate means by national governments of increasing the efficiency of collective decision-making. While supranational delegation undoubtedly creates benefits for governments, the decisions of the Court clearly transcend what was initially foreseen and desired by most national governments (Burley and Mattli, 1993). The 'constitutionalization' of the Treaty of Rome was unexpected. It is implausible, moreover, to argue that the current system is the one to which all national governments would currently consent, as recent explicit limitations on the Court in the Maastricht Treaty demonstrate. Nor is the current institutional form of the Court functionally necessary. Supranational dispute resolution need not take the form, almost unique among international organizations, of a semi-autonomous legal system. Such a system is not *a priori* more appropriate for settling disputes between rival interpretations and applications of a statute than a dispute resolution panel, as exists in the GATT, or the Council of Ministers acting under qualified majority, as exists in EFTA. The Member States might simply have reserved the right to pass legislation to clarify ambiguities. Neither incomplete contracting nor functional analysis can account for the precise form or historical evolution of the ECJ.

The unique role the ECJ has come to play may reflect instead, as Burley and Mattli argue, a number of factors idiosyncratic to the EC. First, the technical complexity of EC law made it difficult to foresee the consequences of early Court decisions, giving those who favoured a strong ECJ some leeway in drafting the treaty (Pescatore 1981). Second, the referral of cases by domestic courts, and their subsequent enforceability in the same forum, render ECJ judgments difficult to ignore. Finally, and most importantly, unanimous consent of Member States would now be required to curb its power. Over the years the Court has pursued a sophisticated strategy, remaining just within a negative consensus that protects it. Any attempt to alter the current arrangements might be challenged by European federalists, by those who favour strong enforcement, and by smaller countries, which would be less well served by a system in which QMV was employed to adjudicate disputes (Burley and Mattli 1993).

While the creation of common rules and procedures in functional regime theory alters only the information and expectations of national governments, the EC goes further, pooling decision-making through arrangements for QMV and delegating authority over representation, formal agenda-setting and enforcement to semi-autonomous institutions. Yet the delegation and pooling of authority in the EC, like the construction of common norms and principles in other regimes, can be explained by extending the central insight of functional regime theory, namely that institutions are means of reducing the transaction costs of identifying, negotiating and enforcing intergovernmental agreements under uncertainty. National governments strike a balance between increased decision-making efficiency and the political risk of uncontrolled issue linkage. The greater the potential gains, the greater the uncertainty about specific decisions, and the lower the political risk, the more likely governments are to delegate power in these ways.

Viewed in light of this trade-off, independent actions by the Commission or outcomes that contravene the interests of a single Member State, taken in isolation, do not constitute decisive evidence against the intergovernmentalist view that the EC is grounded fundamentally in the preferences and power of Member States. Only where the actions of supranational leaders *systematically* bias outcomes away from the long-term self-interest of Member States can we speak of serious challenge to an intergovernmentalist view. While some cases of supranational autonomy, such ascertain actions of the ECJ, may pose such a challenge, most fit comfortably within it.

2   Supranational institutions and 'two-level games'

Traditional regime theory focuses primarily on the role of regimes in reducing the transaction costs of collective decision-making for national governments. Yet EC institutions perform a second function as well, namely to shift the balance of domestic initiative and influence. On balance, this shift has strengthened the policy autonomy of national governments at the expense of particular groups (for a dissenting view, see Marks 1991).[26] Particularly where domestic interests are weak or divided, EC institutions have been deliberately designed to assist national governments in overcoming domestic opposition. Where institutions did not initially serve this purpose in the Treaty of Rome, new institutions were created in order to strengthen this function – the strengthening of the Council bureaucracy in the 1960s, the genesis of the European Council the 1970s, and the reservation of powers over political co-operation to the Member States being prime examples.

National governments employ EC institutions as part of a 'two-level' strategy with the aim of permitting them to overcome domestic opposition more successfully (cf. Putnam, 1988). The EC fulfils this function in two ways: by affording governmental policy initiatives greater domestic political legitimacy and by granting them greater domestic agenda-setting power. Let us briefly consider each. The mantle of the EC adds legitimacy and credibility to Member State initiatives. Domestic coalitions can be mobilized more easily in favour of policy co-ordination. This adds weight in domestic debates to both major reforms and everyday decisions emanating from the EC. Second, the institutional structure of the EC strengthens the initiative and influence of national governments by insulating the policy process and generating domestic agenda-setting power for national politicians. National governments are able to take initiatives and reach bargains in Council negotiations with relatively little constraint. The EC provides information to governments that is not generally available. Intergovernmental discussions take place in secrecy; national votes are not publicized. Domestically, parliaments and publics generally have little legal opportunity to ratify EC agreements and decisions; where they do, there is rarely an opportunity to amend or revise them. National leaders undermine potential opposition by reaching bargains in Brussels first and presenting domestic groups with an 'up or down' choice – just as 'fast track' procedures are employed to speed trade agreements through the US Senate (Destler 1986). Greater domestic agenda-setting power in the hands of national political leaders increases the ability of governments to reach agreements by strengthening the ability of governments to gain domestic ratification for compromises or tactical issue linkages. Whereas governments might be pressured for exemptions, oversight over implementation is placed instead in the hands of the more credible European and national court systems. Ironically, the democratic deficit may be a fundamental source of its success.

From the very beginning, much EC decision-making has been difficult to explain except as a two-level game. The reflexive support of both committed European federalists and those who favour the general economic goals of the EC greatly assisted the early development of specific EC policies. In the initial negotiation of the Treaty of Rome, the liberalization of French industrial trade offers a striking example. In the 1950s Germany, the hub of the European trading system, was engaging in *unilateral* tariff reductions. French exports to Germany were increasing rapidly with little evidence of any protectionist reaction across the Rhine (Milward 1992). The major incentive for France to accept the EC was not to solve an international prisoner's dilemma by assuring access to the German market, as much modern trade theory would have it. Instead, as French leaders made clear at the time and de Gaulle was to reiterate even more forcefully, it was to employ the legitimacy of the EC to force French firms to modernize – a goal that French governments had been promoting for almost a decade without success (Institut Charles de Gaulle 1986).

Today we are witnessing an analogous phenomenon, as the credibility of efforts to achieve macroeconomic convergence in countries like Italy and Spain is bolstered by the impression, deliberately exploited by member governments, that the imposition of anti-inflationary discipline is necessary for full involvement in Europe . . .

The proposed independent Eurofed offers a more recent example of the advantages of insulating agenda-setting policy implementation from domestic pressures – -to an extent that has been widely criticized – in order to achieve go that would otherwise be unachievable. Domestic control over exchange rate policy (as well as the legitimacy of European integration), has permitted German Chancellor Helmut Kohl to pursue a policy of monetary integration without the strong backing of either business or the Bundesbank, although limits imposed by domestic consensus have subsequently become clear. In addition, the proposed European Central Bank will be doubly insulated from domestic pressures in a way designed to make the common European policies credible on domestic and international markets. The Maastricht referendum in France is an exception that proves the importance of secrecy and agenda-setting power, in that it demonstrates the potential consequences when governments lose firm control of domestic agendas or take needless risks in ratification.

VI　Conclusion: Beyond Liberal Intergovernmentalism

The liberal intergovernmentalist view seeks to account for major decisions in the history of the EC by positing a two-stage approach. In the first stage, national preferences are primarily determined by the constraints and opportunities imposed by economic interdependence. In the second stage, the outcomes of intergovernmental negotiations are determined by the relative bargaining power of governments and the functional incentives for institutionalization created by high transaction costs and the desire to control domestic agendas. This approach is grounded in fundamental concepts of international political economy, negotiation analysis, and regime theory.

. . . .

By bringing together theories of preferences, bargaining and regimes, liberal intergovernmentalism provides plausible accounts for many aspects of the major decisions in the history of the EC in a way that is sharply distinct from neo-functionalism. Where neo-functionalism emphasizes domestic technocratic consensus, liberal intergovernmentalism looks to domestic coalitional struggles. Where neo-functionalism emphasizes opportunities to upgrade the common interest, liberal intergovernmentalism stresses the role of relative power. Where neo-functionalism emphasizes the active role of supranational officials in shaping bargaining outcomes, liberal intergovernmentalism stresses instead passive institutions and the autonomy of national leaders. Ironically, the EC's 'democratic deficit' may be a fundamental source of its success.

Moreover, liberal intergovernmentalism provides explanations for some nagging anomalies inherited from neo-functionalism. Variation in the tightness of domestic societal constraints is employed to explain the disruptive role of dramatic-political actors and the distinction between those issues where linkage or compromise is possible and those in which log-rolling or lowest common denominator solution prevails. The distinction between positive and negative externalities helps explain which issues generate common solutions and spark geographical spillover, and which do not. The introduction of a 'two-level' game analysis explains why France sought industrial trade liberalization with Germany in the 1950s, despite the unilateral openness of the German economy at the time.

Critics may challenge the approach proposed here in three ways. First, they may dispute the basic framework, arguing that state behaviour is not purposive and instrumental, that preference formation does not precede the formulation of strategies, or that national preference and intergovernmental bargaining are so completely manipulated by supranational officials as to be meaningless categories. Second, they may challenge the liberal understanding of state preferences employed here, which draws on contemporary theories of economic interdependence to explain national preferences. Alternative conceptions of economic interest are certainly possible, as are (liberal and non-liberal) explanations based on ideology or geopolitics. Third, they may question the Intergovernmental theory of bargaining, with its stress on bargaining power rooted in unilateral alternatives, competing coalitions, the possibilities for linkage, and the controlled delegation of power to supranational institutions under conditions specified by functional theories of regimes and 'two-level' games views of domestic polities. Such debate is to be welcomed.

Yet few would go so far as to deny the importance of preferences and power altogether. Indeed, a strong liberal intergovernmentalist theory is widely seen as a precondition for the development of more complex theories of integration, such as neo-functionalism. Without explicit theories of state interests, interstate bargaining, and international regimes, it is impossible to determine when consequences are truly unintended, the common interest is truly being upgraded or supranational officials are truly acting autonomously. This vindicates Haas's judgement that debate between *general* theories of domestic and international politics is necessary. Such a debate is surely preferable to a clash between intergovernmentalist and 'supranationalist' ideal-types, without any specification of the conditions under which each might be expected to apply.

It is certainly true that liberal intergovernmentalism accords supranational institutions and officials less weight and prominence than neo-functionalism once did. Committed integrationists typically read such conclusions as a disparagement of the unique achievement and future potential of the EC. Yet the real achievement and hope of the Community may lie not in the transcendence of traditional state preferences and power, but in the underlying domestic and international forces that have shaped national preferences and power in the direction of greater co-operation. Liberal intergovernmentalism assimilates the EC to models of politics potentially applicable to all states, thereby specifying conditions under which a similar process of integration may occur elsewhere.

Notes

1 Haas 1976: 183. In Lindberg and Scheingold, there are five alternative models, only one of which is spillover; Nye expanded this to seven process mechanisms or 'actor strategies', only two (1 and 3) of which related to spillover (cf. Lindberg and Scheingold 1970: 134–9; Pentland 1973: 119; Schmitter 1971: 232–64. For an overview, see Nye 1971b: 64–75.

2 An empirical exception is Haas 1966: 93–130. Haas examines other international regimes, but his theoretical explanation if inductive, rather than grounded in micro-analysis of processes.

3 Lindberg's otherwise insightful analysis in *Political Dynamics* largely overlooks this distinction. See also Von der Groeben (1982).

4 Such goals are best seen not as defined across alternative policies or strategies (e.g. a free trade regime, fixed exchange rates), but across alternative future states of the world (e.g. higher levels of economic transactions, exchange rate stability). Rational choices among policies and strategies must generally take into account the expected reactions of other states and the resulting strategic interactions among them, while preference across future states of the world do not. The latter are 'pre-strategic' preferences. On this distinction more generally, see Elster (1986).

5 To avoid confusion, it is important to remember that nested within the domestic definition of the demand function is also a national process of societal demands for and governmental supply of policies. The domestic use of the metaphor of demand and supply is drawn from Shepsle's analyses of legislative politics (Shepsle 1992).

6 Sections IV and V of this article deal respectively with two different aspects of interstate strategic interaction: distributional bargaining and the delegation or pooling of decision-making in international regimes. Regime theory is treated as a theory of strategic interaction, in the sense that the institutional measures for compliance shape the range of potential bargains. The latter might also be thought of not as an element of strategic interaction, but as a separate 'compliance' stage of policy co-ordination. For a model of this kind, see Moravcsik 1989.

7 Moravcsik 1992b from which the argument in this section is drawn.

8 See Gourevitch 1978. To the extent that international factors, such as economic interdependence or external threats to national security influence preference formation, they must pass through the domestic polity.

9 Here I do not mean to imply that all cases in which governments do not serve the interests of particularistic groups should be thought of as 'autonomous' action, but simply that the greater the 'slack' in the relationship between particularistic opponents of co-operation, the greater the possibility of pursuing a policy targeted at a larger domestic constituency or, in some cases, at realizing the preference of these in office.

10 This diverges from the common analysis of regimes as providing public goods. The institutional infrastructure of regimes itself may be thought of as a public good, as can some common goals of regimes. For the most part, however, the benefits of the EC are excludable and, to an extent, rival goods; cooperation stems from interdependence – the effects of national policies on the opportunities for foreigners.

11 This is overlooked by Grieco (1988), but captured by Keohane and Nye (1989), and Krasner (1991).

12 The existence of such a predictive theory distinguishes liberalism from the neo- functionalist tradition of Haas and others (Haas 1964).

13 A more detailed model would take variations in domestic institutions into account.

14 Under conditions of high domestic factor mobility, one would expect coalitions to form between capital and labour; according to the Stolper-Samuelson theory, protection will be sought by factors of production that are relatively scarce – capital in labour-abundant countries, and labour in capital-abundant countries. In the long term, this may be valid (see Rogowski,1989). In the short and medium term, however, many factors are unable to move between industrial sectors, due in part to high fixed investments in human and physical capital. Hence a specific-factors (Ricardo-Viner) approach is more appropriate, in which owners of capital (or land) and labour work together to form sectoral coalitions (Magee et al. 1989).

15 This is the cornerstone of most modern empirical studies of commercial policy. For empirical support see Lavergne (1983).

16 Since protectionist policies can easily be implemented unilaterally, the incentive for international cooperation in these areas typically stems from opportunities to co-ordinate the liberalization of market access.

17 Milner (1988) stresses intra-industry trade.

18 This is not to imply that the two are always in conflict. See the examples drawn from EC regulatory harmonization cited below.

19 Dixit and Nalebuff 1991: 290–2; Keeney and Raiffa 1991; Raiffa 1982: 252–5; Zartman 1991: 69ff. Keohane and Nye (1988)* refer to this as 'vulnerability'; Hirshman develops the same concept. I employed the phrase 'opportunity cost of non-agreement and exclusion' in Moravcsik (1992a) ch. 1. Garrett (1992a) has applied this idea to the EC.

20 Sebenius 1991: 332–4. Where a welfare reducing agreement is reached, it is unlikely to be ratified or implemented. Putnam (1988).

21 While the existence of alternative coalitions has been presented here as a source of power in broad negotiations over the future scope of the EC, it is relevant also to QMV on more specific issues. In bargaining among themselves over the precise terms of a directive or regulation, national governments weigh the costs of compromise, which results in a winning coalition of which they are a member and an outcome closer to their preferred point, against the risks of intransigence, which may result in exclusion from the winning coalition and an outcome more uncongenial to them.

22 This is the Nash bargaining solution whereby a marginal redistribution in either direction between two actor with concave utility functions would lead to an equal percentage change in their utility. This is also the equilibrium of an offer-counteroffer game in which both sides are assumed to be equal in all respects other than their preferences. See Binmore and Dasgupta (1987).

23 This analysis assumes that the transaction costs of institutional creation and reform are relatively low, but the transaction costs of individual decision-making are high. The limitations to more 'optimal' international institutions stem not from transaction costs of creating them, but from the interests of governments in reducing domestic political risk. This leads them to promote a set of decision-making rules consistent with a specific trade-off between efficiency and risk.

24 Some institutions may be biased in a predictable manner, for which a rational government would demand compensation in negotiations.

25 Under unanimity voting, this is less of a problem: each government can compel compromise by vetoing: any proposal that does not accommodate its views, leading to a compromise among proposals. Hence the, sequence in which proposals are voted upon is less essential.

26 Marks argues, on the basis of an analysis of the structural and regional funds, that the EC is catalyzing a process of diffusion, whereby the 'decisional powers' of the state are being shifted both to subnational and supranational institutions.

Chapter 12

The Path to European Integration: A Historical Institutionalist Analysis

Paul Pierson*

The evolution of the European Community (EC) has long fascinated political scientists. For four decades, some of the world's most enduring nation states have conducted an extraordinary political experiment. Progressing sporadically but in a consistent direction, the member states of the European Community have pooled increasing areas of policy authority, introducing prominent collective institutions. The creation of these institutions initiated a process that has transformed the nature of European politics.

How the evolution of these arrangements of collective governance can be explained and the nature of the current system understood remain matters of considerable controversy. Within American political science, students of international relations have maintained the most theoretically driven discussions of the EC. Despite significant internal disputes, the dominant paradigm in international relations scholarship regards European integration as the practice of ordinary diplomacy under conditions creating unusual opportunities for providing collective goods through highly institutionalized exchange (Garrett 1992b; Moravcsik 1993a). From this 'intergovernmentalist' perspective, the EC is essentially a forum for interstate bargaining. Member states remain the only important actors at the European level. Societal actors exert influence only through the domestic political structures of member states. Policy making is made through negotiation among member states or through carefully circumscribed delegations of authority. Whether relying on negotiation or delegation, Chiefs of Government (COGs) are at the heart of the EC, and each member state

* Reproduced by kind permission of Sage Publications, Inc. from Paul Pierson (1996) 'The Path to European Integration: A Historical Institutionalist Analysis', *Comparative Political Studies*, 29(2), 123–63. Copyright by Sage Publications, Inc. The text has been edited, as indicated, to fit the format of this volume. Specifically, a section entailing a case study of European Social Policy has been left out. Some peripheral footnotes have been omitted.

seeks to maximize its own advantage. Debate within this perspective has concerned such questions as why member states desired certain observed outcomes, which member states have the most influence on collective decision making, and which alignment of member-state interests can best explain policy or institutional development in the EC (Lange 1993; Martin 1993; Moravcsik 1991).

. . . .

In practice, the critics of intergovernmentalism have tried to move forward in two ways. Some have continued to investigate particular policy-areas, content to reveal the density and pluralism of actual policy making while simply observing that the focus of international relations theory on grand diplomacy among sovereign member states does not square with what is actually occurring 'on the ground.' However, it is almost always possible, ex post, to posit some set of member-state preferences that reconciles observed outcomes with the image of near total member-state control. Where policy outcomes do not conform to the expected preferences of member states, they may be explained as part of a 'nested game' or as an instance of side payments. Drawing on rational choice theory, intergovernmentalism possesses flexible conceptual tools that can explain why member states would favor the observed outcomes (Green and Shapiro 1994). Thus, absent a theoretically based explanation for the constraints on member states, these detailed investigations will not persuade proponents of intergovernmentalism.

More theoretically oriented critics have drawn on aspects of the neofunctionalist tradition in international relations, showing how spillover processes and the autonomous actions of supranational actors (including the Commission and European Court of Justice) contribute to European policy making. Recent efforts to update neofunctionalism have successfully highlighted important limitations in intergovernmentalist accounts, and I will rely in part on these arguments in developing my own analysis. Yet neofunctionalism has serious problems of its own. Given the strong institutional position of member states in the EC, neofunctionalists seem to attribute greater autonomy to supranational actors than can plausibly be sustained. Although neo-functionalist arguments about the independent action of the Commission and Court of Justice have some merit, there is little doubt that the member states, acting together in the Council, remain the most powerful decision makers. In most cases, it seems equally probable that these decision makers act to secure their own interests, whatever those are deemed to be. Crucially, these principals retain the legal authority to rein in their agents if they find it in their interests to do so. Thus, at any given point in time, the key propositions of intergovernmentalist theory are likely to hold.

This article seeks to lay the foundation for a more persuasive account of member-state constraint. My focus is on why gaps emerge in member state control over the evolution of European institutions and public policies, why these gaps are difficult to close, and how these openings create room for actors other than member states to influence the process of European integration while constraining the room for maneuver of all political actors. The basis for this challenge to inter-governmentalism lies in insights from what I will term historical institutionalism (Ikenberry 1994; Thelen and Steinmo 1992). The label covers a diverse range of scholarship, much of it with little theoretical focus. Indeed, a principal goal of this article is to strengthen the theoretical foundations of historical institutionalism. There are, however, two unifying themes within this broad research orientation. This scholarship is historical because it recognizes that political development must be understood as a process that unfolds over time. It is institutionalist because it stresses that many of the contemporary implications of these temporal processes are embedded in institutions – whether these be formal rules, policy structures, or norms.[1]

The crucial claim I derive from historical institutionalism is that actors may be in a strong initial position, seek to maximize their interests, and nevertheless carry out institutional and policy reforms that fundamentally transform their own positions (or those of their successors) in ways that are unanticipated and/or undesired. Attempts to cut into ongoing social processes at a single point in time produce a 'snapshot' view that is distorted in crucial respects. Central parts of my analysis emphasize temporal aspects of politics: the lags between decisions and long-term consequences, as well as the constraints that emerge from societal adaptations and shifts in policy preferences that occur during the interim. When European integration is examined over time, the gaps in member-state control appear far more prominent than they do in intergovernmentalist accounts.

In contrast to the functional account of institutions that underpins intergovernmentalism, historical institutionalism stresses the difficulties of subjecting institutional evolution to tight control. Two brief historical examples can illustrate the broad point explored in this article. The first concerns the changing institutional position of state governments in the United States (Riker 1955). Because approval of the US Constitution required state ratification, the interests of states received considerable attention in the process of institutional design. The framers intended the Senate to serve as a strong support of state interests. In an arrangement that partly echoes the EC's emphasis on member-state participation in collective deliberations, state legislatures were to appoint senators, who were expected to serve as delegates representing states in the formation of policy. Over time, however, senators seeking greater autonomy were able to gradually free themselves from state oversight. By the early 1900s, the enactment of the 17th Amendment requiring popular election of senators only ratified the result of a lengthy erosion of state legislative control.

The development of Canadian federalism provides another example (Watts 1987). The designers of the Canadian federation sought a highly centralized form of federalism – in part as a reaction to the ways in which decentralization contributed to the horrors of the American Civil War. Yet the Canadian federation is now far less centralized than the American one. Among the reasons: the Canadian federation left to the provinces sole responsibility for many activities that were then considered trivial. With the growing role of government in social policy and economic management, however, these responsibilities turned out to be of tremendous importance.

In both cases, the current functioning of institutions cannot be derived from the aspirations of the original designers. Processes evolving over time led to quite unexpected outcomes. Similarly, I will argue that what one makes of the EC depends on whether one examines a photograph or a moving picture. Just as a film often reveals meanings that cannot be discerned from a single photograph, a view of Europe's development over time gives us a richer sense of the nature of the emerging European polity. At any given time, the diplomatic maneuvering among member states looms large, and an intergovernmentalist perspective makes considerable sense. Seen as a historical process, however, the scope of member-state authority appears far more circumscribed, and both the interventions of other actors and the cumulative constraints of rule-based governance more considerable.

. . . .

2   A Historical Institutionalist Critique

Historical institutionalism is a loose term covering a range of scholarship that has tried to combine social science concerns and methods with a recognition that social processes must be understood as historical phenomena (Ikenberry 1994; Thelen and Steinmo 1992). In my own usage, historical institutionalism cuts across the usual sharp dichotomy between rational choice and nonrational choice work, drawing instead on research within both traditions that emphasizes the significance of historical processes. Thus it includes rational choice analyses that consider issues of institutional evolution and path dependence crucial (Knight 1992; North 1990). It excludes much research in political science that uses history only as a technique for widening the universe of available cases.

The core arguments of historical institutionalism contrast with a more common view in the social sciences, which, as March and Olson (1989: 5–6) observe, assumes (often implicitly) that 'institutions and behavior .

.. evolve through some form of efficient historical process. An efficient historical process ... is one that moves rapidly to a unique solution, conditional on current environmental conditions, and is independent of the historical path'. Given this orientation, Skocpol (1992: 58) notes, 'Analysts typically look only for synchronic determinants of policies – for example, in current social interests or in existing political alliances. In addition, however, we must examine patterns unfolding over time'.

Recent research focusing on institutional evolution and path dependence has challenged the expectation that institutions embody the long-term interests of those responsible for original institutional design (Krasner 1989; North 1990). Where the legal authority of the institutional designers is as unquestionable as that of the member states in the EC, I will argue that such a challenge must be based on two sets of claims. First, there must be an account of why gaps – by which I mean significant divergences between the institutional and policy preferences of member states and the actual functioning of institutions and policies – would emerge. Second, critics must explain why, once such gaps emerge, they cannot reliably be closed. One can find scattered elements of such accounts in recent theoretical treatments of institutional change. When brought together, they provide a compelling response to the claim that institutional development in the EU can be understood in functional terms.

I focus first on the factors that are likely to create considerable gaps in member-state control. Four are of fundamental importance: the autonomous actions of European institutional actors, the restricted time horizons of decision makers, the large potential for unintended consequences, and the likelihood of changes in COG preferences over time. Each of these factors requires more detailed discussion.

The partial autonomy of EC institutions

The main contribution of recent neofunctionalist analysis has been to emphasize the autonomous role of supranational actors, especially the Commission and the Court (Burley and Mattli 1993; Ross 1995; Sandholtz 1993). I begin by summarizing these arguments and suggesting that, by themselves, they constitute an inadequate response to intergovernmentalism.

The central objections raised by neofunctionalists can be cast in terms of the same principal-agent framework used in many intergovernmentalist accounts. Member states created the EC, and they did so to serve their own purposes. In order to carry out collective tasks, however, the member states felt compelled to create new institutions. As Moe has argued, the results are predictable.

> A new public agency is literally a new actor on the political scene. It has its own interests, which may diverge from those of its cre-

ators, and it typically has resources – expertise, delegated authority – to strike out on its own should the opportunities arise. The political game is different now: there are more players and more interests to be accommodated (Moe 1990: 121).

In the European context, the member states' problem has been especially difficult. They have needed to create arrangements that would allow reasonably efficient decision making and effective enforcement despite the involvement of a large number of governments with differing interests, and despite the need for decision making, implementation, and oversight on a wide range of complex and tightly coupled policy areas. These considerations generated pressure to grant those who run these institutions considerable authority. Thus, the political organs of the EC are not without resources; as a result, they are not simply passive tools of the member states.

Over time, EC organizations will seek to use grants of authority for their own purposes, especially to increase their autonomy. They will try to expand the gaps in member-state control, and they will use any accumulated political resources to resist efforts to curtail their authority. The result is an intricate, ongoing struggle that is well-known to students of the EU but would also be familiar to American observers of, say, relations between congressional committees and administrative agencies (Kiewiet and McCubbins 1991; McCubbins and Schwartz 1984; Moe 1987). Member states generally (but not always) seek to rein in EC institutions. They recognize, however, that these crucial collective organizations cannot function without significant power and that the authority required will grow as the tasks addressed at the European level expand and become more complex.

For their part, European institutions such as the Commission, the European Court of Justice, and the European Parliament are always looking for opportunities to enhance their powers. Neofunctionalist analyses have emphasized the significant successes of these supranational actors. The Council, to be sure, continues to stand watch over proposed legislation and actively protects member-state interests. Yet the Commission, Parliament, and Court possess considerable ability to advance their own interests. For the Commission, two assets are particularly important (Ross 1995). The first concerns the setting of agendas, a source of influence it frequently shares with the European Parliament (Tsebelis 1994; Tsebelis and Garrett 1996). Choosing which proposals to consider is a tremendously important (if frequently unappreciated) aspect of politics, and here European institutional actors often have primacy. Obviously, this power is far from unlimited; the Commission cannot expect to pass proposals that ignore the preferences of member states. Usually, however, it will have some room for maneuver (Pollack 1995, 1996). Entrepreneurial European actors, such as the Delors

Commission, may be able to frame issues, design packages, and structure the sequence of proposals in ways that maximize their room for independent initiative (Riker 1986). The expansion of qualified majority voting has widened the range of possible winning coalitions, further increasing the agenda-setting powers of the Commission and Parliament. Neofunctionalists have argued persuasively that the Commission's effective use of agenda-setting powers has advanced European integration and increased its own role in policy reform (Ross 1995).

The Commission's second major asset is its role as what Eichener (1992) calls a process manager (see also Peters 1992). Policy making at the EC level, as many have noted, is heavily tilted toward regulation – a type of policy making with its own distinctive qualities (Lowi 1964; Majone 1992b). The development of complex social regulations requires the assembly and coordination of dense networks of experts. This task falls to the Commission, and with it comes additional room for influence. Especially in the labyrinths of regulatory policy making, this role may give the Commission significant power.

The political resources of the European Court are at least as significant. If the United States in the 19th century had a 'state of courts and parties' (Skowronek 1982), the EC looks at times like a 'state of courts and technocrats' (Leibfried 1992: 249). In the process of European integration, the European Court has taken an active, even forcing stance, gradually building a remarkable base of authority and effectively 'constitutionalizing' the emerging European polity (Alter 1996; Burley and Mattli 1993; Weiler 1991). The Court has more extensive powers of judicial review than most of its national counterparts and fewer impediments to action than other EC decision-making bodies. If the Council is prone to gridlock, the necessity of deciding cases inclines the Court to action. This inclination is strengthened by rules allowing simple majority decisions and by a secrecy (neither actual votes nor dissenting views are made public) that shelters judges from member-state and popular pressures. European Court judges also share a common professional background, legal culture (at least on the continent), and sense of mission that seems to effectively limit the influence of the member states in judicial decision-making.

Neofunctionalist accounts of these supranational institutions have certainly demonstrated their prominent role in the EC, as even some intergovernmentalists have acknowledged (see e.g. Moravcsik 1993a: 513). Yet the true influence of the Court, Commission, and Parliament on policy-making and future institutional development remains uncertain. Do these organizations create genuine gaps in member-state control, or do they simply act as agents, fulfilling monitoring, information-gathering, and implementation roles under tight member-state scrutiny? As Martin, among others, has suggested, autonomy may be more apparent than real:

> Politicians and academic observers often infer from such a pattern [of activity] autonomy of the Commission and/or of government leaders. However, consideration of institutional constraints leads us to examine delegation of authority ... because of the costs of exercising tight control over agents, an optimal structure of delegation may be one with little active oversight or overt interference in the negotiating process from principals. Agents rationally anticipate the responses of those they represent. The law of anticipated reactions suggests that we cannot infer a lack of political influence from a lack of observed oversight activity (Martin 1993: 135).

Thus what appears to be autonomy may simply reflect the principals' deft use of oversight. Relying on the disciplining power of anticipated reactions and the use of 'fire alarms' – signals derived from reporting requirements or interest-group monitoring activity – to identify significant problems, member states can stay in the background while remaining firmly in charge (McCubbins and Schwartz 1984).

Again, given the ease of assembling plausible ex post accounts of why given outcomes served member-state interests, these arguments about delegation are difficult to refute, although they are equally difficult to demonstrate (Garrett 1995; Mattli and Slaughter 1995). To foreshadow a point pursued at length below, the intergovernmentalist claim that supranational actors are agents rather than autonomous actors is strengthened if we believe that member states can react powerfully to observed losses of control. If the Commission, Court, and Parliament anticipate that their efforts to produce or exploit gaps will be detected, punished, and reversed, they are indeed unlikely to strike out on their own. Thus a crucial problem with neo-functionalism is that it lacks a coherent account of why the threat of such a member-state reaction is not always credible. I address this problem below.

Before proceeding to that issue, however, the case for constraints on member-state control can be greatly strengthened if other sources of gaps can be identified. Here, the historical institutionalist focus on the temporal dimension of politics is invaluable. It highlights three additional sources of gaps: the short time horizons of decision makers, the prevalence of unanticipated consequences, and the prospect of shifting member-state policy preferences.

The restricted time horizons of political decision makers

A statement attributed to David Stockman, former President Reagan's budget director, is unusual among political decision makers only for its candor. Asked by an adviser to consider pension reforms to combat Social Security's severe long-term financing problems, Stockman dismissed the idea out of hand, exclaiming that he had no interest in wasting 'a lot of political capital on some other guy's problem in [the year] 2010' (quoted in Greider 1982: 43).

Many of the implications of political decisions – especially complex policy interventions or major institutional reforms – only play out in the long run (Garrett and Lange 1994). Yet political decision makers are frequently most interested in the short-term consequences of their actions; long-term effects are often heavily discounted. The principal reason is that of the logic of electoral politics. Keynes once noted that in the long run, we are all dead; for politicians in democratic polities, electoral death can come much faster. Because the decisions of voters, which determine political success, are taken in the short-run, politicians are likely to employ a high discount rate. They have a strong incentive to pay attention to long-term consequences only if these become politically salient, or when they have little reason to fear short-term electoral retribution.

The gap between short-term interests and long-term consequences is often ignored in arguments about institutional design and reform. As a number of critics have noted, choice-theoretic treatments of institutions often make an intentionalist or functionalist fallacy, arguing that the long-term effects of institutions explain why decision makers introduce them (Bates 1987; Hall and Taylor 1994; Knight 1992). Instead, long-term institutional consequences are often the by-products of actions taken for short-term political reasons. The evolution of the congressional committee system in the US – a central institutional feature of contemporary American governance – is a good example. As Shepsle notes, Henry Clay and his supporters introduced the system to further their immediate political goals without regard to long-term consequences: 'The lasting effects of this institutional innovation could hardly have been anticipated, much less desired, by Clay. They were by-products (and proved to be the more enduring and important products) of self-interested leadership behavior' (1989: 141). In this case, the system's long-term functioning was not the goal of the actors who created it. By the same token, the reasons for the institution's invention cannot be derived from an analysis of its long-term effects.

Recognizing the importance of policy makers' high discount rates raises a challenge for intergovernmentalist theories of the EC. As noted above, most international relations approaches to European integration stress the tenacity with which nation states cling to all aspects of national sovereignty. The design of collective institutions is assumed to reflect this preoccupation. Yet, in democratic polities, sustained power requires electoral vindication. Under many circumstances, the first concern of national governments is not with sovereignty per se but with creating the conditions for continued domestic political success. By extension, where the time horizons of decision makers are restricted, functional arguments that are central to transaction-cost views of international regimes also come into question. Rather than being treated as the goals of policy makers under such circumstances, long-term institutional effects should often be seen as the by-products of their purposive behavior.

Unanticipated consequences

Gaps in member-state control occur not only because long-term consequences tend to be heavily discounted. Even if policy makers do focus on long-term effects, unintended consequences are likely to be widespread. Complex social processes involving a large number of actors always generate elaborate feedback loops and significant interaction effects that decision makers cannot hope to fully comprehend (Hirsch 1977; Jervis 1993; Perrow 1984; Schelling 1978; Van Parijs 1982). Although social scientists possess limited tools for dealing with such outcomes, many models – such as core neoclassical arguments about the dynamics of market systems – are based on them.

Unanticipated consequences are likely to be of particular significance in the EU because of the presence of high issue density (Pierson and Leibfried 1995). In sharp contrast to any existing international organization, the range of decisions made at the European level runs almost the full gamut of traditionally domestic issues, from the setting of agricultural prices to the regulation of auto emissions and fuel content to the enforcement of trade restrictions. In the past decade, there has been a massive expansion of EC decision-making, primarily because of the single market project. The sheer scope of this decision-making limits the ability of member states to firmly control the development of policy.

. . . .

Growing issue density has two distinct consequences. First, it generates problems of overload. As European-level decision-making becomes both more prevalent and more complex, it places growing demands on the gatekeepers of member-state sovereignty. In this context, time constraints, scarcities of information, and the need to delegate decisions to experts may promote unanticipated consequences and lead to considerable gaps in member-state control. Member-state scrutiny will usually be extensive in the formation of the grand interstate bargains that are the favorite subject for intergovernmentalists, such as the Treaty of Rome, the Single European Act, and the Maastricht Treaty. In the intervals between these agreements, however, flesh must be added to the skeletal frameworks. In this context, where much policy actually evolves, the ability of member states to control the process is likely to be weaker. As Marks has put it, 'Beyond and beneath the highly visible politics of member-state bargaining lies a dimly lit process of institutional formation' (1993: 403). Marks, for instance, has demonstrated how the Commission exploited its more detailed knowledge of the policy process and its manager role in policy formation to generate influence over the structural funds that the British government failed to anticipate.

As previously discussed, problems of overload are especially consequential when member states must contend with supranational organizations eager to extend their authority. In the development of complex regulatory judgments and the legal determination of what previous decisions actually require, essential policy-making authority is often in the hands of bodies of experts, where the Commission plays a crucial role, or in the hands of the Court. This is, of course, one of the central insights of principal-agent theory. Agents can use their greater information about their own activities and the requirements connected to their work to achieve autonomy from principals. *Asymmetrical access to information*, which is ubiquitous in complex decision-making processes, provides a foundation for influence (Moe 1984).

The second consequence of issue density is the oft-cited process of spillover: the tendency of tasks adopted to have important consequences for realms outside those originally intended, or to empower actors who generate new demands for extended intervention (Haas 1958a). One of the key arguments in much writing on contemporary political economies stresses precisely the embeddedness of economic action within networks of tightly coupled social and political institutions (Garrett and Lange 1994; Hall 1986; North 1990). Efforts to integrate some aspects of complex modern societies, without changing other components, may prove problematic because the sectors to be integrated cannot be effectively isolated. The more 'tightly coupled' government policies are, the more likely it is that actions in one realm will have unanticipated effects in others (Perrow 1984). McNamara (1993), for example, has demonstrated the significance of such interaction effects in the cases of monetary and agricultural policies. Similar connections between the single-market initiative and social policy development have also been documented (Pierson and Leibfried 1995). As the density of EC policy-making increases, such interaction effects become more prevalent, unintended consequences multiply, and the prospect of gaps in member-state control will grow.

Shifts in COG policy preferences

Intergovernmentalist theories tend to treat the institutional and policy preferences of the member states as essentially fixed. This is one of a number of crucial respects in which intergovernmentalism involves a too-easy translation from the world of economic organizations to the world of politics. It may make some sense to assume stable policy preferences when studying firms, or even when one discusses the enduring issues of grand diplomacy. However, as one moves from traditional foreign policy issues such as national security toward the traditionally domestic concerns where the EC has become quite significant, this becomes a more dubious premise.

The policy preferences of member states may shift for a number of reasons. Altered circumstances or new information may lead governments to question previous arrangements. Equally important, changes in government occur frequently, and governments of different partisan complexions often have quite distinct views on policy matters dealt with at the EC level. Governments come and go. Each inherits a set of arrangements from the past; each tries to place its own imprint on this heritage. The result, over time, is that evolving arrangements will diverge from the intentions of original designers, while any newly arriving COG is likely to find institutional and policy arrangements considerably out of synch with its own preferences.

Thus, there are a number of reasons that gaps in member-state control are likely to emerge. Two general points about these sources of gaps deserve emphasis. First, most of these processes have a temporal quality, which makes them invisible to a synchronic analysis of institutional and policy choice. The role of restricted time horizons, unintended consequences, and shifting member-state preferences will only be evident if we examine political processes over time. Second, most of the processes highlighted are much more likely to be prevalent in the EC than in the more purely international settings that were the subject of original efforts to develop and refine regime theory. Because many of the more domestic issues that the EC considers have significant electoral implications, the time horizons of decision makers are likely to be shorter. Unanticipated consequences are also more prevalent, because unlike a typical international regime, the EC deals with many tightly coupled issues. Electoral turnover is more likely to cause shifts in COG preferences on the more domestic issues that the EC considers than on the traditional diplomatic agenda of most international regimes. In short, the EC's focus on core concerns of traditional domestic politics makes it more prone to all the sources of gaps in member-state control that historical institutionalism identifies.

At this point, however, the claim of member-state constraint is incomplete. Transaction-cost approaches are compatible with the possibility of at least some sorts of gaps, although these are rarely addressed in practice. After all, although it has not emphasized unanticipated consequences (Williamson 1993: 116), TCE is based in large part on how uncertainty about future events provokes particular organizational responses. It is not enough to demonstrate that gaps emerge, one must also show that once such losses of control take place, they often cannot be corrected.

For intergovernmentalists, even where the possibility of gaps is acknowledged, these losses of control are considered theoretically unproblematic. Should outcomes occur that principals do not desire, TCE describes two routes to restored efficiency: competition and learning.[2] Competitive pressures in a market society mean that new organizations with more efficient structures will develop, eventually replacing suboptimal organizations. Learning processes among principals can also lead to correction. According to Williamson, one can rely on

> the 'far-sighted propensity' or 'rational spirit' that economics ascribes to economic actors. . . . Once the unanticipated consequences are understood, these effects will thereafter be anticipated and the ramifications can be folded back into the organizational design. Unwanted costs will then be mitigated and unanticipated benefits will be enhanced. Better economic performance will ordinarily result (Williamson 1993: 116–17).

Both these corrective mechanisms, however, are of limited applicability when one shifts from Williamson's focus on firms in private markets to the world of political institutions (Moe 1984, 1990). This is clearest for the mechanism of competition. Political institutions rarely confront a dense environment of competing institutions that will instantly capitalize on inefficient performance, swooping in to carry off an institution's 'customers' and drive it into bankruptcy. Political environments are typically more permissive (DiMaggio and Powell 1991; Krasner 1989). Within Europe, there is nothing like a marketplace for competition among international regimes in which new market entrants can demonstrate that their efficiency (however that might be defined and measured) is greater than the EC's.

Whereas arguments based on competition are weak, learning arguments would appear to be more applicable to political environments. Indeed, Marks (1993: 403), who has pointed to the significance of unanticipated consequences in limiting member-state control, concedes that the use of such arguments 'is tricky in the context of ongoing political relationships where learning takes place'. The process through which actors learn about gaps in control and how to address them has received little attention (McCubbins and Schwartz 1984). However, at least on the biggest issues, intergovernmentalists can reasonably assert that member states will gradually become aware of undesired or unanticipated outcomes and will become more adept at developing effective responses over time. Learning thus seems to offer an effective mechanism for closing gaps and returning institutional and policy designs to an efficient (from the point of view of the member states) path.

Yet the efficacy of learning argument depends crucially on the capacity of member states to fold new understandings back into the organizational design. Put differently, once gaps appear and are identified, how easy is it for principals to regain control? Here the distinction between economic and political institutions becomes crucial. In economic organizations, owners (or principals) may face few barriers to such efforts. In the political world, however (and in the EC, in particular), incorporating new understandings into institutions and policies is no simple task. The next stage of the argument, then, is to consider why gaps, even when identified, might be hard to close. There are three broad reasons: the resistance of EC institutional actors, the institutional obstacles to reform within the EC, and the sunk costs associated with previous actions. If these barriers are sufficiently high, learning will not provide a sufficient basis for correction, and member-state control will be constrained.

The resistance of supranational actors. To the extent that neo-functionalism has had an implicit argument about the difficulty of closing gaps, it has centered on supranational actors. The Court, Commission, and Parliament have accumulated significant political resources. They can be expected to use these resources to resist member-state efforts to exercise greater control over their activities. Yet neo-functionalism has failed to address the question of why, in an open confrontation between member states and supranational actors, the latter could ever be expected to prevail. Member states, after all, have substantial oversight powers, along with control over budgets and appointments. More fundamentally, they possess the legal authority to determine (and alter) the basic rules of the game, including those affecting the very existence of the EC's supranational organizations. The resources of the Court, Commission, and Parliament, such as the capacity to playoff one member state against another in the agenda-setting process and perhaps exploit information asymmetries, are not trivial, but they are clearly modest by comparison. A persuasive account of member-state constraint must draw on more than the political resources of supranational actors.

Institutional barriers to reform. The efforts of principals to reassert control will be facilitated if they can easily redesign policies and institutions. In the economic realm, principals are generally in a strong position to remake their organizations as they choose. Lines of authority are clear, and the relevant decision makers are likely to share the same broad goal of maximizing profits. In politics, however, the temporal dimension raises distinct problems. Political decision makers know that continuous institutional control is unlikely. This lack of continuous control has implications both for how institutions are designed and for the prospects of changing institutions once they are created. In particular, those designing institutions must consider the likelihood that future governments will be eager to overturn their designs, or to turn the institutions they create to other purposes. As Moe notes, the designers of institutions do not want 'their' agencies to fall under the control of opponents. And given the way public authority is allocated and exercised in a democracy, they often can only shut out their opponents by shutting themselves out too. In many cases, then, they purposely create structures that even they cannot control (Moe 1990: 125).

Thus, political institutions are often 'sticky' – specifically designed to hinder the process of institutional and policy reform. This is, of course, far more true of some national polities than others (Weaver and Rockman 1993). Yet the barriers in most national political systems pale in comparison to the obstacles present in the EC. In principle, the member states decide: They have the authority, if they so choose, to reform or even abolish the Court, Commission, or Parliament. But in fact, the rules of the game within the Community were designed to inhibit even modest changes of course. The same requirements that make initial decision making difficult also make previously enacted reforms hard to undo, even if those reforms turn out to be unexpectedly costly or to infringe on member-state sovereignty.

Efforts to employ the most radical vehicle of institutional redesign, a Treaty revision, face extremely high barriers: unanimous member-state agreement, plus ratification by national parliaments and (in some cases) electorates. Given the chances for disagreements among COGs, let alone the problems connected to ratification, the chances of achieving such a high degree of consensus are generally quite low. Use of this process is now widely recognized to be extraordinarily difficult and unpredictable. As Pollack notes, 'The threat of Treaty revision is essentially the 'nuclear option' – exceedingly effective, but difficult to use – and is therefore a relatively ineffective and non-credible means of member state control' (1995: 30).

Efforts to produce more modest changes in course confront more modest hurdles, but these remain far tougher than the obstacles facing, for example, a congressional committee trying to rein in a rogue federal agency. Member states will often be divided on significant issues, but in many policy areas, change requires a unanimous vote of the member states. In other cases, Qualified Majority Voting (QMV) is the rule. This makes reform easier, but the standard – roughly five sevenths of the weighted votes of member states – still presents a threshold that is considerably tougher to cross than that required in most democratic institutions (Pollack 1995, 1996).

The extent to which these barriers constrain member states has recently been questioned. Where it was once understood that participation in the EC was an all-or-nothing proposition, Maastricht has enhanced the prospects for a Europe a la carte, or a Europe of 'variable geometries'. Britain and Denmark received opt-outs on monetary union; the 11 other member states circumvented the British veto by opting 'up and out' with the Social Protocol. As Anderson (1995: 449) summarizes the new situation, Maastricht 'and attached protocols established an important precedent, opening the door to a multitrack Europe in which the treaties and resulting secondary legislation do not apply uniformly to each member'. This new flexibility, however, refers only to additional treaty obligations. Member-state governments may be able to obtain opt-outs from future treaty provisions. Unless they succeed in navigating the difficult EC decision rules for reversing course, however, they are not free to review and discard the commitments of previous governments, even if those earlier governments were preoccupied by short-term goals, had quite different policy preferences, or acted in ways that produced many unanticipated consequences. And as new policies are enacted, the scope of this restrictive acquis communautaire continues to grow.

The rules governing institutional and policy reform in the EC create what Scharpf (1988) calls a 'joint-decision trap', making member-state efforts to close gaps in control highly problematic. The extent of the institutional obstacles will vary from issue to issue. Obviously, if the benefits of acting are high enough, member states will be able to act. But often the benefits must be quite high. In shutting out their potential successors, COGs have indeed shut themselves out as well.

Sunk costs and the rising price of exit. The evolution of EC policy over time may constrain member states not only because institutional arrangements make a reversal of course difficult when member states discover unanticipated consequences or their policy preferences change. Individual and organizational adaptations to previous decisions may also generate massive sunk costs that make policy reversal unattractive. When actors adapt to the new rules of the game by making extensive commitments based on the expectation that these rules will continue, previous decisions may lock in member states to policy options that they would not now choose to initiate. Put another way, social adaptation to EC institutions and policies drastically increases the cost of exit from existing arrangements for member states. Rather than reflecting the benefits of institutionalized exchange, continuing integration could easily reflect the rising costs of 'non-Europe'.

Recent work on path dependence has emphasized the ways in which initial institutional or policy decisions – even suboptimal ones – can become self-reinforcing over time (Krasner 1989; North 1990). These initial choices encourage the emergence of elaborate social and economic networks, greatly increasing the cost of adopting once-possible alternatives and therefore inhibiting exit from a current policy path. Major initiatives have major social consequences. Individuals make important commitments in response to government actions. These commitments, in turn, may vastly increase the disruption caused by policy shifts or institutional reforms, effectively locking in previous decisions (Pierson 1992, 1993).

Work on technological change has revealed some of the circumstances conducive to path dependence (Arthur 1988, 1989; David 1985). The crucial idea is the prevalence of increasing returns, which encourage a focus on a single alternative and continued movement down a specific path once initial steps are taken. Large set-up or fixed costs are likely to create increasing returns to further investment in a given technology, providing individuals with a strong incentive to identify and stick with a single option. Substantial learning effects connected to the operation of complex systems provide an additional source of increasing returns. Coordination effects occur when the individual receives increased benefits from a particular activity if others also adopt the same option. Finally, adaptive expectations occur when individuals feel a need to 'pick the right horse' because options that fail to win broad acceptance will have drawbacks later on. Under these conditions, individual expectations about usage patterns may become self-fulfilling.

As North (1990: 93–5) has argued, all of these arguments can be extended from studies of technological change to other social processes, making path dependence a common feature of institutional evolution. Path dependence may occur in policy development, as well, because policies can also constitute crucial systems of rules, incentives, and constraints (Pierson 1993: 607–8). In contexts of complex social interdependence, new institutions and policies will often generate high fixed costs, learning effects, coordination effects, and adaptive expectations. For example, housing and transportation policies in the US after World War II encouraged massive investments in particular spatial patterns of work, consumption, and residence. Once in place, these patterns sharply constrained the alternatives available to policy makers on issues ranging from energy policy to school desegregation (Danielson 1976; Jackson 1985). Many of the commitments that locked in suburbanization were literally cast in concrete, but this need not be the case. Social Security in the US became gradually locked in through its financing system, which created a kind of rolling intergenerational contract (Pierson 1992). Institutions and policies may encourage individuals and organizations to develop particular skills, make certain investments, purchase particular goods, or devote time and money to certain organizations. All these decisions generate sunk costs. That is to say, they create commitments. In many cases, initial actions push individual behavior onto paths that are hard to reverse.

Lock-in arguments have received relatively little attention within political science, in part because these processes have a tendency to depoliticize issues. By accelerating the momentum behind one path, they render previously viable alternatives implausible. The result is often not the kind of conflict over the foregone alternative that political scientists would quickly identify, but the absence of conflict. Lock-in leads to what Bachrach and Baratz (1962) called non-decisions. This aspect of politics can probably be identified only through careful, theoretically grounded, historical investigation of how social adaptations to institutional and policy constraints alter the context for future decision making.

Over time, as social actors make commitments based on existing institutions and policies, the cost of exit from existing arrangements rises. Within the EC, dense networks of social, political, and economic activity have grown up around past institutional and policy decisions. In speculating about a hypothetical effort to stem the power of Court and Commission, member states must ask themselves if this can be done without, for instance, jeopardizing the single-market project. Thus, sunk costs may dramatically reduce a member-state government's room for maneuver. In the EC, one can see this development in the growing implausibility of member-state exit threats. Although 'sovereign' member states remain free to tear up treaties and walk away at any time, the constantly increasing costs of exit in a densely integrated polity have rendered this option virtually unthinkable for EC member states.

Williamson's confident assertion that learning allows firms to adjust to unanticipated consequences applies far less well to an analysis of politics. Member-state learning from past events may lead, as it did at Maastricht, to greater restrictions on supranational actors in new initiatives (Dehousse 1994). Recapturing ground in previously institutionalized fields of activity, however, will often be quite difficult. Member states do not inherit a blank slate that they can remake at will when their policy preferences shift or unintended consequences become visible. Decision rules hamper reform, and extensive adaptations to existing arrangements increase the associated costs. Thus a central fact of life for member states is the acquis communautaire, the corpus of existing legislation and practice. As Shackleton notes,

> However much Member States might deplore certain aspects of Community policy, there is no question that all find themselves locked into a system which narrows down the areas for possible change and obliges them to think of incremental revision of existing arrangements. (1993: 20).

As has always been true in domestic politics, new governments in member states now find that the dead weight of previous institutional and policy decisions at the European level seriously limits their room for maneuver.

The need to examine political processes over time is the crucial feature linking all the arguments presented in this section. None of these processes are likely to be captured by a snapshot view. Historical institutionalism provides a clear account of why gaps emerge in member-state authority. Member states are often preoccupied with short-term outcomes. Their decisions are certain to produce all sorts of unanticipated consequences. The preferences of member states may also shift, leaving them with formal institutions and highly developed policies that do not fit their current needs. At least as important, historical institutionalism provides a coherent account of why learning processes and fire alarms may not be sufficient to prompt the reassertion of member-state control. If member states decide that their agents have captured too much authority, they may well seek to rein them in. Gaps, however, open possibilities for autonomous action by supranational actors, which may in turn produce political resources that make them more significant players in the next round of decision making. Decision rules and the proliferation of sunk costs may make the price of reasserting control too high.

In short, historical institutionalist analysis can incorporate key aspects of neofunctionalism while offering a stronger and expanded analytical foundation for an account of member-state constraint. There are important points of compatibility between the two approaches. Both suggest that unintended consequences, including spillover, are likely to be significant for institutional development. Both point to the significance of supranational actors. A crucial difference is that neofunctionalism sees political control as a zero-sum phenomenon, with authority gradually transferred from member states to supranational actors, whereas historical institutionalism emphasizes how the evolution of rules and policies along with social adaptations creates an increasingly structured polity that restricts the options available to all political actors. What has been missing from neofunctionalism – and what historical institutionalist arguments can supply – is a more convincing analysis of member-state constraint. Intergovernmentalists challenge neofunctionalism with two key questions: Why would member states lose control, and even if they did, why would they not subsequently reassert it? Historical institutionalism gives clear and plausible answers to both.

. . . .

4   Conclusion

The arguments advanced in this article present major challenges to an intergovernmentalist account of European integration. By providing explicit microfoundations for an analysis that places much more emphasis on member-state constraint, historical institutionalism increases the pressure on intergovernmentalists to offer convincing evidence that the causal processes they posit are actually at work. Rather than simply inferring policy and institutional preferences post hoc from an examination of outcomes, intergovernmentalists will need to show that the desire to achieve these functional outcomes actually motivated key decision makers.[3]

In principle, important aspects of a historical institutionalist analysis could be integrated with intergovernmentalism. Indeed, this article accepts the starting point of intergovernmentalism: member states are the central institution builders of the EC, and they do so to serve their own purposes. Although it has rarely been done in practice, many intergovernmentalist arguments could incorporate a temporal dimension. Keohane (1984: 117), for instance, has recognized the possibility that COGs might anticipate the potential for preference shifts in successor governments. Other challenges, however, will not be so easy to reconcile, such as the possibility that COGs employ a high discount rate in making decisions about institutional design, unintended consequences are ubiquitous, and gaps that emerge are difficult to close. It is hard to see how these factors could be systematically incorporated into intergovernmentalism without undermining the three pillars of that approach: the emphasis on member-state sovereignty concerns, the treatment of institutions as instruments, and the nearly exclusive focus on grand bargains.

The challenge for those wishing to advance a historical institutionalist account is also daunting. The temporal processes outlined here would have to be carefully specified to generate clear hypotheses concerning such matters as when we should expect policy makers to employ short time horizons, when to expect that unintended consequences will be widespread, or how particular decision rules influence the prospects for closing gaps in control. As Pollack (1995, 1996) has persuasively argued, such analyses should focus on the factors that can explain variation in outcomes across issues and among institutional arenas, as well as over time. To develop the historical institutionalist line of argument will require difficult efforts to trace the motivations of political actors in order to separate the intended from the unintended. Determining the impact of sunk costs on current decision making also represents a considerable challenge. Studying political arenas in detail over long periods of time is arduous. The evidentiary requirements encourage a focus on detailed analyses of particular cases, rendering investigations vulnerable to the critique that the cases examined are unrepresentative. However, if one accepts the conclusion that intergovernmentalists must now show that the processes they hypothesize are actually at work, rather than simply inferring those processes from observed outcomes, it is not clear that their research tasks are any less formidable.

. . . .

Notes

1 Throughout, I rely on North's (1990: 3) definition of institutions: 'the rules of the game in a society or, more formally, . . . the humanly devised constraints that shape human interaction'.

2 An alternative way to discount the significance of unintended effects would be to treat them as random 'noise'. Yet although this may be appropriate in studying mass populations (e.g., the dynamics of public opinion), it seems inappropriate when single unintended effects may be quite large, and processes may be path dependent. There is little reason to think that such effects will somehow 'balance out', leaving an analyst free to study the systematic elements. To take an example discussed later in this article, it would be difficult to examine the dynamics of gender issues in Europe by treating the role of Article 119 as noise.

3 Moravcsik (1991) provides a good example of such an effort. Historical institutionalist arguments, however, suggest the need to go beyond even Moravcsik's ambitious attempt to supplement intergovernmentalism with a liberal theory of COG preference formation. Moravcsik's account considers only the synchronic domestic sources of COG preferences, ignoring the possibility of significant feedback effects from previous rounds of institutionalization. For a critique of his interpretation along these lines, see Cameron (1992).

PART IV

The European Polity: Actors, Multilevel Governance and the 'Low Politics' of Regulation

Featured works

- Simon Hix (1998) 'The Study of the European Union II: The "New Governance" Agenda and Its Rival', *Journal of European Public Policy*, 5(1).

- Gary Marks, Liesbeth Hooghe, and Kermit Blank (1996) 'European Integration from the 1980s: State-Centric vs. Multi-Level Governance', *Journal of Common Market Studies*, 34(3).

- Giandomenico Majone (1994a) 'The Rise of the Regulatory State in Europe', *West European Politics* 17(3).

Europe as a Political System: Comparative Politics and Governance Approaches to Integration

As we have seen in previous chapters, the theoretical study of European integration has with a few exceptions relied primarily on approaches derived from the field of international relations. As integration has advanced, however, some scholars have suggested that the European policy space has been so fundamentally transformed that theories of comparative politics and public policy are now required to replace integration theories anchored in the study of international relations (e.g. Anderson 1995; Armstrong and Bulmer 1998; Caporaso 1998b; Hix 1994, 1998, 2005; Hooghe and Marks 2001a, 2001b; Kohler-Koch and Eising 1999; Marks 1992, 1993; Scharpf 2000, 2002). They argue that the EU's complex institutional structure resembles that of a modern (or, for some scholars, a 'postmodern') state more than a standard international regime. As a result, the most relevant question we can ask about European integration is not 'what are the origins of supranational institutions?' and 'how do they affect the dynamics of integration?'. Rather, the explanatory goal of policy-orientated or so-called 'governance' approaches is to find out how public policies are made in various institutional contexts and with what implications for actors at the subnational, national and regional levels.

As we saw in Part II, the idea of conceiving of the EU as a *polity* rather than an arena for interstate bargaining is not new. Lindberg (1963, 1967) and Lindberg and Scheingold (1970) depicted the EU as a political system that could be analysed in terms of its institutional capacity and policymaking procedures. Puchala (1972: 277–9) conceived the EC as a complex 'concordance system' in which nation states remain the central actors, but where other political actors operate at several levels – subnational, national, transnational and supranational – with differing degrees of autonomy depending on the issue area in question. International relations within this system, he suggested, were better described in terms of 'bureaucracy' than 'diplomacy' (1972: 284). Similarly, Haas (1976: 297) conceived of the EC as a system of 'asymmetrical overlap' in which several decision-making authorities coexist at different levels, often with overlapping competencies. Since the late-1980s, however, a new wave of policy-orientated scholarship has swept the field of European integration studies. This scholarship is to some extent a product of agreement on the SEA in 1986. The SEA endowed the EC with new characteristics – such as qualified majority voting and enhanced legislative and judicial powers – that made it appear more like a polity than the site of diplomatic negotiation among autonomous member states. It also added to the scope and complexity of EU policy-making processes, thereby increasing the relevance of policy-orientated perspectives.

This chapter provides an introduction to so-called 'governance' or policy-orientated approaches in current EU studies. Governance is an umbrella term that covers a range of perspectives from 'policy-network analysis', to 'regulatory policymaking', 'epistemic institutionalism', 'multilevel governance' and 'constitutionalization'. What is common to these approaches is that they focus on the way in which decision-making and administration takes place within the EU system. It is impossible in such a short space to provide an inclusive overview of the multitude of governance perspectives in current integration studies. Instead, I seek to draw attention to some general trends in policy-orientated scholarship. The discussion is divided into two sections. The first addresses what I label 'comparative politics approaches' to studying the EU. These approaches conceptualise the EU as a standard political system whose outputs can be understood by applying the methods and theories of 'standard' political science. The second section addresses so-called 'multilevel governance' (MLG) approaches. These conceive of the EU as a unique system of 'multi-tiered' governance that is conceptually different from either a domestic polity or an international organization and that therefore calls for a different set of theoretical tools.

Comparative Politics Approaches to European Integration

As we saw in Part III, integration theory – especially in its intergovernmentalist forms – has been faulted for focusing primarily on treaty-making bargains among member-state governments. Yet, 'grand bargains' do not exhaust the EU phenomenon. As integration has proceeded, the EU has developed an extensive system of politics and government above the level of the nation state. As a result, it has attracted the attention of comparative politics students concerned with explaining 'normal', day-to-day political phenomena within the EU, such as public opinion, interest group formation, electoral politics, public administration, etc. (see Hix 1994, 1998, 2001; Pierson and

Leibfried 1995). The basic tenet of this literature, which parallels trends in earlier federalist scholarship (e.g. Friedrich 1964) is that the EU's institutional structure resembles that of a modern nation state more than an international organization and that we can therefore improve our understanding of how the EU works by applying our general understanding of the main processes in domestic political systems to the EU (Hix 2005).

One popular way to study the EU as a political system has been to conceive of the EU as a quasi-federal polity and to compare political processes within the Union to those in federal states like Germany, Canada and the United States. Scharpf's (1988) pioneering analysis of 'joint-decision traps' suggests that problems of suboptimal policy design in the EU may be illuminated by reference to some of the institutional problems in German federalism (Scharpf 1988: 244). More recently, Kelemen (2000, 2002, 2003, 2004) has demonstrated the use of comparative federalism in explaining the development and shape of regulatory policy within the EU. While they do not argue that the EU is formally a federal system, these authors argue for the growing relevance of federalist concepts to the evolving EU (see Jupille and Caporaso 1999: 433 – on the uses of comparative federalism; see also Majone 1992b; Sbragia 1992).

While some scholars find the EU can be usefully analysed through comparison with other federal systems, others take a broader view. They stress that the EU does not fit comfortably into the traditional Anglo-American typologies of federal systems, which tend to rely on a clear division of authority between the central government and constituent units. The study of the EU's political system should therefore be linked to the study of government and policymaking in domestic political systems *in general*. The case for a general comparative politics approach to studying the EU is compellingly made by Simon Hix (1994, 1998: see Chapter 13 of this book, 2005). His basic claim is that 'politics in the EU is not inherently different to the practice of government in any democratic system' (1994: 1). Decisions at the EU-level increasingly affect the allocation of values, and influences 'who gets what, where, and how' in European society. As a result, conflict over European integration can no longer be reduced to a single dimension between forces favouring more integration and forces favouring less integration. Rather, political conflict increasingly falls along a traditional left-right dimension familiar to domestic systems (Hix 1994: 2). The upshot is that to understand how the EU works on a day-to-day basis we must reject IR-based integration theories in favour of general theories and methods of political science. This view is elaborated by Hix in his book *The Political System of the European Union* (2005) in which he describes how the EU's everyday political process actually works and demonstrates the relevance of political science theories to understanding discrete policy processes such as electoral politics, regulatory, distributive, monetary and foreign policies. In his later work, Hix also studies patterns of party competition at the EU level (see Hix 2001).

Hix's work has been instrumental in sparking debate concerning appropriate methods of studying the EU. However, he has been criticized both by state-centric scholars and MLG theorists for exaggerating the state-like nature of the EU and for ignoring the continued ubiquity of member-state governments in EU decision-making (see Hurrell and Menon 1996). In Chapter 13 below Hix (1998) explicitly addresses the challenge from intergovernmentalism and MLG theory. He emphasizes that the EU, while not a traditional Westphalian state, possesses the main characteristics of a 'normal' political system. As a result, he argues, we can learn more by comparing the EU to domestic political systems or by using concepts from the field of comparative public policy to study specific European policy processes than we can learn from treating the EU as either an international regime or a fundamentally new form of (multilevel) governance.

Multilevel Governance

Like comparativist integration studies, MLG theory is part of a new wave of thinking about the EU as a political system. But where comparativists portray the EU as a 'normal' political system subject to theories of domestic public policy, students of MLG paint a more ambiguous picture. In their view, the EU is neither reducible to a domestic political system – whether quasi-federal, federal or unitary – nor to a system of interstate bargaining. Rather, the EU is best understood as a new form of complex, multilevel system in which decision-making and implementation authority is shared across multiple 'tiers': sub-national, national, transnational, and supranational (Bulmer 1994; Hooghe 1996; Jachtenfuchs 2001; Marks 1992, 1993; Marks, Hooghe and Blank 1996: see Chapter 14 below). The complex nature of the EU polity implies that EU politics defies explanation either by approaches applied to politics within states or by approaches applied to politics between states but that EU politics are best understood by combining elements from both public policy and IR-based theories (Bache and Flinders 2004: 1; Jachtenfuchs 1995; Hurrell and Menon 1996: 397).

The concept of MLG was first introduced by Gary Marks (1992) to capture developments in EU structural policy that made structural funds subject to administration through partnerships between local, national and supranational actors. Subsequently, the concept has been applied to a broader range of EU decision-making. What unites most MLG theories is the basic assumption that the sovereignty of the

European state has been eroded from several directions. Externally, factors that undermine state sovereignty include the deregulation of trade and financial markets, and the increased volatility of international capital that has deprived the state of much of its traditional capacity to govern the economy (Bache and Flinders 2004: 96; Bulmer 1998: 366). In a regional context, the sovereignty of individual states has been further diluted by collective decision-making within the EU, and by (unintended) consequences of delegation to supranational institutions. Finally, subnational (local and regional) authorities have become more assertive vis-à-vis national governments wearing away executive control in many policy areas (Bulmer 1998: 368; Hooghe and Marks 1996, 2001a; Kohler-Koch 1996, 2002). The result is that decision-making authority is dispersed across different spatial locations.

The alleged dispersion of authority away from state executives toward supranational, regional and local authorities puts MLG sharply at odds with state-centric models. Indeed, Marks, Hooghe and Blank (1996: Chapter 14 below) distinguish intergovernmentalist and MLG approaches as the main competing approaches to European integration. At the same time, MLG approaches also challenge the logic of supranationalism. According to MLG theorists, integration has not resulted in ever-increasing powers for supranational institutions. States remain crucial players in many policy areas (Jachtenfuchs & Kohler-Koch 2004:102). The emerging picture, therefore, is a complex and pluralistic policy-process not firmly under control by member states but not explicable in terms of supranational entrepreneurship either.

It is important to note that the MLG approach does not offer a theory of integration. Rather it is a descriptive approach that depicts complexity as the principal feature of the EU political system and invites us to draw on a combination of other theories – domestic as well as international – to explain European policy outcomes. As is exemplified by the piece by Marks, Hooghe and Blank in Chapter 14, many MLG theorists invoke rational institutionalism to explain delegation to supranational institutions and to demonstrate how collective decision-making can result in a loss of control for individual states. Federalism constitutes another island of MLG theorising. Federalists seek to specify the optimal allocation of authority across multiple tiers of government. Among the terms they adopt to describe systems of diffused authority are MLG or governance (Elazar 1987; Nicolaidis 2001; Simeon and Cameron 2000). A third literature that bears directly on MLG is public-policy analysis. Public policy analysts, like MLG theorists, are concerned with studying how governance works, not only at the national level, but also at the interface between the national and international spheres (see Peters and Pierre 2000). Finally, much of the MLG literature is based on constructivist premises, highlighting the normative effects of European institutions (see Jacthenfuchs 2001; Rosamond 2000: 173).

MLG is primarily a descriptive and analytical approach seeking to draw attention to the complexity of EU governance, but it also has a normative dimension. To MLG theorists, power sharing across multiple jurisdictions is not merely a fact of European governance, it also constitutes an ideal form of political organization since it is thought to be more efficient in reflecting the heterogeneity of preferences of different constituencies situated at different levels. Moreover, multiple jurisdictions allow for jurisdictional competition, which can serve as a stimulus for effective governance and regulatory innovation (see Thompson 2003; also Jachtenfuchs and Kohler-Koch 2004: 97–8). Hence, MLG entails a clear normative commitment to decentralized policymaking.

Characteristics of multilevel governance

When defining multilevel governance, the first step is to understand what is meant by the term 'governance'. According to Webber et al. (2004: 4), 'governance involves the co-ordinated management and regulation of issues by multiple and separate authorities, the interventions of both public and private actors, formal and informal arrangements, in turn structured by discourse and norms, and purposefully directed toward particular policy outcomes'.

As such 'governance' differs in crucial ways from 'government'. 'Government', traditionally understood, reflects a notion of a unified state, comprising a single locus of power. By contrast, 'governance' implies that the regulation of societies has been supplemented by a wealth of political actors other than governments (Webber et al. 2004: 5). Whereas government tends to rely on vertical, hierarchical forms of regulation, governance reflects patterns of horizontally dispersed power, taking various formal or informal institutional shapes.

There is no consensus on how to define the EU MLG system. However, the following characteristics are frequently used to describe EU governance:

- *Multiple actors.* Policymaking and implementation is no longer conducted exclusively by states, but involves a variety of public and private actors at the national, supranational, and international level (Marks , Hooghe and Blank 1996; Kohler-Koch 1996: 191; Peters and Pierre 2004: 82; Caporaso 1996: 32). Key actors may include quasi-governmental agents such as regional authorities, employers and labour associations, and non-state actors such as NGOs and multinational corporations.
- *Differentiation.* Policymaking is functionally differentiated according to distinct policy sectors, such as external relations,

internal market, agriculture and the environment (Hix 1996b; Peterson and Bomberg 1999). Decision-rules and dominant actors vary across policy sectors. Some sectors are characterized by tight government control, while others involve both supranational and non-governmental actors. The way decision-rules and policy procedures are structured in different EU policy sectors determines policy outcomes.

- *Technocracy*. Much EU policymaking is technocratic in nature. Expert policy networks tend to form around specific EU policy sectors, assembling technical and professional expertise, and seeking to shape policy options which are likely to be endorsed by political decision-makers.
- *Non-hierarchical decision-making*. Whereas the domestic relationship between state executives and sub-state actors is typically one of strict hierarchy, there is often no established hierarchy among different policy actors in the EU system. The relationship between state, substate and non-state actors is one of 'mutual dependence' rather than subordination (Marks, Hooghe and Blank 1996: see Chapter 14 below).
- *Informal relations*. EU MLG is characterized by predominantly *informal* interactions between policy actors. While governments generate compliance through formal prerogatives such as sovereignty and constitutional legitimacy, the effectiveness of the EU governance system derives to a large extent from reliance on informal norms and procedures, habits, informal agreements and shared premises that lead actors to comply with directives.

Policymaking in a multilevel system of governance

MLG refers to the particular practice of coordinating the activities of different levels of governance; local, regional, national, supranational and transnational (Thompson 2003: 159). In the absence of a central political authority, this typically requires direct negotiation and bargaining between actors situated at different levels of decision-making. Several kinds of administrative arrangements are said to typify EU decision-making, including 'policy networks', 'expert committees', 'regulatory agencies', 'open methods of coordination' and 'directly deliberative polyarchy'. Among the most frequently stressed arrangements is governance through so-called 'policy networks' (Kenis and Volker 1991; Kohler-Koch and Eising 1999; Mayntz 1993; Peterson 1995a, 2001; Peterson and Bomberg 1999). The concept of 'policy networks' derives from the British policy networks approach, which was developed during the 1980s (see Rhodes 1996, 1997). In contrast to government agencies, policy-networks are characterized by predominantly *informal* interactions between public and private actors who cooperate to solve problems of collective action. A typical policy network may involve semi-autonomous parliamentary committees and bureaucratic agencies inhabited by experts as well as private actors with special expertise and competence in a policy area (Thompson 2003: 151). As such policy networks are similar to 'epistemic communities' as defined by Peter Haas (1992). In the EU context, an often-cited reason for the spread of policy networks is the relative scarcity of EU resources. Because of its limited budget, the only way for the Union to deal with the burden of decision-making and implementation is to encourage the formation of elite policy networks that facilitate exchange of information and ideas and build consensus through informal exchange and backroom bargaining (Peterson and Bomberg 1999).

A second means of policymaking is through delegation to so-called regulatory agencies. According to many scholars, a key aspect of EU governance is that it is orientated toward the regulation of public activities rather than the redistribution of resources (see e.g. Bulmer 1994: 368; Caporaso 1996; Hix 1998; Kohler-Koch 1996: 364; Majone 1994a: 87). Research on the EU as a regulatory state is most prominently associated with the work of Giandomenico Majone (1991, 1993a, 1994a: see Chapter 15 below, 1996, 1999). In contrast to the 'interventionist' state, which relies on taxing and spending to steer the economy, the regulatory state uses rule-making to alter market behaviour (Majone 1997: 139). According to Majone, the EU is particularly well suited to regulatory policymaking. The Union has no real powers of taxation and its budget is too small to support large-scale public-expenditure initiatives (1994a: 87). The only way to increase its competencies, therefore, is to expand its regulatory activities (Majone 1997: 150). The benefit of such activities is that they do not require a large public budget, since the real cost of regulatory programmes is borne by the firms and individuals who have to comply with regulations. Furthermore, by keeping to a regulatory mode of governance, the EU can rely on the existing political and administrative structures of member states to carry out its policies (Majone 1997: 149).

A major consequence of the shift towards regulatory policy-making is the growth in specialized agencies operating quasi-independently from central governments (Dehousse 1997; Majone 1997: 152). Examples include the European Court of Justice, the European Central Bank and a variety of semi-autonomous agencies for the implementation and supervision of economic and social policies (Majone 1994a: 83; Hix 1998: 40). To Majone, the spread of these agencies can be accounted for by a functional logic; the Commission delegates in order to increase its own competences and member states delegate to enhance the credibility of their policy commitments. However, his account also has a normative bend. To Majone, delegation of regulatory powers to independent agencies entails three major benefits. First, regulatory agencies provide decision-makers with technical expertise and specialized information. Second, delegation to agencies separate from the government itself frees administrators from partisan politics thereby introducing greater continuity and stability into policymaking. Third, the delegation of regulatory powers to independent agencies enables credible policy commitments. By transferring enforcement powers to the European Court, for example, member states can commit to regulatory strategies that would not be credible in the absence of delegation (Majone 1994a: 84, 1997: 154). The overall result is greater policy efficiency.

The Legitimacy of Supranational Governance

A major debate within the EU literature concerns the possibility of democratically legitimate government at an EU level. This debate is closely tied to the governance literature insofar as the phenomenon of MLG is held to give rise to special legitimacy concerns. MLG is associated with the delegation of rule-making authority to non-majoritarian and semi-private institutions at both the national and EU level, thereby reducing the impact of democratic input in crucial areas of policy. MLG also gives rise to problems of accountability: as authority is dispersed across multiple levels, the lines of responsibility often become unclear. Moreover, increasing delegation to expert agencies means that many decisions get made as matters of administrative discretion, making it difficult if not impossible to hold supranational institutions and regulatory agencies to political account. This has given rise to a debate on whether the EU suffers from a 'democratic deficit'.

There are two broad positions within the 'democratic deficit' debate. The first position rests on standards derived from analogy with national institutions of liberal parliamentary democracy. The basic tenet of this position is that political outputs must be congruent with democratic inputs. Or, to put it differently, people affected by a policy should have a say in its formulation. This position supports two contrasting views of how to approach the EU's democratic deficit. One view, supported mainly by Euro-sceptics, holds that political authority must remain with the EU member states, since their linking of people, territory and community provides the only viable context for liberal democracy (see especially Moravcsik 1999a). The upshot of this view is that integration should be rolled back. The second view, which is broadly pro-integrationist, holds that the solution to the democratic deficit lies in extending liberal democratic institutions to the European level – for example by enhancing the powers of the European Parliament – thereby making the EU more directly responsive and accountable to its citizens (Burgess 1989). On this view, the solution to the democratic deficit is to move the EU in a more federal direction, giving its citizens a direct role in formulating and controlling EU policy.

The second broad position holds that it is improper to judge the democratic legitimacy of the EU by standards derived from national parliamentary democracy. Unlike national governments, the EU is not underpinned by the existence of a 'demos' or people. It lacks the grounding in a common history, culture, discourse and symbolism on which most national polities can draw to justify majority rule. Without a demos to legitimize majority rule, EU decision-making can only be legitimate if it is non-majoritarian (Dehousse 1995; Majone 1998; Scharpf 1997). This argument is persuasively defended by Fritz Scharpf. In his seminal work *Governing in Europe: Effective and Democratic?* (1999) Scharpf offers a theory of democracy based on 'responsiveness' rather than participation. He presents two conceptions of democratic legitimacy. The first he calls 'input legitimacy' or 'government *by* the people'. Input legitimacy requires that collective decisions 'reflect the general will' of a people as articulated in widely participatory procedures. In a European context, he argues, this is difficult to achieve because of the lack of a European demos. The second conception – 'output legitimacy' or 'government *for* the people' – works via constraints on policy outcomes. This conception does not presuppose any direct input from an European electorate but merely requires the satisfaction of wider classes of 'problem-solving concerns' which can be shared by members of various nested or overlapping groups. On this view, what legitimises EU governance is not democratic representation and control but rather the efficiency of policy output.

Scharpf's defence of 'output legitimacy' is close in spirit to Majone's conception of 'substantive democratic legitimacy', which he outlines in Chapter 15 below. Majone argues that the EU derives *substantive* legitimacy from policy consistency and from the expertise and problem-solving skills of regulators. The main task delegated to regulatory agencies is to correct market failures. In contrast to redistributive policies, which are purely zero-sum, issues of market efficiency are positive-sum games insofar as everybody stands to gain from efficiency-enhancing solutions. Because they tend toward Pareto-optimality, regulatory policies need not be decided by majority rule, but their legitimacy can instead be evaluated by the efficiency gains they secure for people subject to them. On this view, the best way to solve the Union's democratic deficit is to secure maximum capacity for problem-solving. The objective, therefore, is a regulatory state: a large technocracy based on governance by experts (see Majone 1997: 160–1; Kühnhardt 2000: 492).

To Majone and Scharpf the EU is legitimized by its problem-solving capacity and by the fact that its policies have regulatory rather than redistributive effects. If legitimacy is currently lacking, it will grow with the Union's ability to prove its capacity for action. Yet, problem-solving efficiency may not be sufficient to legitimize EU policymaking. First, it is by no means clear that efficiency is of greater importance to the average EU citizens than democratic representation. Second, it is not clear that regulatory policies will necessarily be Pareto-optimal. As Caporaso (1996) argues, regulatory policies are not politically neutral but often have distributive consequences. When deciding among alternative regulatory policies with different distributive effects, policy-makers are likely to be guided not by principles of Pareto-efficiency but by the provision of a politically optimal distribution of rents across groups seeking to influence government policy (Caporaso 1996: 43). This implies that large concentrated, well-organized and well-financed groups will usually win out (ibid.). Moreover, there is a deeper problem with 'output legitimacy' (see Moravcsik and Sangiovanni 2002). In the absence of participatory procedures, how are we to judge what the public wants? How do we know which classes of 'problem-solving concerns' are deemed most pressing by citizens? On an output legitimacy logic, the meaning of 'regulatory efficiency' will depend to a large degree on the interpretation of non-elected officials who are often difficult to hold accountable for any misinterpretations.

The relationship of MLG to existing theories

The intellectual lineage of MLG theory is complex. Several scholars have pointed to a close link between MLG theory and neofunction-alism. Although it does not offer a theory of integration, the MLG approach shares several neofunctionalist premises. Like neofunctional-ists, MLG theorists hold that supranational actors and transnational policy networks play a significant role in shaping regional decision-making (Hooghe 1996; Pollack 1996: 429). Second, the MLG approach, like neofunctionalism, stresses that supranational actors like the Commission and the Court may form policy coalitions with sub-national public actors, bypassing member states (George 2004:112). Finally, MLG theorists, like neofunctionalists, point to important feed-back loops between the Union's day-to-day policy output and the advance of integration. In neofunctionalism, integration is not only advanced through institution building but joint policymaking itself exercises a substantial integrative effect. Similarly, according to MLG theorists, the way policies are made and their impact shapes the institutional framework and changes the overall structure of the European governance system (Jacthenfuchs and Kohler-Koch 2004). As a result of these insights, some scholars argue that MLG has effectively taken the place of neofunctionalism as the alternative theory to intergovern-mentalism (George 2004: 112; Hooghe and Marks 2001b).

There are important similarities between MLG theory and neofunc-tionalism to be sure but it seems to me that a more direct – though widely overlooked – lineage can be traced back to classic functionalism (see Part I). To see why, consider the standard depiction (and indeed normative vision) of MLG. MLG on most descriptions involves a large number of task-specific, overlapping and intersecting jurisdictions. Such jurisdictions are set up to solve particular policy problems, such as managing a common pool resource or setting a technical standard. Hence, their constituencies are often not territorially circumscribed groups but individuals who share a functional space, for example public service users, exporters or software producers (Hooghe and Marks 2001b). The main allure of such task-specific jurisdictions is that they are flexible – they come and go as demands for governance change or as the changing cost and benefit of supplying a particular public good or service impel delegation to another jurisdiction (ibid.). Moreover, as we have seen in the work of governance scholars such as Scharpf and Majone, the delegation of authority to independent agencies is believed to circumvent political conflict by encouraging a focus on (non-controversial) functional 'problem-solving' (Scharpf 1988, 1997). Both these depictions of MLG seem surprisingly close in spirit to Mitrany's functionalism. After all, the goal of Mitrany's functionalism was to diffuse political power through delegation to non-majoritarian, single-issue authorities or agencies, which would rely heavily upon technocratic expertise and in which 'functional problem-solving' rather than political bargaining would dominate.

As a normative approach to international organization, the MLG approach shares many of the basic tenets of Mitrany's functionalism. However, it also suffers from many of the same weaknesses. One weakness derives from the problem of administrative feasibility. A governance system arranged across multiple and intersecting spatial and functional jurisdictions may allow for optimal flexibility but it is also prone to high transaction costs of coordinating multiple jurisdictions. To the extent that the policies of one jurisdiction have negative externalities for other jurisdictions, some form of coordination is necessary to avoid socially perverse outcomes (Hooghe and Marks 2001b). As Fritz Scharpf points out, however, coordination costs tend to increase exponentially as the number of relevant parties or jurisdictions increases and, as a result, 'negotiated solutions incur exponentially rising and eventually prohibitive transaction costs' (Scharpf 1997: 70; see also Hooghe and Marks 2001b). Prohibitive coordination costs was one of the central problems faced by Mitrany, which lead him to concede – albeit reluctantly – that some form of central political authority was necessary to govern international functional jurisdictions. The commitment by MLG scholars to maximum decentralization and flexibility appears to throw up a similar conundrum.

As discussed above, the governance approach – at least in its technocratic version – also runs into similar problems of democratic legitimacy as did classic functionalism. Mitrany saw no problem in rejecting direct democratic participation as a basis for international policy-making. To him participatory democracy was only one possible mechanism of legitimation with a number of possible (functional) alternatives. As we have seen, a similar position is taken by some (but by no means all) governance theorists. The 'output legitimacy' argument of scholars like Scharpf and Majone rests on an explicitly functional basis of legitimation. As long as functional problem solving capacity remains high, legitimacy concerns are satisfied. But if their solution to the problem of legitimacy is similar to Mitrany's – namely to emphasize the satisfaction of welfare goals over democratic participation and control – it also falls subject to the same basic criticisms: 'Regulatory efficiency' is not a neutral term that can be easily separated from politics. As Sol Picciotto (2002: 505) notes, the growth of international regulatory or governance networks entails an attempt to 'depoliticize' issues by deploying scientific managerial or professional techniques. However, such techniques are neither neutral in themselves, nor in the processes of their development and application (ibid.). To operate effectively, they must rest on generally acceptable value judgements and reflect wider public concerns. But without a process of popular participation how will these concerns be articulated?

Of What is the EU an Instance?

The introduction of new comparative politics and governance approaches into the study of European politics raises the fundamental question 'Of what is the EU an instance?'. Is it an international regime, a quasi-federal system or something altogether new? Which aspects of the European integration process should we study and why? In general, the governance literature can be said to represent a move away from 'grand theories' of integration and toward middle-range theories of specific policy processes and phenomena (Scharpf 1997). Substituting the investigation of day-to-day policymaking for the study of long-term integration processes has two advantages. First, studies of this kind contribute to a better understanding of how the European political system actually works. Second, the case for a governance approach is bolstered by the $N = 1$ problem. As the independent variable of governance studies is not the EU as a whole but more concrete parts of its institutional set-up, this type of study opens up a wealth of possibilities for comparison to other political systems (see Jachtenfuchs and Kohler-Koch 2004: 101; Rosamond 2000: 107).

A major critique of the governance literature, which pertains specifically to MLG approaches but not to the comparativist approach of

Hix and others, is that it suffers from a lack of theoretical focus and explanatory power. MLG approaches have been widely faulted for offering a descriptive rather than a theoretical approach to the study of European integration (Bache & Flinders 2004; Jachtenfuchs 2001; Peters and Pierre 2004: 88; Puchala 1999: 323). Terms such as 'multi-level', 'multi-tiered' and 'fragmented' describe the complexity of the EU political system but do not provide a framework for explaining how this system functions and why. The MLG approach also fails to supply an operational framework for policy analysis. As Marks, Hooghe and Blank concede (see Chapter 14), MLG theorists have largely failed to frame clear predictions about the outcomes of the EU governing process. While they have spent considerable energy documenting the complexity of EU policy processes, they have generated few testable hypotheses regarding how this complexity impacts on public decision-making.

A second flaw in the MLG approach pertains to the failure to embed the study of European governance in a wider comparative context. While the policy-centred approach favoured by Simon Hix and others encourages cross-national and cross-regional comparison of policy processes and outcomes, MLG studies tend to be more introspective. Concepts like 'multi-tiered', 'fragmented', 'condominio', etc. capture the complex nature of European institutions but also stress their uniqueness. As Fritz Scharpf argues, this has the adverse effect of carving out a separate and theoretically distinct domain of 'European Community Studies', which is isolated from the general study of policy-making, whether at a domestic or international level (2000: 7–9). Moreover, the international context is often missing from governance studies. MLG approaches have a tendency to view the EU as a closed system, thereby ignoring the role of international factors such as globalization and interdependence in influencing public policy (Hurrell and Menon, 1996: 394–6). These traits – treating the EU as 'unique' and ignoring the role of international factors – were among the key failings that led a generation of scholars to reject neofunctionalist theory during the 1970s. If MLG theory is to constitute a viable successor to neofunctionalism, it must do better on both counts.

Further Reading

Hix, S. (2005) *The Political System of the European Union*, 2nd edn (Basingstoke: Palgrave). An excellent textbook that applies general theories and methods of political science to examine how the EU's everyday political processes actually work.

Hooghe, L. and Marks, G. (2001) *Multi-level Governance and European Integration* (Lanham, MD: Rowman and Littlefield). This book focuses on the emergence of multilevel governance in Europe and discusses its implications for policymaking in national and regional settings.

Peterson, J. and Bomberg, E. (1999) *Decision-making in the European Union* (Basingstoke: Palgrave). An example of policy-network analysis applied to analysing decision-making in different EU policy sectors.

Jachtenfuchs, M. (2001), 'The Governance Approach to European Integration', *Journal of Common Market Studies*, 39(2), 245–64. This article provides an excellent review of the literature on EU governance.

Chapter 13

The Study of the European Union II: The 'New Governance' Agenda and its Rival

Simon Hix*

The New Governance of the EU: Epitaph to a Successful Protest

The study of the European Union (EU) has moved on from the (somewhat artificial) international relations (IR) vs. comparative politics/comparative public policy controversy of the early 1990s (e.g. Hix 1994, 1996b; Rhodes and Mazey 1995; Risse-Kappen 1996). But a general comparative politics/public policy approach has not emerged as the new dominant programme. A popular view is that comparative politics and IR need to be combined to understand the 'new governance' of the EU (Hurrell and Menon 1996; Jachtenfuchs 1995). This label is not directly attributable to any single scholar. Rather, it encompasses a variety of perspective that share some common conceptions, assumptions, and research strategies.

From this new governance perspective, for example, the EU may be more than an international organization, but it will not replicate a state. Governance within this new polity is *sui generis:* through a unique set of multi-level, non-hierarchical and regulatory institutions, and a hybrid mix of state and non-state actors. Comparative politics/public policy is inadequate because it is rooted in the study of domestic states. Instead of replacing IR with an 'old agenda', therefore, the task is to develop a new theoretical and normative programme. Echoing Dahl's (1961) famous 'epitaph to the successful protest' by the behavioural school, this 'new governance' perspective welcomes the comparativist critique of IR, but argues that it is time to sail on to new waters.

. . . .

---

* Reproduced by kind permission of Taylor and Francis Ltd (http://www.tandf.co.uk/journals) from Simon Hix (1998) 'The Study of the European Union II: The "New Governance" Agenda and Its Rival', *Journal of European Public Policy*, 5(1), 38–65. The text has been edited, as indicated, to fit the format of this volume. Some peripheral footnotes have been omitted.

Empirical Interpretation: A Novel form of Governance?

Facts, by definition, are irrefutable. However, facts are inevitably interpreted in different ways. It is in the interpretation of empirical evidence that the first and most basic controversy about the EU emerges. Is the EU a fundamentally new form of governance, or is it simply an unusual version of an old model?

A new governance system

'New governance' has several interrelated characteristics. First, the process of governing is no longer conducted exclusively by the state, but involves 'all those activities of social, political and administrative actors that...guide, steer, control or manage society' (Kooiman 1993: 2). Second, the relationship between state and non-state actors in this process is 'polycentric and non-hierarchical' (Jachtenfuchs 1995: 115) and 'mutually dependent' (Jachtenfuchs 1997: 40). Third, the key governance function is 'regulation' of social and political risk, instead of resource 'redistribution'. The result is a new 'problem-solving' rather than bargaining style of decision-making. In other words, 'new governance' is in stark contrast to the classic state-centric, command-and-control, redistributive and ideological processes of 'government' and 'politics' (e.g. Easton 1953; Lasswell 1936).

Policy-making in the EU is not the same as in a domestic state. There is no central agenda-setting and coordinating actor, like the chief executive in a presidential system or the governing party in a parliamentary system (Peters 1994). The process, from initiation through adaptation to implementation is complex and involves constant deliberation and cooperation between several levels of state and non-state officials In the adoption stage, the need to satisfy a myriad of territorial and functional constituencies requires open 'policy communities/networks', where private interest groups are active and equal participants, alongside European, national and subnational state officials (Mazey and Richardson 1993a, 1995; Peterson 1995a, 1995b; Peterson and Bomberg 1997). The technical nature of market regulation also means that scientific expertise has an unusually high prominence in the policy process (Joerges and Neyer 1997).

In the decision-making stage, *informal* contacts, networks and norms continue to define policy options, provide information and expertise to legislators in the Council and the Parliament, and ultimately shape political outcomes (Kohler-Koch 1994, 1997). For example, policy agreements are usually made long before decisions reach the formal legislative decision-making in the Council (van Schendelen 1996). And, when they do get there, the informal norm that decisions should be by 'consensus' ensures that Council votes are only taken in 25% of cases where only a qualified majority is required (Hayes-Renshaw and

Wallace 1997: 18–19). Finally, in the implementation stage, the problem-solving style, state-private interaction and the interlocking of European and national actors continue in the system of 'comitology' (Joerges and Neyer 1997) and the network of European and national agencies administering EU legislation (Richardson 1996b). With no clear hierarchy of power and competence anywhere in this process, this is 'governance without government' (Rosenau and Czempiel 1992).

Above all, the ability and need to 'regulate' the EU single market is the driving force behind this new governance system.[1] 'As the single market has been progressively completed, a distinctive model of regulation has evolved' (Begg 1996: 527). Regulatory governance, with the aim of positive-sum resource allocation, is a fundamental break from the tradition of redistributive (zero-sum) politics: where state executives allocate resources from electoral losers to electoral winners (Majone 1993a, 1996: 47-60; Müller and Wright 1994; Peltzman 1976)[2]

. . . .

In sum, the new orthodoxy is that the EU has evolved into a unique system of multi-level governance (Marks, Hooghe and Blank 1996). This 'governance *beyond* the state' does not necessarily mean governance *above* the state, thus simply reconstituting the state with all its constituent elements simply on a higher political level (Jachtenfuchs 1995: 124). The EU is *not* a 'rerun' of the processes and policies that earlier made the national state (Schmitter 1996a: 14). Instead, it is 'a web of national and supranational regulatory institutions held together by shared values and objectives, and by a common style of policy-making' (Majone 1996: 217). In other words, it is a 'novel form of political domination' (Schmitter 1991) or a 'post-modern form of state' (Caporaso 1996).

A political system: i.e. 'government' and 'politics' still matter

The EU may not be a state in the Marxian or Weberian sense. But what if the west European state is 'an innovation developed within a specific geographical and cultural context'? (Badie and Birnbaum 1983 [1979]: 135). This would mean that the EU need not be a state to fulfil many of the traditional functions of government. A 'political system' can exist with a low level of centralization, differentiation and institutionalization, by relying on sub-agencies to administer state authority (ibid.: 133–4). And the EU certainly possesses all the classic characteristics of a political system.[3]

The first of these characteristics are the *formal* rules for collective decision-making, the 'government' of the EU. Through the interpretation of these rules, and the 'direct effect' and 'supremacy' of EU law, the European Court of Justice (ECJ) has shaped an EU 'constitution' (Mancini 1989; Stein 1981; Weiler 1991, 1997a). Executive, legislative and judicial powers are exercised 'jointly' by the EU institutions. Nevertheless, instead of a classic 'organic' separation of powers into three different institutions, there is a 'functional' separation of powers across several institutions: with hierarchies *within* each governmental power (see especially Lenaerts 1991). For example, the Council possesses long-term executive authority – e.g. sets the general policy agenda and delegates power to the Commission – whereas the Commission possesses short-term executive authority – e.g. a monopoly on legislative initiation (cf. Cram 1997: 154–77; Pollack 1997a). Similarly, in the execution of policy in the comitology system, the Commission is more powerful under the advisory and management procedures, whereas the Council is more powerful under the regulatory and safeguard procedures (Docksey and Williams 1997; Dogan 1997). Moreover, these principal-agent hierarchies are repeated in the relationships between the Council and the ECJ and between the ECJ and national courts (Alter 1997, 1998; Weiler 1994).

In addition, the EU legislature has become increasingly bicameral as the European Parliament (EP) has gained conditional and unconditional veto powers (Earnshaw and Judge 1995; Garrett 1995; Jacobs 1997; Kreppel 1997; Tsebelis 1994) . . .

The second characteristic is the 'policy' output of the system. The EU redistributes resources through the structural and cohesion funds, which constitute almost 5% of GDP for several member states. However, *direct* redistribution by the EU is small compared with the domestic welfare states. Nevertheless: EU policies and the 'economic constitution' of the EU have an enormous *indirect* redistributional impact (Grahl and Teague 1989; Maduro 1997; Rhodes 1995). Through mutual recognition and harmonization in the single market, state aid and competition rules, the convergence criteria for economic and monetary union: and the emerging social policy regime, the EU severely restricts the redistributional capacity of domestic welfare states (Leibfried and Pierson 1995; Scharpf 1997; Streeck 1995, 1996). In addition to redistribution, through the regulation of social, environmental and health risk, EU citizenship, and competences over food safety, culture, tourism, immigration, combating racism and xenophobia and police and judicial co-operation, the EU is increasingly involved in the allocation of social and political values throughout Europe.

Consequently, Jacques Delors's often quoted prediction that by 1998 80% of economic and social legislation applicable in the member states will be of European origin . . . did not lack solid empirical support (Majone 1996: 265). As in all political systems, the EU now tackles redistribution and stabilization in addition to regulation (Musgrave 1959), undertakes an 'authoritative allocation of values' (Easton 1953), and (at least in part) determines 'who gets what when and how'

(Lasswell 1936). In other words, 'it is beyond dispute that the EU has acquired for itself the political attributes of a modern state' (Richardson 1996c: 26).

The third characteristic is the mobilization of citizens, private groups and office-holders to secure outputs close to their interests, values and ideologies: i.e. the 'politics' of the EU. EU citizens have opinions not only about European integration but also about the issues tackled by the EU (European Commission 1997). And these orientations are increasingly expressed in electoral contests, as in the Maastricht referendum in 1992 and 1993, the European elections in 1994, and the enlargement referendums in 1995 (Franklin et al 1994; Smith 1996) . . .

Furthermore, EU politics is no longer just about institutional integration, where governments, supranational institutions and private interests are located on a single continuum between 'less' and 'more' integration (Garrett 1992a). Despite the rise of 'post-materialism' and the decline of traditional social cleavages (e.g. class and religion), Europe's citizens still care about material issues, such as unemployment and inflation, and take up positions on the classic 'value' questions, such as justice, liberty and equality (Franklin et al. 1992). These traditional economic interests and socio-political values remain the basis of the Left-Right dimension of politics. . . . And as these issues become salient in the EU, through policy-making over redistribution and value allocation, actors are forced to take up position on this dimension at he European level (Hix 1994, 1998; Hooghe 1997; Hooghe and Marks 1997) . . .

In sum, whereas a new governance conception of the EU emphasizes the informal nature of the policy process, the non-hierarchical structure of the institutions and the non-redistributive nature of policy outputs, this alternative conceptions sees politics and government in the EU as 'not inherently different to . . . any democratic political system' (Hix 1994: 1). The EU may not be like a traditional European state, with extensive powers of coercion, a hierarchical bureaucracy and a large welfare budget. But it is a quasi-federal 'regulatory state' (Bulmer 1994; Majone 1993a; McGowan and Wallace 1996), much like the US before the 1930s (Majone 1991). Moreover, it has an integrated and ongoing political system, where the supply of regulatory, redistributive and allocative policies, via the classic executive, legislative and judicial functions of government, feeds back into new demands and competitive struggles.

Method: A 'sui generis' Case?

These rival empirical conceptions have implications for which method should be used to study the EU. If the EU is a completely unique animal, it will be difficult to compare it with other creatures, and new theories will be needed to understand how it behaves. But if it is only a strange variant of an already well-understood species, it can be compared with other members of the species, and theories that explain how the species behave will also apply to the EU.

The 'N = 1' research strategy

. . . .

The *sui generis* method is a logical extension of the new governance empirical conception. If the EU is unique, comparing it with other political systems inherently runs into a 'level of analysis problem'. This means that if two things are treated as comparable when they are actually different levels of the same problem, any inferences are likely to be hugely distorted (Singer 1969[1961]). For example, this problem arises when comparing policy-making in the EU and Germany, where it can often be difficult to separate policy outputs on one level from policy outputs on the other level. Hence, this suggests that the EU could only be compared to another system that is completely unconnected: such as the United States.

However, the new governance approach also sees this cross-systemic method as unsustainable. Governance in the EU is so totally unique that any comparison with politics or policy-making in other systems – states or international organizations – is impossible. As the brochure of the Mannheim University project on the 'Transformation of Governance in the EU' states: 'a dynamic multi-level system...can only inadequately be analysed by social scientific and legal theories and categories relying upon the ideal-typical concept of the state' (SGEU Newsletter 1997: 2).

The classic, yet increasingly artificial, division in political science is between comparative politics/public policy, which seeks to understand political behaviour and institutions *within* states, and international relations, which seeks to understand political behaviour and institutions *between* states. As a result,

> our language for discussing politics – especially stable, iterative, 'normal' politics – is indelibly impregnated with assumptions about the state. Whenever we refer to the number, location, authority, status, membership, capacity, identity, type or significance of political units we employ concepts that implicitly or explicitly refer to a universe featuring sovereign state (Schmitter 1996a: 132).

Yet governance in the EU is no longer between a set of sovereign states, nor is it really within a single state. The solution, therefore, is to invent a whole new body of knowledge, a 'new vocabulary' (Schmitter 1996a: 133). Schmitter (1991, 1996b) consequently proposes a novel typology of possible EU end-points, and gives them 'neo-Latin' labels: stato federato, condominio, confederatio and consortio. Whereas federation and confederation are familiar institutional organizations, condominio and consortio are unknown designs in the current universe of nation states.

The Mannheim University project takes a slightly different tack. Instead of trying to invent new concepts, the aim should be to test existing theories, from comparative politics (CP) and IR, to see which ones fit. In this exercise we must 'leave room for changes, even in the fundamental principles and concepts of political organization with which we are familiar' (Jachtenfuchs 1995: 130). In this method, the study of the EU is an important project for all political science, because it will enable us to drag the old-fashioned disciplines of CP and IR into the complex and unpredictable world of trans-state and non-state governance at the turn of the millenium.

A case study in comparative perspective

But even the strangest cases can and should be compared. As King et al. suggest:

> *the comparative approach – in which we combine evidence from many observations even if some of them are not very close analogies to the present situation is always at least as good and usually better than the analogy.* The reason is simple: the analogy uses a single observation to predict another, whereas the comparative approach uses a weighted combination of a large number of other observations (King et al. 1994: 212).

Only through comparison with several cases, or through the application of concepts developed in the comparison of several cases, are hypotheses secure.

Moreover as Heidenheimer et al. argue: 'By assessing one situation against another, we gain a better perspective on our current situation as well as the options and constraints we face' (Heidenheimer et al. 1990: 1). In other words, comparison is important not only for hypothesis-testing and theory-building, but also for addressing normative problems.

This method does not require explicit comparison between the EU and one or more other cases. The EU can be treated as a single case in 'comparative perspective', simply by applying tools and concepts developed for the study of a general phenomenon to that same phenomenon in the EU. This method hence contributes to the understanding of a specific case, the EU, as well as a general phenomenon, such as constitutional structures (Dehousse 1994). This strategy was explicitly advocated by Lijphart: 'The case study method can and should be closely connected with the comparative method' (1971: 691). However, it was also Tocqueville's approach, when he studied America in an effort to understand democracy in Europe.[4] And this method has produced some of the most celebrated political science works: from Aristotle, via Mill and Bagehot, to Lijphart and Putnam.

Contrary to the new governance suggestion, this 'comparative perspective' method *is* used in much contemporary research on the EU. First, the EU institutions have been compared to other systems and/or studied using concepts from the comparative study of government and governmental institutions. For example, the EU is often treated as a type of 'federal' system, and compared particularly to the US or Germany (Cappelletti et al. 1986; Leibfried and Pierson 1995; Majone 1992b; McKay 1996; Sbragia 1992; Scharpf 1988, 1994, 1997). The EU is also conceptualized as a 'consociational' system (Chryssochoou 1994; Taylor 1991). And most models of EU decision-making use spatial analysis and rational choice methods from the general study of legislative behaviour (Bueno de Mesquita and Stokman 1994; Garrett and Tsebelis 1996; Moser et al. 1997).

Second, EU policy-making is often studied using concepts from the field of comparative public policy (see especially Richardson 1996a). For example, developing out of the study of British and Germany policy-making, the 'policy networks' approach has been applied to the EU in a wide variety of areas, including environmental policy (Bomberg 1994), research and development (Peterson 1992), telecommunications (Schneider et al. 1994) and regulation (Heritier 1993b). Moreover, the EU has been included in several comparative works on the general theory and practice of policy networks (Heritier 1993a; Marin and Mayntz 1991; Marsh and Rhodes 1992). EU policy-making in the areas of social policy (Pierson and Leibfried 1995) and market regulation (Majone 1991, 1993b) has been compared to policy-making in the US. And the implementation of EU legislation has been analysed using techniques from the general study of policy implementation (From and Stava 1993; Siedentopf and Hauschild 1988).

Finally, research into political behaviour is emerging in the EU, using many of the traditional tools of comparative politics. Public opinion in the EU has been modelled using techniques from general public opinion research (Anderson and Kaltenthaler 1996; Eichenberg and Dalton 1993; Gabel 1997; Gabel and Palmer 1995). Interest groups are increasingly analysed within the broader debate between pluralism and corporatism (Falkner 1997; Obradovic 1995; Streeck and Schmitter 1991). Electoral research has developed a general theory of 'second-order' elections from the study of EP elections, which has implications for many political systems (Eijk et al. 1996; Reif and Schmitt 1980). And general theories of party behaviour, competition and cohesion have been applied to the EP Party Groups and the emerging 'EU party system' (Attina 1990; Bardi 1994, 1996; Bay-Brzinski 1995; Hix and Lord 1997).

In sum, mid-range theory in political science is cross-systemic rather than intra-systemic. We have no general theory of American or German government, so why should there be a general theory of the EU? What we do have are particular explanations of phenomena that exist in all political systems: such as executive-legislative relations, policy-making, interest representation, public opinion, voting and party behaviour. If we accept the critique levelled at the new governance empirical conception of the EU, these phenomena can be studied in the EU using methods, concepts and theories from the general fields of comparative politics and comparative public policy.

. . . .

Normative Analysis: Non-majoritarian Democracy?

. . . following the collapse of the so-called 'permissive consensus' in the wake of the Maastricht Treaty, the issues of democracy and legitimacy have been pushed to the top of the EU research agenda. However, there are very different responses to this demand, which derive from the rival empirical conceptions.

The 'no-demos thesis' and non-majoritarianism

From a new governance perspective, because the EU is not a nation state, it does not have a demos. As Weiler explains:

> The nation and its members constitute the polity for the purposes of accepting the discipline of democratic, majoritarian governance. Both descriptively and prescriptively the minority will/should accept the legitimacy of a majority decision because both the majority and minority are part of the same nation (Weiler 1995: 228).

For example, a hypothetical *Anschluss* between Denmark and Germany would be undemocratic because representation of Danes in the German Bundestag would not mean Danish consent for majority Bundestag decisions (Weiler 1995: 228; Weiler *et al.* 1995: 12). With fifteen separate national identities in the EU, majoritarian decision-making at the European level would be similarly illegitimate (Jachtenfuchs 1995: 127–9).

This problem is further compounded by the non-hierarchical nature of executive power in the EU. With power shared by the Council and the Commission, and the selection of Commissioners by national governments, there is no single person or team to 'throw out'. Since the

Maastricht Treaty, the EP has a role in the investiture of the Commission President. However, this is only one part of the EU executive. And because political parties are more interested in winning national government office than this European office, there is little incentive to fight EP elections on European issues. Consequently, European elections are 'second-order national contests': on the performance of national governments, with lower electoral turnouts than national elections, and more protest votes against the governing parties (Eijk and Franklin 1996).

These two factors consequently imply that 'models of democracy developed in the national context cannot be easily transferred to the EU' (Jachtenfuchs 1997: 7). The only solution is a *sui generis* model of representation and accountability. For example, Schmitter (1996a, 1996b) proposes new modes of participation, through a system of vouchers allocated to functional constituencies, and decision-making, through weighting of votes into three separate 'collegii'. Weiler (1997b) adds placing the whole EU decision-making process, 'especially but not only Comitology', on the Internet. And others suggest that EU citizenship should be developed on the basis of (weak) civic rights and obligations, rather than on the classic (strong) national/ethnic ties (Chryssochoou 1996; Weiler 1995; Wiener 1997).

Above all, without a demos to legitimize majority rule or an executive-head to elect, EU decision-making can only be legitimate if it is 'non-majoritarian' (Dehousse 1995; Joerges and Neyer 1997; Obradovic 1996). This normative prescription is directly connected to the new governance analysis of regulation by independent agencies. If regulation is made by a majoritarian institution, such as a parliament, bargaining is between rival legislative coalitions, and the outcome is inherently redistributive/zero-sum: in the interests of the majority, against the interests of the minority. However, by delegating regulatory policy to an independent institution, which is required to act in the 'public interest', outcomes will be positive-sum. Legitimacy will consequently be secured by the universal support for Pareto-optimal outcomes. And this can be supplemented by 'transparency', via media and parliamentary scrutiny and judicial review of the regulator (Majone 1994b, 1996a: 284–301). In other words, through Pareto-efficiency and transparency 'no one controls an agency . . . [but] the agency is under control' (Majone 1996: 300).

Overall, 'the central categories of political theory, such as authority, legitimacy and democracy are implicitly linked to the model of the state' (Jachtenfuchs & Kohler-Koch 1997: 15). The problem for the new governance approach, however, is that public opinion judges governance at the European level by the same (modernist) criteria for legitimacy as at the national level. Rather than abandon the connection between democracy and legitimacy, these scholars consequently argue that democracy needs to be redefined and reconstructed to fit the EU. The favoured solutions are problem-solving rather than competition, efficiency rather than representation, consensus rather than majority, transparency rather than election, and independence rather than partisanship.

Competitive democracy and demos-building

But in Lincoln's famous address, democracy is 'government by the people' as much as 'government for the people'. The support secured by consensual, efficient, transparent and Pareto-optimal *outputs* is thus only one side of the legitimacy equation (e.g. Lipset 1960: 77–96). The other side is democratic participation in, and partisan competition over, *inputs*: the ability of citizens to chose between rival elites or political agendas (see especially Schumpeter 1943; Weber 1942 [1918]). Only this process can lead to a 'mobilization of bias', where every individual, regardless of economic and political resources, can participate equally in setting the boundaries of political action (Schattschneider 1960).

For example, defenders of independent regulatory authorities in the EU ignore the fact that, in most other democratic systems, regulators *are* connected to majoritarian institutions. For example, in the US, 'although *many* administrative agencies are independent of the political branches in theory, they are subject in fact to a considerable measure of political influence by the President and the Congress' (Freedman 1978: 261). It is precisely this interplay between majoritarian and non-majoritarian processes in the American system that guarantees legitimacy for executive agencies (Rose-Ackerman 1992: 187–93; Shapiro 1988: 107–28; Sunstein 1990: 227–35). Similarly, most suggestions of how to legitimize British 'quangos' focus on reconnecting them to majoritarian processes: via selection of the agency chief executives by government ministers, parliamentary committees, regional governments or even direct elections (e.g. Plummer 1994). Indeed, an eminent scholar of the American regulatory state has asserted that one key way of legitimizing the EU regulatory system would be to grant greater scrutiny powers to the EP (Shapiro 1997; see also Everson 1995).

The so-called 'democratic deficit' in the EU was an issue long before the current crisis of legitimacy. And the 'standard version' of the democratic deficit accepts the majoritarian conception of democracy. However, the standard version prescribes a naive recipe of institutional reform, based on increasing the power of the EP, first, in the legislative process (*vis-a-vis* the Council) and, second, over the exercise of executive power (in the investiture of the Commission President) (cf. Weiler et al. 1995). This way, so the argument goes, European elections would have an impact on the 'formation of public policy' and the 'formation of government' at the European level – the two basic functions of elections (King 1981).

But, as the new governance analysis points out, this strategy is flawed. Regardless of the power of the EP, European elections would still not be fought on European issues, because national parties would still treat them as 'second order national contests'. There would consequently be no democratic mandate for a legislative majority, to redistribute resources through EU legislation and capture the Commission and the regulatory agencies. This would be less democratic than consensus decision-making between democratically elected governments and the delegation of regulatory power to agencies required to act in the 'European interest' (see especially Dehousse 1995). Ironically, therefore, increasing the power of the EP in the ways prescribed by the standard interpretation of the democratic deficit may actually reduce rather than increase EU legitimacy (Scharpf 1996b:138).

Nevertheless, this is not the only way to introduce competition and choice into the EU process. The essential requirement is an electoral contest fought on European issues. Under present rules, EP elections do not fulfill this role. But, under different rules, such as candidates selected by pan-European parties, EP elections might become real 'European' contests. However, judging by its plans for a 'uniform electoral procedure', even the EP recognizes that this is far off (European Parliament 1992). But there are two other ways of letting citizens make a choice on EU questions. First, European-wide referendums could be held on European issues, perhaps at the same time as EP elections. Schmitter (1996c) and Weiler (1997b) both propose ways in which this could be done. However, this is surprising given their general sympathies towards a new governance normative analysis.

Second, rather than pushing the EU towards a parliamentary model, where the executive is accountable to a parliamentary majority, the head of the executive could be directly elected, as in a presidential model (cf. Bogdanor 1986; Hix and Lord 1997: 216; Laver et al. 1995). For example, the Commission President could be directly elected, with candidates nominated by at least one party in each member state. This would ensure that one group of elites in each member state would be part of the 'winning team', and no 'nation' would be a collective loser. Also, this would give European citizens someone to throw out, without having to rely on cohesive EP parties to translate voters' preferences into executive selection (Gabel and Hix 1997).

However, these contests would only be fought on European issues if pan-European organizations (i.e. parties) could 'mobilize bias' on either side of the debate (cf. Leonard 1997). Pan-European parties were predicted in the 1970s, in the build-up to the first EP elections (e.g. Pridham and Pridham 1981). This optimism collapsed in the 1980s as the new 'party federations' struggled to survive. But the 1990s witnessed a 'renaissance' of pan-European party activity (Hix 1996a). First, the Socialist, Christian Democratic, Liberal and Green party federations adopted new and more integrated statutes following the Maastricht Treaty 'party article' (Article 138a).[5] Second, these organizations began to mobilize around European Council meetings, holding 'party leaders' summits' in the days immediately before these meetings. This facilitated an increased participation of national party leaders in 'Euro-party' activity (Hix and Lord 1997: 167–97). Third, and perhaps most crucially, as the EU began to tackle issues of redistribution and value allocation, the Euro-parties began to set out coherent agendas for EU action: to construct and compete on a Left-Right dimension of EU politics instead of the more internally divisive pro- and anti-European dimension (Hix 1995, 1998). Consequently, because the EU has developed policy functions of a traditional state, in a 'real' EP election, a contest for Commission President or pan-EU referendum, rival agendas would be put forward by traditional party families.

But the no-demos problem would still remain: in a multinational polity, the losers of a majoritarian contest would not accept the winners as legitimate. But this is only one interpretation. In the evolution from city-states to nation states, electoral contests played a fundamental part in the redefinition and reconstruction of a new demos. Through participation in the democratic process, where rival opinions are legitimately expressed and confronted, new democratic identities were 'constructed'. As the process of majoritarian contestation became accepted as legitimate, so did the outcome, whether on the winning or losing side (cf. Rokkan 1973).

As Habermas consequently argues:

> The ethical-political self-understanding of citizens in a democratic community must not be taken as a historical-cultural *a priori* that makes democratic will-formation possible, but rather as the flowing contents of a circulatory process that is generated through the legal institutionalization of citizens' communication. This is precisely how national identities were formed in modern Europe. Therefore it is to be expected that the political institutions to be created by a European constitution would have an inducing effect (Habermas 1997 [1995]: 264).

Thus, the demos is constructed via democratic 'praxis'. The new governance should hence be reversed: instead of 'no EU democracy with a European demos', we have 'no European demos without EU democracy'. In other words, a real European electoral contest could be the 'democratic baptism of a European democratic community' (cf. Weale 1995: 90–3).

In sum, this alternative perspective has faith in the possibility of designing institutions to create competitive and partisan democracy at the European level, against the new governance view that classic forms of participation are impossible beyond the nation state. However, the crux of the dispute between these two approaches is the age-old tension between majoritarian and consensual models of democracy (Lijphart 1984). Majoritarianism maximizes the connection between a majority's electoral choice and political outputs, but tends to redistribution of resources away from the losing minority. Consensualism, on the other hand, maximizes the protection of the minority, but tends to policy immobilism as a result of too many 'veto players' (Tsebelis 1995b).

Conclusion: Towards a New Duality in EU Research

Never before in the study of the EU has there been such explicit, or even implicit, debate on so many levels of analysis. This is partly a response to the current vogue in political science for ontological, methodological and epistemological arguments. However, this pedantic reason is trivial compared to two other factors. First, as the EU has grown in significance, both internally, to Europe's citizens, and externally, to states, businesses and citizens elsewhere in the world, the need to understand 'how it works' has drawn an ever-larger group of scholars, with broader empirical interests, methods and theoretical expertise. Second, as Europe's citizens have become increasingly skeptical of the EU, the need to address the issue of 'how it can work better' has forced a focus on the normative implications of empirical and theoretical research.

The result is an emerging duality in the study of EU politics and policy. The more popular perspective, which for convenience I have called the 'new governance' agenda, is that the EU is transforming politics and government at the European and national levels into a system of multi-level, non-hierarchical, deliberative and apolitical governance, via a complex web of public/private networks and quasi-autonomous executive agencies, which is primarily concerned with the deregulation and re-regulation of the market. This is best understood as a *sui generis* phenomenon. And because this environment is so complex and unpredictable, institutional and structural factors are more influential than calculated rational action in determining policy outcomes. Finally, without a demos, EU governance can only be legitimized through constraints on the outputs of the system: by ensuring that policy decisions are Pareto-efficient rather than redistributive, through problem-solving rather than bargaining, that the process is transparent, and that individual civic and consume rights are protected.

However, this new governance agenda is problematic. First, traditional 'politics and government' *do* exist in the EU. Executive, legislative and judicial powers are exercised at the European level; EU decisions do alter the allocation of resources and values; and the modern/liberal-democratic questions of freedom, power, wealth, justice, democracy and legitimacy are ever present. Second, all polities are largely unique. However, the EU would only be *sui generis* if it were apolitical. Because the empirical subject (i.e. politics and government) and the normative issues (e.g. democracy) are generalizable, the EU can and should be compared to other political systems. . . . Finally, transparent, efficient and consensual outputs are only one side of legitimacy. The other side is competition over inputs: by allowing Europe's citizens to choose between rival programmes and elites in a partisan European-wide contest. EP elections as contested at present do not fulfil this requirement. Yet only through such a democratic praxis, via EU referendums or even direct election of the Commission President, would a European demos emerge. Drawing these arguments together: only by drawing from our wealth of existing knowledge about institutions, behaviour and democracy, from the study of politics and government in existing political systems, will we be able to understand how the EU works *and* how it could be made to work better.

. . . .

Notes

1 Nevertheless, the term 'multi-level governance' was first coined by Gary Marks (1993) and Liesbet Hooghe (1996) to conceptualize the making of EU regional policy.

2 However, it is worth noting that, contrary to the Peltzman/Majone view that regulation is inherently Pareto-efficient, the classic view is that regulation is simply redistributive politics in another form: where interests compete for 'capture' of the regulator, and then redistribute rewards once they have done so (e.g. Stigler 1971).

3 For the characteristics of a political system, I use Keman's (1993) reformulation of Easton into the more contemporary 'polity-policy-politics triad'. Other conceptions of the EU as a 'political system' include Wallace (1983), Attinà (1992), Andersen & Eliassen (1993), Quermonne (1994) and Wessels (1997).

4 Tocqueville felt that 'without comparisons to make, the mind does not know how to proceed' (1985: 191).

5 Article 138a of the European Community Treaty states that: 'Political parties at the European level are an important factor for integration within the Union. They contribute to forming a European awareness and to expressing the political will of the citizens of the Union.'

Chapter 14

European Integration from the 1980s: State-centric vs Multi-level Governance

Gary Marks, Liesbeth Hooghe, Kermit Blank*

Developments in the EU over the last decade have revived debate about the consequences of European integration for the autonomy and authority of the state in Europe. The scope and depth of policy-making at the EU-level have dramatically increased. The EU has almost completed the internal market and has absorbed the institutional reforms of the Single European Act (1986) which established qualified majority voting (QMV) in the Council of Ministers and increased the power of the European Parliament (EP). The Maastricht Treaty (1993) further expanded EU competencies and the scope of QMV in the Council, and provided the EP with a veto on certain types of legislation. The Maastricht Treaty is a landmark in European integration quite apart from its ambitious plan for a common currency and a European central bank by the end of this century.

Our aim in this article is to take stock of these developments. What do they mean for the political architecture of Europe? Do these developments consolidate nation-states or do they weaken them? If they weaken them, what kind of political order is emerging? These are large and complex questions, and we do not imagine that we can settle them once and for all. Our strategy is to pose two basic alternative conceptions – state-centric governance and multi-level governance – as distinctly as possible and then evaluate their validity by examining the European policy process.

The core presumption of state-centric governance is that European integration does not challenge the autonomy of nation-states (Mann 1993; Milward 1992; Moravcsik 1991, 1993a, 1994; Streeck 1996).

* Reproduced by kind permission of Blackwell Publishing from Gary Marks, Liesbeth Hooghe and Kermit Blank (1996) 'European Integration from the 1980s: State-Centric vs Multi-level Governance', *Journal of Common Market Studies*, 43(4), 341–78. The text has been slightly edited, as indicated, to fit the format of this volume.

State-centrists contend that state sovereignty is preserved or even strengthened through EU membership. They argue that European integration is driven by bargains among Member State governments. No government has to integrate more than it wishes because bargains rest on the lowest common denominator of the participating Member States. In this model, supranational actors exist to aid Member States, to facilitate agreements by providing information that would not otherwise be so readily available. Policy outcomes reflect the interests and relative power of Member State executives. Supranational actors exercise little independent effect.

An alternative view is that European integration is a polity creating process in which authority and policy-making influence are shared across multiple levels, of government – subnational, national, and supranational (Hooghe 1996; Marks 1992, 1993). While national governments are formidable participants in EU policy-making, control has slipped away from them to supranational institutions. States have lost some of their former authoritative control over individuals in their respective territories. In short, the locus of political control has changed. Individual state sovereignty is diluted in the EU by collective decision-making among national governments and by the autonomous role of the European Parliament (EP), the European Commission, and the European Court of Justice (ECJ).

. . . .

Two Models of the European Union

. . . .

The multi-level governance (MLG) model does not reject the view that state executives and state arenas are important, or that these remain the most important pieces of the European puzzle. However, when one asserts that the state no longer monopolizes European level policy-making or the aggregation of domestic interests, a very different polity comes into focus. First, according to the MLG model, decision-making competencies are shared by actors at different levels rather than monopolized by state executives. That is to say, supranational institutions – above all, the European Commission, the European Court, and the EP – have independent influence in policymaking that cannot be derived from their role as agents of state executives. State executives may play an important role but, according to the MLG model, one must also analyse the independent role of European level actors to explain European policy-making.

Second, collective decision-making among states involves a significant loss of control for individual state executives. Lowest common denominator outcomes are available only on a subset of EU decisions, mainly those concerning the scope of integration. Decisions concerning rules to be enforced across the EU (e.g. harmonizing regulation of product standards, labour conditions, etc.) have a zero-sum character, and necessarily involve gains or losses for individual states.

Third, political arenas are interconnected rather than nested. While national arenas remain important for the formation of state executive preferences, the multi-level model rejects the view that subnational actors are nested exclusively within them. Instead, subnational actors operate in both national and supranational arenas, creating transnational associations in the process. States do not monopolize links between domestic and European actors, but are one among a variety of actors contesting decisions that are made at a variety of levels. In this perspective, complex interrelationships in domestic politics do not stop at the nation-state, but extend to the European level. The separation between domestic and international politics, which lies at the heart of the state-centric model, is rejected by the MLG model. States are an integral and powerful part of the EU, but they no longer provide the sole interface between supranational and subnational arenas, and they share, rather than monopolize, control over many activities that take place in their respective territories.

Sources of Multi-level Governance

. . . .

Our starting point in this article is to make clear a division between institutions and actors, i.e. between the state (and the EU) as sets of rules and the particular individuals, groups, and organizations which act within the institutions. This has the decided advantage of leading one away from reified accounts, common in the state-centric literature, of the goals, preferences, desires, and plans of states, towards an actor-centred approach in which one specifies particular actors as participants in decision-making.

When writers refer to the state as an actor, they usually have in mind one or more of the following: public administrators, parliamentarians, judges, the armed forces, subnational executives and, most importantly in the context of EU decision-making, party leaders serving in national governments. From this perspective, the question is not, 'why do states give up sovereignty in the process of European integration? But 'why do particular actors (party leaders in national governments) change institutional rules (e.g. shift Competencies to the EU)?'

. . . .

There are two sets of reasons why government leaders may wish to shift decision-making to the supranational level: the political benefits may outweigh the costs of losing political control or there may be intrinsic benefits having to do with shifting responsibility for unpopular decisions or insulating decision-making from domestic pressures (Pierson 1996 has developed an interesting set of arguments about 'gaps' in state executive control that parallel several points made in this section).

1. *Cost v benefits of decisional reallocation.* Reallocating competencies to the supranational level may be an effective means of providing information and other resources to meet the transaction costs involved in formulating, negotiating, and implementing collective decisions (Majone 1995, 1994a; Moe 1987, 1990; Williamson 1985, 1993). Decisional reallocation may have significant costs for government leaders, but these costs may (a) be less politically salient than the benefits of more efficient delivery of collective policies: or (b) they may be lagged with respect to the benefits, and therefore of less weight for political leaders having a high discount rate. The relative importance of these conditions depends on the potential efficiency gains to be realized by centralizing decisionmaking in a particular policy area, the domestic electoral and party-political context facing government leaders, and their substantive policy goals.

From this perspective, sovereignty is merely one goal among others. To the extent that political leaders have a short time horizon (and thus a high discount rate), and the substantive policy stream of European integration is more salient for powerful domestic constituencies than its decisional implications, so state sovereignty may be sacrificed for efficient policy provision. It is worth stressing that we are not making the argument that supranational empowerment is a Pareto-optimal outcome for Europeans. It suffices that government leaders are able to reap a private gain by instituting a Pareto-suboptimal policy (for example agricultural subsidies) as a means, say, to reward a powerful constituency.

2. *Intrinsic benefits of decisional reallocation.* Government leaders may shift decision-making to the supranational level because they positively wish to do so. In the first place, they may prefer to avoid responsibility for certain policies. A recent highly publicized case where a government was clearly relieved to be impotent was the conflict in the UK in 1995 over the transportation of calves to the Continent in crates for eventual slaughter. In response to the (sometimes violent) demonstrations of animal rights' advocates in British ports, William Waldegrave, the Minister of Agriculture, explained that the British government could not be blamed because effective decision-making was made in Brussels. He advised opponents of the policy to demonstrate in Brussels rather than in the UK, which they promptly did.

Second, government leaders may shift decision-making to insulate it from political pressures. The autonomy of central banks is designed on this premise. The same logic can lead a government to cede competencies to the European Commission or to an independent agency within the EU. Recent examples include the decision on the part of national governments to give the Commission considerable authority over European mergers, and to envisage the creation of an independent European central bank with exclusive responsibility for monetary policy. By insulating policy-making in this way, government leaders seek to control policy after they have left office. To the extent that leaders face a tradeoff between preserving state sovereignty and assuaging a particular constituency, shifting the electoral balance in their party's favour, or institutionalizing deep-seated preferences, they may sacrifice state sovereignty.

. . . .

Limits on individual state executive control

The most obvious constraint on the capacity of a national government to determine outcomes in the EU is the decision rule of QMV in the Council of Ministers for a range of issues from the internal market to trade, agriculture and the environment. In this respect the EU is clearly different from international regimes, such as the UN or WTO, in which majoritarian principles of decision-making are confined to symbolic issues.

State-centrists have sought to blunt the theoretical implications of collective decision-making in the Council of Ministers along two lines of argument.

The first is that while state executives may sacrifice some independence of control by participating in collective decision-making, they more than compensate for this by their increased ability to achieve the policy outcomes they want. Moravcsik has argued at length that collective decision-making actually enhances state executive control because state executives will only agree to participate insofar as policy-coordination increases their control over domestic policy outcomes, permitting them to achieve goals that would not otherwise be possible (1993a: 485). By participating in the EU state executives are able to provide policies, such as a cleaner environment, higher levels of economic growth: etc. that could not be provided autonomously. But two entirely different conceptions of power are involved here, and it would be well to keep them separate.

On the one hand, power or political control may be conceptualized as control over persons. A has power over B to the extent that she can get B to do something he would not otherwise do (Dahl 1961). This is a zero-sum conception: if one actor gains power, another loses it. This conception of power underlies Max Weber's definition of state sovereignty as the monopoly of legitimate coercion within a given territory, and although this definition has been contested, most subsequent theorists of the state have continued to view sovereignty in terms of the extent to which states control the lives of those in their territories.

By contrast, power conceived as the ability to achieve desired outcomes involves not only power over persons, but power over nature in the broadest sense. From this standpoint one would evaluate the power of an institution as a function of its success in achieving substantive goals, rather than in terms of its relations with other actors. Logically, this would lead one to say that a successful national government in a federal European state has more control than a less successful national government in a confederal state.

The latter conception is not invalid, for concepts can be used in any way one wishes to use them. However, it confuses two phenomena that we have already sought to untangle: institutionally rooted relations of power among political actors, and the ability of political actors to achieve substantive policy goals. One of the causal dynamics that may lead government leaders to shift decision-making away from the institution in which they are located, as we have argued above, is precisely that they may achieve desired policy outcomes by so doing.

State-centrists have also claimed that majoritarianism in the Council of Ministers camouflages, but does not invalidate, state sovereignty. They argue that treaty revisions, new policy initiatives, and certain sensitive areas remain subject to unanimity and hence the national veto; that the Luxembourg Compromise gives state executives the power to veto any decision under majority rule that they deem contravenes their vital national interests; and that, ultimately, a state executive could pull out of the EU if it so wished.

The Luxembourg veto is available to national governments only under restricted conditions and even then, it is a relatively blunt weapon. As we detail below, the Luxembourg veto is restricted by the willingness of other state executives to tolerate its use in a particular case. In one famous case, an attempt to veto annual agricultural prices in 1982 by the UK government was actually rejected by the other Member State executives. The Luxembourg veto is a defensive rather than an offensive weapon in that it can only be used to reject a particular course of action, not select another. The German government barred a Council decision to reduce agricultural prices for cereals and colza in 1985, but it was unable to stop the Commission from achieving the required reductions by resorting to its emergency powers (Teasdale 1993).

From the standpoint of physical force, Member states retain ultimate sovereignty by virtue of their continuing monopoly of the means of legitimate coercion within their respective territories. If a national government broke its treaty commitments and pulled out of the EU, the EU itself has no armed forces with which to contest that decision. Here the contrast between the EU and a federal system, such as the US, seems perfectly clear. In the last analysis, states retain ultimate coercive control of their populations.

But monopoly of legitimate coercion tells us less and less about the realities of political, legal, and normative control in contemporary capitalist societies. A Weberian approach, focusing on the extent to which states are able to monopolize legitimate coercion, appears more useful for understanding the emergence and consolidation of states from the twelfth century than for understanding changes in state sovereignty in the latter half of the twentieth century. Although the EU does not possess armed forces, it requires no leap of imagination to argue that a national government is constrained by the economic and political sanctions – and consequent political-economic dislocation – that it would almost certainly face if it revoked its treaty commitments and pulled out of the European Union. Analyses of the ultimate sovereignty of Member States and the sanctions available to the EU under extreme circumstances have an air of unreality about them because, under present and foreseeable circumstances, they remain entirely hypothetical.

Limits on collective state executive control

We have argued that government leaders may have positive grounds for shifting decision-making to supranational institutions and that they do not exert individual control over binding collective decisions in the Council of Ministers. Here we argue that there are reasons for believing that even collectively, national governments are constrained in their ability to control supranational institutions they have created at the European level.

1. The treaty process. In the first place, while state executive control of the big decisions, the treaties, is impressive, it is not complete. State executives play a decisive role in drafting the basic treaties and major legislation underlying the EU, such as the Single European Act and the Maastricht Treaty, but they are far less dominant in most areas of day-to-day policy-making.

Because state representatives are the only legally recognized signatories of the treaties undergirding the EU, they are actually empowered in the process of formulating treaties. If a domestic group wishes to influence a clause of a formal EU treaty it must adopt a state-centric strategy and focus pressure on its national government. Treaty making is the realm of negotiation among national leaders, the national veto, and side-payments to bring recalcitrant national governments on board.

In the pre-Maastricht era, the process of ratification was dominated by state executive leaders through party control of national legislatures. Not only did they determine the content of treaties, but they could be reasonably confident that those treaties would be accepted in their respective domestic arenas.[1] European integration was a technocratic process, involving co-ordination among state executives to achieve limited and contingent policy goals. The course of European integration was pragmatic, not politicized, and state representatives dominated decision-making to the virtual exclusion of other political actors. When this incremental pattern of state executive decision-making was interrupted, as it was by de Gaulle in the 1960s and Thatcher in the 1980s, it was to reassert state sovereignty as a constraint on European integration.

In the wake of the Maastricht Treaty, the process of treaty ratification has shifted beyond the control of state executives to the politicized realms of party-political competition, parliamentary debates and mass referendums. The Maastricht Treaty itself gives only subtle hints to the intensity of response it generated. It lacks any coherent institutional blueprint or constitutional ambition, but is an assembly of discrete and vague policy initiatives that, with the major exception of proposed monetary union, are an extension, rather than an overhaul, of the existing framework. One of the hallmarks of the Treaty, and a clue to the alienation felt by many Europeans, is that it is written in opaque Euro-legalese which is virtually unintelligible to the uninitiated. But whatever the reasons for its tumultuous reception, it has implanted the expectation that state executives must submit future treaties to thorough democratic scrutiny. State executive leaders still have considerable power to frame basic alternatives, but they no longer control the treaty process as a whole.

2. Constraints on the ability of state executive principals to control supranational agents. From a transaction analysis standpoint, it is not feasible for Member State executives to plan for all possible future ambiguities and sources of contention, so they create institutions, such as the European Commission and the ECJ, that can adapt incomplete contracts to changing circumstances (Majone 1995; Pierson 1996). According to agency theory, a principal exerts control by selecting his agent, creating a structure of incentives to induce the required behaviour (Williamson 1985). If a principal finds out at some later date that an agent is not acting in the desired way, he can always fire the agent or reform the incentives. Scholars who have applied principal-agent theory to American political institutions have found that the effectiveness of such incentives and disincentives is limited (Moe 1990). In the EU the ability of principals, i.e. Member State executives, to control supranational agents is constrained by the multiplicity of principals, the mistrust that exists among them, impediments to coherent principal action, informational asymmetries between principals and agents and by the unintended consequences of institutional change. We discuss these briefly in turn.

Multiplicity of principals. It is one thing for a single principal to control an agent. It is quite different for several principals to control an agent. And it is yet another thing for several principals prone to competition and conflict to control an agent. Supranational institutions in the EU are not external to conflicts among Member State executives, but are intimately involved in them and are able to extend their role as a result. One of the consequences of the multiplicity of contending principals is that basic treaties of the EU tend to be ambiguous documents providing ample room for diverse interpretations on the part of both principals and agents. The treaties are hammered out in interstate negotiations in which each state executive wishes to win domestic acclaim for having made collective progress in solving a variety of policy problems, but where each has a veto on the content of the agreement. There is a powerful incentive to ambiguity on points of contention to allow each participating government to claim success in representing national interests.

The basic treaties of the EU have legitimated Commission initiatives in several policy areas, yet they are vague enough to give the Commission wide latitude in designing institutions. This was the case in the creation of structural policy, which, in the wake of the SEA, was transformed by the Commission from a side-payment transferring resources from richer to poorer countries to an interventionist instrument of regional economic development (Hooghe 1996).

The European Court does not act merely as an agent in adapting Member State agreements to new contingencies, but actively adjudicates disagreements among Member State executives, a role that places it in a position of authority not merely as the supreme Judiciary in Europe, but one that is above all Member State actors state executives included (Burley and Mattli 1993; Lenaerts 1992; Volcansek 1992).

Constraints on change. Because the decision rule for major institutional change is unanimity, it is often remarked that this poses a high hurdle for integration. However, unanimity applies for any institutional change in the EU, whether it empowers supranational institutions or reins them in. Supranational actors need only dent the united front of state executives in order to block a proposed change. The logic of lowest common denominator under unanimity voting limits the ability of state executives to shorten their collective leash on supranational institutions, as well as embark on new integrationist measures. Once a supranational institution has a power or powers beyond those necessary to serve as a mere agent of state executives, it needs only gain support from one or more principals to sustain its position.

Informational asymmetries. Agents may gain a potent source of influence if they develop access to information or skills that is not available to principals (Eichener 1992, Majone 1995, 1994a). As a small and thinly staffed organization, the Commission has only a fraction of the financial and human resources available to national governments, but its position as interlocutor with national governments, subnational authorities and numerous interest groups gives it a unique informational base. The Commission's job in reducing transaction costs of policy co-ordination among Member State governments provides it with unparalleled access to information and, therefore, the means for independent influence vis-a-vis those governments.

Detailed regulation as a response to mutual mistrust. It is in the collective interest of Member State executives to enact certain common regulations, but each may be better off if others adhere to them while it defects. To contain defection, state executives have created a Court of Justice with unprecedented powers of adjudication among Member State actors, as described below. A further consequence of mutual mistrust is the highly detailed character of European regulation. While state executives are induced to ambiguity in the high politics of treaty making, they give the Commission latitude to formulate very precise regulations on specific policies. Instead of determining general provisions that are broadly applicable ('relational contracting'), state executives allow the Commission to propose legislation that approximates a 'complete contract', legislation that is designed to straightjacket principals and so reduce their scope for evasion (Majone 1995). This allows the Commission to legitimate its role in technocratic terms, as the hub of numerous highly specialized policy networks of technical experts designing detailed regulations.

Unintended consequences of institutional change. A final limit on the capacity of state executives to control their supranational agents lies in their inability to forecast precisely the effects of their own collective actions. The complexity of policy-making across disparate territories and multiple actors, the changing patterns of mutual interaction among policy arenas, the sensitivity of EU decision-making to international and domestic exogenous shocks – these contribute to a fluid and inherently unpredictable environment which dilutes the extent to which Member State decisions at time T_0 can control supranational actors at T_1.

Policy-making in the European Union

The questions we are asking have to do with who decides what in EU policy-making. If the state-centric model is valid, we would find a systematic pattern of state executive dominance. That entails three conditions. National governments, by virtue of the European Council and the Council of Ministers, should be able to impose their preferences collectively upon other European institutions, i.e. the European Commission, the EP and the ECJ. In other words, the latter three European institutions should be agents effectively controlled by state-dominated European institutions. Second, national governments should be able to maintain individual sovereignty vis-a-vis other national governments. And thirdly, national governments should be able to control the mobilization of subnational interests in the European arena. If, however, the multi-level governance model is valid, we should find, first, that the European Council and Council of Ministers share decisional authority with supranational institutions; second, that individual state executives cannot deliver the outcomes they wish through collective state executive decisions; and, finally, that subnational interests mobilize directly in the European arena or use the EU as a public space to pressure state executives into particular actions.

We divide the policy-making process into four sequential phases: policy initiation, decision-making, implementation and adjudication. We focus on informal practices in addition to formal rules, for it is vital to understand how institutions actually shape the behaviour of political actors in the European arena.

Policy initiation: commission as agenda-setter with a price – listen, make sense, and time aptly

In political systems that involve many actors, complex procedures and multiple veto points, the power to set the agenda is extremely important. The European Commission alone has the formal power to initiate and draft legislation, which includes the right to amend or withdraw its proposal at any stage in the process, and it is the think-tank for new policies (Article 155, EC). From a multi-level governance perspective, the European Commission has significant autonomous influence over the agenda. According to the state-centric model, this formal power is largely decorative: in reality the European Commission draws up legislation primarily to meet the demands of state executives.

At first sight, the practice of policy initiation is consistent with a state-centric interpretation. Analysis of 500 recent directives and regulations by the French Conseil d'Etat found that only a minority of EU proposals were spontaneous initiatives of the Commission. Regulatory initiative at the European level is demand driven rather than the product of autonomous supranational action, but the demands come not only from government leaders. A significant number of initiatives originate in the EP, the Economic and Social Committee, regional governments, and various private and public-interest groups (Majone 1994a).

Such data should be evaluated carefully. For one thing, regulatory initiative at national and European levels is increasingly intermeshed. In its report, the Conseil d'Etat estimated that the European Commission is consulted beforehand on 75–80% of French national legislation. Jacques Delors' prediction that by the year 2000 about 80% of national economic and social legislation would be of Community origin has a solid base in reality (Majone 1994a). Moreover, it is one thing to be the first to articulate an issue, and quite another to influence how that issue will be taken up, with whom, and under what set of rules. And in each of these respects the influence of the Commission extends beyond its formal role, partly because of its unique political and administrative resources, discussed below, and partly because the Council is stymied by intergovernmental competition.

An organization that may serve as a powerful principal with respect to the Commission is the European Council, the summit of the political leaders of the Member States (plus the President of the Commission) held every six months. The European Council has immense prestige and legitimacy and a quasi-legal status as the body which defines 'general political guidelines' (Title 1, Art. 0, Treaty of the EU). However, its control of the European agenda is limited because it meets rarely and has only a skeleton permanent staff. The European Council provides the Commission with general policy mandates rather than specific policy proposals, and such mandates have proved to be a flexible basis for the Commission to build legislative programmes.

More direct constraints on the Commission originate from the Council of Ministers and the EP. Indeed, the power of initiative has increasingly become a shared competence, permanently subject to contestation, among the three institutions. The Council (Article 152, EC) and, since the Maastricht Treaty, the European Parliament (Article 138b, EC) can request the Commission to produce proposals, although they cannot draft proposals themselves (Nugent 1994). Council Presidencies began to exploit this window in the legal texts from the mid-1980s, when state executives began to attach higher priority to the Council Presidency (Nugent 1994). Several governments bring detailed proposals with them to Brussels when they take over the Council Presidency. Another way for the Council to circumvent the Commission's formal monopoly of legislative proposal is to make soft law, i.e. by ratifying common opinions, resolutions, agreements and recommendations (Nugent 1994; Snyder 1994).

The effect of this on the Commission's agenda-setting role is double-edged. On the one hand, the Commission finds it politically difficult to ignore detailed Council initiatives of soft law, even through their legal status is vague (Snyder 1994). On the other hand, state executives are intent on using the European arena to attain a variety of policy goals, and this gives the Commission allies for integrationist initiatives.

The EP has made use of its newly gained competence in Article 138b. In return for the approval of the Santer Commission in January 1995, it extracted from the Commission President a pledge to renegotiate the code of conduct (dating from 1990) between the two institutions in an effort to gain greater influence on the Commission's pen, its right of initiative.

The European Council, the Council, and the EP have each succeeded in circumscribing the Commission's formal monopoly of initiative more narrowly, though none can claim that it has reduced the position of the Commission to that of an agent. Agenda-setting is now a shared and contested competence among the four European institutions, rather than monopolized by one actor.

But the diffusion of control over the EU's agenda does not stop here. Interest groups have mobilized intensively in the European arena and, while their power is difficult to pinpoint, it is clear that the Commission takes their input seriously. The passage of the SEA precipitated a rapid growth of European legislation and a corresponding increase in interest group representation in Europe. Art outpouring of case study research suggests that the number and variety of groups involved is as great, and perhaps greater, than in any national capital. National and regional organizations of every kind have mobilized in Brussels, and these are flanked by a large and growing number of European peak organizations and individual companies from across Europe. According to a Commission report, some 3,000 interest groups and lobbies, or about 10,000 people, were based in Brussels in 1992. Among these there are 500 'Eurogroups' which aggregate interests at the European level (McLaughlin and Greenwood 1995). Most groups target their lobbying activity at the European Commission and the EP, for these are perceived to be more accessible than the secretive Council (Mazey and Richardson, 1993b).

Subnational authorities now mobilize intensively in Brussels. Apart from the Committee of the Regions, established by the Maastricht Treaty, individual subnational authorities have set up almost 100 regional offices in Brussels and a wide variety of interregional associations (Hooghe 1995a; Hooghe and Marks 1996; Marks et al. 1996).

Agenda-setting is therefore increasingly a shared and contested competence, with European institutions competing for control, and interest groups and subnational actors vying to influence the process. This is not much different from the situation in some national polities, particularly those organized federally.

. . . .

The European Commission is a critical actor in the policy initiation phase, whether one looks at formal rules or practice. If one surveys the evidence one cannot, conclude that the Commission serves merely as an agent of state executives. The point is not that the Commission is the only decisive actor. We discern instead a system of multi-level governance involving competition and interdependence among the Commission, Council, and EP, each of which commands impressive resources in the intricate game of policy initiation.

Decision-making: state sovereignty in retreat

According to the Treaties, the main legislative body in the EU is not the EP, but the Council of Ministers, an assembly of Member State executives. Until the SEA, the Council was the sole legislative authority. The thrust of the state-centric argument is to give great weight to the legislative powers of state executives in the decision-making stage. At this stage, state executives may be said to be in complete control. They adjust policies to their collective preferences, define the limits of European collaboration, determine the role of the European Commission and the ECJ and if need be curtail their activities. If previous decisions have unintended consequences these can be corrected by the Council.

There is some plausibility to this argument, but it is one-dimensional. In the first place, one must take into account the serious constraints under which individual governments have operated since the SEA. Second, one should recognize that even collectively, state executives exert conditional not absolute, control. State executive dominance is eroded in the decision-making process by the legislative power of the European Parliament, the role of the European Commission in overcoming transaction problems, and the efforts of interest groups to influence outcomes in the European arena.

The most transparent blow to state sovereignty has come from the successive extension of QMV under the SEA and the Maastricht Treaty: QMV is now the rule for most policy areas covered by the original Treaty of Rome, including agriculture, trade, competition policy, transport, and policy areas concerned with the realization of the international market, though there are important exceptions which include the EU-budget, taxation, capital flows, self-employed persons and professions, visa policy . . . , free movement of persons, and rights of employed persons (Dinan 1994; Nugent 1994; Schmitter 1992b). The decision-making rules are complex, but the bottom line is clear: over broad areas of EU competence individual state executives may be outvoted.

The practice of QMV is complicated by the Luxembourg Compromise and by a 'veto culture' which is said to have predominated in the Council of Ministers. Under the Luxembourg Compromise state executives can veto decisions subject to majority rule if they claim that their national vital interests are at stake. The Luxembourg Compromise features far more strongly in academic debates about the EU than in the practice of European politics. It was invoked less than a dozen times between 1966 and 1981, and it has been used even less frequently since that time.

The Luxembourg Compromise was accompanied by a 'veto culture' which inhibited majority voting if a state executive expressed serious objections. During the 1970s, this led to the virtual paralysis of the Community as literally hundreds of Commission proposals were blocked. But the effectiveness of the veto culture was its undoing. It eroded during the 1980s as a result of growing intolerance with dead-lock on the part of the EP and most national leaders (Teasdale 1993). The turning point was the inability of the British government in 1982 to veto a decision on agricultural prices to extract a larger British bud-getary rebate. A qualified majority vote was taken at the meeting of Council of Ministers despite British objections.

Thereafter, state executives became more reluctant to invoke the compromise or tolerate its use by others . . .

. . . .

State executives have built a variety of specific safeguards into the Treaties. There are numerous derogations for particular states, espe-cially on matters of taxation, state aids, monetary policy and energy policy. The SEA and the Maastricht Treaty preserve unanimity for the most sensitive or contested policy areas.

These qualifications soften the blow to national sovereignty. But a sensible discussion of the overall situation turns on the extent to which national sovereignty has been compromised, rather than on whether this has happened. Even under the doubtful premise that the Council is the sole decision-maker, it is now the case that state sovereignty has been pooled among a group of states in most EU policy areas (Scharpf 1994; Wessels 1992).

Collective state control exercised through the Council has dimin-ished. That is first of all due to the growing role of the EP in decision-making. The SEA and the Maastricht Treaty established co-operation and co-decision procedures which have transformed the legislative process from a simple Council-dominated process into an complex bal-ancing act between Council, Parliament and Commission. Since the Maastricht Treaty, the two procedures apply to the bulk of EU legisla-tion. The procedures are designed to encourage consensual decision-making between the three institutions. It is impossible for the Council to take legislative decisions without the support of at least one of the two other institutions unless it is unanimous. Moreover, the proce-dures enhance the agenda-setting power of the EP (Tsebelis 1994, 1995a).

The co-operation procedure gives the Commission significant agenda-setting capacity (Garrett and Weingast 1993; Schmitter 1992a; Tsebelis 1994; Weiler 1991; compare with sceptical early prognoses: Bieber et al. 1986). It may decide to take up or drop amendments from either the Council or Parliament, a power that makes it a broker – a consensus crafter – between the two institutions.

. . . .

Even though the outcome of the co-decision procedure is likely to be closer to the preferences of the Council than those of the Commission or Parliament (Tsebelis 1995a), it does not simply reflect Council preferences. Under both procedures the Council is locked in a complex relationship of cooperation and contestation with the two other institutions. This is multi-level government in action, and is distinctly different from what would be expected in a state-centric system.

. . . .

Implementation: opening the European arena – breaking the state mould

Multi-level governance is prominent in the implementation stage. Although the Commission has formal executive powers and national governments are in principle responsible for implementation, in practice these competencies are shared. On the one hand, national governments monitor the executive powers of the Commission closely, though they do so in conjunction with subnational governments and societal actors. On the other hand, the Commission has become involved in day-to-day implementation in a number of policy areas, and this brings it into close contact with subnational authorities and interest groups. As in the initiation and decision-making stage, mutual intrusion is contested.

The Commission's formal mandate gives it discretion to interpret legislation and issue administrative regulations bearing on specific cases. It issues 6–7,000 administrative regulations annually (Ludlow 1991; Nugent 1994). However, only a tiny proportion of the Commission's decisions are unilateral. Since the 1980s, with the institutionalization of comitology, the Council and the individual national governments have become intimately involved. Many regulations have their own committee attached to them. Balancing Commission autonomy and state involvement is an open-ended and conflictual process in the EU, and this is also apparent in comitology. Rules of operation vary across policy areas and are a source of contention between the Commission, usually supported by the Parliament, and the Council (St. Clair Bradley 1992). Some committees are only advisory; others can prevent the Commission from carrying out a certain action by qualified majority vote; and a third category must approve Commission actions by qualified majority. In each case the Commission presides.

At first sight, comitology seems to give state executives control over the Commission's actions in genuine principal-agent fashion. But the relationship between state actors and European institutions is more complex. Comitology is weakest in precisely those areas where the

Commission has extensive executive powers, e.g. in competition policy, state aids, agriculture, commercial policy and the internal market. Here, the Commission has significant space for autonomous action (McGowan and Wilkes 1995; Nugent 1994, 1995).

State-centrists may argue that state executives prefer to delegate these powers to achieve state-oriented collective goods, such as control over potential distortion of competition or a stronger bargaining position in international trade. But one result is that state executives have lost exclusive control in a range of policy areas. To mention just three examples among the many discussed in this chapter: they no longer control competition within their borders; they cannot aid national firms as they deem fit; they cannot autonomously conduct trade negotiations.

. . . .

Although comitology involves state actors in the Commission's activities, this intermeshing is not necessarily limited to central state actors. Because the issues on the table are often technical in nature, Member State government tend to send those people who are directly responsible or who are best informed about the issue at home. These are regularly subnational officials, or representatives of interest groups or other non-governmental bodies. Subnational participation in comitology is prevalent for Member States organized along federal or semi-federal lines (see, on Germany, Goetz 1994; on Belgium, Hooghe 1995b). But, in recent years, subnational actors have been drawn into the European arena from more centralized Member States (see, for France, Lequesne 1994).

To the extent that EU regulations affect policy areas where authority is shared among central and subnational levels of government, effective implementation requires contacts between multiple levels of government. Environmental policy is an example of this, for in several European countries competencies in this area are shared across different territorial levels. To speed up implementation of environmental law, the Commission began in 1990 to arrange so-called package meetings to bring together central, regional and local government representatives of a Member State. Such meetings are voluntary, but in the first year of its operation seven countries made use of them. The Spanish central government, for example, was keen to use the Commission's presence to pressure its autonomous provinces into compliance with EU environmentally, but to do so it conceded them access to the European arena.

The majority of participants in comitology are not national civil servants, but interest group representatives (particularly from farming, union, and employer organizations) alongside technical experts, scientists and academics (Buitendijk and van Schendelen 1995). These people are mostly selected, or at least approved of, by their national government. One can plausibly assume that national governments find it more difficult to persuade technical experts, interest group representatives, and private actors than their own officials to defend the national interest. In practice therefore, comitology, which was originally a mechanism for central state oversight over Commission activities, has had the intended consequence of deepening the participation of subnational authorities.

A second development which has received little attention in the literature is the direct involvement of Commission officials in day-to-day policy implementation. The Commission was never expected to perform ground-level implementation, except in unusual circumstances (such as competition policy, fraud, etc.). Yet in some areas this has changed. The most prominent example is cohesion policy, which now absorbs about one-third of the EU budget. The bulk of the money goes to multi-annual regional development programmes in the less developed regions of the EU. The 1989 reform prescribes the involvement of Commission, national, regional, local and social actors on a continuing basis in all stages of the policy process: selection of priorities, choice of programmes, allocation of funding, monitoring of operations, evaluation and adjustment of programmes. ... Such links break open the mould of the state, so that multi-level governance encompasses actors within as well as beyond existing states.

Adjudication: an activist court in a supranational legal order

State-centrists have argued that a European legal order and effective ECJ are essential to state co-operation (Garrett 1995; Garrett and Weingast 1993; Garrett 1995; Moravcsik 1993a). Unilateral defection is difficult to detect, and thus it is in the interest of states to delegate authority to a European Court to monitor compliance. The ECJ also mitigates incomplete contracting problems by applying general interstate bargains to future contingencies. In this vein, the ECJ may be conceptualized as an agent of constituent Member States. However, a number of scholars have argued convincingly that the ECJ has become more than an instrument of Member States (Burley and Mattli 1993). The Court has been active in transforming the legal order in a supranational direction. But the Court could not have done this without a political ally at the European level: the European Commission. Nor could it have established the supremacy of European law without the collaboration of national courts, and this collaboration has altered the balance of power between national courts and national political authorities.

Through its activist stance, the ECJ has laid the legal foundation for an integrated European polity. By means of an impressive body of case law, the Court has established the Treaty of Rome as a document creating legal obligations directly binding on national governments and individual citizens alike. Moreover, these obligations have legal priority over laws made by the Member States. Directly binding legal authority and supremacy are attributes of sovereignty, and their application by the ECJ indicates that the EU is becoming a constitutional regime.

The Court was originally expected to act as an impartial monitor 'to ensure that in the interpretation and application of the treaties the law is observed' (Art. 164 EEC, Art. 136 Euratom, Art. 31 ECSC) but, from the beginning, the Court viewed these interstate treaties as more than narrow agreements. The Court's expansive role is founded on the failure of the treaties to specify the competencies of major EU institutions (Weiler 1991). Instead, the treaties set out 'tasks' or 'purposes' for European co-operation, such as the customs union (Treaty of Rome), the completion of the internal market (SEA) or economic and monetary union (Maastricht Treaty). The Court has constitutionalized European law and expanded European authority in other policy areas by stating that these were necessary to achieve these functional goals (Weiler 1991).

Court rulings have been pivotal in shaping European integration. However, the ECJ depends on other actors to force issues on the European political agenda and condone its interpretations. Legislators (the European Council, Council of Ministers, Commission and Parliament) may always reverse the course set by the Court by changing the law or by altering the Treaties. In other words, the ECJ is no different from the Council, Commission or European Parliament in that it is locked in mutual dependence with other actors.

. . . .

Conclusion

Multi-level governance does not confront the sovereignty of states directly. Instead of being explicitly challenged, states in the EU are being melded gently into a multi-level polity by their leaders and the actions of numerous subnational and supranational actors. State-centric theorists are right when they argue that states are extremely powerful institutions that are capable of crushing direct threats to their existence. The institutional form of the state emerged because it proved a particularly effective means of systematically wielding violence, and it is difficult to imagine any generalized challenge along these lines. But this is not the only, nor even the most important, issue facing the state. One does not have to argue that states are on the verge of political extinction to believe that their control of those living in their territories has significantly weakened.

It is not necessary to look far beyond the state itself to find reasons that might explain how such an outcome is possible. When we disaggregate the state into the actors that shape its diverse institutions, it is clear that key decision-makers, above all those directing the state executive, may have goals that do not coincide with that of projecting state sovereignty into the future. As well as being a goal in itself, the state may sensibly be regarded as a means to a variety of ends that are structured by party competition and interest group politics in a liberal democratic setting. A state executive may wish to shift decision-making to the supranational level because the political benefits outweigh the cost of losing control. Or a state executive may have intrinsic grounds to shift control, for example to shed responsibility for unpopular decisions.

Even if state executives want to maintain sovereignty, they are often not able do so. A state executive can easily be outvoted because most decisions in the Council are now taken under the decision rule of qualified majority, and moreover, even the national veto, the ultimate instrument of sovereignty, is constrained by the willingness of other state executives to tolerate its use. But the limits on state sovereignty are deeper. Even collectively, state executives do not determine the European agenda because they are unable to control the supranational institutions they have created at the European level. The growing diversity of issues on the Council's agenda, the sheer number of state executive principals and the mistrust that exists among them, and the increased specialization of policy-making have made the Council of Ministers reliant upon the Commission to set the agenda, forge compromises, and supervise compliance. The Commission and the Council are not on a par, but neither can their relationship be understood in principal-agent terms. Policy-making in the EU is characterized by mutual dependence, complementary functions and overlapping competencies.

The Council also shares decision-making competencies with the EP, which has gained significant legislative power under the SEA and the Maastricht Treaty. Indeed, the Parliament might be conceived of as a principal in its own right in the European arena. The Council, Commission and Parliament interact within a legal order which has been transformed into a supranational one through the innovative jurisprudence of the EJC. The complex interplay among these contending institutions in a polity where political control is diffuse often leads to outcomes that are second choice for all participants.

The character of the Euro-polity at any particular point in time is the outcome of a tension between supranational and intergovernmental pressures. We have argued that, since the 1980s, it has crystallized into a multi-level polity. States no longer serve as the exclusive nexus between domestic politics and international relations.

. . . .

Notes

1 The only exception was the European Defence Community which was voted down in the French Assemblee in 1954. After that debacle, the European Political Community was quietly dropped as well.

Chapter 15

The Rise of the Regulatory State in Europe

Giandomenico Majone*

Regulation and the Redrawing of the Borders of the State

A paradoxical consequence of the international debate about privatization and deregulation has been to focus the attention of European policy makers and scholars on regulation as a distinctive mode of state intervention in the economy and society. In the words of a legal scholar, regulation has become the new border between the state and the and the battleground for ideas on how the economy should be run (Veljanovski 1991). A political scientist observes that regulation is a pervasive and widely accepted phenomenon in all advanced countries (Dyson 1992). According to an economist, the regulation issue – what, how, and at what level of government to, regulate – is the core of the compromise between the European Community and its member states that made the Internal Market Programme possible (Pelkmans 1989).

This consensus on the significance and distinctiveness of regulation is a relatively new phenomenon. Until recently, European scholars devoted little attention to the special features of regulation that distinguish it from other modes of policy making. Thus, while the American deregulation movement was preceded and prepared by decades of intensive research on the law, economics and politics of the regulatory process, in Europe the terms 'deregulation' and 'privatization' gained sudden currency – even in Great Britain the words were scarcely heard of before 1978 – with hardly any intellectual preparation.

. . . .

The relative neglect of regulatory analysis in the past corresponded to the low visibility of regulatory activities. While in the United States the tradition of regulation by means of independent agencies combining legislative, administrative, and judicial functions goes back to

* Reproduced by kind permission of Taylor and Francis Ltd (http://www.tandf.co.uk/journals) from Giandomenico Majone (1994a) 'The Rise of the Regulatory State in Europe', *West European Politics,* 17(3), 77–101. The text has been edited, as indicated, to fit the format of this volume. References have been changed to Harvard citation style.

the Interstate Commerce Act of 1887 – and even earlier in states like Wisconsin, Massachusetts and New York – the tendency in Europe has been to treat regulatory issues as either purely administrative, and so tasks for central departments or ministries, or as judicial, and so matters for determination by courts or court-like tribunals. In Britain, for example, tribunals like the Railway Commission (created in 1873)

> proved so common that by 1933 the regulation of British public utilities was viewed by some as considerably impaired by this reliance on the quasi-judicial method and by the resulting failure to develop the administrative commission. What was absent was a powerful agency that applied a special expertise, employed its own secretariat and regulated (in the sense of imposing a structure on an industry or social issue). Regulators instead of instituting action, responded to the competing proposals of private interests (Baldwin and McCrudden 1987).

Even these timid beginnings of an autonomous regulatory function were forgotten in the era of nationalisations and municipalisations. In most countries of Europe, public ownership of key industries such as railways, telecommunications, electricity, gas, water, and other natural monopolies was supposed to protect the public interest against powerful private interests. In this respect, nationalisations and municipalisations were the functional equivalent of American-style regulation . . .

Because of these analogies, it has been argued that there is no great difference between public monopolies, like the European Post and Telecommunications Ministries, and privately owned but publicly regulated monopolies like the American Telephone and Telegraph Company before deregulation. However, this argument overlooks one important point: the purpose of public ownership was not simply to regulate prices, conditions of entry and quality of service, but also to pursue many other goals including economic development, technical innovation, employment, regional income redistribution, and national security. While nationalisations and other traditional forms of direct state intervention were thus justified by appealing to a variety of often conflicting goals, regulation has a single normative justification: improving the efficiency of the economy by correcting specific forms of market failure such as monopoly, imperfect information, and negative externalities.

. . . .

. . . Privatization changes the role of the state from a provider of goods and services to that of an umpire whose function is to ensure that economic actors play by the agreed rules of the game. Deregulation often means less restrictive or rigid regulation: a search for ways of achieving the relevant regulatory objectives by less burdensome methods of government intervention, as when command-and-control methods are replaced by economic incentives. Thus, neither American deregulations nor European privatizations can be interpreted as a retreat of the state, but rather as a redefinition of its functions. What is observed in practice is a redrawing of the borders of the public sphere in a way that excludes certain fields better left to private activity, while at the same time strengthening and even expanding the state's regulatory capacity in other fields like competition or environmental and consumer protection.

. . . .

The Growth of Regulation in Europe

Administrative regulation – economic and social regulation by means of agencies operating outside the line of hierarchical control or oversight by the central administration – is rapidly becoming the new frontier of public policy and pubic administration throughout the industrialised world. The absence of an efficient regulatory framework is increasingly seen as a major obstacle to modernisation. Thus, as a 1993 issue of The Economist points out, one of the serious problems of privatization in Russia is that there is no regulatory system to control trading the vouchers or shares. This 'regulatory black hole' has already claimed many victims among uninformed investors, and creates an irresistible temptation for any swindler.

   The growth of administrative regulation in Europe has greatly accelerated during the last two decades . . .

. . . .

. . . the reasons given for the rise of the independent agencies are strikingly similar from country to country. These functional explanations are also strongly reminiscent of the arguments or earlier American writers. Thus it is said that agencies are justified by the need of expertise in highly complex or technical matters, combined with a rule-making or adjudicative function that is inappropriate for a government department or a court; that an agency structure may favour public participation, while the opportunity for consultations by means of public hearings is often denied to government departments because of the conventions under which they operate; that agencies' separateness from government is useful whenever it is hoped to free government administration from partisan policies and party political influence. Agencies are also said to provide greater continuity and stability than cabinets because they are one step removed from election returns; and the exercise of a policy-making function by an administrative agency should provide flexibility not only in policy formation but also in the application of policy to particular circumstances. Finally, it is argued that independent agencies can protect citizens from bureaucratic arrogance and reticence, and are able to focus public attention on controversial issues, thus enriching public debate (Baldwin and McCrudden 1987: 4-9; Guédon 1991: 16–27; Teitgen-Colly 1988; Vesperini 1990: 415–19).

The growth of administrative regulation in Europe owes much to these newly articulated perceptions of a mismatch between existing institutional capacities and the growing complexity of policy problems: policing financial markets in an increasingly interdependent world economy; controlling the risks of new products and new technologies; protecting the health and economic interests of consumers without impeding the free flow of goods, services and people across national boundaries; reducing environmental pollution. It is sufficient to mention problems such as these to realise how significant is the supranational dimension of the new economic and social regulation. Hence the important role of the European Community (now Union) in complementing the regulatory capacities of the member states.

The European Community as Regulator

Apart from competition rules and measures necessary to the integration of national markets, few regulatory policies or programmes are explicitly mentioned in the Treaty of Rome. Transport and energy policies which could have given rise to significant regulatory activities, have remained until lately largely undeveloped. On the other hand, agriculture, fisheries, regional development, social programmes and aid to developing countries, which together account for more than 80% of the Community budget . . . are mostly distributive or redistributive rather than regulatory in nature.

This budget of almost ECU 47 billion represents less than 1.3% of the Gross Domestic Product (GDP) of the Community and less than 4% of the central government spending of member states. Given such limited resources, how can one explain the continuous growth of Community regulation, even in the absence of explicit legal mandates? Take the case of environmental protection, an area not even mentioned in the Treaty of Rome. In the two decades from 1967 to 1987, when the European Single Act finally recognised the authority of the Community to legislate in this area, almost 200 directives, regulations, and decisions were introduced by the Commission. Moreover, the rate of growth of environmental regulation appears to have been largely unaffected by the political vicissitudes, budgetary crises, and recurrent waves of Euro-pessimism of the 1970s and early 1980s. From the single directive on preventing risks by testing of 1969 (L68/19,3.69) we pass to 10 directives/decisions in 1975, 13 in 1980, 20 in 1982, 23 in 1984, 24 in 1985 and 17 in the six months immediately preceding passage of the SEA.

The case of environmental regulation is particularly striking, partly because of the political salience of environmental issues, but it is by no means unique. The volume and depth of Community regulation in the areas of consumer product safety, medical drug testing, banking and financial services and, of course, competition law is hardly less impressive. In fact, hundreds of regulatory measure proposed by the Commission's White Paper on the completion of the internal market represent only the acceleration of a trend set in motion decades ago. The continuous growth of supranational regulation is not easily explained by traditional theories of Community policy-making. At most such theories suggest that the serious implementation gap that exists in the EC may make it easier for the member states and their representatives in the Council, to accept Commission proposals which they have no serious intention of applying. The main limitation of this argument is that it fails to differentiate between areas where policy development has been slow and uncertain (for example transport, energy or research) and areas such as environmental protection where significant policy development has taken place even in the absence of a clear legal basis.

Moreover, existing theories of Union policymaking do not usually draw any clear distinction between regulatory and other types of policies. Now, an important characteristic of regulatory policymaking is the limited influence of budgetary limitations on the activities of regulators. The size of non-regulatory, direct-expenditure programmes is constrained by budgetary appropriations and, ultimately, by the size of government tax revenues. In contrast, the real costs of most regulatory programmes are borne directly by the firms and individuals who have to comply with them. Compared with these costs, the resources needed to produce the regulations are trivial.

It is difficult to overstate the significance of this structural difference between regulatory policies and policies involving the direct expenditure of public funds. The distinction is particularly important for the analysis of Community policymaking, since not only the economic but also the political and administrative costs of enforcing EC regulations are borne by the member states (Majone 1992a, 1992b). As already noted, the financial resources of the Community go, for the most part, to the Common Agricultural Policy and to a handful of distributive programmes. The remaining resources are insufficient to support large-scale initiatives areas such as industrial policy, energy, research, or technological innovation. Given this constraint, the only way for the Commission to increase its role was to expand the scope of its regulatory activities.

Another important element in an explanation of the growth of

Community regulation is the interest of multinational, export-oriented industries in avoiding inconsistent and progressively more stringent regulations in various EC and non-EC countries. Community regulation can eliminate or at least reduce this risk.

A similar phenomenon has been observed in the United States, where certain industries, faced with the danger of a significant loss of markets through state and local legislation, have strongly supported federal regulation ('preemptive federalism'). For example, the American car industry which during the early 1960s had successfully opposed federal emission standards for motor vehicles, abruptly reversed its position in mid-1965: provided that the federal standards would be set by a regulatory agency, and provided that they would preempt any state standards more stringent than California's, the industry would support federal legislation.

Analogous reasons explain the preference for Community solutions of some powerful and well-organised European industries. Consider, for example, the 'Sixth Amendment' of Directive 67/548 on the classification, packaging and labeling of dangerous substances. This amending Directive does not prevent member states from including more substances within the scope of national regulations than are required by the Directive itself. In fact, the British Health and Safety Commission proposed to go further than the Directive by bringing intermediate products within the scope of national regulation. This, however, was opposed by the chemical industry, represented by the Chemical Industries Association (CIA) which argued that national regulation should not impose greater burdens on British industry then the Directive placed on its competitors. The CIA view eventually prevailed.

Similarly, German negotiators pressed for a European-wide scheme that would also provide the framework for an acceptable regulatory programme at home, wanted a full and explicit statement of their obligations to be defined at the EC level. Moreover, with more then 50% of Germany's chemical trade going to other EC countries German businessmen and government officials wished to avoid the commercial obstacles that would arise from divergent national regulations (Brickman et al. 1985).

The European chemical industry had another reason for supporting Community regulation. In 1976 the United States, without consulting their commercial partners, enacted the Toxic Substances Control Act (TSCA). The new regulation represented a serious threat for European exports to the lucrative American market. A European response to TSCA was clearly needed, and the Community was the logical forum for fashioning such a response. An EC-wide system of testing new chemical substances could serve as a model for negotiating standardised requirements covering the major chemical markets. In fact, the 1979 directive has enabled the Community to speak with one voice in discussions with the United States and other OECD countries, and has strengthened the position of the European chemical industry in ensuring that the new American regulation does not create obstacles to its exports. There is little doubt that the ability of the Commission to enter into discussion with the USA has been greatly enhanced by the Directive, and it is unlikely that each European country on its own could do so effectively (ibid.: 277).

Explaining Regulatory Policymaking in the EC

In the preceding section I have considered three variables that are clearly important for explaining the growth of EC regulation: the tightness and rigidity of the Community budget; the desire of the Commission to increase its influence by expanding its competencies; and the preference of multinational firms for dealing with a uniform set of rules rather than with 12 different national regulations. However, these variables are not sufficient to explain the willingness of the member states to surrender important regulatory powers to supranational institutions, not the ability of the Commission to introduce significant innovations with respect to the policies of the member states (Majone 1993a).

As already suggested, available theories of policymaking in the Community do not explain why the member states would be willing to delegate regulatory powers beyond the level required by an integrated market, nor can they explain the policy entrepreneurship of the EC Commission. This is because such theories stress the dominant role of member states in all stages of the policy process, from initiation (which comes from the heads of state or governments in the European Council) to formal adoption (the prerogative of the Council of Ministers), to implementation (in the hands of the national administrations).

A model capable of explaining the above mentioned phenomena must come to grips with two issues that have been overlooked by the traditional theories: first, problems of 'regulatory failure' in an international context, which limit the usefulness of purely intergovernmental solutions; and, second, the fact that regulation, as a very specialised type of policy-making, requires a high level of technical and administrative discretion.

To start with the first issue, market failures with international impacts, such as transboundary pollution, could be managed in a cooperative fashion without the necessity of delegating powers to a supranational level, *provided* that national regulators were willing and able to take into account the international repercussions of their choices; that they had sufficient knowledge of one another's intentions;

and that the costs of organising and monitoring policy co-ordination were not too high. These conditions are seldom, if ever, satisfied in practice. Experience shows that it is quite difficult to verify whether or not intergovernmental agreements are being properly kept. Because regulators lack information that only regulated firms have, and because governments are reluctant, for political reasons, to impose excessive costs on industry, bargaining is an essential feature of the process of regulatory enforcement. Regardless of what the law says, the process of regulation is not simply one where the regulators command and the regulated obey. A 'market' is created in which bureaucrats and those subject to regulation bargain over the precise obligations of the latter (Peacock 1984). Because bargaining is so pervasive, it may be impossible for an outside observer to determine whether or not an international regulation has been, in fact, violated.

When it is difficult to observe whether governments are making an honest effort to enforce a co-operative agreement, the agreement is not credible. For example, where pollution has international effects and fines impose significant competitive disadvantages on firms that comply internationally, firms are likely to believe that national regulators will be unwilling to prosecute them as rigorously if they determine the level of enforcement unilaterally rather than under supranational supervision. Hence the transfer of regulatory powers to a supranational authority like the European Commission, by making more stringent regulation credible, may improve the behaviour of regulated firms. Also, because the Commission is involved in the regulation of numerous firms throughout the Community, it has much more to gain by being tough in any individual case than a national regulator: weak enforcement would destroy its credibility in the eyes of more firms. Thus it may be more willing to enforce sanctions than a member state would be (Gatsios & Seabright 1989). In fact, the Commission has consistently taken a stricter pro-competition stance than national authorities such as the British Monopolies and Merger Commission, the German Bundeskartellamt, or the French Conseil de la Concurrence.

In short, the low credibility of intergovernmental agreements explains the willingness of member states to delegate regulatory power to a supranational authority. At the same time, however, governments attempt to limit the discretion of the Commission by making it dependent on the information and knowledge provided by national bureaucrats and experts. We must now explain how the Commission often manages to overcome these limitations.

The offices of the Commission responsible for a particular policy area form the central node in a vast 'issue network' that includes not only experts from the national administrations, but independent experts (also from non-EU countries), academics, public-interest advocates like environmentalists and leaders of consumer movements, representatives of economic and professional organisations and of regional bodies. Commission officials listen to everybody – both in advisory committees which they normally chair, and in informal consultation – but are free to choose whose ideas and proposals to adopt. They operate less as technical experts alongside other technical experts, than as policy entrepreneurs, that is, as 'advocates who are willing to invest their resources – time, energy, reputation, money – to promote a positions in return for anticipated future gain in the form of material, purposive, or solidary benefits' (Kingdon 1984: 188).

In his study of policy innovations in America, Kingdon identities three main characteristics of successful policy entrepreneurs: first, the person must have some claim to be taken seriously, either as an expert, as a leader of a powerful interest group, or as an authoritative decision-maker; second, the person must be known for his political connections or negotiating skills; third, and probably most important, successful entrepreneurs are persistent (ibid.: 189–90). Because of the way they are recruited, the structure of their career incentives, and the crucial role of the Commission in policy initiation, Commission officials usually display the qualities of a successful policy entrepreneur to a degree unmatched by national civil servants. Actually

> the Commission officials' typical motivational structure is quite different from that of the average national government official. While the staff of the national governments is often recruited from persons who tend to be – compared with their peers who choose an industrial career – solid, correct, security-oriented, conservative, risk-averse and often somewhat narrow-minded, the Commission recruits its staff from people who are highly motivated, risk oriented, polyglot, cosmopolitan, open-minded and innovative . . . From the beginnings in the 1960s and up to the present, it has indeed been officials of a special type who chose to leave the relative security of their national administrations to go to Brussels to do there a well-paid but extremely challenging job . . . The structural conditions of recruitment and career favour a tendency to support new ideas and to pursue a strategy of innovative regulation which attempts to go beyond everything which can presently be found in the Member States (Eichener 1992).

Because of this tendency to favour innovative regulatory solutions, even national experts may find the Community a more receptive forum for their ideas than their own administration. A 1989 directive on the safety of machinery (89/392/EEC) offers a striking example of this phenomenon. The crucially important technical annex of the directive was drafted by a British labour inspector who originally sought to reform the British regulatory approach. Having failed to persuade the policy makers of his own country, he brought his innovative ideas about risk assessment to Brussels, where they were welcomed by Commission officials and eventually became European law (ibid. 52).

Moreover, what is known about the *modus operandi* of the advisory committees suggests that debates there follow substantive rather than national lines. A good deal of *copinage technocratique* develops between Commission officials and national experts interested in discovering pragmatic solutions rather than defending political positions. By the time a Commission proposal reaches the political level, first in COREPER (the committee of permanent representatives of the member states) and then in the Council of Ministers, all the technical details have been worked out and modifications usually leaves the essentials untouched. The Council may, of course, delay a decision or resist the proposal outright, but these options are becoming increasingly problematic under the qualified majority rule and the 'cooperative procedure' between the European Parliament and the Council introduced by the SEA. Fitting together all the variables introduced in this and the preceding section – budget constraints, bureaucratic and economic interests, the poor credibility of purely intergovernmental arrangements and, last but not least, the highly technical nature of most regulatory policymaking – we begin to understand not only the origin and growth of Community regulation, but also its increasingly innovative character.

The Problem of Political Accountability

We just noted the significance of administrative and technical discretion for EU policymaking. Of course, regulatory discretion has important institutional and political implications also at the national level. One obvious consequences is the creation of specialised agencies such as the French *autorites administratives independantes* and the British regulatory offices mentioned above. Such agencies are independent of the central administration, and hence of civil service rules, and often combine legislative, judicial, and executive powers – rule adjudication, and enforcement, in the terminology of American administrative law – in more or less narrowly defined areas of policymaking.

As already suggested, such institutional arrangements represent an important departure from European constitutional and administrative traditions. The implicit, and in some cases explicit, model is the American independent regulatory commission (IRC). The IRCs were created by Congress to ensure agency independence from presidential control and short-term political considerations. Although they cover an extremely wide range of administrative activities – from the control of prices, routes and service conditions of railway companies by the Interstate Commerce Commission created in 1887 to the licensing of nuclear power plants by the Nuclear Regulatory Commission created in 1975 – all IRCs share some organisational characteristics that are meant to protect their decisional autonomy: they are multi-headed, having five or seven members; they are bipartisan; members are appointed by the president with the consent of the Senate and serve for fixed, staggered terms. Unlike the single-headed line agencies, the IRCs operate outside the presidential hierarchy in making their policy decisions. As the US Supreme Court asserted in *Humphrey's Executor vs. United States* (1935) commissions can be removed from office only for official misbehavior, not for disagreement with presidential policy.

In the course of their century-old history, IRCs have been often criticised for violating the principle of separation of powers, for their lack of political accountability, and for an alleged tendency to be captures by private interests. Not surprisingly, the same criticisms are heard now in Europe. Here, regulatory agencies are still seen as 'constitutional anomalies which do not fit well into the framework of controls, checks and balances' (Veljanovski 1991: 16), even as challenges to basic principles of democracy and of the *Rechtsstaat* (Teitgen-Colly 1988: 49). To be sure, it is no easy task to fit the new institutions into the constitutional framework of countries where the diffraction of state power is seen as a direct challenge to parliamentary sovereignty and to the principle of a rigid separation of powers. Expressed in traditional terms the dilemma is: either the regulatory agencies are part of the state administration, and then they cannot be independent; or else they are independent, but in this case to whom are accountable?

It is impossible to escape this dilemma without questioning the relevance of traditional notions such as the constitutional axiom of the tripartite separation of powers, or the political principle that governmental policymaking ought to be subject to control only by persons accountable to the electorate. It is certainly not a coincidence that similar issues are being raised in the ongoing debate about the proper scope of judicial review and judicial policymaking. The rise of judicial review in Europe shows that the triad of government powers is no longer considered an inviolable principle. At the same time, courts find their policymaking role enlarged by the public perception of them as guarantors of the substantive ideals of democracy when electoral accountability in all spheres of government seems to be waning (Volcansek 1992: 5). What connects the discourse about administrative regulation with that about judicial review and policymaking is the issue of the role of non-majoritarian institutions in democratic societies. Again, it is no mere coincidence that the same country has developed both the most advanced system of judicial review and the most extensive network of regulatory institutions.

The American experience shows that a highly complex and specialised activity like regulation can be monitored and kept politically accountable only by a combination of control instruments: legislative and executive oversight, strict procedural requirements, public participation and, most importantly, substantive judicial review. Measured against these standards, regulation in Europe is seen to be highly discretionary, suffering from weak accountability to Parliament, weak judicial review, absence of procedural safeguards, and insufficient public participation (Baldwin and McCrudden 1987; Prosser 1989: 135–65; Veljanovski 1991).

The issue of the political accountability of regulators, who are neither elected nor directly responsible to elected officials, is particularly visible at the EU-level precisely because of the central importance of regulatory policymaking in the Community system. However, the remedies should not compromise the effectiveness of the supranational institutions. The comparative advantage of EU regulation lies mainly in the relative insulation of Community regulators from the short-run political considerations and pressures which tend to dominate national policymaking. As was noted above, the Commission has more to gain by being tough in any individual case than a national regulator. This is because the Commission is involved in the regulation of firms throughout the Community, so that weak enforcement would destroy its credibility in the eyes of more firms. For the same reason the Commission is less likely to be captured by a particular firm or industry than a national regulator. In the language of James Madison, the insulation of the Commission from day-to-day politic is an important safeguard against national and sectoral 'factionalism'.

In fact, as I have shown elsewhere (Majone 1995), many of the arguments developed along Madisonian lines by the American advocates of an 'independent fourth branch of government' – the regulatory branch – apply, *mutatis mutandis,* in the context of the EU and its member states. These writers acknowledge that government by judges and technocratic experts raises serious issues for democratic theory but point out that government by elected officials, too, suffers from defects. For example, in seeking re-election legislators engage advertising and position taking rather than in serious policy-making, or they design laws with numerous opportunities to aid particular constituencies. Thus, re-election pressures have negative consequences for the quality of legislation. On the other hand, pro-regulation scholars ask, if the courts require the regulatory process to be open to public inputs and scrutiny and to act on the basis of competent analyses, are the regulators necessarily less accountable than elected politicians? (Rose-Ackerman 1992).

The procedural remedies suggested here are also relevant to the problem of the 'democratic deficit' of the EU. For example it is well-known that the Treaty of Rome does not structure the executive power of the Community in a single way, applicable to all instances of legislation needing further execution. Instead, it has been left to the Council, in its capacity as legislative decision-maker, to organise case by case, the executive process (Lenaerts 1991). This ad hoc approach is the very negation of the idea of transparency which plays such a large role in the current discussion of regulation. The adoption of something like an Administrative Procedures Act for the EU could do more to make public accountability possible than the wholesale transfer of traditional party politics to Brussels. Any progress along such lines at Union level could have positive spillovers for the member states where, as we saw, accountability of regulators is still an open issue. The fact that regulation is relatively more important at EU than at national level, makes the Union an ideal laboratory for the study of the problems of the regulatory state.

PART V

Non-rationalist Integration Theory

Featured works

- Jeffrey Checkel (1999c) 'Social Construction and Integration', *Journal of European Public Policy*, 6(4).

- Thomas Diez (1999) 'Speaking "Europe": The Politics of Integration Discourse', *Journal of European Public Policy*, 6(4).

- Ernst Haas (2001) 'Does Constructivism Subsume Neofunctionalism?' in T. Christiansen, K. E. Jørgensen, and A. Wiener (eds), *The Social Construction of Europe* (London: Sage).

The Constructivist Turn in European Integration Studies

The most recent contribution to the debate over European integration is the introduction in the 1990s of cultural and sociological perspectives often referred to as 'constructivist'. Constructivist work in EU studies draws on theoretical developments in the wider discipline of IR, where the end of the Cold War was accompanied by a growing dissatisfaction with dominant rationalist theories. In contrast to the materialism and methodological individualism of rationalist models, constructivists point to actors' subjective and intersubjective beliefs – including norms, identities and cultures – as important causes of political outcomes. A key constructivist claim is that political actors do not always make decisions based on calculations of individual utility or material benefit. Instead, they follow socially defined rules and norms – even when doing so may not be directly in their self-interest (Thelen and Steinmo 1992: 8). The focus of constructivist research, therefore, is on the social construction of the collective rules and norms that guide political behaviour.

Constructivism comes in many varieties, ranging from 'soft rationalist' versions or 'thin' constructivism, to more radical 'reflectivist' approaches. The former accept many of the assumptions of rational-choice theories – including the notion that objective truths exist and can be discovered through empirical research – but plead for more attention to the role of intersubjective beliefs in guiding decision-making and action. The latter – which encompasses post-structuralist, postmodernist, critical and feminist theories – challenge the notion that an objective reality exists outside our knowledge. A key reflectivist claim is that material causes are meaningless in separation from social interpretation and language (Checkel 1998: 325–7). Material things only acquire meaning through the structure of shared knowledge and understandings in which things are embedded. Hence, the social world can only be understood through the study of ideas and of language and communication through which the ideas are transmitted. The primary focus of this introduction is to highlight key differences between rationalist theories and so-called 'soft' or 'thin' constructivist approaches which tend to dominate the field. However, I also include an example of post-structuralist or reflectivist scholar-

ship (Diez 1999) that focuses on the constitutive role of language in
international politics.

The use of constructivist analysis in European studies is fast growing
and many scholars contend that constructivism offers a more
promising way to understand current EU politics than rationalist
debates between intergovernmentalists, supranationalists and comparativists (Christiansen, Jørgensen and Wiener 1999: 537; see also Ben
Rosamond's contribution in Part VI). It is important to stress,
however, that – unlike neofunctionalism or liberal intergovernmentalism – constructivism does not offer a substantive theory of European
integration. Much like rational-choice, constructivism is not a theory
of politics per se but an ontological perspective or 'metatheory' on
which middle-range theories of international relations can be based
(Adler 1997: 323; Checkel 1998: 325). Hence, a constructivist
approach may be coupled with an intergovernmentalist focus on interstate negotiations as the key to understanding EU policy, but it may
equally be joined with a neofunctionalist emphasis on supranational
entrepreneurship, or a multilevel governance approach (Risse 2004:
160).

Defining Social Constructivism

There is no single shared constructivist approach either in IR theory or
in European integration studies. Instead of a general theory of international politics, constructivism must be seen as an umbrella approach
under which various theoretical interests and research strategies merge
(Shaw and Wiener 1999: 2). In ontological terms, constructivism is
often described as a 'middle ground' between rationalist and reflectivist
approaches (see Adler 1997: 319; Christiansen, Jørgensen and Wiener
1999: 535–7; Katzenstein, Keohane and Krasner 1998; Wendt 1992).
At one extreme, rationalist models (whether neorealist or neoliberal)
treat norms and subjective beliefs as causally epiphenomenal to more
fundamental (material) influences on state behaviour (Moravcsik
1999b: 674). Ideas and beliefs are seen as 'transmission belts' for
underlying material interests – they are not instrumental in defining
those interests. At the other extreme, reflective theories build on an
interpretivist sociology of knowledge, which sees knowledge/beliefs as
constitutive of the social world. Such theories reject the material
empiricism of rationalist accounts; in the social world only ideas and
beliefs matter and can be studied (Adler 1997: 321).

Social constructivism establishes a middle ground between these
extremes. Constructivists side with rationalists in accepting that social
reality does not simply depend on our way of interpreting or theorising
it (Christiansen, Jørgensen and Wiener 1999: 535). However, they insist

that the structures of international politics are not entirely determined by material factors but depend on socially constructed norms and identities that shape the interests and identities of agents (Adler 1997: 329; Wendt 1992). Hence, constructivism focuses on how the material and subjective worlds interact in the construction of social reality (Adler 1997: 324–30; Katzenstein, Keohane and Krasner 1998: 675). Moreover, according to Thomas Risse, constructivists are generally sceptical of what they see as a 'positivist' striving among many rationalists toward a 'covering law' approach to social science that applies irrespective of time and space (Risse 2004: 160). Instead they strive toward middle-range theories within carefully circumscribed domains.

Sociological Institutionalism

Constructivists take a very different view of institutions than the rational-choice theories presented in the previous parts. Whereas rational-choice studies focus on the formal attributes of European institutions – such as policy initiation and amendment rules – constructivists hold that the key to explaining policy outcomes is not the formal attributes of European institutions but rather the informal rules, norms, and shared systems of meaning, which shape the interests of actors (March and Olsen 1998; Risse 2000: 4–5). Second, whereas rational-choice theories focus on how institutions (i.e. collective norms, rules and procedures) regulate or 'constrain' behaviour by altering actors' cost-benefit calculations, constructivists contend that institutions are likely to alter not only material incentives but also the very identities, self-images and preferences of actors. When actors act according to appropriate rules, they do so not because there are external sanctions that compel them, but rather because they have internalized the duties and obligations that define an institutional identity (Sending 2002: 449). Hence, institutions have not merely a regulative but a *constitutive* role in politics (DiMaggio and Powell 1991: 11; Hall and Taylor 1996: 940; Checkel 1998: 325–7; Wendt 1999: 165–6; Aspinwall and Schneider 2000).

The constitutive effects of institutions work through two main mechanisms. The first is through processes of 'socialization' by which actors internalize rules and norms, which then influence how they see themselves and what they perceive as their interests (Risse and Wiener 2001: 202). Such socialization is typically a gradual process, which alters the attitudes and beliefs of actors over time in often imperceptible ways. The second, and more direct, mechanism is via processes of 'social learning' by which actors acquire new interests through argumentation, deliberation and persuasion (Checkel 1999c; Risse 2000: 3). When actors interact with and within European institutions they come into contact with new ideas and arguments which may change their understanding of their own roles and interests. As a result, they may alter their behaviour in ways that are unexplained by material incentives. It is important to stress that the idea that social interaction can cause actors to adopt new identities and interests stands in sharp contrast to rational-choice models, which treat interests and preferences as exogenous and fixed prior to interaction. On a rationalist view, social interaction may lead to changes in strategies, but identities and interests remain fixed. On a constructivist view, social interaction and argumentation is the very basis for interest and identity formation.

The emphasis on the constitutive role of international institutions may seem to suggest a strongly structuralist view in which institutions fundamentally determine actors' behaviour. This is not the case. A key constructivist premise is that social structures and agents are mutually co-determined. Collectively held norms and rules do not confront agents as social facts that are fixed and unchangeable. Rather, constructivists view the development of institutions as an ongoing process of mutual constitution or 'structuration' (see Giddens 1984) in which institutions shape the identities and preferences of actors, and actors in turn reshape institutions through their social interactions (Adler 1997: 330–9; Jupille, Caporaso and Checkel 2003: 14; Kelemen 2003).

Constructivism also leads to a different model of decision-making and action than do rational-choice models. Rationalist theories conceptualize international relations as a series of strategic interactions in which the actors' primary goal is to maximize their own interest ('utility'). To the extent that the maximization of individual utility is only possible through cooperative behaviour, egoistic utility-maximizers are expected to collaborate or coordinate their actions with others. Cooperation, on this view, remains purely instrumental, and compliance with collective rules and norms is strictly the result of calculated reasoning and expected future benefits. As long as the expected benefits from compliance exceed the potential gains from non-compliance, states will comply – otherwise they will not (Aspinwall and Schneider 2000: 11; March and Olsen 1998: 949; Risse 2000: 3). Constructivists, by contrast, hold political actions to be driven not by a logic of utility maximisation but by a 'logic of appropriateness' and by a strong sense of identity. In this view, actors are thought to choose specific policies not because they maximise their calculated self-interest but rather because they resonate with deeper, collectively held norms, ideas and values (March and Olson 1989: 159; 1998: 949–51; Marcussen et al. 1999: 617; Risse 2000: 4). According to March and Olson (1989: 23) decisions derived from a 'logic of appropriateness' are based on the following considerations: What kind of situation is this? Who am I? How appropriate are different actions for me in this situation? Rather than act in accordance with their calculated self-interest, actors will do what they feel is most appropriate given their socially defined role.

To sum up: Moderate constructivism rests on three core claims:

- institutions (understood as collective norms, rules and procedures) are constitutive for actors' identities rather than acting as constraints on behaviour (rationalism);
- agents and structures are mutually constitutive;
- changes in ideas and identities lead to changes in political practice.

Constructivism as an Approach to European Integration

A substantial literature has emerged during the 1990s which uses constructivist analysis to study aspects of European integration (see Christiansen et al. 1999, 2001). The boom in constructivist research on the EU may be partly explained by the fact that the EU constitutes a particularly good case for studying the constitutive effects of international institutions. As Checkel notes the EU is an institutionally dense environment with plenty of repeated interaction of the kind that constructivists expect to have a 'socializing effect' on actors (Checkel 1999c; also Jupile and Caporaso 1999: 440). Some constructivists have sought to analyse the creation of political identities in Europe (see e.g. Risse 2004). Others have focused on the role of ideas in the integration process (e.g. Jachtenfuchs 1995; Parsons 2002, 2003). A large literature also focuses on 'Europeanization' in terms of how interaction with and within European institutions socialize domestic agents and alter their behaviour over time. The basic thrust of this literature is that integration has a transformative impact on the European state system and its constituent units (Christiansen, Jørgensen and Wiener 1999: 529; Risse and Wiener 2001: 202).

An example of constructivist work that focuses on the socializing effect of European institutions is Jeffrey Checkel's article on social constructivism and integration (1999: see Chapter 16 below). In this article, Checkel accepts key insights from both rationalist and historical institutionalism but insists that these dominant 'isms' must be supplemented by a constructivist understanding of institutions that stresses their interest and identity-forming role. To demonstrate how interaction within European institutions 'constructs' the identities and interest of state and social actors, he examines how norms are constructed at the European level and how, once they reach the national level, they interact with and socialize agents. He finds that the successful construction of new norms at the European level is most likely when decision-makers are faced with a crisis or policy failure, which creates a window of opportunity for re-evaluating existing beliefs. Hence, socialization is most likely to work in conditions where existing identities and interests are in flux.

While Checkel stresses the identity-forming role of European institutions, other scholars have analysed the specific role of ideas in the integration process (e.g. Jachtenfuchs 1995; Parsons 2002, 2003). Parsons (2002) makes the strong case that ideas are crucial in determining policy choices – often more so than economic factors. Ideas are most likely to matter when material pressures are indeterminate or when multiple outcomes are consistent with underlying structural conditions. This, he argues, was the case in Europe before 1958. Post-war structural conditions created pressure for integration but they did not push Europe in a particular direction. Only certain visionary ideas led Europe to be structured in the way it is today (2002: 47–55). To demonstrate the causal effect of ideas, Parsons examines settings where ideas cross-cut prevailing lines of organization – i.e. where political actors in similar objective positions hold different ideas. Such settings, he argues, can confirm the autonomous impact of ideas by ruling out diverging preferences and interests that are a mere reflection of different structural circumstances. He stresses, however, that ideas are one among many causal factors and that ideational accounts must therefore be seen as a supplement, not an alternative, to rational-choice models (2002: 50).

As both Checkel's and Parsons' work demonstrates, soft constructivism is quite compatible with rationalist-choice theory. Indeed, a number of scholars have urged a synthesis of rationalism and constructivism, suggesting that the two approaches may apply within different domains and therefore complement rather than contradict each other (see e.g. Checkel 2003: 2; Jupille, Caporaso and Checkel 2003: 21). Suggestions for a synthesis of rationalism and constructivism take several forms. Some scholars have proposed a distinction between 'high stake' and 'low stake' issues as a way to separate domains of application. They suggest that high substantive stakes may invite rational calculation, whereas low-stake issues are subject to non-calculative decision-making (see Aspinwall and Schneider 2000: 27; March and Olsen 1998: 952–3). Others have suggested a domain division based on the relative strength and clarity of material interests vs identities. They suggest that in situations where preferences and consequences are precise and identities ambiguous, instrumentalist reasoning will prevail over rule-based choices and vice versa (March and Olsen 1998: 952).

A third proposal is a 'sequencing approach' in which variables from both approaches work together over time to explain policy outcomes in a given domain. For example, one might grant that EU treaty negotiations tend to be dominated by rational, lowest-common denominator, interstate bargaining but take a constructivist view of subsequent processes of 'Europeanization'. This would suggest that actors enter into new institutional relationships for purely instrumental reasons but develop new identities and interests as a result of their experience, thus shifting increasingly toward actions based on a 'logic of appropriateness' (Jupille, Caporaso and Checkel 2003: 22–3; March and Olsen 1998: 953) Yet, the opposite might also be true. For example, Cooley (2003: 681) suggests that constructivist approaches might go a long way in explaining the generation of a number of transnational governance mechanisms. However, he argues rationalist theories are more effective at identifying and specifying the incentive structures and their behavioural consequences once these governance mechanisms have become institutionalized (ibid.). Checkel's article in Chapter 16 appears to provide an example of a 'sequencing approach' applied across the history of European integration. He accepts that the historical process of integration has been primarily market driven, dominated by actors whose motivations are best understood within a rationalist framework. Yet, he insists that the relevance of constructivism is growing. As the EU has developed from a single market to a comprehensive political union, we are witnessing the emergence of a European civil society dominated by domestic NGOs, churches, etc., whose goals are better understood within a constructivist frame.

Discursive Approaches

Moderate constructivism shares much in common with rationalist theory. However, some constructivists take a more radical, postmodern perspective, arguing that reality in its objective form cannot be known or seen to exist outside human interpretation or language. Unlike natural objects social facts are established through human agreement, which can only be achieved through language. As a result, social reality is best conceived as a linguistic construct, which can only be understood through textual and discourse analysis. The object of such analysis is to reveal how certain meanings that are assigned to material reality come to be fixed for some period of time and hence confront us as 'social facts' (Adler 1997: 332; see also Diez 1997, 1999; Rosamond 1999; Wæver 1997b).

One of the clearest examples of a 'discursive' approach to European integration is provided by the work of Thomas Diez (1999: Chapter 17 below). Diez explores the role of language in the construction of the EU. His central proposition is that attempts by academics and politicians to capture the nature of the EU polity are not mere descriptions of an existing reality but take part in the construction of that reality. In other words, language does not simply confirm the existence of an EU polity – it is *through* language that the EU polity is constructed. Indeed, Diez argues, the entire history of European integration can be understood as a history of performative 'speech acts' establishing a system of governance. For example, the 'democratic deficit' is constructed discursively through the prevalent institutional language of neofunctionalism, which provides the ground to continuously reconstruct the EU as a monster bureaucracy deciding on technical matters that affect citizens' lives without their active consent. Similarly, the widespread conceptualization of the EU as a system of 'multilevel governance' establishes a notion of politics working on separate planes as if it were an objective fact. The development of the EU toward such a system that way becomes a self-fulfilling hypothesis (Diez 1999: 604–5).

Social Constructivism and Neofunctionalism

As is pointed out in several of the articles featured in this part, constructivism shares several aspects of neofunctionalist theory – most importantly a focus on socialization, learning and transfers of loyalty, as well as the possibility that actors may redefine their interests as a result of interaction within European institutions (see Checkel 1999c: Chapter 16 below; Diez 2001; Haas 2001: Chapter 18 below; Wendt 1994). In the article below, Haas goes as far as to suggest that neofunctionalism is in fact a precursor to what he labels the 'soft rational choice' version of constructivism. Like constructivism, he notes, neofunctionalism does not assume that actors' preferences are fixed. Instead neofunctionalists accept the possibility of a transformation of interests within the integration process. Moreover, neofunctionalists, along with constructivists, assume that actors derive their interests from their notions of political causality rather than from structural pressures.

There are certainly important overlaps between neofunctionalist and constructivist concerns. For example, both neofunctionalism and constructivism assume that integration leads to a high degree of actor socialization. In Part II we saw how early neofunctionalists sought to document how political elites adopt multiple identities and redefine their interests as a result of interaction within EU institutions. However, neofunctionalism itself does not pay much attention to the actual processes of socialization within European institutions. Once integration is underway, socialization and learning are thought to be relatively automatic. The focus, in short, is on demonstrating an outcome – changed identities and interests – rather than theorizing or empirically documenting the causal mechanisms through which these changes come about. It is thus possible to argue that constructivism builds on and refines neofunctionalism by adding an explicit theory of identity and its transformation. Yet there are also grounds to be sceptical of the claim that neofunctionalism and constructivism are close theoretical cousins. While neofunctionalism stresses the possibility of socialization and learning through interaction, it remains based on a fundamentally consequentialist logic. As Haas explains in Chapter 18, integration in a neofunctionalist view is expected to occur when societal actors examine their interests and decide that those interests are better served by supranational institutions than by reliance on their own governments. To the extent that actors 'learn' new interests it is thus in response to actual or anticipated pay-offs from supranational institutions rather than due to an internalization of new norms and practices. Similarly, while neofunctionalism presupposes a 'transfer of loyalties' to regional institutions (which Haas argues is similar to a change in identity), such transfers depend on the perception by actors that their (exogenously derived) interests are better served by European than by national solutions. Integration, by this logic, seems to be driven not so much by a sociologically driven redefinition of interests and identities as by a rational reassessment of how existing interests can best be realized.

Finally, it is worth emphasizing that neofunctionalism is premised on a utilitarian-individualistic logic. Successful integration depends on 'overlapping' rather than 'collective' or 'shared' interests (see Part II). Indeed, Haas in 1968 explained the slowdown of European integration by the fact that integration was based on 'converging pragmatic interests', concerned chiefly with economic welfare, and not reinforced by a deep ideological or philosophical commitment to cooperate on common goals and values (Haas 1968: xxiii). In other words, integration, on a neofunctionalist view, has been shaped by the convergence of individual preferences rather than by 'intersubjectively' defined values or interests. Given these fundamental differences, it is hard to see how neofunctionalism can be defined as a precursor to constructivism or indeed how neofunctionalism can find a 'home' within a constructivist approach as Haas suggests below. Indeed, it seems more relevant, in many ways, to trace the line of intellectual descent back to Karl Deutsch (see Part I), whose transactionalist approach stresses the crucial importance of shared identities and intersubjective beliefs as a basis for successful integration.

The Methodological Foundations of Constructivism

Constructivist research promises to make an important contribution to European integration studies, not only by focusing attention on the role of non-material interests in the integration process, but also by seeking to account for what remains that is exogenous in rationalist theory, namely the production of and changes in the interests of actors over time (see Adler 1997; Sending 2002). The chief problem with constructivist analyses, however, is the relative weakness of their methodological foundations (see Checkel 2001: 223; Jupile and Caporaso 1999; Moravcsik 1999b). Take the role of ideas. A key constructivist claim is that ideas play an independent causal role in decision-making. Yet, it is often difficult in practice to distinguish ideas as independent causes. Many constructivist scholars simply look for a correlation between ideas or norms and individual behaviour and actions as proof that 'ideas matter'. The obvious danger with such an approach is that it overlooks what Parsons calls the 'Janus-faced' nature of ideas: sometimes actors' beliefs guide their actions, sometimes apparent beliefs only rationalize strategies chosen for other reasons (Parsons 2002: 49). The preferred method for getting around this problem is to use a technique of 'process tracing', designed to 'reconstruct actual agent motivations' by carefully 'investigating the decision process by which various initial conditions are translated into outcomes' (Checkel 2001: 223–4). Unfortunately, such techniques often fail to clearly demonstrate the causal power of ideas. Relying on interviews and cross-checking findings through close readings of official documents and reports, such as Checkel suggests, is rarely sufficient to establish whether new ideas are due to socialization or to a rational understanding of changed circumstances. Apart from the obvious problem that political actors may have incentives to falsely report their motivations, the actors may themselves find it difficult to determine whether their changed preferences are a result of persuasion and learning rather than strategic adaptation in the face of changed incentives or simple imitation. To strengthen constructivist claims, hypotheses must therefore be systematically tested against competing theories. Demonstrating that given social outcomes are consistent with constructivist assumptions while they cannot be accounted for by changes in material circumstances would lend strong support to constructivist propositions. Yet, many scholars have noted a 'characteristic unwillingness of constructivists to forward distinctive testable hypotheses . . . and to test those hypotheses against the best alternative theories' (Moravcsik 1999a, 2001: 177; Wiener 2004). Too often, constructivists reject rationalist theories out of hand on ontological grounds, rather than seek to systematically test constructivist theories against conventional rationalist alternatives.

One possible reason for the lack of systematic testing of constructivist assumptions may be the lack of clear and distinctive constructivist hypotheses. Checkel, among others, concedes that constructivists have spent too much effort exploring ontological distinctions between rationalist and constructivist perspectives, and not enough time deriving hypotheses and subjecting them to empirical testing. As a result, he argues, constructivism has yet to develop a set of middle-range propositions that could compete with conventional integration theories such as neofunctionalism and liberal intergovernmentalism (Checkel 1999c; see also Risse 2004: 174). Checkel's own attempt at developing a theory of social learning in the EU, and Parson's attempt to theorize on the role of ideas and to specify the conditions in which ideas influence political choices probably come closest to advancing testable mid-range propositions. For example, Checkel hypothesizes that social learning is most likely to occur when actors are faced with a crisis or policy failure, thereby identifying a clear observable implication of his theory. Yet, as Andrew Moravcsik notes, the assumption that underlying ideas and norms change only at 'critical junctures', which arise in response to political crises, is not distinct to constructivism (1999b: 674). Indeed, this assertion seems to counter the notion that subjective beliefs, rather than material circumstances, are causally central. This points to a basic problem in much constructivist research, namely a lack of observationally distinctive hypotheses. Competitive testing can only be successful if evidence permits adjudication between rival propositions. If, however, rival propositions are observationally equivalent in terms of relevant evidence, then we cannot judge between theories. For example, if both rationalism and constructivism expect the interests of political elites to shift as a result of membership in European institutions, then it will not be enough to simply point to the end result of reshaped preferences. The challenge is to empirically demonstrate the social interaction processes through which interests are changing. Unfortunately, much constructivist research has tended to emphasize end states where 'socialization' or 'learning' is complete instead of documenting the causal mechanisms through which it comes about. (For a critique along these lines, see Checkel 2004).

A second critique pertains to the ability of constructivism to account for political change. A central claim in constructivist theory is that it is able to account for change in international politics beyond the changes in behaviour that rationalist theories can account for (Finnemore 1996b; Ruggie 1998; Sending 2002: 459). Whereas rationalists take interests as exogenous givens, constructivists argue that changes in intersubjectively defined ideational factors such as norms and beliefs lead to changes in the identities and interests of actors and hence to changes in political behaviour/outcomes (Adler 1997). Yet, this argument simply pushes the burden of explanation one step back; namely accounting for changes in ideational structures. In a cogent critique, Sending argues that constructivism cannot account for the process by which the changes in ideational structures and norms come about (Sending 2002: 459–60). According to the logic of appropriateness to which constructivists subscribe, political action is motivated by the demands of norms, duties and obligations which have been internalized and which are therefore constitutive of actors' identities.

As a theory of individual action, the logic of appropriateness thus depicts actors as being institutionally programmed to act in certain appropriate ways (Sending 2002: 450–5). In order for institutions/ideational structures to change, actors would have to be in a position to evaluate, reflect upon and choose regarding what rules to follow and how to act. This would require a motivational externalist position in the sense that actors are never fully motivated to follow a certain rule by any constitutive and internalized norm (Sending 2002: 458–9). Yet, despite claiming to be based on a structurationist logic (whereby institutions shape the identities of actors, and actors in turn reshape institutions through their social interactions) constructivism fails to provide such an externalist position. It does not explain why actors follow some rules and bend or break others. As a result, constructivism is no better at accounting for political change than rationalist alternatives.

Finally, one may criticize constructivist students of European integration for having failed, along with MLG theorists, to add a comparative dimension to their analyses. So far, constructivist scholars have focused more on demonstrating that normative structures matter than on accounting for variation in the impact of norms and ideas across polities or policy domains. The result, in the words of two proponents of the approach, has been 'a rich collection of descriptive analyses of events but with little theoretical generalisation' (Aspinwall and Schneider 2000: 24). It is therefore easy to agree with Checkel when he argues below that the central challenge for constructivists is theory development (Checkel 1998: 324). Having demonstrated that social construction matters, constructivists must now address when, how, and why it occurs, clearly specifying the actors and mechanisms that bring about change, and the scope conditions under which they operate.

Further Reading

Christiansen, T., Jørgensen, K. and Wiener, A. (eds) (2001) *The Social Construction of Europe* (London: Sage). Originally published as a special issue of the *Journal of European Public Policy*, this collection of essays provides a variety of social constructivist perspectives on the study of European integration.

Jørgensen, K. (ed.) (1997) *Reflective Approaches to European Governance* (London: Macmillan). An excellent discussion and illustration, through a series of essays, of what the social constructivist and critical approaches can bring to the study of European integration.

Wæver O. (1998) 'Explaining Europe by Decoding Discourses' in A. Wivel, (ed.), *Explaining European Integration* (Copenhagen: Copenhagen Political Studies Press) 100–46. A detailed discussion of the uses of discourse analysis in European studies.

Chapter 16

Social Construction and Integration

Jeffrey T. Checkel*

Introduction

Over forty years after the European project began, it is striking how little we know about its socialization and identity-shaping effects on national agents. Indeed, prominent Europeanists are themselves deeply divided on this question, with some arguing that integration has led to a fundamental shift in actor loyalty and identity, while others claim the opposite. The basic premiss of this article is that both schools are right: constructing European institutions is a multi-faceted process, with both rationalist and sociological toolkits needed to unpack and understand it (for the diverging views among Europeanists, compare Wessels 1998 and Laffan 1998).

Put differently, much of European integration can be modelled as strategic exchange between autonomous political agents with fixed interests; at the same time, much of it cannot. Constitutive dynamics of social learning, socialization, routinization and normative diffusion, all of which address fundamental issues of agent identity and interests, are not adequately captured by strategic exchange or other models adhering to strict forms of methodological individualism. For these constitutive processes, the dominant institutionalisms in studies of integration – rational choice and historical – need to be supplemented by a more sociological understanding of institutions that stresses their interest- and identity-forming roles.

After briefly addressing definitional issues and the literature on integration, I argue that social construction, a growing literature in contemporary IR, can help students of integration to theorize and explore empirically these neglected questions of interest and identity. Specifically, the article shows how a social constructivist cut at institu-

* Reproduced by kind permission of Taylor and Francis Ltd (http://www.tandf.co.uk/journals) from Jeffrey Checkel (1999c) 'Social Construction and Integration', *Journal of European Public Policy*, 6(4), 545–60. The text has been slightly edited, as indicated, to fit the format of this volume. Where possible, references have been changed to Harvard citation style.

tion building explains key aspects of Europeanization – social learning and normative diffusion – better than its rationalist competitors, with the practical goal being to elaborate the specific methods and data requirements for such work.

Before proceeding, three comments are in order. First, my analytic starting point is that research on integration should be problem-, and not method-, driven; the goal is to encourage dialogue and bridge building between rationalists and social constructivists. By itself, each school explains important elements of the integration process; working together, or at least side-by-side, they will more fully capture the range of institutional dynamics at work in contemporary Europe. Indeed, too many constructivists are themselves method-driven, ignoring the obvious empirical fact that much of everyday social interaction is about strategic exchange and self-interested behaviour (e.g. Christiansen 1997).

Second, and following on the above, the constructivism favoured in this article belongs to what has been called its modernist branch. These scholars, who combine an ontological stance critical of methodological individualism with a loosely causal epistemology, are thus well placed, within the integration literature, 'to seize the middle ground' (Adler 1997) – staking out a position between positivist and agent-centred rational choice, on the one hand, and interpretative and structure-centred approaches on the other (on the different schools within constructivism, see Adler 1997: 335–7. Checkel 1998 provides a critical overview of the modernist branch).

Third, the article's central focus is theoretical and methodological, and not empirical. My concern is how one could develop and apply, in a systematic manner, constructivist insights to key puzzles in the study of integration. Empirically, I seek only to establish the plausibility of such propositions, and do so in two ways: (1) by drawing upon arguments and evidence from a wide range of existing studies on European integration; and (2) by reference to my own work in progress.

Institutions and European Integration

Of the many institutionalisms floating around these days in economics, political science and sociology, I need briefly to discuss three: rational choice institutionalism, historical institutionalism, and sociological institutionalism. For rational choice scholars, institutions are thin: at most, they are a constraint on the behaviour of self-interested actors – be they interest groups or unitary states in IR. They are a strategic context that provides incentives or information, thus influencing the strategies that agents employ to attain given ends. In this thin conception, institutions are a structure that actors run into, go 'ouch', and then recalculate how, in the presence of the structure, to achieve their interests; they are an intervening variable (on various forms of institutionalism, see DiMaggio and Powell 1991: ch. 1; Finnemore 1996b; Hall and Taylor 1996; Kato 1996; Katzenstein 1996: ch. 2; Koelbel 1995; Longstreth et al. 1992: ch. 1).

For historical institutionalists, institutions get thicker, but only in a long-term historical perspective. In the near-term here and now, they are thin – structuring the game of politics and providing incentives for instrumentally motivated actors to rethink their strategies; they are a constraint on behaviour. Over the longer term, however, institutions can have deeper effects on actors as strategies, initially adopted for self-interested reasons, get locked into and institutionalized in politics. Institutions thus can be both intervening and independent variables. (For historical institutionalists employing a thin conception of institutions, see Immergut 1992; Pierson 1994. Thicker conceptualizations are found in Goldstein 1993; Hattam 1993.)

Sociological institutionalists are unabashedly thick institutionalists. Not only in the distant future, but in the near-term, institutions constitute actors and their interests. What exactly does it mean for institutions to constitute? It is to suggest that they can provide agents with understandings of their interests and identities. This occurs through interaction between agents and structures – mutual constitution, to IR scholars. The effects of institutions thus reach much deeper; they do not simply constrain behaviour. As variables, institutions become independent – and strongly so (see DiMaggio and Powell 1991 *passim;* Dobbin 1994; March and Olsen 1998).

In our research and theorizing about Europe, should one of these institutionalisms be favoured, serving as the baseline? The answer here is 'no', for ultimately this is an empirical question. No doubt, there are many situations and aspects of integration where agents operate under the means-end logic of consequences favoured by rationalist choice and some historical institutionalists (meetings of the European Council or the hard-headed interstate bargaining that features prominently in intergovernmentalist accounts). At the same time, the less static perspective favoured by sociologists reminds us that much social interaction involves dynamics of learning and socialization, where the behaviour of individuals and states comes to be governed by certain logics of appropriateness (informal communication in working groups of the Council of Ministers, European-level policy networks centred on the Commission). Unfortunately, these latter logics, while equally compelling and plausible, have received little systematic theoretical attention in studies of Europeanization.

Indeed, to students of international politics well versed in the neverending neorealist-neoliberal controversy, the debates over Europeanization and European integration produce an eery feeling of *deja vu*. On the one hand, the discussion has helped advocates of opposing approaches to sharpen their central arguments and claims; similar intellectual clarifications have occurred over the past decade in the debate between neorealists and neoliberals in IR.

At the same time and in a more negative sense, the debate over Europeanization, like any academic discourse, has emphasized certain methods and actors at the expense of others. To my reading, much of the discussion has been about institutions – be they encompassing governance or federal structures, historically constructed organizational and policy legacies, or, more narrowly, bodies of the EU such as the Commission or European Council. Moreover, in most cases, the analysis is about how such institutions structure the game of politics, provide information, facilitate side payments or create incentives for agents to choose certain strategies.

Such an emphasis, however, comes at a cost. It short-changes the role that institutions can play in politics, or, more to the point, in European integration. In particular, their constitutive role, typically stressed by sociologists, is neglected. If the neo-debate in contemporary IR can be accused of neglecting fundamental issues of identity formation, much of the current discussion about European integration can be accused of bracketing this constitutive dimension of institutions. Put differently, the great majority of contemporary work on European integration views institutions, at best, as intervening variables. Missing is a thick institutional argument, derived from sociology, that demonstrates how European institutions can construct, through a process of interaction, the identities and interests of member states and groups within them.

Social Construction and Integration

In this section, I develop an approach that addresses the above-noted gaps, and do so by drawing upon a growing and vibrant body of IR scholarship: social constructivism. As presently elaborated, constructivism – at least the modernist branch of concern here – is an argument about institutions, one which builds upon the insights of sociological institutionalism. It is thus well suited, in a conceptual sense, for expanding our repertoire of institutional frameworks for explaining European integration. Moreover, modernist social constructivists remind us that the study of politics – or integration – is not just about agents with fixed preferences who interact via strategic exchange. Rather, they seek to explain theoretically both the content of actor identities/preferences and the modes of social interaction – so evident in everyday life – where something else aside from strategic exchange is taking place. (For detailed overviews of the epistemological, ontological and methodological emphases in the work of modernist constructivists, see Adler 1997; Checkel 1998; Ruggie 1998: 35–6.)

So defined, constructivism has the potential to contribute to the study of integration in various areas. Below, I consider two: learning and socialization processes at the European level; and the soft or normative side of Europeanization at the national level. In each case, I explore what a constructivist approach entails, how it could be carried out empirically and its value added compared to existing work on integration. I also address and counter the argument that my results cannot be generalized. The section concludes by noting how a constructivist approach to integration can build upon and systematize theoretical arguments and descriptive insights advanced by a growing number of Europeanists; I also argue that the whole exercise is not one of reinventing the wheel.

Learning and socialization

What does it mean for an agent to learn? Social learning involves a process whereby actors, through interaction with broader institutional contexts (norms or discursive structures), acquire new interests and preferences – in the absence of obvious material incentives. Put differently, agent interests and identities are shaped through interaction. Social learning thus involves a break with strict forms of methodological individualism. This type of learning needs to be distinguished, analytically, from the simple sort, where agents acquire new information, alter strategies, but then pursue given, fixed interests; simple learning, of course, can be captured by methodological-individualist/rationalist accounts (on learning, see Levy 1994).

Consider small group settings: it is intuitively obvious that there are times when agents acquire new preferences through interaction in such contexts. This is not to deny periods of strategic exchange, where self-interested actors seek to maximize utility; yet, to emphasize the latter dynamic to the near exclusion of the former is an odd distortion of social reality. Now, the perhaps appropriate response is 'so what?'. In an abstract sense, it readily can be appreciated that social learning takes place at certain times, but how can one conceptualize and empirically explore whether and when it occurs? Luckily, there is a growing literature in contemporary IR – by constructivists, students of epistemic communities and empirically oriented learning theorists – that performs precisely this theoretical/empirical combination. More specifically, this research suggests four hypotheses on when social learning occurs; these could be translated to empirical work conducted at the European level.

1. Social learning is more likely in groups where individuals share common professional backgrounds – for example, where all/most

group members are lawyers or, say, European central bankers.

2. Social learning is more likely where the group feels itself in a crisis or is faced with clear and incontrovertible evidence of policy failure.
3. Social learning is more likely where a group meets repeatedly and there is high density of interaction among participants.
4. Social learning is more likely when a group is insulated from direct political pressure and exposure (see Checkel 1997a: chs. 1, 5; DiMaggio and Powell 1991; Haas 1990; P. Haas 1992; Hall 1993; Risse-Kappen 1996).

Clearly, these hypotheses require further elaboration. For example, can a crisis situation be specified a priori and not in a *post-hoc* fashion as is typically done? When is the density of interaction among group participants sufficiently high for a switch to occur from strategic exchange to interactive learning? These are difficult issues, but they are only being raised because a first round of theoretical/empirical literature exists. Europeanists could build upon and contribute to this work – for example, by exploring and theorizing the impact, if any, of different EU voting rules (unanimity, qualified majority voting) on these group dynamics.

The deductions also point to a powerful role for communication. However, in keeping with this article's attempted bridging function, it is a role between that of the rationalists' cheap talk, where agents (typically) possess complete information and are (always) instrumentally motivated, and the postmodernists' discourse analyses, where agents seem oddly powerless and without motivation. Yet, this role itself requires further unpackaging: underlying my communication/learning arguments are implicit theories of persuasion and argumentation (see Johnson 1993).

On the latter, students of integration can and should exploit a rich literature in social psychology, political socialization and communications research on persuasion/ argumentation. At core, persuasion is a cognitive process that involves changing attitudes about cause and effect in the absence of overt coercion; put differently, it is a mechanism through which social learning may occur, thus leading to interest redefinition and identity change. The literature suggests three hypotheses about the settings where agents should be especially conducive to persuasion:

1. when they are in a novel and uncertain environment and thus cognitively motivated to analyse new information;
2. when the persuader is an authoritative member of the in-group to which the persuadee belongs or wants to belong; and
3. when the agent has few prior, ingrained beliefs that are inconsistent with the persuader's message (see Johnston 1998: 16–25; Zimbardo and Leippe 1991).

While these deductions partly overlap with the first set, further work is still needed – for example, how to operationalize 'uncertain environments' and integrate political context. On the latter, my strong hunch is that persuasion will be more likely in less politicized and more insulated settings. All the same, both sets of hypotheses do elaborate scope conditions (when, under what conditions persuasion and learning/socialization are likely), which is precisely the promising middle-range theoretical ground that still awaits exploitation by both constructivists and students of European integration (Checkel 1998. On the insulation/persuasion connection, also see Pierson 1993: 617–18).

What are the data requirements for research based on the above hypotheses? Essentially, you need to read things and talk with people. The latter requires structured interviews with group participants; the interviews should all employ a similar protocol, asking questions that tap both individual preferences and motivations, as well as group dynamics. The former, ideally, requires access to informal minutes of meetings or, second best, the diaries or memoirs of participants. As a check on these first two data streams, one can search for local media/TV interviews with group participants. This method of triangulation is fairly standard in qualitative research; it both reduces reliance on anyone data source (interviewees, after all, may often dissimulate) and increases confidence in the overall validity of your inferences (see also Zürn 1997: 300–2).

For students of integration, is this a feasible undertaking? Drawing upon my own work in progress, I suggest that the answer is 'yes'. In a larger project, I am studying the appearance and consolidation of new European citizenship norms; an important concern is to explain, at the European level, whether and how new understandings of citizenship are emerging. To date, my focus has been on Strasbourg and the Council of Europe (CE), for this has been where the more serious, substantive work has occurred. When the CE is trying to develop new policy, it often sets up committees of experts under the Committee of Ministers, the intergovernmental body that sits atop the Council's decision-making hierarchy. In a sense, then, these committees are the functional equivalent of the working groups of the EC's Council of Ministers.

I have been examining the Committee of Experts on Nationality, the group that was charged with revising earlier European understandings of citizenship that dated from the 1960s. My particular interest was to describe and explain what occurred in this group as it met over a four-year period: for example, why did it revise existing understandings on dual citizenship to remove the strict prohibition that had previously existed at the European level? To address such issues, I did the following. First, three rounds of field work were conducted in Strasbourg;

during these trips, I interviewed various individuals who served on the Committee – members of the Council Secretariat and experts. Second, I conducted interviews in several member state capitals, meeting with national representatives to the committee of experts. Third, as a cross-check on interview data, more recently I was granted partial access to the confidential meeting summaries of the Committee (Checkel 1999b: 94–6 provides full documentation for the claims advanced in this and the following paragraphs).

This was a considerable amount of work, but the pay-off was high. Over time, particular individuals clearly shifted from what they viewed as a strategic bargaining game (for example, seeking side payments to advance given interests) to a process where basic preferences were rethought. This shift was particularly evident on the question of dual citizenship, where a growing number of committee members came to view the existing prohibition as simply wrong. Processes of persuasion and learning were key, and such dynamics were greatly facilitated by a growing sense of policy failure – the number of dual nationals was climbing rapidly despite the existing prohibition – and the committee's insulation from publicity and overt political pressure. Indeed, the committee benefited from the public perception of Strasbourg as a quiet backwater of Europeanization – with the real action occurring in Brussels. This allowed it to meet and work out revised understandings on citizenship prior to any overt politicization of its work.

At the same time, it should be stressed that not all committee members learned new interests. Indeed, the national representative of one large European state held deeply ingrained beliefs that were opposed to arguments favouring a relaxation of prohibitions on dual citizenship. Consistent with the above deductions, there is no evidence that this individual was persuaded to alter his/her basic preferences.

The point of this example is not to dismiss rationalist accounts of strategic bargaining. Rather, it is to note the value added of a middle-range constructivist supplement to these more standard portrayals: it led me to ask new questions and employ a different set of research techniques. The result was to broaden our understanding of how and under what conditions new European institutions norms – are constructed through processes of non-strategic exchange.

. . . .

Socialization/diffusion pathways

Constructivists view norms as shared, collective understandings that make behavioural claims on actors. When thinking about norms in the EU context, two issues must be addressed: (1) through what process are they constructed at the European level; and (2) how do such norms, once they reach the national level, interact with and socialize agents? Now, the distinction between European and national levels is false, as multiple feedback loops cut across them; at the same time, the dichotomy can be justified analytically as it helps one to unpack and think through different stages in the process of European norm construction. In what follows, I am less interested in formal legal norms developed and promulgated, for example, by the ECJ; a growing body of literature in both law and political science already addresses such understandings and their impact (see Mattli and Slaughter 1998). Rather, the constructivist value added comes from its focus on the less formalized, but pervasive social norms that are always a part of social interaction (see Katzenstein 1996: ch. 2).

On the first issue – the process of norm development – constructivists have theorized and provided empirical evidence for the importance of three dynamics. First, individual agency is central: well-placed individuals with entrepreneurial skills can often turn their individual beliefs into broader, shared understandings. The importance of this particular factor has been documented in case studies covering nearly a one-hundred year period and a multitude of international organizations and other transnational movements. In the literature, these individuals are typically referred to as moral entrepreneurs; in the language of my earlier discussion, they are the agents actively seeking to persuade others (see Finnemore 1996a; Finnemore and Sikkink 1998; Nadelmann 1990).

Second, such entrepreneurs are especially successful in turning individually held ideas into broader normative beliefs when so-called policy windows are open. This means that the larger group, in which the entrepreneur operates, faces a puzzle/problem that has no clear answer, or is new and unknown. In this situation, fixed preferences often break down as agents engage in cognitive information searches. While the policy-window concept was first elaborated by public policy (agenda-setting) and organizational theorists (garbage-can models), it was only more recently that constructivists applied its insights in the international realm to explain norm formation. (The epistemic and ideational branches of constructivism are especially helpful here. See Checkel 1997a: ch. 1; P. Haas 1992.)

Third, processes of social learning and socialization (see the previous section) are crucial for furthering the norm creation process first begun by individual agents exploiting open policy windows. The basic point is that individual agency is insufficient to create durable social norms. A brief example clarifies the point. In the mid-1980s, several close advisers to Soviet leader Gorbachov played the part of entrepreneurs seeking to advance new ideas about international politics. In the near-term, such individually held beliefs, which were influential in shaping Gorbachov's own preferences, were decisive in bringing the Cold War to a dramatic, peaceful and unexpected end. Yet, once the USSR collapsed and Gorbachov was swept from power, these ideas largely vanished, as many analysts of Russian foreign behaviour have noted. Put differently, absent social learning among a larger group of actors – that is, the development of norms – the particular ideas held by specific agents had no real staying power (Checkel 1997a: chs 5, 6).

When and if new European norms emerge, one must still theorize about the mechanisms through which they diffuse to particular national settings and (perhaps) socialize agents. Here, constructivists have identified two dominant diffusion pathways: societal mobilization and social learning. In the first case, non-state actors and policy networks are united in their support for norms; they then mobilize and coerce decision-makers to change state policy. Norms are not necessarily internalized by the elites. The activities of Greenpeace or any number of European non-governmental organizations (NGOs) exemplify this political pressure mechanism (Keck and Sikkink 1998: ch. 1 *passim*; Risse and Sikkink 1999. See Checkel 1999a: 3–8, for a full discussion of these two diffusion pathways).

The second diffusion mechanism identified by constructivists is social learning, where agents – typically elite decision-makers – adopt prescriptions embodied in norms; they then become internalized and constitute a set of shared intersubjective understandings that make behavioural claims. This process is based on notions of complex learning drawn from cognitive and social psychology, where individuals, when exposed to the prescriptions embodied in norms, adopt new interests (Risse-Kappen 1995b; Stein 1994).

A key challenge is to develop predictions for when one or the other of these mechanisms is likely to be at work. To date, constructivists have been silent on this issue; however, my work on European citizenship norms suggests a possibility. I hypothesize that the structure of state-society relations – domestic structure – predicts likely diffusion pathways, with four categories of such structures identified: liberal, corporatist, statist and state-above society. From these, I deduce and predict cross-national variation in the mechanisms – social mobilization and social learning – through which norms are empowered (see Checkel 1999b: 87–91).

A brief example highlights the utility of the approach as well as the attendant data requirements. In the project on European citizenship norms, I have explored whether and in what way they diffused to several European states, including the Federal Republic of Germany. Consider this German case. I first did research on the basic structure of state-society relations in the country; like many others, I concluded that the polity is corporatist. That is, it possesses a decentralized state and centralized society, with a dense policy network connecting the two parts; both state and society are participants in policy-making, which is consensual and incremental.

Given this coding of the German structure, I next advanced predictions on the expected process whereby norms would have constitutive effects, arguing that societal pressure would be the primary and (elite) social learning the secondary mechanism empowering European norms in Germany. The logic is as follows. In a corporatist domestic structure, state decision-makers play a greater role in bringing about normative change than in the liberal case, where policy-makers are constantly pressured by social actors; however, this does not mean that they impose their preferences on a pliant populace. A hallmark of corporatism is the policy networks connecting state and society, with the latter still accorded an important role in decision-making. In this setting, I thus hypothesize that it is both societal pressure (primary) and social learning (secondary) that lead to norm empowerment.

With these predictions in hand, I then conducted extensive field work in the Federal Republic. To date, this research has confirmed my working hypotheses: emerging European norms on citizenship are diffusing and being empowered in Germany primarily via the mobilization of societal pressure; social learning at the elite level has been secondary. More specifically, these norms are connecting to a wide variety of social groups and individuals: NGOs favouring the integration of Germany's large resident foreigner population; activists in the churches and trade unions; and immigrant groups. At the decision-making level, one finds isolated evidence of elites learning new preferences from the norms (for example, a small group of Christian Democratic Bundestag deputies) (for extensive documentation of these points, see Checkel 1999b: 96–107, where I also consider alternative explanations for the results presented here).
. . . .

What is the value-added of all this work? It convincingly demonstrates that a rational choice institutionalist understanding of the role that norms play in social life (norms as constraint) missed an important part of the story in the Federal Republic. I indeed found instances where domestic agents simply felt constrained by the European norms (for example, a number of officials in the Federal Interior Ministry); yet, in many other cases, I uncovered evidence of non-strategic social learning where agents, in the norm's presence, acquired new understandings of interests . . .

Extending the argument

Perhaps, though, my constitutive analysis of European institutions only works because of the particular organization and policy area from which I drew empirical examples: the Council of Europe and human rights. Such arguments are largely irrelevant for the EU – a special type of institution with very different policy domains. Two responses counter such a critique.

First, there are well-established theoretical reasons for suspecting that Europe, especially Western Europe, is a most likely case for international institutions to have constitutive effects. Most important, it is an institutionally dense environment, one where theorists predict high levels of transnational and international normative activity. This logic, precisely because it is a particular way of viewing the social world, is in principle equally applicable to a variety of European institutions whether their focus is human rights (CE) or political and economic affairs (EU). (See Adler and Barnett 1996: 97 *passim*; Risse-Kappen 1995a: ch. 1; Weber 1994).

Second, assume, despite the foregoing, that differences in policy domains do matter. That is, arguments about social learning or the constitutive effects of European norms just do not work when applied to the EU. After all, the process of European integration has largely been about market integration, where national and transnational business interests have played key roles. Such groups are quite different in structure and goals from the actors of civil society – domestic NGOs, churches – highlighted in several of my examples. However, if the institutional (enhanced role of the European Parliament) and substantive (third pillar of justice and home affairs) innovations of Maastricht and Amsterdam continue to evolve, new actors and policy issues are increasingly likely to make themselves felt. Moreover, the current interest in Brussels, London and elsewhere in moving the EU away from a strict regulatory role to one emphasizing standard-setting and so-called 'soft law' plays to the strength of social actors like NGOs: it is precisely the promotion of such informal practices and norms where they are most influential.[1]

In fact, human rights pressure groups have begun utilizing the European Parliament as a means of generating precisely the sort of normative pressure-from-below documented in my CE example. Moreover, immigration, which is now on the third pillar agenda, is an issue where previous studies have documented the extensive degree to which European state interests are constituted by broader international norms. On the related issues of citizenship and racism, recent work establishes that the 1996–7 Intergovernmental Conference (IGC) saw extensive mobilization by NGOs and other transnational movements, and their qualitatively different, when compared to the past, interaction with EU institutions, as well as the IGC itself. Thus, even if differences in policy domains are important, these are at present being blurred if not erased.

Summary

My purpose in the foregoing was constructive. The goal was not to dismiss rational choice or historical institutionalist work on integration; those literatures are rich and offer many insights. Yet, because of their adherence to variants of methodological individualism, certain analytic/empirical issues – interest and identity formation, most importantly – are bracketed. A more sociological and constructivist understanding of institutions as constitutive allows one to address such questions.

. . . .

A final issue is not so much one of new theoretical directions for analyses of integration, but, instead, a look back. Simply put, is my call for bringing constructivist insights to bear on the study of the EU a short-sighted reinventing of the neofunctionalist wheel? After all, over thirty years ago, Haas and others were writing about the identity-shaping effects of the European project. Indeed, collective identity was to emerge via a 'process whereby political actors in several distinct national settings are persuaded to shift their loyalties, expectations and political activities towards a new centre, whose institutions possess or demand jurisdiction over the pre-existing nation-states' (Haas 1958a: 16).

While references to social learning and socialization are evident in the work of many early neofunctionalists and regional integration theorists, the differences with constructivism are significant. Most important, the latter is not a general substantive theory that predicts constant learning or a growing sense of collective identity; rather, its aspirations are more modest. As currently being developed, it is a middle-range theoretical approach seeking to elaborate scope conditions for better understanding precisely when collective identity formation occurs. Constructivism is thus agnostic as to whether the endpoint of social interaction is greater common interests and identity. Neofunctionalists, at least implicitly, were not neutral on this question; there was a clear normative element to their scholarship. (On neofunctionalism's in-built bias toward viewing integration as a 'perpetual [forward] motion machine,' see Caporaso 1998a: 6–7.)

In addition, despite the strong allusions to identity formation and change, neofunctionalists failed to develop explicit micro-foundations that moved them beyond an agent-centred view of social interaction. In fact, there is a strong element of rational choice in their research. While considerable work remains, constructivists are attempting to elaborate such alternative foundations – their stress on logics of appropriateness and communicative action, for example. (On the rational choice foundations of neofunctionalism, see Burley and Mattli 1993: 54–5; see also Pollack 1998 *passim*.)

Conclusions

My arguments throughout this article were based on an obvious but too often neglected truism about our social world: the most interesting puzzles lie at the nexus where structure and agency intersect. The real action, theoretically and empirically, is where norms, discourses, language and material capabilities interact with motivation, social learning and preferences – be it in international or European regional politics. Research traditions such as rational choice, postmodernism and, more recently, large parts of constructivism, which occupy endpoints in the agent-structure debate, have life easy: they can ignore this messy middle ground. Yet, the true challenge for both rationalists and their opponents is to model and explore this complex interface; this article has suggested several ways in which this could be done (see Hix 1998: 55–6. More generally, see Checkel 1997b).

As one scholar recently put it, 'regional integration studies could uncharitably be criticized for providing a refuge to homeless ideas' (Caporaso 1998a: 7). While constructivism is certainly not homeless, Europeanists should resist the temptation simply to pull it off the shelf, giving it a comfortable European home in yet another N = 1, noncumulative case study. Rather, these scholars have the opportunity – given their immensely rich data set – to push forward one of the most exciting debates in contemporary international and political theory.

Note

1 The issue and actor expansion noted here has already begun. See Hooghe and Marks 1996, and, more generally, the entire literature on MLG. Indeed, the June 1997 Amsterdam Treaty, by incorporating the social policy articles of Maastricht directly into the TEU, codified the access of various non-state actors to EU decision-making in that area (Obradovic 1997) . . .

Chapter 17

Speaking 'Europe': The Politics of Integration Discourse

Thomas Diez*

Naming the 'Beast'

Suppose a zoologist reveals the existence of an animal so far unknown to mankind. In an article, she describes its features and gives the beast a name. It is classified and categorized, put into the framework of zoological knowledge. In recent years, there have been many attempts at 'exploring the nature of the beast' (Risse-Kappen 1996) in European integration studies. In many of them, the European Union (EU) is dealt with as if it were our zoologist's unknown animal. It is compared to other polities and international organizations, its organizational mechanisms are described and categorized. And there is much effort to name this unknown beast. Debates abound as to whether it is a 'postmodern' or 'regulatory state' (Caporaso 1996), a 'confederatio', 'consortio' or 'condominio' (Schmitter 1996b), a system of 'multi-level governance' (Marks 1993) or a 'multi-perspectival polity' (Ruggie 1993).

But as long as there is such a proliferation of names, and conceptualizations of what the name 'EU' means, the EU remains beyond the framework of our political knowledge. While the efforts of categorization and naming are most often presented as pure descriptions, i.e. as mirrors of reality, the discrepancy between the existence of the beast and our knowledge of it suggests that reality is not so readily observable as it may seem. Instead, even the zoologist needs a given system of language, constituting the body of zoological knowledge, for her categorizations. Language is thus central to our knowledge of reality. It does not only serve as a 'mirror of nature' (Rorty 1979). Rather, it is possible to know of reality through linguistic construction only.

This article explores the role of language in the construction of the EU. Its main argument is that the various attempts to capture the

* Reproduced by kind permission of Taylor and Francis Ltd (http://www.tandf.co.uk/journals) from Thomas Diez (1999) 'Speaking "Europe": The Politics of Integration Discourse', *Journal of European Public Policy*, 6(4), 652–68. The text is reproduced in full. Some peripheral footnotes have been omitted.

Union's nature are not mere descriptions of an unknown polity, but take part in the construction of the polity itself. To that extent, they are not politically innocent, and may themselves become the subject of analysis, along with articulations from other actors. My plea is therefore to include discourse analysis in the canon of approaches in European studies. With a few exceptions, and in contrast to the field of international relations, such work is currently missing. Closing that gap would both enlarge our understanding of the integration process, and insert a reflective moment in our analyses. First, it adds an important dimension to the predominant focus on ideas and institutions within social constructivist studies of European integration, arguing that they cannot exist apart from discourse. Second, it introduces a new 'face of power'. Analyses of European integration have so far by and large focused on (absolute or relative) material capabilities as power, and on the interests behind the application of such power. Against such an understanding, Steven Lukes once put his 'radical' view of power that works through preventing individuals or classes from realizing their 'real' interests in the first place (Lukes 1974). The notion of power employed in this article follows the line of Lukes but doubts that there is such a thing as a 'real' interest independent from the discursive context in which interests emerge. The power of discourse then becomes crucial.[1] Third, it allows for an analysis of the contestedness of certain concepts, and thus points towards possible integration alternatives. Finally, it brings with it a reflective dimension to the research processes, particularly necessary in a field in which many researchers have traditionally been directly entangled with the political process of integration.

Throughout the article, I will restrict myself to providing some illustrations of the argument and not conduct a discourse analysis as such. Instead, my aim is to lay down the theoretical groundwork that relates a constructivism focusing on language (variously called 'radical' or 'epistemological' constructivism, among other labels) to European studies.[2] The argument proceeds in three moves, each of which I associate with the name of a certain philosopher or social/political theorist whose writings have contributed to the elaboration of these moves. The first move is labelled 'Austinian' and introduces the notion of a performative language. The second move is called 'Foucauldian' and points to the political implications of the performativity of language through the definition of meaning. The third move takes up 'Derridarean' themes and discusses the possibilities of change, opening up space for the articulation of alternative constructions of European governance.

I introduce these moves as a way of developing and introducing a certain approach. There are various problems attached to such a procedure. Most importantly, it is not at all clear whether the work of the respective theorists is compatible. On the contrary, it has been claimed that lumping together Foucault and Derrida, for instance, is to ignore the disagreements both of them expressed *vis-a-vis* each other (see Marti 1988: 167, n. 2). The exchange between Derrida and Searle (who uses an Austinian understanding of language) has become a linguistic classic (Derrida 1977; Searle 1977). It is, however, also the case that the works associated with each of the three moves are, at least in part, shaped by the others. The order in which they are presented here roughly follows the historical chronology of their development, in particular in relation to when each move was taken up by the social sciences in general, and international relations in particular. Thereby, it will become clear how the debate proceeded from insisting on the relevance of language *per se* to clarifying its power and potentials to change. Each move will therefore refine, transform and thus move somewhat away from the insights gained from earlier steps. All of them push the argument in a certain direction, with other paths available. Readers may thus want to leave the proposed tour of inquiry at a certain point, and prefer other possibilities opened up by then. Nonetheless, I propose that the approach I will have elaborated in the end is valuable in that it provides a new perspective on the development of European governance.

The Austinian Move: The Performative Language

The common sense of language is that it describes or takes note of a reality outside language. It is, in other words, 'constative' (Austin 1975: 3). The search for the nature of the beast EU is in this tradition: European governance is something 'out there', the nature of which needs to be captured by language, i.e. by the definitions and observations entailed in our analysis. But there are several cases in which language, even to the casual observer, seems to go beyond its constative function. Examples are the declaration of a child's name at her baptism, the issuing of an order, or the formulation of a treaty through which a new political organization comes into existence. In his lectures at Harvard in 1955, J. L. Austin thus introduced the notion of 'performative' sentences (Austin 1975: 6). In the examples above, language is performative in that it does not only take note of, say, the founding of the European Economic Community (EEC). Instead, it is *through* language that this founding is performed. Apart from the act of speaking itself (which Austin labelled a 'locutionary act'), in these cases it is '*in* saying something [that] we do something' (Austin 1975: 94). There is an 'illocutionary force' to language. Furthermore, what we say may have an effect on other people; by saying something, we may not only act ourselves, but also force others to do so.

Austin and his student John Searle contributed significantly to the development of a theory of 'speech acts' – acts performed through speech. On the basis of this theory, Jurgen Habermas was later to develop his theory of communicative action (Habermas 1984), the influence of which one may trace to his current concerns for a European citizenship linked to a European politico-communicative space (Habermas 1992a, 1992b). It is, however, important to note the 'through' in the above definition of speech acts. In contrast to the following moves, the Austinian move does not locate action on the level of language as such. Instead, language serves as an instrument of will and intention: the question posed by Austin is, 'how to do things *with* words', and not, 'how are things done *by* words'. To the extent that this presupposes language as a carrier of meaning, the 'principle of expressibility', formulated by Searle (1969: 19–21), is of crucial importance: It is 'in principle' possible to say what one means. Habermas's discursive ethics, after all, relies upon exactly this possibility of expression in a discursive space ideally situated outside coercive power relations (Habermas 1990).

Although speech acts are never purely particularistic but rule-governed and thus performed within a certain social context, they none the less flow, seen from this perspective, from the individual. But to the extent that they are conceptualized as rule-governed, meaning in Searle's work is already 'at least sometimes a function [and not the origin] of what we are saying' (Searle 1969: 45). Speech act theorists are concerned with politics *through,* not politics *of* discourse. But they recognize that language is not always a neutral and purely descriptive device. Instead, it may contain evaluations and serve political purposes (Searle 1969: 132–6).

When it comes to politics, it is probably uncontested that most articulations, in the form of negotiation statements, laws, treaties or the like, do or at least intend to do something. Introducing speech act theory to international law, Nicholas Onuf cites the statement of rules as an example of typical illocutionary acts (Onuf 1989: 83–4). The signing of the treaty on the ECSC, for instance, founded the first European institution on the way to what is now the EU, and served France's interest of controlling an important base of German industry, while it helped Germany to return to the international scene. The system of governance established since then can be presented as a remarkable collection of speech acts and their effects, be it in the form of declarations, further treaties, decisions by the ECJ, or Community legal acts.

In contrast to other attempts to analyse European governance, an approach informed by speech act theory would pay more attention to language. In looking for the nature of the beast, Thomas Risse-Kappen, for instance, is mostly concerned with the domestic structure of certain policy fields and their degree of 'Europeanization' (Risse-Kappen 1996). The role of language in governance seems to be as much underplayed as it is in social constructivist scholarship in international relations more generally speaking, starting with Alexander Wendt's focus on state interaction through 'gestures', not speech (Wendt 1992: 404; see Zehfuss 1998: 125–8).[3]

A most interesting story in this respect is how citizenship developed from concerns about Europe's political future and role in the world, via the necessity to regulate membership of a single market, to being a response to questions about legitimacy and democracy within the EU. During this process, speech acts performed by a variety of actors, often with different intentions, not only led to the establishment of EU citizenship, but also to the reformulation of the concept of citizenship, with consequences for the shape of the Euro-polity. More generally speaking, the whole history of European integration can be understood as a history of speech acts (following Onuf: rules) establishing a system of governance (which, after all, is about rules that are binding for the members of the system; see Kohler-Koch 1993).

We should not, however, overstate the distinction between locutionary and illocutionary acts. In fact, one of Austin's central propositions concerned the practical difficulties in distinguishing between constative and performative sentences (Austin 1975: 94). First, even locutionary acts are performative to the extent that to state something is to do something: it is to locate something in a specific context, following certain rules and depending on the given circumstances (Austin 1975: 146–7; Searle 1969: 22). Second, the notion of locutionary and illocutionary acts is an abstraction. Speaking more generally includes both acts (Austin 1975: 147). In the same vein, Searle insisted that the idea that descriptive statements could never entail evaluative ones amounted to what he called the 'naturalistic fallacy fallacy' (Searle 1969: 132).

Consider that it was common in the British debate of the 1960s to refer to the EEC as the 'Common Market', whereas in Germany the term most often used was *'Gemeinschaft'* (*'Community'*). One can reasonably assume that, to most people, the utterance of these words seemed innocent and descriptive, but they were not. First, in locating the EEC in different contexts according to the rules and circumstances of their respective national debates, they established a specific reading of the Treaties of Rome. Second, in the case of Britain, this partial fixation of meaning, together with a referendum as a means of legitimization, served to structure the evolving debate about possible European Community membership, dividing the broad spectrum of opinions into two simple camps: 'pro-' and 'anti-marketeers'.

Even if their illocutionary force is not as readily visible as in the case of rules, such speech acts have important social and political consequences. Whereas the Austinian move helped us to understand that speaking Europe is to do something, the Foucauldian move will help us to understand better the political force of such performative language.

The Foucauldian Move: Discourse, Power and Reality

The British example is, of course, well known and not very original. But it seems that its implications are rarely understood. More often than not, the British are taken to be 'natural' Eurosceptics, owing to their history or geographical status (see Diez 1999: ch. 1). But on closer inspection, the problem is less to do with different attitudes towards Europe, but with the concept of 'Europe' itself. It has to be stressed that neither the 'Common Market' nor the *'Gemeinschaft'* conception was 'correct' or 'false'. Rather, they were possible readings of the system of Western European governance. In other words, 'Europe' is not a neutral reality but a 'contested concept', the meaning of which is not (yet) fixed (Connolly 1983; see Schäffner et al. 1996: 4). Even assuming (as I will do in the following) that it is somehow related to a system of governance does not help that much: there are still numerous ways to construct such a system, in content, nature and scope. It is such constructions that the speech acts discussed at the end of the last section were about.

'Europe' might be one of the most typical examples of contested concepts, but the argument can be made on a more general level. The central proposition is that 'reality' cannot be known outside discourse, for the moment broadly defined as a set of articulations. In the words of Michel Foucault:

> We must not imagine that the world turns towards us a legible face which we would have only to decipher; the world is not the accomplice of our knowledge; there is no prediscursive providence which disposes the world in our favor. We must conceive discourse as a violence which we do to things, or in any case as a practice which we impose on them (Foucault 1984: 127).

In many ways, this is merely a more radical reformulation of Austin's observation that to state something is to do something. But to phrase it in such radical terms brings to the fore the political relevance of language beyond the concept of rhetoric as a means to political ends, and towards a power that rests in discourse itself. This power makes us understand certain problems in certain ways, and pose questions accordingly. It thereby limits the range of alternative policy options, and enables us to take on others. The contest about concepts is thus a central political struggle (Connolly 1983: 30), not only between individuals and groups defending one meaning against another, but also between different ways of constructing 'the world' through different sets of languages. (These different languages are not employed by actors in a sovereign way. It is the discursive web surrounding each articulation that makes the latter possible, on the one hand (otherwise, it would be meaningless), while the web itself, on the other hand, relies on its reproduction through these articulations.)

Discourse in this Foucauldian reformulation is thus more radical than the speech act tradition in that more emphasis is put on the context in its relation to the individual actor. Although it is 'we' who impose meaning, 'we' do not act as autonomous subjects but from a 'subject position' made available by the discursive context in which we are situated (Foucault 1991: 58). The speech act tradition emphasized the rules and contexts of speaking; the discursive tradition furthermore emphasizes the constitutive role of discourse in the production of subject identities. Discourse then takes up a life of its own. It is not a pure means of politics – instead, politics is an essential part of discourse. The struggle to impose meaning on such terms as 'Europe' is not only a struggle between politicians but also between the different discourses that enable actors to articulate their positions (Larsen 1997a: 121–2).

In a way, this notion amounts to what one may call a 'linguistic structurationism', adding to Giddens' theory the crucial importance of language (see Giddens 1984). Giddens' central aim, shared by Foucault, was to move beyond structuralism and to reconceptualize the duality of structures and agency. His theory of structurationism, imported into international relations by Alexander Wendt (1992), argues that both, structure and agency, were mutually dependent on each other. Whether Giddens was successful in this endeavour is contested. It has been argued, for instance, that structurationists eventually privilege structure by making it their ontological starting point whereas, in a Foucauldian perspective, more emphasis is put on practice in that structures are always reinterpreted and thereby transformed (Ashley 1989: 276–7). The major point in the present context, though, is that Giddens does not take language seriously enough (Zehfuss 1998), whereas a focus on discourse attributes a central importance both to the practice of speaking and the linguistic context in which articulations emerge and are read.

Before I move on to show the relevance of this to European integration studies by way of some more examples, I need to clarify that to say that any talk about reality will always be a specific construction of the latter is not to deny the existence of reality itself (Laclau and Mouffe 1985: 108; Potter 1996: 7). When entering a different country, confronted with very 'real' physical barriers, one has to present a passport. While the Schengen agreement has eliminated borders between some of its signatory states, it has led to the intensification of such controls at the outside borders of 'Schengenland'. But there is no 'neutral language' to convey the meaning of these 'real' borders. Their construction as guarantees of welfare provisions or illegitimate walls depriving people of their right to move are both speech acts within a specific discursive context. Furthermore, discourse itself is part of reality. In that sense, discursive approaches do not fit into the old dichotomy of idealists versus realists. In fact, the example of 'Schengenland' nicely illustrates this: it emanates from and reifies a specific discursive construction of European governance.

'Euro-speak'

After the Foucauldian move, any 'description' of European governance participates in the struggle to fix the latter's meaning, and thus is a political act. This is hardly ever recognized. Philippe Schmitter, for one, explicitly acknowledges the role of language in European integration. He identifies the development of a 'Euro-speak' defining the space for political action within the EU, while often being hardly comprehensible to an outsider (Schmitter 1996b: 122–7; see also Schäffner et al. 1996: 8). Elements of this 'Euro-speak' range from *'acquis communautaire'* to 'codecision', from 'subsidiarity' to *'supranationalite'* (Schmitter 1996b: 137). At the same time, however, Schmitter sees a need 'for labels to identify the general configuration of authority that is emerging' in the case of the EU, and doubts that this can be done by a mere aggregation of currently existing 'Euro-speak' (Schmitter 1996b: 137).

But following the Austinian and Foucauldian moves, the 'new vocabulary' that Schmitter is looking for cannot be used simply to 'pick up such developments' as the emergence of a new form of multi-layered governance', and to 'describe the process of integration' (Schmitter 1996b: 132–3). Instead, such developments are only knowledgeable to us within specific discursive contexts, and to label them from our various subject positions is to engage in the 'struggle for Europe' (Wæver 1997b). This struggle is not restricted to the realm of political 'practitioners' – as academics dealing with matters of European integration, we are also part of it.

Consider the conceptualization of the EU as a system of 'multi-level governance' (e.g. Christiansen 1997; Marks 1993). The image created by this account is one of a set of various separated levels of governance (local, regional, national, European) that interact with each other in some issue areas and follow their own course in others. This has by now become something of a 'textbook image' of the EU. It would be naive to assume that this image directly becomes the ground on which politicians in the EU base their decisions. This is not what is claimed here. Rather, the point is that such conceptualizations are part of a wider discursive context and do not 'stand aside' from their object of analysis. They take up the claims made by German *Länder* about their role in the overall system, or by various national governments leading to the specific construction of subsidiarity in Art. 3b TEC.[4] It is these 'multi-level' representations *taken together* that reify a notion of politics working on separate planes. The development of the EU towards such a system that way becomes a self-fulfilling hypothesis.

The power of discourse is that it structures our conceptualizations of European governance to some extent, rather than us simply employing a certain language to further our cause. The multi-level language gives preference to actors on various 'state' levels and is linked to an extension of the classical federalist practice of territorial representation on the 'highest' organizational level, now with three representational bodies instead of two. What happens if for a moment we employ a different language and speak of a 'network polity' instead? Our conception of the EU changes, and instead of 'levels', we find a more open political space, both geographically and functionally diversified, undermining the territorial notion of politics that is still upheld by the multiple levels concept (Kohler-Koch 1999).

Which of the two languages should be preferred is contestable, and need not be discussed at this point. Both have their own political consequences in that they enable different kinds of political actors to claim legitimate existence in different kinds of decision-making processes. A functional body such as the Economic and Social Committee does not, of course, simply disappear once the multi-level language is employed. But it does not figure too prominently in our representations of the EU, and this quasi non-existence is being reified.

The language of neofunctionalism provides a second illustration. One of the distinctive features of neofunctionalism was its proposal to bridge the gap between functional and political association in classic functionalism by transforming the concept of 'spillover' (i.e. the notion that integration processes, once started in a field of 'low politics', will create a dynamic of their own and sooner or later affect other policy fields) by adding to it an explicit political content and agent, working towards the eventual establishment of an overall federal, or at least supranational, system (Caporaso and Keeler 1995: 33–4; Kelstrup 1998: 29; Zellentin 1992: 70–1). Again, the question is not whether those expectations were right or misplaced. Instead, my proposition is that while neo-functionalism might thereby have closed one gap, it opened up another one, and that this is because of the language employed.

On the one hand, the reformulated spill-over concept had to include democratic processes at one point or another. Economic policy might well be legitimized by references to economic output – the guarantee of welfare. But this leads to the construction of Europe as an 'Economic

Community' (Diez 1999; Jachtenfuchs 1997; Jachtenfuchs et al. 1998). While legitimation through output is already a position hardly accepted universally in relation to economic policy, things become even more problematic if one moves into other policy fields. Thus, the inclusion of participatory elements was unavoidable if spill-over was to be sustained. But, on the other hand, the language of neo-functionalism was all very technical, the name of the approach itself being no exception. Accordingly, the central institution in the emerging polity was given the name of a 'commission', and the means of governance were called 'directives' and 'regulations' (Art. 189 TEC). Such terms are hardly reconcilable with the current language of democracy without a redefinition of democracy itself. That, however, was not what was proposed – in fact, classic functionalism might have been more apt to such a redefinition by changing the territorial organization of societies into a functional one, whereas neofunctionalism proposed using the latter to achieve the former.

The 'democratic deficit' charge that has haunted the EU ever since its inception at Maastricht seems to be directly connected to this problematic. Its citizens claim that the EU is far too bureaucratic, technical, distant, and its decision-making procedures too intransparent (see Weiler 1998: 78). This might be the case or not – it seems at least questionable whether politics in any of the national capitals is more transparent. But the institutional language of neofunctionalism has prevailed until today, and provides the ground to continuously reconstruct the EU as a monster bureaucracy concerned with technical matters that increasingly affect the everyday life of its citizens without their formal consent, while the nation state carries with it the ideals of self-determination and democracy.

In such a setting, it is hard to make the case that the initiative for a substantial number of directives can be traced back to member state governments, or that the size of the EU administration is smaller than that of a single member state such as Germany's federal bureaucracy (Wessels 1996: 182–4), or that non-governmental organizations are heavily involved in the making of EC policies (Jachtenfuchs and Kohler-Koch 1996: 24; Kohler-Koch 1998). Surely, none of this makes the EU a heaven of democracy – not on the basis of the predominant current understanding of democracy, in any case. Instead, the point of this discussion is that the language of neo-functionalism enables one reading of the EU rather than another. And furthermore, this language seemed right and innocent (in the sense of being the objectively best available way) at one point – much in the same way as the language of multi-levelism today. In each case, the Foucauldian move points to the politics involved in discourse, a politics that we are often unaware of and that does not come to our attention as long as we equate politics with interests and intentions.

The Derridarean Move: Conceptualizing Change and Options for Alternatives

Within a universe of discourses, change is only possible if meaning is not eternally fixed and if the lines of contestation between various discourses are allowed to shift. Only if this is the case will there be a chance for the development of a new 'Euro-speak', and thus for the development of alternative constructions of European integration. On the other hand, the meaning of words needs to be relatively stable in a given context for communication to be possible. In his structural theory of language, Frederic de Saussure argued that national languages 'work' because they represent crystal grids in which each word has its proper place. It takes on meaning through the firm opposition in which it stands towards another word in this grid (Frank 1983: 32–4). In such a 'crystal grid' model, change is hard to conceive of. But we all know that meaning is not eternally fixed: dictionaries provide us with contested meanings of a single word, and, once in a while, such entries have to be changed because the word is now used in a different or additional sense. Furthermore, we do experience breakdowns of communication.

This is the reason for a third and final move, which I will call Derridarean. Change was not absent from the Austinian and Foucauldian moves. They emphasized the role of action in a continuous reconstruction of and struggle for meaning. But in order to conceptualize the interplay of structure and agency in linguistic terms, the Derridarean move will be more helpful. In contrast to Saussure, French philosopher Jacques Derrida conceptualized language not as a closed and more or less rigid grid, but as a series of open-ended chains (Derrida 1977). With each articulation, there is at least a potential of adding new oppositions to the already existing chain, and thereby of altering it (see Potter 1996: 84). This does not necessarily result in a breakdown of communication. In fact, communication does not have to rest on a concept of 'understanding', assuming the correspondence of what is said and received in the speaker's and receiver's minds. Instead, it can be conceived of as operating on the level of language, where the decisive factor is the affinity of discourses and thus their mutual translatability. Furthermore, change and continuity always go hand in hand with each other. Although the overall discursive space is not as volatile as Derridareans sometimes suggest, and each addition to a linguistic chain seems to be minor at first, it may indeed be part of a major transformation, the importance of which becomes clear only in the long run.

An example of such a change is the development of the construction of European governance as an economic community in the form of a 'common market' in the British case. There, the predominant concept of European integration in the 1950s was indeed a classic 'Eurosceptic' one of pure intergovernmental co-operation. But at the same time, economic considerations played an increasing role in the overall political debate. This led to the reformulation of co-operation as a free trade area. The language in which this area was constructed centred around economic output. Its basic mechanism was still intergovernmental, but this economic focus laid down a trace that soon made it possible to articulate supranational governance in the economic realm. And indeed, this is how Macmillan presented his 'bid for membership' in August 1961 (Hansard 1961: 1481, 1490; see Diez 1999: ch. 3).

Put in a simple way, we all enter into a conversation with a set of preconceptions from which we set out to reconstruct other articulations. Thus, we not only receive them passively, but regularly add to the linguistic chain unless our set of preconceptions (or at least those relevant for the given conversation) are exactly the same as the ones of the speaker. Borrowing a conceptualization from the radical constructivist branch of systems theory (Hejl 1987), we may think of ourselves as being situated in, and our preconceptions resulting from, a node of discourses providing the basis for our interaction in communication. In other words, our preconceptions are nothing other than objects of particular discourses, which in turn are linked to a number of other discourses in what I call a 'discursive nodal point' (Diez 1998a, 1998b, 1999: ch. 2). There is a simple reason for such linkages between discourses: the conceptualization of objects in one discourse follows a set of rules, which, in turn, result from 'metanarratives' providing meaning to the latter, etc. This creates a web in which discourses are bound up with each other, and which is held together by nodal points.

The latter, given the Derridarean move, are potentially unstable, but will usually not change in a radical way. Shifts seem most likely if there is a considerable overlap between the rules (and therefore the metanarratives) of the two discourses in question, both in terms of content (that is, concerning the objects of the metanarratives) and in terms of structure (that is, some overall principles to which the rules adhere). This overlap makes articulations translatable. On the basis of such similar 'languages', it is possible from one nodal point to make sense of articulations resulting from another one, so that the latter are not rejected right away, opening up the possibility of (ex)change. Seen from such an angle, the language of a free trade area in the British case facilitated the move towards the articulation of an economic community that would otherwise have been much harder, if not impossible.

Finally, the Derridarean move also allows us to address possible alternatives to the federal state and economic community conceptions that currently dominate the debate (see Jachtenfuchs et al. 1998). Recent years have witnessed an emerging 'Euro-speak' that focused on subsidiarity and flexibility (see Adonis 1991; Endo 1994; Hüglin 1994;

Stubb 1996; van Kersbergen and Verbeek 1994; Wilke and Wallace 1990; Wind 1998). Most well known are the introduction of the principle of subsidiarity into the Treaty of Maastricht, accompanied by the establishment of the Council of the Regions, and suggestions ranging from the *'Kerneuropa'* and 'concentric circle' visions of German Christian Democrats Karl Lamers and Wolfgang Schäuble and former French Prime Minister Eduard Balladur to the demands for more flexibility by former British Prime Minister John Major. All of them, in one way or another, are set in opposition to 'centralization' and a further unitary development of the EU, either because the latter are linked to hindrances for further deepening and widening of integration, or because they are associated with a neglect of nation state identities. While potentially undermining the *acquis communautaire,* the emergence of this new 'Euro-speak' in parts also serves to reify the 'nation state' as a central concept in politics. Nowhere is this clearer than in the way 'subsidiarity' is invested in legal discourse through Art. 3b and its sole stress on member states' competences.

In terms of the centrality of territorial statehood in political discourses, the change brought about by these terms thus seems to be of a rather marginal kind. It is easier to see the problems they pose to the construction of European governance as a federal state in the making than to the territorial organization of politics as such. Rather, their usage seems to follow rules similar to those of 'multi-level' constructions. But seen from the perspective outlined above after the Derridarean move, these seemingly marginal changes might bring with them more fundamental transformations in that they layout a linguistic trace that can be seized upon by alternative constructions.

Consider the rules of the network discourse. It, too, is set against centralization, but also against purely territorial politics, and includes both territorial and functional divisions. Network-like constructions of European governance have traditionally been marginalized in the overall integration debate. Members of the Integral Federalists, for instance, argued at the Congress of The Hague in 1948 for the encouragement, 'regardless of frontiers, [of] the spontaneous articulation of interests, energies and hopes' (Lipgens and Loth 1985: 49), and stated their 'wish to be as far as possible decentralized, both regionally and functionally; not a superstate but a real democracy, built up of self-governing communities' (Lipgens and Loth 1985: 45). But their influence within the federalist movement was never strong, and if anything became weaker over time. Their construction of 'federalism' was too far apart from that of the dominant discourse, the discursive nodal point from which they argued too different and outlandish for those used to talking in terms of modern territorial statehood. The language of the latter is clear, orderly and relatively parsimonious – the waters of the network discourse are much more muddied. They do not provide a clear outlook and focus on terms such as 'spontaneity' or 'living, supple complexity' (Lipgens and Loth 1985: 50). From the discursive nodal point of a federal state conception, it is hard not to see this as a deficiency. To put it simply, the language of vagueness did and does not translate well into a language of clear borders, hierarchy and uniformity. The language of neofunctionalism, in contrast, was in a much better position, having a clear overall programme. In the same vein, 'multi-level governance' is still a pretty much ordered one in that it implies, for instance, the clear separation of a minimum number of levels.

But remember that the exact meaning of a term is context-bound, while at the same time it can be transformed through the reinvestment of the terms in question from different discursive positions. Hence, it may turn out to be of some significance that the terms 'subsidiarity' and 'flexibility' are contested concepts that are not alien to the network language. Instead, they are much closer to it than, for instance, neo-functionalist language. This increases the translatability of network articulations into dominant 'Euro-speak'. Much like the movement from free trade area to economic community in the British case, there is a trace that can be seized upon by actors working from the network's discursive nodal point.

This is, of course, not to say that, in due course, the debate will have changed so much that it becomes common to construct European governance in such terms. The notion of 'linguistic structurationism' reminds us of the need for these terms to be reinvested by actors from such a discursive position. What is important, however, is that the current transformations in 'Euro-speak' allow for such a reinvestment. Thus, the language of day-to-day politics may well be ahead of our minds in trying to figure out the 'nature of the beast'.

The Importance of Language

My attempt in this article was to make a case for the importance of language in the process of European integration. By way of three moves (Austinian, Foucauldian and Derridarean), I argued that language does more than describe; that all our accounts of the world (and thus of European governance) are embedded in certain discourses; that the meaning of words is dependent on their discursive context; that this context is not rigid but in constant, if only slow, flux; and that recent transformations of the discursive context enable the construction of Europe as a 'network'. I have illustrated this string of arguments with a number of examples, but there is no doubt that there needs to be more research into the workings of each of the moves in the context of European integration. Among the research questions that emanate from the above line of argument are the following:

- What are the terms with which we speak about European integration? How did 'Euro-speak' evolve?
- What are the political pre-decisions implied in those terms?
- What are the alternative meanings of these terms in various contexts?
- How are these terms invested? Which rules do they follow? From which contexts do they emanate?

Substantiated by such research, there are at least two further 'practical' implications, besides the enablement of the network alternative.

First, the future development of the EU will not depend solely on member states' interests, but also on the translatability of the discourses on European governance that the relevant political actors are embedded in. It seems that the EU is a 'multiperspectival polity' not only because of its lack of a single centre of decision-making, but also because it allows for conceptualizations from various angles. The issue for institutional development is not whether these conceptualizations are identical, but whether they can make sense of the Treaties and other basic texts at the core of integration (Wæver 1990).

Second, there might be too much focus these days on the change of institutions in the narrow, organizational sense of the term. The change of institutions, from the perspective developed above, is not interesting as a fact in and of itself, but as part of a broader set of practices in which language plays a crucial role. Institutions cannot be separated from the discourses they are embedded in, and rather than a formal change of institutions, what seems necessary is a change in the discursive construction of these institutions, of which the former would only be one particular component. Such change is obviously problematic, for no one can control language, but everyone contributes to it in each new articulation.

The academic attempts to categorize the EU and give it a place in our order of political systems are nothing but such contributions. They are attempts to fix the meaning of European governance, so that we know what the latter 'is', but they are not just 'objective' analyses of a pre-given political system. This does not make them worthless; on the contrary, they are as essential for our knowledge as the zoologist's classification of her 'beast' is, and they are probably more relevant to our daily lives.

Eventually, a further difference to what the zoologist does with her words is that while it may be relatively easy for her to take the lead in constituting the first dominant discourse on the newly discovered animal, the many voices involved in the construction of European governance will ensure that the fixation of meaning in this case is much harder.

What is the politics involved here? On one level, the answer that this article has given is that it is a politics of discourse, that within the language in which we operate lies a set of choices about the political decisions of our day. Since I started out from the observation that this discursive dimension is largely neglected, it was my attempt to bring the latter to our attention by focusing on these pre-decisions. But are we then, according to the above line of argument, *dependent* on the discourses of the nodal points in which we are situated? Addressing these questions is a thorny undertaking, and I can only sketch my (preliminary) answer. But however thorny, they are of the utmost theoretical and practical relevance. After all, the poststructuralist work in the theory of international relations, from which my argument is largely derived, set out as a critique both of individualized conceptions of political agency and of the structuralism of neo-realism, which seemed to undermine any attempts to change the anarchical international system (Ashley 1989: 273–4).

My sketch draws on two distinctive features of discourse at it was set out above. First, I pointed out that discourses do not 'cause' but *enable*. They do have a structural quality in that they are more than the sum of individual acts, but they are at the same time dependent on the latter. They set limits to what is possible to be articulated (Wæver 1998: 108), but do also provide agents with a multitude of identities in various subject positions, and are continuously transformed through the addition and combination of new articulations. In spite of all the epistemological and ontological differences, their work is thus none the less similar, for instance, to the structures in Robert Cox's work on international relations, in which structures predispose, but do not determine (Mittelman 1998: 76). There is room for creativity on behalf of political actors in the model of discursive nodal points. In Ernesto Laclau and Chantal Mouffe's conceptualization, stressing the practice of articulations, the latter are even the means to link various meta-narratives in order to fix meaning (Laclau and Mouffe 1985: 113). But this creativity is not unlimited, and it does not *originate* within the individual because the latter operates from a subject position that is in itself discursively produced (Laclau and Mouffe 1985: 109, 115), and so each articulation will already flow from a discursive nodal point. Neither needs articulations that lead to a reformulation to be consciously conceived of as such. Their meaning cannot be fixed, and thus they might induce changes beyond original intentions – actors, as Foucault once remarked, may well know what they do, 'but what they don't know is what they do does' (quoted in Dreyfus and Rabinow 1982:187).

Second, it needs to be recalled that, following the Derridarean move, discourses are different from traditionally conceptualized structures in that they are not rigid. Their contents can thus only be approximated, and not be once and for ever determined. The concept of discourse itself might help us to think in novel ways of structure and agency, since each articulation (a political *act)* is in itself a constitutive part of discourse. It is essential to note the extent to which articulations combine linguistic elements in novel ways, or whether they largely reproduce the prevailing rationalities. In that respect, the social constructivisms of Alexander Wendt (1992), or Jeffrey Checkel (1998), stressing the co-constitution of structure and agency and asking for greater attention to be paid to the processes of this coconstitution, are closer to the discursive constructivism espoused in this article than is often assumed, again despite their differences. Surely, I cannot claim to have finally solved the general puzzle of transcending the duality of structure and agency. But the purpose of this article was a more limited one. It was to foster in European studies, on the ground of theoretical reflections largely taken from the current debate in international relations, the awareness of the power of language, and of the discursive situatedness of our articulations and their readings. Speaking 'Europe', I hope I have shown, is always to participate in a struggle, as much as is practices from within a discursive context. The political of integration discourse should not be underestimated.

Notes

1 For a discussion of these various kinds of power, see Hindess 1996. The latter are not necessarily mutually exclusive, but my point in this context is to introduce the notion of discursive power. A discussion of how the different 'faces of power' are related is an interesting task beyond the scope of this article.
2 It should be noted that discourse is not reducible to language. But since the latter is a crucial element of the former, I will restrict myself in this article to the role of language.
3 Generally, though, the use of speech act theory is more widespread in IR than in European integration studies. Examples are the already quoted work by Nicholas Onuf on international norms, Friedrich Kratochwil's study on international law (Kratochwil 1989), or more recently the conceptualization of security as a speech act called 'securitization' by Ole Wæver and the so-called Copenhagen School (Wæver 1995; Buzan et al. 1998; see Huysmans 1998). Wæver and his colleagues have also been among the so far few to analyse the role of language in constructing European governance (Holm 1997; Larsen 1997a, 1997b; Wæver 1990, 1997b, 1998a).
4 TEC: Treaty establishing the European Community, as amended by the Treaty on European Union.

Chapter 18

Does Constructivism Subsume Neofunctionalism?

Ernst B. Haas*

Why Compare Neofunctionalism with Constructivism?

A case can easily be made that the Neofunctionalist approach, developed in order to give the study of European regional integration a theoretical basis, is a precursor of what has lately been called Constructivism. Both clearly reject realism, neorealism, and world systems theory as useful interpretations of international relations; but both retain affinities to other IR theories such as neoliberal institutionalism, pluralist liberalism, decision-making schemes and peace theory. Both feature the importance of ideas and values as explanations of behaviour and accept the constraining power of multilateral institutions, even if such constraints were not anticipated by actors at the time such organizations were set up. And both see important continuities between domestic and foreign policy decision-making.

But others object to the notion that the two are ontologically part of the same family. Neofunctionalists accept a kind of soft rational choice ontology which puts them closer to utilitarianism than most constructivists consider acceptable. The core epistemologies which neofunctionalists have featured are more akin to positivism than many constructivists consider legitimate. At least, neofunctionalists do not make positivism a target for the contempt which many constructivists heap upon that view.

It is my intention to sort out these differences and similarities to show that Neofunctionalism is indeed a precursor of a certain type of Constructivism, but not of all the IR studies that currently claim that label. I justify the comparison, in part, because I wish to clarify lines of intellectual descent. But, more important, I wish to demonstrate the need to disaggregate that non-theory called Constructivism in order to

* Reproduced by kind permission of Sage Publications Ltd from Ernst Haas (2001) 'Does Constructivism Subsume Neofunctionalism?' in T. Christiansen, K. E. Jørgensen and A. Wiener (eds), *The Social Construction of Europe* (London: Sage), 22–31. The text is reproduced in full. Where possible, references have been changed to Harvard citation style. Some peripheral footnotes have been omitted.

rescue a 'softly rational' ontology from its fuzzy embrace. First, I summarize the ontological essence of Neofunctionalism.

Neofunctionalism: Evolving Ontologies

Neofunctionalism (NF) originated as a theory explaining the process of European integration; efforts were made to extend its usefulness to the exploration and – we hoped – the successful explanation of regional integration in general (See Haas 1967: 315–43; Haas and Schmitter 1964: 705–37).[1] Finally, I tested the power of NF in a global setting in which no supranational institutions were active and where governments remained the core actors – and found it wanting (see Haas 1964).

The theory was self-consciously designed to reject the ontological assumptions realism. NF differs from Marxist theories by holding groups to be the core actors, not classes with fixed interests. It rejects the utopianism of idealist-liberal theories because of its insistence that group interests are rationally determined and defended, and hence not subject to ready change by mere persuasion.

States, instead of struggling for power, are expected to defend their preferences and to cooperate when cooperation was deemed necessary for their realization. State preferences are seen as resulting from changing domestic competitions for influence; there is no fixed and knowable national interest. Preferences of political actors are formulated on the basis of the values held; they, in turn, determine an actor's sense of interest. In short, NF carried the assumptions of democratic pluralism over into policy formulation relating to international matters by disaggregating the state into its actor-components.

Regional integration was expected to occur when societal actors, in calculating their interests, decided to rely on the supranational institutions rather than their own governments to realize their demands. These institutions, in turn, would enjoy increasing authority and legitimacy as they become the sources of policies meeting the demands of societal actors. Originally, NF assumed that integration would proceed quasi-automatically as demands for additional central services intensified because the central institutions proved unable to satisfy the demands of their new clients. Thus, activities associated with sectors integrated initially would 'spillover' into neighbouring sectors not yet integrated, but now becoming the focus of demands for more integration.

The ontology is 'soft' rational choice: societal actors, in seeking to realize their value-derived interests, will choose whatever means are made available by the prevailing democratic order. If thwarted they will rethink their values, redefine their interests, and choose new means to realize them. The alleged primordial force of nationalism will be trumped by the utilitarian-instrumental human desire to better oneself in life, materially and in terms of status. It bears repeating that the ontology is *not* materialistic: values shape interests and values include many non-material elements.[2]

The rational component of the original version of NF bears a strong resemblance to what later became known as path-determination. Choices, once made, carried their own internal logic for producing specific eventual outcomes; the rationality imputed to the actors' choices initially made it likely, in later decisions, that branching points consistent with the initial objectives be chosen. This, of course, turned out to be wrong. By 1970 neofunctionalists were amending NF in significant ways (see Haas 1968: preface; Haas 1975; Lindberg and Scheingold 1970, 1971). The spillover became neither automatic nor irreversible; nationalisms were given their due; governments were conceded to retain the preponderance of power over supranational actors; extraregional practices and institutions in which European countries are embedded were given more causal significance than was true in the original NF. Most important, outcomes other than a federal state were envisaged; the notion of political community was drastically reconceptualized (see especially Haas 1971: 26–32*, 1995: 72–85*).

Neofunctionalism Revisited

Some commentators on the European *relance* after 1985 conclude that these events bear out the analysis provided by a revised NF (see Keohane and Hoffmann 1991; Michelmann and Soldatos 1994, especially the essay by Mutimer; Ojanen 1998: ch. 3). Others do not. Thus, the treatments of European integration that rightly stress the role of law and of legal actors in advancing the process, make generous use of NF ideas in explaining the motives and tactics of litigants, and occasionally even the reasoning of judges. Sandholtz and Zysman mix NF reasoning about actor motives with emphasis on global political economy trends. Pierson's historical institutionalism is easily combined with NF as is Hix's emphasis on the increasing relevance of concepts derived from comparative politics rather than international relations.

Several authors argue that NF was the most appropriate theory for dealing with the first fifteen years of European integration, but is no longer. They maintain that the name of the game in Europe is 'multi-level governance'. Demands for the improvement of participatory democracy at all levels of governance go hand in hand with controversy over the extent of subsidiarity, or of centralization, thus allowing for a Europe *a plusieurs vitesses,* asymmetrical commitments to central institutions and more decentralized decision-making. Neither NF nor

Jean Monnet imagined these refinements (Hooghe and Marks 1999; Marks, Hooghe and Blank 1998: 273–93; Schmitter 2000: 2–3).

However, some scholars reject NF altogether. Some do so because they consider that rational choice via formal modeling makes unnecessary the concern with variable actor preferences because it allows a stylized mode of explanation that achieves analytic independence from historical contexts. Others do so because they deny the importance of supranational institutions as shapers of new actor expectations.[4] Committed federalists, of course, persist in rejecting NF because of its instrumentalist ontology and its gradualism (for examples, see Pinder and Tsoukalis 1998: 189–94, 335–44*).

Given these core characteristics of NF and its lingering appeal to current scholarship, we must now face the question of NF's fit with constructivism.

Dimensions for Comparing Neofunctionalism with Constructivism

Neofunctionalism did not originate as a theory of international relations; its purpose was more modest: to explicate and possible predict the prospects of political integration, first in Europe, then in other regions, and eventually in a global setting. The name of the game was to understand how human collectivities can move 'beyond the nation-state'. Constructivism, on the other hand, was devised as an explicit theory of general international relations. It was not linked to the attainment of a specific outcome, such as the creation of supranational political community. Despite these different origins and purposes the two theories share many common commitments: they stress the causal role of ideas and values in defining actor preferences (interests) rather than more abstract structural features enshrined as social facts by theorists.

Why does it matter whether NF and Constructivism are close kin or not? Suppose we conclude that NF and Constructivism are not closely related and that NF should not be subsumed by a more general Constructivism. Such a finding would enable us to consider NF a manifestation of a type of theorizing that stresses disaggregation of the state in the search for explanations, the tradition we might all 'liberal-pluralist'. While getting rid of 'the state' as the core actor, this tradition retains the 'soft rationalist' assumption that actors, whatever their values and interests, act deliberately in pursuing what they want. Their preferences do not result from random choice; their selection of means are the result of calculation; they can and do change their minds, and hence their preferences and thus whatever passes for the 'national interest' of their state. NF would find a home, but not among the constructivists.

But what if NF can be reasonably subsumed by Constructivism? In that case it retains its lease on life by gaining legitimacy within the family of constructivists as lore that explicates the phenomenon of transnational political integration. NF would become a theory of international relations by virtue of such an affiliation. It would gain generality, lose its specificity.

Before we make a systematic comparison of the two we have to specify the dimensions along which the comparison is to proceed. We want to know whether the two are, or are not, compatible with respect to these ontological issues:

1. How important is the fact that the dependent variables are not the same (even though many of the independent ones are)?
2. How is the agent-structure problem resolved? If structures are held to matter, how are they defined and identified?
3. Is there a level-of-analysis problem to be resolved? If all action is presumed to 'take place at the level of 'the second image' there is no issue. But what if the respective theorists hold that the first and/or third images matter as well? How can explanation proceed if action takes place by using several images at the same time?
4. How are actors expected to define their preferences? How much choice do actors have in the selection of preferences?
5. Do the two use identical epistemologies? Are they both tied to positivism in some way even though some constructivists explicitly reject it?

Any putative clustering of attributes we might be tempted to undertake at this stage must await a more careful delineation of the universe of Constructivism.

Types of Constructivism

Constructivism, said its originators,

> is a constructive response to the challenge of the 'post' movements. It rejects the 'slash-and-burn' extremism of some post-modern thinkers who leave nothing behind them, nowhere to stand, nothing even for themselves to say. . . . While constructivists join the 'post' movements in calling into question much of the orthodoxy of postwar IR scholarship, they reject neither empirical research nor social science as such. Instead, constructivism maintains that the sociopolitical world is constructed by human practice, and seeks to explain how this construction takes place (Kubalkova, Onuf, Kowert 1998: 20, 42–3).

This much all constructivists accept, though some persist in including the 'post' movements in their own typologies, albeit shunted off into the ghetto. However, if we look at the all-important issue of *how actors construct their own interests,* the field breaks down into three quite different schools of thought.

1. The 'systemic school' holds that interests result from the definition of actor identities, which in turn result from the role played by the actor in the global system. State-actors are constituted by that system and take their roles from their perceived positions in it. Leading theorists include Alex Wendt and David Dessler, who, however, acknowledge a kinship to such world-society British theorists as Hedley Bull, Anthony Giddens, and Barry Buzan (See Ruggie 1998: 32ff).

2. The 'norms and culture' school maintains that interests derive from the cultural matrix in which actors live. This setting generates the norms which underlie collective choices. Prominent theorists include John Meyer, Friedrich Kratochwil, Christian Reus-Smit, Keith Krause, and Bill McSweeney. Much empirical work on the role of norms in shaping foreign policy derives from this school. International society is the preferred site for finding embedded norms.

3. The 'soft rationalist' school holds that actors derive their interests from their notions of political causality. Their ontological understanding of what makes 'their' world tick informs their definition of interests. This school subsumes the scholars who look for the origins of interest in consensual knowledge and in epistemic communities of knowledge-purveyors. Soft rationalists find the origin of interests within nation-states, but also look to transnational movements as stimulants. Prominent theorists include Peter Katzenstein, Emanuel Adler, Peter Haas, Harvey Starr and Andrew Farkas.

Why do I refer this typology to other now being discussed? Hollis and Smith familiarized us with the juxtaposition of two approaches to IR theorizing: 'explanatory' (realist ontology with positivist epistemology) efforts as against attempts at 'understanding' (idealist ontology with a hermeneutic epistemology). Constructivism is the prime exhibit of the hermeneutic approach. This typology is a very dangerous oversimplification because it denies constructivists the right to attempt explanatory and predictive statements. According to Hollis and Smith any effort to use ontologies other than individualistic and interest-maximizing ones precludes the use of methods associated with scientific inquiry (Hollis and Smith 1990). I insist, along with most other constructivists, that we all remain part of social science. Therefore I reject the Hollis-Smith dichotomy.

So do several others. Katzenstein, Keohane and Krasner show that rationalism and constructivism are by no means always incompatible. However, their own typology muddies the waters by including postmodern approaches as one branch of constructivism even though this school strongly identifies with a hermeneutic view about epistemology. In Ruggie's view there are three kinds of constructivists distinguishes by their epistemologies: postmoderns who reject social science notions of causality, neo-classicals who espouse Webrian and Durkheimian methods and concepts, and naturalistic scholars who adhere to scientific-realist notions of truth. He identities with the second (as do I) even though he also believes in the mutual constitution of the world's norms by ideas and structures, a position closer to the naturalistic strand (Katzenstein, Keohane and Krasner 1998: 680–2; Ruggie 1998: 32ff).

Which Type of Constructivism Resembles Neo-functionalism?

The main characteristics of NF and our three kinds of Constructivism are summarized in Table 4.

NF characteristics coincide exactly with those of Soft Rationalism three times and partially twice. On the other hand, they do not coincide at all, fully or in part, with systemic constructivism, and only twice, partially, with constructivists of the cultural persuasion. The verdict is clear: NF has a great deal in common with one type of Constructivism only, the type which remains unwilling to break completely with the utilitarian/individualistic tradition and insists on softening the anti-positivism of many constructivists by embracing the pragmatist epistemology.

I highlight the similarities. There is a common commitment to an ontology of 'soft' rational choice. Actors are expected to choose in terms of their perceived interests and to select means deemed most appropriate for realizing them. They are also expected to change interests if and when the ideas and values inspiring them undergo alteration, and to substitute new means for old ones found to be unsatisfactory by the actor . In short, a utilitarian-individualistic mode of behavior prevails. Actors are conceptualized as actual or potential learners.[4] Ideas inspire interests, or, as Weber might have put it, ideas *are* interests.[5]

Moreover, the epistemologies of the two schools are strikingly similar. They rely heavily on ideal types. These, in turn, are derived mostly by following the mode of abductive reasoning made familiar by American Pragmatist philosophers, though hardly invented by them. NF and Soft-Rationalist Constructivism both reject positivism as the

Table 4   *Comparison of neofunctionalism and three constructivisms*

Dimension	Neofunctionalism (Haas version)	Organizational	Systemic	Norms/Culture
Dependent Variable	political community	international cooperation-value/policy integration	types of anarchy and conflict	international cooperation; value integration
Agent/ structure Relationship	agency favoured	structuration; agency favoured	structuration; structure favoured	structuration; agency favoured
Chief Actors	organizations (all kinds)	organizations (all kinds)	states	states, groups governments
Level of analysis	second image favoured	third/second image tension, 2nd -image favoured	third image favoured	unresolved tension between 3rd and 2nd images
Derivation of actor interests	values and material needs	collectively-defined values and needs	socially-values, norms defined identities	
Dominant Epistemology	Weberian; pragmatism	Weberian; Durkheirnian: pragmatism	scientific realism; Durkheimian	unclear

sole road to knowledge and are willing to settle for the less determinative and less magisterial guidance of the pragmatist philosophy of science.

The overlap is not quite as clean when it comes to the issue of whether agency trumps structure as a source of actor conduct. The emphasis on ideas as sources of perceived interest dictates a concern with actor motivations on the part of both schools, in contrast to the other Constructivisms. Still, my NF has no concern with structures at all, while that of Lindberg and Scheingold, for example, does. 'Soft Rational' Constructivism shows more concern about a possible interaction between structural and agential forces than NF did. Nevertheless, the concern with motivation as cause makes the two quite similar, though a constructivist who takes the principle of structuration very seriously, without bending it in favour of agency as most of us do, will part company with NF.

Similarly, commitment to the second image is not a totally consensual matter. NF is concerned with regional institutions, national governments, political parties and interest groups as the main actors. Soft Rational Choice constructivists are also, especially with these actors as they impinge on multilateral institutions and negotiations. But some are more attuned to the constraining influence of international structures – or what counts as such – than was true of my NF, though not of others'.

The main lack of congruence derives from a disagreement about the dependent variable. There is an overlap, but not an identity of concerns. Constructivists can easily subsume NF's concern with political community formation under their more general interest in processes of international cooperation and value integration. But NF cannot expand its focus to the much more general interest of Constructivism in processes of value integration that are not expected to end up as political communities, either at the regional or the global level. Perhaps I was right after all when, in 1975, I argued that NF was obsolescent because actor concerns have shifted to global interdependence and our disciplinary interests should follow them.

Notes

1 We predicted successfully that regional integration would not readily occur in Latin America and I explained in the preface of *The Uniting of Europe* (1958a), that the explanatory power of NF in leading to new political communities was confined to settings characterized by industrialized economies, full political mobilization via strong interest groups and political parties, leadership by elites competing for political dominance under rules of constitutional democracy accepted by leaders and followers. My reasons for limiting the explanatory scope of NF are illustrated with reference to most regional integration efforts then ongoing in Haas 1971.

2 I chose the label 'soft rational choice' because most of the criteria for the 'hard' variety cannot be satisfied. Green and Shapiro hold that 'rational choice theorists generally agree on an Instrumental conception of individual rationality, by reference to which people are thought to *maximize their expected utilities in formally predictable ways. . . . The further assumption [is] that rationality is homogeneous across individuals under study'*. (1994: 16). The italicized words and phrases refer to ideas I do not share. The maximization of utilities is a microeconomic concept of intentionality which excludes values as shapers of preferences; revised NF makes possible retrodiction, not formal prediction of anything more specific than a range of possible outcomes; and if values differ, preferences will vary non-homogeneously. Jon Elster's (1986: 16) criteria of rational choice that considers intentions as causes also cannot be met. It requires optimality in the search for solutions to choices, absence of contradictions among beliefs, and the action must be 'caused' by desires and beliefs, not merely rationalized, and the results must have been intended by the agent. Agents in NF are assumed to be acting consistent with their desires and beliefs but cannot meet the other conditions of rationality.

3 Examples of rational choice argumentation include Mattli 1999. Andrew Moravcsik is the most visible defender of the continuing centrality of the nation-state and its government as the engine of integration. See Moravcsik 1998. For a scathing critique of this argument see Saeter 1998: 49–61. I find it at least very curious that despite great similarities in both ontological and epistemological assumptions my treatment and Moravcsik's turn out to be so different. His ontology is described in detail as 'liberalism' in Moravcsik 1997. Its core assumptions are identical with those of NF and seem quite compatible with certain kinds of constructivism as well. It is difficult to understand why he makes such extraordinary efforts to distinguish his work from these sources.

4 The theory of collective learning developed to work out the changes state policy undergoes in response to interactions within international organizations and negotiations is a direct outgrowth of the ontology of 'soft' rational choice first elaborated in the context of NF and subsequently applied in the larger context of international cooperation which constructivists like to study. See Haas 1980: 357–405, 1990.

5 Those who follow Durkheim's lead rather than Weber's would argue that ideas take shape as norms guiding actors, and thus become social facts. Some constructivists advance such an ontology, notably Ruggie and Adler, while also adhering to the soft rational choice argument about interests I associate uniquely with 'my' school of Constructivism. Hence my concept of 'actor dissatisfaction' – essentially a utilitarian notion – is not congruent with theirs.

Part VI

The Future of European Integration Studies

The preceding parts of this volume have looked at the past history of European integration studies. In this final part we take a look ahead to consider where the field may be going from here. The first chapter by Ben Rosamond highlights the merits of classical integration theory and considers the perennial question of how to secure analytical leverage when studying a single case such as the EU (Chapter 19). The second chapter is a set of concluding remarks by the editor, in which I reflect on the relative merit of various possible future approaches to the study of European integration (Chapter 20).

The Future of European Studies: Integration Theory, EU Studies and Social Science

Ben Rosamond*

Introduction

There is an inherent danger for those of us who choose to write about integration theory. Our focus, quite reasonably it has to be said, is on a subfield ('EU studies', to use the contemporary label) and its internal theoretical jousts. The danger is that we might fall prey to a form of intellectual isolationism in which we think of a conceptual cleavage structure that is self-generated and self-generating. While a field obviously has its own specific ecology that influences theoretical evolution, it is not an isolated ecology. Rather, the space occupied by EU studies is and always has been a venue for theoretical immigration and emigration. EU studies has its own indigenous theoretical culture, but, as this volume demonstrates consistently, it is impossible to understand that culture without reference to how it is shaped by (and perhaps shapes) the broader evolution of the social sciences in general and the political sciences in particular. It is easy to forget this important point. For one thing, the EU is strikingly peculiar; on the face of it, there is and has been nothing quite like it. In addition, scholars of comparative regional integration – a field that has undergone a significant revival in the past decade or so – have tended to treat the EU and the insights of EU studies with considerable caution. One net effect of this is the danger of the vibrant and populous field of EU studies becoming largely self-referential on the one hand and largely ignored by other scholars of international relations and political science on the other. While this portrayal of the contemporary situation is undoubtedly stylized and is perhaps an inevitable consequence of the highly compartmentalized and specialized nature of contemporary social enquiry, it is nevertheless striking how far away we seem

* I am grateful for constructive comments on earlier versions of this piece by Mette Eilstrup-Sangiovanni, William Paterson and an anonymous reviewer.

to have moved from the ambitions of the founding scholars of classical integration theory.

In this chapter I want to supplement Mette Eilstrup-Sangiovanni's excellent introductions to the pieces presented in this book by thinking explicitly, in light of the foregoing, about where the theoretical treatment of European integration/the EU might go from here. I want briefly to develop three interrelated arguments. The first section of this chapter revisits one of the enduring conundrums of integration theory: how to secure analytical leverage where the object of study appears to have no obvious comparators. It accepts that there are potentially several ways to deliver this necessary condition of 'good' social science, but suggests that constructivism offers an especially productive pathway. The second and third arguments share a common root in that they both proceed from the central claims (a) that mainstream interpretations of past integration theory are often simplistic and partial and (b) that the production and reproduction of these interpretations close off analytical possibilities for the present and the future. The second section seeks to show how a vital component of present theoretical health in EU studies involves the systematic rereading of the field's past theoretical texts. It assumes that theoretical health is obtained via the preservation of openness in terms of both epistemology and methodology and that discernible attempts to identify EU studies in terms of a particular conception of 'good' political science are misplaced. Moreover, such moves often follow from heavily stylized readings of past theoretical efforts. The third section of this chapter is concerned with rethinking the possibilities for bringing together EU studies with other fields of enquiry. In short, this contribution seeks to remind us that EU studies is a field whose identity is struggled over and where these identity struggles are played out through theoretical jousts and through the deployment of foundational theoretical claims. This raises important and ongoing questions about the disciplinary coordinates of EU studies and the vexed question of what kind of social scientific enterprise it is. A recurring theme throughout this chapter is the promise of a constructivist form of analysis. This, emphatically, does not represent an argument on behalf of constructivism as 'the only way ahead' for EU studies. Rather, the intention is to offer one example of how some perennial problems of theorizing the EU might be addressed.

Solving the Problem of Analytical Leverage in EU Theory

Everybody agrees that European integration is empirically exciting. This innate characteristic has attracted a generation of chroniclers, whose work has been described variously as 'thick description' (Wallace 2000: 103) or as 'a historicist attempt to capture an epochal transformation in the European order and its corresponding political lexicon' (Wæver 1998: 724). Even the thickest descriptive work can only proceed via the deployment of some kind of conceptual vocabulary. The selection of particular events or phenomena in the EU's history is in and of itself a theoretical choice. The social scientific mind is pretty much automatically prompted to ask 'of what is this an instance?' (Rosenau and Durfee 1995). So one way of understanding theories of the EU/integration is to think of them ultimately as rival answers to this very question. Two problems immediately present themselves. The first, of course, is that the question might be loaded. It presumes that the EU is like other things that might be familiar to social scientists – an international organization, a regime, a security community, a polity (federal or otherwise), whatever. In other words, the 'of what is this an instance?' reflex presumes that we possess an off-the-peg conceptual vocabulary. If the EU is like nothing before or since, if – to borrow from former Commission President Jacques Delors – it is 'un objet politique non-identifié' (an unidentified political object), then how should social scientists engage with the EU? If the EU is a *sui generis* phenomenon it follows that investigators might fall into the famous $n = 1$ elephant trap, where analytical leverage and explanatory power are markedly absent.

Continuing with the theme of elephants, the second problem was captured memorably in Puchala's (1972) discussion of the difficulties of capturing the integration process and the Communities through the medium of a single theoretical apparatus. The EU might be conceived of as many things simultaneously, and most scholars would accept that it more desirable to look at components of the EU and treat these, rather than the totality, as dependent variables. However, the selection of appropriate facets of the EU brings with it automatically (a) understandings of how analytical leverage is achieved and thus (b) particular theoretical toolkits.

The first of these two problems has been addressed consistently throughout the history of social scientific engagement with the EU. The integration theory project of the 1950s and 1960s associated with neofunctionalism was a large-scale attempt to develop a generalizable hypothesis about regional integration from the study of the European experience. Meanwhile, comparativists prefer to treat the EU as a political system that can be studied through the conceptual lenses of conventional political science. Constructivists of various hues are able to think of the EU as an institutionalized venue for the negotiation of interests and identities and the development of intersubjectivities and norms. Each of these analytical strategies is premised on the idea that the EU or elements of the EU are in some way familiar; that the 'of what is this an instance?' question can be answered. The extent to which any or all of these represent successful solutions to the *sui generis* problem is, of course a matter for academic exchange and debate. That said, it does not always follow that these rival images of the EU are complementary. They may – as in the distinction between rationalist versions of political science and constructivist understandings of social processes – represent quite different ontological starting points. This inevitably raises questions about the extent to which rival interpretations of the nature of social reality and strategies for accumulating and verifying knowledge are allowed to coexist within a field. I return to this point in the third section below.

The second perennial problem with the study of the EU – the idea that it is not amenable to capture through a single theory – is a little more difficult to negotiate and has rather more bearing on how EU theory might move on in the future. There seems to be four potential responses to this. The first involves recasting EU studies (and thus the theorization of the EU) as the investigation of one particular facet of EU activity. This might be an extreme version of the comparativists' strategy: treat the EU as a political system and 'mainstream' EU studies into the 'normal science' of political studies (Dowding 2000; Hix 1994; Schneider 2000). The danger with this kind of move is that it is potentially exclusionary of those approaches to the EU that fall outside of the designated political science mainstream and would certainly militate against the view that EU studies need to be attentive to a much broader range of disciplinary, epistemological and methodological insights (Manners 2003; Rosamond 2005a, Rumford and Murray 2003). The presumption of this first way of thinking is not that EU studies should be a zone of theoretical innovation, but that its practice should be renovated and (literally) 'disciplined' to bring it into line with the mainstream norms of political science. The rationalization of such a move downgrades and largely eschews those approaches to politics – some forms of constructivism and virtually all varieties of post-positivism – that depart from the standard norms of explanatory political science theorizing.

The second way ahead follows Peterson's (1995a) suggestion of a division of theoretical labour so that alternative theories are used to explain distinct parts of the EU enterprise. In Peterson's formulation this roughly corresponds to 'IR' theories being used to account for the EU's supersystemic context, institutionalist theories being deployed at the institutional level and the tools of policy analysis operating at the 'meso' level of day-to-day decision-making. This might be read as provoking a 'Balkanization' of EU studies into a set of (potentially non-communicating) subfields, although this outcome might be prevented if the repertoire of theories used have much in common at the metalevel.

Again this carries with it the dangers of closure and the adjudication of 'legitimate' analytical boundaries for EU studies. This is not to argue that neither of these ways ahead should proceed. However, it needs to be understood that each seeks to secure analytical leverage through conceptualizing the EU in terms of the familiar.

The third strategic response involves reflection on how the EU might take a role within forms of comparative analysis. To be comparative need not involve the rigidities of approaches that assume the EU (or parts of the EU) to be definitive cases of a familiar problem. It could also be about the comparative study of indeterminacy, novelty and the un-familiar. I discuss below some of the reasons for the demise of the EU as a primary case in studies of comparative regional integration. Yet the relaxation of the assumption that the EU constitutes some sort of benchmark case of regional integration could well facilitate a productive dialogue between political economists interested in region building across the world on the one hand and the established corpus of work in EU studies on the other. Alex Warleigh (2006) has provided the most eloquent expression of this line of reasoning to date. Recognizing tendencies within both EU studies and IR/ International Political Economy (IPE) to auto-define the present in ways that place past theoretical efforts into a category of backwardness, Warleigh suggests that EU studies has much to offer the contemporary scholar interested in transformations in world politics or the emergence of a global polity. The failure of such scholarship to cite cognate work in EU studies speaks volumes about field and disciplinary specialization, and Warleigh's point is to show how ideas generated by conceptual reflection on the EU can have a broader application. Thus, the EU studies-generated notion of 'multilevel governance' might assist scholars grappling with transformations in international organizations. Work on problems of authority and governance under conditions of globalization might learn much from the huge body of work on EU institutions and decision-making. 'Europeanization' – suitably adapted – could help research on how domestic transformations relate to new post-national forms of governance.

The fourth response requires the use of more 'critical' approaches and attendant concepts that are comfortable with the idea of the EU as 'multi-perspectival' (Ruggie 1998). By focusing on actors' perceptions and the importance of ideas, norms, identities and language in the EU context, constructivists (Christiansen, Jørgensen and Wiener 2001; Risse 2004) and discourse analysts (Diez 2001; Wæver 2004) move away from the rationalist-objectivist concern with identifying what the EU is and toward an account that re-imagines the EU as an arena for the practice of multiple subjectivities where there are many rival answers to this basic ontological puzzle. In other words, constructivism has at its heart a quite radical interpretation of some of the analytical dilemmas that have beset EU studies since its birth. As noted above, one of the ways out of the $n = 1$/*sui generis* problem is to make analytical choices in ways that allow scholarship to proceed on the basis of familiar categories. The acquisition of analytical leverage becomes a matter of rethinking particular elements of the EU experience as instances of phenomena that are studied elsewhere within the social sciences. Constructivism does this, but it also (potentially) identifies the EU as a subject of political argument and disagreement in its own right. It offers a set of tools to investigate the different ways in which actors themselves conceptualize the EU, its normative substance and its location within the global political economy. In short, this approach recasts the social scientific enterprise as the study of human subjectivities and the consequences of those subjectivities rather than simply the identification of the most appropriate objective descriptions of phenomena.

It follows that these more 'dissident' approaches are regarded by their proponents as innovative and mould breaking, not simply within EU studies, but within political science more generally (Manners 2006). It is perhaps more enlightening to look at contemporary EU studies as an arena for a clash between these two broad approaches to social science (mainstream rationalism vs critical approaches); and interestingly many of these contests are presently being played out within the broad constructivist project. Risse (2004: 159) is right to say that EU-studies constructivism represents a kind of spillover from the constructivist movement in IR. However, there are some important qualifiers, which may ultimately distinguish EU-studies constructivism from its IR cousin. Within IR, constructivism's primary voice (Wendt 1999) has sought to keep the approach within the epistemological mainstream of the political sciences. This project certainly has its adherents within EU studies (Checkel 2001; Jupille, Caporaso and Checkel 2003), but work on the EU that operates beneath the banner of constructivism is altogether more variegated and, in some cases, quite epistemologically distinct (varieties of constructivism in EU studies are discussed by Christiansen, Jørgensen and Wiener 2001 and Risse 2004). Work on the constitutive effects of discursive practices and some studies of communicative action within supranational institutions mark out EU-studies constructivism as a distinctive project, somewhat different from the American and Anglophone mainstream (Smith 1999). If nothing else, constructivist approaches to the EU represents (out of necessity) a departure from mainstream-IR constructivism's preoccupation with the dynamics of interstate interaction, the security dilemma and the nature of 'anarchy' as a defining structural condition. Indeed, EU-studies constructivism's efforts have been directed hitherto to three distinctive projects. The first is the treatment of EU institutions (be they formal or informal) as venues for deliberation, persuasion and socialization and within which actors' interests may be actively constructed. The second is a focus on the exchange of norms between the EU and domestic polities, with an emphasis on the (potentially) mediating role played by institutionalized and embedded national discourses. The third project focuses on the constitutive power of discourses both of European space and the structures within which that space is imagined. These in turn are investigated as constructions that may constrain or enable particular conceptions of policy choice. Therefore, as well as one of many ways forward for EU studies, constructivism *within* EU studies might yet prove to be a rival for what some see as a rather formulaic and mainstream version of constructivism that has taken root within US political science and IR.

EU Theory and Social Scientific Propriety

We have seen that the story of (conventional) political scientific engagement with European integration can be read as either (a) efforts to secure analytical leverage by anchoring the EU within the standard imagination/conceptual vocabulary or (b) efforts to use the EU as a case for the generation of hypotheses that might then be applied to other putative cases. Strategy (a) is more deductive than (b), but (b) is not wholly inductive, drawing as it does on a 'normal' conception of social scientific propriety utilizing standard technologies of enquiry. Perhaps the best exemplar of (b) is neofunctionalism, but standard accounts of its rise and fall tend to neglect this characteristic. Recent years have seen efforts to generate clear blue water between 'old' and 'new' approaches to integration. EU studies is not unique in this regard (see the discussion in the next section about 'new' approaches to regionalism). Scholars have a habit of announcing progress in their fields and a precondition of this assertion is a demonstration that past scholarly efforts were in some way misplaced or erroneous. The argument here is that this type of claim in EU studies is at best misconceived and at worst simply wrong.

Needless to say, the story of theoretical effort tends to be presented chronologically. But it is crucial that characterizations of 'old theory' do not amount to stereotyping (this volume, it ought to be said, is clearly 'not guilty' on this charge). One of the key tenets of good research is that scholarship should be based upon close inspection of primary sources, not upon secondary renditions of what primary sources supposedly say. The same is surely true of those seeking to map the theoretical contours of a field. Secondary and tertiary claims about 'classical' integration theory are prone to stylize and strip nuance from a body of literature. Neofunctionalism, for example, was not only more complex than many standard textbook treatments allow, but also much more dynamic and reflexive (Rosamond, 2005b). In particular neofunctionalism has suffered from the accusation that it did little more than successfully discover a dynamic ('spillover') that applied to a small phase of the EU's experience and which was not reproduced elsewhere. At worst, neofunctionalism is characterized as a *description* of certain elements of the early phase of European institution building. What this caricature misses is the way in which neofunctionalists (a) wrestled with this problem, (b) focused on the issues of integration's 'background conditions' and in so doing (c) made successful negative predictions about the prospects for integration elsewhere (Haas and Schmitter 1964). Moreover, later neofunctionalism paid significant attention to the role of cognitive variables in the integration process (Nye 1971a). Old/pre-theories have been too readily dismissed because they supposedly failed the test of analytical leverage, but we should also be certain to inspect 'new theories on the block' lest they be exaggerated in their auto-definition of 'self' (new) as distinct from 'other' (old). The simple lesson is that we (as scholars and students) should read the original integration theorists more than we habitually do.

Thus, moves to discredit the integration theory of the past on behalf of a more rigorous present underplay the degree to which neofunctionalism in particular conformed to a model of social scientific rectitude. A further claim is that early integration theory – and here the debate between neofunctionalists and intergovernmentalists is implicated – was an IR enterprise that cannot speak to the political systemic character of the present EU. Haas (2004) described this distinction as 'silly', and closer inspection shows that scholars in this tradition were among the very first to start conceptualizing the EU as a polity (Lindberg 1967; Lindberg and Scheingold 1970). Again, closer inspection of the original texts might prevent us from needlessly reinventing conceptual wheels. Also, standard narratives of old integration theory as moribund need to be read in the context of broader debates in contemporary political science. Part of what might be going on here is an attempt to push EU studies further toward the disciplinary norms of (US) political science. There is no space here to discuss the merits or otherwise of such a move other than to say that those norms are felt by many to be restrictive and stifling of intellectual creativity (Lustick 1997; Wæver 1998). Awareness of the relevance of such debates to our field is an important side effect of theoretical literacy – and theoretical literacy in our field must involve the routine inspection of the 'classics'.

But where might we go with this insight? The argument presented here could be taken as nothing more than a plea to secure a more reliable theoretical archaeology of our field or as an entreaty to retell the story of EU studies in ways that recognize the complexity (as opposed to the stereotypical simplicity) of past theoretical schools. I suggest that this insight is important because it puts into sharp focus the very notion of 'progress' in European/EU studies. Disciplinary histories can be narrated in quite 'Whiggish' ways; that is to say, we think of ourselves as located in the theoretical present as somewhat 'further on' or closer to the truth than our predecessors. Students of the sociology of knowledge and the philosophy of science will be aware of how contentious this assumption is. Moreover, it presupposes, by and large, that disciplinary/theoretical progress covaries with both (a) the evolution of our object of study (the EU) and (b) more rigorous social scientific insights. The notion of progress in EU studies needs to be rethought to take account of the problematic status of point (b), while utilizing wide ranging conceptual tools to present a more dynamic account of (a).

In practice, this involves thinking through the linkages between past theoretical contributions and present concerns. A textbook example was Haas's careful consideration of the possibilities for linkage between the 'soft rationalism' of a rehabilitated neofunctionalism and certain forms of constructivism (Haas 2004). Constructivism also provided the stimulus for Adler and Barnett's attempt to regenerate the study of Deutschian security communities in comparative perspective (Adler and Barnett 1998). In both cases the promise of constructivism facilitated a re-evaluation of supposedly 'old', allegedly moribund theoretical schools. What is perhaps still missing is more systematic work on the history and evolution of the EU polity using both 'new' theoretical insights and revived versions of 'old' patterns of thinking. A startling exception, which perhaps shows the way, is the interdisciplinary marriage of political science and legal scholarship within a broadly constructivist frame. This, as Shaw and Wiener (2000) have pointed out, has revived the study of European law as the investigation of the dynamic constitutive power of norms and their role in polity building. That this takes a special form in the EU case does not disqualify comparative analysis. Indeed the normative aspects of international law have been integral to some of the more creative discussions of region building (where the EU is presented as one case among several; see particularly Duina 2006).

Émigré Theories? EU Studies' Contribution to Wider Social Science

To what extent can the theoretical practice of EU studies continue to contribute to the broader social scientific project? The discussion of theories of integration tends to focus the question on the disciplines of political science and International Relations (IR). For the most part this is more a question of how approaches, ideas and concepts imported from other fields have matured and taken on a life of their own in the context of studying European integration. EU studies – certainly in its formative phases – has never really been a venue for the isolated generation and maturation of theoretical discourses. The rise and (supposed) fall of neofunctionalism did occur within the context of EU studies – the boundaries are normally held to be two works by Haas 1958a and 1975 – but the inspiration for neofunctionalism, its modes of reasoning and its approach to social scientific rigour, were already firmly established in US political science by the mid-1950s. So while, to all intents and purposes, neofunctionalism was a 'new' theory in the late 1950s and early 1960s, its intellectual coordinates were familiar. Neofunctionalists were committed to 'professionalized' Weberian social scientific norms involving a commitment to theory building and the robust testing of hypotheses using the latest intellectual technologies (De Vree 1972; Kaiser 1965; Rosamond 2005b; Ruggie et al. 2005). If anything, early neofunctionalism in European studies brought together a collection of the brightest political science minds in the US, motivated not only by the exciting empirical experiment taking place in Western Europe, but also by the analytical leverage that might be obtained for the broader study of regional integration.

Yet the most prominent victim of integration theory's self-declared 'obsolescence' and the subsequent tendency to draw a line underneath classical theory was the EU's status as a legitimate case in the study of comparative regional integration. The resurgence of interest in integration (or regionalism) has coincided with the creation of a new auto-defined school of political economy – usually labelled the 'new regionalism' (see Hettne and Söderbaum 2000; Hettne, Inotai and Sunkel 1999; Söderbaum and Shaw, 2003). Much of the work in this field relies upon a semantic-conceptual differentiation between the 'new' and 'old regionalism' as analytical schools, with the European case looming overly large in the latter, but appropriately and sceptically contextualized in the former. The various objections to/complaints about the EU may be summarized briefly as follows. The use of the EU as a paradigm case of regionalism propagates the assumption that all cases of regional integration will come to resemble the form taken by the (west) European variant (something which is mimicked by much of the policy debate over whether the EU provides an appropriate 'model'). Using the EU as a benchmark, runs the argument, biases the analysis and prevents a proper, grounded analysis of post-Cold War regional forms. Indeed the EU is read as a particular path-dependent consequence of a remarkably specific set of imperatives confronted by west European political elites in the aftermath of the World War II. Newer regional projects like NAFTA have emerged from a different historic conjuncture and thus should be analysed differently. It follows that EU theories are also unsuitable because they are designed to account for this particular case rather than the generic phenomenon. Indeed, integration theory (EU style) is part of the 'old regionalism' and newer non-Eurocentric theories informed especially by developments in IPE should prevail.

There is much merit in such arguments, but the empirical and analytical differentiation between 'old' and 'new' regionalisms is not as easy to sustain for reasons discussed both above and in the next section. The seductive claim that 'new regionalism' as a field of enquiry should be different from 'old regionalism' relies upon a set of assumptions about the analytical potential (or otherwise) of the 'old', within which a stylized narrative of EU studies takes centre stage. There is, at the very least, a case for some intellectual archaeology to investigate whether established and (supposedly) discredited theories have been stereotyped or stripped of nuance. As suggested already, closer reading than is customary of these original texts might allow us to extract some useful ideas for the study of contemporary regionalism.

We can certainly trace lines of descent from theoretical work originally conducted in EU studies to other domains. Simple pursuit of the intellectual trajectories of the main early integration theorists will demonstrate this (Rosamond 2000: 96–7). One influential review of the growth of IPE makes clear the intellectual debt that field has to the early efforts of integration theorists (Katzenstein, Keohane and Krasner 1998). But, if anything, the broader impact of (EU) integration theory is not what it might be, in part because it is thought about in a particular way and in part because EU studies as a field has been so successful that many of its discourses take place in endless intra-disciplinary loops.

Of course, the incentives to remain within these intradisciplinary loops are compelling, not least because EU studies has acquired sufficient maturity to be treated as a field by those who work within it. A critical mass of scholars, a set of professional associations, a conference circuit and numerous journals devoted to the study of the EU all tend to allow for the making of scholarly careers within EU studies and thus for the confinement of insights to this self-sustaining field. This is a quite distinct environment from that of the late 1950s and the 1960s within which the earliest theoretical contributions were fashioned. The recent revival of comparative integration studies has occurred without significant attention either to the EU as a relevant case or to EU studies as a supplier of concepts and ideas. This suggests that work is proceeding with a rather static and stereotypical view of the conceptual and empirical content of EU studies, which in turn is an invitation for some cross-field entrepreneurship. This would not simply be a matter of (re)introducing the field of EU studies and demonstrating the range of academic goods it has to offer. It should also involve a critical engagement with conventional narratives about the place of EU studies scholarship within comparative integration studies.

Conclusions

EU studies is a field that is by and large self-sustaining, characterized as it is by its own professional associations, conference circuits and journals as well as characteristic intra-disciplinary discourses (Rosamond, 2006). There is always the danger that we think about fields solely in their own terms. It is obviously vital that considerable scholarly resources are devoted to conceptualizing the EU and understanding the dynamics that drive integrative processes. Yet perhaps the most important lesson to be drawn from discussing theories of the EU and integration is that they are derivatives of broader patterns of social scientific practice. Moreover, this chapter has tried to show that this relationship is far from benign. EU studies is – and always has been – a venue in which alternative approaches to political science are contested. This is partly about the discussion of rival hypotheses, but also about strategies to secure analytical leverage and, more recently, about some rather bigger metatheoretical questions cutting to the very heart of what social science is and should be. The cosmopolitan character of the EU-studies community amplifies this debate and in many ways prevents the field from entering an introverted 'normal science' phase.

This contribution has sought to make an argument about the virtues of looking back carefully at past theoretical efforts as an essential precondition for thoroughgoing and creative theoretical work in the present. How we think about the *future* of EU studies always relies on a set of understandings about the *past* of the field. We can think about past theoretical work as a closed chapter or as an open book. The 'closed chapter' strategy has negative consequences for our capacity to think about how genuine theoretical innovation can generate insightful work about the EU. To remain open minded about 'old' approaches not only saves us from unnecessarily reinventing old wheels, but also provokes thinking about what questions we might ask about the EU and how the EU can be used as a comparator in wider studies of region building and polity formation. A vital prerequisite is a critical approach to the way in which we tell stories about theory and theoretical progress in our field.

This chapter has also argued that approaches such as constructivism have a particular part to play within this broad set of aspirations. Constructivism not only adds an alternative voice to the rationalist mainstream within EU studies; a positive development if we regard theoretical pluralism as an essentially healthy sign. The fact that constructivist work has come to occupy such a significant place in the contemporary study of the EU also helps to identify EU studies as a primary venue for the discussion of some of the main debates within the political sciences broadly defined. Whether this means striving for some kind of theoretical synthesis between rationalism and constructivism as approaches to political phenomena (Checkel 2001) or carving out a distinct 'European' variant of the constructivist project (Diez 2001), the arrival of constructivism has added a significant degree of theoretical impetus to EU studies. Moreover, constructivism's core ontological insight – that the world 'out there' is social rather than material – not only encourages us to think about elements of the EU as socially constructed or about the institutions of the EU as venues for argument, deliberation, socialization and persuasion, but also invites us to move away from the the perennial question of what the EU is toward an engagement with the way in which actors themselves imagine 'Europe' and the possibilities for its construction and transformation.

Chapter 20

The Future of European Integration Studies: The Road Ahead

The previous chapters have chronicled the past history of European integration theory. They bear witness to a rich and complex field, which has struggled with all of the fundamental issues in politics – issues of power and authority, of trade and prosperity, of democratic legitimacy, of war and peace. Looking to past theories continues to be of great relevance to the contemporary student of European integration. Although the nature of the EU is constantly changing, the fundamental issues – how to strike a balance between delegation and sovereignty; how to enhance problem-solving capacity through cooperation while retaining control over key domestic policy issues; how to weigh up technocratic efficiency against democratic participation – are enduring, and the careful inspection of past theoretical works may prevent us from travelling down dead ends or reinventing conceptual wheels. Too often, 'classic' integration theories are either dismissed as 'pre-theoretical' or interpreted and recounted in ways that are simplistic and one sided. However, as this book has attempted to show, close reading of past theoretical texts contains important lessons for those seeking to theorize the European project today. Still, to understand the nature of the constantly evolving European integration process, we must go beyond extant theory. In this final chapter I take a brief look ahead to the future of European integration studies.

Today it is increasingly common to argue that regional integration theory is moribund. The failure of previous grand theories to explain or predict the empirical development and shape of the European integration project, it is often said, raises important questions about the merits of regional integration studies. On what social scientific basis can we continue to make reliable predictions about the future of European integration or about integration elsewhere? At the same time, new influences from comparative politics, public policy and international relations theory make it increasingly difficult to describe European integration studies as a separate discipline from the general study of international and comparative politics. Can EU studies meaningfully be regarded as a separate subfield or has it been reincorporated within the wider study of international relations and comparative politics?

Whether EU studies today can be described as a disciplinary subfield whose boundaries with other fields such as international relations, comparative politics and international political economy can be clearly distinguished, I believe, is of little consequence for the future of integration studies. In fact, it is questionable whether there has ever been such a thing as specifically 'European integration theory'. Rather, as we have seen throughout this book, the European integration project has traditionally served both as a testing ground for theories developed in other contexts – such as transactionalism, rational institutionalism, realism and constructivism – as well as a fertile framework for the generation of novel theoretical tools and hypotheses with application far beyond the EC/EU. This was as true during the 'heyday' of regional integration theory in the 1950s as it is today when European generated theories of multilevel governance, regulatory cooperation and benchmarking are beginning to produce important insights about the development and functioning of international organizations in general. Consider not only how the study of European integration fed into general theories of custom and currency unions but also how the functionalist ideas of spillover and politicisation were applied to a broad range of international institutional venues. The view taken here is that theoretical innovation and progress is most likely if we continue to treat European integration studies as part of mainstream social-scientific inquiry. This requires us to resist the temptation of treating the EU as a unique phenomenon that neither holds insights for nor can be illuminated by political phenomena and processes outside Europe. While the extent and depth of cooperation in the EU may be exceptional, the various components and dimensions of the European integration project are consistently comparable to similar political phenomena elsewhere.

So how should we study the EU and its continuing integration process? There are several ways forward for those who choose not to regard the EU as a unique case, which requires its own peculiar theoretical vocabulary. Historically three main routes have been followed: scholars have treated the EU as an instance of an international organization, as a polity, or as an example of regionalism in the global political economy. These are still today the most common avenues of research. In the previous chapter, Ben Rosamond offers constructivism as an alternative and particularly fruitful way to tackle the $n=1$/*sui generis* problem. Instead of getting bogged down with the perennial question 'of what is the EU an instance?', constructivism focuses on the way in which actors perceive 'Europe' and imagine its future trajectory. Constructivist scholars do not approach the EU as a set of objective institutional structures but rather conceptualize the Union as an institutionalized venue for the construction of ideas, identities and norms. This shifts the focus of inquiry from the study of a particular set of institutions to the more general study of human (inter) subjectivities and thus provides an alternative and potentially broader perspective on the ongoing process of integration.

Insofar as it provides a set of tools to study the construction of ideas, norms, interests and identities in different structural conditions, a constructivist approach is indeed well situated to offer a novel interpretation of how to secure analytical leverage when studying the process of European integration. By shifting the focus from a concrete set of institutions to human understandings and intersubjectivities, a constructivist approach opens up a range of questions with universal scope: How are norms and identities created and sustained through interaction? How do processes of socialization and learning work in different structural and institutional settings? How do actors update or redefine their causal beliefs in response to different material or social stimuli? A constructivist research agenda addressing these questions in the context of European integration is indeed promising. Moreover, constructivists can draw on rich literatures in sociology, social psychology and communications research to enhance and broaden their analyses of individual and group interaction in different social and political settings. Yet, it is important to remember that constructivism tackles only one aspect of the complex reality of the EU – the construction of norms and identities – and tends to pay less attention to other features such as strategic interaction among states or external factors. It will therefore only ever provide a partial picture of the complex reality of European integration. Moreover, and more problematically, whereas a constructivist approach in *principle* enables scholars to gain analytical leverage by studying the impact of norms and ideas across various cases and policy domains and by drawing on broader sociological studies, in practice there is a tendency among many constructivist EU scholars – especially those of post-structuralist hue – to treat European integration and the processes of social construction associated with it as somehow exceptional. The claim is that European integration is a special phenomenon, which can in turn only be captured by 'critical' perspectives. Yet, it is widely accepted that the move to portraying European integration as *sui generis* led to theoretical stagnation in the 1970s, and present calls for seeing the EU as a novel political form that can only be captured by 'critical' theories carries similar dangers. If constructivist and post-structuralist theories are to present a solution to the $n = 1$ problem proponents must not only show a stronger commitment to the development of distinct testable hypotheses and to evaluating their propositions against competing theories (see discussion in Part V), but they must also be committed to generalization across social and geographical settings.

The alternative to a constructivist research agenda is to rely on more conventional (i.e. rationalist) political-science approaches, which seek to recast particular components of the EU as instances of general phenomena that are studied elsewhere within the social sciences and which rely on systematic comparison across a variety of different cases. In particular, the use of international relations and international political economy literatures to study the EU alongside other regional processes of political, economic and social integration is promising. Undisputedly, processes of political and economic integration have gone much further in Western Europe than anywhere else, but similar patterns have been developing in other regions such as the Americas and East Asia. Looking across geographic regions and across history, we can ask questions with a general scope: What are the factors that promote regional political cooperation and economic integration? Are there common forces encouraging integration in different geographical settings and at different moments in history? To what extent do different regions respond in similar ways to current pressures of globalization? Or, more narrowly: What governs patterns of enlargement within regional trade unions? How are relations with outsiders mediated by regional agreements? Although many so-called 'new regionalism' studies do not include European integration as a case for comparison, there are also many examples of integration studies which do take a broad comparative perspective. For example, there is a growing literature comparing political and economic integration in Europe and East Asia. Although such studies often highlight differences above similarities, they nonetheless provide valuable insights into the forces that govern the emergence and shape of regional integration.

A second promising strategy is to treat the EU as a standard political system whose functioning can be analysed using the methods and theories of 'normal' political science. This strategy has been successfully pursued for decades, but much work still remains to be done in terms of spelling out how various European-level institutions influence the specification, organization and representation of interests at both the European and national level. This includes work on the role of national parliaments, political parties and general publics. Conceptualizing the EU as a fully-fledged political system similar in operation to a modern nation-state naturally creates rich opportunities for comparative studies. But also those who conceptualize the EU merely as an *emergent* polity can find a comparative basis for their studies. History offers numerous examples of independent states merging together to form new political systems – think only of regional trade and currency unions such as the German Zollverein or the United Dutch Provinces, which evolved into single polities, or the United States, which started out as a loose confederation but evolved into a fully-fledged federal system. In this context, the literature on confederation, federation and nation building offers an abundant source of comparative data for students interested in 'polity building'.

Finally, we can choose to look at the EU as an instance of an international organization. From this perspective we can compare the EU to other international organizations along dimensions such as voting procedures, the strength of central institutional mandates, degrees of legalized dispute resolution, distribution of power among member states, etc. This in turn enables us to gather valuable information about the factors governing variation in patterns of bargaining, negotiation outcomes and compliance across different institutional settings. Similarly we may explore, in this way, how the impact of ideas, beliefs and norms varies across different institutional contexts.

Due to their predisposition to theoretical importation and exportation and their inherent inclination to test theories against evidence from a variety of different geographical and historical cases, I find that the above moves are generally healthier than recent attempts by some students of European integration to recast the European project as a unique endeavour, which can only be captured by 'critical' or 'post-structuralist' perspectives. A note of caution, however, is in order. Ben Rosamond is right to warn that the above strategies tend not to be inclusive of unorthodox perspectives which fall outside the political science mainstream. Certainly, it would be regrettable if efforts to anchor European studies more firmly within the political science mainstream should lead to a systematic exclusion of approaches that depart from the standard norms of explanatory political science theorizing. Yet, a determined effort by EU scholars to draw on and contribute to scholarship in other fields such as public policy, international organization and international political economy would in many ways represent a significant broadening of the current scope of inquiry. Additionally, a certain 'mainstreaming' of European integration studies would entail clear analytical advantages as I discuss below. To my mind, there is little danger that such a move should lead to 'theoretical closure'. As long as the EU remains a theoretical and empirical playing ground for both students of political science, international relations, international political economy and international law, a broad range of competing theoretical perspectives is guaranteed. Moreover, there is no reason why mainstream perspectives should not be able to co-exist with dissident approaches, which depart from different epistemological and ontological starting points. Certainly, a greater degree of engagement with and adherence to the analytical principles of mainstream political science does not imply that dissident approaches cannot continue to operate alongside more conventional approaches.

Methodological Pluralism

Clearly, there are many ways in which to study the EU. No single method or approach is likely to lead, on its own, to a complete understanding of the European integration process. Ben Rosamond has stressed in the previous chapter the importance of methodological pluralism and warned against epistemological 'mainstreaming' along American lines, where a largely consensual approach to analysis has emerged along broadly positivist themes. Whether or not one agrees with the depiction of American political science as united in this way, there is little doubt that analytical openness is important. A plurality of approaches and methods will make it easier to discover new empirical developments and devise provisional ways to deal with them. At the same time, it is also important to take seriously the problems that may arise from a lack of agreement on basic analytical approaches and methods. After some 70 years, the subfield of European integration theory is still in a stage of paradigmatic conflict. There is no consensus on major theories, methods, analytical perspectives, or, for that matter, even on what the important questions are. Rather there is competition among different macrotheoretical models – liberal intergovernmentalism supranationalism, and multilevel governance – each of which takes a different analytical approach and asks a different set of questions. A multitude of paradigms is appropriate when dealing with complex developments such as regional integration. Yet, pluralism can also be a hindrance, if there is no underlying consensus on what constitutes good social science. While it is both unlikely and undesirable to aim for a unified method of analysis across the field, a greater degree of shared disciplinary norms might help to reduce the present lack of interperspectival cooperation and mutual appreciation of the work that is being done. Greater agreement on analytical standards would both encourage and enable scholars to build upon previous work, rather than defining themselves in opposition to it. In turn, this would pave the way for greater accumulation of knowledge.

One way to ensure that various theoretical perspectives complement each other rather than work at cross-purposes would be to encourage a greater degree of division of theoretical labour. As noted in the introduction, previous attempts at constructing competing 'grand theories' have increasingly given way to an appreciation that different theories can be used to explain different aspects of the EU enterprise. This in turn opens up possibilities for syntheses or sequencing techniques, where various middle-range theories work in tandem to explain particular processes and outcomes. In particular, much could be gained from combining rationalist and soft constructivist approaches. It may be true, as Ben Rosamond argues in the previous chapter, that rationalist and critical constructivist theories offer fundamentally rival interpretations of social reality. However, more mainstream constructivism is quite compatible with rationalist approaches, as illustrated in Part V. As we have seen, both rationalism and soft constructivism share the basic premise that the world is 'social' as well as material but simply differ on how malleable social reality is. Hence, the two perspectives face a common theoretical challenge in terms of discovering when, how and why social change occurs, and specifying what actors and mechanisms bring about the change. A fruitful division of labour, however, can only ensue if there is a common language that allows followers of the two approaches to compare and to share their findings. Establishing such a language will require greater openness and methodological transparency on both sides and a greater willingness to accept mutual methodological criticism.

A New Research Agenda

Whether we treat the EU as unique or approach its various components as specific instances of more general phenomena, and whether we subscribe to rationalist, soft constructivist or critical approaches, there are some common theoretical challenges which confront all students of European integration. Perhaps the greatest theoretical challenge facing the field today is to understand the simultaneous interaction of domestic-level and regional-level factors in determining European integration outcomes. So far, most theories have sought to work out dynamics at one level, while holding the other level constant. Models seeking to explain interstate bargaining have tended to treat domestic preferences as exogenous and fixed. Preferences are either observed or deduced from existing theories, then plugged into models aimed at analysing international interaction. On the other hand, models of domestic interest politics have focused on how domestic institutions affect the generation and aggregation of preferences at the national level while leaving aside the question of how domestic institutions and interests are shaped by European-level factors. What is missing so far is a dynamic model of domestic-international interaction which seeks to determine the impact of domestic institutions and interests on international interaction and vice versa.

Modelling the simultaneous interaction between domestic and regional-level factors is extremely complex. Two-level models, introduced into the study of international relations in the late 1980s (Putnam 1988) and subsequently taken up by European integration theorists have begun to address the issue. This work concentrates on defining 'win-sets' specified by domestic interests. The idea is that those negotiation outcomes, which can be expected to be ratified or generally accepted at the domestic level in all participating states, define the sphere of possible international bargains. At the same time, it is also acknowledged that international bargains and commitments can serve to shape domestic interests and control domestic interest groups. A prominent example of this approach is the work of Andrew Moravcsik, which demonstrates how the preferences of key domestic groups constrain EU intergovernmental negotiations and how intergovernmental bargains in turn condition domestic preference formation. However, most such models are still too crude to address the complex simultaneous interaction effects that operate at both the domestic and international levels (Martin and Frieden 2002). Moreover, many models of the domestic–international interface offer at best a partial picture of domestic–regional interaction effects. For example, domestic interests are often reduced to those of dominant social groups (e.g. organized producers) and domestic institutions to those of national executives. In a similar manner, analyses of international interactions are often limited to looking at major international treaty bargains. If we wish to understand the complex interrelations between domestic and international politics, future work will need to allow for more nuance by incorporating other domestic institutions such as parliaments, political parties, courts, general publics, etc. and by broadening the focus on international interactions to include day-to-day institutional relations as well as major treaty-making bargains.

A better understanding of how domestic and international factors interact requires a firm foundation in theories both of domestic politics and international relations (Martin and Frieden 2002). At the domestic level scholars must specify the interests at stake in determining foreign policy, characterize the organization of these interests and investigate how interests are mediated through political institutions. At the international level, scholars must specify how different strategic settings, levels of uncertainty, power distributions and institutionalized rules and norms influence interstate negotiation and policy outcomes. Then they must then determine how one impacts on the other. Today work on domestic–international interaction within the EU is able to draw on well-established building blocks at both the domestic and regional levels. Students of domestic politics are getting steadily better at determining how the interests of domestic economic and political actors are translated into foreign policies. They are also increasingly attentive to the fact that European integration affects both domestic interests and domestic institutions in ways that reshape and constrain national policies. Students of interstate interactions on the other hand are getting more sophisticated when it comes to determining how different institutional settings and rule sets impact patterns of interstate bargaining. They are also increasingly aware of how norms, beliefs and roles entrenched at the European level condition states' interests and constrain their behaviour. Putting the parts together requires dialogue across disciplinary boundaries. It is also likely to require, as I have already argued, some basic agreement on analytical standards and approaches.

A second major challenge is to secure better empirical testing. If the field is to advance, abstract theoretical work must be underpinned by rigorous empirical testing. Here there is a hope as well as a danger. The general move away from traditional, all-embracing 'grand theories' of integration toward more partial theories concerned with specific aspects of the integration process holds out a promise for better empirical testing, since the application of theories within carefully circumscribed domains lends itself to in-depth case studies. However, this trend also entails a danger, namely of poor testing across cases. Few proponents of middle-range theories engage in comparative analysis; most rely on single-case studies, which marshal evidence for a few instances of the phenomenon in question instead of comparing across cases. (For a critique along these lines, see Burgess 2000: 47; Moravcsik 1997.) Moreover, it is increasingly rare for EU scholars to devote attention to systematic testing of hypotheses against competing theories. Too often, theorists focus on lining up evidence to support their own theories but are far less concerned with demonstrating how their theories fare against alternative explanations. This lack of comparing and contrasting between theories and across different cases is a serious hindrance to effective theory selection. The standard view of theory testing is that strong confirmation of a theory requires not only that we evaluate hypotheses against the statistical (null) hypothesis but also that we seek to rule out alternative explanatory variables. This is particularly important in single-case studies where we cannot boost confidence in our own explanation by replicating our findings across several cases. In such research, demonstrating that a theory provides a more convincing or more comprehensive explanation than the best available alternatives is crucial for producing theoretical confidence.

Better empirical testing also requires careful attention to the selection and use of sources. Reliance on 'hard' primary evidence (including internal government reports, legal documents, records of confidential deliberations among decision-makers, diary entries and structured interviews with policymakers) is generally more reliable than secondary or 'soft' sources (e.g. newspaper reports, public statements, political memoirs) which are based on a large degree of subjective interpretation and which may be deliberately manipulated or distorted *ex post* for personal gain. (On the reliability of different types of primary and secondary sources, see Moravcsik 1998: 81–2. For a critique of Moravcsik's selection criteria and use of sources, see Lieshout, Segers and van der Vleuten 2004.) While it is increasingly rare to come across scholarship that relies primarily on newspaper articles or personal memoirs as evidence, there is still room for improvement with respect to securing an unbiased selection and treatment of sources. In particular, it is important to appreciate that fair adjudication between rival theories depends on a broad and representative selection of sources.

The above areas are by no means exhaustive of the manifold challenges confronting students of the European Union. There are many additional areas of promising future research, including theorizing the EU as an international actor (i.e. analysing and explaining the making of European foreign policy) or addressing the normative implications of growing social and political integration. By highlighting the above challenges, I do not wish to suggest that these are the only or even the most pressing challenges facing today's students of European integration. However, tackling these challenges would be a good starting point and would go a long way toward securing the future success of the field.

Conclusion

The EU offers a unique setting for studying many of the problems of politics – both international and domestic. As the most integrated and highly institutionalized area in the world, the EU presents a unique opportunity to study the functions of international institutions, the complex links between domestic and international political processes, and the role of international law. It is for this reason that European integration studies in the past have been an area for both importation and emigration of ideas, concepts and theories. However, the status of the EU as both an empirical testing ground and a source of theoretical innovation cannot be taken for granted. Historically the field has gone through periods of isolation and introspection, during which it was shut off from the general study of international organization and domestic politics. The continued status of European integration studies as an area of theoretical innovation and refinement therefore requires a self-conscious engagement with wider debates in international relations and political science. As students of a particular region, European integration scholars cannot afford to be inward looking but must remain open to ideas and developments in the broader social science environment. On the other hand, integration scholars must also make a conscious effort to export their concepts and ideas to a broader audience of scholars outside the field of European integration studies. This was the strategy of the classical integration theorists, and current and future integration scholars would do well to follow their example.

Bibliography

Adler, E. (1997) 'Seizing the Middle Ground: Constructivism in World Politics', *European Journal of International Relations*, 3, 319–63.

Adler, E. and Barnett, M. (1996) 'Governing Anarchy: A Research Agenda for the Study of Security Communities', *Ethics and International Affairs*, 10, 63–98.

Adler, E. and Barnett, M. (eds) (1998) *Security Communities* (Cambridge: Cambridge University Press).

Adonis, A. (1991) 'Subsidiarity: Theory of a New Federalism?' in P. King and A. Bosco (eds), *A Constitution for Europe: A Comparative Study of Federal Constitutions and Plans for the United States of Europe* (London: Lothian Foundation Press), 63–73.

Alger, C. F. (1961) 'Non-resolution Consequences of the UN and Their Effect on International Conflict', *Journal of Conflict Resolution*, 5, 128–45.

Alter, K. (1996) 'The European Court's Political Power', *West European Politics*, 19(3), 458–87.

Alter, K. (1997) 'The European Court's Political Power', *West European Politics*, 19, 458–87.

Alter, K. (1998) 'Who are the "Masters of the Treaty"? European Governments and the European Court of Justice', *International Organization*, 52(1), 121–47.

Alter, K. and Meunier-Aitsahalia, S. (1994) 'Judicial Politics in the European Community. European Integration and the Pathbreaking Cassis de Dijon Decision', *Comparative Political Studies*, 26, 535–61.

Andersen, S. S. and Eliassen, K. A. (1993) 'The EC as a Political System' in S. S. Andersen and K. A. Eliassen (eds), *Making Policy in Europe: The Europeification of National Policy-Making* (London: Sage).

Anderson, C. and Kaltenthaler, K. (1996) 'The Dynamics of Public Opinion towards European Integration', *European Journal of International Relations*, 2, 175–99.

Anderson, J. J. (1995) 'The State of the (European) Union: From the Single Market to Maastricht, from Singular Events to General Theories', *World Politics*, 45, 441–65.

Anderson, P. (1996) 'Under the Sign of the Interim' in P. Gowan and P. Anderson (eds), *The Question of Europe* (London: Versus), 51–76.

Angell, N. (1910) *The Great Illusion: A Study of the Relation of Military Power in Nations to their Economic and Social Advantage* (London: Heinemann).

Armstrong, K. and Bulmer, S. (1997) *The Governance of the Single European Act* (Manchester: Manchester University Press).

Armstrong, K. and Bulmer, S. (1998) *The Governance of the Single European Market* (Manchester: Manchester University Press).

Aron, R. (1962) *Paix et Guerre entre les Nations* (Paris: Calmann-Lévy).

Arthur, B. (1988) 'Self-reinforcing Mechanisms in Economics' in P. W. Anderson, K. J. Arow, and D. Pines (eds), *The Economy as an Evolving Complex System* (Reading, MA: Addison Wesley).

Arthur, B. (1989) 'Competing Technologies, Increasing Returns, and Lock-in by Historical Events', *Economic Journal*, 99, 116–31.

Ashley, R. K. (1989) 'Living on Border Lines: Man, Poststructuralism, and War' in J. Der Derian and M. J. Shapiro (eds), *International/Intertextual Relations: Postmodern Readings of World Politics* (New York, NY: Lexington Books).

Ashworth, L. M. (1999) *Creating International Studies. Angell, Mitrany and the Liberal Tradition* (Aldershot: Ashgate).

Aspinwall, M. and Schneider, G. (2000) 'Same Menu, Separate Tables. The Institutionalist Turn in Political Science and the Study of European Integration', *European Journal of Political Research*, 38, 1–36.

Aspinwall, M. and Schneider, G. (eds), (2001) *The Rules of Integration: Institutionalist Approaches to the Study of Europe* (New York: Manchester University Press).

Attinà, F. (1990) 'The Voting Behaviour of European Parliamentary Members and the Problem of Europarties', *European Journal of Political Research*, 18, 557–79.

Attinà, F. (1992) *Il Sistema politico della Communità Europea* (Milan: Giuffrè).

Austin, J. L. (1975) *How to Do Things with Words: The William James Lectures Delivered at Harvard University in 1955*, ed. J. O. Urmson and M. Sbisà (London: Oxford University Press).

Austin, M. and Milner, H. V. (1999) 'Strategies of European standardization', *Journal of European Public Policy*, 8(3), 411–31.

Bache, I. and Flinders, M. (2004) 'Themes and Issues in Multi-level Governance', in I. Bache and M. Flinders (eds), *Multi-level Governance* (Oxford: Oxford University Press), 1–11.

Bachrach, P. and Baratz, M. (1962) 'The Two Faces of Power', *American Political Science Review*, 56, 947–52.

Badie, B. and Bimbaum, B. (1983 [1979]) *The Sociology of the State*, tr. A. Goldhammer (Chicago: Chicago University Press).

Balassa, B. (1961) *Theory of Economic Integration* (Homewood, IL: R. D. Irwin).

Balassa, B. (1965) *Economic Development and Integration* (Mexico City).

Baldwin, R. and McCrudden, C. (1987) *Regulation and Public Law* (London: Weidenfeld).

Barav, A. (1980) 'The Judicial Power of the European Economic Community', *Southern California Law Review*, 53, 461–525.

Bardi, L. (1994) 'Transnational Party Federations, European Parliamentary Party Group, and the Building of Europarties' in R. S. Katz and P. Mair (eds), *How Parties Organize: Adaptation and Change in Party Organization in Western Democracies* (London: Sage).

Bardi, L. (1996) 'Transnational Trends in European Parties and the 1994 Elections of the European Parliament', *Party Politics*, 2, 99–114.

Baron, E. (1989) *Europe 92: Le Rapt du Futur* (Europe 92: Kidnapping the future) (Paris: Edition Bernard Coutas).

Bates, R. (1987) 'Contra Contractarianism: Some Reflections on the New Institutionalism', *Politics and Society* 16, 387–401.

Bates, R. and Lien, H.D. (1985) 'A Note on Taxation, Development and Representative government' *Politics and Society*, 14, 53–70.

Baun, M. J. (1996) *An Imperfect Union: The Maastrict Treaty and the New Politics of European Integration* (Boulder, CO: Westview Press).

Bay-Brzinski, B. (1995) 'Political Group Cohesion in the European Parliament, 1989–1994' in C. Rhodes and S. Mazey (eds), *The State of the European Union*, vol. 3 (London: Longman).

Beach, D. (2005) *The Dynamics of European Integration: Why and When EU Institutions Matter* (Basingstoke: Palgrave Macmillan).

Begg, I. (1996) 'Introduction: Regulation in the European Union', *Journal of European Public Policy*, 3, 525–35.

Bettati, M. (1989) 'Le "law-making power" de la Cour', *Pouvoirs*, 48, 57–70.

Bickel, A. (1970) *The Supreme Court and the Idea of Progress* (New York: Harper & Row).

Bieber, R., Pantalis, J. and Schoo, J. (1986) 'Implications of the Single Act for the European Parliament', *Common Market Law Review*, 23, 767–92.

Binmore, K. and Dasgupta, P. (1987) *The Economics of Bargaining* (Oxford: Blackwell).

Bogdanor, V. (1986) 'The Future of the European Community: Two Models of Democracy', *Government and Opposition*, 21, 161–76.

Bomberg, E. (1994) 'Policy Networks on the Periphery: EU Environmental Policy and Scotland' *Regional Politics and Policy*, 4, 45–61.

Brickman, R., Jasanoff, S. and Ilgen, T. (1985) *Controlling Chemicals* (Ithaca, NY: Cornell University Press).

Brown, N. L. and Jacobs, F. (1977) *The Court of Justice of the European Communities* (London: Sweet and Maxwell).

Buchanan, J. M. and Tullock, G. (1962) *The Calculus of Consent: Logical Foundations of Constitutional Democracy* (Ann Arbor, MI: University of Michigan Press).

Buchanan, W. and Cantril, H. (1953) *How Nations See Each Other* (Urbana, IL: University of Illinois Press).

Bueno de Mesquita, B. and Stokman, F. N. (eds) (1994) *European Community Decision-Making: Models, Applications and Comparisons* (Yale: Yale University Press).

Buitendijk, G. J. and van Schendelen, M. P. (1995) 'Brussels Advisory Committees: A Channel for Influence', *European Law Review*, 20, 37–56.

Bulmer, S. (1983) 'Domestic Politics and European Community Policy-Making', *Journal of Common Market Studies*, 21(4), 349–63.

Bulmer, S. (1994) 'The Governance of the EU: A New Institutionalist Approach', *Journal of Public Policy*, 23(4), 351–80.

Bulmer, S. (1998) 'New Institutionalism and the Governance of the Single European Market', *Journal of European Public Policy*, 5(3), 365–86.

Burgess, M. (1989) *Federalism and European Union: Political Ideas, Influences and Strategies in the European Community, 1972–1987* (London: Routledge).

Burgess, M. (2000) *Federalism and the European Union: The Building of Europe, 1950–2000* (London: Routledge).

Burley, A-M. (1992) 'Liberal States: A Zone of Law', presented at the annual meeting of the American Political Science Association, Chicago, 3–6 September.

Burley, A. M. and Mattli, W. (1993) 'Europe Before the Court: A Political Theory of Legal Integration', *International Organization*, 47(1), 41–76.

Buzan, B. (1991) *People, States and Fear: An Agenda for International Security Studies in the Post-Cold War Era*, 2nd edn (London: Harvester-Wheatsheaf).

Buzan, B., Wæver, O. and de Wilde, J. (1998) *Security: A New Framework for Analysis* (Boulder, CO: Lynne Rienner).

Cameron, D. (1992) 'The 1992 Initiative: Causes and Consequences' in Sbragia, A. (ed.) *Euro-Politics: Institutions and Policymaking in the 'New' European Community* (Washington, D. C: The Brookings Institution).

Caplow T. and Finsterbusch, K. (1968) 'France and Other Countries: A Study of International Interaction', *The Journal of Conflict Resolution*, 12(1), 1–15.

Caporaso, J. (1971) 'Theory and Method in the Study of International Integration', *International Organization*, 25(2), 228–53.

Caporaso, J. (1996) 'The European Union and Forms of State: Westphalian, Regulatory, or Post-Modern', *Journal of Common Market Studies*, 34(1), 29–52.

Caporaso, J. (1998a) 'Regional Integration Theory: Understanding our Past and Anticipating our Future', *Journal of European Public Policy*, 5, 1–16.

Caporaso, J. (1998b) 'Regional Integration Theory: Understanding Our Past and Anticipating Our Future' in W. Sandholtz and A. Stone Sweet (eds), *European Integration and Supranational Governance* (Oxford: Oxford University Press).

Caporaso, J. and Keeler, J. (1993) *The European Community and Regional Integration Theory*, paper presented at the Third Biennial International Conference of the European Community Studies Association, Washington, DC, 27–29 May.

Caporaso, J. and Keeler, J. (1995) 'The European Community and Regional Integration Theory' in Rhodes, C. and Mazey, S. (eds), *The State of the European Union: Building European Unity?* (Boulder, CO: Lynne Reinner).

Cappelletti, M., Secombe, M. and Weiler, J. H. (eds) (1986) *Integration Through Law: Europe and the American Federal Experience* (Berlin: Walter de Gruyter).

Carr, E. H. (1939) *The Twenty Years' Crisis, 1919–1939* (New York: Harper & Row).

Carr, E. H. (1965[1945]) *Nationalism and After* (London: Macmillan).

Cecchini, P. (1988) *The European Challenge, 1992: The Benefits of a Single Market* (Hounslow, UK: Wildwood House).

Checkel, J. (1997a) *Ideas and International Political Change: Soviet/Russian Behavior and the End of the Cold War* (New Haven, CT: Yale University Press).

Checkel, J. (1997b) 'International Norms and Domestic Politics: Bridging the Rationalist–Constructivist Divide', *European Journal of International Relations*, 3, 473–95.

Checkel, J. (1998) 'The Constructivist Turn in International Relations Theory', *World Politics*, 50(2), 324–48.

Checkel, J. (1999a) 'International Institutions and Socialization', paper presented at the International Studies Association Annual Convention, 1999.

Checkel, J. (1999b) 'Norms, Institutions and National Identity in Contemporary Europe', *International Studies Quarterly*, 43, 83–114.

Checkel, J. (1999c) 'Social Construction and Integration', *Journal of European Public Policy*, 6(4), 545–60.

Checkel, J. (2001) 'A Constructivist Research Programme in EU Studies? *European Union Politics*, 2(2), 219–49.

Checkel. J. (2003) 'Social Constructivisms in Global and European Politics: A Review Essay', Arena Working Papers 15/03, Oslo.

Checkel. J. (2004) 'Social Constructivisms in Global and European Politics: A Review Essay', *Review of International Studies*, 30(2), 229–44.

Christiansen, T. (1997) 'Reconstructing European Space: From Territorial Politics to Multilevel Governance' in K. E. Jørgensen (ed.) *Reflective Approaches to European Governance* (Basingstoke, UK: Macmillan), 51–68.

Christiansen, T., Jørgensen K. and Wiener, A. (1999) 'The Social Construction of Europe', *Journal of European Public Policy*, 6(4), 528–44.

Christiansen, T., Jørgensen, K. E. and Wiener, A. (eds), (2001) *The Social Construction of Europe* (London: Sage).

Chryssochoou, D. N. (1994) 'Democracy and Symbiosis in the European Union: Towards a Confederal Consociation?', *West European Politics*, 17, 1–14.

Chryssochoou, D. N. (1996) 'Europe's Could-be Demos: Recasting the Debate', *West European Politics*, 19, 787–801.

Claude, I. (1956) *Swords Into Plowshares: The Problems of Progress of International Organization* (London: University of London Press).

Cohen, S. (1983) 'Informed Bewilderment' in Cohen, S. and Gourevitch, P. (eds), *France in a Troubled World Economy* (London: Butterworth).

Connolly, W. E. (1983) *The Terms of Political Discourse* (Princeton, NJ: Princeton University Press).

Cooley, A. (2003) 'Thinking Rationally about Hierarchy and Global Governance', *Review of International Political Economy*, 10(4), 672–84.

Cooper, R. N. (1972) 'Economic Interdependence and Foreign Policy in the Seventies' *World Politics*, 24, 159–81.

Cooper, R. N. (1986) 'Interdependence and Co-ordination of Policies' in R. N. Cooper, (ed.) *Economic Policy in an Interdependent World: Essays in World Economics* (Cambridge, MA: MIT Press).

Corbey, D. (1995) 'Dialectical Functionalism: Stagnation as a Booster of European Integration', *International Organization*, 49(2), 253–84.

Cornett, L. and Caporaso, J. (1992) 'And it still moves! State Interests and Social Forces in the European Community' in Rosenau, J. and Czempiel, E-O. (eds), *Governance without Government: Order and Change in World Politics* (Cambridge: Cambridge University Press).

Coudenhove-Kalergi, R. N. (1923) *Pan-Europe* (Vienna: Pan-Europa-verlag).

Cram, L. (1997) *Policy-Making in the European Union; Conceptual Lenses and the Integration Process* (London: Routledge).

Crombez ,C. (1996) 'Legislative Procedures in the European Community', *British Journal of Political Science*, 26, 199–218.

Curtin, D. (1990) 'Directives: The Effectiveness of Judicial Protection of Individual Rights', *Common Market Law Review*, 22, 709–39.

Dahl, R. A. (1961) 'The Behavioral Approach in Political Science: Epitaph for a Monument to a Successful Protest', *American Political Science Review*, 55, 763–72.

Danielson, M. N. (1976) *The Politics of Exclusion* (New York: Columbia University Press).

David, P. (1985) 'Clio and the Economics of QWERTY', *American Economic Review* 75, 332–7.

Debre, M. (1960) 'Statement Made by Michel Debre at Metz on 2 October 1960' in *France and the European Community*, occasional paper 11 (London: Political & Economic Planning, January 30 1961).

De Gaulle, C. (1960) 'Statement by de Gaulle at his Paris Conference of 5 September 1960' in *France and the European Community*, occasional paper 11 (London: Political & Economic Planning, January 30 1961).

Dehousse, R. (1994) 'Community Competences: Are there Limits to Growth?' in R. Dehousse, (ed), *Europe after Maastricht: An Ever Closer Union* (Munich: Beck).

Dehousse, R. (1995) 'Institutional Reform in the European Community: Are there Alternatives to the Majoritarian Avenue?', in J. Hayward (ed.), *The Crisis of Representation in Europe* (London: Frank Cass).

Dehousse, R. (1997) 'Regulation by Networks in the European Community: The Role of European Agencies', *Journal of European Public Policy*, 4(2), 246–61.

Deniau, J. F. (1960) *The Common Market: Its Structure and Purpose* (London: Barrie & Rockliff).

Derrida, J. (1977) 'Limited inc. abc . . .' , *Glyph*, 2, 162–254.

Destler, I. M. (1986) *American Trade Politics: Systems Under Stress* (New York: Institute for International Economics).

Deutsch, K. W. (1953a) *Nationalism and Social Communication. An Inquiry into the Foundations of Nationality* (Boston: The Technology Press of the MIT).

Deutsch, K. W. (1953b) 'The Growth of Nations: Some Recurrent Patterns of Political and Social Integration', *World Politics*, (January), 168–196.

Deutsch, K. W. (1954) *Political Community at the International Level: Problems of Definition and Measurement* (Garden City, NY: Doubleday).

Deutsch, K. W. (1956) 'Shifts in the Balance of Communication Flows: A Problem of Measurement in International Relations', *Public Opinion Quarterly*, 20(1), 143–60.

Deutsch, K. W. (1966) 'Integration and Arms Control in the European Political Environment', *American Political Science Review*, 60(2), 428–45.

Deutsch, K. W. et al. (1957a) *Political Community and the North Atlantic Area: International Organization in the Light of Historical Experience* (Princeton: Princeton University Press).

Deutsch, K. W. et al (1957b) *Political Community at the International Level: Problems of Definition and Measurement* (Garden City, NY: Doubleday).

Deutsch, K. W. et al. (1967) *France, Germany and the Western Alliance* (New York: Scribner).

Deutsch, K. W. (1969) *Nationalism and its Alternatives* (New York: Alfred A. Knopf).

De Vree, J. K. (1972) *Political Integration: The Formation of Theory and its Problems* (The Hague: Mouton).

Diebold, W. (1955) 'The Relevance of Federalism to Western European Economic Integration' in A. Macmahon, (ed.) *Federalism Mature and Emergent* (Garden City, NY: Doubleday), 433–57.

Diez, T. (1997) 'International Ethics and European Integration: Federal State or Network Horizon?', *Alternatives, 22,* 287–312.

Diez, T. (1998a) 'Discursive Nodal Points and the Analysis of European Integration Policy', paper presented at the Third Pan-European Conference on International Relations, 1998.

Diez, T. (1998b) 'The Economic Community Reading of Europe: Its Discursive Nodal Points and Ambiguities towards "Westphalia", COPRI working paper 6 (Copenhagen).

Diez, T. (1999) 'Speaking "Europe": The Politics of Integration Discourse', *Journal of European Public Policy,* 6(4), 652–68.

Diez, T. (2001) 'Europe as a Discursive Battleground: European Integration Studies and Discourse Analysis', *Cooperation and Conflict,* 36(1), 5–38.

DiMaggio, P. and Powell, W. (eds) (1991) *The New Institutionalism in Organizational Analysis* (Chicago: University of Chicago Press).

Dinan, D. (1994) *An Ever Closer Union? An Introduction to the European Community* (Basingstoke, UK: Macmillan).

Dixit, A. and Nalebuff, B. (1991) *Thinking Strategically: The Competitive Edge in Business, Politics and Everyday Life* (New York: Norton).

Dobbin, F. (1994) 'Cultural Models of Organization: The Social Construction of Rational Organizing Principles' in D. Crane (ed.), *The Sociology of Culture: Emerging Theoretical Perspectives* (Oxford: Blackwell).

Docksey, C. and Williams, K. (1997) 'The Commission and the Execution of Community policy' in G. Edwards and J. Spence (eds), *The European Commission,* 2nd edn (London: Catermill).

Dogan, R. (1997) 'Comitology: Little Procedures with Big Implications', *West European Politics,* 20, 31–60.

Dowding, K. (2000) 'Institutional Research on the European Union: A Critical Review', *European Union Politics,* 1(1), 125–144.

Dreyfus, H. and Rabinow, P. (1982) Michel Foucault: Beyond Structuralism and Hermeneutics (Chicago: University of Chicago Press).

Duina, F. (2006) The Social Construction of Free Trade: The European Union, NAFTA and Mercusor (Princeton, NJ: Princeton University Press).

Dumon, F. (1976) La Jurisprudence de la Cour de Justice. Examen Critique des Methodes d'interpretation (Luxembourg: Office for Official Publications of the European Communities).

Dyson, K. (1992) 'Theories of Regulation in the Case of Germany: A model of Regulatory Change' in K. Dyson (ed), *The Politics of German Regulation* (Aldershot, UK: Darthmouth), 1–28.

Earnshaw, D. and Judge, D. (1995) 'Early Days: The European Parliament, co-decision and the European Union Legislative Process post-Maastricht', *Journal of European Public Policy,* 2, 624–49.

Easton, D. (1953) *The Political System* (New York: Knopf).

Easton (1961) 'An Approach to Analysis of Political Systems', in R. C. Macridis, and B. E. Brown, (eds), *Comparative Politics* (Homewood, IL: Dorsey Press).

Eichenberg, R. C. and Dalton, R. J. (1993) 'Europeans and the European Community: The Dynamics of Public Support for European integration', *International Organization,* 47, 507–34.

Eichenberg, R. C. and Dalton, R. J. (1995) 'Europeans and the European Community: The Dynamics of Public Support for European integration', *International Organization,* 47, 507–34.

Eichener, V. (1992) 'Social Dumping or Innovative Regulation? Processes and Outcomes of European Decision-making in the Sector of Health and Safety at Work Harmonization', European University Institute Working Paper 92–28.

Eijk, C. van der and Franklin, M. (eds), (1996) *Choosing Europe? The European*

Electorate and National Politics in the Face of Union (Ann Arbor, MI: Michigan University Press).

Eijk, C. van der, Franklin, M. and Marsh, M. (1996) 'What Voters Teach us about Europe-wide Elections: What Europe-wide Elections Teach us about Voters', *Electoral Studies*, 15, 149–66.

Eilstrup-Sangiovanni, M. and Verdier, D. (2005) 'European Integration as a Solution to War', *European Journal of International Relations*, 45(4), 193–206.

Elazar, D. J. (1987) *Exploring Federalism* (Tuscaloosa, AL: University of Alabama Press).

Elazar, D. J. (1998) *Constitutionalizing Globalization. The Postmodern Revival of Confederal Arrangements* (Boston, MA: Rowman & Littlefield).

Elster, J. (ed.) (1986) *Rational Choice* (New York: New York University Press).

Emerson, M. (1988) *1992 and After* (Brussels: EEC).

Emerson, R. (1962) *From Empire to Nation* (Cambridge, MA: Harvard University Press).

Endo, K. (1994) 'The Principle of Subsidiarity: From Johannes Althusius to Jacques Delors', *Hokkaido Law Review*, 44, 552–652.

Etzioni, A. (1964) *Political Unification: A Comparative Study of Leaders and Forces* (New York: Holt, Rinehart and Winter).

Europe 1990 (Brussels: Chez Philips S.A., no date).

Everling, U. (1981) 'Das Europiiische Gemeinschaftsrecht im Spannungsfeld von Politik und Wirtschaft', in W. G. Grewe, H. Rupp, and H. Schneider (eds), *Europiiische Gerichtsbarkeit und nationale Verfassungsgerichtsbarkeit Festschrift zum 70. Geburtstag von Hans Kutscher* (Baden-Baden: Nomos), 155–87.

Everling, U. (1984a) 'The Member States of the European Community Before Their Court of Justice', *European Law Review*, 9, 215–41.

Everling, U. (1984b) 'Europaische Politik durch Europaisches Recht?', *EG-Magazin*, (February).

Everling, U. (1984c) 'The Court of Justice as a Decisionmaking Authority', *Michigan Law Review*, 82, 1294–1310.

Everson, M. (1995) 'Independent Agencies: Hierarchy Beaters?', *European Law Journal*, 1, 180–204.

Falkner, G. (1997) 'Corporatist Governance and Europeanisation: No Future in the Multi-level Game?', *European Integration Online Papers*, vol. 1 (http://eiop.or.at/eiop/index.php/eiop).

Feldstein, H. S. (1967) 'A Study of Transaction and Political Integration: Transnational Labour Flow Within the European Economic Community', *Journal of Common Market Studies*, 6(1), 24–55.

Finnemore, M. (1996a) *National Interests in International Society* (Ithaca, NY: Cornell University Press).

Finnemore, M. (1996b) 'Norms, Culture and World Politics: Insights from Sociology's Institutionalism', *International Organization* 50, 325–47.

Finnemore, M. and Sikkink, K. (1998) 'International Norm Dynamics and Political Change', *International Organization*, 52, 887–918.

Fisher, W. E. (1969) 'An Analysis of the Deutsch Sociocausal Paradigm of Political Integration', *International Organization*, 23(2), 254–90.

Forman, C. (1988) 'European Firms Hope Swapping Stakes Gives Them 1992 Poison Pill Protection', *Wall Street Journal*, 18 October.

Forsyth, M. (1996) 'The Political Theory of Federalism: The Relevance of Classical Approaches' in J. Hesse and V. Wright (eds), *Federalizing Europe? The Costs, Benefits, and Preconditions of Federal Political Systems* (Oxford: Oxford University Press).

Foucault, M. (1984) 'The Order of Discourse' in M. J. Shapiro (ed.), *Language and Politics* (Cambridge, MA: Blackwell).

Foucault, M. (1991) 'Politics and the Study of Discourse' in G. Burchell, C. Gordon and

P. Miller (eds), *The Foucault Effect: Studies in Governmentality* (Hemel Hempstead, UK: Harvester Wheatsheaf).

Frank, I. (1961) *The European Common Market: An Analysis of Commercial Policy* (New York: Praeger).

Frank, M. (1983) *Was ist Neostrukturalismus?* (Frankfurt: Suhrkamp).

Franklin, M., Mackie, T. and Valen, H. (1992) *Electoral Change: Responses to Evolving Social and Attitudinal Structures in Western Countries* (Cambridge: Cambridge University Press).

Franklin, M., Eijk, C. van der and Marsh, M. (1994) 'Referendum Outcomes and Trust in Government: Public Support for Europe in the Wake of Maastricht', in J. Hayward (ed.), *The Crisis of Representation in Europe* (London: Frank Cass).

Freedman, J. O. (1978) Crisis and Legitimacy: The Administrative Process and American Government (Cambridge: Cambridge University Press).

Frieden, J. A. (1991a) *Debt, Development and Democracy: Modern Political Economy and Latin America* (Princeton, NJ: Princeton University Press).

Frieden, J. A. (1991b) 'Invested Interests: The Politics of National Economic Policies in a World of Global Finance', *International Organization*, 45, 425–52.

Friedrich, C. J. (1953) *Man and His Government. An Empirical Theory of Politics* (New York: McGraw Hill).

Friedrich, C. J. (1964) 'International Federalism in Theory and Practice' in E. Plischke, (ed.), *Systems of Integrating the International Community*, 117–55.

Friis, L. (1998) 'Approaching the "Third Half" of EU Grand Bargaining—The Post-negotiation Phase of the "Europe Agreement game"', *Journal of European Public Policy*, 5(2), 322–38.

From, J. and Stava, P. (1993) 'Implementation of Community Law: The Last Stronghold of National Control?' in S. S. Andesen and K. A. Eliassen (eds), *Making Policy in Europe: The Europeification of National Policy-Making* (London: Sage).

Gabel, M. (1997) *Interests and Integration: Market Liberalization, Public Opinion, and European Union* (Ann Arbor, MI: Michigan University Press).

Gabel, M. and Hix, S. (1997) 'The Ties that Bind: The European Parliament and the Commission President Investiture Procedure', unpublished mimeo.

Gabel, M. and Palmer, H. (1995) 'Understanding Variation in Public Support for European Integration', *European Journal of Political Research*, 27, 3–19.

Garrett, G. (1992a) 'International Cooperation and Institutional Choice: The European Community's Internal Market', *International Organization*, 46(2), 533–560.

Garrett, G. (1992b) 'Power Politics and European Integration' (Stanford, CA: Unpublished MS).

Garrett, G. (1995) 'The Politics of Legal Integration in the European Union', *International Organization*, 49(1), 171–81.

Garrett, G. and Lange, P. (1994) 'Internationalization, Institutions, and Political Change', unpublished MS.

Garrett, G. and Tsebelis, G. (1996) 'An Institutional Critique of Intergovernmentalism', *International Organization*, 50(2), 269–99.

Garrett, G. and Weingast, B. (1991) 'Interests and Institutions: Constructing the EC's Internal Market', paper presented at the American Political Science Association Meeting, September.

Garrett, G. and Weingast, B. (1993) 'Ideas, Interests, and Institutions: Constructing the European Community's Internal Market' in J. Goldstein, R. O. Keohane, *Ideas and Foreign Policy* (eds), (Ithaca, NY: Cornell University Press), 173–206.

Garrett, G. and Kelemen, R. and Schulz, H. (1998) 'The European Court of Justice, National Governments, and Legal Integration in the European Union', *International Organization*, 52(1), 149–76.

Gatsios, K. and Seabright, P. (1989) 'Regulation in the European Community', *Oxford Review of Economic Policy*, 5(2), 37–60.

Gehrels, F. and Johnston, B. F. (1955) 'The Economic Gains of European Integration' *Journal of Political Economy*, (August) 275–92.

George, S. (1996) *Politics and Policies in the European Union*, 3rd edn (Oxford: Oxford University Press).

George, S. (2004) 'Multi-level Governance and the European Union' in I. Bache and M. Flinders (eds), *Multi-Level Governance* (Oxford: Oxford University Press), 107–26.

Giddens, A. (1984) *The Constitution of Society: Outline of a Theory of Structuration* (Cambridge: Polity Press).

Goetz, K. (1994) 'National Governance and European Integration: Intergovernmental Relations in Germany', *Journal of Common Market Studies* 33, 91–116.

Goldman, G. (1993) 'National Courts, Governments, and the European Court of Justice: A Bargaining Model of EC Legal Integration', mimeograph (Stanford, CA: Stanford University).

Goldstein, J. (1993) *Ideas, Interests and American Trade Policy* (Ithaca, NY: Cornell University Press).

Gormley, L. (1990) 'Recent Case Law on the Free Movement of Goods: Some Hot Potatoes', *Common Market Law Review*, 27, 825–57.

Gourevitch, P. (1978) 'The Second Image Reversed', *International Organization*, 32, 881–912.

Gourevitch, P. (1986) *Politics in Hard Times: Comparative Responses to International Economic Crises* (Ithaca, NY: Cornell University Press).

Gowa, J. (1994) *Allies, Adversaries and International Trade* (Princeton, NJ: Princeton University Press).

Grahl, J. and Teague, P. (1989) 'The Cost of Neo-liberal Europe', *New Left Review* 17, 33–50.

Green, A. W. (1969) *Political Integration by Jurisprudence* (Leiden: Sijthoff).

Green, D. P. and Shapiro, I. (1994) *Pathologies of Rational Choice: A Critique of Applications in Political Science* (New Haven, CT: Yale).

Greider, W. (1982) *The Education of David Stockman and other Americans* (New York: Dutton).

Grieco, J. M. (1988) 'Anarchy and the Limits of Cooperation: A Realist Critique of the Newest Liberal Institutionalism', *International Organization*, 42(3) 485–507.

Grieco, J. M. (1995) 'The Maastricht Treaty, Economic and Monetary Union and the Neo-Realist Research Programme', *Review of International Studies*, 21(1), 21–40.

Grieco, J. M (1999) 'Realism and Regionalism: American Power and German and Japanese Institutional Strategies During and After the Cold War' in E. Kapstein and M. Mastanduno (eds), *Unipolar Politics: Realism and State Strategies After the Cold War* (New York: Columbia University Press).

Groom, A. J. R. and Taylor, P. (eds) (1975) *Functionalism. Theory and Practice in International Relations* (London: University of London Press).

Grosser, A. (1965) *La politique exterieure de la V Republique* (Paris: Seuil).

Guédon, M-J. (1991) *Les Authorités Administratives Indépendantes* (Paris: Librairie Générale de Droit et de Jurisprudence).

Guetzkow, H. (1955) *Multiple Loyalties: Theoretical Approach to a Problem in International Organisation* (Princeton: Centre for Research on World Political Institutions, publication no. 4).

Haas, E. B. (1958a) *The Uniting of Europe: Political, Social and Economic Forces 1950–1957* (London: Stevens and Sons).

Haas, E. B. (1958b) 'The Challenge of Regionalism', *International Organization*, 12(4), 440–58.

Haas, E. B. (1958c) 'Persistent Themes in Atlantic and European Unity', *World Politics*, 10, 614–29.

Haas, E. B. (1960) *Consensus Formation in the Council of Europe* (Berkeley: University of California Press).

Haas, E. B. (1961) 'International Integration: The European and the Universal Process', *International Organization*, 15(3), 366–92.

Haas, E. B. (1964) *Beyond the Nation-State: Functionalism and International Organization* (Stanford, CA: Stanford University Press).

Haas, E. B. (1966) 'International Integration: The European and the Universal Process', in *International Political Communities: An Anthology* (New York: Doubleday), 91–130.

Haas, E. B. (1967) 'The Uniting of Europe and the Uniting of Latin America', *Journal of Common Market Studies*, 5(4), 315–43.

Haas, E. B. (1968) *The Uniting of Europe: Political, Social and Economic Forces 1950–1957*, 2nd edn (Stanford, CA: Stanford University Press).

Haas, E. B. (1970) 'The Study of Regional Integration: Reflections on the Joy and Anguish of Pretheorizing', *International Organization*, 24(4), 607–46.

Haas, E. B. (1971) 'The Study of Regional Integration: Reflections on the Joy and Anguish of Pretheorizing', in L. Lindberg and S. Scheingold (eds), *Regional IntegrationL Theory and Research* (Cambridge, MA: Harvard University Press).

Haas, E. B. (1975) 'The Obsolesence of Regional Integration Theory' (Berkeley: Institute of International Studies).

Haas, E. B. (1976) 'Turbulent Fields and the Theory of Regional Integration', *International Organization*, 30(2), 173–212.

Haas, E. B. (1980) 'Why Collaborate? Issue-Linkage and International Regimes', *World Politics*, 32(2), 357–405.

Haas, E. B. (1982) 'Words Can Hurt You; Or, Who Said What About Regimes?', *International Organization*, 36(2), 141–72.

Haas, E. B. (1990) 'Reason and Change in International Life – Justifying a Hypothesis', *Journal of International Affairs*, 44(1), 209–40.

Haas, E. B. (2001) 'Does Constructivism Subsume Neofunctionalism?' in T. Christiansen, K. Jørgensen and A. Wiener (eds), *The Social Construction of Europe* (London: Sage), 22–31.

Haas, E. B (2004) 'Introduction: Institutionalism or Constructivism?' in E. B. Haas, *The Uniting of Europe: Politics, Social and Economic Forces 1950–1957*, 3rd ed. (Notre Dame, IN: University of Notre Dame Press).

Haas, E. B. and Schmitter, P. (1964) 'Economics and Differential Patterns of Political Integration: Projections about Unity in Latin America', *International Organization*, 18(4), 705–37.

Haas, E. B. and Schmitter, P. (1965–66) *The Politics of Economics in Latin American Regionalism: The Latin American Free Trade Association after Four Years of Operation*, monograph series in world affairs, III (Denver).

Haas, E. B. and Whiting, A. S. (1956) *Dynamics of International Relations* (New York: McGraw-Hill).

Haas, P. (1990) *Saving the Mediterranean: The Politics of International Environmental Cooperation* (New York: Columbia University Press).

Haas, P. (1992) 'Knowledge, Power and International Policy Coordination', *International Organization*, 46, special issue.

Habermas, J. (1984) *The Theory of Communicative Action*, vol. 1: *Reason and the Rationalization of Society* (Boston: Beacon Press).

Habermas, J. (1990) *Moral Consciousness and Communicative Action* (Cambridge: Polity Press).

Habermas, J. (1992a) 'Citizenship and National Identity: Some Reflections on the Future of Europe', *Praxis International*, 12, 1–19.

Habermas, J. (1992b) 'Staatsbürgerschaft und nationale Identität' in J. Habermas (ed.), *Faktizität und Geltung: Beiträge zur Diskurstheorie des Rechts und des demokratischen Rechtsstaats* (Frankfurt: Suhrkamp), 632–60.

Habermas, J. (1997 [1995]) 'Reply to Grimm' in P. Gowan and P. Andeson (eds), *The Question of Europe* (London: Verso).

Hall, P. (1986) *Governing the Economy: The Politics of State Intervention in Britain and France* (Cambridge, UK: Polity Press).

Hall, P. (ed.) (1987) 'European Labor in the 1980s', *International Journal of Political Economy*, 17.

Hall, P. (1993) 'Policy Paradigms, Social Learning and the State: The Case of Economic Policymaking in Britain', *Comparative Politics*, 25, 279–96.

Hall, P. and Taylor, R. (1994) 'Political Science and the Four New Institutionalisms', paper presented at the American Political Science Association Meeting, New York.

Hall, P. and Taylor, R. (1996) 'Political Science and the Three New Institutionalisms', *Political Studies*, 44(5), 936–57.

Hansard (1961) Parliamentary Debates, House of Commons, Official Report, Fifth Series, vol. 645 (2–3 August): European Economic Community.

Hansen, R. (1967) *Central America: Regional Integration and Economic Development* (Washington).

Hansen, R. (1969) 'Regional Integration: Reflections on a Decade of Theoretical Efforts', *World Politics*, 21(2), 242–71.

Harsanyi, J. (1977) *Rational Behavior and Bargaining Equilibrium in Games and Social Situations* (Cambridge: Cambridge University Press).

Hassner, P. (1965) 'Nationalisme et relations internationales', *Revue francaise de science politique*, XV(3), 499–528.

Hattam, V. (1993) *Labour Visions and State Power: The Origins of Business Unionism in the United States* (Princeton, NJ: Princeton University Press).

Hayes-Renshaw, F. and Wallace, H. (1997) *The Council of Ministers* (London: Macmillan).

Heidenheimer, A. J. Heclo, J. H. and Adams, C. T. (1990) *Comparative Public Policy: The Politics of Social Choice in America, Europe, and Japan*, 3rd edn (New York: St Martins).

Hejl, P. M. (1987) 'Konstruktion der sozialen Konstruktion: Grundlinien einer konstruktivistischen Sozialtheorie' in S. J. Schmidt (ed.), *Der Diskurs des radikalen Konstruktivismus* (Frankfurt: Suhrkamp), 303–39.

Heritier, A. (ed.) (1993a) *Policy-Analyse: Kritik und Neuorientierung* (Opladen, Germany: Westdeutscher Verlag).

Heritier, A. (1993b) 'Policy-Netzwerkanalyse als Untersuchungsinstrument im europäischen kontext: Folgerungen aus einer empirischen Studie regulativer Politik' in A. Heritier (ed.), *Policy-Analyse: Kritik und Neuorientierung* (Opladen, Germany: Westdeutscher Verlag).

Hettne, B. and Söderbaum, F. (2000) 'Theorising the Rise of Regionness', *New Political Economy* 5(3), 457–73.

Hettne, B., Inotai, A. and Sunkel, O. (eds) (1999) *Globalism and the New Regionalism* (Basingstoke, UK: Macmillan).

Hillman, A. L. (1989) *The Political Economy of Protection* (New York: Harwood).

Hindess, B. (1996) *Discourses of Power: From Hobbes to Foucault* (Cambridge, MA: Blackwell).

Hirsch, F. (1977) *The Social Limits to Growth* (Cambridge, MA: Harvard University Press).

Hirschman, A. (1970) *Exit, Voice, and Loyalty-responses to Decline in Firms, Organizations, and States* (Cambridge, MA: Harvard University Press).

Hix, S. (1994) 'The Study of the European Community: The Challenge to Comparative Politics', *West European Politics*, 17(1), 1–30.

Hix, S. (1995) 'Parties at the European Level and the Legitimacy of EU Socio-Economic Policy', *Journal of Common Market Studies*, 33, 527–54.

Hix, S. (1996a) 'The Transnational Party Federations' in J. Gaffney (ed.), *Political Parties and the European Union* (London: Routledge).

Hix, S. (1996b) 'CP, IR and the EU! A Rejoinder to Hurrell and Menon', *West European Politics*, 19(4), 802–4.

Hix, S. (1998) 'The Study of the European Union II: The "New Governance" Agenda and Its Rival', *Journal of European Public Policy*, 5(1), 38–65.

Hix, S. (2001) 'Legislative Behaviour and Party Competition in European Parliament: An Application of Nominate to the EU', *Journal of Common Market Studies*, 39(4), 663–88.

Hix, S. (2002) 'Parties at the European Level' in P. Webb, D Farrell, and I. Holliday (eds), *Political Parties in Advanced Industrial Democracies* (Oxford University Press), 280–309.

Hix, S. (2005) *The Political System of the European Union*, 2nd edn (Basingstoke, UK: Palgrave).

Hix, S. and Lord, C. (1997) *Political Parties in the European Union* (London: Macmillan).

Hodges, M. (ed.) (1972) *European Integration. Selected Readings* (Harmondsworth, UK: Penguin Books).

Hoffmann, S. (1963) 'Discord in Community: The North Atlantic Area as a Partial International System', *International Organization*, 17(3), 521–49.

Hoffmann, S. (1965a) 'Rousseau on War and Peace' in S. Hoffmann (ed.) *The State of War* (New York: Pall Mall).

Hoffmann, S. (1965b) 'The European Process of Atlantic Cross Purposes', *Journal of Common Market Studies*, 3(2), 85–101.

Hoffmann, S. (1966) 'Obstinate or Obsolete? The Fate of the Nation-state and the Case of Western Europe', *Daedalus*, 95(3), 862–915.

Hoffmann, S. (1982) 'Reflections on the Nation-state in Western Europe Today', *Journal of Common Market Studies*, 21(1–2), 21–37.

Hoffman, S. and Keohane, R. (eds) (1991) *The New European Community: Decision-making and Institutional Change* (Boulder, CO: Westview Press).

Hoffmann et al. (1963) 'Paradoxes of the French Political Community' in S. Hoffmann et al., *In Search of France* (Cambridge, MA: Harvard University Press).

Hollis, M. and Smith, S. (1990) *Explaining and Understanding International Relations* (Oxford: Clarendon Press).

Holm, U. (1997) 'The French Garden is no Longer What it Used to Be' in K. E. Jørgensen (ed.), *Reflective Approaches to European Governance* (Basingstoke, UK: Macmillan), 128–45.

Hooghe, L. (1995a) 'Subnational Mobilisation in the European Union', *West European Politics*, 18, 175–98.

Hooghe, L. (1995b) 'Belgian Federalism and the European Community' in M. Keating and B. Jones (eds), *Regions in the European Union* (Oxford: Clarendon Press), 135–66.

Hooghe, L. (ed.) (1996) *Cohesion Policy and European Integration: Building Multi-level Governance* (Oxford: Oxford University Press).

Hooghe, L. (1997) 'Serving "Europe": Political Orientations of Senior Commission Officials', *European Integration Online Papers* (http://eiop.or.at/eiop/texte/1997-008a.htm).

Hooghe, L. (2003) 'The Renaissance of European Integration Studies', unpublished paper (www.unc.edu/~hooghe/downloads/Europeanintegration.pdf).

Hooghe, L. and Marks, G. (1996) 'Territorial Restructuring in the European Union: Regional Pressures' in S. Cassese and V. Wright (eds), *La restructuration de l' Etat dans les pays d'Europe occidentale* (Paris: Editions La Decouverte, Collection 'Recherches').

Hooghe, L. and Marks, G. (1997) 'The Making of a Polity: The Struggle over European Integration', *European Integration Online Papers* (http://eiop.or.at/eiop/texte/1997-004a.htm).

Hooghe, L. and Marks, G. (1999) 'The Making of a Policy' in H. Kitschelt, G. Marks and J. Stephens (eds), *Continuity and Change in Contemporary Capitalism* (New York: Cambridge University Press).

Hooghe, L. and Marks, G. (2001a) *Multi-level Governance and European Integration* (Lanham, MD: Rowman and Littlefield).

Hooghe, L. and Marks, G. (2001b) 'Types of MLG', *European Integration Online Papers*, 5(11) (http://eiop.or.at/eiop/texte/2001-011a.htm).

Hubschmid, C. and Moser, P. (1997) 'The Co-operation Procedure in the EU: Why was the European Parliament Influential in the Decision on Car Emissions Standards?', *Journal of Common Market Studies*, 25, 225–42.

Huelshoff, M. G. (1994) 'Domestic Politics and Dynamic Issue-linkage: A Reformulation of Integration Theory', *International Studies Quarterly*, 38(2), 255–79.

Hüglin, Thomas (1994) 'Federalism, Subsidiarity and the European Tradition: Some Clarifications' *Telos*, 100, 37–55.

Hurrell, A. and Menon, A. (1996) 'Politics Like Any Other? Comparative Politics, International Relations and the Study of the EU', *West European Politics*, 19(2), 386–402.

Huysmans, J. (1998) 'Revisiting Copenhagen, or: About the "Creative Development" of a Security Studies Agenda in Europe', *European Journal of International Relations*, 4, 479–508.

Ikenberry, G. J. (1994) *History's Heavy Hand: Institutions and the Politics of the State*, unpublished MS.

Immergut, E. (1992) *Health Politics: Institutions and Interests in Western Europe* (New York: Cambridge University Press).

Inglehart, R. (1967) 'An End to European Integration?', *American Political Science Review*, 61, 91–105.

Inglehart, R. (1968) 'Trends and Non-trends in the Western Alliance: A Review', *Journal of Conflict Resolution*, 12(1), 120–8.

Jachtenfuchs, M. (1995) 'Theoretical Approaches to European Governance', *European Law Journal*, 1(2), 115–33.

Jachtenfuchs, M. (1997) 'Democracy and Governance in the European Union', *European Integration Online Papers*, 1997–002a (http://eiop.or.at/eiop/index.php/eiop).

Jachtenfuchs, M. (2001) 'The Governance Approach to European Integration', *Journal of Common Market Studies*, 39(2), 245–64.

Jachtenfuchs, M. and Kohler-Koch, B. (1996) 'Regieren im dynamischen Mehrebenensystem' in M. Jactenfuchs and B. Kohler-Koch (eds), *Europäische Integration* (Opladen, Germany: Leske & Budrich), 15–44.

Jachtenfuchs, M. and Kohler-Koch, B. (1997) 'The Transformation of Governance in the European Union', updated version of MZES working paper no. 11, http://user page.fu-berlin.de/~jfuchs/current/transfo.htm.

Jachtenfuchs, M., and Kohler-Koch, B. (2004) 'Governance and Institutional Development' in A. Wiener and T. Diez (eds), *European Integration Theory* (Oxford: Oxford University Press), 97–115.

Jachtenfuchs, M., Diez, T. and Jung, S. (1998) 'Which Europe? Conflicting Models of a Legitimate European Political order', *European Journal of International Relations*, 4, 409–45.

Jackson, K. T. (1985) *Crabgrass Frontier: The Suburbanization of the United States* (Oxford: Oxford University Press).

Jacobs, F. (1997) 'Legislative co-decisions: A Real Step Forward?', paper presented at the 5th Biennial Conference of the European Community Studies Association, 29 May–1 June.

Jacob, P. E. and Toscano, J. V. (eds) (1964) *The Integration of Political Communities* (Philadelphia: J. B. Lippincott).

Jervis, R. (1993) 'Systems and Interaction Effects' in J. Snyder and R. Jervis (eds), *Coping with Complexity in the International System* (Boulder, CO: Westview), 25–46.

Joerges, C. and Neyer, J. (1997) 'Transforming Strategic Interaction into Deliberative Problem-solving: European Comitology in the Foodstuffs Sector', *Journal of European Public Policy*, 4, 609–25.

Joffe (1984) 'Europe's American Pacifier', *Foreign Policy*, Spring, 64–82.

Joffe, J. (1992) 'Collective Security and the Future of Europe: Failed Dreams and Dead Ends', *Survival*, 34(1), 36–50.

Johnston, A. I. (1998) 'Socialization in International Institutions: The ASEAN Regional Forum and IR Theory', paper presented at the Workshop on 'The Emerging International Relations of the Asia-Pacific Region', University of Pennsylvania, May.

Johnson, H. (1966) 'Trade Preferences and Developing Countries' *Lloyds Bank Review*, 80, 1–18

Johnson, H. (1967) *Economic Policies Toward less Developed Countries* (Washington, DC: The Brookings Institution).

Johnson, J. (1993) 'Is Talk Really Cheap?: Prompting Conversation between Critical Theory and Rational Choice', *American Political Science Review*, 87, 74–86.

Jørgensen, K. (ed.) (1997) *Reflective Approaches to European Governance* (London: Macmillan).

Jupille, J. and Caporaso, J. A. (1999) 'Institutionalism and the European union: Beyond International Relations and Comparative Politics', *Annual Review of Political Science*, 2, 429–44.

Jupille, J., Caporaso, J. A. and Checkel, J. C. (2003) 'Integrating Institutions: Rationalism, Constructivism and the Study of the European Union', *Comparative Political Studies*, 36(1–2), 7–40.

Kaiser, K. (1965) 'L'Europe des Savants. European Integration and the Social Sciences', *Journal of Common Market Studies*, 4, 36–46.

Kato, J. (1996) 'Review Article: Institutions and Rationality in Politics – Three Varieties of Neo-institutionalists', *British Journal of Political Science*, 26, 553–82.

Katzenstein, P. (1989) 'International Relations Theory and the Analysis of Change' in E-O. Czempiel and J. Rosenau (eds), *Global Changes and Theoretical Challenges* (Lexington, MA: Lexington Books).

Katzenstein, P. (ed.) (1996) The *Culture of National Security: Norms and Identity in World Politics* (New York: Columbia University Press).

Katzenstein, P., Keohane, R. O., and Krasner, S. (1998) 'International Organization and The Study of World Politics', *International Organization*, 52, 645–86.

Keck, M. and Sikkink, K. (1998) *Activists Beyond Borders: Transnational Advocacy Networks in International Politics* (Ithaca, NY: Cornell University Press).

Keeney, R. L. and Raiffa, H. (1991) 'Structuring and Analysing Values for Multiple-issue Negotiations' in H. Peyton Young (ed.) *Negotiating Analysis* (Ann Arbor, MI: University of Michigan Press), 131–51.

Kelemen, R. D. (2000) 'Regulatory Federalism: EU Environmental Policy in Comparative Perspective', *Journal of Public Policy*, 20(2), 133–67.

Kelemen, R. D. (2002) 'The Politics of Eurocratic Structure and the New European Agencies', *West European Politics*, 25(4), 93–118.

Kelemen, R. D. (2003) 'The Structure and Dynamics of European Union Federalism', *Comparative Political Studies*, 36(1–2), 184–208.

Kelemen, R. D. (2004) *The Rules of Federalism: Institutions and Regulatory Politics in the EU and Beyond* (Cambridge, MA: Harvard University Press).

Kelstrup, M. (1998) 'Integration Theories: History, Competing Approaches and New Perspectives' in A. Wivel (ed.), *Explaining European Integration* (Copenhagen: Copenhagen Political Studies Press), 15–55.

Keman, H. (1993) 'Comparative Politics: A Distinctive Approach to Political Science?' in H. Keman (ed.), *Comparative Politics: New Directions in Thoery and Method* (Amsterdam: VU Press).

Kenis, P. and Volker, S. (1991) 'Policy Networks and Policy Analysis: Scrutinizing a

New Analytical Toolbox' in B. Marin and R. Mayntz (eds), *Policy Networks. Empirical Evidence and Theoretical Considerations* (Boulder, CO: Westview Press), 25–62.

Keohane, R. O. (1983) 'The Demand for International Regimes' in S. Krasner (ed.), *International Regimes* (Ithaca, NY: Cornell University Press), 325–55.

Keohane, R. O. (1984) *After Hegemony: Cooperation and Discord in the World Political Economy* (Princeton, NJ: Princeton University Press).

Keohane, R. O. (1988) 'International Institutions: Two Approaches', *International Studies Quarterly*, 32, 379–96.

Keohane, R. O. and Hoffmann, S. (1990) 'Conclusions: Community Politics and Institutional Change' in W. Wallace (ed.), *The Dynamics of European Integration* (London: Pinter).

Keohane, R. O. and Hoffmann, S. (1991) 'Institutional Change in Europe in the 1980s' in R. Keohane and S. Hoffmann (eds), *The New European Community: Decision-making and Institutions Change* (Boulder, CO: Westview).

Keohane, R. O. and Nye, J. S. (1975) 'International Interdependence and Integration' in F. Greenstein and N. Polsby (eds), *Handbook of Political Science* (Andover, MA: Addison-Wesley), 363–414.

Keohane, R. and Nye, J. S. (1977) *Power and Interdependence: World Politics in Transition* (Boston, MA: Little, Brown).

Keohane, R. and Nye, J. (1989) *Power and Interdependence*, 2nd edn (New York: Harper Collins).

Kerr, P. (Lord Lothian) (1935) 'Pacifism is not Enough nor Partiotism either', Burge Memorial Lecture, 28 May (http://www.federalunion.org.uk/archives/pacifism.shtml).

Kiewiet, D. R. and McCubbins, M. D. (1991) *The Logic of Delegation: Congressional Parties and the Appropriations Process* (Chicago: University of Chicago Press).

King, A. (1981) 'What Do Elections Decide?' in D. Butler, H. R. Penniman and A. Ranney (eds), *Democracy at the Polls: A Comparative Study of Competitive National Elections* (Washington, DC: American Enterprise Institute).

King, G., Keohane, R. O. and Verba, S. (1994) *Designing Social Inquiry: Scientific Inference in Qualitative Research* (Princeton, NJ: Princeton University Press).

King, P. (1982) *Federalism and Federation* (London: Croom Helm).

Kingdon, J. W. (1984) *Agendas, Alternatives and Public Policies* (Boston, MA: Little, Brown).

Kissinger, H. (1965) *The Troubled Partnership: A Reappraisal of the Atlantic Alliance* (New York: McGraw-Hill).

Knight, J. (1992) *Institutions and Social Conflict* (Cambridge: Cambridge University Press).

Koelbel, T. (1995) 'The New Institutionalism in Political Science and Sociology', *Comparative Politics*, 27, 231–43.

Kohler-Koch, B. (1993) 'Die Welt regieren ohne Weltregierung' in C. Böhret and G. Wewer (eds), *Regieren im 21. Jahrhundert – zwischen Globalisierung und Regionalisierung* (Opladen, Germany: Leske & Budrich) pp. 109–41.

Kohler-Koch, B. (1994) 'Changing Patterns of Interest Intermediation in the European Union', *Government and Opposition*, 29, 166–80.

Kohler-Koch, B. (1996) 'Catching up with Change: The Transformation of Governance in the European Union', *Journal of European Public Policy*, 3(3), 359–80.

Kohler-Koch, B. (1997) 'Organized Interests and the European Parliament', *European Integration Online Papers*, 1997–009a (http://eiop.or.at/eiop/index.php/eiop).

Kohler-Koch, B. (1998) 'Die Europäisierung nationaler Demokratien: Verschleiß eines europäischen Kulturerbes?' in M. Greven (ed.) *Demokratie – eine Kultur des Westens?* (Opladen, Germany: Leske & Budrich), 262–88.

Kohler-Koch, B. (1999) 'The Evolution and Transformation of European Governance' in B. Kohler-Koch and R. Eising (eds), *The Transformation of Governance in the European Union* (New York, NY: Routledge), 14–35.

Kohler-Koch, B. and Eising, R. (eds) (1999) *The Transformation of Governance in the European Union* (New York, NY: Routledge).

Kohler-Koch, B. and Jachtenfuchs, M. (2004) 'Multi Level Governance' in A. Weiner and T. Diez (eds), *European Integration Theory* (Oxford: Oxford University Press), 97–115.

Kohnstamm, M. (1964) 'The European Tide' in S. R. Graubard (ed.), *A New Europe?* (Boston, MA: Houghton Mifflin), 140–73.

Kooiman, J. (1993) 'Social-Political Governance: Introduction' in J. Kooiman (ed.), *Modern Governance: New Government-Society Interactions* (London: Sage).

Krasner, S. (1983) 'Structural Causes and Regime Consequences: Regimes as Intervening Variables' in S. Krasner (ed.), *International Regimes* (Ithaca, NY: Cornell University Press), 1–22.

Krasner, S. (1989) 'Sovereignty: An Institutional Perspective' in J. A Caporaso, ed., *The Elusive State: International and Comparative Perspectives* (Newbury Park, CA: Sage).

Krasner, S. (1991) 'Global Communications and National Power: Life on the Pareto Frontier', *World Politics*, 43, 336–66.

Kratochwil, F. (1989) *Rules, Norms and Decisions: On the Conditions of Practical and Legal Reasoning in International Relations and Domestic Affairs* (Cambridge: Cambridge University Press).

Krause, A. (1988) 'Many Groups Lobby on Implementation of Market Plan', *Europe*, (July/August).

Krause, L. B. (1967) *European Economic Integration and The United States* (Washington, DC: The Brookings Institution).

Kreppel, A. (1997) 'The European Parliament's Influence over EU Policy Outcomes: Fantasy, Fallacy or Fact?', paper presented at the 5th Biennial Conference of the European Community Studies Association, 29 May–1 June.

Kubalkova, V., Onuf, N. and Kowert, P. (1998) *International Relations in a Constructed World* (Armont, NY: M. E. Sharpe).

Kühnhardt, L. (2000) 'Globalization, Transatlatic Regulatory Cooperation, and Democratic Values' in G. Bermann, M. Herdegen and P. Lindseth (eds), *Transatlantic Regulatory Cooperation: Legal Problems and Political Prospects* (Oxford: Oxford University Press), 481–94.

Laclau, E. and Mouffe, C. (1985) *Hegemony and Socialist Strategy: Towards a Radical Democratic Politics* (London: Verso).

Laffan, B. (1998) 'The European Union: A Distinctive Model of Internationalization', *Journal of European Public Policy*, 5, 235–53.

Lange, P. (1993) 'The Maastricht Social Protocol: Why did they do it?', *Politics and Society*, 21, 5–36.

Larsen, H. (1997a) *Foreign Policy and Discourse Analysis: France, Britain and Europe* (London: Routledge).

Larsen, H. (1997b) 'British Discourses on Europe: Sovereignty of Parliament, Instrumentality and the non-Mythical Europe' in K. E. Jørgensen (ed.), *Reflective Approaches to European Governance* (Basingstoke, UK: Macmillan), 109–27.

Lasswell, H. D. (1936) *Politics: Who Gets What and How* (New York: McGraw-Hill).

Laursen, F. (1990) 'Explaining the EC's New Momentum' in F. Laursen (ed.), *EFTA and the EC: Implications of 1992* (Maastricht: European Institute of Public Administration), 33–52.

Laursen, F. (ed.) (2003) Comparative Regional Integration: Theoretical Perspectives (London: Ashgate).

Laver, M. J., Gallagher, M., Marsh, M., Singh, R. and Tonra, B. (1995) 'Electing the President of the European Commission', Trinity Blue Papers in Public Policy, 1 (Dublin: Trinity College).

Lavergne, R. (1983) *The Political Economy of US Tariffs: An Empirical Analysis* (New York: Academic Press).

Lax, D. A. and Sebenius, J. K. (1986) *The Manager as Negotiator: Bargaining for Co-operation and Competitive Gain* (New York: Free Press).

Lecourt, R. (1976) *L'Europe des Juges* (Brussels: E. Bruylant).

Leibfried, S. (1992) 'Towards a European Welfare State? On Integrating Poverty Regimes into the European Community' in Z. Ferge and J. E. Kolberg, eds., *Social Policy in a Changing Europe* (Boulder, CO: Westview), 245–79.

Leibfried S. and Pierson, P. (1995) 'Semi-sovereign Welfare States: Social Policy in a Multi-tiered Europe' in S. Leibfried and P. Pierson (eds), *European Social Policy* (Washington, DC: Brookings Institution).

Leleux, P. (1982) 'The Role of the European Court of Justice in Protecting Individual Rights in the Context of Free Movement of Persons and Services' in E Stein and T. Sandalow (eds), *Courts and Free Markets*, vol. 2 (Oxford: Clarendon Press), 363–427.

Lenaerts, K. (1991) 'Some Reflections on the Separation of Powers in the European Community', *Common Market Law Review*, 28, 11–35.

Lenaerts, K. (1992) 'The Role of the Court of Justice in the European Community: Some Thoughts about the Interaction between Judges and Politicians', University of Chicago Legal Forum, 93.

Leonard, M. (1997) *Politics Without Frontiers: The Role of Political Parties in Europe's Future* (London: Demos).

Lequesne, C. (1994) 'L'administration central de la France et Ie systeme politique europeen: mutations et adaptations depuis l' Acte unique' in Y. Meny, P. Muller and J-L. Quermonne (eds), *Politiques publiques en Europe* (Paris: L'Harmattan).

Levi, L. (1991) 'Recent Developments in Federalist Theory' in L. Levi (ed.), *Altiero Spinelli and Federalism in Europe and in the World* (Milano: Franco Angeli).

Levy, J. (1994) 'Learning and Foreign Policy: Sweeping a Conceptual Minefield', *International Organization*, 48, 279–312.

Levy, M. (1991) 'The Greening of the United Kingdom: An Assessment of Competing Explanations', paper presented at the APSA Convention.

Levy, M., Keohane, R. O. and Haas, P. M. (1992) 'Conclusions; Improving the Effectiveness of International Environmental Institutions', in P. Haas, M. Levy and R. Keohane (eds) *Institutions for the Earth* (Cambridge, MA: MIT Press), 397–426.

Lieshout, R. H., Segers, L. L. and van der Vleuten, A. M. (2004) 'De Gaulle, Moravcsik, and the Choice for Europe: Soft Sources, Weak Evidence', *Journal of Cold War Studies*, 6(4), 89–139.

Lijphart, A. (1971) 'Comparative Politics and the Comparative Method', *American Political Science Review*, 65, 682–93.

Lijphart, A. (1984) *Democracies: Patterns of Majoritarian and Consensus Government in Twenty-One Countries* (New Haven, CT: Yale University Press).

Lindberg, L. (1963) *The Political Dynamics of European Economic Integration* (Stanford, CA: Stanford University Press).

Lindberg, L. (1965) 'Decision Making and Integration in the European Community', *International Organization*, 19(1), 56–80.

Lindberg, L. (1966) 'Integration as a Source of Stress on the European Community System', *International Organization*, 20(2), 237–56.

Lindberg, L. (1967) 'The European Community as a Political System: Notes towards the Construction of a Model', *Journal of Common Market Studies*, 5(4), 344–88.

Lindberg, L. and Scheingold, S. (1970) *Europe's Would-Be Polity: Patterns of Change in the European Community* (Englewood Cliffs, NJ: Prentice-Hall).

Lindberg, L. and Scheingold, S. (eds), (1971) *Regional Integration: Theory and Research* (Cambridge, MA: Harvard University Press).

Lindblom, C. E. (1977) *Politics and Markets: The World's Political-Economic Systems* (New York: Basic Books).

Lipgens, W. (1985) *Documents on the History of European Integration.* Vol. 1: *Continental Plans for European Union 1939–1945* (Berlin: de Gruyter).

Lipgens, W. and Loth, W. (eds) (1985) *Documents on the History of European Integration* (Berlin: de Gruyter).

Lipset, S. M. (1960) *Political Man: The Social Bases of Politics* (Garden City, NY: Doubleday).

Lodge, J. (ed.) (1989) *The European Community and the Challenge of the Future* (London: Pinter).

Longstreth, F. et al. (eds) (1992) *Structuring Politics: Historical Institutionalism in Comparative Analysis* (New York: Cambridge University Press).

Lowi, T. (1964) 'American Business, Public Policy Case Studies, and Political Theory', *World Politics*, 16, 667–715.

Ludlow, P. (1991) 'The European Commission' in R. O. Keohane and S. Hoffmann (eds), *The New European Community: Decisionmaking and Institutional Change* (Boulder, CO: Westview Press).

Lukes, S. (1974) *Power: A Radical View* (London: Macmillan).

Lustick, I. S. (1997) 'The Disciplines of Political Science: Studying the Culture of Rational Choice as a Case in Point', *PS: Political Science and Politics*, June, 175–9.

Macmahon, A. (1955) *Federalism Mature and Emergent* (New York: Doubleday).

Maduro, M. P. (1997) 'Reforming the Market or the State? Article 30 and the European Constitution: Economic Freedom and Political Rights', *European Law Journal*, 3, 55–82.

Magee, S. et al. (eds), (1989) *Black Hole Tariffs and Endogenous Policy Theory* (New York: Cambridge University Press).

Majone, G. (1991) 'Cross-National Sources of Regulatory Policymaking in Europe and the United States', *Journal of Public Policy*, 11(1), 79–106.

Majone, G. (1992a) 'Market Integration and Regulation: Europe after 1992', *Metroeconomica*, 43(1–2), 131–56.

Majone, G. (1992b) 'Regulatory Federalism in the European Community', *Government and Policy*, 10, 299–316.

Majone, G. (1992c) 'Cross-National Sources of Regulatory Policy-making in Europe and the United States', *Metroeconomica*, 11, 79–106.

Majone, G. (1993a) 'The European Community between Social policy and Social Regulation', *Journal of Common Market Studies*, 31(2), 153–70.

Majone, G. (1993b) 'The European Community: An "Independent Fourth Branch of Government"', EUI working paper SPS 93/9 (Florence: European University Institute).

Majone, G. (1994a) 'The Rise of the Regulatory State in Europe', *West European Politics*, 17(3), 77–101.

Majone, G. (1994b) 'Independence and accountability: non-majoritarian institutions and democratic government in Europe' EUI Working Paper SPS 94/3, Florence: European University Institute.

Majone, G. (1995) 'Controlling Regulatory Bureaucracies: Lessons from the American Experience' in H. U. Derlain, I. Gerhardt and F. Scharpf (eds), *Systemnationalitat und Parteillintereste* (Baden-Baden, Germany: Nomos), 291–314.

Majone, G. ed. (1996) *Regulating Europe* (London: Routledge).

Majone, G. (1997) 'The New European Agencies: Regulation by Information', *Journal of European Public Policy* 4(2), 262–75.

Majone, G. (1998) 'Europe's Democratic Deficit: The Question of Standards', *European Law Journal*, 4(1), 5–28.

Majone, G. (1999) 'The Regulatory State and its Legitimacy Problems', *West European Politics*, 22(1), 1–24.

Majone, G. (2000) 'The Credibility Crisis of Community Regulation', *Journal of Common Market Studies*, 38(2), 273–302.

Malcolm, N. (1995) 'The Case Against Europe', *Foreign Affairs*, March/April, 52–68.

Mance, O. (1946) *Frontiers Peace Treaties, and International Organization* (London: Oxford University Press).

Mancini, G. F. (1989) 'The Making of a Constitution for Europe', *Common Market Law Review*, 26, 595–614.

Mann, C. (1972) *The Function of Judicial Decision in European Economic Integration*, (The Hague: Martinus Nihjoff).

Mann, M. (1993) 'Nation-States in Europe and Other Continents: Diversifying, Developing, Not Dying', *Daedalus*, 13, 115–40.

Manners, I. (2003) 'Europaian Studies', *Journal of Contemporary European Studies*, 11(1), 67–83.

Manners, I. (forthcoming) 'Critical Perspectives on European Union Politics', in K. E. Jørgensen, M. Pollack and B. Rosamond (eds), *The Handbook of European Union Politics* (London: Sage).

Mansfield, E. and Milner, H. (eds), (1997) *The Political Economy of Regionalism* (New York: Columbia University Press).

March, J.G. and Olson, J.P. (1989) *Rediscovering Institutions: The Organizational Basis of Politics* (New York, N.Y: Free Press).

March, J. G. and Olsen, J. P. (1998) 'The Institutional Dynamics of International Political Orders', *International Organization* 52(4), 943–69.

Marcussen, M., Risse, T., Engelmann-Martin, D., Knopf, H. J., and Roscher, K. (1999) 'Constructing Europe? The Evolution of French, British and German Nation State Identities', *Journal of European Public Policy*, 6(4), 614–33.

Marin, B. and Mayntz, R. (eds). (1991) *Policy Networks: Empirical Evidence and Theoretical Conclusions* (Frankfurt: Campus).

Marks, G. (1991) 'Structural Policy, European Integration and the State', mimeo (Chapel Hill, NC: University of North Carolina).

Marks, G. (1992) 'Structural Policy in the European Community', in A. Sbragia (ed.), *Euro-Politics: Institutions and Policy Making in the 'New' European Community* (Washington, DC: Brookings Institution).

Marks, G. (1993) 'Structural Policy and Multilevel Governance in the European Community' in A. Cafruny and G. Rosenthal (eds), *The State of the European Community II: The Maastricht Debates and Beyond* (Boulder, CO: Westview Press), 391–410.

Marks, G. (1997) 'Does the European Union Represent an *n* of 1?' *ECSA Review*, 10(3) (http://www.eustudies.org/N1debate.htm).

Marks, G., Scharpf, F., Schmitter P. and Streeck, W. (eds) (1996) *Governance in the European Union* (London: Sage).

Marks, G., Hooghe, L. and Blank, K. (1996) 'European Integration from the 1980s: State Centric vs Multi-Level Governance', *Journal of Common Market Studies*, 34(3), 341–78.

Marks, G., Hooghe, L. and Blank, K. (1998) 'European Integration from the 1980s: State-centric vs Multi-level Governance', in B. Nelsen and A. Stubbs (eds), *The European Union: Readings on the Theory and Practice of European Integration* (Boulder, CO: Lynne Rienner).

Marsh, D. and Rhodes, R. A. W. (eds), (1992) *Policy Networks in British Government* (Oxford: Clarendon Press).

Marti, U. (1988) *Michel Foucault* (Munich: C. H. Beck).

Martin, L. (1993) 'International and Domestic Institutions in the EMU Process' *Economics and Society*, 5, 125–44.

Martin, L. (2000) *Democratic Commitments: Legislatures and International Cooperation* (Princeton, NJ: Princeton University Press).

Martin, L. and Frieden, J. (2002) 'International Political Economy: The State of the Sub-discipline', *The Political Economist*, X(2), 1–8.

Mattli, W. (1999) *The Logic of Regional Integration. Europe and Beyond* (Cambridge: Cambridge University Press).

Mattli, W. and Slaughter, A-M. (1995) 'Law and Politics in the European Union: A Reply to Garrett', *International Organization*, 49(1), 183–90.

Mattli, W. and Slaughter, A-M. (1998) 'Revisiting the European Court of Justice', *International Organization*, 51(1), 177–209.

Mayall, J. (1975) 'Functionalism and International Economic Relations' in A. J. R. Groom and P. Taylor (eds), *Functionalism. Theory and Practice in International Relations* (London: University of London Press).

Mayntz, R. (1993) 'Modernisation and the Logic of Interorganizational Networks' in M. Child, R. Crozier and R. Mayntz (eds), *Social Change Between Market and Organization* (Aldershot, UK: Avebury).

Mazey, S., and Richardson, J. (1993a) *Lobbying in the European Community* (Oxford: Oxford University Press).

Mazey, S. and Richardson, J. (1993b) 'EC Policy-Making: An Emerging European Policy Style?' in D. Liefferink and P. Lowe (eds), *European Integration and Environmental Policy* (Scarborough, UK: Belhaven Press).

Mazey, S. and Richardson, J. (1995) 'Promiscuous Policymaking: The European Policy Style?' in C. Rhodes and S. Mazey (eds), *The State of the European Union*, vol. 3: *Building a European Polity?* (London: Longman).

McCubbins, M. and Schwartz, T. (1984) 'Congressional Oversight Overlooked: Police Patrols versus Fire Alarms', *American Journal of Political Science*, 28, 165–79.

McGowan, F. and Wallace, H. (1996) 'Towards a European Regulatory State', *Journal of European Public Policy*, 3, 560–76.

McGowan, L. and Wilkes, S. (1995) 'The First Supranational Policy in the European Union: Competition Policy', *European Journal of Political Research*, 28, 141–69.

McKay, D. (1996) *Rush to Union: Understanding the Federal Bargain* (Oxford: Clarendon Press).

McLaughlin, A. and Greenwood, J. (1995) 'The Management of Interest Representation in the European Union', *Journal of Common Market Studies*, 33(1), 143–56.

McNamara, K. R. (1993) 'Common Markets, Uncommon Currencies: Systems Effects and the European Community' in J. Snyder and R. Jervis (eds), *Coping with Complexity in the International System* (Boulder, CO: Westview), 303–25.

Mearsheimer, J. (1990) 'Back to the Future: Instability in Europe after the Cold War' *International Security*, 15, 5–56.

Merritt, R. L. and Russett, B. M. (1981) 'Karl W. Deutsch and the Scientific Analysis of World Politics' in R. L. Merritt and B. M. Russett (eds), *From National Development to Global Community: Essays in Honor of Karl W. Deutsch* (London: George Allen and Unwin), 1–21.

Michelmann, H. J. and Soldatos, P. (eds), (1994) *European Integration* (Lanham, MD: University Press of America).

Milner, H. (1997) *Interests, Institutions and Information: Domestic Politics and International Relations* (Princeton, NJ: Princeton University Press).

Milner, H. V. (1988) *Resisting Protectionism: Global Industry and the Politics of International Trade* (Princeton, NJ: Princeton University Press).

Milward A. S. (1984) *The Reconstruction of Western Europe, 1945–51* (London: Methuen).

Milward, A. S. (1992) *The European Rescue of the Nation-State* (London: Routledge).

Milward, A. S. (2000) 'A Comment on the Article by Andrew Moravcsik', *Journal of Cold War Studies*, 2(3), 77–80.

Milward, A. S. and Sørensen, V. (1993) 'Interdependence or Integration? A National Choice' in A. S. Milward, F. M. B. Lynch, R. Ranieri, F. Romero, V. Sørensen (eds), *The Frontier of National Sovereignty. History and Theory 1945–1992* (London: Routledge), 1–32.

Mitrany, D. (1930) 'Pan-Europa – A Hope or a Danger?', *The Political Quarterly*, 1(4), 457–78).

Mitrany, D. (1932) 'The Progress of International Government', The William Dodge

Lectures, Yale University (London: Allen and Unwin). Reproduced in Mitrany, D. (1975) *The Functional Theory of Politics* (London: Martin Robertson).

Mitrany, D. (1939) 'Agenda of Peace-Making'. Reproduced in Mitrany, D. (1975) *The Functional Theory of Politics* (London: Martin Robertson).

Mitrany, D. (1941) 'Territorial, Ideological, or Functional International Organisation'. Reproduced in Mitrany, D. (1975) *The Functional Theory of Politics* (London: Martin Robertson).

Mitrany, D. (1943) 'A Working Peace System; An Argument for the Functional Development of International Orgaization'. Reprinted in Mitrany, D. (1975) *The Functional Theory of Politics* (London: Martin Robertson).

Mitrany, D. (1948) 'The Functional Approach to World Organisation', *International Affairs*, 24(3), 350–63.

Mitrany, D. (1965) 'The Prospect of Integration: Federal or Functional', *Journal of Common Market Studies*, 4, 119–49.

Mitrany, D. (1969) 'The Making of the Functional Theory. A Memoir'. Reproduced in Mitrany, D. (1975) *The Functional Theory of Politics* (London: Martin Robertson).

Mitrany, D. (1971) 'The Functional Approach in Historical Perspective', *International Affairs*, 47(3), 532–43.

Mitrany, D. (1975), 'Retrospect and Prospect'. In Mitrany, D (1975) *The Functional Theory of Politics* (London, Martin Robertson).

Mittelman, J. H. (1998) 'Coxian Historicism as an Alternative Perspective in International Studies', *Alternatives*, 23, 63–92.

Moe, T. M. (1984) 'The New Economics of Organization', *American Journal of Political Science*, 28, 739–77.

Moe, T. M. (1987) 'Interests, Institutions and Positive Theory: The Politics of the NLRB', *Studies in American Political Development*, 2, 236–99.

Moe, T. M. (1990) 'The Politics of Structural Choice: Toward a Theory of Public Bureaucracy' in Williamson, O. E., (ed.), *Organization Theory from Chester Barnard to the Present* (Oxford: Oxford University Press).

Moravcsik, A. (1989) 'Disciplining Trade Finance: The OECD Export Credit Arrangement', *International Organization*, 43, 173–205.

Moravcsik, A. (1991) 'Negotiating the Single European Act: National Interests and Conventional Statecraft in the European Community', *International Organization*, 45, 19–56.

Moravcsik, A. (1992a) *National Preference Formation and Interstate Bargaining in the European Community, 1955–86* (Cambridge, MA: Harvard University Press).

Moravcsik, A. (1992b) 'Liberalism and International Relations Theory', CFIA working paper no. 92–6 (Harvard University).

Moravcsik, A. (1993a) 'Preferences and Power in the European Community: A Liberal Intergovernmentalist Approach', *Journal of Common Market Studies*, 31(4), 473–524.

Moravcsik, A. (1993b) 'Armaments among Allies: Franco-German Weapons Cooperation, 1975–1985' in P. Evans, H. Jacobson and R. Putnam (eds), *Double-Edged Diplomacy: International Bargaining and Domestic Politics* (Berkeley, CA: University of California Press).

Moravcsik, A. (1994) 'Why the EC Strengthen the State: Domestic Politics and International Cooperation', (Harvard University: Center for International Affairs) paper no. 52.

Moravcsik, A. (1997) 'Does the European Union Represent an *n* of 1?', *ECSA Review*, 10(3) (www.eustudies.org/N1debate.htm).

Moravcsik, A. (1998) *The Choice for Europe: Social Purpose and State Power from Messina to Maastrict* (Ithaca, NY: Cornell University Press).

Moravcsik, A. (1999a) 'A New Statecraft? Supranational Entrepreneurs and International Cooperation', *International Organization*, 53(2), 267–306.

Moravcsik, A. (1999b) 'Is Something Rotten in the State of Denmark? Constructivism and European Integration', *Journal of European Public Policy*, 6(5), 669–81.

Moravcsik, A. (2001) 'Federalism in the European Union: Rhetoric and Reality' in K. Nicolaidis and R. Howse (eds), *The Federal Vision: Legitimacy and Levels of Governance in the United States and the EU* (Oxford: Oxford University Press)

Moravcsik, A. (2002) 'In Defence of the Democratic Deficit: Reassessing Legitimacy in the European Union', *Journal of Common Market Studies*, 40(4), 603–24.

Moravcsik, A. and Sangiovanni, A. (2002) 'On Democracy and Public Interest in the Europe Union', Center for European Studies working paper no. 93, (Cambridge, MA: Harvard University).

Morgenthau, H. (1993 [1948]) *Politics Among Nations. The Struggle for Power and Peace*, ed. K. Thompson (New York: McGraw-Hill).

Moser, P. (1996) 'The European Parliament as a Conditional Agenda-setter: What are the Conditions? A Critique of Tsebelis (1994)', *American Political Science Review*, 90, 834–8.

Moser, P., Schneider, G. and Kirchgässner, G. (1997) 'Decision Rules in the European Union – A Rational Choice Perspective', special issue of *Aussenwirtschaft*, 52, 1–321.

Müller, W. C. and Wright, V. (1994) 'Reshaping the State in Western Europe', *West European Politics*, 17, 1–11.

Musgrave, R. A. (1959) *The Theory of Public Finance: A Study in Political Economy* (New York: McGraw-Hill).

Mutimer, D. (1992) 'Theories of Political Integration' in H. Michaelmann and P. Soldatos (eds), *European Integration: Theories and Approaches* (Lanham, MD: University Press of America), 13–42.

Myrdal, G. (1957) *Economic Theory and Under-Developed Regions* (London: Duckworth).

Nadelmann, E. (1990) 'Global Prohibition Regimes: The Evolution of Norms in International Society', *International Organization*, 44, 479–526

Nau, H.R. (1979) 'From Integration to Interdependence: Gains, Losses and Continuing Gaps', *International Organization*, 33, 119–47.

Nentwich, M. and Falkner, G. (1997) 'The Treaty of Amsterdam: Towards a New Institutional Balance', *European Integration Online Papers*, 1997–015 (http://eiop.or.at/eiop/index.php/eiop).

Nicolaidis, K. (2001) 'Conclusion: The Federal Vision Beyond the State', in K. Nicolaidis and R. Howse (eds), *The Fedeeral Vision: Legitimacy and Levels of Governance in the United States and the European Union* (Oxford: Oxford University Press), 442–70.

Noll, R. (1992) 'The Economics and Politics of Deregulation', Jean Monnet Chair papers, (The European Policy Unit, European University Institute, San Domenico, Italy).

North, D. O. (1990) *Institutions, Institutional Change, and Economic Performance* (New York: Cambridge University Press).

North, R. C., Koch, H. E. and Zinnes, D. A. (1960) 'The Integrative Functions of Conflict', *Journal of Conflict Resolution*, 4, 355–74.

Nugent, N. (1989) *The Government and Politics of the European Community* (Durham, NC: Duke University Press).

Nugent, N. (1994) *The Government and Politics of the European Community* (Basingstoke, UK: Macmillan).

Nugent, N. (1995) 'The Leadership Role of the European Commission: Explanatory Factors', paper presented to the Research Conference of the University Association for Contemporary European Studies, University of Birmingham, 18–19 September.

Nye, J. S. (1965) 'Patterns and Catalysts in Regional Integration', *International Organization*, 19, 870–84.

Nye, J. S. (1966) *Pan-Africanism and East African Integration* (Cambridge, MA: Harvard University Press).

Nye, J. S. (1968a) 'Comparative Regional Integration: Concept and Measurement', *International Organization*, 22(4), 855–80.

Nye, J. S. (1968b) *International Regionalism* (Boston: Little, Brown).

Nye, J. S. (1970) 'Comparing Common Markets: A Revised Neofunctionalist Model', *International Organization*, 23, (Autumn) 161–6.

Nye, J. S. (1971a) 'Comparing Common Markets: A Revised Neofunctionalist Model', in L. N. Lindberg and S. A. Scheingold (eds), *Regional Integration: Theory and Research* (Cambridge, MA: Harvard University Press), 192–231.

Nye, J. S. (1971b) *Peace in Parts: Integration and Conflict in Regional Organization* (Boston, MA: Little, Brown).

Nye, J. S. (1971) *Power and Interdependence: World Politics in Transition* (Boston, MA: Little, Brown).

Obradovic, D. (1995) 'Prospects for Corporatist Decision-making in the European Union: The Social Policy Agreement', *Journal of European Public Policy* 2, 261–84.

Obradovic, D. (1996) 'Policy Legitimacy in the European Union', *Journal of Common Market Studies*, 34, 191–221.

Obradovic, D. (1997) 'Eligibility of Non-state Actors to Participate in European Union Policy Formation', paper presented at the workshop in 'Non-state Actors and Authority in the Global System', University of Warwick.

Odell, J. S. (1982) *U.S. International Monetary Policy* (Princeton, NJ: Princeton University Press).

Ojanen, H. (1998) *The Plurality of Truth* (Aldershot, UK: Ashgate).

Onuf, N. (1989) *World of Out Making: Rules and Rule in Social Theory and International Relations* (Columbia, SC: University of South Carolina Press).

Olson, M. (1965) *The Logic of Collective Action: Public Goods and the Theory of Groups* (Cambridge, MA: Harvard University Press).

Padoa-Schioppa, T. (1987) *Efficiency, Stability and Equity* (Oxford: Oxford University Press).

Parsons, C. (2002) 'Showing Ideas as Causes: The Origins of the European Union', *International Organization*, 56, 47–84.

Parsons, C. (2003) *A Certain Idea of Europe* (Ithaca, NY: Cornell University Press).

Patterson, B. (1965) 'Would Tariff Preferences Help Economic Development?', *Lloyds Bank Review*, 76, 18–30.

Peacock, A. (ed.) (1984) *The Regulation Game* (Oxford: Basil Blackwell).

Pederson, T. (1992) 'Political Change in the European Community: The Single European Act as a Case of System Transformation' in M. Kelstrup (ed.), *European Integration and Denmark's Participation* (Copenhagen: Copenhagen Political Studies Press), 184–209.

Pedersen, T. (1998) *Germany, France and the Integration of Europe. A Realist Interpretation* (London: Pinter).

Pelkmans, J. (1989) 'Regulation and the Single market: An Economic Perspective' in H. Siebert (ed.), *The Completion of the Internal Market* (Tubingen: J. C. B. Mohr), 91–117.

Pelzman, S. (1976) 'Towards a More General Theory of Regulation', *Journal of Law and Economics*, 19, 211–40.

Pentland, C. (1973) *International Theory and European Integration* (New York: Free Press).

Pentland, C. (1975) 'Functionalism and Theories of International Political Integration' in A. J. R. Groom and P. Taylor (eds), *Functionalism: Theory and Practice in International Relations* (London: University of London Press).

Perrow, C. (1984) *Normal Accidents* (New York: Basic).

Pescatore, P. (1974) *The Law of Integration* (Leiden: Sijthoss).

Pescatore, P. (1981) 'Les travaux du "Groupe juridique" dans la négotiation des Traités de Rome', *Studia Diplomatica*, 43, 159–78.

Peters, B. G. (1992) 'Bureaucratic Politics and the Institutions of the European Community', in A. Sbragia (ed.), *Europolitics: Institutions and Policymaking in the 'new' European Community*, (Washington, DC: Brookings Institution), 75–122.

Peters, B. G. (1994) 'Agenda-setting in the European Community', *Journal of European Public Policy*, 1, 9–26.

Peters, B. G. and Pierre, J. (2000) 'Developments in Intergovernmental Relations: Towards Multi-Level Governance', *Policy and Politics*, 29, 131–5.

Peters, B. G. and Pierre, J. (2004) 'Multilevel Governance and Democracy: A Faustian Bargain?' in I. Bache and M. Flinders (eds), *Multi-Level Governance* (Oxford: Oxford University Press), 75–89.

Peterson, J. (1992) 'The European Technology Communty – Policy Networks in a Supranational Setting' in D. Marsh and R. A. W. Rhodes (eds), *Policy Networks in British Government* (Oxford: Clarendon Press).

Peterson, J. (1995a) 'Decision-making in the European Union: Towards a Framework for Analysis', *Journal of European Public Policy*, 2(1), 69–93.

Peterson, J. (1995b) 'Policy-networks and European Union Policy Making: A Reply to Kassim', *West European Politics*, 18, 389–407.

Peterson, J. (2001) 'The Choice for EU Theorists: Establishing a Common Framework for Analysis', *European Journal of Political Reseach*, 39, 289–318.

Peterson, J. (2003) 'Policy Networks', IHS Political Science Series, 90.

Peterson, J. and Bomberg, E. (1993) 'Decision-making in the European Union: A Policy Networks Approach', mimeo (York).

Peterson, J. and Bomberg, E. (1997) 'Rationality, Structure and Power in EU Governance: A Process Dominant Approach', paper presented at the 5th Biennial Conference of the European Community Studies Association, 29 May–1 June.

Peterson, J. and Bomberg, E. (1999) *Decision-making in the European Union* (Basingstoke, UK: Macmillan).

Piciotto S. (2002) 'Introduction: Reconceptualizing Regulation in the Era of Globalization', *Journal of Law and Society*, 29(1), 1–11.

Pierson, P. (1992) '"Policy Feedbacks" and Political Change: Contrasting Reagan and Thatcher's Pension-reform Initiatives', *Studies in American Political Development*, 6, 361–92.

Pierson, P. (1993) 'When Effect Becomes Cause: Policy Feedback and Political Change', *World Politics*, 45, 595–628.

Pierson, P. (1994) *Dismantling the Welfare State? Reagan, Thatcher and the Politics of Retrenchment* (New York: Cambridge University Press).

Pierson, P. (1996) 'The Path to European Integration: A Historical Institutionalist Analysis', *Comparative Political Studies*, 29(2), 123–63.

Pierson, P. (2000) 'Increasing Returns. Path Dependence and the Study of Politics', *American Political Science Review*, 94(2).

Pierson, P., and Leibfried, S. (1995) 'Multi-tiered Institutions and the Making of Social Policy' in S. Leibfried and P. Pierson (eds), *European Social Policy: Between Fragmentation and Integration* (Washington, DC: Brookings Institution), 1–40.

Pinder, J. (1986) 'European Community and Nation-state: A Case for a Neo-federalism?', *International Affairs*, 62(1), 41–54.

Pinder, J. (1991) *European Community: The Building of a Union* (Oxford: Oxford University Press).

Pinder, J. (1993) 'The New European Federalism: The Idea and Achievements', in M. Burgess and A. G. Gagnon (eds), *Comparative Federalism and Federation* (London: Harvester Wheatsheaf), 62–4.

Plummer, J. (1994) *The Governance Gap: Quangos and Accountability* (London: Joseph Rowntree Foundation).

Pollack, M. (1995) 'Obedient Servant or Runaway Eurocracy? Delegation, agency, and agenda setting in the European Community', unpublished MS, WCFIA, Harvard University.

Pollack, M. (1996) 'The New Institutionalism and EC Governance: The Promise and Limits of Institutional Analysis', *Governance*, 9(4), 429–58.

Pollack, M. (1997a) 'Delegation, Agency and Agenda Setting in the EC', *International Organization*, 51(1), 99–134.

Pollack, M. (1997b) 'Does the European Union Represent an *n* of 1?', *ECSA Review*, 10(3) (www.eustudies.org/N1debate.htm).

Pollack, M. (1998) 'Constructivism, Social Psychology and Elite Attitude Change: Lessons from an Exhausted Research Program', paper presented at the 11th International Conference of Europeanists.

Pollack, M. (2003) *The Engines of European Integration: Delegation, Agency and Agenda-setting in the EU* (New York: Oxford University Press).

Pollack, M. (2004) 'New Institutionalism' in A. Wiener and T. Diez (eds), *European Integration Theory* (Oxford: Oxford University Press).

Potter, J. (1996) *Representing Reality: Discourse, Rhetoric and Social Construction* (London: Sage).

Pridham, G. and Pridham, P. (1981) *Transnational Party Co-operation and European Integration: The Process Towards the Direct Elections* (London: Allen & Unwin).

Prosser, T. (1989) 'Regulation of Privatized Enterprises: Institutions and Procedures' in L. Hancher and M. Moran (eds), *Capitalism, Culture and Economic Regulation* (Oxford: Clarendon Press).

Pryce, R. (1987) 'Past Experience and Lessons for the Future,' in R. Pryce and W. Wessels (eds), *The Dynamics of European Union* (London: Croom Helm), 273–96.

Puchala, D. (1970a) 'Integration and Disintegration in Franco-German Relations, 1954–1965', *International Organization*, 24(2), 183–208.

Puchala, D. (1970b) 'International Transactions and Regional Integration', *International Organization* 24(4) 732–63.

Puchala, D. (1972) 'Of Blind Men, Elephants, and International Integration' *Journal of Common Market Studies*, 10(3), 267–84.

Puchala, D. (1975) 'Domestic Political and Regional Harmonization in the European in the European communities', *World Politics*, 27, 496–520.

Puchala, D. (1997) 'Does the European Union Represent an *n* of 1?', *ECSA Review*, 10(3) (www.eustudies.org/N1debate.htm).

Puchala, D. (1981) 'Integration Theory and International Relations', in R. L. Merritt and B. M. Russett (eds), *From National Development to Global Community: Essays in Honor of Karl W. Deutsch* (London: Allen & Unwin), 145–64.

Puchala, D. (1999) 'Institutionalism, Intergovernmentalism and European Integration: A Review Article', *Journal of Common Market Studies*, 37(2), 317–31.

Putnam R. (1988) 'Diplomacy and Domestic Politics', *International Organization*, 42, 427–61.

Quermonne, J. (1994) *La Système politique de l'Union européene* (Paris: Montchretien).

Raiffa, H. (1982) *The Art and Science of Negotiation* (Cambridge, MA: Harvard University Press).

Rasmussen, H. (1980) 'Why is Article 173 Interpreted Against Private Plaintiffs?', *European Law Review*, 5, 112–27.

Rasmussen, H. (1986) *On Law and Policy in the European Court of Justice: A Comparative Study in Judicial Policymaking* (Dortrecht: M. Nijhoff).

Rasmussen, H. (forthcoming) 'The Role of the Court in the European Community: Towards a Normative Theory of Interpretation of Community Law', *University of Chicago Legal Forum*.

Reif, K-H. and Schmitt, H. (1980) 'Nine Second Order National Elections: A Conceptual Framework for the Analysis of European Election Results', *European Journal of Political Research*, 8, 3–44.

Revzin, P. (1988) 'Italians Must Change Their Business Style in Integrated Europe', *Wall Street Journal*, 21 November.

Rhodes, M. (1995) '"Subversive Liberalism": Market Integration, Globalization and the European Welfare State', *Journal of European Public Policy*, 2, 384–406.

Rhodes, R. A. W. (1996) 'The New Governance: Governing without Government', *Political Studies*, 44(4), 652–67.

Rhodes, R. A. W. (1997) *Understanding Governance. Policy Networks, Governance, Reflexivity and Accountability* (Buckingham, UK: Open University Press).

Rhodes, C. and Mazey, S. (1995) 'Introduction: Integration in Theoretical Perspective' in C. Rhodes and S. Mazey (eds), *The State of the European Union*, vol. 3: *Building a European polity?* (London: Longman).

Richardson, J. (1996a) 'Policy-making in the EU: Interests, Ideas and Garbage Cans of Primeval Soup' in J. Richardson (ed.), *European Union: Power and Policy-Making*, (London: Routledge).

Richardson, J. (1996b) 'Eroding EU Policies: Implementation Gaps, Cheating and Re-steering', in J. Richardson (ed), *European Union: Power and Policy-Making*, (London: Routledge).

Richardson, J. (1996c) 'Actor-based Models of National and EU Policy-making' in H. Kassim and A. Menon (eds), *The European Union and National Industrial Policy* (London: Routledge).

Riker, W. (1955) 'The Senate and American Federalism', *American Political Science Review* 49, 452–69.

Riker, W. (1994 [1964]) *Federalism: Origin, Operation, Significance* (Boston: Little, Brown).

Riker, W. (1986) *The Art of Political Manipulation* (New Haven, CT: Yale University Press).

Risse, T. (2000) '"Let's argue!" Communicative Action in World Politics', *International Organization*, 54, 1–40.

Risse, T. (2004) 'Social Constructivism and European Integration' in A. Wiener and T. Diez (eds), *European Integration Theory* (Oxford: Oxford University Press),159–76.

Risse, T. and Sikkink, K. (1999) 'The Socialization of International Human Rights Norms into Domestic Practices: Introduction' in T. Risse, S. C. Ropp and K. Sikkink, (eds), *The Power of Human Rights: International Norms and Domestic Change* (Cambridge: Cambridge University Press), 1–38.

Risse, T. and Wiener, A. (2001) 'The Social Construction of Social Constructivism', in T. Christiansen, K. E. Jørgensen, and A. Wiener (eds), *The Social Construction of Europe* (London: Sage).

Risse-Kappen, T. (ed.) (1995a) *Bringing Transnational Relations Back In: Non-state Actors, Domestic Structures and International Institutions* (Cambridge: Cambridge University Press).

Risse-Kappen, T. (1995b) 'Democratic Peace – Warlike Democracies? A Social Constructivist Interpretation of the Liberal Argument', *European Journal of International Relations*, 1, 491–517.

Risse-Kappen, T. (1996) 'Exploring the Nature of the Beast: International Relations Theory and Comparative Policy Analysis Meet the European Union' *Journal of Common Market Studies*, 34(1), 53–80.

Rogowski, R. (1989) *Commerce and Coalitions: How Trade Affects Domestic Political Alignments* (Princeton, NJ: Princeton University Press).

Rokkan, S. (1973) 'Cities, States and Nations: A Dimensional Model for the Study of Contrasts in Developemnt', in S. N. Eisenstadt and S. Rokkan (eds), *Building States and Nations: Models and Data Resources* (London: Sage).

Rorty, R. (1979) *Philosophy and the Mirror of Nature* (Princeton, NJ: Princeton University Press).

Rosamond, B. (1999) 'Discourses of Globalization and the Social Construction of European Identities', *Journal of European Public Policy*, 6(4), 652–68.

Rosamond, B. (2000) *Theories of European Integration* (Basingstoke, UK: Palgrave).

Rosamond, B. (2005a) 'Globalization, the Ambivalence of European Integration and the Possibilities for a Post Disciplinary EU Studies', *Innovation: The European Journal of Social Science Research*, 18(1), 25–45.

Rosamond, B. (2005b) 'The Uniting of Europe and the Foundation of EU Studies: Revisiting the Neofunctionalism of Ernst B Haas', *Journal of European Public Policy*, 12(2), 237–54.

Rosamond, B. (forthcoming) 'The Political Sciences of European Integration: An Intellectual History of EU Studies', in K. E. Jørgensen, M. A. Pollack and B. Rosamond (eds), *Handbook of European Union Politics* (London: Sage).

Rose-Ackerman, S. (1992) *Rethinking the Progressive Agenda* (New York: The Free Press).

Rosenau, J. N. and Czempiel, E.-O. (eds), (1992) *Governance Without Government: Order and Change in World Politics* (Cambridge: Cambridge University Press).

Rosenau, J. N. and Durfee, M. (1995) *Thinking Theory Thoroughly: Coherent Approaches in an Incoherent World* (Boulder, CO: Westview).

Rosenstiel, F. (1962) *Le principe de 'Supranationalite'* (Paris: Pedone).

Ross, G. (1992) 'European Community Politics and the New Europe', mimeo (Cambridge, MA).

Ross, G. (1995) *Jacques Delors and European Integration* (New York: Oxford University Press).

Ruggie, J. G. (1993) 'Territoriality and Beyond: Problematizing Modernity in International Relations', *International Organization*, 47(1), 139–74

Ruggie, J. G. (1998) *Constructing the World Polity: Essays on International Institutionalization* (New York: Routledge).

Ruggie, J. G., Katzenstein, P. J., Keohane, R. O. and Schmitter, P. C. (2005) 'Transformations in World Politics: The Intellectual Contributions of Ernst B. Haas', *Annual Review of Political Science*, 8(1), 271–96.

Rumford, C. and Murray, P. (2003) 'Globalization and the limitations of European Integration Studies: Interdisciplinary Considerations', *Journal of Contemporary European Studies*, 11(1), 85–93.

Russett, B. (1963) *Community and Contention: Britain and American in the Twentieth Century* (Cambridge: Cambridge University Press).

Russett, B. (1970) 'Interdependence and Capabilities for European Cooperation', *Journal of Common Market Studies*, 9(2), 143–50.

Russett, B. (1971) 'Transactions, Community, and International Political Integration' *Journal of Common Market Studies*, 9(3), 224–45.

Sabel, C. and Piore, M. (1984) *The Second Industrial Divide* (New York: Basic Books).

Saeter, M. (1998) 'Beyond the Nation-state. Functionalism and International Organization', *Internasjonal Politikk*, 56(2), 282–94.

Salter, A. (1919) 'The Organisation of the League of Nations' in W. Arnold-Forster (ed.), *Sir Arthur Salter: The United States of Europe and Other Papers* (London: Allen and Unwin, 1933).

Salter, A. (1921) *Allied Shipping Control* (Oxford: Clarendon Press).

Salter, A. (1929) 'The United States of Europe Idea', in W. Arnold-Forster (ed.) *The United States of Europe and Other Papers* (London: Allen and Unwin, 1933).

Sandholtz, W. (1989) 'Crisis and Collaboration in European Telematics'. PhD dissertation, Department of Political Science, University of California, Berkeley.

Sandholtz, W. (1992) *High-Tech Europe: The Politics of International Cooperation* (Berkeley, CA: University of California Press).

Sandholtz, W. (1993) 'Choosing Union: Monetary Politics and Maastricht', *International Organization*, 47 (1), 95–128.

Sandholtz, W. (1996) 'Membership Matters: Limits of the Functional Approach to European Institutions', *Journal of Common Market Studies*, 34(3), 403–29.

Sandholtz, W. (1998) 'The Emergence of a Supranational Telecommunications Regime' in W. Sandholtz and A. Stone Sweet (eds), *European Integration and Supranational Governance* (Oxford: Oxford University Press).

Sandholtz, W. and Stone Sweet, A. (eds), (1998) *European Integration and Supranational Governance* (Oxford: Oxford University Press).

Sandholtz, W. and Zysman, J. (1989) '1992: Recasting the European Bargain', *World Politics*, 42(1), 95–128.

Sbragia, A. (1992) 'Thinking about the European Future. The Uses of Comparison' in A. Sbragia (ed.), *Euro-Politics: Institutions and Policymaking in the 'New' European Community* (Washington, DC: The Brookings Institution).

Schäffner, c. et al. (1996) 'Diversity and Unity in European Debates' in A. Musolff et al. (eds), *Conceiving of Europe: Diversity in Unity* (Aldershot, UK: Darthmouth).

Scharpf, F. (1988) 'The Joint Decision Trap: Lessons from German Federalism and European Integration', *Public Administration*, 66, 239–78.

Scharpf, F. (1994) 'Community and Autonomy: Multilevel Policy Making in the European Union', *Journal of European Public Policy*, 1(2), 219–42.

Scharpf, F. (1996b) 'Democratic Policy in Europe', *European Law Journal*, 2, 136–55.

Scharpf, F. (1997) 'Introduction: The Problem-Solving Capacities of Multi-Level Governance', *Journal of European Public Policy*, 44, 520–38.

Scharpf, F. (1999) *Governing in Europe: Effective and Democratic?* (Oxford: Oxford University Press).

Scharpf, F. (2000) 'Notes Towards a Theory of Multi-Level Governance in Europe', discussion paper 00/5 (Berlin: Max-Planck-Institut fur Gesellschaftforschung).

Scharpf, F. (2002) 'The European Social Model: Coping with the Challenges of Diversity', *Journal of Common Market Studies*, 40(4), 645–70.

Schattschneider, E. E. (1960) *The Semisovereign People: A Realist's View of Democracy in America* (Hinsdale, IL: Dryden Press).

Scheingold, S. (1965) *The Rule of Law in European Integration* (New Haven, CT: Yale University Press).

Scheingold, S. (1970) 'Domestic and International Consequences of Regional Integration', *International Organization*, 24(4), 978–1002.

Scheingold, S. (1971) '*The Law in Political Integration: The Evolution and Integrative Implications of Regional Legal Processes in the European Community*', occasional papers in International Affairs 27, (Cambridge, MA: Center for International Affairs, Harvard University).

Schelling, T. (1978) *Micromotives and Macrobehavior* (New York: Norton).

Schermers, H. (1990) 'Special Foreword'; *Common Market Law Review*, 27, 637–8.

Schimmelfennig, F. (2004) 'Liberal Intergovernmentalism' in A. Wiener and T. Diez (eds), *European Integration Theory* (Oxford: Oxford University Press), 75–94.

Schmitter, P. (1969) 'Three Neofunctionalist Hypotheses about International Integration', *International Organization* 23(1), 161–6.

Schmitter, P. (1970) 'A Revised Neofunctionalist Theory', *International Organization*, 24(4), 836–68.

Schmitter, P. (1971) 'A Revised Theory of Regional Integration', in L. Lindberg and S. Scheingold (eds), *Regional Integration: Theory and Research* (Cambridge, MA: Harvard University Press), 232–64.

Schmitter, P. (1991) 'The European Community as an Emergent and Novel Form of Political Domination', estudio/working paper 1991/26 (Madrid: Juan March Institute).

Schmitter, P. (1992a) 'Interests, Powers and Functions: Emergent Properties and Unintended Consequences in the European Polity', MS (Center for Advanced Study in the Behavioral Sciences, Stanford University, CA).

Schmitter, P. (1992b) 'The Emerging Europolicy and its Impact upon Euro-capitalism' in R. Boycr (ed.) *Contemporary Capitalism: the Embeddedness of Institutions* (Cambridge: Cambridge University Press).

Schmitter, P. (1996a) 'Examining the Present Euro-polity with the Help of Past Theories' in G. Marks, F. Scharpf, P. Schmitter and W. Streeck (eds), *Governance in the European Union* (London: Sage).

Schmitter, P. (1996b) 'Imagining the Future of the Euro-polity with the Help of New

Concepts' in G. Marks, F. Scharpf, P. Schmitter and W. Streeck (eds), *Governance in the European Union* (London: Sage), 121–50

Schmitter, P. (1996c) 'How to Democratize the Emerging Euro-polity: Citizenship, Representation, Decision-making', Institute Juan March, Madrid.

Schmitter, P. (2000) *How to Democratize the European Union . . . And Why Bother?* (New York: Rowman & Littlefield).

Schmitter, P. (2004) 'Neo-Neofunctionalism' in A. Wiener and T. Diez (eds), *European Integration Theory* (Oxford: Oxford University Press), 45–74.

Schmitter, P. (forthcoming) 'Interests, Powers and Functions: Emergent Properties and Unintended Consequences in the European Polity' in P. Lange and G. Marks (eds), *The Future European Polity*.

Schneider, G. (2000) 'European Union Politics Editorial Statement', *European Union Politics*, 1(1), 5–8.

Schneider, V., Dang-Nguyen, G. and Werle, R. (1994) 'Corporate Actor Networks in European Policy-making: Harmonizing Telecommunications Policy', *Journal of Common Market Studies*, 32, 473–98.

Schokking, J. and Anderson, N. (1960) 'Observations on the European Integration Process', *Journal of Conflict Resolution*, 4, 385–410.

Schumpeter, J. (1943) *Capitalism, Socialism and Democracy* (London: Allen & Unwin).

Searle, J. R. (1969) *Speech Acts: An Essay in the Philosophy of Language* (Cambridge: Cambridge University Press).

Searle, J. R. (1977) 'Reiterating the Differences', *Glyph*, 1, 198–208.

Sebenius, J. K. (1991) 'Negotiation Analysis' in V. Kremenyuk (ed.), *International Negotiation. Analysis, Approaches, Issues* (San Francisco, CA: Jossey Bass), 203–15.

Sending, O. J. (2002) 'Constitution, Choice and Change: Problems with the "Logic of Appropriateness" and its use in Constructivist Theory', *European Journal of International Relations*, 8(4), 443–70.

Sewell, J. P. (1966) *Functionalism and World Politics* (London: Oxford University Press).

Shackleton, M. (1993) 'The Delors II Budget Package' in N. Nugent (ed.), *The European Community 1992: Annual Review of Activities* (Oxford: Basil Blackwell), 11–25.

Shapiro, M. (1978) 'The Constitution and Economic Rights' in M. J. Harmon (ed.), *Essays on the Constitution of the United States* (Port Washington, NY: Kennikat Press).

Shapiro, M. (1980) 'Comparative Law and Comparative Politics' *Southern California Law Review*, 53(2), 537–42.

Shapiro, M. (1988) *Who Guards the Guardians? Judicial Control of Administration* (Athens, GA: University of Georgia Press).

Shapiro, M. (1991) 'The European Court of Justice' in A. Sbragia (ed.), *Euro-politics: Institutions and Policymaking in the New European Community* (Washington, DC: Brookings Institution).

Shapiro, M. (1997) 'The Problems of Independent Agencies in the United States and the European Union' *Journal of European Public Policy*, 4, 276–91.

Shaw, J. and Wiener, A. (1999) 'The Paradox of the "European Polity"', Jean Monnet working paper, no. 10 (New York University School of Law).

Shaw, J. and Wiener, A. (2000) 'The Paradox of the European Polity', in M. Green Cowles and M. Smith (eds), *The State of the European Union: Risks, Reform, Resistance and Revival*, (Oxford: Oxford University Press).

Shepsle, K. (1979) 'Institutional Equilibrium and Equilibrium inMultidimensional Voting Models', *American Journal of Political Science*, 23: 27–59.

Shepsle, K. (1986) 'Institutional Equilibrium and Equilibrium institutions' in H. Weisberg, ed. *Political Science: The Science of Politics* (New York: Agathon Press).

Shepsle, K. (1989) Studying Institutions: Some Lessons from the Rational Choice Approach', *Journal of Theoretical Politics*, 1(2), 131–47.

Shepsle, K. (1992) 'Congress is a "They", Not an "It": Legislative Intent as Oxymoron', *International Review of Law and Economics*, 12, 239–56.

Siedentopf, H. and Hauschild, C. (1988) 'Part I: The Implementation of Community Legislation by the Member States: A Comparative Analysis' in H. Siedentopf and J. Ziller (eds), *Making European Politics Work: The Implementation of Community Legislation in the Member States,* vol. 1 (Maastricht: European Institute for Public Administration).

Signorini, C. (1989) 'The ECU, a Success Factor for the 1993 Community Market' address in Madrid, 12 January.

Simeon, R. and Cameron, D. (2000) 'Intergovernmental Relations and Democratic Citizenship', in B. G. Peters and D. V. Savoie (eds), *Governance in the 21st Century* (Montreal: McGill/Queens University Press), 58–118.

Singer, D. (1969 [1961]) 'The Level-of-analysis Problem in International Relations', in J. Rosenau, (ed.) *International Politic and Foreign Policy: A Reader in Research and Theory*, rev. edn (New York: Free Press).

Skocpol, T. (1992) *Protecting Soldiers and Mothers: The Political Origins of Social Policy in the United States* (Cambridge, MA: Beklknap Press of Harvard).

Skowronek, S. (1982) *Building a New American State* (Cambridge: Cambridge University Press).

Smith, D. L. and Wanke, J. (1993) 'Completing the Single European Market: An Analysis of the Impact on the Member States', *American Journal of Political Science*, 37, 529–54.

Smith, J. (1996) 'How European are European elections?' in J. Gaffney (ed.), *Political Parties and the European Union* (London: Routledge).

Smith, S. (1999) 'Social Constructivism and European Studies; A Reflectivist Critique', *Journal of European Public Policy*, 6(4), 682–91.

Snyder, F. (1994) 'Soft Law and Institutional Practice in the European Community' in S. Martin (ed.), *The Construction of Europe: Essays in Honour of Emile Noel* (Dordrecht: Kluwer).

Söderbaum, F. and Shaw, T. (eds) (2003) *Theories of New Regionalism: A Reader* (Basingstoke, UK: Palgrave).

Soskice, D. and Vitols, S. (1993) 'Financial Deregulation in the New European Community', MS, (Berlin: Wissenschaftszentrum).

Spinelli, A. (1957) 'La beffa del Mercato comune', in *L'Europa non cade dal cielo* (Bologna: Il Mulino), 282–7.

Spinelli, A. (1966) *The Eurocrats* (Baltimore, MD: Johns Hopkins Press).

Spinelli, A. (1944) *For a Free and United Europe. A Draft Manifesto.* (Edizioni del Movimento Italiano per la Federazione Europe).

St. Clair Bradley, K. (1992) 'Comitology and the Law Through a Glass, Darkly' *Common Market Law Review*, 29, 693–721.

Stacey, J. and Rittberger, B. (2003) 'Dynamics of Formal and Informal Institutional Change in the EU', *Journal of European Public Policy*, 10(6), 858–83.

Stein, E. (1981) 'Lawyers, Judges, and the Making of a Transnational Constitution,' *American Journal of International Law*, 75(1), 1–27.

Stein, J. (1994) 'Political Learning by Doing: Gorbachev as Uncommitted Thinker and Motivated Leader', *International Organization*, 48, 155–83.

Steuenberg, B. (1994) 'Decision Making under Different Institutional Arrangements: Legislation by the European Community' *Journal of Institutional and Theoretical Economics* 150, 642–69

Stigler, G. J. (1971) 'The Theory of Economic Regulation', *Bell Journal of Economics and Management Science*, 6, 114–41.

Stone Sweet, A. (1994) 'What is a Supranational Constitution: An Essay in International Relations Theory', *Review of Politics*, 56, 441–74

Stone Sweet, A. (2003) 'European Integration and the Legal System', in T. Börzel and

R. Cichowski (eds), *The State of the European Union: Law, Politics and Society* (Oxford: Oxford University Press), 18–47.

Stone Sweet, A. and Sandholtz, W. (1997) 'European Integration and Supranational Governance', *Journal of European Public Policy*, 4(3) 297–317.

Stone Sweet, A. and Sandholtz, W. (1998) 'Integration, Supranational Governance, and the Institutionalization of the European Polity' in W. Sandholtz and A. Stone Sweet (eds), *European Integration and Supranational Governance* (Oxford: Oxford University Press), 1–26.

Stone-Sweet, A. (2000) *Governing with Judges: Constitutional Politics in Europe* (Oxford: Oxford University Press).

Stone-Sweet, A. (2004) *The Judicial Construction of Europe* (Oxford: Oxford University Press).

Streeck, W. (1995) 'From Market Making to State Building? Reflections on the Political Economy of European Social Policy' in S. Leibfried and P. Pierson (eds), *European Social Policy: Between Fragmentation and Integration* (Washington, DC: Brookings Institution).

Streeck, W. (1996) 'Neo-Voluntarism: A New European Social Policy Regime?' In G. Marks, S. Scharpf, P. C. Schmitter and W. Streeck (eds), *Governance in the Emerging Euro-Polity* (London: Sage).

Streeck, W. and Schmitter, P. (1991) 'From National Corporatism to Transnational Pluralism: Organized Interests in the Single European Market', *Politics and Society*, 19, 133–64.

Streit, C. (1939) *Union Now: A Proposal for a Federal Union of Democracies of the North Atlantic* (New York: Harper and Brothers).

Stuart, M. (1977) *The European Communities and the Rule of Law* (London: Stevens).

Stubb, A. (1996) 'A Categorization of Differentiated Integration', *Journal of Common Market Studies*, 34, 283–95.

Sunstein, C. R. (1990) *After the Rights Revolution: Reconceiving the Regulatory State* (Cambridge, MA: Harvard University Press).

Taylor, P. (1968) 'The Concept of Community and the European Integration Process', *Journal of Common Market Studies*, 7(1), 83–101.

Taylor, P. (1975a) 'Functionalism and Strategies for International Integration' in A. J. R. Groom and P. Taylor (eds), *Functionalism. Theory and Practice in International Relations* (London: University of London Press).

Taylor, P. (1975b) 'Introduction' in D. Mitrany, *The Functional Theory of Politics.* (London: Martin Robertson & Co.).

Taylor, P. (1983) *The Limits of European Integration* (New York: Columbia University Press).

Taylor, P. (1989) 'The New Dynamics of EC Integration in the 1980s' in J. Lodge, (ed.), *The European Community and the Challenge of the Future* (London: Pinter).

Taylor, P. (1991) 'The European Community and the State: Assumptions, Theories and Propositions', *Review of International Studies*, 17, 109–25.

Teasdale, A. (1993) 'The Life and Death of the Luxembourg Compromise', *Journal of Common Market Studies*, 31(4), 567–79.

Teitgen-Colly, C. (1988) 'Les Autorites Administratives Independantes: histoire d'une Institution' in C-A. Colliard and G. Timsit (eds), *Les Autorites Administratives Independantes* (Paris: Presses Universitaires de France).

Thelen, K. and Steinmo, S. (1992) 'Historical Institutionalism in Comparative Analysis' in S. Steinmo, K. Thelen, and F. Longstreth (eds), *Structuring Politics: Historical Institutionalism in Comparative Analysis* (New York: Cambridge University Press), 1–32

Thompson, G. F. (2003) *Between Markets and Hierarchy: The Logic and Limits of Network Forms of Organization* (New York: Oxford University Press).

Tocqueville, A. de (1985) *Selected Letters on Politics and Society*, ed. and tr. R. Boesche (Berkeley: University of California Press).

Tranholm-Mikkelsen, J. (1992) 'Neofunctionalism: Obstinate or Obsolete?, *Millennium: Journal of International Studies*, 20(1), 1–22.

Tsebelis, G. (1992) 'The Power of the European Parliament as a Conditional Agenda Setter', paper presented at the Annual Meeting of the APSA, September.

Tsebelis, G. (1994) 'The Power of the European Parliament as a Conditional Agenda Setter', *American Political Science Review*, 88(1), 128–42.

Tsebelis, G. (1995a) 'Conditional Agenda Setting and Decision-Making Inside the European Parliament', *Journal of Legislative Studies*, 1(1), 65–93.

Tsebelis, G. (1995b) 'Decision Making in Political Systems: Veto Players in Presidentialism, Multicameralism and Multipartyism', *British Journal of Political Science*, 25, 283–325

Tsebelis, G. (1996) 'More on the European Parliament as a Conditional Agenda Setter', *American Political Science Review*, 90(4), 839–44.

Tsebelis, G. and Garrett, G. (1996) 'Agenda-setting Power, Power Indices, and Decisionmaking in the European Union', *International Review of Law and Economics*, 16, 345–61.

Tsebelis, G. and Garrett, G. (2001a) 'Legislative Politics in the European Union' *European Union Politics*, 1(1), 9–36.

Tsebelis, G. and Garrett, G. (2001b) 'The Institutional Foundations of Intergovernmentalism and Supranationalism in the European Union', *International Organization*, 55(2), 357–90.

Usher, J. (1981) *European Community Law and National Law* (London: Allen & Unwin).

van Kersbergen, K. and Verbeek, B. (1994) 'The Politics of Subsidiarity in the European Union', *Journal of Common Market Studies*, 32, 215–36.

van Parijs, P. (1982) 'Perverse Effects and Social Contradictions: Analytical Vindication or Dialectics?', *British Journal of Sociology*, 33, 589–603.

van Schendelen, M. (1996) '"The Council Decides": Does the Council Decide?', *Journal of Common Market Studies*, 34, 531–48.

van Tulder, R. and Junne, G. (1988) *European Multinationals in Core Technologies* (New York: John Wiley).

van Wagenen, R. (1952) *Research in the International Organization Field; Some Notes on a Possible Focus* (Princeton, NJ: Center for Research on World Political Institutions).

van Wagenen, R. (1965) 'The Concept of Community and the Future of the United Nations', *Institutional Organization*, 19(3).

Veljanovski, C. (1991) 'The Regulation Game' in C. Veljanovski (ed.), *Regulators and the Market* (London: Institute of Economic Affairs), 3–28.

Vesperini, G. (1990) 'Le Funzioni delle Autorita Amministratuve Indipendenti', *Diritto della Banca e del Mercato Finanzario*, 4(4) 415–30.

Vogel, D. (1992) 'Environmental Protection and the Creation of a Single European Market', mimeo, University of California, Berkeley.

Volcansek, M. L. (1986) *Judicial Politics in Europe* (New York: Peter Lang).

Volcansek, M. L. (1992) 'Judges, Courts, and Policy-Making in Western Europe', *West European Politics*, 15(3), 109–21.

Von der Groben, H. (1982) *Aujbaujahre der europaiischen Gemeinschaft: Das Ringen um den Gemeinsamen Markt und die politische Union (1958–1966)* (Baden-Baden: Nomos).

Wallace, H. (2000) 'Studying Contemporary Europe', *British Journal of Politics and International Relations*, 2(1), 95–113.

Wallace, H. and Wessels, W. (1989) 'Towards a New Partnership: The EC and EFTA in the Wider Western Europe', occasional paper no. 28 (EFTA, Economic Affairs Department).

Wallace, W. (1983) 'Less than a Federation, More than a Regime: The Community as a

Political System' in H. Wallace, W. Wallace and C. Webb (eds), *Policy Making in the European Community*, 2nd edn (London: John Wiley), 403–36.

Waltz, K. (1979) *Theory of International Politics* (New York: McGraw-Hill).

Waltz, K. (1986) 'Reflections on Theory of International Politics A Response to My Critics' in R. Keohane (ed.), *Neorealism and Its Critics* (New York: Columbia Univesity Press).

Warleigh, A. (2006) 'Learning from Europe? EU Studies and the Re-thinking of "International Relations"', *European Journal of International Relations*, 12(1), 31–51.

Watts, R. L. (1987) 'The American Constitution in Comparative Perspective: A Comparison of Federalism in the United States and Canada', *Journal of American History*, 71, 769–91.

Weale, A. (1995) 'Democratic Legitimacy and the Constitution of Europe' in R. Bellamy, V. Bufacchi and D. Castiglione (eds), *Democratic and Constitutional Culture in the Union of Europe* (London: Lothian Foundation).

Weale, A. (1997) 'Environmental Rules and Rule-making in the European Union', *Journal of European Public Policy*, 3, 594–611.

Weaver, R. K. and Rockman, B. (1993) *Do Institutions Matter? Government Capabilities at Home and Abroad* (Washington, DC: Brookings Institution).

Webb, C. (1977) 'Theoretical Perspectives and Problems' in H. Wallace, W. Wallace, and C. Webb (eds), *Policy Making in the European Community* 1st edn (London: John Wiley).

Webb, C. (1983) 'Theoretical Perspectives and Problems' in H. Wallace, W. Wallace, and C. Webb (eds), *Policy Making in the European Community* (London: John Wiley).

Webber, M., Croft, S., Howorth, T., Terriff, T. and Krahmann, E. (2004) 'The Governance of European Security', *Review of International Studies*, 30, 3–26.

Weber, M. (1942 [1918]) 'Politics as a Vocation' in H. H. Gerth and C. W. Mills (eds and trs), *From Max Weber: Essays in Sociology* (Oxford: Oxford University Press).

Weber, S. (1994) 'Origins of the European Bank for Reconstruction and Development', *International Organization*, 48, 1–38.

Weiler, J. (1981) 'The Community System: The Dual Character of Supranationalism', *Yearbook of European Law*, 1, 268–306.

Weiler, J. (1982) 'Community, Member States, and European Integration: Is the Law Relevant?', *Journal of Common Market Studies*, 21, 39–56.

Weiler, J. (1991) 'The Transformation of Europe', *Yale Law Journal*, 100, 2403–83.

Weiler, J. (1994) 'A Quiet Revolution: The European Court of Justice and Its Interlocutors', *Comparative Political Studies*, 26, 510–34.

Weiler, J. (1995) 'Does Europe Need a Constitution? Demos, Telos and the German Maastricht Decision', *European Law Journal*, 1, 219–58.

Weiler, J. (1997a) 'The Reformation of European Constitutionalism', *Journal of Common Market Studies*, 35, 97–131.

Weiler, J. (1997b) 'The European Union Belongs to its Citizens: Three Immodest Proposals', *European Law Review*, 22, 150–6.

Weiler, J. (1998) 'Ideals and Idolatry in the European Construct' in B. McSweeney, (ed.) *Moral Issues in International Affairs: Problems of European Integration* (Basingstoke, UK: Macmillan), 55–82.

Weiler, J., Haltern, U. R. and Mayer, F. C. (1995) 'European Democracy and its Critique' in J. Hayward (ed.), *The Crisis of Representation in Europe* (London: Frank Cass).

Wendt, A. (1992) 'Anarchy is What states Make of it: The Social Construction of Power Politics', *International Organization*, 46(2), 391–425.

Wendt, A. (1994) 'Collective Identity Formation and the International State', *American Political Science Review*, 88(2), 384–7.

Wendt, A. (1999) *Social Theory of International Politics* (Cambridge: Cambridge University Press).

Wessels, W. (1992) 'Staat und (westeuropaische) Integration. Die Fusionsthese', *Politische Vierteljahresschrift*, Sonderheft 23, 36–60.

Wessels, W. (1996) 'Verwaltung im EG-Mehrebenensystem: Auf dem Weg zur Megabürokratie?' in M. Jachtenfuchs and B. Kohler-Koch (eds), *Europäische Integration* (Opladen, Germany: Leske & Budrich), 165–92.

Wessels, W. (1997) 'An Ever Closer Fusion? A Dynamic Macropolitical View on Integration Processes', *Journal of Common Market Studies*, 35, 267–99.

Wessels, W. (1998) 'Comitology: Fusion in Action. Politico-administrative Trends in the EU System', *Journal of European Public Policy*, 5, 209–34.

Wheare, K. C. (1963 [1946]), *Federal Government*, 4th edn (Oxford: Oxford University Press).

White, L. C. (1949) 'Peace by Pieces. The Role of Non-governmental Organizations' in E. M. Paterson (ed.), *World Government* (Philadelphia: The American Academy of Political and Social Sciences).

Wiener, A. (1997) *Building Institutions: The Developing Practice of 'European' Citizenship* (Boulder, CO: Westview Press).

Wiener, A. and Diez, T. (2004) *European Integration Theory* (Oxford: Oxford University Press).

Wilke, M. and Wallace, H. (1990) *Subsidiarity: Approaches to Power-sharing in the European Community* (London: Chatham House).

Williamson, O. E. (1985) *The Economic Institutions of Capitalism* (New York: Free Press).

Williamson, O. E. (1993) 'Transaction Cost Economics and Organization Theory', *Industrial and Corporate Change*, 2, 107–56.

Wincott, D. (1995) 'Institutional Interaction and European Integration: Towards an Everyday Critique of Liberal Intergovernmentalism', *Journal of Common Market Studies*, 33(4), 597–609.

Wind, M. (1998) 'Flexible Integration: The European Union as a Polycentric Polity?', paper presented at the conference on 'Rethinking Constitutionalism in the EU'.

Wionczek, M. (1967) 'La Communidad Economica de Africa Oriental', *Commercio Exterior*, XVII, 837–40.

Woolcock, S. et al, (1991) *Britain, Germany, and 1992* (London: Pinter).

Woolcock, S. et al, (1992) *Britain, Germany, and 1992* (London: Pinter).

Wæver, O. (1990) 'Three Competing Europes: German, French, Russian' *International Affairs*, 66, 477–93.

Wæver, O. (1995) 'Securitization and Desecuritization' in R. D. Lipschutz (ed.) *On Security* (New York: Columbia University Press), 46–86.

Wæver, O. (1997b) 'Discourse as Foreign Policy Theory: The Case of Germany and Europe', mimeo, Center for German and European Studies, University of California, Berkeley.

Wæver, O. (1998a) 'Explaining Europe by Decoding Discourses' in A. Wivel (ed.), *Explaining European Integration* (Copenhagen: Copenhagen Political Studies Press), 100–46.

Wæver, O. (1998b) 'The Sociology of a Not So International Discipline: American and European Developments in International Relations', *International Organization*, 52(4), 687–727.

Wæver, O. (2004) 'Discursive Approaches' in A. Wiener and T. Diez (eds), *European Integration Theory* (Oxford: Oxford University Press), 197–216.

Yondorf, W. (1965) 'Monnet and the Action Committee: The Formative Period of the European Communities', *International Organization*, 19, 885–912.

Zartman, W. (1991) 'The Structure of Negotiation' in V. Kremenyuk (ed.), *International Negotiation. Analysis, Approaches, Issues* (San Francisco, CA: Jossey Bass), 65–77.

Zehfuss, M. (1998) 'Sprachlosigkeit schränkt ein: Zur Bedeutung von Sprache inkon-struktivistischen Theorien', *Zeitschrift für Internationale Beziehungen*, 5, 109–37.

Zellentin, G. (1992) 'Der Funktionalismus – eine Strategie gesamteuropäischer Integration?', in M. Kreile (ed.), *Die Integration Europas* (Opladen, Germany: Westdeutscher Verlag), 62–77.

Zimbardo, P. and Leippe, M. (1991) *The Psychology of Attitude Change and Social Influence* (New York: McGraw-Hill).

Zürn, M. (1997) 'Assessing State Preferences and Explaining Institutional Choice: The Case of intra-German Trade', *International Studies Quarterly*, 41, 295–320.

Zysman, J. (1983) *Governments, Markets, and Growth* (Ithaca, NY: Cornell University Press).

Index

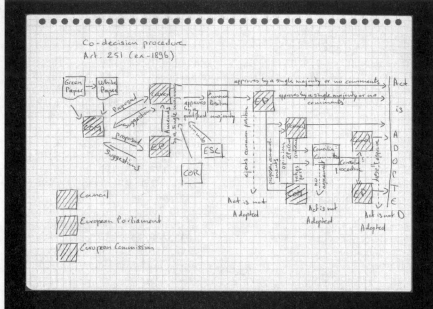